REAL ESTATE FINANCE & INVESTMENT MANUAL

REVISED & EXPANDED

JACK · CUMMINGS

PRENTICE HALL
Paramus, New Jersey 07652

Library of Congress Cataloging-in-Publication Data

Cummings, Jack.
    Real estate finance & investment manual / by Jack Cummings.
       p.   cm.
    Includes index.
    ISBN 0-13-493396-6 (cloth)—ISBN 0-13-493388-5 (pbk.)
     1. Real estate business—Finance—Handbooks, manuals, etc.   2. Real estate
investment—Finance—Handbooks, manuals, etc.   3. Mortgage loans—Handbooks,
manuals, etc.   4. Mortgages—Handbooks, manuals, etc.   I. Title.
HD1375.C8537   1997   96-29527
332.7′2′0973—dc21   CIP

Printed in the United States of America

10 9 8 7 6 5 4 3 2 1 *(cloth)*

10 9 8   *(pbk)*

To Anne Marie & Robert
No one said success was easy, only that it is possible
when you set worthy goals, then let them lead the way.

ISBN 0-13-493396-6 (cloth)

ISBN 0-13-493388-5 (paper)

ATTENTION: CORPORATIONS AND SCHOOLS

Prentice Hall books are available at quantity discounts with bulk purchase for
educational, business, or sales promotional use. For information, please write to:
Prentice Hall Special Sales, 240 Frisch Court, Paramus, New Jersey 07652. Please
supply: title of book, ISBN number, quantity, how the book will be used, date needed.

PRENTICE HALL
Paramus, NJ 07652

On the World Wide Web at http://www.phdirect.com

TABLE OF CONTENTS

Chapter 3
The Power of Negotiating—34

Chapter 4
How Leverage and Risk Affect the Value of Real Estate—51

Chapter 5
Conventional Financing of First Mortgages: Where to Find Them and How to Negotiate the Best Terms—70

Chapter 6
How to Use Creative Financing to Maximize Your Benefits—113

Chapter 7
How to Use Government-Insured Loans to Finance Real-Estate Purchases and Sales—129

Chapter 8
How to Get Land Development
and Construction Loans—155

Chapter 9
How to Use Blanket Mortgages—185

Chapter 10
How to Use the Wraparound Mortgage Effectively—196

Chapter 11
How a Sale-Leaseback Works for
Both Buyer and Seller—230

Chapter 12
The Last Loophole to Build Wealth:
Real-Estate Exchanges—243

Chapter 13
How to Use Pyramid Financing—282

Chapter 14
How and When to Use a Discount Sale + Buy-back—314

Chapter 15
When, Why, and How to Discount a Mortgage—325

Chapter 16
Two Prime Insider Techniques:
Preferred Income Sweeteners and Options—340

Chapter 17
Three Secondary Financing Techniques That Close Deals—364

Chapter 18
Eleven Creative Financing Techniques That Make Your Deals Fly—381

Chapter 19
Four Techniques Where You Keep Part
and Sell Part—415

Chapter 20
How to Use Hidden Benefits to Barter Your Way Into Real Estate—432

Chapter 21
The Five Stages of Every Real-Estate Transaction—452

Chapter 22
The Four Most Asked Questions About Real-Estate Financing—488

Chapter 23
How to Keep the Wolf from the Door: Dealing with Foreclosure—501

Appendix—513

Index—537

INTRODUCTION

To be a success in real-estate investing you should keep in mind the following tenets:

1. Formulate goals you want to achieve.
2. Establish then implement an investment plan to take you where you want to go.
3. Learn how to maximize your bottom line, take-home profits.
4. Continually reduce your risk while increasing your exposure to opportunities.
5. Develop an exit strategy that will complement your plan and goals.
6. Establish timetables and deadlines to reach your goals.
7. Do not rationalize why you did not achieve them, learn your errors and move forward.
8. Reach self-established plateaus then pat yourself on your own back.
9. Then set higher plateaus and more worthy goals and work for them.
10. Achieve financial independence.

Armed with this book, you can attain all of this.

This book is devoted to every aspect of real-estate investment. It is designed and written to give readers a single one-stop source for the best real-estate investing advice and information possible. This book, and its hundreds of financing and investment strategies and techniques, is specifically written for real-estate investors, developers, bankers, buyers, sellers, tenants, salespeople, mortgage brokers, land planners, lawyers, and other professional advisors.

The material contained in this book is offered so that each chapter can be used as a stand-alone reference guide for the specifics that are covered within that chapter. This will enable the reader to turn to that chapter or chapters that can provide a source for solutions to existing problems as they occur. In this way, the book can become an instant tool for all readers. As a total source of information, the book is compiled in such a way that all readers can build their knowledge of real-estate investing and financing in a smooth progression of information. As with any comprehensive book, the reader will find that an initial reading of the entire book will enable the reader to obtain maximum use of the material for many years to come.

This book will become indispensable to buyers and sellers who are looking to improve their chances in the marketplace. It gives each side of the real-estate transaction all the elements that are essential to a successful conclusion of a transaction. Best of all, this book shows you how to become the expert within your own comfort zone, and how to get the edge in the market and keep it.

The hundreds of examples contained within are to spark your own imagination. Every kind of transaction from the purchase of a timeshare week, to the financing of a multimillion dollar shopping center are covered. The simple strategies that have worked for others are here, waiting for you to discover just how simple it is to become a true *real-estate investment* insider.

In the presentation of this book, I have looked back over my past thirty-plus years as a real-estate investor, broker, and developer. I have reviewed mistakes I have seen other people make, and those which I have made along the path to success. I can tell you that the cliché of *learning from the mistakes of others* is a sound bit of advice, and this book offers you a shortcut around the pain and financial disaster of having to make your own mistakes.

As the author of many books on the subject of real-estate investing, brokerage, and financing, I have been able, in the drafting of this book, to bring to the forefront the best of the techniques and strategies that have been presented in my earlier books. As an avid reader and constant student of just about everything dealing with real estate, I have made sure that the material contained in this book is fresh, full of concepts that work, and offers techniques that can make a beneficial difference in your investment plan, that you will be able to implement immediately. Any single chapter of this book can give you a positive edge in your investment plan. Just one, of the hundreds of techniques and strategies I have presented, can give you financial success.

Have you ever wondered why some people seem to excel at everything they do? Have you wanted to know how some people seem to find success in every real-estate investment they make? The answer is one of the first elements of this book you will discover. You will succeed because you learn how to maximize the bottom-line, take-home profits, and you reduce risk in your investments because you have *discovered how to recognize opportunities*.

This book is easy to use. Study it from chapter to chapter and you will be well on your way to being one of the most knowledgeable real-estate investors in town. All you will need after that is to begin to implement your own plan, which this book will help you design. Or, use the book for the chapters that interest you the most. This book is, after all, structured for that purpose too. Take any chapter that fits your current needs and refresh yourself with what you need to get and keep the upper edge in each kind of transaction.

Everything from wraparound mortgages to very creative 1031 real-estate *tax-free* exchanges is at your beck-and-call. The chapter on goal setting, that starts you on the right track for success, will put everything you do into proper perspective.

The goal of this book is to help you get the most from your efforts, and hard earned money. Each of you, depending on your specific goals or real-estate aspirations, will find a wealth of material to fit your own specific needs.

REAL-ESTATE INVESTORS. No matter how much experience you have, this book will offer you a keen insight on how to increase your productivity, reduce your risk, and maintain your edge even when you sell in a buyer's market or buy in a seller's market. Dozens of checklists will help you quickly and simply calculate data that you might have been missing before, or which came in too late to be of any real use to you. This book will show you how you can anticipate which property is going to go up in value, and even better, which properties are going to go down in value, then turn up again. If you already consider yourself a successful real-estate investor, then get ready to have an injection into your system that will take you to higher plateaus.

DEVELOPERS. You are special to the real-estate market. You make the market out of nothing, but you can also get caught in a down-turning trend over which you cannot control. This book will show you that even in the worst market there is a way to go to find success. All it takes is understanding your goals and applying the techniques and strategies offered to you in this book. In this book you will find many key elements to solve your specific problems. As financing is often the most illusive factor for the real-estate developer, you will discover this book will be indispensable to you in your next project, and the potential sale, at even bigger profits than you anticipated, of your last project. Much of this book is devoted to obtaining financing in real-estate transactions. This means everything from learning how to improve your chances at the local savings and loan association, to cutting a great deal with a seller who, because you are now thinking more creatively, agrees to a proposal you make.

BANKERS. Bankers and loan officers will find this book will offer them a very special look at what's beyond the other side of the fence. This book will help anyone who is in the business of making loans, either for or as a part of a major institution or for his or her own private account. As a lender you will develop a new understanding of what it takes to do deals that work for both parties, and how to take creative concepts and apply them to very sound transactions.

BUYERS.   The ultimate profit of every deal depends on an initial purchase that fits the investor's plan. This does not mean that your ultimate success is attained by beating the seller over the head to the point that you walk away from the table with a bargain. Bargains are obtained by knowing what will work for you. This book will show you that to get the edge in the deal does not pit you against the seller. Often you and the seller have the same goals in mind. *You want to buy, and the seller wants you to buy.* By creative and constructive use of financing, and incorporating many other aspects of investment strategies, both you and the seller can come out winners, every time. You must open the door to what you need to do to make the deal work for you. This book is your key to that door.

SELLERS.   Over the long haul, the seller is the king of the game. You are in possession of the property, and can, if financially strong enough, keep the property. However, buyers often control the market, because when you *need* to sell, nothing happens until you find a buyer who wants your property. When there are fewer buyers than sellers the marketplace can be very slow. Often values have very little to do with this concept. This book will show all sellers how to overcome a buyer's market and achieve your goals. Do this once and this book will be worth many hundred times what it cost you. All you have to do is to read on, build a plan that fits your needs, and go for it.

TENANTS.   Most real-estate investment books don't say much about tenants. As a rental property owner I can tell you that were it not for tenants there would not be much of a real-estate market. The key for you as a tenant is to be able to ascertain when you should buy, and when you should rent. The key to both situations is found in this book. You will find many examples of how to maximize lease terms to your favor, and many special lease terms that you will want to insist on in your next lease.

SALESPEOPLE.   If you sell real estate, you know how tough the profession is. As a realtor for over thirty years I know how the market can rise and fall. In some parts of the country there seem to be more real-estate salespeople than trees. To become a top real-estate salesperson in any part of the world means you have to be the best, and to offer your clients the best service possible. This book will open your eyes to how you can be of greater service to your buyers and sellers. If you can accept the fact that *by helping your buyers and sellers attain their goals, you will be successful as a salesperson*, then this book is for you. The idea is to expand your own reference point so that you are better able to put yourself into your clients' shoes. This will enable you to see beyond the standard way of doing things, and be creative in many new ways not possible before. By the way, creative financing often scares people. That is because the word *creative* is often confused with the word *complicated*. All creativity really is, is keeping your eyes and mind open to new ideas and concepts, and understanding where and when they fit to help someone. Take advantage of the tools contained in this book. Your clients will be glad you did.

MORTGAGE BROKERS.   Will find this book to be a great tool in building a stronger client base. As a reference work it will be your guide to how to build better presentations, and how to apply simple and creative techniques to make the loan package stronger. We are all in this boat together, and the more the mortgage broker knows about what the real-estate investor needs, the greater the success for each of us.

LAND PLANNERS.   Every real-estate investor and for that matter, just about anyone connected with real estate will feel the touch of the city, county or state land planning staff, at one time or another. My own experience in this direction is considerable. I have had the experience of making hundreds of presentations before planning boards and city commissioners on subjects that deal with planning and ordinance matters. I have found that the more knowledgeable the planner is about the needs of the real-estate investment community, the closer the two sides can work together. This book will be a unique tool to aid all land planners.

LAWYERS AND OTHER PROFESSIONAL ADVISORS.   Law, tax matters, accounting, and estate planning, just to name a few important factors that demand specialization, continue to become more and more complicated and diverse. No single person in any profession can be expected to know everything about his or her own field. That is why the best advisors read a lot. When it comes to matters dealing with real-estate techniques, FHA mortgages, wraparound mortgages, exchanges, including the Starker *tax-free* exchange and so many other complicated financing techniques, this book will become an extraordinarily useful resource. Scan the Table of Contents and you will quickly discover that this book will be indispensable to any transaction that deals with any aspect of real estate, both your clients' and your own portfolio.

Everyone has a need for this book. At present, you either own or rent. It is likely that in the near future you may make a change in your current status. When it comes time for you to sell, you will be faced with many decisions you need to make. Buyers are faced with many different kinds of decisions that can have a major impact on the future of their investments. Some of these decisions are shared by both buyer and seller, such as the tax basis of a new property, or the correct way to formulate a

Starker exchange so that the IRS will not disavow the 1031 tax-free exchange status. This book will help you make the right decision no matter what the problem is that faces you. For the senior population of America, one of the most important aspects that need be considered is the tax liability that we will be faced with in an ultimate sale, or in establishing an estate. This book deals with this aspect in detail, and gives you many different strategies that are designed to reduce or eliminate the tax you may otherwise pay in a sale. The IRS will not tell you that you could have legally avoided paying them all that tax, but this book will. Not only that, I will show you in clear-to-follow examples and checklists how to beat the IRS at its own game.

Very simply, *you should own this book*; it is an essential "cooking" book of real estate. It is filled with recipes for success.

Jack Cummings

Chapter 1

HOW REAL ESTATE INVESTING GOALS DIRECT FINANCING STRATEGIES

There are six simple and undeniable truths to success in real estate investing. They are:

THE SIX TRUTHS TO SUCCESS IN REAL ESTATE

1. Know what you want to accomplish: Your Goal.

2. Find the specific type of real estate that will take you to your goal: Your Vehicle.

3. Learn everything you can about that kind of property in the areas you want to own it: Mastering the Vehicle.

4. When you find the property that seems to meet your investment criteria, tie it up: Taking Action and Gaining Control.

5. When you have entered into a contract that binds the seller to terms you think will work for you, you spend time and effort to ascertain if this is truly the property for you to purchase: Due Diligence Period.

6. If you discover anything that suggests the property will not meet your goals, then either: Withdraw from the transaction, or adjust the price and/or terms to the point where the transaction will meet your original criteria: Final Decision Time.

While these six simple elements may appear to be very basic and overly simplified, they are a specific and important part of real estate financing. I can assure you that these six elements are so very important that they should be the essence of every chapter in any book written about real-estate investing.

THE ESSENCE OF ACCOMPLISHMENT

Ultimate success in real-estate investing depends on a clear focus of the desired result. As an example, the builder of hotels avoids being sidetracked to the green pastures of another category of real-estate development. Hotel development requires a very specific and dedicated approach to the economics that make that type of real-estate venture work. The same applies to rental apartment developers, shopping center developers, and so on.

In my thirty plus years as a broker and developer, I can attest to the fact that the truly successful investors are those who stay firmly within a narrow focus of interest and knowledge. They are the shopping center giants who do nothing but regional malls, or the rental apartment owners who dominate a local or national market. Size and importance of investment has little to do with this idea. The focus is directed to becoming an expert on the category of real estate where the investor wants to buy. For the rental home investor this means knowing what is available, what prices are offered, and how to deal with rental homes; then you will suddenly begin to see opportunity surfacing long before other, less knowledgeable investors recognize a good buy.

The trick is to recognize that real estate is universal in nature, but its trends are local. This paradox occurs because real estate is not as dependent on national trends as many investors believe. What causes real estate to go up or down in value is usually something that is occurring in or around the location of the real estate. This simple statement goes unnoticed to many thousands of would be real estate investors, to the great delight of those of us who are very dedicated real estate investors. This is an important factor in both the purchases and financing of real estate. For this reason, it is critical that you develop a system or operating procedure that allows you flexibility. With a set program you can move quickly and decisively when you recognize a property that fits your investment criteria.

HOW TO BE AT THE RIGHT PLACE AT THE RIGHT TIME

Just about every person has made the comment at one time or other, "Boy, that guy sure was lucky to be at the right place at the right time." Timing is very important to just about every decision you can make, and when it comes to investment decisions, timing is the most important aspect of the entire process. But for timing to work there must be the recognition of opportunity. Unless you see a way to reach for your goals the right time just never seems to come around. As for being at the right place, that is up to you. Your gold mine is likely to be found wherever you want to look for it; that is, if you truly want to take the time and effort to learn everything you can about the kind of property you want to buy.

THE BEST TIME AND PLACE ARE LOST WITHOUT ACTION

To benefit from being at the right place at the right time you must act. You must make a decision to move forward in a decisive way. For a pilot the act of taking off requires a decision to pull back on the yoke some time before arrival at the end of the runway. Fortunately, the real estate investor can act without having to make an all or nothing decision. But there is a right way and a wrong way to go, and unfortunately the vast majority of real estate buyers or sellers only think they are acting decisively. In reality they make decisions by default, or they spend time trying to decide what to do without having control over the situation. The key to having control over the situation is to get the other party to commit to a price and terms that seem to work for you. While they are bound to these terms you still are not firmly committed to the transaction.

Generally, you would be a buyer in this example. It will be up to you to discover the truth about the property and to make educated decisions accordingly. In real estate terms, you have a period of *due diligence*, where you can make inspections, make studies, and so on, whatever is essential for you to make a final decision. Should you buy or go back to the negotiating table and attempt to restructure the deal, or should you walk away from the transaction.

Timing plays its most important role in the step just prior to gaining control over the situation. Follow this example: You have made a decision that rental apartments are what you want to buy. Your goal is to own enough rental apartments to allow you to hire full outside management and to support the kind of lifestyle you want for yourself and your family. You have hired a good real estate lawyer, and a good tax accountant to advise you on those specific matters. Your lawyer has given you a good purchase agreement that allows for adjustment to different situations, but that covers all the possible due diligence you would want to accomplish. This means full property inspections. These inspections will include all building elements, such as plumbing, electrical, structural, roof, foundation, termites, radon gas, and most important of all, environmental problems. In addition to these situations you have the right to request a City Inspection. Most cities will send out a code enforcement inspector to decide if there are any building code violations. You will also want to check out all other governmental restrictions such as zoning, and possible limitations due to platting or possible building moratoriums. These situations require time to check out, and usually require some outside assistance, which you would need with the environmental inspections.

Time and money are spent in the accomplishment of these studies and they should be done only if you have the property locked up; that is, the Seller firmly tied into a deal while you spend the time and money to properly make a decision. You are armed with the knowledge that allows you to recognize a potential opportunity. This is the right place, now is the right time. You act by moving quickly to tie up the property. After all, if the property looks good to you, there may be other possible buyers who are about to come to the same conclusion. You act, and now that the property is in your control, you can spend the time and money to make your thorough inspections before making the final decision.

All of this assumes that you are acting with a goal in mind. A clearly seen goal is the destination to all your effort and will allow you, or force you to stay on the right road as you head toward the goal. Yet not all investors have the same result in mind, and your own goals are likely to vary over a period of time. Therefore, it is important to recognize that ownership structure and debt may also vary. These changes may allow goal adjustments without having to deviate from the actual type of property chosen in the first instance. Any specific property can help its owner attain different goals, depending on the structure of debt, and the terms of that debt. This chapter is designed to help you develop a clear understanding of the relationship between financing and the attainment of your financial goals, as they relate to real estate. Through this understanding you should be able to use the financing tools and techniques described in this book, to enhance your success in real estate investing.

All success must begin somewhere, and in real estate financing it begins with the Ten Goals of Financing. You will find that you can approach any problem using these ten goals to decide whether financing can provide a solution or direction to attain your specific goal. If, after reviewing each goal and applying them to a given situation to achieve a desired result, no benefit or clear direction can be obtained, you can stop looking to financing as the source of the solution.

To help you decide how to use financing as a purchase or sales tool, review the following ten goals of financing. As you continue through this book and learn the many different financing techniques, you will see how each technique benefits the buyer or seller in different ways, depending on how they are applied. The idea is to gain as much flexibility in moving closer to your desired investment goal or strategy.

THE TEN GOALS OF FINANCING AND WHAT THEY WILL DO

1. Enhance the value of a property.
2. Consolidate existing debt into more manageable debt.
3. Attract more "buyers" to a property for sale.
4. Increase the market potential of a property.
5. Increase the cash return from a marginal property.
6. Generate immediate cash that is often tax free.
7. Help solve tax problems.
8. Create tax-deferred transactions.
9. Open new doors for the investor to expand his or her investment portfolio.
10. Provide the professional touch to a good marketing plan.

Review each of these goals carefully. It is important to realize that the improper use of any financing tool can negate the positive result needed. It is important to look at all the different techniques that this book provides. You will be able to ascertain the best approach to solving the problem, and to attainment of the desired goal. The use of any technique for the sake of using that technique should be avoided if other financing tools are available that can improve the result.

1. ENHANCE THE VALUE OF A PROPERTY.   When properly used, financing can enhance the value of a property to the owner or buyer. From a buyer's standpoint, financing should provide the best terms that fit the ownership goals. These terms can vary between different owners and buyers, dependent solely on what they expect from that investment. It is possible that for one buyer or owner the best terms may be a high beginning interest rate that declines over the mortgage term. Another investor may find a mortgage with a deferred payment plan where either interest, or interest and principal are reduced during the initial payment term of the mortgage. A third investor may want to incorporate a land lease as part of the financing strategy for reasons that are unique to his or her situation. Whatever the situation, the amount of principal payments could be the same, the only difference may be the adjustment of when the actual payments are made and what they are called (principal, interest, rent, percent of gross sales, and so on). You should recognize that while the total payments may or may not vary for one party (either paying or receiving), the benefits or penalties can differ for the other party. Interest and rent may be tax deductible for the payer, but taxable as income for the receiver.

The term *value* is relative to the goal one wants to attain. From the Seller's point of view, the financing that attains the Seller's most important goal works best and establishes the highest value even if the monetary amount is less. If the Seller needed to attain the highest possible market price for tax or other reasons, the terms the seller provided to the buyer may soften the economic impact to counterbalance the high price. This could occur by a lower than market interest rate or another condition of the payback. Because the concept of *best value* is likely to differ between the parties, the method of financing used often helps bring the two parties together to maximize mutual benefits. The compromise aspect of negotiations is enhanced when each party has a wide range of options to view. The buyer or seller who has only one fixed agenda in drafting a contract, will not be as successful in attainment of his or her investment goals as the investor who has a strong understanding of the tools of finance. When the market is buyer driven, which is to say, a *Buyer's market*, the most important goals are the buyer's goals. On the other hand, when the market is strong and there are more buyers than sellers, then the seller can call the shots. In a *Seller's market*, the seller's goals receive the highest priority.

Usually the market is never clearly oriented to the buyer or the seller. Savvy investors understand this and no matter if they are buyers or sellers, they work to make the terms of the deal work for each party. Real insider buyers recognize the value of this well-worn adage: "I'll pay your price, if you'll take my terms." In other words, price can often be a fluctuating factor, solely dependent on the terms of the sale.

It should be clear that a property can be difficult to sell if the seller feels that he or she must receive all cash to effect the sale. There is, however, a potential market for the property at an all cash price. Yet the seller does not want to reduce the price to that level. This is a typical situation that often can be solved by a hard look at the seller's most important goals. By doing this, it may be possible that the original plan of action was not the best one to follow. In chapter two you will see more on this aspect of goal orientation and investment strategy achievement.

It is critical, as a Buyer, to realize that the importance of the cash to the seller may be more critical than the highest possible price. Yet, it is equally critical to recognize that some sellers will find their goals are better attained if they get less cash at closing, and a higher price. It is important for sellers to understand that there are reasons for this disparity in payment schedule, and in price determination. Often transactions are lost because none of the parties to the deal, buyer, seller or brokers, could grasp this truth. Therefore, using the tools of financing to solve their problems, all parties involved should look at the principal goals more closely. The final aspect of this goal is that the technique used enhances the idea of value that is important to the buyer and seller.

2. CONSOLIDATE EXISTING DEBT INTO MORE MANAGEABLE DEBT. Financing can be used to consolidate existing debt that is overburdening the owner of a property into a more manageable payment. The goal here is to reduce the total annual (or monthly) payment of the existing debt or the combination of all forms of debt on the property. When this is the desired result, it is necessary to examine the owner's or buyer's options. You may discover that by using one or more financing techniques you can obtain several potential solutions to the problem.

The simple refinancing of a property can work wonders in a market where interest rates have dropped. In this situation the owner or buyer may find the opportunity to convert a high-interest loan into a newer, more affordable loan. If there has been an increase in the value of the property, the added value may also provide the opportunity to increase the loan amount, without a reduction of the bottom line benefits of the property. For example, a buyer purchases a ten-unit apartment complex for $500,000. There is an existing first mortgage of $250,000 with an annual debt service of $41,240 (principal and interest as would result with a 12-year term at 13% interest). The buyer obtains a new loan of $350,000 payable over a 20-year term at 8.75% interest. The new annual payment on the new mortgage would be $37,117.50.

Two important things have happened in the above example. First, the investor has obtained an additional $100,000 over the previous debt, which could be used to pay off other debt. Interestingly, that other debt might have been the down payment needed to give to the seller. Secondly, by refinancing at a lower overall payment, additional cash flow has resulted. This additional cash in the pocket of $4,122.50 ($41,240.00 less $37,117.50) may be the single element that makes this transaction work. An important benefit in this transaction is that the additional $100,000 comes to the mortgagor tax free.

Consolidation of debt extends beyond real estate investing and should be an important part of anyone's personal financial planning. We live in an age of high credit charges. It is not very smart to carry high credit card or installment loan interest rates. Such rates can exceed 18%. This is not a good idea when you have the potential of refinancing your real estate through more modest rates. In the early 90s there was a rash of refinancing going on. It was not uncommon for people to have refinanced their homes several times between 1989 and 1997. A small spread in interest rates may not produce any real savings. You must look at the overall picture to see if there is any real benefit.

The interest rates are not the only criteria to examine when you are looking into total debt payments. You may owe on several different loans at various repayment terms. The most specific item to note is the combined constant rate of payment of the loans. The term *constant rate of payment* is used within the lending industry, and you should become aware of what it is and how it is used. In Chapter 3, I provide you with details of how to use the constant rate of payment in analyzing mortgage situations.

Consolidation of debt has many different benefits as you will see as you combine its effects with some different financing tools illustrated in this book. The key to using any of the consolidation techniques is to make sure that you keep your ultimate goal in clear focus. For example, if you simply want to reduce your monthly debt payments that currently satisfy several loans (home, car, credit card company, and so on), you could consider refinancing your home to produce the added cash to retire all outstanding loans. This may look attractive at first, but it is important that you look at other alternatives. One of the most basic forms of reduction of debt payments, that is the most overlooked, is to pay off the overburdening debt. Instead of refinancing to pay off the debt, where you simply extend your current debt by a period of time, you dig down deeply into your pockets and pay what you owe. From a financial point of view this may be nothing more than sound economic practice. In essence, do not overextend your ability to pay debt.

This is often easier said than done, and once you are in the trap of consumer debt (high interest rates), the solution can be hard to come by. The critical point to consider in any form of consolidation is to take a hard look at how the remedy will affect your long-term goals. If a longer payback at lower interest rates benefits you in comparison to paying off debt, then the proper thing to do is to look to consolidation. On the other hand, a very low rate existing loan may be kept in place if the new real estate loan that replaces it produces a greater payback, even if the monthly payments seem lower. For example, you have a total of $20,000 in short-term consumer loans at an interest rate of 18%. At the same time you owe $120,000 on a first mortgage on your home, at 7.5% interest per annum. If current new rates on real estate loans are higher than your present 7.5%, say 9.5%, you would not find any benefit to a refinance and consolidation of the two debts. This would be the situation even though the consumer debt was more than double the interest rate of the potential of your new loan. Review the current payments: Interest on the $20,000 consumer loan is 18% of $20,000 or $3,600 per year. Interest payment on the real estate loan is 9.5% or $9,000. This gives you a total current interest obligation of $12,600. If you refinanced, with the idea to consolidate your debt, so that you could cover your loan cost, and then pay off the existing consumer loan, you may discover that your new loan balance is $141,500 ($120,000 existing loan, and $20,000 consumer loan, and $1,500 in loan origination cost and out of pocket). If the interest rate on this new loan was 9.5% then your interest cost the first year would be over $13,000. The general result is not favorable. On the other hand, if the $20,000 is due now, or there is some other pressing need for cash, refinancing, even if it increases the previous payment schedule may be the only solution. If this is the case, you should review all the different possible refinancing tools available to you. You must look at the total picture.

KEY POINTS TO USING CONSOLIDATION TECHNIQUES

- There is a need to reduce existing debt payments through the refinancing of any or all of the existing debt so that the total future payments will not exceed those payments under the old finance situation.

- There is an inability to meet current debt payments, and refinancing is the only way to meet the current payments, though the total payments will exceed those of the current debt structure.

- The property is not readily marketable with the present financing structure. A change in this situation through refinancing may provide a more favorable result in the marketplace.

- A cash-out situation is needed in which the owner can mortgage above the present financing levels and put cash in his or her pocket. This must be done so that the property will not become overburdened.

- There is the immediate need to create cash, and no other option is viable at the present.

There are many ways to consolidate existing financing. Almost any form of financing will lend itself to consolidation of an existing debt. Naturally, some forms of financing will give better results than others.

3. ATTRACT MORE "BUYERS" TO A PROPERTY FOR SALE.   One of the major aspects of financing is the ability to make property more salable. This goal may seem to be the same as Goal 1, but through a careful analysis of the former you will see some very important, though subtle differences.

In the real-life approach to the sale of real estate, creative financing may be the only way to take a property that is difficult to sell into the marketplace. The actual contract of sale may contain more than one form of financing to bring the buyer and seller together. For example, consider a sale then lease-back. Here the seller holds secondary financing (with or without additional security for the lease). This reduces the buyer's risk and is an example of multiple techniques that can be used to simplify the sale. In this and every other situation, the goals of both the buyer and the seller are weighed, then balanced on which is the most critical to solve.

Even great properties are difficult to sell because of high interest rates in the finance market or low buyer demand. In these circumstances the seller must find techniques to make his or her property stand out as a property that is both attractive, and affordable. For example, to get the buyer in the door of a model apartment or home, it is not unusual for a builder to offer mortgage financing at well below the marketplace interest rate and at attractive principal pay-back for the first several years of the mortgage. Once the buyer has been attracted to the property, the buyers may discover, (or be led down the path by the seller) that if they can pay more cash up front they can get a better price (use of the first goal).

We are all accustomed to the leader ad that brings us to the store. Financing terms attract buyers to cars, computers and homes. The importance, when it comes to real estate, is that you recognize that when the seller offers great terms, that this is a seller who understands the concept of good marketing. This is the right kind of seller to be, and to deal with, if you are a buyer.

In commercial real estate there are many different techniques that can be offered that look more attractive than they actually are. If you keep your own goal firmly in focus you can be more likely to stick to the techniques that take you closer to your goal rather than farther away. The key to this is to keep your goal clearly in your mind and not to deviate from any technique that will lead you away from the ideal. While you may give in or compromise in the end, it is best to leave that concession to the final moment. You should attempt to visualize the entire deal before you need to learn exactly where to make compromises.

4. INCREASE THE MARKET POTENTIAL OF A PROPERTY.   This is another seller-oriented financing goal. Here, the goal is to expand the market potential of the property, which is more than just making the property more salable. It is possible, of course, that by doing one you will also do the other. Review the following case study.

Mr. Wallace wanted to sell his 25-unit apartment house for a price of $500,000. He had an opportunity to buy another property in another town and needed the cash for that purpose. The price he was asking was within the market range with a net operating income (NOI is gross rents less operating expenses, which do not include any debt service) of $53,000 out of a gross rent roll of $76,000. However, the city was about to launch a major road and sewer project right in front of the apartment house, and it was likely that the apartment complex would lose all of its tenants for part of the year. Once the work was finished there would be a newly planted median with wide sidewalks where none had previously existed. This kind of improvement could cause the value of the apartment complex to quickly recover if not increase.

For Mr. Wallace, the approach to his first goal (to sell the property) was to find a solution to the pending problem of the loss of tenants. A simple answer was for Mr. Wallace to indemnify a potential buyer for any possible loss of revenue during the construction period. This was accomplished by establishing a format for a sale and lease-back for one year. Wallace became the master tenant, with the existing tenants his subtenants. By assuming the risk for the year during which the road work was to take place, the seller was taking no greater risk than if he put the building up for sale and was unable to sell it during the same time period. As the specific need of the seller was to sell the building, holding onto the building was a hardship that he could not afford to take as he was sure to lose the opportunity to buy the other property. By offering an indemnity a buyer would not suffer from any loss of tenants, and Wallace would only be liable for any lost rent. Wallace calculated that the most rent he would have to make up would be around $40,000. If he cut the monthly rent to the tenants he felt that some of them would tough out the construction mess. Thus far, the goal served was to help make the property salable. Now the task was to increase the market potential for the property.

To this end, Mr. Wallace could have taken a number of directions. Keep in mind that one form of increasing the market potential of a property is to make it available to more ready, willing, and able buyers. As seller of the apartment building, Mr. Wallace could have turned the building into a condominium or a cooperative apartment building, seeking twenty-five different buyers at much reduced prices. It is likely that in some market areas this has been the direction that many sellers have taken, producing a greater sales price than would have been realized had the building been sold to a single investor.

Another way to increase market potential is to be more flexible in the terms one is willing to accept in the sale of the property. By the way, this flexibility is difficult for many sellers to attain because they have not properly established their own investment goals. If you have clear goals and know exactly where you want to be at any given time in the relatively near future, and you constantly review those goals, you will begin to realize that it is the attainment of the goals that is important, not the attainment of any specific terms of a sale.

Let's go back to our apartment-building seller, Mr. Wallace. If part of his long-term goal was to retire to the mountains of North Carolina with a nice cabin and 10 acres of apple trees, he might look for an exchange that would take him directly to that goal. It is possible that somewhere in the North Carolina mountains there is a property owner who would like to own the Wallace apartment complex.

No matter what Mr. Wallace's long-term goal is, by viewing it clearly he will begin to see that there are additional "things" to help him entice more buyers to his apartment building. At the same time, these "things" or avenues to approach, would accomplish the critical task of "getting rid of the apartment building" while moving Mr. Wallace closer to his long-term goals.

By utilizing Internal Revenue Code 1031, a buyer or seller may enter into an agreement that will have more specific benefits than a more conventional transaction because of the reduced tax liability to one or more of the parties. This option is open to you only if you know how it works and how it fits into your goals. A later chapter in this book will illustrate the strategic moves you can make as a buyer or seller (or broker) to use the IRC 1031 to obtain marvelous benefits.

Mr. Wallace decided that another available option was to reduce the amount of cash needed to take control of the property. With his accountant, he worked up an attractive package that, when coupled with the sale lease-back technique, would allow a buyer with little cash to purchase the property. This technique enticed more buyers and produced the desired results of selling the property.

5. INCREASE THE RETURN ON CASH INVESTED IN INCOME PROPERTIES. This goal is usually the most important goal for owners or potential buyers of income property. Due to its importance to buyers, it also becomes important criteria of *market appeal* to sellers. The potential effect of financing on cash flow can be very important to the ultimate success in the sale of a property. For example, consider an office building that is free and clear of any debt. The NOI (gross income less operating expenses), is $100,000. If the current market for such properties required that the invested capital give the buyer an 11% return, then an all cash purchase price would require the buyer to come up with $909,090 in cash. In essence, the return on the cash invested ($909,090 would be 11% per annum). Now consider the effect of financing. Assume the buyer could borrow (or the seller arrange for it as a part of the offering package) new financing on the property of $800,000 at a constant rate (the combined rate which is interest and principal repayment) of 10% interest per annum. Now there would be a debt service of $80,000 deducted from the NOI giving a CASH flow of $20,000. The resulting $20,000 is the return that the investor would obtain on his or her investment of $109,090. ($909,090 less the new debt of $800,000 = $109,090). A $20,000 return on an investment of $109,090 is a return of 18% per annum.

When cash flow is the desired effect, the investors goal is to maximize immediate return, instead of equity build up, or other benefits; then an increase of cash flow will appeal to that investor. All things being equal, a cash oriented buyer will pay more for a property that produces a greater cash flow, whereas an equity motivated buyer will adjust financing (on this same deal) to maximize debt pay-off and equity enhancement. The bottom line, which is so important to most investors, is clearly a function of the kind of financing that is placed on the property.

If local or currently available financing is not viable at the best rate or terms, the ultimate payments would reduce the potential cash flow that the investor could realize. This would dictate more creative measures might be necessary for the seller to sell the property.

Most creative financing tricks learned by real estate investors are designed to soften the overall blow of the property debt. There was a time, not so long ago, when it was deemed that the ideal situation for an investor was when the investor could buy a property without putting up any of his or her own money. This use of OPM (other peoples money) would create a deal that was 100% financed, or at least 100% purchased, without the buyer digging around for cash.

Before you jump to conclusions that such a transaction can be counterproductive to your healthy attitude about buying or selling real estate this way, let me state that buying real estate without putting up any cash is not difficult to do. The hard part is being able to make money doing it. In any city in the world there are sellers of real estate who would gladly accept a solid promise of payment as a down payment to a property that they could not sell, or that was grossly overpriced. Let this statement be a warning to you before you rush out and invest in a quick way to fame and riches as promised by some promoters of their Investment Programs.

As the goal to increase cash flow from marginal properties serves the buyer best, it is essential that you recognize that buying from a seller who is inflexible and who only wants cash over his or her existing mortgage, may not give you much room to be creative. In these circumstances, and assuming that, as a buyer you want that property and none other, it may be that the brick wall in the way of the deal is that the seller is ignorant of the benefits of creative financing. As a broker I have had to educate many sellers to the benefits of using sound economic investment planning that saved them money, time and produced the desired result: the sale of their property. This is important for every potential seller to review, because there are important tax and reinvestment criteria that should be considered. Buyers and/or brokers often must help in the learning process of stubborn sellers.

Investors will look for sellers who are flexible and with whom the investor can mix and match one or more of the techniques that will be discussed in detail within this book.

6. GENERATE IMMEDIATE CASH THAT IS OFTEN TAX FREE.   Often this goal is overlooked. Since the principal owed in existing mortgages may decline over the

years, and the value of the property may increase, generally it is possible to refinance and obtain additional cash after repayment of the old loan. This becomes very attractive when this can be accomplished without affecting the cash flow on a property. For example, the mortgage payment for $150,000 over 15 years at 9 $1/_2$% per annum is $1,554 per month. If a new mortgage can be obtained at 10 $1/_2$% per annum but the term is 25 years, the same payment of $1,554 would allow the owner to get $179,275. This would produce $29,275 (less loan costs) in immediate cash. Naturally, if the interest rate was lower the benefits for refinancing would be greater.

While this may not appear to be dramatic, if cash is essential at that moment of need, the opportunity to get cash and use cash may be worth the increased term and interest in the debt payment. While the amount paid each month has not increased and in fact remains the same, the investor has an additional ten years to make those same payments at his or her cost to get ready cash. This would add $186,480 to the total payment (the last ten years of the 25-year term total this amount). However, this sum could be offset by the yield or need for the $29,275 gained now.

When a borrower obtains money through financing, such as getting a loan from the local savings and loan association, there may be no income tax liability on that money. In essence, the money was not "earned" but borrowed. The borrower can in many circumstances renew loans from time to time, increasing amounts borrowed as the values of the real estate go up, pulling out capital that is tax free, at least for the moment. When the borrower ultimately sells the property an adjustment would be made to determine what amount of the loan still outstanding exceeded the basis (book value) of the property. This excess would be treated as earned income at that time and taxed accordingly. Under present IRS rules the real estate investor is able to deduct the interest paid on many real estate loans, which makes this technique a very positive aspect to real estate investing. For example, if you refinanced a property you had depreciated down to $100,000 but was actually valued by the lender at $500,000, you might be able to borrow $350,000 or more on that property. If the actual loan was $350,000, your loan is $250,000 more than your book value, or depreciated basis. If you sold the property for $500,000 any time prior to repayment of the loan to a level below your basis, the IRS will calculate that the excess funds are now taxable. This may not be a problem; however, it needs to be considered before you end up selling at a down payment that does not provide sufficient cash to pay your tax. If you sold for $500,000 and took a $50,000 down payment, and held onto the balance in the form of a wraparound mortgage, you would think you had an installment sale with no tax to pay on principal except as it is paid back to you. Wrong. As your loan of $350,000 was $250,000 over basis, and tax free at the time of the loan, it becomes taxable the year you close the sale. Your tax liability on this borrowed money could be over $75,000.

Your use of financing to produce cash in a transaction will depend on your ultimate goals and what it is that you are trying to accomplish at the time you desire this cash. As you learn more of the creative techniques of financing, you will discover that getting cash in refinancing is not always the most productive or best route to take. For example, in this book you will discover a technique called *pyramiding*. With it, you will be able to take the cash needed to buy property from the first property you own by giving the seller of the second property a second mortgage on the first property. You will do this, and variations thereon, at interest rates well below those offered by the institutional lenders in your marketplace.

7. HELP SOLVE TAX PROBLEMS.   This goal serves two masters: the buyer and the seller. When you use a form of financing to solve a tax problem, you often create a problem for the other party to the transaction. It is at this time that the most critical item that comes into play is the motivation of the parties. If the most motivated party is the seller and his or her goals are better met by selling the property, the transaction may be slanted to the buyer in tax benefits and still be able to close. On the other hand, if the most motivated party is the buyer, there may be an opportunity for the seller to find additional solutions to his or her tax problems. On some occasions, both parties can gain benefits from careful review of the transaction and the tax laws.

The items to review will vary, depending on the circumstances and needs of the parties. However, there are ten items that should be part of your checklist when either buying or selling real estate. A review of each item with careful attention to your own goals and circumstances will aid you in determining if there are any tax advantages you need to consider prior to either making the offer or at least prior to closing.

THE TAX ADVANTAGES CHECKLIST

- What items are to be depreciated within the investment property? Buyers generally want maximum values established; sellers often want lower values set. In exchanges, both parties may want to have the depreciable items considered with different base values.

- Should you take title to land and building and personal property equally? There are advantages to taking it differently if it fits your circumstances.

- On what date should you close? This can have a specific advantage to one party or both if the date can be split between two tax years.

- How should an option payment be established? This can create cash to the seller that is not taxed right away and can be highly effective in nailing down a deal.

- Review the advantages of the wraparound mortgage, as it might apply to the transaction contemplated.

- In an IRC 1031 exchange, should the property be directed against the land, the building, or both?

- What are the one-time capital gains exclusions available to you under the current tax laws?

- If the seller is to hold financing, should part of the down payment include the maximum advance interest allowed by the IRS? (The maximum allowed as of this writing is the interest that would be earned during the balance of the year.)

- Should the buyer buy the property or the personal interest in a corporation or trust that owns the property? This and similar questions about form of ownership can give the investor a lot to think about when he or she buys so as to establish the best form of selling interest.

8. CREATE TAX-DEFERRED TRANSACTIONS.   Sometimes, the only major benefit from a financing technique might be to pass on the possible tax consequence to some future date. There are, of course, other nonfinance options available to the investor that may have similar results. The idea is to examine what benefit the investor or the seller may have and at what cost. For example, if the technique used by a buyer was to acquire a property by entering into a long-term lease with an option to buy, the seller would not have a capital gain tax to pay until the sale took place. If part of the rent paid was *option money* that was paid each year or month to the seller to keep alive the option to buy, and part of that money was to be applied toward the ultimate purchase, it is possible that some or all of the option money would not be taxed as income or as capital gain until the sale actually took place no matter how many years in the future that was.

In the IRC 1031 exchange, which is covered in detail in this book, it is possible to have a lifetime of investing and still not trigger any capital gains tax; with an installment sale provision you can sell a property and only pay the gains tax on the portion of the actual gain you get, and in the year you get it. Both the exchange and the installment sale allow creative tax planning, and as with any provision that deals with the Internal Revenue Codes you must make sure that you have gotten the most recent up-to-date advice possible. All IRS rules and regulations are subject to change and different interpretations to what appear to be similar transactions. While this often intimidates people, you should not let the fear of the IRS stand in your way for using totally legal and often creative means to build or keep your wealth.

Keep in mind that many techniques have an effect on the benefits of real estate and change the long-range tax, which may be payable at some time in the future. The more you know about your own tax consequences and your future goals, the better you will be at using the laws and finance tools to your best advantage.

9. OPEN NEW DOORS FOR THE INVESTOR TO EXPAND HIS OR HER INVESTMENT PORTFOLIO.   As a real-estate investor, you would learn quickly that profit in real estate is not a function of buying real estate. It depends on use and utility of the property and the final disposition of the property.

This signifies that to be successful in real-estate investing, you will benefit the most when the complete plan fits the goal. You will not succeed in investing by buying this and/or that without knowing what to do with the property after you have acquired it. There is no doubt that with sound study of the area and with the development of expertise you could recognize opportunities that other people would overlook. Soon you will be able to take advantage of those properties. In those cases, the use or utility of the property is simply that of a good sound investment spawn out of your unique knowledge in the area and your grasp of the opportunity.

The more you understand about the tools of financing the better equipped you will become to use them to expand your portfolio. In developing your knowledge, you are reducing your risk in the investment game. Some of the benefits of finance are to assist in the sale or disposition of property. Through your knowledge of these tools you will move through your portfolio to other properties and investments.

Risk, which will be discussed in greater detail throughout this book, is similar to the term *value*. Both risk and value are relative to the investor's ability and capability. Savvy investors make things look easy because they recognize opportunity, therein reducing or removing the aspect of risk. They create value because they know what they want, and where they are going.

10. PROVIDE THE PROFESSIONAL TOUCH TO A GOOD MARKETING PLAN. In selling your most difficult property, the maximum appeal to the marketplace and the maximizing of your goals will be in covering all possible bases. Investors who look after details are generally the most successful investors. Your devotion to the use of the tools of finance will demand that you anticipate your ultimate marketing plan, which should include various financing approaches to suit the probable investors who will buy your property.

When the time comes for you to "need" heavy financing for a large transaction or the development of some upcoming project you have been wanting to build, success could well depend on your past history of dealing with lenders.

KNOW THE LIMITATIONS OF THE TOOLS OF FINANCING

The preceding ten goals are the keys to your use of financing as a problem solver. Yet from time to time there will be situations that you cannot solve by using any of the financing techniques. In fact, at best you will simply maintain the status quo by using these tools. In the worst case you can ruin the property and the investment by applying the wrong technique.

The knowledge that you develop of the financing techniques covered in this book cannot be considered absolute. There will be many tips and suggestions to help you expand your knowledge, and you should recognize that there is no single source of knowledge in any field.

In the chapters to come, I will approach many of the techniques by reviewing their advantages and their disadvantages to the buyer and seller of any property. In your review of these different points of view, you should ask yourself how you would approach a particular technique in your own circumstances. If you are reviewing this book to brush up on some of these techniques in anticipation of some specific transaction you are trying to nail down, I recommend that you also review the Table of Contents to spark additional recollections of other techniques as well.

It is rare for a real estate investor to use any single technique offered, countered, or refined into the final document of sale. One party buys hoping to have made the best investment possible, and another sells with a similar hope in mind. Each party to the transaction may have still held onto a card that he would have thrown into the pot to sweeten the transaction were it necessary. But no more cards were required, so the deal stands as executed.

Here are some important points to remember when approaching a situation that you feel may be solved with one of the financing techniques covered in this book:

FIVE TIPS TO SOLVING REAL-ESTATE FINANCING NEEDS OR PROBLEMS

1. At least one of the ten goals described in this chapter should be met for financing to have any real benefit to the parties involved.

2. Different points of view will be held by the buyer and the seller in their interpretation of these goals. The results of the form of financing used often will affect these two parties differently.

3. Theories that work on paper are valid only if they work in real life. Remember, there often are many parties to a transaction even when only two or three are apparent. The visible ones are the buyer and seller, and often the broker. The not-so-visible ones are the lawyers, wives, boyfriends, bankers, bartenders, and so on, each party having some relationship to the deal. Each party has to be dealt with when he or she impedes on the desired results of a transaction.

4. To achieve constant success in real-estate investing stay as close to your long-range goals as possible. Since so much does depend on this goal-setting ability, I have provided a detailed chapter on goal setting and development of your comfort zone. Each chapter will become a foundation to your future as a real estate investor.

5. If your role in the game of financing is that of a real-estate broker, you will have the added burden of acting as fiduciary in the transaction. However, you will also have the advantage in the investment game and will find that all of the techniques covered in this book will become useful tools in helping your clients buy and sell properties.

Chapter 2

HOW TO SET GOALS FOR SUCCESSFUL REAL-ESTATE INVESTING

The importance of setting your own investment goals is critical to getting the maximum benefit out of your time and effort. Once you have your goals firmly established, every decision you make about your investments will be directed to one ultimate result: the attainment of your goals. As real estate financing has an immediate as well as a long-term effect on those investments, clear goals will help you select the best financing tool to get the most out of the investment. Because the actual goal selection process is important, I have devoted an entire chapter to this topic.

A WORD OF CAUTION ABOUT GOAL SETTING

Proper goal setting is difficult. It should not be contemplated halfheartedly, but instead should be given thought and deliberation. Your goals should come under constant review, and you should not hesitate to alter or revise your goals once you are sure they need changing. Resist however, the urge to make a change in a goal just because you are having difficulty reaching it. It could be that the method you are following is either lacking in some foundation, or you are moving in the wrong direction although the goal is a good one.

The fact that you may set goals does not ensure success or happiness. Some people attain wealth and happiness without having gone through any specific goal-setting process. Yet, motivation within these people often is at a very high level. While they may not have made a conscious effort to set goals, they often are driven by high ideals or are out to prove something to someone.

Having said that, if you take a look at the truly successful people around you, or in the news, you will find one trait that links them all. The ability to stay focused on a task at hand. The kind of focus I am talking about allows the person to have an actual vision of what the end results will be. This is not easy and is not something people are born with. It requires work and self-confidence. You will discover that your level of self-confidence will begin to climb once you start setting goals which you then attain.

The kind of goal setting that I refer to relates to the prudence of setting your priorities straight. You would not get much out of training to be an Olympic swimmer by spending all your energy on the ski slopes. It is the same with any business or investing arena. A computer designer needs to establish his or her foundation that will build to the desired end result that person is shooting for. A real-estate investor needs to set a foundation of knowledge and experience in much the same way, but directed to a different topic and different end result in mind.

Time management, the acts that will be required of you to achieve the most efficient task at the time to attain the desired results, depends on your knowing what the desired results should be. The goal of this chapter is to help you find and set goals that will work for you. Keep in mind that the progression of setting goals is a multiple-step process.

BEFORE YOU CAN GET TO YOUR DESTINATION YOU MUST MAKE THE DECISION OF WHERE YOU WANT TO GO

It's similar to going on vacation by car. You have to make the following determinations:

1. Do you actually want to get down the road?
2. Do you know where you want to go?
3. Do you have some mode of transportation in mind?
4. Do you know how to drive that vehicle?
5. Do you have the staying power, both physical and economic, to keep it on the road?
6. Do you have the willpower to avoid being detoured from your desired destination?
7. Will you recognize when you have arrived at your destination?
8. Will you set new destinations and start over again?

The foregoing sequence should be easy to follow. It is all a matter of goal setting and then formulating the plan to get you to your goals. It starts with the selection of the destination. Let's begin there.

DEVELOP A VISION OF THE FUTURE

In one of my all-day seminars, I go through the following session with the audience. Read over the following material and then let your own mind take over. Better yet, have someone read this section to you.

Get comfortable. Find everything about your position that is not comfortable and change it. Then, when you feel you have a comfortable position, tense every muscle in your body in any random order that works for you, then return to that comfortable position. Do this for about ten minutes, then relax. Now close your eyes and have someone read the following to you.

I want you to clean the slate in your mind. I want you to think only about the things I tell you to think of, remembering things from your past only to make the scenes I describe be more vivid to you.

Erase the mixture of colors in your mind, just as a child would wipe the blackboard with a dusty eraser. Now, all you see is that misty white slate; a white mist fills your mind. Unlike dusty chalk the mist is cool, damp, like a friendly fog rolling in off a calm lake.

You will relax even more now. See the cool, fresh-smelling milky white fog in your mind as it changes from the white on the blackboard to a misty morning. You are somewhere where it is cool and pleasant, you are very relaxed, your mind very clear, and you now see clearly that the mist is over a lake or pond. The water is very still, and you are very relaxed. You are thinking at this very moment how relaxed you are. You are very relaxed.

You are actually in a time machine, and you are passing ahead into the future. Somewhere below as you are flying through this cool, pleasant mist you see things going on. It's as though you are in the clouds and cannot quite see what is going on below you.

It is clearing now and you realize that you are beginning to see where you are. You look around within your mind. You see yourself and you note on the wall there is a calendar. The date is nearly ten years into the future. You look around and see what is going on.

Take careful note as to what you are doing, who you are with, where you are. What kind of clothes do you have on? When you are satisfied that you can fully describe the setting, you will return to the mist and return to the present.

When I finish this, I let the audience relax for a few minutes. Then I ask several of them to describe to me, and to the audience, what it was they saw.

When you look into your future like this, you have the tendency to see your own self-image of your future. To some degree, it might be the dream of what you would want, or hopes for the future. These are the natural goals that live within you. Like computer programs that can be altered, these goals may well be the default parameters that drive you.

The critical part of these visions are that they are not accepted by you as goals but as dreams. For some people, these visions are not pleasant at all, as if some more dramatic force were taking them into the future without much hope, without much self-esteem.

VISUALIZING THE FUTURE IS ESSENTIAL TO SOUND GOALS

An athlete knows the power of visualizing winning. The runner who is able to demonstrate that she "sees" herself winning can demoralize her opponent. Likewise, the salesperson who "sees" the sale being closed and assumes that his or her efforts will be rewarded knows that his or her success in selling will be increased. So it is with goals. If you can't clearly see the end result, you may never attain the desired goals, or at best you will not attain them with the ease and satisfaction that will come through goal setting.

Are Your Goals Realistic?

Proper goal setting is critical because it is easy to "see" the wrong future. You must realize and accept the fact that you can change your self-image, and can set your own goals. You are not bound by the vision you first saw when you looked into the milky mist.

Is What You See What You Want?

In this vision, there are elements that you will want to work on. It is critical that you constantly recall this vision because you will be making changes as you get closer to it. However, the most important aspect to pay attention to is the vision, and not the specifics as to how you got to the vision.

Most people have the wrong concept about goals, and when they set them they look more to the mode of transportation rather than to the destination itself. For example, if your vision is of you and your family living on an island paradise with dozens of close friends around you at all times with nothing to do but lounge around, the first element you would establish as your goal would be the money it will take to buy this lifestyle. Money is the mode of transportation, not the destination. The goal of having lots of money, "I want to be a multimillionaire," is an improper goal as it directs you to the vehicle of transport rather than to the items you think money will buy.

Mind you, money and the desire for it are very strong motivators and can drive many people so strongly that they get money but little else. It is far better for you to understand that there are people so motivated, and to use their motivation to your own benefit. Money is relative and its worth changes. The amount of money you think it might take to attain your goals can be much more than your goal requires.

To understand this last statement, you need only look at what has happened to the value of money in some countries. If you were looking into your own vision twenty years ago in Turkey, your concept of the amount of money needed to become "independent" would just about buy you breakfast today. In the early 1930s in Germany, boxes of money wouldn't buy you the boxes the money was in.

The best goals then are those that follow these guidelines:

TIPS TO HELP YOU SET THE RIGHT KIND OF GOALS

1. Define your goals in terms of what you want to attain, where you want to be, what kind of lifestyle you want to live. Avoid establishing a monetary value to either the effort or the results. The money aspect of goal setting will play its part later on.

2. Make sure that your goals fit into your abilities or the abilities you plan to attain. It should be obvious that if your vision has you doing heart transplants and you are not yet out of high school, you have a lot of work ahead of you and you must plan accordingly.

3. Goals should be set in stages. You will have to establish these visions in increments of future time zones. In other words, the greater the distance you put between now and your first vision, the tougher it will be to attain that goal. It is far better to establish deadlines that are closer together and work for those intermediate goals, attain them and move on toward the greater goal down the road. For example, for a car trip to the West Coast from New York City, you want to know exactly where you want to go (say, Beverly Hills, not just California), but equally important you want to know where you need to stop for gas along the way, and where you plan to stop for the night. Investing, just like this car trip, will come easier if you do not push either. Plan ahead, and attain each step along the way before going on to the next. If it takes a bit longer to get halfway, don't worry about it; after all, you have already attained that part of the goal, and that is worth your own pat on your back before you move forward.

4. Accept the fact that *failure is essential to success*. This is important because it is a realistic view of life. You have to plan for setbacks so that when they occur you will be able to move on without becoming disillusioned about your ultimate success. Learn by your failures to the extent that you review your own goals to make sure they are attainable. Remember that if your goals are too distant, it is very difficult to be able to find the opportunity to adjust in midstream. Failure is not the opposite of success.

5. Continue to "fine-tune" your vision of yourself in the future. This will be a constant ongoing process. The clearer your vision, the easier it will be to attain that image. You will modify and enhance the goals as you advance toward them.

6. Be so specific that you can write down the significant elements of your goals as you visualize them. This is important because it will later give you proof that you have attained your goals. Nothing is better for your self-esteem than the personal satisfaction of attaining something you have set out to obtain. The written-down evidence is important because it is too easy to remember a goal slightly less than or greatly more than its actual realization. Some people always believe they are right on target when they are way off base, and others continually fail because they are too harsh on themselves. Be honest with yourself and write down the goal.

7. When you have attained the goal, celebrate. You will enjoy the success more this way and let these moments offset the moments of failure you are bound to encounter along the way.

HOW YOUR GOALS WILL HELP YOU PROPERLY FINANCE YOUR REAL-ESTATE INVESTMENTS

Let's tie everything together and make sure we keep the continuity of goals with the concept of using the tools of real estate finance to make for better real estate financing.

As you develop goals, you will begin to visualize how the other side of the forest should look, even while you are still deep in the woods. This ability allows you to anticipate what you will need to do, what abilities you will have to attain, and just how much money you may need to accomplish the current and upcoming tasks. You will also begin to see other ways to obtain your desired goals without using cash.

Let me give you an illustration of how this can work for you. Assume that you are a "fresh-out-of-law-school" graduate who has just started to work for some big law firm in Miami, Florida. You have worked hard to get where you are at the moment, and you want to build a future for yourself using all of your abilities. This includes taking the plunge into real estate investing.

Examine All of Your Abilities

One of the first stages in setting your goals is to look at exactly what you are good at and what you might want to be good at (and therefore could take a course to learn). As a budding lawyer, you might have made the following list:

ABILITIES

1. Good at law.
2. Can study well.
3. Know and enjoy working around the garden.
4. Have painted inside and outside houses before.

5. Can come up with $10,000 in cash to invest.
6. Can carry a moderate mortgage (rent?) payment of $1,000 per month.
7. Have a high energy level.
8. Have weekends partially free for other self-investment work.
9. Want to specialize in real-estate law.
10. Need to develop contacts in all real-estate areas for my legal work.

As the list is being composed, your mind is running on the back lot side of the fence. When the abilities list is completed, you begin to look at your liabilities.

LIABILITIES

1. Have to be very conservative because of the new job and lack of security.
2. Can only spend a few hours per weekend to look for or keep up investments.
3. Have car payments.
4. Have a six-month lease I can't get out of.

Once these two elements have been taken care of, you then sit back and let yourself be immersed into that milky-white substance of the clearing of the mind. You work on your vision for several weeks and decide that your destination in about ten years is to:

WANTS

1. Own your own office building and law practice.
2. Own your own home, somewhere in the Boca Raton area.
3. Have a forty-foot (or better) sailboat.
4. Be financially set for life.

In a review of these four goals, you notice that you have not been specific enough concerning the levels of debt that might occur. Owning an office building, home, sailboat, and being set for life are relative to how much you want to owe (in order to buy them) and what you mean by "set for life." So you sharpen your pencil and come up with these more specific goals:

FINE-TUNING GOALS OUT OF WANTS

1. Owning an office building where you can have your own offices without expense, sufficient income to support any debt on the building, and a minimum of a current market rate return on your cash invested.
2. Own a home on the water in Boca Raton where you can dock your boat and own the home free of any debt.

3. Own a forty-foot sailboat free of any debt.

4. Have sufficient "outside" income to support all insurance needs, and all costs to keep and maintain a home.

On the Way to Setting Intermediate Goals

Once the revised goals are established, you can set your intermediate goals to guide you along the way. These intermediate goals may include a number of items that may not be necessary at first, but may at the outset go down on the list. Your preliminary list of steps to attain your goals could look like this:

STEPS TO ATTAIN GOALS

1. Need to build a specialty in my law field that will support my other interests. This specialty should be within the real estate field in the geographic areas in which I want to live and invest.

2. I need to develop insight into the techniques of investing in real estate and specific contacts in the area where I want to live and invest.

3. I may want to buy some vacant land on which I can build my office building and/or home in the future.

4. I should anticipate learning how to operate a forty-foot sailboat.

5. My first step is to stop renting and start owning and building equity.

6. I shall begin Monday.

Your approach to setting your goals should follow similar stages in real life. This need not be an overnight event, and if you are married or have dependents they should be a part of this process.

WHO DO YOU SHARE YOUR GOALS WITH?

Your goals have to be your own goals and not your friends' goals that have been superimposed on you. This goes for your family goals too. But what then? Whom do you entrust with this personal information? Who do you let know your secret?

The answer is: Keep your goals to yourself and only the most important members of your "advancement" team.

DEVELOP AN ADVANCEMENT TEAM

Every person who has a plan should have as part of that plan an advancement team. This team is made up of people who can advance your interests toward your goals. The available members to the team are many, and best of all their services may be totally free.

Others may charge you only for their performance, while others will charge you by the hour. In any event, to attack a future without an advancement team is foolhardy.

Your advancement team consists of the following people:

GENERAL TEAM MEMBERS	SPECIFIC TEAM MEMBERS
Realtors	Your specific and loyal lawyer
Bankers	Your own true-and-true accountant
Insurance companies	Your own banker
Loan officers at savings and loans	A trusted financial advisor
A handyman you know and trust	
Local governmental officials	

Of these advancement team members, you will entrust your goals only to specific team members. The general team members should be told only what they need to know, as they need to know it. (It's like sending them behind the lines; you never know whether the enemy will get to them.)

GET YOUR GOALS, TEAM MEMBERS, AND YOUR ABILITIES AND PUT THEM TO WORK

The total picture now comes together: You have your goals, you see your abilities and your liabilities, and you begin to develop your team members and your techniques at the same time. The only thing that is keeping you from success and attainment of your goals is fear of failure, or just fear itself. There is still one element you need to attend to. It's the development of your comfort zone. Once you have finished this last task, risk will be minimized and success is just around the corner.

PROFIT IN REAL ESTATE THROUGH YOUR COMFORT ZONE

The comfort zone is a category of knowledge and ability that is directed to any given task. In the case of real estate it will become a geographic area where the type of real estate you plan to invest in will be found. The real-estate comfort zone will be your specific niche in which you will live and invest. It is your zone of reference, your zone of total comfort and knowledge. It will be within this zone that you will reduce or eliminate all risk in activity. It will become your financial security blanket.

Why Is a Comfort Zone Important?

Every form of investing or activity has its comfort zone. If you were to make your fortune investing in stamps or coins, you would have to have an area of interest and expertise. Just as in other fields, people first become proficient and then expert in any specific talent. The singer, the dancer, the pilot; each requires something unique, something oriented to one area of risk. To intrude into another's field can be highly risky, even deadly. For the jazz singer to try to sing hard rock could be suicide, as could be true for the Sunday afternoon pilot who tries to land a 747.

All forms of investing have comfort zones in which the participants succeed once they understand the rules, the regulations, and most importantly the pitfalls of what they are doing. Just as the windsurfer makes that sport look easy (when in reality it is almost impossible until you have spent many hours of practice), the investor with a comfort zone can create the illusion that making money is easy and simple.

What is simple is the technique. What is easy is the concept of how to make money. What is fun is the development of the comfort zone. What is difficult is making money without knowing what you are doing.

How the Comfort Zone Will Make You Successful

Nothing lends itself to a comfort zone as much as does real estate. Of course, you can develop a comfort zone in any kind of field or interest, but when it comes to making money in your backyard, real estate is it.

Basically, the reason the comfort zone works so well for real estate investing is this: Real estate is local in nature. Local real estate has very little relationship to real estate that is across the country or in another, distant town. It is specifically here and not there. It has appeal because of that fact. Its value or lack of it is due solely to where it is located. It is said that "location, location, location" are the three most important aspects of real estate. While this statement is not entirely true, location plays a very important role in the importance of real estate. Remember in Chapter 1 I said that value was a relative aspect of real estate. This is where the location comes into the picture. Real estate value is less dependent on the actual location as it is on the value of that location to you. Your intended need for a tract of land, for example, may allow you to pay much more for a main intersection of two highways than another investor would be willing to pay. On the other hand, that other investor may place a greater value on a different location for reasons that pertain solely to the use that investor has for the other site. Value then becomes a function of how important a location is to the investor who is ready, willing and able to buy it at any given moment of time. All of this is strictly local.

Due to real estate's purely local nature, you cannot devise an accurate national statistic on what is going on in the market. The only important fact to keep in mind about national statistics and real estate is to understand that some people will believe a national statistic which is published in the newspaper. Take for example the statement that indicates a major drop in housing starts. This is a popular statistic that may have importance to the lumber industry more than it will to the values of property in your neighborhood. But people run scared when they hear such news. Savvy investors take advantage of this and make their move. If you have been watching what is going on in your neighborhood you would know that values are going up or down all the time. Act on what is real in your area, and not some national trend.

The stock market expert can watch the market and become the national expert in gold, silver, or pork bellies. But someone in Chicago can never be an expert on Asheville, North Carolina, real estate unless that town is part of his or her comfort zone. Only in real estate can you become an absolute expert in record-breaking time.

There can be a million experts in real estate, each having a different comfort zone, each knowing more about a particular area than any other person, and yet none of them ever infringe on the others. Your comfort zone then will be the totality of where you are comfortable in the opportunity to use your techniques and abilities within the real estate game. Some of you will become multinational investors who think nothing of building high-rise buildings, while others will be single-home investors who never buy any further than two miles from where you live. The whole idea is to be pleased with yourself, to have confidence in what you are doing, to achieve the goals you set for yourself, and to sleep soundly at night.

BUILDING YOUR COMFORT ZONE

Prior to building your comfort zone, you should develop the goals that I discussed earlier. Without a clear set of goals, you will not be able to formulate or benefit from your comfort zone properly.

To establish your comfort zone, begin with your goals. Remember when you role-played the lawyer, the list of four goals were the office building, the home, the sailboat, and certain economic freedom. A comfort zone would be devised to help you attain those goals. However, in getting started the comfort zone may have little relationship to the final product.

If you, as a young lawyer, began at a stage in your life where you wanted to buy office buildings and have waterfront homes in Boca Raton, Florida, you would develop as your comfort zone the specific areas that contain exactly the kind of property that you want to buy. This means that you would geographically locate a zone or territory that consists of office buildings and waterfront homes in Boca Raton.

You then would define that area in specific terms. It might be all the property along three main commercial streets in town, or all the waterfront properties along five or six canals. Whatever the area, it would begin small and work into a comprehensive area. However, because you are just starting out, you may begin with your more immediate needs, your intermediate goals. To this end, you still devise a geographic area, and you will follow the same techniques you will use later on as you advance to the higher, more specific areas of your dreams and goals.

How to Get Started with Your Comfort Zone

You might want to establish your first ownership of real estate, or find a good investment in apartment buildings. These final types of properties that you decide you want to buy should take you closer to your final goal.

First, you have to learn how to set your priorities to the kind of property you want to own within the geographic area we now call your comfort zone. Since you cannot know everything about every area of town, you need this specific area to be well chosen and clearly defined. So decide right now that you will never stray from your comfort zone.

This "never stray out of the comfort zone" rule is not a limiting element. The concept is that you must start somewhere, and that as you develop the comfort zone you will be adding to your own confidence and therefore reducing your risk. As this process develops, the comfort zone is expanded little by little. So instead of being limiting, it is constantly allowing you to expand your opportunity awareness safely.

Six Steps to Setting Up Your Comfort Zone

1. Review your goals.

2. Review with your specific team members what kind of property can move you closer to your goals.

3. Pick a part of town where you can:
   a. Find the kind of property you want to own.
   b. Feel comfortable.
   c. Be able to get to easily.

4. Begin to learn all you can about that part of town:
   a. Start by driving around in the area. Do you like what you see?
   b. Walk and/or jog in the area during all times of day.
   c. Get your team members to help. They can provide:
      (i) Maps.
      (ii) Zoning books and regulations.
      (iii) Local officials names and addresses.
      (iv) Local tax laws.
      (v) Property ownership information.
      (vi) Introductions to important people.
      (vii) Invaluable contacts.
   d. Go to the town hall meetings.

e. Meet city, county and state municipal planners:
   (i) Learn what is going on, where roads, bridges, new highways are to be built.
   (ii) What are the busy areas in town?
f. Meet the building and zoning officials in town:
   (i) They know what is going on long before the newspapers.
   (ii) The officials will tell you what is going on.
g. Be observant.

5. Get your knowledge together:
   a. Get the data on the properties you want to own.
   b. Contact the owner.
   c. Demonstrate that you know more about that property than anyone.

6. Put your other talents to play:
   a. You will have more confidence in your own abilities.
   b. You will reduce risk in your investment portfolio by:
      (i) Knowing what is going on in your area
      (ii) Being able to recognize a good buy in your area.
      (iii) Have more deals come to you because you are becoming known as the "expert" in the area.

THIS CONCEPT WORKS WELL FOR INVESTORS AND REAL-ESTATE SALESPEOPLE

Using the comfort-zone concept, you can actually feel the power gained through knowledge. Knowledge, by the way, is the same kind of foundation that makes one real-estate salesperson stand out over another. Smart real-estate salespeople will learn all that they can about the area in which they want to list and sell real estate. Their demonstration of being experts in the area enables them to dazzle owners into the realization that the best person to list and sell their property is someone who knows the property like the back of his or her hand.

The investor who has established goals, has picked out a comfort zone, and is proceeding to become an expert in the area, will equally demonstrate to the participants that he knows what he is doing.

The effect of all of this is multilevel. Not only will sellers be more receptive to buyers who are so knowledgeable, but lenders also will lean toward doing business with this kind of person. Much of the art of using the tools of finance depend on your being able to convince the other side of the deal that what you propose is sound, good business for all persons involved, and should be accomplished.

The prospective investor who shows up at the local savings and loan without confidence in himself and without assurance that he can back up the property will not be well received.

We Live in a World of Nameless, Faceless Neighbors

The comfort zone works simply because people have a tendency to live in a world in which they keep to themselves. We don't know the names of our neighbors, we don't know values across the street, and we don't even care if the house down the block is rented, or if so, for how much. Investors buy for many reasons, often taking the word of their realtor or salesperson as to what is going on in the area. This fact may not hamper their success, since many investors obviously do succeed with this tactic of investing.

However, this involves taking more risk than is necessary for the majority of investors, and most certainly for the investor who doesn't have a lot that can be placed at risk. The "lack of knowledge" that most people have of where they live and invest can then work for the investor who has developed his or her own comfort zone and works it properly.

MAKE YOUR COMFORT ZONE WORK WITH CREATIVE TOOLS

Once your goals are firmly established in your mind and you are underway with your plan, the critical steps are just around the corner. You must implement your plan with the financing techniques, and how you use them will become an important aspect of your success in real estate investing. All the financing techniques and tips described in this book can be utilized in combination with each other, giving you nearly endless opportunities to best solve a problem at hand or seek the best format to buy or sell your real estate to take you closer to your desired goal. The subtleties of these techniques will begin to become evident as you use them. Each will have a slightly different effect on each deal and for each user. A sale lease-back in one transaction could work wonders for you, whereas in the next deal it could be the least attractive format.

You should approach each real-estate investment with the question, "Do I need to buy this?" If the answer is yes, your whole approach to the transaction may be greatly altered. In essence, you would be "forced" to find a technique that solved that basic need (to buy that property), with the secondary benefit of doing so at the best terms possible. On the other hand, if the answer was no, but that you would buy it only if it was clearly a good deal, you can be far more selective in the use of your financing techniques and can walk away from those deals that cannot be made on terms that enable you to "own" that property in such a way that it moves you closer to your desired goals.

Keep your goals constantly in your mind. Review them, update them, and work toward them. They are what will help keep you out of trouble. Your goals will keep you on the right track. The following list will show you many opportunities to the end result of disposing of real estate. Review this list from time to time to remind yourself that disposition of real estate is not just selling, and in some cases not even a transfer of title. Real-estate ownership can be considered the use and benefit of the real estate as much as the holding of a fee simple title.

FIFTY-FOUR METHODS FOR OBTAINING OR GETTING RID OF REAL ESTATE

1. Acquisition (of additional property).
2. Adverse possession.
3. Bankruptcy.
4. Build to suit.
5. By will.
6. Charitable contribution.
7. Chattel.
8. Condemnation
9. Conversion.
10. Demolition.
11. Development.
12. Discount sale with lease-back.
13. Discount sale with recapture.
14. Easement lease.
15. Easement sale.
16. Eminent domain.
17. Escheat.
18. Exchange all the property.
19. Exchange a portion of the property.
20. General corporation.
21. Gift.
22. Joint venture.
23. Holding company.
24. Insurance lease.
25. Insurance mortgage.

26. Improvement of building.
27. Lease of air rights.
28. Lease of all rights.
29. Lease, Sub.
30. Limited partnership.
31. Mortgage out, foreclose.
32. Option-lease.
33. Option-sale.
34. Partition sale.
35. Prescription.
36. Pyramid.
37. Reclamation.
38. Refinancing.
39. Rent.
40. Rezoning.
41. Sale, Air rights.
42. Sale, Improvements only.
43. Sale, Land only.
44. Sale, Auction.
45. Sale/Lease riparian.
46. Sale, Leaseback with a recapture.
47. Sale or lease of leasehold.
48. Sell option back.
49. Subdivide.
50. Subordination.
51. Subordination of the mortgage.
52. Syndicate.
53. Tax sale.
54. Trusts.

All of the foregoing methods to obtain or to dispose of real estate can be accomplished by using the techniques contained in this book. Once you have finished this book, plan on going over this chapter again to remind you of the importance of goals and your comfort zone.

Chapter 3

THE POWER OF NEGOTIATING

There was a time, not too many years ago, when buying real estate, and making money doing it, were as simple as throwing a dart at a map of the area. This is not the way it is now. Now you have to be on your toes from the day you pick up the map of the area until you close on the transaction. What has happened over the years to turn real estate investing into the bundle of bureaucracy that it has become? People, that is what.

Take for example, almost any city that has grown, and that is just about any city in the U.S. As growth was taking place, the local government was also growing. City ordinances were getting less developer-friendly. Land planners, straight out of the State University system began to make their mark. That generally meant putting the clamps on growth. Then came scores of different environmental groups and protection laws that look good on paper, but when you are being eaten alive by mosquitoes on a nice summer evening, you wonder why no one has done anything about the swamp next door.

But this is the good news of the story. The tougher it is to deal with the bureaucracy the less your competition. There is even better news too. Because each city comes with its own set of building codes and city ordinances, if you decide to specialize in one or two towns, very quickly you will have the edge on any outside buyers. Better yet, with a little effort, very quickly you will know more about what is going on in the community. This means you know and understand more about property values than most real estate brokers in the area, and certainly the majority of sellers. By following a comfort zone program as was discussed in the previous chapter, you will start to see opportunities popping up all around you.

Timing is everything when it comes to getting the best deal. This means being early to spot the opportunity, and being early to take control of the property, before you actually close on the transaction. The steps that fall between each of those two events are the subject of this chapter. The goal of this chapter is to introduce you to some of the critical aspects of what it takes to take control of the property. The key word to this process is that you want to be in control before you actually must commit to buy. The reason for this is simple. You want to have control to allow you time to make a complete inspection of the property and all possible elements that affect the property. To spend the time, money and effort on this kind of detailed due diligence without being in control is a waste. To get into control takes a combination of talents. These talents combine to describe the *art of negotiating*. The route to success in real estate is through good negotiating. Nothing happens within the closed doors of bankers, buyers, sellers, and developers that is not won or lost on the finesse of the participants to negotiate properly, or, for that matter, to negotiate at all.

When it comes to being a success in real estate, you must develop good negotiating skills, or find someone who can do that important task for you. This is as important if you are a buyer as it is if you are a seller.

Timing, by the way, has little to do with the clock, or a date on a calendar. It is the simple element that at any given moment, the motivations of a buyer or a seller can change. This change can be so dramatic that an opportunity is born. Many buyers fail to grasp this concept of good timing. I have seen buyers turn down a property that truly suited their investment portfolio because it had been on the market for a long time. They were confusing timing with the lapse of time. "How can this be any good?" they would argue, "Look at all the time the seller has tried to sell this property. Why, everyone in the world has turned this down." Suddenly there is a change in the seller's motivations, and the buyer who grasps that this has opened the doors to the property by allowing a change in price or terms, is the person at the right place at the right time.

But all the best timing will not put you into control unless the negotiations work. If you accept this, then you are on the way to learning what most real estate investors never learn. Keep in mind that this chapter is not meant to teach you all you could learn about the art of negotiation. But this chapter and this book are more than a first-aid course that can only save your life in an emergency. This chapter and this book will give you the knowledge of what to look for, and how to develop the critical insight to what motivates the other party. Start with the understanding that you will win in negotiations if you approach every contract confrontation with the idea that you will succeed only if you help the other party attain all or most of his or her goals. Sound revolutionary? Just wait and see how this works.

THE STEPS TO SUCCESSFUL NEGOTIATING

The following steps will guide you through the early stages of getting your act into proper gear so that you can present your case in a businesslike way, and move into the close of the transaction. As you move through these four steps, you will find that the most essential part of any negotiating is to have an absolutely clear vision of your goal. If you don't know what it is you are negotiating for, your end result is apt to be far different from your original desire. Also critical is your understanding that winning doesn't mean coming out ahead of the other party. Winning is achieving your goals.

The best part of dealing with these four steps and then succeeding in the art of negotiating is that you don't require a degree or any education other than the ability to demonstrate empathy and to keep your cool. The homework that you may need to do from time to time will be easy, and there will be many people ready to help you. Sometimes the most help comes from the other side.

1. THE FOUNDATION OF THE DEAL.   The first step in any negotiation is to review your goals, or if you are negotiating for someone else, make sure you have a clear understanding of the goal to be served. Each situation may present a different set of circumstances, but the end result should be clearly in mind. Assume, for example that you are in the hospitality business, and want to add to your existing holdings of hotel properties. Long before you sit down with a seller of a property you want to buy, you must be sure you understand what kind of property and the criteria of that property that will work for you.

If the property must be purchased to allow redevelopment of an adjoining property, there will be different tactics used in the acquisition of the site than if the goal was to land bank a future development site. Write down the goal, and the way in which a successful negotiation will help attain that goal. This will help you stay on track during the negotiation process.

On the other hand, suppose you want to buy an apartment building for yourself. Within step 1 of negotiating, you must examine the various elements involved: What is the long-range goal you plan to reach through the purchase or acquisition of the apartment building? Is it to buy the property for a potential conversion to a condominium or other use some time in the near future? Or do you want to maximize equity build-up and plow as much of the cash flow back into the property to attract a wealthy prospect? The investment plan is important because this will dictate the direction you go in developing the financing for the acquisition. Both the long-term and short-term goals are important, and must be kept clearly in sight. It is too easy to overlook the original objective and to attain the desired result in such a way that you jeopardize your long-term position.

Assume that your long-term goal is to establish a steady income at the end of a fifteen-year period and that the apartment complex will fill that need at that time by paying off its debt by then. Once the total goal is seen, visualized, and written down, you can move deeper into the foundation in preparation for your negotiations. One of the next stages is the review of options open to you to meet this goal. How many apartment buildings have you seen? Where do you want your apartment building?

And so on. Each move toward the end result will take you deeper into more alternatives that can sway you from your intended path. It is important that you be flexible so that as you move into this jungle you won't overlook the fact that other pathways that present themselves to you might lead to improved goals. However, do not let the greener grass syndrome take you into an ambush by the local natives (brokers or other sellers). Many a would-be investor has lost his or her head over something that looked too good, too easy, too quick.

Look at and examine the alternatives. If you have done your homework and know the marketplace, your clear focus on what works for you leads you to the right property. Still, you will want to ask yourself these questions prior to entering into negotiations. Does this property appear to meet or exceed my minimum criteria? Are there circumstances that suggest that this represents an opportunity? Have I arrived at the point in time that I need to take control of this property? Will this property help me achieve my investment goals? Is this property in my comfort zone? Or do I need to change my goals or expand my comfort zone? All investors who succeed ask themselves these questions over and over again. They listen to the answers, then act.

You are ready to proceed to the next step in negotiating when you are comfortable that you know just how far you are willing to go in the acquisition of the property. Even at this stage you must be flexible. The other participants may have some elements available that you don't know about, and these elements might get you where you want to go quicker than you thought. But remember this word of warning: The best negotiator is the one who makes you believe that you have just won when in fact you both have.

The foundation, therefore, is:

- Know your goals.
- Find properties that will take you closer to your goals.
- Set the maximum economic cost that you feel you can afford on any specific property, based on the information you believe to be factual.
- Keep an open mind as to how that economic cost can be handled.
- Get ready to move to the next step.

Some of the best examples of real-estate investors who follow all these elements illustrated in step 1 are the national fast-food franchises. They know what works for them, what they need, and generally must act quickly when they decide to saturate a market area. But not all national companies are so smart. Poor long-range planning and the inability to make a decision often causes many investors to lose.

2. DOING YOUR HOMEWORK.   There are two basic kinds of negotiation: (a) blind, and (b) open.

BLIND.   This is the most common kind of negotiation. Blind is when you have no idea who you are dealing with, and make little or no effort to find out the motivations that steer the other side of the deal. Blind negotiations occur much of the time because of blocks in the way of your finding out anything about the other side. Real estate brokers or salespeople are one such roadblock. In real estate transactions, they frequently represent the sellers and like to keep control of the situation. They want to keep the buyer and seller apart and generally feel that each party should know as little about the other party as possible. This situation is founded on the premise that many transactions are lost when the buyer and seller get together. This is a very valid basis too, as most buyers or sellers let personality get in the way of sound negotiations. "What do you mean 'who picked out that carpet?' I did." Just about every real estate broker who has been on the job for a couple of weeks can tell you horror stories of buyers and sellers going at each other with kitchen knives.

However, it is a good idea that you know as much as possible about the other party, whether you are the buyer or the seller. This will help you put together a deal that will work. If you want to let the broker keep you apart, that's just fine. There is a school of international negotiations that is sometimes called *English School of Negotiation Method* that works very well in real-estate transactions. The theory is that, blind or open, it is critical that the negotiator be talking with someone who can make a decision. In real estate terms this might be the actual buyer or seller. However, the negotiator is not someone who can make decisions. This kind of negotiation is difficult and the negotiator must be very calm under stress. The key to this kind of success is that one side is always committing to each point discussed, whereas the other side must always go back to the principal, to get confirmation. "My brother has controlling interest" is a more Americanized version of this same tactic where no matter what your actual control of the deal, there is always someone else who has to make the decision. Many an only child has used this tactic.

Blind negotiation is not a waste of time, however. The speed with which you can make an offer makes blind negotiation work when speed is the most critical element of the transaction. If you know your comfort zone well and recognize that the property offered is a bargain, you have already done your homework and that additional information on the other party may not be necessary. This points out the importance of knowing all you can about the property you want to buy or the market in which you want to sell. That homework is the most essential.

OPEN.   This form of negotiation involves a lot of homework. The idea is to know as much as possible about your counterpart so that when it comes time to make the deal you won't have any surprises or anything outstanding to keep you from closing the transaction. In essence, you have made the decision that this is a deal you want and that you will do all that you can to make the deal within reason and legality. This kind of negotiation isn't as difficult as it might seem. Most of the homework you can and will do will fall into your lap, if you let it. Of course, you should rely on the help of your broker, lawyer, or accountant whenever he or she can be of assistance. Let me give you an example of one such transaction where the homework made the difference.

Charles wanted to own a home that he saw on Center Avenue. It was just a few blocks from the beach; he could walk to his office on nice days, and he liked the look of the house from the street. After only two blind offers, the seller stood firm at a price that Charles didn't think was realistic. In essence, price was standing in the way of the deal. Instead of giving up on the transaction, Charles decided to ask the broker to look into the motivations of the seller. Keep in mind that the broker worked for the seller, so he already knew some things about him.

Charles was interested in knowing what would turn the reluctant seller into a willing participant to the transaction. This was the critical stage of the transaction, because the broker didn't want to betray any secrets, but at the same time he wanted to make a deal.

Charles wants to buy the property, the broker wants him to buy the property, and the seller wants someone to buy her property. But so far, neither the seller nor any buyer has been able to get together to make the deal work. Charles knows that in good negotiations there is always a way to make a deal if one side makes a greater effort than the other. Since Charles is a good businessman, he knows that there is a limit to the economic cost of the transaction for the deal to make sense to him, and he would like to get in as inexpensively as possible. Therefore, Charles wants to discover if there is some factor that will help put the deal together. Sometimes the road blocks in putting a deal together is that one side or the other cannot see how to attain his or her own goal other than follow one direction. In Charles' case it might be the seller needs to be shown alternative directions to follow.

The homework Charles must consider may take a different tack than that which you may require to make your next deal. But all homework must be comprehensive and to the point.

THE HOMEWORK FACTORS THAT MAKE DEALS COME TOGETHER

1. WHY DOES THE OTHER PARTY WANT TO BUY OR SELL? Simple logic will tell you that this is the toughest question to answer. If you are the buyer, you want to know the reason the seller wants to sell. The reason the broker comes up with is apt to be a figment of the broker's imagination or the seller's invention. You need to look deeper. Do some homework. Find the answers to such questions as: What are the economic factors of the property? Is there a mortgage foreclosure, are there liens filed against the property or the people? Has the owner lost his job? What is it that occurred that causes this property to be up for sale?

This is an overall review of the circumstances. The seller just bought a new home. He just divorced his wife. He lost everything he owned in the storm and wasn't insured. He drew into an inside straight. He just doesn't know what he is doing. Or whatever. If you are the seller, knowing why the other party wants to buy is helpful too. The answer to this question is a bit more difficult to find since the motivations of those who have money or who are in the "taker" position might be more difficult to inspect. However, there are very obvious reasons some buyers want to buy. The fast-food franchise company that needs a location in the area, the hospital next door that wants to expand, and so on. When you have this kind of insight you can act accordingly. Generally, sellers can get sufficient information about the buyer by finding out who the buyer is.

Much of the homework you do is a matter of being aware of what is going on around the transaction. That information must then be tied into the form of negotiations you devise to meet any objection that stands in your way of successfully concluding the transaction. Other parts of the homework fall into the comfort zone that we have discussed in earlier sections of this book. So far, each of these two tactics is a question of awareness and comfort. The facts are often public knowledge and easy to obtain once you know how to find them.

For example, in your community there are sources of information that can tell you a lot about the person with whom you are dealing. Some of these are:

- *A city cross-reference directory*. This is a book much like a telephone book but it contains other data, such as place of employment, name of spouse and children. You also can check addresses to match phone numbers if you have one and not the other. Once you know where your counterpart lives and works, you can go deeper into the background of that person.

- *A city social directory*. If you are dealing with one of the social cream, you can bet that he or she will be listed in the social directory. This book often tells you things such as the clubs the person belongs to, the name of his or her yacht, the person's summer or winter address, the names of children, where the children are going to school, and so on. A check of some of these key items can be rewarding.

- *County court house*. Here, you can find a great deal of information about many people in your community. What real estate do they own, how much tax do they pay, what did they pay for the real estate they own? Do they have mortgages on their real estate? Is there a foreclosure in the wings? How much? Have they been sued? When and for what? Are they divorced? Married? And so on.

- *Credit reports*. You can obtain a credit report on anyone. Look in your phonebook for companies that provide this service. If you are a member of Dun and Bradstreet, this is a good place to start. But be careful of the institutional kind of report. It often only shows up the shine, and unless the person has had a lot of bad news lately, that part may not be available for the usual D and B report.

- *Better Business Bureau.* Give this organization a call if your counterpart in the deal is a businessperson in the community. What about his or her reputation anyway? If you find a long list of complaints, be warned that you may soon be following with one of your own.

Relying on reports such as those mentioned will give you some insight into the person and the potential problems you might have. But by themselves they will not make your deal for you. You will have to make your deal based on the final play of this game as it develops. Homework only gives you the edge; the actual play is up to you.

2. WHO IS HE OR SHE TRYING TO IMPRESS? Almost everyone has someone he or she is trying to impress. The loan officer wants to impress his boss, the guy down the street wants to impress his wife or his girlfriend, and your next-door neighbor may want to impress you. Whom do you want to impress?

While you may never discover the person the other party is trying to impress most, it should be obvious to you that knowing that information would be very important. For example, some people want to impress their parents more than anything else in the world. Other people want to impress their bosses, or employees, while others are constantly trying to impress their husbands or boyfriends. Possessing this information would allow you to present an offer that would allow the person to impress that person most. If it was the mother, a casual remark made in front of the party such as, "I'll bet your mother would be proud of your making a deal like this" would do no harm.

Try to find out something about the other party if you can. Sometimes you can get enough insight from the real estate broker, or if the deal is big enough, and important enough, some homework in the way of research into the other party's motives or interests will help. Knowing who the other party wants to impress, and why, could be the difference between a closed deal and wasted effort.

3. KNOW THE TIMING OF THE TRANSACTION BETTER THAN THE OTHER PARTY. How much can you know about the time elements that the other person must face up to? Time often gets in the way of many deals. If it is the loan officer: When does she have to meet her quota? If it is the seller: When does he have to own up to his foreclosure? Or the buyer: When does she have to move out of her current home? Or office? When must she meet some deadline? Find out the deadline of the other person by asking the following types of questions:

"When do you need this property?"
"Is the first of March okay?"
"Can you get an okay by June 15?"

By itself, the time element is not critical unless there is a specific urgency, such as the buyer's lease is up on the first of next month. What is important is acknowledgment of the transaction. Any statement, either positive or negative may be a buying or selling acknowledgment. Time is no exception. For example, if the buyer asks, "Can you move out by the first of next month?" then the seller should ask, "Can you close on the title that soon?" If the buyer replies positively then the contract may be all but signed. If the buyer replies negatively, "You're right, that might be too soon for me to come up with the money." The deal is still on track, and you know what factor to work on.

Any time urgency works in favor of the opposing party. The party with the time urgency will make a deal that is realistic, even one that costs more than he wants to pay or gets him less than he wants to get. However, some participants will end the deal if they feel they are being delayed: "Look Mr. Broker, I can't fool around with that seller any longer. Get me another deal, even if I have to pay a little more. Okay?"

In negotiations with a loan officer, there are some important facts to know. These include the time periods for submission to loan committees, quotas that the loan officer has to meet, and other time traps that affect you in your need for money. For example, a 90-day delay while your credit is being checked when you only have 60 days to meet some contract provision to keep your deal alive can be disastrous.

4. VERIFY THE FACTS.   This sounds like good, sound business practice. However, you would be surprised to learn that most deals are completed without the major factors being tested out. In many transactions, the end result is that those factors might not have mattered anyway. However, if you are trying to make the best deal you can, you owe it to yourself to make sure that the following items are verified.

TIPS FOR THE BUYER

1. PRICE.   Is the price quoted to you the lowest price quoted in the most recent period? Sometimes brokers get old brochures; in reality, the price may have gone down. I don't ever recall a seller telling the offering party that he had just reduced the price from $300,000 to $250,000 when the would-be buyer has just offered $275,000. Make sure your broker has double-checked the price the day you go to make the offer.

2. THE LEGAL DESCRIPTION.   The legal description can be, as an example "Lot 1, Block 7 of the Cummings Plat Number 1" (often followed by other information such as a tax folio number to make it easy to find the property through tax rolls). Be sure that the legal description you put in the offer is in fact the property you want to buy. This error sometimes occurs, and people have bought the wrong property. It is critical that you do this for vacant land and improved property. In addition

to any legal description, I suggest that the property be described in lay terms as well: "That property located at 2671 East Commercial Blvd., Fort Lauderdale, Florida, 33308, a two-story office building consisting of 3,100 square feet on a lot sized 36' frontage on East Commercial Blvd., at a depth of 150' to an alley to the north, which are the present offices of Cummings Realty, Inc." It would be difficult for a problem to arise if you take this simple step. There is one additional step to add to this protection: "As is shown on the attached survey and plat map."

To illustrate what can happen if you don't pay attention, let me give you an example. I purchased a vacant lot (and later built a home on it) in Fort Lauderdale. The property was the last vacant lot in an area of homes that fronted canals leading to the ocean. It was very odd to find a vacant lot in this area, and on walking the lot I realized that the reason it had remained vacant was its odd shape and the small amount of water frontage it had on the canal. The lot seemed unattractive due to vegetation on two sides of the lot (the lot itself was a corner, so it had streets on two sides, and neighbors on two sides, with a fifth side facing the canal). Along its northern boundary were a massive hedge and a tree line that ran down to the canal retaining wall to a point where there was a marker nail driven into the concrete with a yellow circle around it. The amount of canal frontage that seemed to belong to this lot was only about 20 feet, whereas all of the neighbors had 100 feet or more of dock space. However, on reviewing the plat, it turned out that the lot actually was larger than it appeared and had about 60 feet of canal frontage with riparian rights that gave the lot an ideal dockage for boats up to 70 feet. Also, all of the hedges, trees, and barbecue, and most of the lawn sprinklers and yard of the home to the north belonged to this lot, which I bought.

I also discovered that the home to the north had gone through five owners in the past seven years. I surmised that each owner made the discovery of just where their south lot line really was located and sold out to someone else.

The current owner of the property to the north had no idea, of course. When he purchased the property he asked his lawyer to check the title, plat and survey of the lot. The only problem was the lawyer failed to do the most critical check of all. Neither the attorney nor the current owner had walked the property with a tape measure to locate the actual corners and side boundaries and to compare them to the descriptions in the title, plat and survey. Had either of them done so, they would have known that the nail and yellow circle were the figment of an overly anxious seller.

The lesson learned here is to be sure of everything that relates to the specific property in question.

3. THE MORTGAGES.   Whether you are taking out or assuming a mortgage, be sure you understand all of its terms. The mortgage documents should be in your possession prior to your final acceptance of any offer and your lawyer should go over the mortgage with you to explain it fully. Do not let him or her slip by a clause by

saying, "That's common." You should know what it means, and be sure you will agree to its terms.

For new mortgages, you will be able to negotiate some terms and conditions. You should question any part of a mortgage you don't like or that sounds unfair. If it doesn't sound fair, it probably isn't.

Many mortgages have clauses and conditions that can be confusing to anyone, including wise and educated lawyers and real estate brokers. These clauses include, but are by far not limited to:

- Term of payment. How many payments? When can the mortgage be paid off ahead of schedule? Is it principal plus interest, or interest and principal? How is amortization calculated? Are the payments monthly, or what?

- Balloon payments. One balloon or two? When? How much exactly?

- Assumption by other parties.

- Pay-off penalty.

- Acceleration.

- Form of payment. In U.S. dollars? Monthly with principal and interest? Is the escrow included or added in a lump?

- Escrowing. Why? How much? Exactly what is included?

- Insurance included or required. Can you get your own? Why is it required?

- Title insurance. Can you provide your own and coinsure the lender?

4. WHAT IS INCLUDED WITH THE PROPERTY? Is a comprehensive inventory attached to the contract, or do you at least have the right to make up an inventory and approve it? If you don't approve it, can you get out of the deal prior to the closing? If not, you may be making a bad deal. The only time you will get everything you think you are getting is to have it in writing. Make sure that you get an inventory that is specific: not just chairs and tables and beds, but specific chairs and tables and beds. A good idea is to go through the property with a red marker and number each item of furniture and each fixture (provided the mark does not detract from the value of the property). If you cannot mark the property itself, place a stick-on tab on the item with your initial and that of the seller. Then make a detailed list of each item. The hazard of not doing this early in the negotiation or shortly after the contract is that items will disappear and/or will be replaced with less valuable items.

The same goes for the landscaping. If there are valuable plants in the garden and you want to make sure that they remain, do an inventory of the gardens (preferably with a camera). I can tell you many sad stories of sellers taking plants with them.

5. ARE THERE ENVIRONMENTAL PROBLEMS? This requires professional help. Yet it is very critical to include in a contract a clause that the seller warrants there is no environmental problem at all. Most people think that it is the law for sellers and brokers to disclose this and other kinds of known problems. In reality this may not be the case at all. If you ask the question, however, and the seller, broker or any other party to the deal says there is not a problem, they will have broken the law if you can prove they did know.

TIPS FOR THE SELLER

1. EXACTLY WHEN WILL THE CLOSING OF THE TRANSACTION OCCUR? If you think that the closing date is the one that is filled into the blanks following the words "The closing will occur on the _____ day of _____ in the year 19___ ," then you might be in for a surprise. Sharp buyers have a tendency to insert provisions in the agreement that may, at their option and often at their control, delay the closing well beyond the established date indicated on the contract. You should examine the agreement carefully to determine whether such conditions exist and what delays they may cause. One safe thing to do is to put an outside date in the agreement with wording such as: "All parties agree that under no circumstance whatsoever shall the closing occur after the following date, providing the seller is not in default in this agreement and has used due diligence to meet all obligations herein contained, and that if the buyer elects not to close on that date and the seller does not extend the closing date then this agreement will terminate and any and all deposits placed in escrow pending the closing will become liquidated damages to the favor of the seller." Keep in mind that this is just a part of what you will need in your agreement. The wording is not as critical as the effect.

2. HOW IS THE PRICE DETERMINED, AND EXACTLY HOW MUCH IS IT? I have seen agreements that showed a price that the seller would never get due to other conditions that took away from that price. If the agreement calls for you, the seller, to pay certain costs; cover certain expenses; make repairs, additions, refurbish; give credit for changes; allow for interest to be included; have moratoriums on interest or principal or both, these are all deductions from the price.

As long as you agree with these deductions, there is no problem; but watch out if you don't. By the way, don't assume that your lawyer will tell you about these items. He is apt to look at the agreement with a legal eye instead of a business eye, thinking that whatever terms or conditions are contained in the agreement are acceptable to you.

3. WHAT ARE YOU SELLING?   For the same reason the buyer wanted to know what he or she was buying, you need to check very carefully what it is you are about to sell. I can tell you from firsthand experience that it is easy to slip up in this area if you own a lot of property or have complicated legal descriptions on the property being sold. The solution to this problem is exactly that as was provided for the buyer. Review that section once more.

4. HOW ARE THE MORTGAGES PAID?   The same situation that befalls the buyer will befall you, only you as seller have other considerations to look after. If you have a large taxable income or capital gain as a result of this sale, the method of payment of the mortgage could have a major impact on your tax considerations. You may want to make some adjustments in that area prior to final agreement.

GET STARTED ON THE RIGHT FOOT

In the art of negotiation, it is important to begin properly. You should establish, right up front, the tone of the negotiation and the pattern you wish to follow. This will be your game plan, and like all good game plans it will be flexible enough to allow you to make adjustments along the way to meet any objections.

It is my opinion that in buying real estate a direct confrontation between the buyer and the seller is not wise. Now by this I do not mean that the buyer and the seller should not know each other, nor that they should not be in communication during the negotiation process. I mean that all confrontation should be left to intermediaries. This works for both the buyer and the seller.

KEYS TO GETTING STARTED

1. If you already know the other party, maintain the same relationship as before if it is friendly; if it is not friendly, do nothing to aggravate the circumstances. Don't make any rash changes in the friendship. Under the circumstances, you are apt to appear to be insincere and may discredit your proposal or counterproposal.

2. As a buyer, do not criticize the property or give it praise. Be polite in complimenting the owners on their good taste, beautiful view, and other obvious elements of the home just as you might had you been invited to tea that afternoon.

3. As a seller, do not knock yourself out to sell the property. You have a salesperson or broker to do that. If you are called on to give information, do so without adding postscripts: "Yes, but you know. . . ."

4. Do not criticize the agents or brokers representing the deal. You never know whether the agent is the other party's brother- or sister-in-law, mother, or friend. Even if he or she is not, there is no reason to find fault with the people the other party has hired as representatives. Some buyers do this in the belief that they can divide the broker from the seller and therefore make some gain.

5. Explain why you want to buy or sell the property if you can do this without disclosing any secrets or important strategies. "I want to acquire a vacant tract to build an industrial park. I have had this dream for several years now and believe that now is the time for me to act on that goal. My timing is such that I wish to have a property under contract within the next 30 days so that I can lock up my financing, get my building permits, and start construction as soon as possible." How the seller responds to a statement like this can give you some clue if you are dealing with a seller who will be receptive to your offer, or not.

6. Do everything you said you would do on time, or sooner. If you promised the seller that you would have your lawyer call his lawyer by Friday, make sure the call takes place on Thursday. If you said you would be there at 3:00 P.M. be there by 2:55 P.M. at the latest. This sets a theme that you value your time enough to get things done and that you value other people's time so as not to waste it. This is the single factor where many buyers go wrong. When you promise you will deliver an offer by Friday and Wednesday of the following week rolls around and you have not even bothered to make a phone call to explain the reason for the delay, then you are jeopardizing the future of these negotiations. This is true even if there is a very good reason for the delay. Many institutional buyers are the worst violators of this simple rule. Remember that by doing what you say, when you promised it, you are establishing a good example for more important things later on such as "Sure, I'll pay off the $5,000,000 in two years, no problem."

7. Critical elements to remember:

   • Avoid using the other party's phone or taking calls that are about other business while in the presence of the other party. If you are at a place of business or home of the other party or his lawyer and you must use the phone for some other business, wait until you have concluded your business with that party.

   • Do not say "We are tired of dealing with people who waste our time. I want you to know we aren't like that," or any other statement that only your actions can prove.

   • Do not praise yourself. However, feel free to let others mention your past successes or point out your professionalism. All you have to do is be professional.

- Do not lie. If you can't think of any good truth, say nothing. Many people lie and never get caught. However, it is the quickest way to end a negotiation or, at best, discredit everything you have said.

UNDERSTAND THE FUNDAMENTALS OF NEGOTIATION

Communication becomes a step to understanding any form of negotiation. Like an argument, it is very difficult to have lasting problems if there is no communication. It is the same in negotiations. It is better to have no communication at all than to have no understanding, or bad communication. But you must get your point across. And you do that by demonstration more than by talk. Talk is the murderer of negotiation.

How then do you negotiate? As a buyer of real estate, you do it through an offer to buy, or a letter of intent to buy. This occurs after you have concluded many elements of the transaction that less informed people want to "negotiate" their way through.

The actual negotiation should not occur until there is a confrontation. After all, if you offer $100,000 on a property that the seller has been asking $200,000 for, there is nothing to negotiate if the seller accepts. (Except you won't sleep well wondering if he would have accepted $90,000.) Only when the other party balks at what you want does negotiation begin.

Take into consideration the other form of buying and selling. In bartering, where one person asks (talks) "Would you take $100,000?," the rest of the conversation might go like this:

"Are you offering $100,000?"
"No, just wondering if I did, would you take it?"
"If I said yes, would you want to buy it?"
"If you said yes, I'd think about it."
"So why not offer the $100,000 then?"

Nothing is going on here that resembles negotiation, yet each party thinks they are negotiating pretty well.

Some years ago I was in a rug merchant shop in Tangier, Morocco. I asked "Would you sell that for $200?"

"Would you like to own this rug?" was the reply.
"I might if you'd sell it for $200."
"Do you want only one?"
"Yes. One is all I can afford at the moment."

"Will you take it with you, or must I ship it to you?"
"I'll take it with me."
"You have very good taste, sir. And for only $200 you have made a very good buy."

How I love to meet good salesmen like that! Not only is he negotiating pretty darn well, he lets me sell myself by giving me simple decisions to make. Every time I respond positively the sale has moved closer to a closed transaction.

Know who the enemy is in the game. Both the buyer and the seller are actually on the same side. They both want the same ultimate goal: the sale of the property. The enemy is that raft of truths such as the following:

1. Taxes.
2. Death.
3. Government.
4. Rejection.
5. Hate.
6. Fear.
7. Failure.
8. Desire for immortality.
9. Intimidation.
10. Indecision.

To win any game, you must know who you are playing against, so try to let other game players help you rather than block you. It's like having your star player on the bench right when you need him or her in the game. The only thing you have to remember to do is not let on that you know the others are really on your team; better to let them think you are on theirs.

Winning in negotiation is not a matter of intimidation. Intimidation is one of the enemies to establishing good rapport in any kind of negotiation process. It is poise and diplomacy that win the game. All participants in the game of negotiation want to feel that they are the winners. Good participants know just how far they can go to get the points they feel are essential and still let the other side walk away satisfied.

It is possible to nail someone's back to the wall when all their chips are down, or to play a dirty game putting them into a position where there are no other participants. I won't judge you nor will I claim there is a special morality in the matter of business or negotiation that you are bound to follow. Each player must find the kind of game they want to play. I have known very successful businesspeople who are ruthless and cunning, who had no friends, and who won their business deals by pushing their counterparts to the wall. Some of these "successful" people have hung themselves, filed bankruptcy, or fled to Rio, and they are usually sad cases. Were they successful? Only in their minds.

In the real-estate field, success tends to be related to fair dealing. Much of what really goes on between the people who will help you, occurs without contract, without obligation, because all of us need people we can trust. So you will spend much of your business life finding out who you cannot trust and therefore cannot deal with. Some of the difficult-to-negotiate-with people are just frightened or unsophisticated men and women who are in trouble and don't know who to turn to for help. These people don't want to appear to be frightened or unsophisticated, so they delay, balk, or just become uncommunicative. You may batter down those kinds of doors, but it can be a very slow and unpredictable process. Sometimes the best negotiator has to throw in the towel and give up. If you do enough deals there will be some failures. The key to the failures is to size up the deal as soon as possible and not waste time in closing down the negotiations. Just remember to do so without burning the bridge in case the road block suddenly comes down due to something unexpected that happens.

It is a good idea to remember that the sweetener of success is failure. After all, without failure there would be no pleasure to success. I call this to your attention because in any negotiation you will be under the pressure of "failing" at your intended task. In the case of real estate investment, the task is generally to make the best investment possible to meet or take you closer to your desired goals. To do this requires you to: (1) find properties you would want to own which serve your needs, and (2) make offers and attempt to negotiate the acquisition of those properties. All successful real estate investors fail at step 2 some of the time. Your failure in this task should not be discouraging to you, nor should you let it deter you from moving along to another property. You should fail from time to time in step 2 because, if you don't, you are doing one of two things.

1. You are buying property on terms that are not favorable to your goals. This could be because of your inexperience, or lack of clear understanding of your goals.
2. You aren't making enough offers to buy property. If you pick the property, and stick to terms that you know will help you reach your goal, you will not be able to buy every property you find. Not all sellers will be that cooperative.

Analyzing your failures will help you improve your future negotiations. Never avoid a conflict because you fear you can not succeed. But never let a failure go by without it being a learning process.

Chapter 4

HOW LEVERAGE AND RISK AFFECT THE VALUE OF REAL ESTATE

Leverage is the affect of financing on any investment. When used properly it can increase the yield on cash invested. It is an important factor in real estate financing. With it you can reduce investment risk, adjust a transaction to better fit your goals, and ultimately change the value of the property. This chapter will show you how these three elements can dramatically be altered by the structure of the financing of a transaction. The goal of this chapter is to give you a detailed look at how to use leverage to your maximum advantage.

WHAT ROLE DOES RISK PLAY IN THE USE OF LEVERAGE?

Risk is present in any and/or all investments. Most certainly, any real estate deal can fail to achieve its projected end result. This does not mean that the transaction fails completely or at all. Failure to achieve goals can mean the goals were overly optimistic. Falling short on a timetable can be a fault of the business plan, and not the goal. Risk is present for these reasons as well as that all the best plans that can be made will most likely depend on certain events over which you have no control. These uncontrollable, or unforeseen circumstances or events can present problems that may spell disaster, unless you can deal with them, one way or the other. Because of this, there is an amount of risk associated with every real estate venture. The level of risk is important to at least two parties to the transaction: The buyer and the lender, and often the seller as well. The buyer looks at the level of risk to mean at what jeopardy he or she has placed the invested capital. The buyer would view a purchase with only 10% down as highly leveraged. The lender looks at the level of risk in a repayment of the loan. In this situation a 90% loan is seen as a highly leveraged transaction.

Sellers can have a stake in the success of a venture too. You will see later on in this chapter that the difference of point of view between these parties can shift between what might be highly leveraged for the buyer and *not* be highly leveraged for the primary lender.

Lenders associate risk differently than the owner of the property would. For example, the most important element of security to a lender is the combination of value plus owner strength. Lenders will vary on which of these two factors is the most important. Some lenders look to the loan-to-value ratio as a primary criteria to making a loan. For example, if the value of a property is a conservative $100,000 and the lender's loan-to-value comfort level is 80%, then the lender may look harder at the borrower. Large loan amounts usually cause the lenders to look more to the owners strength, and may require additional security or collateral.

Review the following two examples:

Example 1

Winkle wants to purchase a small apartment building that contains five apartments. The value, that would be accepted by a lender, is $200,000. Winkle has an agreement to purchase provided he pay the seller $120,000 in cash, plus give the seller a second mortgage of $80,000.

Example 2

Jones wants to purchase an office building that any lender would value at $1,000,000. His purchase agreement requires him to pay $800,000 in cash, and the seller will hold additional financing for the balance ($200,000). Can you tell what the level of risk is for the buyer, seller or lender in either example? No, not based on the above information.

Review Example 1

If the seller were to hold an $80,000 second mortgage on the five apartments Winkle is buying it is very doubtful that any lender would loan him the $120,000 which would be the balance of the price. Because the total price is made up of a first mortgage and a seller held second mortgage there is a combined 100% loan-to-value ratio. Not impossible, mind you, but the lenders (both of them), would be looking to the strength of the buyer as the primary security to the deal.

If this was your first real-estate transaction, and unless you could meet the obligations the lender might impose on you, this transaction might slip past you. After all, from the lender's point of view the prospect of a 100% loan to value has increased the lender's risk for repayment considerably. The seller, being in a secondary position carries the majority of the risk, but even the first mortgage holder would feel uneasy.

Risk for the buyer is another thing altogether. Unless there is a requirement of personal obligation on the loan, the actual risk to Winkle is limited to his time and effort to put the deal together and keep it together as he meets the obligations of the mortgage. If he is confident in that ability, and has a sound plan for the property which will allow him to increase rents, thereby increasing value, that risk may fade away to little or none.

One creative approach, and this book will give you many, would be for Winkle to increase the security to the seller by giving him an $80,000 first mortgage on another property. As long as the property was worth $80,000 or more, the seller would have improved his position.

In doing this, the first mortgage lender's position has improved dramatically. Now a loan-to-value ratio of 60% will allow the lender to make the loan of $120,000. Carry this one step more, Winkle can ask for a new first mortgage of $140,000, which is a loan to value ratio of only 70%. He can sweeten the deal to the lender by showing that he will spend $15,000 of the new money to upgrade each of the apartments. At this point what has happened is the deal now has gone to 120% loan to value, and is a workable deal.

Review Example 2

Jones has the similar opportunity to obtain 100% financing. All he has to do is to get the seller to shift the secondary financing to something else, or to take an exchange in lieu of the added payback in the form of a mortgage. If the seller were to accept other real estate worth $200,000 then Jones has invested the real equity into the property and the only debt he would have to pay back would be the $800,000. While Jones did not come out of pocket the $200,000, the new first mortgage lender would treat this as cash invested and would look at the new $800,000 loan as a loan-to-value ratio of 80%. If this risk was acceptable to the lender then the loan would be obtainable. For Jones, this deal has more risk to him than the Winkle's example. Winkle didn't invest any cash. His sole investment was the promise to payback, putting the property he purchased, and perhaps his own personal signature on the line.

Each of these examples shows varying levels of leverage in action. If Winkle was able to get a lender to make a 60% loan-to-value loan without the need for personal signatures then Winkle's actual risk would be limited. High leverage without great financial risk. Jones' deal equally could end up high leverage, but if he gave the seller another property (worth $200,000), then his deal is zero cash, with moderate leverage.

INTRODUCE LEVERAGE INTO THE EQUATION

Leverage is one of the most misunderstood factors of real estate financing, and its understanding is a prerequisite to the application of the tools of financing. While it often is thought that leverage and risk go hand in hand, and that the greater you have of one the greater you have of the other, this is not always the case. In fact, once you realize just how leverage works, you will see that if this financing tool has been used to its maximum benefit, the greater the leverage the lower the risk.

The concept of highly leveraged properties as being risky will continue to be deemed as investments to avoid. When you run into this kind of viewpoint, you will have the leisure of knowing that you are dealing with someone who operates under the myth rather than the reality of this factor of financing.

WHAT IS LEVERAGE?

Leverage is the result of borrowing money at a constant rate lower than the net operating income rate generated by the property. If the property is not income producing but is going up in value at an establishable rate, then leverage can be applied. In general, however, leverage works best when lenders can see income from the property as a source to repay the loan. For example, suppose you buy a small shopping center. The store price is $400,000 and as it is owned free and clear (free of any debt), the seller wants all cash. The net operating income is $44,000 each year, you would have a return on your investment, prior to income tax computations, of 11% of your cash invested.

Example 3

The Shopping Center Transaction. You purchased a modest shopping center. Take a look at what you did: Price paid: $400,000. Cash return before taxes: $44,000. Return on your invested cash: ($400,000) 11% per annum.

As there is no mortgage in this deal there is no financing effect (either beneficial or otherwise). No leverage is found in this example. Without financing, therefore, nothing is leveraged. Leverage only occurs when there is borrowed money.

If you purchase this same property and had used one or more of the financing tools available to you, there would have been one of three possible results from leverage: positive leverage, negative leverage, or no leverage at all. Of these three elements, it is very rare to have no leverage effect.

Assume that you put $25,000 down on this strip store, and obtain a total of $175,000 in financing. This financing might be in one new mortgage obtained from the First Forever Savings and Loan Association, or a combination of mortgages you finesse out of the transaction. The transaction might have one mortgage that is held by the seller in the amount of $350,000. The terms of this mortgage are one annual payment per year of $36,000 until the mortgage is paid off. This payment of $18,000 per year now represents a constant annual payment of 10.28% per annum. (Remember, the constant payment takes into consideration both principal and interest, and the rate is an initial percentage which reflects the payment in relation to the original amount of the principal owed.)

Since the total purchase price is $400,000 and the net operating income is $44,000, if you now have a mortgage payment of $36,000 there will be a sum of $8,000 left over after all expenses and debt payments.

The leverage factor is viewed as follows: In this case, we have a debt of $350,000 that has a constant payment of 10.28%, or $36,000 per year. The net operating income is $44,000 when based on free and clear property; this would give a return on the all cash investment of 11%. When financing is introduced into the investment, you will notice that there is to be a change in the interest yield of the cash invested.

In the financed deal, you paid $50,000 down (assume that came from your savings), and had a cash flow (gross income less all expenses and all debt service payments) of $8,000, you have a cash yield of 16% (16% of $50,000 = $8,000). This means that in this transaction you have created a positive leverage by increasing the yield on the invested capital from 11 to 16%. This increase has come solely from the effect of the financing applied. It is possible that you may have created even greater increase in yield through the use of other financing techniques. There are many different kinds of financing that you could apply in a situation such as this previous one.

However, as attractive as high leverage is, the maximum effect may not be to create the highest possible leverage. You will soon see that *overleverage* or *negative leverage* has disadvantages. What you want to do is to use the highest leverage that allows you to meet your goals, while at the same time keeping the financial obligation of the investment within your control. Investments that are very highly leveraged may reduce the investor's risk, because there is a smaller percentage of investment to risk.

In the balance of this chapter, I delve into leverage to show you how to put it to work. I also cover the elements of over leverage. As in all aspects of anything good, there are pitfalls that must be discussed. They are overextension.

UNDERSTAND THE COMBINED EFFECT OF THE CONSTANT RATE ON THE MORTGAGE TO CASH FLOW

The effect of leverage is always examined with its relationship to the constant rate of the mortgages and the constant cash flow rate of the net operating income. As has been mentioned, the combined principal and interest payments of the total mortgages make up the constant rate. This constant rate is fixed at the time of the mortgage for that investor.

For example, if you bought the strip store and had one loan for 30 years, with an interest rate of 8.47% per annum and the principal balance of the mortgage at the closing of the purchase was $175,000, your annual payment would be $16,000, with a monthly payment each month for 30 years of $1,333.33. The constant rate would be found by dividing the total annual payment by the amount of principal owned ($16,000 divided by $175,000 = 0.0914). To show this as an interest rate, move the decimal two places to the right to get 9.14%.

The constant rate is important as a way to gage the overall effect of financing. Since interest rates only tell you the economic cost of the money you have borrowed, they cannot be the final criteria in the overall cash payment. As the constant rate contains both interest and principal pay-back, its rate is an effective guide to determine your final cash-flow circumstances.

The constant rate is a function of time and interest and as one changes the constant rate changes. As shown in the following table, a $100,000 loan has a combination of constant rates, depending on the functions of time and interest.

Constant Rates for a $100,000 Loan

Interest	Years	Monthly payment	Annual constant rate
10%	25	$ 901.13	10.814%
11%	30	$ 943.65	11.324%
9%	10	$1,256.93	15.083%
8%	4	$2,423.76	29.086%

Review the above table. You quickly notice that while the lowest interest rate is 8%, due to the short payout of four years it has the highest constant payment and therefore the highest constant payment rate.

When refinancing older properties, it is not uncommon to discover mortgages that can be assumed at rates well below the current market conditions. These mortgages may be attractive to assume on first glance at their interest rate. Yet when you discover the actual cost, the sacrifice to get the attractive interest rate may not be worth the loss of cash flow due to the excessive constant rate.

Your review of the options available to you, and the creative way in which you reduce the overall constant rate, can mean additional cash flow to you and increased value in the property. Each of these two elements satisfy financing goals covered in the first chapter of this book.

VALUE AND RISK IN LEVERAGE:
THE BOTTOM LINE CAN BE THE MOST IMPORTANT
CRITERIA TO DETERMINE BOTH VALUE AND RISK

Investment properties are valued to a great extent by the cash flow they produce. A buyer will pay a price based on the yield he or she gets from the cash invested. If the risk demand for the investment for this investor is 10%, the maximum amount of money the investor may be willing to spend would be the amount that would then earn that desired rate.

While the amount of cash flow is not always the most important economic criteria for an investor, it is generally the safest guide to market value for income-producing properties. Some investors want fast debt reduction and sacrifice cash flow for some other benefit because it fits their business plan. Low or even zero cash flow would be the case of an investment in vacant nonincome-producing or low-income property. As there is little or no income to be leveraged into a higher yield, the relative yield must be based on the potential increase in value when the property is either sold, or developed. In the meantime, debt, and holding cost, must be met by reaching into your own pocket. If the property were to be developed within a year or so, short-term financing costs may be absorbed into the transaction even though it might have an excessive constant rate in comparison to the actual market conditions of financing.

You purchase a lot on which you are going to build a fast food restaurant for a national company. It has signed a triple net lease (where the tenant generally pays all expenses including real estate taxes, insurance, and maintenance). The period of time you pay the debt and carrying cost out of your own pocket or finance them into a final development loan should be considered as part of the gross investment. Any tax advantage you may obtain by deduction of interest, and so on may lessen that financial drain. In this kind of situation a very high negative leverage would result, but would not be detrimental to the deal if you have the financial staying power. The end result (the goal is to build a fast food restaurant), should have a positive leverage once rents begin to come in. If the leverage still shows as negative (in comparison to a free and clear ownership), then you need to rework the plan, or reassess your goals.

Six Key Factors in Real-Estate Leverage

1. THE STRUCTURE OF FINANCING WILL AFFECT THE AMOUNT OF LEVERAGE YOU RECEIVE.   A short payout of a mortgage may have a very high constant and may eliminate the cash flow entirely. On the other hand, an interest-only mortgage will reduce the constant rate to a lower level for the early term of the loan, even though it may create havoc in the cash flow of later years. The goals of the investor form the basis of the way to establish the leverage best suited for the transaction if the investor has the option available to alter the financing at all.

2. LEVERAGE CALCULATIONS THEMSELVES ARE MERELY A COMPARISON OF THE YIELD CHANGES, AND SHOULD BE USED ONLY TO SHOW THE DIFFERENCES BETWEEN THE FINANCING METHODS THAT COULD BE USED.   The actual amount of yield that is increased or decreased is not the specific criteria for the use of the financing tool. However, it is helpful to see how the leverages can be increased or decreased, and know what element is affecting the outcome. Some of the discount transactions you will have available to you will enable you to increase the amount of loan at zero or very low constant rate. This kind of financing can enable you to average out very low rates.

3. MAXIMUM LEVERAGE MAY NOT BE POSSIBLE UNDER THE CIRCUM-
STANCES.   Then, it may not be the most advisable either. The options available to
the buyer or to the seller in the actual structure of the deal are limited by the circumstances and the goals of both parties. In the give-and-take of the negotiations,
each party may give in to some demand of the other party. In addition to these
demands, the lender may require some changes in the overall deal. It is generally the
buyer who is the lender's target and buyer's flexibility is increased tremendously when
the lender is the seller.

In the trade-off between obtaining the maximum benefits of price and terms
the following elements should be considered by the buyer.

- *Appreciation.* Appreciation is the increase in the value of a property over a period of time. While financing has only a passive affect on appreciation, it is
  nonetheless very real. As income properties are valued as per their income based
  on the desired yield, a mortgage or set of financing tools that reduce or eliminate the increase of income and set for a long term the yield an investor could
  earn, the appreciation of this property would be slowed or eliminated. Some
  financing tools can maximize the immediate cash flow and hold back future
  increases of value. If the immediate cash flow were the most important aspect
  of the purchase, that loss would not be a sacrifice at all.

On the other hand, for some investors appreciation is the most important
aspect and whole estates are planned on the ultimate growth of a portfolio.

- *Equity build-up.* This is the slow-and-steady pay-off of the principal owed on the
  debt against the property. An interest-only mortgage would have no principal
  pay-back and would therefore have no equity buildup at all. Other mortgages
  that have a negative payment, which is one where the monthly payment is not
  sufficient to pay the interest due so unpaid interest is added to the principal
  owed, actually reduce equity by building onto the amount owed. This kind of
  financing is good only where the need for cash and the assumed appreciation of
  the property support taking out the future equity now through greater cash flow.
- *Cash flow.* This usually is the desired goal for many investors. However, when
  the existing financing is at a low interest rate, despite the high constant rate of
  a short-term pay-back, the sacrifice might well be the cash flow to obtain greater
  yields later on by increasing the equity buildup for the early years.
- *Tax credits.* Some investors want greater tax credits and lower immediate cash
  flow. These investors would want to see financing tools that would provide for
  maximum tax credits at a sacrifice of cash flow. Some of the tools that increase
  cash flow have the effect of reducing tax credits. This is all a part of the balance
  between these four elements.

- *Use of funds available.* The maximum use of your investment funds may demand that you get the highest mortgage you can and invest the least cash possible. This frequently is done with the idea that eventual income levels can be increased. This causes investors to go in on a shoestring. Great fortunes can be made this way . . . and lost.

Nonetheless, if you know your comfort zone and have strong and visible goals, you will find that the risk you would have on such an investment may be well below that of the typical investor in the marketplace.

4. THE AMOUNT OF LEVERAGE YOU GENERATE IN THE USE OF FINANCING IS NOT THE FINAL CRITERIA. Remember, while you can make a marginal deal acceptable, you cannot turn a bad deal into a good deal. Overworking a transaction generally means you are looking for some rationalization to enable you to make the investment. While it may be okay for you to make the investment, do not kid yourself that something that looks good on paper (using figures you have forced) is, in reality, not good at all. This points out the importance of having good facts on which to base your final decision. In all my thirty plus years as a commercial real estate broker I stress to buyers that the only economic figures of a transaction that they can rely on will be the ones they arrive at through due diligence, and the application of their own experience. This is not because sellers lie about the data, although many do, but the simple fact that the present owner may be running the property (or business), to a different drummer than you would.

5. REMEMBER THAT THE ABILITY TO LEVERAGE YOUR INVESTED CASH IS GREATER IN REAL ESTATE INVESTING THAN MOST ANY OTHER FORM OF INVESTMENT. Naturally there are exceptions from truly anxious and motivated sellers (usually a former lender). This is due to the ease and acceptability of real estate as a collateral for mortgage financing. However, we often take this for granted without realizing that in many areas of the world, long-term loans on real estate are unheard of. In some countries, the land and real estate is state owned. In other countries, much of the land is "leasehold" and all users are tenants on land owned by the Crown, State, or old families who have handed down townships over generations. In other parts of the world, land and other real estate may be private ownership but have no value as a security on a mortgage due to the lack of confidence the banks would have in "taking that land" as a security.

Real estate has proven itself in the United States as the single most secure form of security for a loan. For this and other reasons, institutional lenders have no hesitation making a loan based on some reliable estimate of value. This fact has given rise to a strong secondary market for real estate loans. Of all the secondary loan market, the best for the buyer, and often the most motivated to make the loan, is the seller.

6. LEVERAGE IS A FUNCTION OF FINANCING, BUT IT IS THE TEMPERA-
TURE GAUGE OF WHAT YOU ARE DOING. Understanding financing means
understanding the overall picture of what happens when mortgages are paid down
and equity is built up. As the term suggests, leverage is a fulcrum where the weight
of the loan offsets the absence of weight of the investment. Many multimillionaires
are defined as people who owe millions of dollars.

THE PITFALL OF LEVERAGE: OVEREXTENSION

Overextension occurs when the cost of the debt exceeds the abilities of the borrower.
This event can occur with the most conservative approach to a mortgage on one
property when the borrower has gotten in over his or her head on another property.
In fact, this seems to be true for many foreclosures.

In the case of income properties, the proper approach to financing is to try not
to overexpose the ability of that property. Naturally, there are times when you are
looking for increases in rents to support the added debt to the property, and sometimes those increased rents just don't occur.

While there is no single test for you to use to keep from going in deeper than
you can swim, there are some guidelines you can follow that would help you stay out
of overextension.

SEVEN GUIDES TO AVOID OVEREXTENSION

1. Make sure you are investing within your comfort zone. This means a comfort
   zone you have been working and know like the back of your hand. The fastest
   way to become overextended is to buy something out of your comfort-zone area.

2. Be very sure the investment will move you closer to your goals. That means do
   not fool yourself. Does the purchase of that property bring you closer to your
   goals? Can you write down why?

3. Is it within your physical abilities? Don't take on anything that you cannot handle just because it looks good.

4. Have you "worked" the purchase negotiations? This means: Have you been a
   part of the transaction, or was it brought to you? If you have worked it or have
   been involved with the transaction for awhile, it is likely you will have a better
   understanding for items 1, 2, and 3 above.

5. Can you carry the property for the estimated time plus an additional 50% of
   the estimated time needed to generate the income it would take to support the
   property 100%? In short, a low down payment and tons of leverage won't help
   if you promptly go bankrupt because it took nine months to get the tenants you
   anticipated you would have in six months.

6. Are you jeopardizing everything for this one deal? If so, you had better make sure you are all set on items 1, 2, 3, 4, and 5.

7. If things go astray, be sure you don't hold onto the sinking ship for too long. Too many investors fail because they tried to save something they were incapable of saving. If they had simply stepped out of the deal at the time they knew the ship was actually going to sink, they would have been a lot wiser.

THE FINAL ELEMENT: HOW LEVERAGE AFFECTS THE INCREASE OF VALUE IN REAL ESTATE

There are six reasons property values go up. Often more than one of the six factors are working at the same time, some to a positive way, others negative. Each of the following six factors can be enhanced or detracted from by the total effect of financing. First look at the six factors.

The Six Factors That Cause Property Values to Go Up in Value

1. Inflation.
2. Improved infrastructure.
3. Economic conversation.
4. Increased cash flow.
5. Capital improvements.
6. Supply and demand.

Review each of these factors in detail.

INFLATION

Inflation increases the monetary value of a property by the effect of two different, but related events. The first is the general decline of buying power of money, also called the effect of the increase in the cost of living. The increased cost of living is a widely studied economic circumstance that is the result of many different things going on. The end result of this effect is that the same item that cost $10 a few years ago, may now cost $30. The cause of inflation is the trend for more complicated and sophisticated apparatus to be a part of our lives. The equipment we take for granted, such as Boeing 747s, main-frame computers, wide-screen television sets, ultrasophisticated life-saving equipment, and so on. All are far more expensive than what our Grandfathers were used to. As a nation becomes used to this modern and sophisticated world, we actually develop a need for things that cost more because they do more. This is a price we pay for having a high standard of living.

Income property has the potential of offsetting the effect of inflation. This single factor can make a real estate investment worthwhile even if there is no immediate cash flow return. The investor's opportunity to enhance this potential even more, through positive leverage or other beneficial financing techniques, can turn a modest investment into a real winner.

Example

The following is an example of how inflation and financing techniques affect the value of an investment.

Frank York has owned a 20-unit apartment building for the past twenty-five years. The original purchase price was $200,000. He was able to obtain new financing when he purchased the building in the amount of $160,000 and invested a total of $40,000 in the down payment. The mortgage payments over those twenty-five years consisted of approximately $14,000 per year, payable in monthly installments of $1,166.67. Over the term of the loan (25 years) he has paid $370,480 in payments, around $210,480 of which was interest, the balance was principal.

The first year of his ownership Frank pocketed around $6,000 in cash flow after making all payments for operations and debt. This was a 15% annual return on his $40,000 investment. (Actual return would be found by the formula: $6,000 (Return) divided by $40,000 (Investment) equals 15% (Yield).

Over the years the monthly rents kept pace with the cost of living and what began as $150 per month is currently $550 per month. Gross rents increased from $36,000 per year to $132,000. The annual operational expenses also rose, keeping pace with the cost of living, averaging 40 to 45% of gross revenue. Current net operating income is $72,600.

If Frank had purchased this property using 100% cash, his return would have been 10% of his investment from day one. The increase in income and the increase in expenses would have kept pace with the rise in the value of the building so that at any given point of time the property would have been giving Frank a return of only 10%, and not the 15% bonus he had.

Because Frank had borrowed $160,000 to purchase the property he benefitted in two ways over an all-cash buyer. First he was able to buy a property he might not have been able to afford otherwise. Second, he let his tenants pay off the $160,000 so that at the end of the 25th year he now has a property that is worth over $700,000. His investment never changed. The yield on that $40,000 grew each year until presently with a $72,000 net operating income, and zero mortgage payments, the yield on cash invested (with no other things taken into account) is 180%. Now that's how to make money.

The effects of the cost of living for Frank were buffered by this steady increasing spendable cash flow. As has been my experience in similar investments, the rental income increase from $150 per month to $550 per month could easily counterbalance other costs, say Frank's health insurance, or real-estate tax on his home, or his monthly electric bill at his own home. As this is the way it works, for Frank, his electric bill for his home has actually not gone up over the past twenty-five years because one apartment's rent covered it. For Frank, and other income property owners, this is a considerable benefit. As all benefits contribute to value, this is one of the best sources of wealth you will ever find.

IMPROVED INFRASTRUCTURE

Changes in the infrastructure within a community can produce a very predictable effect on the value of real property. Not all of these effects are beneficial.

Community infrastructure is a combination of many different things. New roads, bridges, new hospitals, water systems, schools, and so on, all contribute to the infrastructure within a city or area. Some of these elements are publicly built and financed, others are privately owned and financed. Each can have an immediate impact on the value of a property. Each can present an investment opportunity by pointing to a time and place to buy, or signal an urgent need to sell.

Positive impacts of improved infrastructure are relatively easy to anticipate, when you look at a long time period. Immediate or short-term benefits may not materialize however, and some values may go down, only to recover dramatically later on. This dive-and-recovery of property values is an important factor and many savvy investors look for these situations.

For example, a new bridge is planned to replace an old one. The approach roads from both sides will be widened. The reasons for the new bridge and widened road system is to meet the growing traffic demands for the next twenty years or more. The logical long-term benefits would include increased values of some of the property on both sides of the bridge. However, not all property is likely to go up in value, and may actually go down in value, with no short-term recovery possible. Other property will dive in value for a short time, then recover nicely.

Consider a potential of eighteen months of construction time. During that period there is likely to be a considerable amount of road work, noise, detours, dust, and so on. This often causes major disruption in the existing commercial properties along or near the work area. If there has been a long build-up to the construction, as is often the case, even prior to the construction actually beginning, a year or two of preliminary work may have occurred. This may or may not include the taking of additional road right-of-way, actual condemnation of properties for new approach ramps and other needed land areas to support the new bridge. Tenants may have run for the hills in search of new sites for their businesses. Few companies and businesses can weather this kind of storm. And what about the property owners who own the commercial properties? Don't they have mortgage payments to make?

The argument that all they need to do is hang in and wait out the construction until the values go up may not be good enough for every property owner. These properties might be ripe picking for the investor who has a new use for the property to take advantage of the soon-to-be-increased traffic flow.

New roads cut off entire sections of the previous subdivision. This might cause one part of the area to suddenly be the in spot, whereas the other, now hard to get to, or suddenly on the wrong side of the tracks, goes down in value.

As a seller, you want to be very alert to any changes that are going on that have any effect on property you own, no matter how small the effect might appear to be. Even very small changes from the previous status quo may only be the start of a trend of changes. As a buyer, being alert to these same potential changes on a broader scale, will lead you into investment potential.

The best part of this, from each point of view, is that virtually every change in infrastructure requires a long lead time. Government projects might be in planning for years, city and other local development follows long-range planning and often the need to have special public vote prior to funding. You will be surprised to discover that the majority of people are not aware of even very major construction or other changes to their city or neighborhood until the work actually begins. Apathy about what is going on in your backyard will cost you dearly, and you will miss many opportunities to sell, before the crash, or buy before the jump in values.

Your approach to either situation may require some fancy footwork and creative financing strategies. As a seller the key is time. Get the property sold prior to the bottom dropping out. As a buyer, make sure you take into account that there may be a delay in the rise of values.

ECONOMIC CONVERSION

Economic conversion occurs when there is a change in the use of a property. If you cause the change to take place, then this is *voluntary economic conversion*. For example, you buy an old home that is in an area where the zoning permits professional offices (or you get the zoning changed). Your economic conversion would happen when you convert the old home into offices. If the change is *involuntary*, as might occur with a government action, such as rezoning, or the taking of part of the land (to widen a road or other use), then the present use must be changed.

Voluntary economic conversion is the best immediate real estate investment strategy available to investors. It is immediate because you generally don't do it until you are ready to act. This is the opposite of buying vacant land to sit on for the next ten years. Because it is immediate, every decision you need to make can be based on facts as they actually will affect what you want to do. Rental market studies, construction costs, zoning rules and regulations for example, will apply today to what you are doing. Planning to do the same thing, some time in the future, can be met with a future of changes that may prevent you from following your desired plan.

Mostly economic conversion is creating something new from something old. This has certain appeal because the key word *new* seems to bring with it *added value.* This concept spills over into the financing aspects of the property or venture. Because you are approaching a property with change in mind, the prefinancing package or loan presentation will need to demonstrate the soundness of the plan. This is where your homework will pay off handsomely.

INCREASED CASH FLOW

The value of every income-producing property is greatly affected by small changes in certain aspects of the property. The cash flow of any property, either before or after taxes, is one of the important criteria to the investment. Your specific goal may not depend or even require an increased cash flow. Yet, because cash flow sets the cash on cash yield (the return on your actual cash invested in the deal), anything that increases the cash flow will generally increase the value of the property.

STEPS NECESSARY TO INCREASE CASH FLOW. You can increase cash flow by doing any of the following. The steps shown below may be combined or acted on individually. It is possible that the result will be immediate with some, and slower in coming with others. To accomplish some of these, such as increasing rent, you may have to spend money in improvements and maintenance to upgrade the property. Each of the following four items may be within your control.

- Increased collected revenue
- Reduced operating expenses
- Reduced fixed expenses
- Reduced cash invested

How to Increase Collected Revenue

- *Increase monthly rent.* If you study your competition closely, you may discover that your rents are lagging behind. Stay up with the market whenever possible.

- *Increase occupancy.* Be aggressive in looking for good tenants, even when you don't have a vacancy. You may help a would-be tenant plan ahead for a scheduled vacancy you will have coming up in the near future.

- *Introduce "added income."* With residential income properties you can introduce add-on rents for services, or benefits, a supplement for pets, kids, extra cars, cable TV, and so on. Social functions can prove to be profitable too. In commercial properties these extra services might include security alarms and service, janitorial, executive services and the like.

- *Enforce rent penalties.* Many landlords overlook or forgive the penalties that are built into the leases. When tenants are late, or damage a property, they should be held accountable. Failure to collect can come back and punch you in the nose by encouraging people to get away with murder.

How to Reduce Operating Expenses

- *Get competitive prices.* If you have a lot of services then get competitive prices from different providers.
- *Charge the tenants for some of the "free" services.* If you don't have a *common area maintenance* (also called CAM), then add it. It is always quoted extra from rent, and may vary according to the actual common area expenses.
- *Practice prevention maintenance.* Major repairs and replacements may be cut down dramatically by having better prevention maintenance. Good planning generally is the key to getting more out of your appliances, roof, air-conditioning equipment and so on.

How to Reduce Fixed Expenses

- *Reduce annual real estate taxes.* Appeal to the taxing authority and request a reduction in the tax assessment. There are companies you can hire who will charge you only a percentage of what you save.
- *Reduce your debt service.* This may be nothing more than refinancing to a lower interest rate, or if your existing loan is two/thirds into its term of years, then a new longer term loan may reduce your monthly payments even if the interest rate is higher than the existing one. Remember, it is the constant rate that you need to look at.

How to Reduce Cash Invested

- *Take out cash.* The key word here is *tax-free cash.* If you can refinance the property you may find that by increasing the debt you can pull out some of your investment. If nothing else changes, if you cut your previously invested cash in half, you will have doubled your cash yield.
- *Bring in a partner.* The partner may not get the same split for his or her half of the cash as you do.

- *Sell off part.* This technique is often overlooked. You might find that a sale and lease-back of part or all of the property can free up capital, get your investment back and still give you cash on top of that. If you don't need part of the property at all, then sell it, or find a way to get income from it.

CAPITAL IMPROVEMENTS

While not all capital improvements increase value overnight, you will find that any capital improvement that allows you to accomplish one of the previously mentioned items, will increase value. Capital improvements that are nothing more than catch-up of poor maintenance may not have any immediate benefit to value.

A sound investment plan will include a schedule of capital improvements that are designed to enhance and upgrade a property. One of the most productive forms of improvement to a property is decorative landscaping. As landscaping will vary in price depending on the age and size of the plants when they are purchased, the sooner the plan gets underway the less expensive the ultimate five-year (for example) goal can be. One word of warning about landscaping. Get professional help in the plant selection, time of the year to plant, and overall design. Good landscapers are worth their weight in saffron.

When you purchase any real estate, the future capital improvements you anticipate, might be included in the initial financing package. Instead of putting off improvements that will increase revenue, get the money up-front and get the work done sooner, rather than later. To accomplish this may not require you to add any more invested capital, as the projected new or increased income may warrant the purchase money lender to add it to the loan. Keep in mind that the key word is new, as new hints at more income and greater value.

SUPPLY AND DEMAND

When there are only one or two vacant corners in town where the zoning will allow a gas station to be built, then the reduced supply of such sites is bound to increase the value. When the demand for fast food locations is high, any kind of property that will fit that need is going to be priced at a premium. The other side of this equation dictates that when there are a thousand residential lots or condos on the market, and few buyers, then the values will come down, or at least not go up, unless one of the other factors works its magic on the situation.

Often the only way to deal with a big supply and a low demand is to try to get the property out of the category that is not in demand. This is where savvy investing comes in handy, and the knowledge of the local market is important. When there is a large supply of something, say for example, old homes, but a short supply of nice professional office space, find an old home that can be converted into a nice professional office building. This is very simple economics, and best of all, it actually works.

Moving from one kind of property that is a buyer's market to another that is a seller's market may not be possible when there are few alternatives to follow. When your options are few, and you are a seller, then the only thing you may have going for you is to either change the direction you are going; that is, stop being a seller and become a buyer.

How can you sell a property in a buyer's market by becoming a buyer? I realize that this appears to be a paradox, but in reality it is most simple. Take for example a really strong buyer's market for exactly the same kind of property you need to sell. You have toughed out the market, endured bottom-scraping offers that just did not work, and are ready to make a change. Remember back in Chapter 1 the importance of knowing where you want to end up? Remember your goals? Now is one of those times you can put them to use.

Selling a property is less an economic benefit than it is the attainment of some other need or goal. This does not subtract from the fact that money may be at the center of your motivation. Yet, often the need for money, or for that matter, the need to sell the property is because you have not reviewed all the other alternatives open to you. This frequently is because you do not have a clear goal in mind. Assume the goal is to maintain or improve your present living standard while living within your fixed income. Presently, you are living in a 4,500 square foot apartment that is double the living area you actually need or think you can afford and you believe that one step to your goal is to down-size your living accommodations. Sell the big place, move into something more to your actual needs. Doing this you would have some cash left over to invest to increase your income. Not a bad approach either: save money on expenses and have more money to invest. The only problem is that big apartments are very hard to sell, and there are few buyers in the marketplace.

Become a buyer. Turn the tables on the poor market to sell your apartment and start looking for a purchase that can help you get closer to your goals. Remember, attaining your goal is what is important, not just the idea of selling the apartment.

One of several approaches would be for you to start looking for an investment that would strengthen your annual income. To acquire this new investment you will want to incorporate the equity you have in your apartment. If the value of the apartment was $800,000 and it was free and clear, it is likely that you could purchase a property worth well over $2,000,000. If your total down payment was $800,000 this would indicate that to borrow the balance would create a loan to value ratio of only 60%. (60% of $2,000,000 is a $1,200,000 loan with your equity of $800,000 as the balance).

A $2,000,000 income-producing property should have a viable NOI of around $220,000. If you could get a loan or combination of first and seller-held second loans of a pay-back with a constant rate of 10%, your total debt payment would be $120,000 per year. This would give you a cash flow of $100,000. This additional income may allow you to go back to the marketplace and buy a new place to live. You are benefitting because it is a buyer's market in all instances. Your large apartment becomes a part of a bigger deal, and may actually help the seller of the income property you acquire by taking that person closer to their own goal.

Leverage is like the foot in the door for the encyclopedia salesperson. It gives you opportunity. It is not a reason, by itself, to make the purchase, nor is it a solution to any specific problem, if the deal is a bad deal to begin with. You will maximize its benefits only when you use it to move closer to your goals.

Chapter 5

CONVENTIONAL FINANCING OF FIRST MORTGAGES:

Where to Find Them and How to Negotiate the Best Terms

This chapter deals with the complex world of institutional mortgages and other financing called *conventional financing.* The goal of this chapter is to give you the edge in finding the best mortgage to fit your specific needs. I will show you where to go and how to negotiate the best terms available in the market at the time you need the loan.

Conventional financing is financing obtained from savings and loan associations, commercial banks, pension funds, insurance companies and other similar institutional lenders. However, conventional financing terms can be from any other source that will lend on the same terms and standards as these institutions.

For this reason, the term conventional financing is misleading. "Conventional" need not be "institutional." It simply must be a loan along the same general terms and conditions as one provided by one of the institutional sources. This factor in itself is not that significant, unless the purchase agreement requires that you obtain financing from an "institutional lender." In that situation you would be excluded from finding the funds from a private source, even if the private loan was on better terms and conditions offered by an institutional lender.

A seller may have good reasons for requiring the buyer to use "institutional loan sources," such as if the seller was holding a substantial second mortgage, or offering a subordinated land lease that tied him or her to the deal after the closing. Forcing the buyer to go to a local savings and loan association, for example, may offer some insurance to the seller that the buyer and the lender were dealing at arms length.

Less than arms length deals have happened. For example, a buyer offers an above market price and gets the seller to take back a very large second mortgage subordinated to new financing. The buyer goes to his brother-in-law, (or someone else in on the caper), and borrows more than the purchase price. A year later the buyer

70

lets the loan go into default. The brother-in-law (and his partners) foreclose on the loan, all according to the plan. The seller either has to step in and cover the excessive loan, or lose his position.

This chapter covers the different types of first mortgages offered by the institutional lenders and examines some of the advantages of dealing with private "conventional" sources over lending institutions. In all instances, however, there are different techniques and strategies in dealing with the different kinds of lenders. I will give you a full and comprehensive procedure to follow which will aid you in obtaining any kind of a first mortgage.

WHEN IS A FIRST MORTGAGE A FIRST MORTGAGE?

A first mortgage, or first deed of trust, as it is called in some states, is a document that gives the lender a right, or lien, to the title of the property that is pledged as security to the loan. These rights, by the way, are an application of law, which may vary slightly from state to state.

The mortgage document itself is not evidence of the amount of money owed, as it is only the evidence of the security to the mortgage. The document that describes the amount of money owed, the method of payments, and other terms of pay-back is called the *mortgage note* (or just *note*) and is sometimes attached to the mortgage document. If you do not locate the mortgage note then you will not have the complete picture of what the lender expects.

FOLLOW THESE STEPS TO OBTAIN A MORTGAGE

When a borrower goes to a lender to apply for a loan, the borrower must provide information requested by the lender on the loan application. This application requests details about the property to be pledged as security, as well as considerable other data, such as the reason for the loan, and the borrower's personal background and financial strength. If the lender approves the loan application a commitment of the lender's willingness to make the loan is given. This loan commitment generally contains the full terms and conditions of the loan and the pay-back terms of that loan. Some lenders will not issue a loan commitment unless the borrower has paid a *loan origination fee*. This fee may have many different names, and will range from a very small amount to cover credit reports, to as much as two or three points of the total loan requested. The term *points* is just another term for "interest percent." Two points of $50,000 is $1,000 ($50,000 × .02 = $1000).

If the borrower needed $3,000,000 the commitment fee could be $90,000 or more. If the borrower was not a triple prime borrower, then the commitment fee, or loan origination fee may be much higher. The lender will tell the borrower that if a loan is offered along the terms requested, then the fee will apply to the closing of the loan. In some situations this fee may be built into the loan or added on top of the amount required by the borrower. This is to ensure that the project or purpose of the loan will not be diluted. Also it will ensure to the lender that the fee for making the loan will be covered.

If there is new construction or development involved, there are often two different loans. The original *construction loan* covers the cost of the actual acquisition and development. Then, within a prescribed period of time, sufficient to allow development and rent-up, the construction loan needs to be paid off. Prior to actual issuance of the construction loan the lender usually requires the borrower to have a *take-out loan*, or a *permanent loan commitment* already arranged. This loan will step in and pay off the construction loan and become the first mortgage or financing of record. Each of these two loan types may come from the same lender, or two or more different lenders may participate to make this all happen.

At the closing of the loan, the lender advances the money, and the borrower executes the mortgage note and the mortgage. The lender will generally require that the title of the property that is to become the security to the loan be rechecked by a title company and/or lawyers working for the lender prior to releasing any funds. This title is frequently checked prior to the issuance of the loan, and then once again after the mortgage document and note have been executed (and/or recorded). This final check is to ensure that the borrower has not managed to "hit" several lenders using the same property as security on several loans. Until the lender is secure that was not the case, it will generally hold up on giving the borrower the proceeds of the loan.

As title has not passed to the lender, the borrower still owns the property and has full use of it. The lender however, has obtained the right or lien against the property and should the borrower default on the note the lender can exercise its rights as would be provided for in the mortgage and by state and federal law. The rights to foreclose or to accelerate the demand of repayment are two of the rights the lender has to govern the force it can exert on the borrower to "get" its money back.

There is one form of mortgage agreement where title is retained by the lender. This is generally a seller-held mortgage, although sellers sometimes sell these mortgage agreements to third parties. This is the *contract for deed*, or *land contract*. There could be other terms used by sellers or realtors in your area that would be in fact the same kind of mortgage. No matter what it is called, if it fits the example I will give in the next paragraph, be aware of its conditions.

The contract for deed or land contract occurs when the seller and the buyer enter into an agreement where the buyer puts a down payment in the hands of the seller, and then makes a series of monthly payments over a period of time. At the end of this payment period, the amount owed on the purchase price would then be paid up and the property title would be delivered to the buyer. This resembles the mortgage you might get if you bought a home and owed the seller for the balance of the purchase price after making a down payment. The difference is who holds the title of the property. In the contract for deed or land contract, the seller retains title to the property until the terms of the sale have been met. In a mortgage situation, the borrower holds the title and pledges that title as security. In the contract for deed the buyer only gets the actual title when all the payments have been made, according to the terms of the agreement.

Some states have specific laws that deal with this kind of contract, because it has been a favorite kind of sales agreement by land developers and timeshare sales efforts, two kinds of development and sales operations that often have specific laws to govern sales practices, to protect buyers. Because of this you must be specially careful when this kind of mortgage or purchase/sales provision is used.

Most investors would avoid the contract for deed as it has a number of problems that become more evident the longer the term of payment. Sellers might "sell" bulk packages of collections (a $1,000,000 or so, worth of contracts for deed) or simply go out of business. If the buyer was still making payments for another fifteen to twenty years, it is possible that when the loan was paid off, there would be no entity to get the title from. Private deals using the contract for deed and short payoff are okay as long as you follow the advice of your lawyer. It is sound practice, to keep the pay-back term to fewer than five years. Even in those instances, as a buyer, you would want to limit this technique to vacant land. Because you don't get title until the last payment, you do not want to put capital into land, by building a building, or other equity, unless you were very sure you would eventually get title. Be sure to use a very good real estate lawyer, who knows about this kind of agreement as local laws apply.

A conventional first mortgage can be satisfied simply by paying off the amount owed, plus any interest or other assessments that are due. When the mortgage is paid off, the lender gives the borrower (or whomever holds title to the property at that time) a document titled *mortgage satisfaction*, or *satisfaction of mortgage*. It is up to the borrower to be sure that he or she gets this document from the lender and that it is properly executed by the lender. The borrower then has the document recorded in the county records, where the property is located. Unless this satisfaction of mortgage is recorded, there could be a *cloud on the title* at a later date as to the status of this mortgage. A cloud on the title is any possible glitch that shows up in the title. This can be an outstanding judgment against you, or some previous owner, or some other problem that suggests or illustrates that the present owner does not have all the rights to the title that are possible. Some clouds exist that may be okay, for example a utility easement, or drainage ditch. In the case of the missing mortgage satisfaction, unless there is clear evidence that a mortgage was actually paid off, (as the recorded mortgage satisfaction would illustrate), a prospective buyer or future lender, would insist that such evidence be produced. This can be a costly circumstance several years later if the principals to the loan have died, or cannot be found, or take the position that the loan has never been repaid.

If the borrower fails to make payments to an existing mortgage on time, nothing happens until the grace period has expired. This grace period can be any time period that the parties establish, but in general use it is 15 to 30 days. Remember, there may be no automatic grace period in your state, and while mortgages often provide for such a period of grace to take into account delay in mail, or other reasonable events, you can be held accountable if you do not pay on time.

If the payments due are not made by the last day of the grace period, the mortgage is in default and subject to the wrath or pleasure of the lender. In Chapter 23, I look into the horrors of this event. I suggest it as required reading by every person who may be using this book for research only. In this chapter I will comment briefly on foreclosure.

Foreclosure is very cumbersome and expensive for lenders. Usually a lender will avoid taking a borrower into foreclosure if at all possible. It is not uncommon for savings and loan associations to let their borrowers get well behind in their payments prior to actually filing foreclosure documents. Nonetheless, as the final step they will do all they can to collect the amounts owed. No lender likes foreclosure, but they all have gotten so they can do it with the least possible inconvenience. Still, almost all of them will work with the borrower who is in trouble and who comes to them and presents his or her case.

The position the lender has in a first mortgage exceeds any right of any other lender. This is the *primary loan. Secondary loans* are loans that are made behind the rights of the first mortgage or that were actually made prior to the first mortgage but subordinated to the rights of the lender. *Subordination* is the circumstance where one person agrees to let the rights of another person (or entity) move ahead of his or her rights. An example follows.

I sell you a property and hold a mortgage on the property. While my mortgage is a first mortgage simply because there is no other mortgage yet recorded, I can give you the right to go to another lender to borrow more money and let the rights of the other lender move ahead of my former first mortgage. Secondary financing of any nature has more risk to it than the primary loan. This is because these second loans are junior to the rights of the first mortgage. In the event of a foreclosure against the borrower, the primary or first loans get paid off first, and the junior or secondary loans come next, in their order of rank (second, third, fourth and so on). If there is not sufficient equity or value in the property it is possible that all junior mortgages will go unpaid. Even some first mortgages may not be fully paid. This assumes that the borrower has not filed bankruptcy, which would upset this sequence and in those events the end result may be that a court decides who gets what.

The position of the mortgage with respect to this junior or superior rank is not always what appears and should be examined carefully. For example, the document that says "This is a first mortgage" is not always a first mortgage. The rank of a mortgage with respect to the position of rights of the lender has to do with the time of recording and possible subordination provisions.

When a mortgage is executed, the lender will take that document, along with the mortgage note, and record it in the county or township of the state where the property is located. The intention of the lender may be to have a first mortgage; however, if the borrower has given another mortgage to another party (thinking it was a second mortgage) and the mortgage that was to be the second mortgage was recorded ahead of the mortgage that was to be the first mortgage, the time of recording becomes the critical element and not the intention or the title of the document.

In taking back a mortgage, as a lender (if you were to sell your own property or to make a loan to another party), you would want to be absolutely sure that the mortgage is indeed what it has been reported to be. In short, no matter how much you trust the people, make sure that the actual recording dates are verified. Errors by lawyers, title companies, or county recording offices could have positioned another mortgage ahead of that "first mortgage" you thought you were holding.

This situation explains the requirements of most lenders to check the title of a property after they have actually made the loan, but prior to funding the money.

WHO IS THE MORTGAGOR AND WHO IS THE MORTGAGEE?

The mortgagor is the person who gives the mortgage document to the lender. The lender is the mortgagee. The mixup in these words comes from the common practice to say "I will go to the bank and get a mortgage." In actual fact, you go to the bank to "get money" and by doing so to "give a mortgage." The key to this and any other "give" or "take" terms is that any words that end in "-er" or "-or" generally denote the "giver of the item." For example, the mortgagor, lender, grantor, lessor, and so on, are all people who have given something to someone else. That someone else is the "ee," of the same term: mortgagee, lendee, grantee, lessee, and so on is the person who "gets" the item. So the mortgagee is the person who gets the document called a mortgage . . . and in return is the grantor of the funds, therefore, the money.

Still not clear? Okay, think of it this way. When you borrow money from a lender who demands security in the form of a mortgage, you give that lender a right to your property by giving the lender a mortgage document. This makes you the mortgagor. That document says that if you don't make your payments on time or default in any other way, you risk actions by the lender that are not pleasant and where the end result is that you can lose your property. In essence, you pay up on time "or else." You give others rights to your property and you have to make good, or else. Remember that you are the mortgagor when you get money, and all else will fall into place.

STANDARDS THAT MAKE A LOAN "CONVENTIONAL"

When you are dealing with the conventional loan market, you will find a standard that tends to prevail throughout the country. There is little variance in the basic format of the loan once you are within the same category. However, many aspects of the loan can differ between states and even within the same city. Lending is a business, and a very big business at that. The people who make loans and the organizations who provide money are open to negotiation. If you know what you want and what the competition is offering, you usually can improve your position.

It may be as basic as understanding the difference between government restriction and lender policy. Each aspect is critical for you to know just how far you can go in hammering out good terms. Start with the fundamentals. The lender's policy is the flexible part of the equation. The inflexible part of any institutional transaction lies within governmental restrictions.

Savings and loan associations are governed by either state or federal regulations or both, and these regulations often restrict the percentage to a category of loan the lender can give. The restriction will not hamper your ability to negotiate with the lender as long as it still has room to make the loan within its portfolio requirements. However, when the lender is nearly out of its allocation for commercial loans, things begin to get tough for that lender. When things are tough the lender begins to get very picky about where to place funds.

To improve your success in loan presentations, make sure the lender has money to lend prior to knocking yourself out to win one or two points. Remember the old vaudeville phrase, "Yes we have no bananas." The fundamentals are simply that "yes" the lender will loan you money at the best rate and terms, but "no" they don't have any funds available at the moment.

Other restrictions that affect you, as a borrower, are the percentage of loan-to-value ratio that the lender is allowed to lend. This percentage depends on the kind or category of loan and may vary between lenders. For example, most savings and loans (both state and federal) are allowed to lend up to 95% of the value of the property if the property is to be owner-occupied, and the amount of the loan does not exceed $150,000. Yet many of these same institutions will have an internal policy that will restrict this amount to a lower figure. To some degree, this depends on the market for the area. Beverly Hills, California, is apt to have loans in the upper percentage while Camden, South Carolina, will have loans in the middle range of what is allowed.

MAKE CONTACTS WITH LOAN OFFICERS

One of the best ways to obtain information about the policy of a lending institution is to sit down with one or more loan officers within that institution and have the rules, regulations, and policy explained to you. You may discover that the loan officers are discovering which is which at about the same time you are, because policy is regulation to the employees and they often don't attempt to distinguish between the two until someone else forces the issue.

Use every meeting as an opportunity to make contact at a learning session. If you sincerely approach every contact as if they can "teach you something" you will be giving them a compliment while establishing good rapport. A secondary benefit is that you will get updated data on these regulations and policies at the same time. Remember, the key to this exercise is to discover the policy; it is here that you will be able to win points and obtain better loan conditions and terms from one lender over the other. But you must know policy. For example, the regulation may limit the maximum investor-nonresident owner loan on a single-family home to 80% of the value of the property, yet the loan officer may tell you that the maximum the bank will loan is 75% of the loan value. In this case, the policy is 75%, not the regulation. Policy can be negotiated, whereas regulation is fixed. Another element of this example is the loan value percentage. The regulation generally states that the percentage of the loan is based on the value of the property. Value is somewhat of an opinion, and to help smooth out this potential problem, many lenders temper this regulation and add policy that should be something like the following:

" . . . and value will be determined as the lower of the contract price or the appraisal." The wording can be rephrased a thousand different ways, but the idea should be clear to you. The lender wants to see your contract of purchase and will reserve the right to use its price as the value.

Yet, you know that loan percentages are dependent on value and not price so you can push the lender to make the loan based on real value and not a contract price on a property you are buying. If you bought the property for a song, you should be able to utilize the real value for the basis of the loan and not the "contract value" as the limitation to the deal. After all, if you already owned the property (say you bought it ten years ago), the actual price you paid would have no bearing, would it?

OVER ONE HUNDRED PERCENT FINANCING USING REGULATIONS AGAINST POLICY

I was reviewing the needs of a friend and client one day when he told me that he wanted to buy a small industrial building in Fort Lauderdale, Florida. He was very familiar with the building since he had worked as manager of an industrial parts distribution business that had occupied the structure for nearly seven years. The owner of the distribution business (who was at that time the owner of the building) acquired another company in Miami and moved the distribution business to that city. In the meantime, he leased out the Fort Lauderdale building to another firm, which was about to move out, leaving the building vacant. The owner had no real interest in owning the Fort Lauderdale building, and he did not want to get into the problems of management at a distance.

My friend suggested to the owner that he buy the building. He would then relocate the business that had moved to Miami back into the building and operate as the firm's representative rather than as a company-owned outlet. The concept made economic sense to the owner. He could rid himself of a real-estate problem and at the same time remove the management headaches of the company store in Miami.

With my help, my friend worked out a contract to buy the building for what was a very good price of $105,000. In a review of the capital needs of my friend, we determined that he would need all of his capital to get the business going and would not have sufficient funds to pay the $105,000 price unless that sum could be financed. From the way the numbers looked, I didn't think there would be any problem financing not only the purchase price, but the loan costs and some improvement money as well.

To accomplish this, I developed a pro forma and an evaluation of the building as it would be as of the time of sale. I was not interested in the actual current value of the building, only what the value would be under the upcoming circumstances and use.

In doing this study my back-up material showed that the value of this building, after the sale and with the fix up intended and the new use of the facility, would be $175,000. I had followed the *mortgage request outline*, which is shown on page 72. I was satisfied that I had sufficient material to support the following request:

Value of the Structure

Loan requested: $122,500
Use of the funds:

To seller	$105,000
Remodel	10,000
Loan costs	3,850
To borrower	3,650

Total of loan $122,500
Loan to value
$122,500 divided by $175,500 = 70%

What I had not anticipated was being thrown out of the first two savings and loan associations because the loan officer could not understand how he could request a loan based on value and not just the contract price. The end result: My friend got his building without having to spend any of his own money, and the lender got a good deal. The value of the building was as it had been represented, so the parties made a very good loan-to-value ratio. Once the contact had been made with the loan officer at the lending institution, it was a matter of "educating the lender" as to policy versus regulation.

No matter what your current needs in real estate financing, if you plan to become an investor you will need to shop for a loan. Since lending is a very big business, you will want to have friends in as many places as you can find to ease your way into the loan committee's good graces. Visit several potential lenders now and make the proper contact well before you need it.

Loan Conditions Common to Savings and Loan Associations

Maximum loan (%)	Term (Years)	Type of property	Conditions
90	30	Single family and condos	Percent of loan is based on the contract price or an appraisal, whichever is the lower amount. The total loan is usually under $45,000.
95	30	Single family and condos	Same as above, except private mortgage insurance is required. These loans usually are below $40,000.
80	30	One to four multifamily dwelling units	Appraisal value will take market conditions of rental area and vacancies into account.
75	25	Five or more units Commercial real estate	Greater emphasis on the person behind the loan. Appraisals will also be more detailed and the term of years reduced.
75	3	Developed lots	Terms for builders of more than two lots.
	5	Developed lots	Terms for individuals are longer. Usual provisions on which the lots are built within the term of loan.
100	12	New mobile homes	Based on invoice price.
100	8	Used mobile homes	Wholesale value.

MODIFICATIONS LENDERS FREQUENTLY IMPOSE ON THE ABOVE LOANS

1. It is interesting to note that almost all loans over 80% of loan monthly payments must include principal, interest, and a pro-rata buildup for an escrow of taxes and hazard insurance.

2. If the property is a residence of the borrower (and therefore qualifying for a better term mortgage), there must be a certification that the property will indeed be the borrower's home. Most lenders will limit the years and offer more restrictive interest rates and payback terms on investment property.

3. At the time of the loan, no secondary or junior loans can be made or placed on the property. This is standard for all primary lenders, but is more policy than regulation. Creative investors know that you can have secondary financing that makes the deal work, if the secondary loan is on another property. Land leases are a common form of secondary loan that is actually on the same property which secures the primary loan, provided that the loan is either subordinated, or of such a long term that the lender is comfortable with the loan situation.

4. Depending on the market, many lenders seek to shorten the pay-back terms of loans. It is not uncommon for these repayment terms to be five to ten years. The lender wants to shorten the exposure to the property and market conditions by having this short repayment term. To encourage the borrower to agree with this shortened term, a lower interest rate may be offered.

5. Most institutional lenders will offer a variety of repayment programs. In Chapter 5 a number of these different programs are discussed. They will include straight amortization, where the loan is repaid over a term of years, where equal monthly payments will satisfy the loan by the end of the term. Shorter pay-back schedules, but with a long amortization schedule requires a balloon payment to retire the still outstanding debt at the end of the term. These are just two of the many different repayment schedules that may be offered.

All lenders will negotiate any term or condition it considers reasonable or obtainable in the market. Banks, savings and loan associations, and other lenders are in the business of providing loans to borrowers for a specific business reason: profit. If the lending institution cannot make a profit, it is apt to slip slowly but surely into the oblivion of bankruptcy. As any business can go out of business, it should not be a surprise that in the economic world competition can have the same effect as in any other business.

The effect of competition on the borrower's ability to obtain loan terms that are better from one lender to another is something that has been around for a long time. One of the goals of this book is to assist any lender to recognize what the options are in seeking these better terms, and how to distinguish what is better instead of just different.

INTEREST, POINTS, AND COST

Interest rates are not regulated except by state law, which sets usury, which then establishes the maximum rate that can be charged. Interest charged is generally somewhat competitive, and on the surface it may not seem to vary much between lenders. However, as the jargon of finance is somewhat concealing, the total outcome of one loan that looks to be close to another can be most costly in the end.

The actual cost per $1,000 loaned is the best way to determine the overall cost of the total term of the loan. By comparing overall cost to actual cost, you gain a composite view of the potential economic picture. I say potential picture as some loan terms are not possible to forecast accurately. For example, if you take out a loan that is adjustable in the future, the lender has a formula that allows them to adjust the interest charged against the outstanding balance owed. This adjustment is frequently tied to the interest charged on an average of the U.S. Treasury Bills, or a specific "T" Bill rate. If this is the case, the interest can go up or down (but generally up) from the original loan rate. Some lenders attract borrowers to their institutions by offering interest rates below the market for the first year or so and then "bank" on the adjustment being sufficiently beneficial to the lender to make up for the "come on" rate. In this ploy to lend money, different lenders will offer different packages in their adjustment loan package. Maximum adjustments each year, or over the life of the loan, as well as different terms for adjustments do more to confuse the borrower (and make it far more difficult to calculate the actual cost in comparison to another lender) than to serve the public. One way to combat this is to take a "best" and a "worst" appraisal of specific loans. In essence, look at the actual cost to you if the loan rates are adjusted to the maximum rates. This will then give you the parameters for any specific loan, and in the end the absolute comparison between different loans.

Fixed-rate loans were once the only kind of loan available. However, even then the kinds of fixed interest rates were varied. For example, automobile loans often are quoted at an "add on" interest rate and the final cost of an add-on rate is nearly double that of the same rate on a common interest loan. The reason for this is the way interest is calculated. In a typical real estate mortgage or loan, interest is quoted as an annual percent charged against the amount of the loan (the principal) outstanding for the term that the interest is paid.

For example: If the principal of a mortgage was $100,000 at the start of the year, and no payments were made to reduce the principal during the year, and there was an annual interest payment due at 12% per annum, at the end of the year the interest due would be $12,000. If the interest payments were due each month, the borrower would owe $1/12$th of the interest rate monthly, which in this case would result in 1% per month being due. In a mathematical sense, the monthly $1,000 appears equal to the annual $12,000, but economically it is not. As a borrower, you would find it to your benefit to pay annually at $12,000 rather than monthly at $1,000. The situation should be obvious as you could take the $1,000 each month and put it to work for you at the same interest rate of 12%; at the end of the year you would have accumulated $682.25 of interest. If you then made your mortgage payment, you would pay a net of $11,317.75 as the interest in your account goes to you and not the lender. The actual cost of the annual payment (if you can earn 12%) of this mortgage is not 12% but only 11.3175%. While this may not sound like a lot of difference, it can add up.

On the other hand, the way the game is played by lenders is reversed. Lenders want interest as often as once a month. As you saw in this example, your bank account earned an interest of $682.25 by paying the interest monthly; therefore the lender will be able to earn that rate instead of you. So the lender gets your 12% in this example, plus a bonus of $682.25. As the amount of the principal has not changed due to the lack of principal payments, the bonus is 0.68225% for the year. In real terms, the lender makes 12.68225% on the loan in comparison to your paying 11.31775% on an annual payout.

Let's review the mathematics involved in the previous paragraph: $682.25 interest divided by the principal of $100,000 equals 0.0068225, which is the mathematical decimal for 0.68225%. Remember that whenever you divide dollars you will get the mathematical percentage and not the actual rate, which first must be multiplied by 100. Equally, when you want to multiply a number, say $50,000 by 12%, you must first translate that percentage to the mathematical decimal by dividing by 100 to make it 0.12.

The relation to the interest you pay and the method of payment should be clearly understood. Only by having it clear in your mind will you be able to make maximum use of the loans offered, and obtain the best terms to suit your goals.

Interest then becomes another of the elements of the mortgage that can be negotiated between the borrower and the lender. Not just the rate of interest is involved, but how it is paid. As we have just seen, the frequency of payment during the year has a relationship to the total cost of the mortgage. This cost should be considered in the complete relationship of the circumstance.

For example, if the interest is a deductible expense and will reduce another out-of-pocket cost, such as income tax, then the increase of the interest cost, if offset by some other element, may cause the borrower to give in on the higher interest (thereby increasing the yield to the lender at no net cost to the borrower). An example of this would be in a tradeoff to a lender who might be holding out for some other factor besides the interest. One such factor is participation in the transaction. This hidden interest is commonplace in large commercial transactions where the lender not only gets paid in interest, but also takes a percentage of ownership of the property or a percentage of gross income from the venture.

If this were the case, the wise borrower takes a hard, cold look at the potential cost of that participation and calculates the overall cost of a higher interest rate, which will have a definite termination point: that being when the mortgage is finally paid off, whereas the participation may be for the duration of ownership of the property. Another example of a tradeoff in which the tax advantages of higher interest may be desirable is in situations where the amount of the loan is higher than that loan possible at a lower interest rate. The borrower again has to weigh the cost of the money, and in this case the use of the funds, or in many events, the need for the funds to complete the transaction at hand.

INTEREST AND PRINCIPAL PAYMENTS COMBINED

As interest rates increase, the combined effect of interest and principal make for high monthly payments. To counterbalance this, lenders have come up with a form of mortgage that has negative amortization. Amortization is that element of a mortgage that is the reduction of the principal owed. In most mortgages, the monthly payment does not change during the base term of the mortgage. If the mortgage had a 25-year term with no balloon, over the period of 25 years, which may be seen as 300 months, the monthly payment would contain two amounts of money that would total one steady monthly payment. For example, if the amount of the loan was $100,000 and the rate of interest was 12% per annum, over a 300-month mortgage with regular amortization the payment would be $1,042.79 per month (a total of $312,837 over 300 months.)

If the lender was unable to lend sufficient money to meet its lending requirements with these terms, it could reduce the payback sum by either reducing the interest or increasing the term of the loan to cut the payments and therefore attract more borrowers. However, by increasing the term from 25 to 35 years, the payment only drops to $1,005.49.

This would mean that the borrower would pay back a total of $422,307.82 if he or she lived those 35 years and still owned the property. As you can see, spreading out the total term doesn't help, and the lender will not want to reduce the interest if there is another alternative. Thus, negative amortization mortgage is born. In this kind of mortgage, the payment is set at an attractive amount. How about $600 per month for the first two years, $700 per month for another two years, and so on, increasing the monthly payment every few years until the mortgage reaches the end of the tenth year, at which time the whole thing balloons.

Negative Amortization Mortgage Table

Principal at the start of the term: $100,000
A ten-year mortgage with 12% interest and monthly payments shown.

Year	Monthly payments	Amount of unpaid interest added to the principal	Principal at the end of the year
1	$ 600 per month	$4,996.91	$104,996.91
2	600 per month	5,630.64	110,627.55
3	700 per month	5,063.81	115,691.36
4	700 per month	5,706.03	121,397.39
5	800 per month	5,148.77	126,546.16
6	800 per month	5,801.76	132,347.92
7	900 per month	5,256.63	137,604.55
8	900 per month	5,923.37	143,527.86
9	1,000 per month	5,393.60	148,921.46
10	1,000 per month	6,077.64	154,999.10

Total payments made over 120 months: $96,000 on the $100,000 loan and the borrower still owes $154,999.10.

Most lenders have discovered that with this kind of lending two catastrophic things often occurred. The first was that many borrowers found that they were obligated to a debt greater than the property would support. The second event was that the property often didn't keep pace with the increased principal owed on the mortgage. If the original loan had been at a 90% loan-to-value ratio, the original value would have been $111,111 (90% of $111,111 is $100,000). At the end of the third year, if the actual value of the property had not increased, the borrower would have no "profit" in the property and foreclosure by the lender would soon follow. Many investors operate by spending the cash flow, and almost no one builds a reserve for replacements anymore. The concept of reserves for ultimate replacements, is a sound accounting practice, when used. However, most investors simply go back to the lender to get the needed funds, when replacements are needed. This works too, but can have major setbacks if the lending market drys up just when you need to make some major replacements. The negative amortization compounded this potential problem.

In looking at negative interest mortgages, you must be critically aware of the overall effect. If you take all of these elements into consideration, you will then be able to proceed to make value judgments that will direct you closer to your goals.

When we get to secondary financing, I will show you how many of these aspects discussed will be put to play to give you the advantage as either buyer or seller. When you are dealing with the institutional market, and therefore the conventional form of financing, you have less creativity available to you in private dealings.

DEALING WITH THE POINTS AND CLOSING COSTS OF CONVENTIONAL FINANCING

All lenders seek to cover their expenses in any transaction. The first line of defense of such costs and expenses comes in the way of "points." The origin of the "points" that lenders charge was to discount the amount lent so that when you paid back the total amount the lender would get an additional yield.

For example: If I borrow $10,000 and the lender charges $500 in points (5% of the amount borrowed), I only get $9,500 but have to pay back the $10,000. All interest is calculated on the $10,000, so you can see the lender's advantage.

When we get to FHA loans, you will see that the "points" charges have this effect. The lender gets a higher yield because FHA charges the seller for some of these points. This "cost" is the seller's expense because the seller can sell his property with a lower interest rate than available from the general market.

Points have become so commonplace in the conventional market that it has become a situation of the lender getting back from the borrower as much as it can to increase its yield and to make the interest rate appear lower. Points are an up-front deduction or expense from the borrower. If the lender wants five points and the loan is $1 million, we are talking about a lot of money.

However, most lenders will talk about reducing their points just as they will talk about other factors of their loans with which they have some leeway.

Another cost for conventional lenders and secondary lenders are "out-of-pocket expenses." In essence, lenders make a list of expenses they have incurred over the last year and charge it to you as out-of-pocket expenses. So far, competition in the industry has kept this list down to a minimum, but you should question every item that is going to be charged to you prior to signing the mortgage and note. The list is apt to include items such as the following.

OUT-OF-POCKET-LOAN EXPENSES
1. Abstract review.
2. Credit report.
3. Document preparation.
4. Environmental inspection and review.
5. Field investigation.
6. Legal expenses.
7. Loan origination fee.
8. Miscellaneous expenses.
9. Mortgage insurance.
10. Postrecording title check.
11. Preloan title check.
12. Property inspection.
13. Recording of title and other documents.
14. Review of credit report.
15. Staff review of documentation.
16. Survey check.
17. Title review.
18. Title insurance.

Many of these items are duplicates of other things you may be doing through other activities of the transaction. You need to ask about each item because the lender's list may have some very creative titles to describe some of the expenses. You will end up paying for most of the expenses the lender wants to charge. However, there are apt to be some expenses that will save you money if you know about them in advance, and others that may be eliminated.

For example, lenders often charge you for a title insurance policy to cover the amount of the loan. If you are not careful and observant you could end up paying for two policies: one for the lender which would be insufficient to cover the total value of the property, and a separate one in a greater amount to cover the amount of your investment. The proper and least expensive way is to make sure you get one policy to cover the value of your investment, and provide (at a small expense) for a coinsured provision in the policy to cover the lender.

Find out all of the items the lender wants to charge you for. Ask if you can have them done elsewhere, and then get a price quote from several other sources. You might find that the lender is the best price around, or the worst.

Some lenders try to sell you all sorts of other insurance. Extra insurance comes in two forms: Hazard insurance covers the property against storms, fire, and other disasters, and mortgage insurance pays back the lender should you die before the mortgage has been paid in full. Mortgage insurance is usually very expensive for what you get, and you may already have life insurance that can be partially assigned to the lender in the unlikely event of your death. Even if you don't have any other insurance, make sure to ask an independent insurance agency for the price of life insurance that will pay off your mortgage, if necessary.

Another factor that comes to play in these costs is the loan-to-value ratio. This is one of the strongest factors in lending. Is the loan 50% of the value, or 95%, or somewhere in between? The lender likes a large spread in the loan-to-value ratio. If you have done your homework well and utilized all of the steps provided in this book, you can maximize your loan and at the same time minimize the pay-back cost of the loan by showing a low loan-to-value ratio.

One step in that direction will be to do all you can to show the maximum value of the property you are buying. Remember the industrial building that was discussed. Your contract doesn't establish the value of the property, and you must provide back-up data to support the real value, which you believe to be higher than your contract price (if it is a new property), or provide as much detail to support the appreciated value if you have held the property for some time.

Later in this chapter you will find an outline for a loan request. Follow its guides for all loans except for development loans, which are discussed in Chapter 8.

WHERE DO CONVENTIONAL LOANS COME FROM?

You will find conventional loans from these following sources:

Savings and Loan Associations	Thrift Savings Associations
Credit Unions	Commercial Banks
Mortgage Bankers	Mortgage Brokers

HOW TO DETERMINE WHICH SOURCE TO APPROACH

Which lender in your area will be the best for you? That is a difficult question to answer. The economic market in lending fluctuates greatly from time to time, and the lender with the best secondary market going for it will be apt to be the most liberal lender. The majority of the money that you borrow comes from the secondary marketplace. This is the market to which the lenders sell their loan packages. Savings and loans, credit unions, and commercial banks maintain the added advantage of having their depositors' money as well, but the secondary market rules as king. Unfortunately this secondary market is not available to you unless you need to borrow large sums of money for development, and even then the possibility of your entry into the secondary market is slight. What this secondary market is and how it affects your determination of who to go to for your loan is simply this: insurance companies, the Federal National Mortgage Corporation, and the Government Insured Mortgage Corporation buy mortgages in large packages. Mutual funds are being formed also to buy mortgages.

THE BEST SOURCE WILL BE THE ONE
THAT LIKES YOU MOST

In all business dealings, the element of like and trust mean a lot. Naturally, there must be good, sound business principals at work, and in the moment of compromise between you and someone else the soundness of the loan might weigh more than friendship. However, never underestimate the power of your contacts. What this means, of course, is if you don't have any contacts you had better start establishing them. Your contacts should not be only in the banking field, but in all areas where one person could mean the difference between your success and your failure. In this book, you will find that lesson brought out constantly, as I feel very strongly about the power of personal attraction. There is more on this aspect in Chapter 8.

THE PERSON YOU TALK TO IS NOT LOANING
YOU HIS OR HER MONEY

You will rarely, if ever, sit down with someone who will give you money out of his or her own pocket in the conventional mortgage market. You will be dealing at a distance through the institution's agents, employees, or whatever. You will be dealing with people, and no matter what the institution is or how small or large it is, the person you meet face to face is an obstacle on your way to a loan.

It is rare for any mortgage or loan board in any institution to grant a loan that the loan officer has a "funny feeling" about. Somewhere along the way between your first encounter with the institution and that person, you will be judged in a variety of ways. Many of these judgments will have nothing to do with your ability to pay back the loan. Some simply are personal, others are purely business or even based on envy, jealousy, or hate.

It's people business: the attitude one person has towards another, or how well a prospective borrower is prepared to meet any objection the loan officer can throw his or her way. Power players in any game or business abound. These people will cause or invent problems to test and pressure you. For example, your loan officer might try to improve the loan-to-value ratio, thereby increasing the security to the lending institution, and to test your vulnerability he might spring something like this on you: "You know, Mr. Cummings, in the preliminary review of your loan request several questions came up that centered around the magnitude of your request. Do you suppose you could reduce your request by $1 million?"

There are several reasons for this kind of approach, one is as I suggested and another is to set me up for some other term consideration that I would not want to give in on unless absolutely necessary, such as "Of course, Mr. Cummings, I realize how important it is for you to keep the loan at the requested amount. I offered one suggestion as a compromise to the committee. What do you think, Mr. Cummings, of a $300,000 reduction instead of $1 million, and you accept a small increase in the interest rate to 11%?"

You'll be better equipped to handle this type of approach by the time you finish this book. You must understand that all of these people that you deal with need to have some personal satisfaction from their job, just as you must from yours. It isn't critical that you understand what position the other person has taken in his or her own mental game, but only that you do not infringe on that position.

We all play some kind of mental game in our business dealings, and while some of us are quarterbacks in that game, others are owners of the team. Loan officers are not the owners of the team, but they often act as though they are.

The reality is that in the lending business, loan officers get lots of red marks when loans they have recommended go sour. It doesn't matter if the reason for the loan going sour had nothing to do with them. They get the red marks just the same. They will avoid red marks whenever possible and will do everything they can to show that they did everything they could have (or should have), to make a loan that should not have gone bad.

However, loan officers must make loans because they also get red marks when they aren't doing the business for which they are hired. When the institution has money and word has come down to lend out the money, the loan officer is anxiously looking for you to help him or her avoid red marks. You will do that by knowing how to deal with different institutions, and what it is that they need.

Part of your success then will be in making sure that you have developed some kind of relationship that is on the professional and business level. You can socialize with the loan officer, but if you had to socialize with anyone at the bank try the president first, vice presidents second, and so on. Remember that the higher your contacts, the easier it is in dealing with the lower echelons.

DEALING WITH THE SAVINGS AND LOAN ASSOCIATIONS

When you are in the market for a first mortgage, the first source you should turn to is the savings and loan association closest to that property. We have already seen some of the basic restrictions of the savings and loan associations, but it is not the restrictions that will affect you the most, it is the policy that institution has that will determine just how far you might get with the loan you want or need.

If the savings and loan closest is not one with which you are familiar, go in and establish your position as an investor of real estate. I don't care what your job is, you can and most likely will become an investor of real estate. For your original and first encounter, you should dress in neat business apparel. There is an old axiom in lending, "If you need it, you don't get it; if you don't need it, you'll get it."

Walk right up to some employee other than the person seated behind the desk that says "Information" and ask where to find the president's office. The reason you don't go to the Information Person is that the sign is only to mislead you. The person sitting behind the "Information" sign is really a traffic cop. His or her real job is to direct you to the person he or she wants to send you to, no matter who you want to see. Specially if you want to see the president of the company. Information people will not send you to the president except as a last possible choice.

Other signs say something like "Vice President Commercial Loans" or whatever, simply to get rid of you; the quickest way to do that is to tell you what you want.

On the way to the president's office, ask someone else the name of the president's secretary. Armed with this information, you are on your way to making your first and most effective contact: the secretary of the president of the institution.

Six Advantages in Dealing with a Savings and Loan

1. LOCAL IN NATURE.   Unlike some sources, the savings and loan is local in nature. Granted, the savings and loan association may have branches all over the country, but the office you deal with is on the spot. The loan officers are on the spot too, and you will find them easy to get to and for the most part very helpful. You usually have direct contact with the savings and loan official and are not dealing through some other party, such as a real estate broker or mortgage broker. If you develop a success pattern, this local aspect of the savings and loan will be far more visible than at a more distant lender. It is critical, however, to make sure that the decisions for the loan are as local as possible. With the branch banking that is found in most states, the savings and loan two blocks away from the home you want to buy could be in the direct control of an institution 3,000 miles away. This may not work against you, but

your approach and the details you provide would be different if you knew that. As you shop for a loan, make sure that all of the savings and loans you visit are not controlled from a great distance. Find out by asking the direct and obvious question: "Where is the loan committee, who sits on it, and are they all from this area?"

Like most local businesses, the savings and loans and commercial bank like to pride themselves on community spirit. You can and should take advantage of that whenever possible and whenever there is something unique about the loan request that has some specific benefit to the community.

In rough times, savings and loans don't like to spoil their community spirit and friendly neighbor image. If you keep your rapport with the institution, it can be most understanding. This is one of the most rewarding advantages and one of the reasons for its success. But this is not the way it is with all savings and loans. Some are cold and distant in more ways than one. You will find great differences in personnel, attitude, and service. However, if it is truly local in thought, policy, service, and attitude, find a loan officer in that institution with whom you can work.

2. INEXPENSIVE APPRAISALS.   This is a side benefit of the local nature of a savings and loan. Since it is in the community, it usually has its own appraisal division or department. This department keeps up-to-date records on what is going on in the community and on the evaluations of property in that area. But more than that, it is aware of what is happening with future growth, new developments that you may not be aware of that can have some positive effect on your loan. You will note this difference far more positively when you deal with a distant lender who knows nothing about your area (or assumes it doesn't) and needs to be taught everything that is going on. Appraisals to satisfy these lenders can be expensive and long in coming. Naturally, the accuracy of the appraisal made by the savings and loan can work against you if it lowballs it. Give it all necessary data. This will only lend credence to the fact that you are on top of the game.

3. CONFIDENCE IN AREA.   Lenders must have confidence in the growth potential of an area. In essence, they are forced into this confidence. Remember, the savings and loan exists because of the need to loan money. Naturally, areas can change, and more than one savings and loan was closed due to bad loans and a declining number of depositors. Like all businesses, savings and loans are not immune to failure and they can and do go out of business. Nonetheless, their desire to be in business works for you.

4. ATTRACTIVE TERMS.   For all lending institutions, the amount of competition for borrowers will vary with the circumstances of the market. In the middle 1980s, for example, the lending business grew with a multitude of companies vying

for borrowers. For the first time in a long while, there seemed to be competition for the lenders. Along with competition usually come benefits for the consumer in the form of lower prices or, in the case of lending, better borrowing terms. When it comes to this kind of competition, the savings and loans are well-equipped to match any of the other lenders, or better them, and quite often they do. However, you still must shop around not only between the savings and loans, but with other lenders as well.

5. BETTER LOAN-TO-VALUE RATIOS IN THE FAVOR OF THE BORROWER. With the exception of government loan programs such as VA and FHA loans, the 90 to 95% of the value that can be borrowed on many types of property and circumstances is most attractive to some borrowers. Keep in mind that the maximum loan from any institution or any lender will generally carry with it a penalty of higher interest than a lower loan-to value ratio. This is because of the added risk to the lender, or to cover the insurance the lender puts into the transaction to cover the upper limits of the loan in the event of a default. This added risk or cost gets passed on to the borrower, who may, as many do, still find that loan to be the one that enables him or her to reach his goal.

6. LOWER QUALIFICATION STANDARDS. Among local S & Ls, there seems to be a drive to provide loans wherever possible, often making the local savings and loan the most lenient of all sources. However, I do expect this to change and for the savings and loans to pay much more attention to the credit of their borrowers and to the appraisals and evaluations of the properties they take as security on their loans in the future. From the middle 1970s to early 1980s, savings and loans lost money with some of the creative lending techniques they devised that did little more than encourage borrowers to maximize their loans. The lending institutions took the blunt of a decline in growth in many areas and a real decline in property values in some parts of the country.

Let's face it, as branch banking takes hold of an area, the local nature of the S & L is going to slip to some degree. Different areas of the country within the same savings and loan association will vie to be the top lender, with the lowest foreclosure rate of all other branches. As that kind of competition takes hold, the qualifications for a loan will go up, and savings and loans will be as tough as other lenders.

Another factor to consider is the growing demands of the secondary market. For example, insurance companies buy portfolios of loans totaling millions of dollars on a regular basis from savings and loans and other lenders. As these companies increase their standards or impose restrictions on the kind of loan they will buy or the area in which they will buy, lenders who must rely on these secondary markets to bank their loans will quickly comply with that secondary market demand.

ELEVEN STEPS IN APPROACHING AND DEALING WITH LENDERS

1. GET TO KNOW THE SAVINGS AND LOANS AND OTHER KINDS OF LENDERS WITHIN YOUR COMFORT ZONE.   This should include commercial banks and mortgage brokers. Begin by looking in the Yellow Pages to get the names of the institutions and their branch offices. Make note of those that are closest to your area, keeping in mind that any of the institutions in your county and most in the state may actually be able to serve your needs. However, you will begin with three different institutions and follow each of the next ten steps with them until you have a working relationship with a minimum of three such savings and loan offices.

2. MAKE YOUR FIRST CONTACT THE MOST IMPORTANT ONE.   This means you should call on the president or manager of that association. Find out the person's title by calling the savings and loan and asking the receptionist to connect you with the secretary for the president of that facility. Be sure to ascertain first that you have reached the facility you want, and not a central phone number that was answered five hundred miles away. This can happen, and it is very frustrating when it does. It only demonstrates a slipping away from the local, friendly neighbor policy savings and loans have prided themselves on over the years.

The receptionist will give you the proper title to use, and it will frequently be "president." The ultimate contact is, of course, the president. However, from a practical point of view, it is the secretary of the president that you want to win over to your side. We shall assume that by going to the top of the line with bosses, we have also gotten to the best secretary available for the position. Once you take that position and treat her accordingly, you will find that no matter how slight your relationship with the president, you will have access to him or her through the secretary.

Your quest to know the president shouldn't be more than a professional visit. Call, make the appointment (through the secretary), and introduce yourself as a real estate investor who plans to buy property in the area. State that you have been told (by me) that meeting the president would be productive for you both. Oh . . . no. You don't have an account at that savings and loan just yet. Perhaps that can come later, if there is to be a mutual understanding. (If you have a small savings account somewhere and don't have much action in the deposit side, why have that prejudice the loan officer when he wants to know about your account history.)

Begin at the top, but move quickly into the ranks because it is here that you will find the loan officer who will help you get the money you need. To keep you from wasting time, ask your friend, the president's secretary, if she could recommend one of the loan officers that she feels would be good for you to meet.

Word from the secretary, no matter if it is to the President of the United States or the manager of the branch office, has a sting that is not unlike that of the top guy himself. After all, who passes on the president's words if not his secretary.

A call from you to "Fran," with a simple request that sounds like this, is very effective: "Oh, Fran, seems like I remember you liked concerts. Well, could you do me a favor? My wife and I can't make the Pavarotti concert next week and I'm going to drop in the mail two tickets to the concert. Please see they get good use, would you? Oh yes, Charles (the president) said I should call if you could help with any introductions. Anyway, I would like to meet with one of the loan officers. You know, Fran, I like dealing with an officer who isn't one of the old-timers or the new guy in the department. Who would you recommend I meet with?"

When Fran comes up with a name or two, follow up with: "Fran, look, I don't want to bother Charlie about this, would you please call this fellow you just recommended and ask him when it would be convenient to meet with him? I've got next Tuesday at 10 or Wednesday at 2 open. Can I call you back on this tomorrow?"

What happens now is Fran will call the loan officer she recommended, and her request to meet with you will sound like an absolute order directly from the president of the association himself. This is all rather simple.

The next part of this step is to make the meeting, find out for yourself if this is indeed someone with whom you can work. If for any reason you feel uncomfortable with the loan officer, give your friend, the secretary, a call: "How was the concert . . . ?" Thank her for setting up the meeting and let her know that you would now like to meet another loan officer so that you can meet as many officers in the association as possible to better determine which would work well with you.

Finally, make sure you have at least two meetings with the loan officer of your choice. It will be in these meetings that you set the foundation for the loan requests you may submit in the future.

3. LEARN THE PROCEDURES OF THE INSTITUTION.   The procedures of each savings and loan will vary slightly. Some require very detailed forms to be filled out for any loan request; others are less complicated. Collect all of the forms you must ultimately fill out and go over them so you understand exactly what the institution wants, and why.

You will want to know these things:

- How often does the loan committee meet?
- What day do they meet?
- What is the deadline to get a request in any meeting?
- Does the association do its own appraisals?
- If not, who does?
- What are the current loan rates, terms, and policy?
- What kind of property does the association not like to lend on?
- What kind of property does the association like to lend on?

You will be collecting a lot of data by visiting the institution, and as you make calls on several savings and loans and other kinds of lenders you will find you are receiving quite an education. In fact, it is a good idea to make two practice calls on savings and loans that are on the other side of town to get the feel for things. Play as dumb as you want on those calls. Ask the loan officer to explain anything and everything until you are absolutely sure you understand the terms he or she is using and the reasons behind everything.

4. When you get ready to ask for a loan, plan your submission well.   Later in this chapter, you will find an outline for a loan request. It contains all of the information the lender would need to know about you and the property except some very minor details it may want to know just because of some local quirk. You should have already discovered through your contacts with the loan officers what data that association will look at most. If one institution looks very hard at the loan-to-value ratio, it is critical that you pay more attention to that aspect of the request. Another loan officer may have told you that the economics of the transaction and proforma are the key factors for the kind of property you know you want to buy. It is important, however, that you pay some attention to all of the items in the loan request. In the lending business, it is impossible to provide too many answers. Remember, the more detailed your request and back-up data, the heavier your report, the more time you have spent on specifics and background, the better your loan officer will feel about backing you in the loan committee. Don't forget that loan officer doesn't want to get red marks against him, and the best way to avoid this is to give the impression that he or she did the job, so do yours.

5. Make your loan requirements known.   You should be able to support that request fully, of course, but be as specific as possible, and have a margin for negotiations in the request: small, but some margin.

What I mean here is you have to ask for an amount of money and show the terms you expect to be able to pay based on the project or property. For example, you might ask for $125,000 with a payback over 18 years, with a monthly payment not to exceed $1,319.22. In this way, you have established what would be an 11% mortgage for eighteen years with a normal payback to amortize the mortgage for that term. The lender has room to match many of the criteria of the mortgage and still better its position if it can and if you will let it. For example, if it said okay to the monthly payment and total amount of the loan, but that at the end of the eighteen years you will have a balloon of $6,000, it will have increased its yield to 11.12%. This balloon may not mean that much to you since you don't plan to keep the property for the full eighteen years anyway, and by keeping the constant payment rate the same for the term you may agree to that slight increase in interest.

As you go through this book, you will see that it is designed to allow you the opportunity to use it as a reference tool in later years. You will become aware that the more you know about the functions of finance and where the tradeoffs lay, the better you will be at developing more attractive loan portfolios for yourself and your property.

6. DON'T RUSH THE LOAN COMMITTEE.   You will know its schedule and the general policy with which it functions from earlier contacts. Plan your submission well and submit it on time so you don't have to use up any of your "credits" by asking the loan officer to "please get this processed for me." The presentation is important also. If your package is complete and up to date, and you have anticipated all of the loose ends that might occur, the approval will be sped up anyway. Loan requests often are held up due to many items that the applicant could have taken care of in the beginning. The savings and loan association will have to go back and ask an applicant again and again for this or that document that is lacking in the files. Don't let that happen to you. If you do leave out something, make sure that you take care of it the moment it comes to your attention.

7. DON'T TAKE NO FOR AN ANSWER.   Not everything you do is going to succeed. The same is true with loan requests. If the loan committee comes back with a direct turndown on a request, which is unusual, go back to the loan officer and ask if the head of the department could sit in on the meeting to explain what happened and why the loan was turned down.

As I said, a direct turndown is unusual. Generally, the loan officer will come back to you with some change in the terms you requested. It might be a decrease in loan amount, an increase in interest rate, a shorter term, a balloon payment, or all of these changes. Some loan officers will give you an idea about what went on in the committee. Just before leaving his office, you might turn to him and say:

"Oh, I have a lot of confidence in you, Frank. Let me give this some thought for a couple of days. I know you have spent a lot of time and effort on this, and if there is any way we can work something out we will." As you start to leave, turn to him and say, "Only it's hard to understand how your institution could be so much below the others," and slowly let the door close.

Some lenders just won't make the loan no matter what. It might be that they don't have the funds or that they have filled that kind of loan in their portfolio for the month. Most likely, it is that they must change to meet the needs of their secondary market.

If the lender won't give you the loan, don't beat a dead horse. It is far better just to shop around for another lending institution. There will be another time you may want to ride this horse.

8. USE YOUR INFLUENCE.   You either already have some, or you can develop some quickly. If you don't now belong to some success-oriented kind of organization, take a look at the partial list below and select one that sounds good and is located in your area. Pay it a visit. You will find that within these organizations are the leaders of the community or the future leaders of the community.

Toastmasters International	SME International
DECA	Junior Achievement
Junior Chamber of Commerce	United Way

Of course, there are other such organizations but they are social fraternal organizations. I have nothing against the Lions, the Elks, or the Italian-American Clubs and the like, they are important too. But, if you want to develop influence and do it in a hurry, pick one or several of the organizations listed, or one that is specially *in* in your community, to get things moving.

If more than one such club exists in your area, pick the one that meets for breakfast. Remember the adage: The early bird gets the worm.

As you develop your comfort zone, you will be following a pattern also designed to expand on your potential influence. One of the steps in comfort zone development is attending city and county council meetings, going to the city hall, court house, and building departments to meet key people. As you are doing this, you should also be making sure that the people you meet are also meeting you. Through proper follow up, you will find that they will remember you, so if you have left a good impression you're on your way.

Be careful not to abuse your hospitality or influence. If you work for a company that has an account with a potential lender, don't threaten to remove your company's account unless (1) it is absolutely the final straw and you are so burned up you don't care about burning your bridges behind you, or (2) you are so secure in your position that you don't care what your boss thinks about that threat.

9. REMAIN CALM.   It is not the end of the world, and there will be another opportunity along in a few minutes. There are times when you have to step back and take a hard, cold look at what it is you are trying to do. One turndown doesn't mean you need to make any changes, but if you are consistently being turned down then something you are doing isn't winning people over to your cause. So back off. Don't push the cause until you have the opportunity to sift out the bugs. Your friendly loan officer should help here if he or she can and will. Ask. If you're turned down, he or she should be replaced.

However, never fade into the background. Send a thank-you note to the loan officer and anyone else who worked on your project. Tell them you appreciated their sincere help and that you are sorry things didn't work out with that lending institution on that project (never admit that you were wrong or that you failed in getting the loan somewhere else). Tell them you will keep in touch and that because of their efforts you will contact them on your next transaction.

10. KEEP UP YOUR RAPPORT WITH THE INSTITUTION BETWEEN LOAN REQUESTS AND PROJECTS.   Maintain some kind of contact from time to time: a lunch, a note in the mail, a copy of a book you have read about the decline of the savings and loans, whatever might give you the opportunity to keep your name in front of the people who may help you out when you need it.

11. AVOID DIRECT CONFRONTATION AND COMPARISON OF ONE LENDER TO THE OTHER.   There is a temptation to invent offers that you have had from other lenders, such as, "Yeah! Well, you know that American National Federal has offered me $125,000 at 7%?"

However, as long as you have made it clear in a sound business way that you are talking to at least one other lender, you will keep them on their toes. If you are talking with twenty lenders, don't let that get around. In fact, talk about your loan with no fewer than four lenders, but do not let them know you are dealing with more than two. You don't want to give the impression that you fear the failure of one lender, but simply that you want to get the best terms from the best lenders around.

These eleven steps are not easy to follow, and apply to other kinds of lenders as well as the savings and loans. As you follow the eleven steps, you will learn more about the lending business than you could in any book. Best of all, you will be giving yourself a better foundation to deal with other aspects of the real estate finance and investment arena.

As you progress in this book and in your own experiences in real estate investing and financing, you will discover that the creativity of bankers and lenders is often quite shallow. Perhaps that was not a fair statement because you will find several bankers or lenders who are progressive and most astute at what they do. However, they must limit that progressive and astute behavior to their own industry. As an independent investor, you have far more tools at your disposal to attack the problem of financing or investing. Your creative power and finesse then will exceed the ability of many lenders to provide compatible responses to your circumstance. This is not to be viewed as a detriment to you, but as a challenge for you to expand on your own opportunities.

To best take advantage of those opportunities, you must be open to all of your options and attempt to utilize a particular tool or option that is best suited to take you closer to your goals. By becoming proficient with the eleven steps in approaching lenders, you will quickly see that there are ways to use the institutional lender to the maximum benefit.

Example

One financing tool we have not yet covered, but will in great detail, is open to you through the very best lender of all, the seller. As we get into seller-held financing, you will see that there are times when you can utilize the institutional lender with a conventional loan and the seller to provide you with more money than you need to acquire the property.

Several years ago, I helped a client of mine do exactly that when he was buying an expensive single-family property. The property consisted of two ocean-front lots in Fort Lauderdale, Florida. On the two lots, there was one single-family home. The home was livable, but was 35 years old and in great need of remodeling. The most conservative cost estimate to put the home into livable shape was $150,000.

The buyer was very well-qualified financially and had a good personal statement; however, he wanted to keep his cash in reserve for his business and for any unforeseen event.

His intention was to build a modern home on the same location as the existing one, either through extensive remodeling or new construction. He had correctly concluded that the price he paid for the property was just for the lots, and it was a good buy at that. Like a lot of home buyers, my client owned another home that he was living in at the moment. His existing home was to go on the market for $150,000. As that home had a first mortgage of $30,000, he had $120,000 of equity in his present home. After the sale and deduction of all expenses, he could count on a profit of about $105,000.

His need at the moment was to buy the ocean-front property without putting any cash into that deal, sell his existing home, and prior to moving rebuild the ocean-front property for his own use. Since he didn't know at this time how extensive the remodeling or construction would be, he could not apply for a development loan.

The savings and loan association that he had a good relationship with had indicated that it would lend 75% of the contract price now, and when he knew what his plans would be it would renew the loan to include the new construction.

This 75% loan would account for $150,000 of the purchase of the ocean-front land, but my client still would have to come up with $50,000 out of his own pocket, and he didn't want to part with that cash.

So in the negotiations with the seller of the ocean-front property, the following deal was worked out.

The seller agreed to sell the ocean-front property for $200,000, taking a $100,000 cash down payment at the closing. The balance of $100,000 was to be held by the seller in a mortgage secured by my client's existing home. There was a stipulation that on the sale of the existing home the $100,000 would be paid off.

Now we went back to the savings and loan and borrowed the $150,000 that they said they would lend in the first place. They had the first mortgage on the ocean-front lots, and out of the proceeds of the mortgage my client gave the seller of the lots $100,000, paid the lender for the costs involved in the mortgage, and put about $46,000 cash in his pocket.

Everything about this transaction was legal and ethical. However, the savings and loan that made the loan first objected to the concept. When I pointed out that they did have the first mortgage on the ocean-front property and that there was no secondary financing on that property, they realized that they had made a good loan.

In a follow-up some eight years later, my client decided that living on the ocean was nice, but he wanted to move to a waterfront location on one of the Fort Lauderdale canals. In the eight years that had gone by the values had gone up substantially and he ended up selling the home for over $1,200,000.

DEALING WITH COMMERCIAL BANKS

While savings and loans are the major source of first mortgage funds, there are times when the commercial banks, both state and federal chartered banks, will be the most interested in your submissions. Commercial banks and savings and loans often look alike and offer many of the same services; however, commercial banks differ in many ways and are one of the sources for conventional real-estate loans. FHA and VA loans are generally arranged through commercial banks and mortgage bankers. No matter who else you contact, you will want to know what is available from the commercial bank you deal with.

Unlike the savings and loans, commercial banks are very protective of their clientele. This means that unless you are looking for a major development loan or plan to shift your commercial account to another bank, you will stick to the commercial bank you deal with. This is, by the way, an important lesson in why it is good to have accounts in more than one commercial bank.

THE PLUS FACTORS OF THE COMMERCIAL BANK

Many of the same features found in savings and loans are also found in the commercial bank. Nonetheless, take a look at the four big reasons that commercial banks can be a good choice for real estate loans.

1. THEY ARE LOCAL IN NATURE.   To some degree, the commercial bank is actually more local in nature than the savings and loan. At least they used to be until the savings and loans around the country began to offer checking accounts.

However, commercial banks are still the heaviest suppliers for checking accounts, so the average person will visit or in some way use the services of the commercial bank several times a week.

The commercial bank is in the primary business of loaning money to many commercial ventures of which real estate is just one factor. Because of this, the bank gets involved with many of the community's basic foundations: Car loans, inventory financing, home improvement loans, boat loans, business lines of credit, letters of credit, and so on. The more access you have had to any of these kinds of services, the greater your awareness of how commercial banks operate.

2. THEY HAVE GOOD INSIGHT INTO THE REAL ESTATE MARKET IN THE COMMUNITY.   Perhaps they do not have as broad an approach as the savings and loan when it comes to total business in that sector of their operation, but they do keep on top of things that are important to them. The closer the property is to their front door, the better they like it. Mind you, some commercial banks will lend on projects around the world and can do so without any security other than a line of credit or personal signature.

3. THEY OFFER LOWER LOAN FEES THAN FOUND IN MANY SAVINGS AND LOANS.   Now be careful about this one: The banker can find some way to offset this lower cost by finding a higher cost somewhere else. However, commercial banks can be most competitive in any of their usual services.

4. THEY OFFER A WIDER RANGE OF PROJECTS THEY WILL LOAN ON.   In real estate, this becomes critical as the savings and loan associations will rarely lend on vacant land unless it is tied into a development program. The commercial bank, however, can be a big source of funds for developers as well as investors who want to tie up a lot or two for the future.

DISADVANTAGES OF DEALING WITH COMMERCIAL BANKS FOR CONVENTIONAL LOANS

1. Commercial banks are older than savings and loans and often have a more conservative approach to lending. This conservatism can present some distinct disadvantages to the borrower. Some of the more pronounced are:

   - A low loan-to-value ratio. The bank will look hard at the loan and examine the value of the property very carefully. It would rather be conservative and lose the loan than produce a high loan-to-value ratio and risk taking back a property. Commercial banks do not like to lend their own funds above the 75% loan-to-value ratio. Of course, when it comes to FHA- or VA-insured loans, that is another matter and the bank will go all the way on those.

- They generally require that the borrower be a client of the bank. This sometimes means that the borrower also has to keep a substantial deposit in the bank during the term of the loan. This goes back to the concept that if you have it you don't need it so that's when we'll give it to you.
- Interest rates can be higher than current rates from other sources. However, as the commercial bank is usually the fastest lender on any kinds of properties, the extra interest paid can be worth the cost later on down the line.

2. Prepayment of mortgage loans will generally carry a penalty or some other stipulation that limits the amount of principal that can be paid off at any given time or during any year. This may not seem to be a problem, but if you want to sell the property in a few years and the new buyer must refinance to make the transaction work for him or her, a penalty to get the old loan off the books can get in the way of a successful closing or can come out of your pocket.

3. The term of years a mortgage is amortized is generally shorter with commercial banks than with savings and loans. However, this aspect is changing as many savings and loans are using loan instruments that have a seven-year call term on a longer amortization basis. For example, this means that even though the loan looks as though it is good for twenty-five years, the lender or the company that the lender has sold the mortgage to can call the loan at the end of seven years. If that is the comparison loan at the local savings and loan, the seven- to ten-year term at the commercial bank will look attractive.

HOW TO DEAL WITH THE MORTGAGE BROKER

Mortgage brokers and mortgage bankers can be worth their weight in gold. It is a very good idea to have at least one or two contacts with a mortgage brokerage firm in your area. These companies either act as a "finder" for money for you or actually bank the loan with their own sources. They deal with many of the prime money sources around, with which you would have no direct contact were it not for these brokers or bankers. These sources are the pension funds, insurance companies, large out-of-the-area commercial banks and savings and loan associations, offshore money, real estate investment trusts, and so on.

When you deal with a mortgage broker, it is similar to going to a real estate broker who'll find you a house, only the mortgage broker finds a lender who will make your loan for you. Since the mortgage broker shops around for you, you sometimes can save time and effort by using his or her services. However, any benefit can come at a high penalty because you may be lax in seeking other sources for the funds. You may find in the end that the mortgage broker was unable to make your loan or does in fact place it with the savings and loan around the corner from where you work.

However, there are many loans that cannot be made without the help of a good mortgage broker. So make a contact with a mortgage broker in the same way you would with a loan officer of a savings and loan. Do it well before you need to borrow the money.

PRIME SOURCES FOR CONVENTIONAL LOANS

The following sources for conventional money may or may not be available to you on a direct basis. Most often, the following lenders are buyers of mortgage packages from savings and loans, commercial banks, or mortgage bankers. However, sometimes you do have access to them, and if that is the case these lenders can offer the very best terms for your borrowing needs.

Insurance Companies

Insurance companies are a good source for funds and supply a major amount of cash outside the governmental reserves into the conventional lending systems. Unless you are a major borrower (in need of $1 million or more), it is unlikely that you will have a loan directly placed with an insurance company. However, some insurance companies will look at smaller loan requests through their representative mortgage brokers and mortgage bankers.

Insurance companies have very strong motives to lend out money if they have it. Unlike savings and loans who may be packing loans to sell to secondary buyers, insurance companies have their own cash and they must put it somewhere. The investments the insurance companies make include a wide range of items, of which mortgages are just a part. However, if you need a lot of money, this is usually where you will get it.

Dealing through a representative, such as the mortgage broker, is different than dealing with the loan officer at the local commercial or savings and loan association. As the lender is usually distant from you and your property, loan committees generally require far more details and information than the local lender.

There are several drawbacks in dealing with insurance companies other than their distance. These drawbacks may not be a problem for you, and if not you should make sure that your mortgage broker has included one or more insurance companies in his or her search for a lender to take your loan. Naturally, this assumes that your loan request meets the minimum loan requirements by the specific insurance company.

The most notable drawback is the problem of good news-bad news. Since insurance companies are a good source for major loans, they frequently have a lot of requests for the funds available. This enables the institution to be selective and that makes their money difficult to get at times. This also leads to a time element that can be the killer for most borrowers who have a need to get the funds relatively quickly. Of all lenders, insurance companies can be the slowest to approve a loan. Of course, this time factor varies between different lenders and projects, but when you couple the extra data needed, frequently the requirement of having an M.A.I. appraisal in addition to all the other back-up material, plus a thirty- to sixty-day shuffle through loan committee, you can see that the commercial bank or savings and loan can be a good alternative.

Real-Estate Investment Trusts (REITS)

There are three basic types of REITS:

1. THE EQUITY REIT. This is similar to a mutual fund except the investors own an interest in whatever real estate the organization acquires. The form of ownership is like a corporation, only the income and losses are treated, for the investor, as though this were individual ownership of that percentage of the transaction. The equity REIT is a major buyer of office buildings, shopping centers, and the like. It takes part in joint ventures, develops, builds, and otherwise is involved in many forms of real-estate investing.

2. THE MORTGAGE REIT. This form of real-estate trust is designed for lending. They vary in size but are very potential in the lending game. They got into trouble in the early 1970s by being overly zealous with their lending practices. Many of their loans went bad and they ended up owning property through foreclosures. Some of the mortgage REITS found themselves in irreversible trouble as they made construction loans on projects that failed prior to the permanent loan paying off the REIT. As the earlier mortgage REIT based its success on a shorter duration loan, i.e., the development loan, it was not a surprise that these REITS have undergone the greatest change over the years. Where they still exist, they are more often found as a part of the third form of REIT.

3. THE HYBRID REIT. This is a mixture of the two earlier forms of REITS. Some of these REITS were formed by accident, others by design. They have found the best and worst of both worlds, but in a counterbalance they seem to now make up the majority of REITS. Hybrids generally participate in the project, lending money and taking a percentage of ownership or override on income.

REITS fall into the same category as insurance companies in that they are prime sources for funds, but their access is generally remote and distant unless you are a major borrower or developer. Nonetheless, keep them in mind. When they have money to lend, they can be very aggressive to lend it. As a joint venture partner, the REITS can be one of the first lenders to call.

Pension Funds and Credit Unions

These organizations collect massive amounts of funds and then make investments to suit their charters and goals. They act much like insurance companies but are often more accessible to fund or union members than other larger lenders. For example, if you are a member of a credit union there are many services that organization can provide to you besides lending money. Pension funds vary in the services they offer their members; find out what services they offer, if any.

General Comments About Institutional Lenders

The whole finance game seems to revolve around major lenders. The secondary market that buys packages from savings and loans, commercial banks, and the United States government plays a big roll through the Federal Reserve Monetary Policy.

The economics of government intervention in the free enterprise system is subject to argument by just about any economist you will find. The problem seems to be that no two economists seem to agree as to the exact definition of the problem or its potential solution. The theory of control by the government to provide checks and pushes to the nation's economy are based on the principal that if nothing is done things will work out.

The United States is both a lender and a borrower. It is a lender in that its insurance to banks, savings and loans, and for FHA and VA loans makes a marketplace for borrowers that may not exist otherwise. The money borrowed through the sale of bonds and the like is a real debt that is repaid through new loans made (more bonds sold).

The government is such an enormous borrower that it affects the market by taking out of it money that might go into other resources.

If You Are a Big Borrower, the Pension Fund Can Be the Only Way to Go

No one will disagree with this statement, except the other lenders hoping to make the same loan. The only answer, of course, is to shop around and find out for yourself just who is the best source for you at the time you need the money.

A Summary of Advantages and Disadvantages of Loan Sources

	Advantages	*Disadvantages*
Savings and Loans	Local and on the spot Know property and area Have confidence in area Long pay-out High percent of loan to value More lenient in qualifying both the property and the borrower	High points Personal liability Nonassumable at times Prepayment penalty
Commercial Banks	Local and on the spot Know property and area Have confidence in area Lower points Construction and land loans	Low percent of loan to value Want other business Higher interest rate Sometimes prepayment penalty Shorter term of years
Insurance Companies	Have ample money Like big borrowers Lower interest rate Low points Permanent loan usually not personally guaranteed	Not local Can be impersonal Highly selective Demand greatest qualification on property and borrower Long processing time
REITS	Same as insurance companies Less conservative Loan terms more flexible	Not local Can be impersonal Generally short-term lender Long processing time
Pension Funds	Same as insurance companies	Same as REITS
The Seller	Depends on the situation and the seller No points at all Usually best rate No processing time to worry about	Seller may be limited in the amount he or she can hold Term usually shorter

AN OVERLOOKED SOURCE FOR FIRST MORTGAGES

One of the best sources for first mortgages is the seller. There are many advantages to this source, and oddly enough it is the seller that is often the first source that is overlooked. The biggest advantage to you is that there is no middleman. You are the middleman, and the saving of loan points and time are valuable to all parties of the transaction. This chapter will not deal with the methods of approaching the seller. Other chapters will cover this aspect in greater detail. Yet you should never overlook this as perhaps the best source of all.

Mortgage Source Checklist

What kind of loan needed	Where to go to get the money	When to use this source to its best advantage	How to get the most from this source
	Start with the local savings and loan association and make at least two or three applications.	When you need between an 80 to 90% loan and total loan is under $50,000.	Follow the procedure given in this chapter.
Single family residence (first mortgage under $80,000 in value)	Your commercial banks. Pick one you deal with. Insurance companies: Deal with your mortgage broker. Often, they will be in the market for single family loans.	For loans over $50,000. Or when you are well-respected by commercial bank or you struck out at the savings and loan. When you cannot get anywhere with the other sources. Or, if you know the mortgage broker is hot to make a deal.	Follow the procedure given in this chapter. Remind them how much they respect you. Deal only with a reputable mortgage broker. Do not try to deal directly with an insurance company.
Single family residence (first mortgage over $80,000 in value)	Start with the local savings and loan and make at least three applications.	When you need no more than 80% loan to value ratio and total loan is under $100,000.	Give more of your financial details, as well as comprehensive sales data.
Residential lots for ready development, single buyer	Commercial banks. Same as previous mortgage.	For loans over $100,000 you may find the commercial bank the best bet.	Negotiate for good terms and use your financial statement.
Multifamily (up to 5 units)	Start with the local savings and loan. Make as many applications as possible.	Maximum loan possible is 80%, but your chance is improved if you ask for only 75%.	Have detailed loan request ready for each savings and loan.
Residential lots for builder-developer use	Talk to commercial banks first. If they have money available, make several applications.	When you need only 70% loan to value ratio or less.	Have detailed loan request and stress the buyer as much as the property.
Multifamily (6 to 20 units)	Start with the local savings and loan. Make at least three applications.	When the loan to value ratio does not exceed 75%.	Have detailed loan request with past years' statements available.

Mortgage Source Checklist *continued*

What kind of loan needed	Where to go to get the money	When to use this source to its best advantage	How to get the most from this source
Commercial properties up to $500,000 in value	Commercial banks may be good market here; but this will depend on the bank, the property, and the person. Check around. Insurance companies: REITS and funds.	If you can get the seller to hold some paper and only need a 50% loan. When the value is over $300,000 these sources may be interested.	Show strong management capability of buyer and good past history. Use good mortgage broker and detailed loan request.
Multifamily (20 to 100 units)	Savings and loans. Make at least three applications.	Will find 70% of economic value with conservative approach the best loan ratio.	Do your homework and have detailed loan request.
Commercial properties ($500,000 to $2,000,000 in value)	Insurance companies, REITS and pension funds.	If the value is over $1,000,000 these may be the only source.	Mortgage broker and loan requests are necessities.
Multifamily (over 100 units) and Commercial properties (over $2,000,000 in value)	Insurance companies, REITS, pension funds, and trust funds.	You have little choice: these are about the only sources you have.	Mortgage broker and very detailed loan request.
Shopping center development with major tenants (over $1,000,000 in value)	Commercial banks	Very rare; but if you are close to one you might have luck.	Pray.
Restaurants and special single-use properties	Insurance companies	Loan to value ratio 50%.	Detailed loan request, and heavy input on ability of buyer and past records.

PRIVATE MONEY: WHERE IT IS AND HOW TO FIND IT

Because private money is not institutional, it is often not classified along with conventional financing. But as conventional financing is a type of loan, and not limited by the source, I have chosen to include a brief section on private money. Because the use of private money varies greatly in its advantages and disadvantages, it is safe to say that it can have both the advantages and the disadvantages of all other sources.

Each private lender is an independent lender, and reacts to a loan request by seeking the most profitable deal based on what the market and his or her requirements dictate. In general, rates will be the highest and the amounts limited. Some private sources seem to be well-financed, but these are few.

However, finding the private money is easier than getting it. A look in the Yellow Pages or newspaper classifieds will be a good start. Many mortgage brokers and stock brokers know of private money. Deal with private money very carefully. It is best to have any and all mortgage documents examined by an attorney.

HOW TO PUT TOGETHER A LOAN INFORMATION PACKAGE WHICH WILL GET THE BEST TERMS AND THE MOST MONEY

Whenever you have a loan request in excess of $100,000, and always when you are putting a commercial venture together, you should develop a loan request package. This folio of information will be used by the lending institution to help justify the loan. The approach is to demonstrate your professionalism. Every point you can win up until the final vote of the loan committee will be a point in your favor. Give them something they can look back at and will make them feel good about their decision to give you the money.

The information you provide should be data already known to you. Your investment team should be alert to the need for a pending loan request and start obtaining the necessary information the moment you begin planning for the purchase, or the project.

I have included in this chapter an outline which you can follow in the preparation of a Mortgage Loan Request (Figure 5-l). The request you formulate should be as complete as possible. Because the outline can become the index to all your loan applications and requests, you should make several copies of this outline. Highlight the sections that your different investment team members need to work on. A review of the first five chapters of this book might be excellent brush up before any formal presentation is presented.

Figure 5-1. Outline of Your Mortgage Loan Request

   I.   The Property

       A.   General Description

B. Legal Description
C. Location
D. Location Sketch
E. Aerial Photo
F. Location Benefits
G. Location Drawbacks
H. General Statistics
   (1) Demographics
   (2) Average Rent
   (3) Traffic Count
I. General Site Data
   (1) Legal
   (2) Size and Square Feet of Land and Site Coverage
   (3) Use of Site
   (4) Zoning
   (5) Utilities
   (6) Access
   (7) Sketch of Lots Sharing Building Location
   (8) Survey
J. Land Value
   (1) Estimated Value of Site
   (2) Comparable Land Sales and Values

II. The Improvements
A. Description
B. General Statistics
   (1) Date Built
   (2) Year Remodeled
   (3) Type of Construction
   (4) Other Structural and Mechanical Data
   (5) Floor Area
   (6) Parking
   (7) Other Data
C. Sketch/Ground Floor
   (1) Show Tenants
   (2) Show Square Feet

    (3) Show Approximate Sizes

    (4) Building Plans (if new building, if lender is not in area, or if requested)

D. Sketch/Second Floor

    (1) Show Tenants

    (2) Show Square Feet

    (3) Show Approximate Sizes

    (4) Building Plans (if new building, if lender is not in area, or if requested)

E. Sketch/Third Floor

    (1) Show Tenants

    (2) Show Square Feet

    (3) Show Approximate Sizes

    (4) Building Plans (if new building, if lender is not in area, or if requested)

F. Personal Property

    (1) Inventory

    (2) Value

G. Statement of Condition of Property

    (1) Copies of general inspection reports

    (2) Copies of Environmental inspections and recommendations if any.

Note: If there are environmental problems, you need to address these with a business plan on how they will be dealt with, cost estimates from reliable contractors experienced in dealing with clean-up or treatments, and so on.

H. Replacement Cost of Structure

    (1) Original Cost

    (2) Replacement Cost

I. Comparable Sales of Improved Property of Similar Nature in the Area

J. The Economics (Actual)

    (1) Income

    (2) Expense

    (3) Net Operating Income

    (4) Economic Value

    (5) Rent Roll

    (6) Sample Lease

    (7) Past Records of Income and Expense

K. Opinion of Economics
  (1) Relationship to Average Square Foot Rent for Area
  (2) Average of Square Foot for this Building
  (3) General Opinion
  (4) Estimated Future Income

L. General Summary of Value
  (1) Land Values
  (2) Replacement Value
  (3) Personal Property Value
  (4) Estimated Present Value
  (5) Economic Value at Present Income
  (6) Comparable Value
  (7) Contract Price
  (8) Copy of Contract
  (9) Value Justified

III. The Person
  A. Name
  B. Address
  C. Occupation
  D. General Data
  E. Net Worth
  F. Supporting Documents
    (1) Net Worth Statement
    (2) Schedule of Assets
    (3) Schedule of Liabilities
    (4) References
    (5) Position of Employment
    (6) Verification of Salary
    (7) Estimated Annual Earnings
    (8) Credit Report of Applicant
    (9) Other Forms Supplied for Application

IV. The Loan Request
  A. Amount
  B. Terms and Conditions

FOUR KEY STEPS IN FORMULATING THE LOAN PACKAGE

1. Keep your sales material up-to-date and accurate. This will mean knowing all there is to know about the property you are to sell.

2. Accumulate the various sketches, photographs, past records, and other supporting documents you will use. These are shown in the Presentation Index as you go from listing to marketing.

3. Develop an understanding with the lenders you will approach to make sure what parts of the presentation they want emphasized. Remember, some lenders pay more attention to the person, others the property. You will want to know just how far you should go with the economics on the property. I prefer to limit the economic data to a minimum. Past records going back two or three years are helpful, and of course current data is a must. Expenses are almost more important than income and should be realistic. In most cases, you will have to increase the expenses the seller gives you. Avoid proforma showing the next five years or more. Some of the new computer printouts enable you to run a ten year, or longer, projection of income and expenses. This is a waste of time on two counts. First, no one will read them with any real belief that they are correct. Second, they will not be correct. You cannot effectively project into the future, so don't go beyond one or two years at most.

4. Get into the habit of using the package on all your loan applications.

Chapter 6

HOW TO USE CREATIVE FINANCING TO MAXIMIZE YOUR BENEFITS

Real-estate financing can be much more creative once you are outside the conventional financing world. Your success in dealing with conventional financing will often be by using it with one or more of the unconventional techniques discussed in this book.

Unconventional real-estate financing consists of elements that often appear not to be financing at all. For example, land leases are not usually thought of as a financing technique nor would a banker call a timeshare hotel a financing tool. Nonetheless, both of these two methods of shifting equities are exactly that: financing tools that are available to you when the right moment comes along.

Once you understand the idea of shifting equities you will have a much easier time using the more complex techniques displayed in this book. Best of all, you will find that you will begin to combine different techniques to fit your specific situation and transaction.

FINANCING IS A SHIFT OF EQUITY

If you owned a home that had no mortgage and was worth $100,000, your total equity would be $100,000. If you go to a local savings and loan and give them a mortgage, and they lend you $60,000 against your home, your equity is still $100,000. You have shifted part of it ($60,000) into your pocket as the cash. The remaining equity of $40,000 is still in the house. This means that if you do not count the cash in your pocket, your home equity is only $40,000.

113

Example

Assume that you want to acquire a farm on the outskirts of town. When you meet the seller's broker, you discover that the seller may be interested in taking your mortgaged house as partial payment against the farm. The farm is priced at $70,000. You have $40,000 equity in your home (value $100,000 but there is an existing mortgage of $60,000). To balance this exchange you would owe the seller $30,000. The seller indicates he will lend you the $30,000 by taking a mortgage back from you secured by your equity in the farm. What happened to your original $100,000 equity? Nothing, except that it has been divided and spread around. You have $60,000 cash, and owe $30,000 on the farm that is worth $70,000. Your $40,000 equity in the farm, and the $60,000 in cash means your original equity of $100,000 is still in place. However, as your goals were to get rid of the house and purchase a farm, you have moved toward that goal in a very positive way.

The critical part of this example is that you must keep open all of your options in using financing to your best benefit. You will find that you can shift equity and ownership at the same time to get closer to your goals. Or you could have taken another tact, such as might occur in a land lease with option to recapture. Using this combination you give up ownership, but keep the use of the property until you decide if you want ownership back again. All of this is shifting equity.

One reason this concept is important is that many people look at real estate as a two-sided affair. You buy it, and you sell it. Many people think that the immediate step to buying one property is to sell the property they currently own. For many people, this is the exact pattern they should follow. There are other ways to attain your goals than just selling one property to be able to buy another. I will show you techniques that will help you buy two properties easier than you could buy one, and other techniques that help you get the maximum value out of your investments.

Most new single-family financing is through conventional lenders. The money market favors single family homes because institutional lenders can sell these loans to larger investment banks or funds. Portfolios of several million dollars worth of loans are packaged together with loan service included in the deal. In this way the savings and loan or other lender can make loans, make a profit on selling the loan package, and retain an annual servicing fee. These loan packages must meet the institutional buyer's criteria, and for the moment, all loans that fall into this category are first mortgages, and the vast majority are on single family owner occupied homes and apartments.

RANKING OF MORTGAGES

As we get into the nonconventional financing arena, we will find that we for the most part are now dealing with a mixture of first and second mortgages. This topic has been touched on in the previous chapter, and will be brought up when it is important in later chapters. There will be times when the mortgage looks like a conventional mortgage and appears to be a first mortgage just as its savings and loan counterpart would be. But if you go by the label and you are the seller in the situation, you might find yourself on the losing end of that rope pull.

As you develop the basics of secondary and other creative financing, take a look at how mortgages are ranked and the significance of those rankings.

A FIRST MORTGAGE COMES FIRST, BUT IT ISN'T ALWAYS

The rank of a mortgage is its position to the other mortgage liens recorded against the property. The important word here is *position*. When a mortgage is given to a lender, it is taken down to the courthouse and the document is recorded as a lien against the property.

Example

You have just sold your home for $100,000, and after getting $30,000 cash at the closing you took back a mortgage for the balance of $70,000. The buyer had the standard forms, and the document said *first mortgage* right on the top line. In fact, the buyer was so nice that he said he would drop the papers off at the courthouse for you. He did so the day after he recorded his title, and he took out another mortgage in the amount of $80,000 from his brother-in-law. If the brother-in-law was able to get his mortgage document recorded prior to yours, it would have the first mortgage position and you would have a second position.

WATCH OUT FOR SUBORDINATION TO A LATTER RECORDED MORTGAGE

This following example is not the only scenario in which this problem can occur, but it is a frequent pattern. Assume that there are several mortgages on a property. This is the order in which they were recorded:

1. A $30,000 mortgage.
2. A $25,000 mortgage.
3. A $50,000 mortgage.

Since the recording was in the order indicated, the first mortgage is the $30,000 mortgage, unless something else had also happened; that something is subordination.

Subordination is a term that relates to holding rank in order or time recorded in the public records, to such an extent that one mortgage is given priority over others that would normally have superior rank. For example, at one time there was only one mortgage on the above property. When the property was sold to Mr. Smyth, it was done so on the specific terms that he could get a total of $25,000 in additional financing, which would be ranked ahead of the existing mortgage. (Naturally, this provision would have to be either already in the existing mortgage terms or the mortgagee would have to agree to its conditions for the agreement with Smyth). The $50,000 mortgage may have been put on the property at a later date when Smyth sold it to a third party.

The significance of this subordination is the position of the mortgages and to illustrate that in some circumstances the position and rank can change. The $30,000 mortgage was a first mortgage at one time, and it was ranked ahead of any other mortgage until the subordination provision was inserted. When the second mortgage was recorded in the amount of $25,000, it actually became the first mortgage. The last mortgage remained the third mortgage. However, the wording of the subordination provision could have been something like the following:

> ". . . and the mortgagee does herein agree that during the life of this mortgage and until such date that all principal and unpaid interest shall be satisfied to the benefit of the mortgagee, this mortgage will be, at the option of the mortgagor or his successors in title, subordinated to a debt of up to but not to exceed $25,000, provided that the payment of that debt shall not be at an interest rate to exceed ___ percent per annum, with total payments of interest and principal per year not to exceed $_____ in any given year."

It isn't the form of the statement that is important. What you want to look for is an open-ended form of subordination. What would happen here is that if the second recorded mortgage of $25,000 was to be paid off, an amount of $25,000 of what was the third-ranked mortgage could then become the first mortgage. The point is that rank can change because of the terms and conditions in other mortgages no matter what is said within a specific mortgage.

Knowing the whole story when you buy or sell property or deal in discounting of mortgages, which will be a separate chapter in this book, it becomes critical for you to read and then understand the terms of all the underlying mortgages.

Please make careful note: Never rely on the mortgagor or the mortgagee to give you the whole story or even the truth when it comes to the terms and conditions of a mortgage that person, company, bank, or savings and loan may be holding. It has been my sad experience that lending institutions give out information about mortgages they hold that is wrong, misleading, incorrect, and, in general terms, a lie.

That is a strong statement, but it has been true in the majority of situations and circumstances involving my clients. There are reasons for this that do not include intent to commit fraud, such as inexperienced staff, change in loan policy and loan forms, the de-neighborhoodization of the institute or bank so it is possible that the forms are a thousand miles away, and so on. But if you have not read the terms, get them and don't even bother to ask the lender.

Make sure your lawyer has read them too. And be sure he has understood what they said. There are many ways to write mortgage terms, and those terms can sound so similar to methods used by lawyers that they too could slip up.

SECONDARY FINANCING IS A DEAL MAKER

In the purchase or sale of real estate it is not unusual for a seller to be asked to take back a second mortgage. This second mortgage in its usual form is nothing more than an additional mortgage that runs concurrent to the existing financing.

It will be the terms of the secondary mortgage that give you the flexibility to use financing to adjust the benefits of the real estate investments so that it fits your needs. The secondary financing that you develop will follow the same techniques that will work for first mortgages or in conjunction with several techniques. It could well be that you establish both conventional and secondary financing at the same time.

I WILL PAY YOUR PRICE IF YOU ACCEPT MY TERMS

By adjusting the form of financing you use in your offers to acquire real estate or in the methods used to negotiate to sell your own real estate, you will find that price can be the least important aspect of a transaction.

Many transactions have failed to go to agreement form even though both the buyer and the seller already had a meeting of the minds; only they didn't know it.

Example

Bob has made up his mind that he will never take less than $50,000 for a vacant lot he wants to sell. Along comes Charlie who has made up his mind that he will not pay more than $45,000 for the property. However, out of this seemingly impossible transaction Bob has indicated that one or more of the following factors apply to the deal:

1. He wants to take $25,000 of the sale and travel around the world on a cruise ship with his wife.
2. Since he paid only $5,000 for the lot five years earlier, he will have a heavy gains tax to pay and needs some tax planning.
3. He plans to buy a yacht with the cash, expecting to add more money to the deal.
4. He will take as little as $10,000 down and get the balance over a period of up to 15 years (putting that in the bank for his grandson's future college education).

Working with any of the above factors would have made this transaction work. Let's look at each one in more detail:

1. Charlie gets additional information from the broker about the desired cruise. Charlie then goes to a travel agency and makes the following deal with the owner. "I plan to buy real estate by giving away cruises that you sell. I want you to pay me a top commission. Give me a list of cruises that pay maximum commissions." The travel agent shows Charlie some cruises that would earn Charlie 20% commission. Charlie picked out a couple of the voyages and booked space in the name of Bob and his wife. These cruises ranged from $20,000 to $30,000 (for double occupancy and all air and ship transportation). He then makes his offer to Bob showing that he will pay cash over and above the price of any of the cruises to match Bob's asking price of $50,000. Bob says okay and picks a $25,000 package. Charlie now closes the deal with the travel agent to lock in the deal and closes with Bob. The actual commission Charlie gets is $5,000. He writes out two checks, one to the travel agent for $20,000 and the balance to the closing agent on the vacant lot of $25,000. This means that the transaction will now close with Charlie actually paying only $45,000 while Bob got his full value of $50,000.

2. Realizing that the seller has a capital gains problem, the buyer approaches the situation with an installment sale. This is a provision where the seller takes the purchase price spread over more than one year. He saves on tax as he does so since the total gain does not increase his income to the point that his overall tax rate is increased excessively.

   This technique can be coupled with the "split payment" method, where the actual price is shown as $50,000 but the payments are divided into several years. If the buyer's cash can earn him extra dividends elsewhere, the ability to spread the total payment of the purchase over one or two additional years may make up part or all of the $5,000 over the desired payment of $45,000, and the seller will end up the same "after tax."

3. The boat deal is even easier to handle than the cruise around the world. The buyer pays a visit to one or more boat brokers or companies and makes a deal to "sell" one or more of their boats. The buyer puts $50,000 in the bank, and whenever the deal goes through he can collect the $5,000 or more that would be his commission from the yacht deal. Other benefits might include interest on the $50,000, which was in the bank during the decision process.

4. Any time a seller indicates that he or she will hold secondary financing and spread the payments on the balance over time, it tells the buyer that the most critical aspect of the deal is the price, but that the terms are somewhat flexible.

As financing is simply adjustment of values to interest rates over time, the buyer can make up his needed $5,000 over a ten- to fifteen-year term. In fact, this could be done in a much shorter time period.

Example

A $40,000 mortgage at 8% interest per annum over 7 years (84 months) will have a monthly payment of $623.46. A $35,000 mortgage for 7 years with a monthly payment of $658.55 has an interest rate of 12.25% per annum. By getting the seller to agree to accept a payment of $658.55 over the term, it becomes a matter of point of view as to the actual amount. Is it $40,000 at 8%, or $35,000 at 12.25%? Keep in mind that from the seller's point of view he's apt to want to look at it as $40,000 at 8% since his goal was to get a total of $50,000. The buyer can rationalize that he got his deal the way he wanted it, and why not? A deal was made when it might not have been made otherwise.

The basic structure of the financing technique used should then be devised to meet your goal and close the transaction.

All transactions must have a proper and satisfactory close or there is no transaction. Real estate investors who build substantial wealth through their investments know that there is a time and place for talk, and a time for action. Between the two it will be action that closes the deal, and not talk. Too much talk makes a deal drag along until all parties lose interest. Reluctant sellers and difficult situations that cannot be resolved simply or quickly, or buyers who cannot make up their minds, cause more deals to be lost than any single deal breaker.

Real estate salespeople know the power of "now" and act to nail down deals while the decision process is working. In any secondary financing, a good real estate salesperson will help you take advantage of this power, whether you are the buyer or the seller.

ADVANTAGES AND DISADVANTAGES OF SECOND MORTGAGES

This is how the second mortgages look to lenders and borrowers.

THE INSTITUTIONAL OR PRIVATE LENDER	THE BORROWER
1. More risky the higher the position (seconds more than firsts, thirds more than seconds, and so on).	1. Can reduce equity in the property and leverage up the return.
2. The more the risk, the higher the rate.	2. Can mean a high rate on the money borrowed.
3. Borrower should be strictly qualified.	3. May be hard to get.

THE INSTITUTIONAL OR PRIVATE LENDER	THE BORROWER
4. Keep the term short.	4. Term too short to make a reasonable payment schedule.
5. Obtain other security.	5. Other security can tie up other property.
6. Be quick to foreclose.	6. Even slight default can bring pressure.

A lender will examine all superior financing when considering making a loan on a property. The value of the property and the percentage of existing financing will dictate the amount of risk he or she is taking. Obviously, the lower the percentage of existing financing to total value, the lower the risk to the lender. If the property is valued at $50,000 and the first mortgage is $20,000, a second mortgage of $10,000 is a fairly safe gamble for the lender. The rate and term of years can be adjusted to account for the level of risk.

Lower-ranking mortgages, such as third or fourth mortgages, will command even higher rates as the risk increases and as the position or rank decreases. From a practical point of view, there are few institutional or private money sources that will lend on third or fourth mortgages.

WHEN SECONDARY LOANS ARE NEEDED

Because not all real estate transactions involve the use of secondary financing, it will be helpful for you to know when you should look to this form of financing as a deal maker. The first step in ascertaining when the secondary form of financing is needed is to fully understand what the second loan can do.

SIX THINGS A SECONDARY LOAN CAN DO

1. It can enable the buyer to structure the total financing so that he or she can afford the required equity down payment. Because the terms of the secondary financing may vary, the overall debt service may require lower monthly payments due to the combined financing, when compared to other alternatives. Of course, there are times when the new first mortgage money market will not permit the loan-to-value ratio needed, and the secondary financing may be the only way to achieve that ratio.

2. It can increase the cash flow yield on the cash invested in an income property transaction by reducing the amount of cash to be invested, and by establishing a constant rate of payment on the secondary financing which is lower than the prior cash flow yield, then the new cash flow yield will be increased.

3. It can leverage a seller's return on the paper. If the seller were to receive $50,000 in cash, where could (or would) he or she invest the sum or money and at what interest rate? On the other hand, if the seller were able to obtain a 15% return or better from a secure second mortgage on previously owned property, he or she might be interested. The wraparound may do this, and is one of the better forms of secondary financing.

4. It can spread risk and separate values. Because secondary financing covers such a broad spectrum, it includes such creative forms of financing as: land leases, wraparound mortgages, blanket mortgages, cross-collateralized purchase money financing, subordinated interest, interest-only payments, moratorium on all payments, percentage override sale of divided interest, and on and on. These various techniques that are covered in this book, are used in secondary financing. You will be able to sell a building, for example, but keep the land, which is then leased to the purchaser (this is a form of secondary financing).

5. There may be a limit to other choices. If the new money market is tight, seller-held secondary money may be the only possibility for structuring a high loan-to-value ratio.

6. The secondary loan can substantiate value. If the seller will hold a substantial second or third mortgage, at good terms, a sale at a higher price may be attained. There is normally a trade-off in this situation. The seller accepts lower than current interest over the term of the mortgage and the buyer pays more for the property than he or she might have if more cash were invested. The judgment of which is better for the buyer or the seller depends on the alternatives that are actually present. It will do no good to assume it would be better to take cash instead of a mortgage, unless someone actually is offering cash and someone else is offering a mortgage.

Of the six things that secondary financing can do, not all may be present in every situation. In fact, to have two or three would be exceptional. Now that you have seen what secondary financing can do, look at the circumstances that will cause you to look to it as the most effective method of financing a transaction.

WHEN TO USE DIFFERENT TYPES OF SECONDARY MORTGAGES

The Circumstances/Example 1

New money is tight and expensive. Closing costs and points are high, and loan to value ratios are 75% or less. The property has an existing financing that totals 50% of the property value and has a reasonable constant rate of payment. The buyer has a limited amount of cash to invest and must raise the loan-to-value ratio.

The Types of Secondary Financing to Use/Example 1

- Start with seller-held secondary financing. If the seller won't hold a normal secondary loan, then approach him with a wraparound structure.
- A land lease subordinated to existing financing will separate values and reduce the cash needed for the down payment.
- If the seller will not take the paper, look to other markets for the secondary loan.
- Possible cross-collateralization of other property may provide sufficient equity to support the loan for the seller or other lenders.

The Circumstances/Example 2

New money is tight and expensive as in the previous situation. Loan-to-value ratios are not sufficient to give the amount of financing needed, and the lender will not permit secondary financing on the property. The existing mortgage is very low (below 30% of value) or the property is free and clear.

The Types of Secondary Financing to Use/Example 2

- Use other property the buyer has for the security of the secondary financing, and go into the new money market for a first mortgage.
- In some situations the lender will not look at a land lease that is subordinated to the first mortgage as secondary financing, and this alternative can be used.
- Leaving the seller in the deal, with a right to buy him or her out in the future, is a form of secondary financing.
- Establishing a royalty fee on overages of income can provide income to a seller, and will not affect the lender's restrictions on new money.

The Circumstances/Example 3

New money is available at reasonable rates. Loan-to-value ratios are high, and the property is free and clear or has a low percentage of existing financing. However, the buyer still needs extra financing.

The Types of Secondary Financing to Use/Example 3

- Look to the seller as the prime secondary lender.
- If the amount of the secondary financing needed is small, and the commission substantial, the broker will often hold the paper.

- The land lease and other provisions mentioned earlier may be useful in this type of situation.

The above three situations are most frequently encountered. There are many variations, of course, and secondary financing can be used in any deal. However, there are times when secondary financing is not effective and you should be aware of these.

WHEN SECONDARY FINANCING SHOULD BE USED ONLY AS A LAST RESORT

1. Avoid using secondary financing when the buyer is financially weak and the transaction must be forced to meet his or her economic ability. If a buyer is putting down a last dime on an income property, he or she may be destined for trouble. Overextension of loan-to-value ratios will create debt service that may be more than the property or the buyer can handle.

2. Avoid seconds if the new money market is good, the existing financing on the property is low, and the equity needed with this type of financing is available from the buyer. Do not use secondary financing simply to increase this extension at the sacrifice of leverage. You should, however, first analyze the leverage and extension of a property to be sure you are arriving at a proper level. Use the Leverage Calculation Chart discussed earlier.

3. If a property has several existing secondary loans, you may still use secondary financing, but see if it is possible to eliminate some of the current loans with the cash down or by refinancing the entire package with a new first mortgage.

4. Avoid a package of combined financing that has a constant rate which is more than 3 points above the possible existing financing, unless there is a good reason (such as an existing mortgage that is to retire in a few years, and the cash flow can be sacrificed for the period of time for future gains).

Remember that the greater the percentage of loan-to-value ratio, the more risky the secondary loans become. There are exceptions to every rule mentioned about secondary financing. The needs of the parties involved, their capabilities, and their willingness to risk capital need to be considered.

WHERE TO GO TO FIND SECONDARY FINANCING

The few sources of secondary financing are listed below:

1. **The seller.** The best. (See sections of this chapter which follow for more detailed information.)

2. **Commercial banks and savings and loans.** These sources are available for secondary financing in the form of home improvement loans. These loans should not be overlooked, because the buyer often anticipates additions to a property and plans on using cash after the sale for these improvements. Transfer cash to the down payment and finance the improvements with a home improvement loan. Some commercial banks are good sources for personal loans secured by real estate. This is a changing market, however, and will depend on the bank and the person.

3. **Mortgage companies.** Most communities have several mortgage companies that deal in the secondary loan market. They are effective, although often expensive. Check your area to locate them. Then use the same methods of establishing rapport with them as you would for a lender (discussed in the previous chapter).

4. **Private investors.** This source is hard to find, and often there are investors that deal with the mortgage companies. Sometimes, however, you will find them advertising in the classified section of the local newspaper. They should be found before you need them. Your commercial bank may know of some. Many mortgage brokers have a list of private investors who supply funds for loans. Make a few calls to some of the local mortgage brokers and inquire what private funds they might represent.

5. **The real-estate broker.** In the large commercial transactions, brokers are often asked to hold a part of the risk in the transaction by holding some of the paper. Some brokers will, and others will not.

HOW TO DEAL WITH SECONDARY LOAN MAKERS

Each of the preceding five sources will require a slightly different approach. Not all five will be available for all transactions. The banks, for example, will not be very useful in secondary financing over a first mortgage that represents at least 75% of the value. The effectiveness of mortgage companies diminishes when there is existing financing of at least 80% of the value.

Therefore, in the order of their acceptability to the transaction, look at the major sources of secondary loans and learn how to deal with them.

Dealing with the Seller on Secondary Financing

The seller is the most motivated of all possible lenders. When you deal with the seller, you don't have to justify the value or pay points. But sellers require special handling.

Third-party loans, made by outside lenders, banks, or private parties, are not highly negotiable. The end result will be a loan in the amount and at the terms the lender feels he or she can live with. The seller, on the other hand, is not bound by the same restrictions and can be more flexible. Some brokers mistakenly feel that the sellers who don't need the money (wealthy sellers) are the best candidates for purchase money secondary financing. Naturally, these sellers are good sources and are often receptive to this form of financing. However, they can sometimes be very independent. They may take the attitude that they will hold out until a cash buyer comes along. Wealthy sellers sometimes expect all buyers to have money.

The seller who doesn't have money and needs money from the transaction is generally the one who is most motivated to take the secondary financing. Why? Look back at the motivation. If he or she needs money, the sale of the property becomes the important aspect. It could be that the person is being transferred, or just cannot afford to keep the home or property being sold. The desire to get money (that seller's goal), may really be the need to get off the current debt. The transaction can provide some of both benefits. By selling there are no more debt payments to make, and a small down payment with secondary financing provides sufficient cash to meet that part of the deal. In this situation, the need to make the sale will motivate the seller to hold some reasonable paper. Many sales are lost because the broker assumes the seller will not hold secondary paper. The fact may be that the seller cannot afford not to be flexible.

How to Lay the Groundwork for Secondary Financing to Be Held by the Seller

1. **First make sure you know the difference between the goals and the needs of the seller.** If the seller needs a quick sale or money in a hurry, then your entire marketing program may take on a different approach than if he or she were not pressed. You may find secondary financing becomes more important and crucial as the motivation of the seller increases. However, because most people associate needs as their goals, the direction the seller (or buyer for that matter) follows may be shortsighted to attaining the real goal. Remember that either party may not know or understand how to use the different creative financing tools, or realize there are different benefits that can be obtained. This is one of the reasons a broker or other intermediary is worth its weight in closed deals.

2. **Examine the property carefully.** If you believe the first or existing financing is good and adds to the salability of the property, start talking about the possibility of the seller holding paper or other forms of secondary financing rather than new financing. When the money market does not provide suitable or reasonable terms for new financing, then seek a form of secondary financing as a solution to the marketing problems. Remember, the seller is the best such source.

3. **Know the options you have in providing secondary financing.** Do not forget that it is not a first mortgage, it is a secondary or junior loan, and secondary financing is not just mortgages. It can be a land lease or building lease. The combinations are many, and you can utilize this book as a reference source for reviewing those options.

How to Deal with Commercial Banks and Savings and Loan Associations for Secondary Financing

There are usually two forms of commercial banks in any area, state and federal. There are slightly different regulations that govern each of them, and the individual bank policy on secondary financing may vary widely. It is necessary, therefore, that you review the following guide in order to obtain good secondary financing from these institutions.

The savings and loans also follow similar guidelines, so you may consider this section as a combined guide for both these institutions. Keep in mind, however, that each loan situation is different and, as with all loans, one bank or association will look for different criteria in its analysis of the risk. Here are five important guidelines:

- Know the policy of the institution before you go in to talk about a loan.
- When you make a loan presentation, have all the necessary back-up material you know the institution will require in order to reach a decision.
- Precondition your buyer to the possibility that he or she may need a cosigner for the note. Sometimes a relative will be glad to do this.
- Do not approach this form of secondary financing unless you could not arrange satisfactory financing with the seller or get new money.
- Find out, ahead of time, what additional collateral your buyer has that can be used as security on the loan needed. Often, stocks can be pledged, eliminating the need for a second mortgage on the property, or at least assuring the availability of a second mortgage.

How to Deal with Mortgage Companies

Mortgage companies are also regulated, but not to the same degree as normal banks or savings and loan institutions. These companies are either private firms or credit institutions. They may be a branch of a union dealing primarily with its own members, or backed by insurance companies or trust funds. Their interest rates vary, from higher than any other source to lower.

The first step is to locate them and the best place to start is the Yellow Pages of your phone book. They will be listed under "Mortgages," "Loans," and sometimes

"Trust Funds-Credit Unions." If you fail to locate any this way, contact your commercial bank and ask if it has a list of the public as well as private mortgage companies that are in the area.

Once you have found them, learn what their lending policies will be in various types of deals. Some of these lenders will not touch anything but single family, while others will go into hotels and other commercial transactions.

This source is large and seems to have a lot of money most of the time. However, before you deal with any such lender do the following:

- Sit down with one of its representatives and find out how the operation works.
- Ask if he or she will give you information on the company.
- Get a list of references.
- Check out the references given, but also ask others about them.
- A check with the Better Business Bureau may disclose some interesting facts about the firm.
- Get a clear understanding of its charges and interest rates.
- Be sure that the mortgage company is indeed reputable.

Finding Private Lenders and Dealing with Them

This is the most difficult source of all to find, but can be one of the best. These investors are usually wealthy persons who have substantial cash and/or the ability to borrow cash at better rates than you can. They will then lend the cash out at a higher rate, picking up the leverage. Secondary loans that are secure are a good form of investment for many people and those who are in that field seem to do well. It is not, however, a market for the occasional investor, and you should avoid the casual investor who says he or she will take a second mortgage on a property if it is exceptional. Look for the full-time investor.

These investors are found in the most unlikely places. They will normally deal with mortgage brokers or mortgage lenders to some degree, but the mortgage broker or lender will guard the identity of this investor and you will not find out who he or she is. Sometimes they work from leads they cultivate with commercial banks, and this contact is more accessible to you.

Some private lenders advertise in the newspaper, usually in the classified section under "Venture Capital" or "Capital Available." Various newspapers have different headings for this type of ad so look around. You can, of course, advertise for this source yourself, but this is rarely very productive. About the only way is to keep your eyes and ears open and to ask your commercial bank president and other lenders.

Because the private lender uses a lawyer in closing transactions, you may find that if you send a letter to attorneys in your area, asking them if they know of private investors dealing in first and second mortgages, you may locate this elusive investor.

The private lender has an advantage over you and your buyer, and takes advantage of that situation. After all, this is often the last person you and other borrowers will turn to. Because of this fact, the private lender will either take the loan or not, and the initial presentation is critical. The terms and conditions the lender offers will depend on many different aspects of course. Some private lenders stick to one type of property, others are less selective. The harshness of the terms will depend mostly on the general market for other investments. If the investor is able to obtain investments that have little risk elsewhere at a good rate, then the rate he or she will demand on a second loan will be considerably higher, depending on the risk involved. You can do very little to change the outcome of a loan from such a lender. Nonetheless, you may find that the need for the money will be great enough to warrant the cost.

There are times when the private lender will lend at comparative terms when all things are considered. Usually, the closing costs are a fraction of those available from commercial banks and mortgage companies.

When dealing with private lenders, keep in mind the following two warnings:

- Be sure the lender's attorney does not represent you (as the borrower) in closing the real estate transaction.
- Have your own attorney go over the loan document before you sign it.

WHEN AND HOW THE BROKER CAN HOLD SOME OF THE PAPER

If the transaction has a substantial commission, and the buyer is just a little short of cash to close the deal, the broker may be asked to take some of the paper as a deferred commission. Of course, this situation can come up in almost any transaction, and this becomes an individual matter that some brokers will agree to do while others will not. It is important, however, that certain factors be understood about deferred commissions.

- If the broker takes a note or other form of loan equivalent to a deferred commission, it is likely the IRS will tax the full amount of the commission the year the note was taken, rather than in subsequent years when payment is received.
- A fee conditioned on the future collection of a debt held by the seller may avoid the tax situation shown above, as the future payments are in a sense based on continued performance.

Chapter 7

HOW TO USE GOVERNMENT-INSURED LOANS TO FINANCE REAL-ESTATE PURCHASES AND SALES

There is considerable mortgage financing available to buyers, sellers and builders through the Federal Mortgage Insurance Programs. The United States Government provides these insurance and lending programs that will help you buy and sell your properties. These programs vary tremendously and are available in every state. They help buyers who do not have the larger down payment required for more conventional loans. Equally these loan programs aid sellers who may not be able to sell their properties were it not for this easy to come by financing. When it comes to providing options to finance your investments and to aid in the sale of your properties, you will want to learn as much as you can about government-insured loans and programs.

The VA and FHA have loan programs for single-family home buyers. However, government loan programs are wide reaching and take into account a substantial amount of loans for many different kinds of residential and commercial ventures.

When it comes to government programs, you will want to deal with a good mortgage broker who is up to date in this kind of market and who deals with the specific type of loan you may want or that will best suit your needs. The information provided in this chapter is as up to date as possible, and while there may be no changes by the time you read it, government loan programs are constantly reviewed for alterations. Generally, the changes that may be enacted will improve the programs since the loan amounts are revised upward on a frequent basis. The first step, however, is to have a general understanding of what the government programs do and how you can benefit from them.

Keep in mind that you should think of two factors of each loan program: (1) how it will help you to buy a given property, and (2) how you can use that technique to sell a property you own. Since not all of the loan programs are applicable to everyone, it is possible that you cannot use some of the loan programs offered. However, as a seller, many of your properties will find an increased market through the VA or FHA programs to be discussed.

Once you have reviewed this chapter, go out and find a good mortgage broker who is familiar with these types of programs. You will find mortgage brokers listed in the Yellow Pages under that title, and the answers to a few simple questions will tell you if you are talking with someone who may be worth meeting.

QUESTIONS AND ANSWERS TO FIND A QUALIFIED MORTGAGE BROKER

Q. One.   Does your company have a loan officer who specializes in FHA loans, VA loans?

A. One.   Yes. (If any other answer is given, you need to call another broker.)

Q. Two.   (To that specialist.) Do you specialize in single-family loans and investment loan programs within the VA and FHA programs?

A. Two.   Yes. (Or better: No, I specialize only in the single-family loans. Mr. Jones of our office is the government loan specialist for investments.)

Q. Three.   I would like to sit down and discuss my investment needs. Would there be any charge for the opportunity to discover if you can help me?

A. Three.   No. When would you like to get together? If you want to include investments as well as single-family homes, I'll ask Mr. Jones to join us.

You will find that while there may be programs on the books that look as if they are exactly what you need, the actual availability of that program will depend on the determination of the area's needs and the amount of money that has been allocated to that specific area of loan assistance. For example, there are loan programs that are designed to assist in the construction of low-cost housing for the poor or the elderly. These programs open and close for specific areas of the country on the needs for housing in those areas. Some builders and investors follow these programs around the country, looking for opportunities when they open up.

GOVERNMENT PROGRAMS PROVIDE INSURANCE, NOT LOANS

The first thing you should know about government loans is that in most instances the government does not make the loan. Instead it merely insures a portion of the loan, thereby reducing the risk to the lender who actually provides the funds. This insurance then makes more money available from conventional lenders for these programs since the loans are more secure than uninsured loans in the same category.

In addition, since such loans are less risky, the lender is willing to increase the amount of the loan. Some government loans provide 100% of the funds needed for the buyer to acquire the property. In turn, this increases the number of ready and willing buyers, which enables many real estate developers to find an easy market for their properties. As a buyer, this is good news if you can qualify for the program; as a seller, this is great news if your property meets the requirements for the program.

The insurance premium is paid by the buyer. The mortgage insurance premium (MIP) was implemented as a lump sum in 1983 and two methods of payment are allowed. One hundred percent of the payment can be financed, or the borrower can pay a percentage of the premium in cash at the closing, with a monthly add on paid over a period of years. This period of years will vary depending on the initial up-front payment and the loan-to-value ratio (LTV) of the loan.

The following two charts illustrate the up-front and annual MIP rates for mortgages closed on or after April 17, 1994.

MORTGAGE INSURANCE PAYMENT CHART

Up-Front and Annual MIP Chart
for Mortgage Terms Greater Than Fifteen Years

Up-Front Percent Paid Down	Loan-To-Value Ratio	MIP (Mortgage Insurance Premium)	Term of Years for Payment of Insurance
2.25%	89.99% & under	.50%	7
2.25%	90.00 to 95.00%	.50%	12
2.25%	95.01 & over	.50%	30

Up-Front and Annual MIP Chart
for Mortgage Terms of Fifteen Years or Less

Up-Front Percent Paid Down	Loan-To-Value Ratio	MIP (Mortgage Insurance Premium)	Term of Years for Payment of Insurance
2.00%	89.99% & under	None	Not Available
2.00%	90.00 to 95.00%	.25%	4
2.00%	95.01% & over	.25%	8

Suppose that Abercoumbe took out a loan through one of the government programs in the amount of $80,000. The term was 25 years. At the closing of the loan, he could either pay cash or have the loan financed. If he had decided to finance the amount of the loan, it would be added to the total loan, and he would then pay back the loan based on the larger amount. First, he calculated the two different amounts:

100 Percent Finance Amount

Amount of the loan	$80,000	
Multiplied by	× .005	(found in the 100% finance line under the over 15-year table)
Insurance due	$ 400.00	(per year, payable $33.33 per month for full term)

Paid at Closing Amount

Amount of the loan	$80,000	
Multiplied by	× .0225	(see up-front section of chart)
Insurance due		
in cash at closing	$ 1,800.00	

WHO MAKES THE GOVERNMENT LOANS?

Loans that are insured by the government are obtained from most institutional lenders. Local savings and loans, commercial banks, and other forms of mortgage bankers make these loans. These loans are then frequently sold to major investors such as insurance companies, pension funds, mutual funds, as well as back through government securities funds, which hold large blocks of these mortgages and sell shares to investors.

HOW DO THE INVESTORS MAKE OUT?

The lender or investor who buys the loan portfolio finds that usually it is going to benefit from ownership of the loan in two areas. First, a contract rate is paid by the borrower to the lender. This rate usually is slightly lower than the same conventional rate that would have been offered for the similar loan. However, as the risk is less, some investors feel this rate, and the next item to come, makes these loans very attractive investments. When the loan is made, a discount is paid by the seller. This discount is a cost that is required to be paid by the seller and adjusts the yield to the lender to increase the actual percentage earned by the lender above the contract rate. For example, if the contract rate were 10% on a loan of $80,000, the interest paid by the buyer the first year would be approximately $8,000. On this same loan, the seller may have paid a discount (points) of 4%, or $3,200, which would have reduced the actual amount of the funds provided by the lender by the same amount. The lender then actually paid out only $76,800. However, the loan is set at a contract rate of 10% on $80,000. In this case, the actual interest yield to the lender is about

10.54% if the loan was a 25-year loan and was not prepaid. Since the lender gets an additional bonus if the loan is prepaid, and as most loans are prepaid within seven to twelve years, the lender could earn an average yield of 11% or more on this example.

When you review the chapters on mortgage discounts and wraparound mortgages, you will find other examples of how this discount can be put to use.

THE VETERANS ADMINISTRATION AND THE GI LOAN

Veterans of the United States Armed Forces number well over 30 million. This is a sizable number of prospective applicants for loans, and many have not taken advantage of the opportunities available to them through the VA loan programs offered. The veteran loan is often referred to as the GI loan, and it will be discussed here in detail. As in all aspects of government loan programs, the requirements and loan amounts and costs are subject to change.

Who Is Eligible for a GI Loan?

According to the most recent guidelines available from the VA, the following people are eligible for guaranteed or insured GI loans:

1. A veteran who has served a minimum of at least 90 days active service between September 16, 1940 and July 25, 1947 (WW II vets); 180 continuous days between July 26, 1947 and June 26, 1956 (Peacetime Vets); June 27, 1950 to January 31, 1955 (Korean vets); 181 continuous days between February 1, 1955 and August 4, 1964 (Post-Korean Vets) and August 5, 1964 to May 7, 1975 (Vietnam vets); 181 continuous days between May 8, 1975 and September 7, 1980 (Post-Vietnam Vets); two years of active duty between September 1, 1980 and August 1, 1990 for enlisted men; two years active duty between October 17, 1981 and August 1, 1990 for officers; two years or period longer than 90 days called to active duty after August 2, 1990 to (at writing this date has not ended, so check with VA office), provided that the veteran was not discharged dishonorably. If the veteran within the above dates was discharged due to a service-incurred disability, the active service could be less than 90 days.

2. A veteran who served active duty for a period of 181 days or more and any part of which occurred after January 31, 1955, who does not meet the exact dates shown above for the 90 days active duty, and who was discharged or released under conditions other than dishonorable or who was discharged or released after such date for a service-connected disability.

3. Widows of men who served during the stated periods and who died as a result of the service.

4. Any member of the Women's Army Auxiliary Corps who served for at least 90 days and who was honorably discharged for a disability incurred in the conduct of service causing her to be unable to physically perform service in the Corps or in the Women's Army Corps. (*Note:* This provision is applicable only to discharges prior to the integration of that Corps into the Women's Army Corps, pursuant to Public Law 110, 78th Congress.)

5. Certain United States citizens who served in the Armed Forces of a government allied with the United States in World War II.

6. A serviceman or -woman who served on active duty for 181 days or more not already covered, provided that the enlistment into active service occurred prior to September 7, 1980, and that any discharge or release was other than dishonorable.

7. An enlistment after September 7, 1980, would require the serviceman or -woman to have served two years of active duty except if discharged for a disability whether or not service connected; discharged for a hardship; or any case in which it is established that the person is suffering from a service-connected disability not the result of willful misconduct and not incurred during a period of unauthorized absence.

8. Unremarried widows of veterans of service personnel described in items (2) (6) and (7) above, who died as a result of service.

9. The wife of any member of the Armed Forces serving on active duty who is listed as missing in action or is a prisoner of war and has been so listed for a total of more than 90 days.

10. A serviceman or -woman who is on active duty at present and has served at least 181 days but not the full two years of duty will be granted an eligibility certificate conditioned on the veteran remaining on continuous active duty.

These categories indicate those persons who may be entitled to obtain a GI loan. this ability depends on the criteria mentioned and the prior use of this opportunity. Once a veteran has met the aforementioned rules or requirements, he or she automatically obtains an entitlement. This means that he or she can "draw" on his or her right for a GI loan. The entitlement is a term that relates to the amount of a loan the government will insure. At the moment, this amount is $50,750 (Bill H.R. 995 was signed by President Clinton on October 13, 1994 and is effective for all loans closed on or after October 13, 1994). This amount is the new maximum for loans above $144,000 that are used to purchase or construct a home, or refinance an existing VA-guaranteed loan to a lower interest rate. The basic entitlement for all other loans is $46,000.

Keep in mind that the entitlement is not the loan amount, but the insured amount. Lenders look at the entitlement as the top portion of the loan and will issue loans in multiples of this amount. In general, the lender will advance a loan equal to four times the entitlement. That means that at present the maximum loan on the GI program that *would not require the buyer to put any money down* would be $203,000 (4 x $50,750).

REINSTATEMENT OR RESTORATION OF THE VA ENTITLEMENT

A veteran who has previously purchased a property with a GI loan may be eligible for a second loan if he or she meets the following specific conditions:

- The previous property must have been sold and the original loan paid off.
- Another veteran assumed the GI loan and substituted his or her entitlement, thereby freeing the first veteran's eligibility for another loan.

In addition to these two circumstances, it is possible that the veteran didn't use all of the entitlement that he or she has obtained. One reason for this possibility is that the amount of the entitlement has continually increased over the years. You can see from the following chart the dates and amounts that established these increases. If you used the total entitlement available to you during an early year and then the entitlement was increased, you now have new entitlement coming to you.

Entitlements and Dates They Were Established

Date		Amount
Prior to	September 1, 1951	$ 4,000.00
Changed	September 1, 1951	7,500.00
Changed	May 7, 1951	12,500.00
Changed	December 31, 1974	17,500.00
Changed	October 1, 1978	25,000.00
Changed	October 1, 1980	27,500.00
Changed	February 1, 1988	36,000.00
Changed	January 1, 1990	46,000.00
Changed	October 14, 1994	50,750.00[*]

[*] The $50,750 amount is limited to certain mortgages; see previous text.

By following the chart, it would be obvious that a veteran who obtained a mortgage on July 1, 1951, has only used $4,000 of his or her entitlement. The veteran would now have a new entitlement of up to $50,750 less the $4,000 already used. If he or she met the requirements of the reinstatement, $46,750 would be available to him or her at this time. As the actual loan amount could be 4 times that amount, there is substantial borrowing power available.

In addition to the automatic restoration or reinstatement of the entitlement to the veteran, there are three other ways in which the entitlement can be renewed. These occur when the security for the loan has been:

1. Taken by the United States or any state, or local government agency for public use (through condemnation or otherwise).

2. Destroyed or damaged by fire or other natural hazard to the extent that occupancy, use or restoration is impractical, which destruction or damage is not a result from an act or omission willfully designed by the veteran to bring about such destruction or damage.

3. Disposed of because of other compelling reasons devoid of fault on the part of the veteran. These reasons may include health, employment, voluntary conveyance in lieu of condemnation, or other reasons felt to be compelling.

The VA loan can be used for a variety of real estate ventures and is not limited just to single-family homes. The following is a list of the different kinds of properties the veteran can purchase using the GI loan program:

1. A single-family home.

2. A residential unit in an approved condominium project.

3. New construction of a single family home.

4. Repair, alterations, or improvements of a home.

5. Refinancing of an existing home loan.

6. A mobile home.

7. Farm land.

8. Business land, buildings provided that the property is primarily for residential purposes and there is not more than one business unit. The nonresidential area may not exceed 25% of the total floor area.

9. Apartment buildings up to four units (plus one additional unit for each additional veteran living on the property who cosigns on the mortgage). Vet must demonstrate his or her ability to manage rental property and knowledge of landlord expenses.

10. Refinance property so it may be sold with improved financing.

INCOME REQUIREMENTS TO OBTAIN A LOAN

The VA has set a basic qualification formula that must be met by every applicant for a GI loan. This formula sets the maximum loan available in most cases. The essence of this formula is to assure the lender that the borrower has reasonable income and credit to repay the loan. Therefore, in addition to being declared eligible for a GI loan based on his or her period of service, the veteran must meet the requirements of the governing law in respect to income and credit. This income and credit takes into consideration more than the property and the respective mortgage payments that will become due as a result of the financing. It also takes into account other obligations confronting the veteran, which include dependents and other expenses that he or she may have. At the time an applicant is filing for a loan, the pertinent data will be used in the final calculations as to the credit of the borrower. The wife's or spouse's income will also be included in the total family income. Prior to going for an interview for an application, there is some specific information that you should have available.

DATA NEEDED FOR ANY MORTGAGE APPLICATION

1. The veteran and spouse's name and current address.
2. Entitlement amount. (Obtain through the VA office.)
3. Entitlement certificate. (Obtain through the VA office.)
4. Place of employment for veteran and spouse, with name for verification.
5. Internal Revenue Service 1040 or other form for the last two years.
6. All sources of income, with documentation.
7. Bank, savings and loan, investment brokerage account, thrift institution address, and account number, and exact name on the account.
8. Loan information, lender's address, amount owned, and loan number.
9. Credit card numbers.
10. List with values of all major assets, and amounts owed against each.
11. Total (with breakdown) of all loan payments.
12. Details on any unusual expenses, which may be temporary or permanent.

THE PROCEDURE WITH A VA OR GI LOAN

Under the current law, there are several elements about the GI loan that both the buyer and the seller need to be aware of. The VA is very specific about what costs the veteran can pay and which costs he or she is not allowed to pay. The importance is that the seller is required to pay certain costs with respect to a sale to a veteran through the GI loan. The seller's cost is limited to 4% of the loan amount. It is critical that the seller understand that if the contract calls for the veteran to pay for cost the VA will not allow him or her to pay, the contract will not close in accordance with its provisions. At or prior to the closing, the parties will have to have an understanding based on the following items:

ITEMS THE VETERAN CAN PAY
IF HE OR SHE IS THE BUYER

1. The veteran's lawyer.
2. Title insurance (if no charges for abstract).
3. Survey.
4. Credit report.
5. Appraisal (if obtained in his or her name).
6. Intangible tax on mortgage.
7. State stamps on note, if any.
8. Repairs.
9. Funding fee (see next chart).

ITEMS THE VETERAN CANNOT PAY
IF HE OR SHE IS THE BUYER

1. Discount (points).
2. Photographs.
3. Preparation of deed.
4. Surtax on deed.
5. Assignment of mortgage.
6. Mortgage satisfaction.
7. Recording of item 6.
8. Documentary stamps on deed.
9. Inspections.
10. Appraisal in another's name.

VA funding fees as of April 12, 1994

Loan type	Active duty or veteran	National Guard/reserves
Purchase/construction—0% Down	2.00%	2.75%
Purchase/construction—5% Down	1.50%	2.25%
Purchase/construction—10% Down	1.25%	2.00%
Cash-out refinance	2.00%	2.75%
Rate reduction refinance	0.50%	0.50%
Native American direct loan	1.25%	1.25%
Manufactured homes	1.00%	1.00%
Assumptions	0.50%	0.50%
Vendee loans	1.00%	1.00%
Second or subsequent use (some limits)	3.00%	3.00%

All properties on which a GI loan application is to be made must be properly appraised by an appointed and approved appraiser. The VA will only appraise property for veterans. The appraisal fees are apt to vary but will be approximately $275 for single-family homes; $295 for duplexes; $300 for triplexes and four-unit apartments.

FHA appraisals cost a little more, but they can be used in the VA loan process. This is important for sellers who are not veterans and who wish to get the appraisal to facilitate a sale through the GI loan program, or one of the FHA loan programs.

There are a variety of types of loans the veteran can obtain with this program. Most follow conventional patterns similar to those loans offered by savings and loan associations to the general public. GI loans are limited in amount and have restrictions that make them available only to qualified veterans. Lenders benefit because of the reduced risk; sellers are able to sell property they might not have been able to without the GI loan (even though it cost them more to do this), and veterans get the opportunity to purchase a property they may not have been able to buy otherwise.

All veterans need to understand that when they take out a GI loan, they are on that loan until either it is paid off or they are replaced by another veteran. The significance of this is that loan remains as an outstanding liability to the original veteran no matter how the loan is assumed on the specific property. If the buyers are not veterans, or if a buying veteran has no entitlement to replace the original, then the vet is there for the duration. This may not present any economic hardship for anyone, but when the veteran sells the property he or she would be best advised to sell to another veteran who can remove him or her entirely, and thereby restore and reinstate the entitlement back to the original veteran.

FHA LOAN PROGRAMS

The Federal Housing Administration provides loans that are similar to GI loans, except there is a required down payment by the borrower. The most-used FHA program is the Section 203 (b) loan, which is open to anyone, including a non-United States citizen. The property being purchased can be owner-occupied or investment property. The basic terms would be 30-year payback on the mortgage, with loan amounts as follows:

FHA 203 (B) Loan Program

Loan maximums * (check local office for limitations)

Single-family homes	$ 78,660 to $155,250
Duplexes	100,000 to 198,550
Three-family buildings	121,600 to 240,000
Four-unit apartments	151,500 to 298,350

Down payment required minimums

3% of the first $25,000 purchase price

3% of everything over the first $25,000

	Appraisal fees
Single-family homes	$275
Duplexes	295
Three-family buildings	300
Four-unit apartments	325

In keeping with the institutional lenders' creative form of financing, the FHA has developed the Section 245 (a) program, which is a graduated payment mortgage. As in all graduated payment mortgages (G.P.M.), the initial monthly payment is less than would cover the interest and insurance costs of the loan. The unpaid interest and insurance is added to the principal owed, making the total amount owed on the mortgage increase in the early years of the G.P.M. As the amount of payment is increased, this trend reverses and the payment begins to cover all costs on the mortgage and amortization of principal owed.

The 245(a) offers the borrower three different loan programs depending on the initial term and the increases in payment. All three programs have a total 30-year payout term, and are as follows:

Plan 1   Five years of monthly payments that increase 2.5% annually, then remain constant for the remainder.

Plan 2   Five years of monthly payments that increase 5% annually, then remain constant for the remainder.

Plan 3   Five years of monthly payments that increase 7.5% annually, then remain constant for the remainder.

Specific Elements of the245(a)

1. Cannot be used to refinance a present-level mortgage.
2. Maximum amounts set for specific areas of the country by HUD.
3. Can be assumed as with other FHA programs.
4. Down payment is greater than with the 203 (b) program and is reviewed on a case-by-case basis.
5. Maximum mortgage amount is $155,250 but some areas may be limited to less.

HOW TO GET INFORMATION

The following list includes all the regional offices of the Veterans Administration. Any correspondence should be sent to the director of the corresponding office in your area. You may request additional data from the office to assist you in your use of the VA loan program. One caution, however. Much of the material they will send you is out-of-date, and you should not rely on this information if it applies to interest rates, dollar amounts, and current programs. Local lenders dealing with loans can provide this up-to-date information. The VA sends notices on minor changes on a very frequent basis, and there is no way you can keep abreast of these changes unless you have the time to sift through all the notices which the VA sends out.

VA Regional Office
Aronov Building
474 South Court Street
Montgomery, AL 36104

VA Regional Office
Federal Building
230 North First Avenue
Phoenix, AZ 85025

VA Regional Office
Federal Office Building
700 West Capitol Avenue
Little Rock, AK 72201

VA Regional Office
Federal Building
11000 Wilshire Boulevard
Los Angeles, CA 90024

VA Regional Office
211 Main Street
San Francisco, CA 94105

VA Regional Office
Denver Federal Center
Denver, CO 80225

VA Regional Office
450 Main Street
Hartford, CN 06103
Note: *Loan guaranty consolidated with Philadelphia.*

VA Center
1601 Kirkwood Highway
Wilmington, DE 19805

Veterans Benefits Office
Veterans Administration
2033 M. Street, NW
Washington, DC 20421

VA Regional Office
P.O. Box 1437
144 First Avenue, South
St. Petersburg, FL 33731

VA Regional Office
730 Peachtree Street, NE
Atlanta, GA 30308

VA Regional Office
P.O. Box 3198
680 Ala Moana Boulevard
Honolulu, HI 96801

VA Regional Office
Federal Building and U.S. Courthouse
550 West Fort Street
Box 044
Boise, ID 83724

VA Regional Office
2030 West Taylor Street
Chicago, IL 60680

VA Regional Office
36 South Pennsylvania Street
Indianapolis, IN 46204

VA Regional Office
210 Walnut Street
Des Moines, IA 50309

VA Center
5500 East Kellogg
Wichita, KS 67218

VA Regional Office
600 Federal Place
Louisville, KY 40202

VA REGIONAL OFFICE
701 Loyola Avenue
New Orleans, LA 70113

VA CENTER
Togus, ME 04330

VA REGIONAL OFFICE
Federal Building
31 Hopkins Plaza
Baltimore, MD 21201

VA REGIONAL OFFICE
J.F.K. Federal Building
Government Center
Boston, MA 02203

VA REGIONAL OFFICE
801 West Baltimore at Third
P.O. Box 1117-A
Detroit, MI 48232

VA REGIONAL OFFICE
252 Seventh Avenue (at 24th St.)
New York, NY 10001

VA CENTER
Federal Building
Fort Snelling
St. Paul, MN 55111

VA CENTER
1500 East Woodrow Wilson Avenue
Jackson, MS 39216

VA REGIONAL OFFICE
Room 4705, Federal Building
1520 Market Street
St. Louis, MO 63103

VA CENTER
Fort Harrison, MT 59636

VA REGIONAL OFFICE
220 South 17th Street
Lincoln, NE 68508

VA REGIONAL OFFICE
1201 Terminal Way
Reno, NV 89502

Note: *Loan Guaranty consolidated with San Francisco. Loan Guaranty activities for Clark and Lincoln Counties, Nevada consolidated with Los Angeles.*

VA REGIONAL OFFICE
497 Silver Street
Manchester, NH 03103

VA REGIONAL OFFICE
20 Washington Place
Newark, NJ 07102

VA REGIONAL OFFICE
500 Gold Avenue, SW
Albuquerque, NM 87101

VA REGIONAL OFFICE
Federal Office Building
111 West Huron Street
Buffalo, NY 14202

VA REGIONAL OFFICE
Wachovia Building
301 North Main Street
Winston-Salem, NC 27102

VA CENTER
Fargo, ND 58102

Note: *Loan Guaranty consolidated with St. Paul.*

VA REGIONAL OFFICE
Federal Office Building
1240 East Ninth Street
Cleveland, OH 44199

VA REGIONAL OFFICE
Second and Court Streets
Muskogee, OK 74401

VA REGIONAL OFFICE
426 Southwest Stark Street
Portland, OR 97204

VA CENTER
P.O. Box 8079
5000 Wissahickon Avenue
Philadelphia, PA 19101

VA REGIONAL OFFICE
1000 Liberty Avenue
Pittsburgh, PA 15222

VA CENTER
Barrio Monacillos
GPO Box 4867
Rio Piedras, PR 00936

VA REGIONAL CENTER
Federal Building, Kennedy Plaza
Providence, RI 02903
Note: *Loan Guaranty consolidated with Boston.*

VA REGIONAL OFFICE
1801 Assembly Street
Columbia, SC 29201

VA CENTER
Sioux Falls, SD 57101
Note: *Loan Guaranty consolidated with St. Paul.*

VA REGIONAL OFFICE
U.S. Courthouse
801 Broadway
Nashville, TN 37203

VA REGIONAL OFFICE
515 Rusk Avenue
Houston, TX 77061

VA REGIONAL OFFICE
1400 North Valley Mills Drive
Waco, TX 76710

VA REGIONAL OFFICE
125 South State Street
Salt Lake City, UT 84138

VA CENTER
White River Junction, VT 05001

VA REGIONAL OFFICE
211 West Campbell Avenue
Roanoke, VA 24011

VA REGIONAL OFFICE
Sixth and Lenora Building
Seattle, WA 98121

VA REGIONAL OFFICE
502 Eighth Street
Huntington, WV 25701

VA REGIONAL OFFICE
342 North Water Street
Milwaukee, WI 53202
Note: *Wyoming consolidated with Denver.*

VA and FHA Programs

Because there are so many different programs, and these programs are constantly undergoing updates and replacement by other programs, a list of all the current programs would not be of any real use to you. The important thing for you to remember is that there is likely to be a VA or FHA financing program that would be available to you as a buyer or developer. This does not mean that the program will be the best in the marketplace, as there are drawbacks to these programs.

It would be important for you, as a buyer, seller or developer, to become aware of what the VA and the FHA has to offer you. As with any loan source, getting to know your way around the VA and FHA loan programs can come in handy when you might need that kind of loan.

Mortgage bankers and mortgage brokers that deal with both the VA and FHA loan programs will generally be the best place for you to go for information and ultimately, the loan itself. You will become very frustrated trying to find anyone at the VA or FHA office. It is becoming increasingly difficult just to get past the voice mail system.

Naturally, it is not necessary for you to deal with a mortgage broker. You can handle the applications yourself. However, unless you plan to devote a major part of your time to keeping up-to-date with FHA and VA regulations, do not attempt to handle your own applications or the applications of your clients.

HOW TO USE THE FHA PROGRAMS TO CLOSE MORE DEALS

The FHA covers far more ground than the VA. Therefore, it will offer more opportunities for selling real estate.

The Federal Housing Administration was created by the National Housing Act, which was approved on June 27, 1934. The purpose of the FHA was to encourage improvement in housing standards and to offer lenders incentives to have a broader lending policy, thereby stabilizing the mortgage market. All these things were needed in 1934; in retrospect, the FHA programs first offered to the public had considerable impact on lending policies.

In 1965, the office of the Federal Housing Administration was transferred to the Department of Housing and Urban Development. As a result, the FHA is now an organizational unit within the Department of Housing and Urban Development (HUD). Like the VA loan program, the FHA does not give loans, but insurance on loans. The FHA provides insurance for private lenders against loss on mortgages that they give to finance homes, multifamily projects, land development projects, and other programs that will be discussed in this chapter.

Here is a list of some of the current, existing programs that indicate the involvement of the FHA in mortgage assistance.

Homes and Units Up to 4-Plex

Title II

Section 203 (b)	One to 4-family housing units
Section 203 (h)	Disaster housing
Section 203 (I)	Low-cost homes in outlying areas
Section 203 (k)	Home improvement loans
Section 203 (m)	Seasonal, leisure, or vacation homes
Section 213	Sales of individual housing cooperative units
Section 220	Urban renewal housing
Section 220 (h)	Home improvement loans in urban renewal areas
Section 221 (d) (2)	Low-cost homes for families displaced by urban renewal, and so on
Section 221 (h)	Low-income rehabilitation housing
Section 222	Servicemen's and women's homes
Section 233	Experimental homes
Section 234 (c)	Sales of individual condominium housing units
Section 235	Home ownership for lower-income families
Section 237	Marginal credit risk
Section 245 (a) (b)	Graduated payment mortgages

FHA Program Chart

Figure 7-1 on page 146 illustrates the more useful FHA programs, showing the VA or GI loan as a comparison. You will find this chart helpful as a quick reference to the program number and the general aspects of that program.

Keep in mind that this chapter is not designed to make you an expert in FHA or VA financing. Books containing far more pages than this one could not accomplish that. The more you work with the VA and the FHA, the greater your understanding will be of the workings of these government programs. There can be no doubt that both VA and FHA are more complex than conventional financing. And generally, the time periods required to obtain the commitments and funding can be greater than those required in obtaining conventional financing.

In viewing the chart, take the minimums and maximums shown as the amounts or periods that can be obtained under ideal conditions. In some cases, those maximum amounts can be altered upward, but such circumstances would be highly unusual and cannot be counted on. A lot of the actual funding has to do with the favor in which the particular program finds itself at any given point of time. For example, if the FHA has decided to cut back on the Title XI program for medical facilities, you can have the finest presentation and the worthiest cause and not get anywhere. On the other hand, if Section 207 is pushing mobile home parks and money is flowing into this area, it might be to your advantage to know this and to look for clients who may want to build mobile home parks.

The Advantages and Disadvantages of Dealing with VA and FHA Financing

In the first place, it is necessary to find out the advantages and disadvantages of the three parties involved: the buyer, the seller, and the broker.

The pros and cons of VA-FHA for the buyer. Since financing has a long-range effect on the property, the buyer will generally see the majority of the advantages and disadvantages. Nonetheless, it is necessary to compare the VA or the FHA loan with alternatives. In many cases, there are no alternatives, and hence no real comparisons to make. The VA, for example, is the only way to buy with no down payment, since no conventional financing is available to match that capability. On the other hand, if you have a buyer who has between 5 and 10% that she can put down, and she insists on going ahead with a VA loan, then you should show her the effect of going with a conventional loan, having coinsurance which will allow 10% down. Since the seller is to pay the discount under VA and FHA, the savings that can accrue to the buyer may make it feasible and desirable to buy conventionally, even though she must put cash down.

The long-term pay-out provided for in most VA and FHA loans can be most advantageous. Once the loan is placed with an interest rate (due to the discount policy) below the market rate, the loan becomes valuable in its own right.

FIGURE 7-1 USEFUL FHA & VA PROGRAMS

SECTION 203 (B)

a. Type of property: 1 to 4 family homes, either existing, under construction or proposed.

b. Maximum loan amounts: 1-family, $155,550; 2-family $198,550; 3-family $240,000; 4-family, $298,350.

c. Down payment required: Construction approved by FHA—3% of first $25,000 with 5% over $25,000. Existing construction not approved by FHA—10% of total cost.

d. Maximum term of years: 30 years.

e. General information: Owner occupied only.

Section 203 (h)

a. Type of property: Disaster housing.

b. Maximum loan amounts: 1-family, $155,550; 2-family $198,550; 3-family $240,000; 4-family, $298,350.

c. Down payment required: None required.

d. Maximum term of years: 30 years of 3/4 of the remaining life (as established by FHA).

e. General Information: Mortgages given to finance the purchase of homes destroyed or damaged by major disasters.

Section 203 (v) with veteran buyer

a. Type of property: 1-family homes existing or under construction or proposed.

b. Maximum loan amounts: $155,250.

c. Down payment required: No down payment on first $25,000, and 5% above $25,000.

d. Maximum term of years: 30 years.

e. General information: S & Ls can loan $5,000 without secured high first mortgage. Veteran must have had 90 days of continuous service on active duty at any branch at any time. Eligibility never expires. There is a minimum investment of $200 on the first $25,000 and this can be applied toward costs. National Guard and Reserves are eligible.

Section 207

a. Type of property: Mobile homes and mobile parks.

b. Maximum loan amounts: Mobile homes up to 100% of value, and mobile home parks up to $2,500 per pad, and $1,000,000 per park.

c. Down payment required: No down payment required by FHA. Some lenders may require equity.

d. Maximum term of years: 40 years.

e. General information: Limitations will be placed by the lenders depending on the area. Loan amounts may be increased.

Section 207

a. Type of property: Rental housing of eight or more family units or new or rehabilitated units.

b.   Maximum loan amounts: 90% of face value with a maximum amount to be established by each project.

c.   Down payment required: 10%.

d.   Maximum term of years: 40 years

e.   General information: No discrimination permitted against families with children.

SECTION 213

a.   Type of property: Coops of 5 units or more.

b.   Maximum loan amounts: Varies, follows a very complicated formula.

c.   Down payment required: Varies as to maximum loan requirements.

d.   Maximum term of years: 40 years.

e.   General information: Mortgagor must be a nonprofit organization. Individual units to be owned by a closely defined group, usually a part of the nonprofit organization.

SECTION 220

a.   Type of property: Improvement loans for one to four unit properties.

b.   Maximum loan amounts: Usually follows 203(b).

c.   Down payment required: Usually follows 203(b).

d.   Maximum term of years: 40 years.

e.   General information: Mortgagor can seek funds through FNMA under this program when local lenders are not available.

SECTION 221 (D) (2)

a.   Type of property: 1 to 4 family existing or proposed, rehabilitated properties that are for low- and moderate-income families.

b.   Maximum loan amounts: 1-family, $36,000; 2-family $45,000; 3-family $57,600; 4-family, $68,400.

c.   Down payment required: Minimum of 3% of total acquisition cost (unless 221 Certificate holders which would be a minimum investment of $200).

d.   Maximum term of years: 40 years.

e.   General information: Single people not eligible unless mortgagor is 62 or older. Some FHA offices have income limits others do not.

SECTION 222

a. Type of property: 1 family; existing or proposed; home or condo, provided that the condo is insured under FHA Section 234 (c).

b. Maximum loan amounts: 1-family, $155,550.

c. Down payment required: For Construction approved by FHA 3% of first $25,000 and 5% over $25,000.

d. Maximum term of years: 30 years.

e. General information: For members of the armed forces on active duty.

The value of low interest and long terms is seen when the property is placed back on the market in a few years. If you buy a property worth $50,000 and have a $50,000 mortgage, and in three years hope to get $60,000, you can offer the property for sale with excellent financing already on it. Your VA-FHA loan will still have nearly $48,500 in principal, and will have up to twenty-seven years to go at an interest rate which should be well below the market rate. In essence, you have over 80% financing available which can be assumed at no cost to close the loan. This type of financing on a home may well mean a better opportunity to sell at a higher price.

The ups and downs for the seller. The seller takes the big bite when he or she pays the discount on the VA-FHA loan. A minor disadvantage comes in taking the property off the market while the appraisal is made and the buyer is undergoing the qualification process. Time thus becomes the major nonmonetary stumbling block for the seller. Nonetheless, the sale via VA or FHA may still be the best way to go, or the only way to go. The arguments made by the seller over discount are usually unwarranted, since he or she would have dropped the price anyway. But this usually means that sellers increase the price to cover the cost. Of course, the appraisal should include this price, and history has indicated that it generally does.

The biggest problem for the seller in this whole transaction is the waiting period, or worse, having taken the property off the market while the buyer is going through the approval period. In addition, the seller will not know the exact amount of the discount at the times he or she places the property on the market, nor know the totality of repairs that the VA or FHA appraisal will indicate must be made.

The advantage to the seller is the obvious expansion of the marketplace for this property. There are many buyers who would not qualify for any other form of loan except the VA or FHA loan, and if that is the only way to sell that property then there are no drawbacks, only benefits.

The broker's problems come in two packages. First, the problem for both the buyer and seller is that unless they are dealing with a broker who is qualified and knowledgeable with the ins and outs of the government insurance programs then a lot of time can be lost. Second, as this kind of loan program is complicated, many brokers shy away from getting involved. Rather than bring in someone who does know, brokers often will try to divert the clients to a more conventional program or will give bad advice.

WHERE TO OBTAIN FHA INFORMATION

The following shows the addresses for the regional offices of the Department of Housing and Urban Development (HUD). Drop one of their offices a card, ask for their current literature and to be put on their mailing lists.

Note: Begin each address with Department of Housing and Urban Development

ALABAMA STATE OFFICE
Beacon Ridge Tower
600 Beacon Parkway West, Suite 300
Birmingham, AL 35209-3144
Phone(205) 290-7607
Fax(205) 290-7502

ALASKA STATE OFFICE
University Plaza Building
949 East 36 Avenue, Suite 401
Anchorage, AK 99508-4399
Phone(907) 271-4610
Fax(907) 271-3667

ARIZONA STATE OFFICE
Two Arizona Center
400 North Fifth Street, Suite 1600
Phoenix, AZ 85004-2361
Phone(602) 379-6704
Fax(602) 379-3985

ARKANSAS STATE OFFICE
TCBY Tower
425 West Capitol Avenue, Suite 900
Little Rock, AR 72201-3488
Phone(501) 324-5283
Fax(501) 324-5900

CALIFORNIA STATE OFFICE
Phillip Burton Federal Building
450 Golden Gate Avenue
P.O. Box 36003
San Francisco, CA 94102-3448
Phone(415) 556-3880
Fax(415) 556-8500

COLORADO STATE OFFICE
First Interstate Tower North
633 17 Street
Denver, CO 80202-3607
Phone (303) 672-5313
Fax(303) 672-5071

CONNECTICUT STATE OFFICE
3300 Main Street, First Floor
Hartford, CT 06106-1860
Phone (203) 240-4553
Fax (203) 240-4549

FLORIDA STATE OFFICE
Gables One Tower
1320 South Dixie Highway
Coral Gables, FL 33146-2911
Phone(305) 662-4530
Fax(305) 662-4584

GEORGIA STATE OFFICE
Richard B. Russeel Federal Building
75 Spring Street, SW
Atlanta, GA 30303-3388
Phone(404) 331-4127
Fax(404) 730-2364

HAWAII STATE OFFICE
Seven Waterfront Plaza
500 Ala Moana Boulevard, Suite 500
Honolulu, HI 96813-4918
Phone(808) 522-8190
Fax(808) 522-8194

IDAHO STATE OFFICE
Plaza IV
800 Park Boulevard, Suite 220
Boise, ID 83712-7743
Phone(208) 334-1886
Fax(208) 334-9648

ILLINOIS STATE OFFICE
Ralph H. Metcalfe Federal Building
77 West Jackson Boulevard
Chicago, IL 60604-3507
Phone(312) 886-9762
Fax(312) 886-9763

INDIANA STATE OFFICE
151 North Delaware Street
Indianapolis, IN 46204-2526
Phone(317) 226-7654
Fax(317) 226-6317

IOWA STATE OFFICE
Federal Building
210 Walnut Street, Room 239
Des Moines, IA 50309-2155
Phone(515) 284-4840
Fax(515) 284-4743

KANSAS/MISSOURI STATE OFFICE
Gateway Tower II
400 State Avenue
Kansas City, KS 66101-2406
Phone (913) 551-6864
Fax(913) 551-5468

KENTUCKY STATE OFFICE
601 West Broadway
P.O. Box 1044
Louisville, KY 40201-1044
Phone(502) 582-6255
Fax(502) 582-6549

LOUISIANA STATE OFFICE
Ninth Floor
Hale Boggs Federal Building
501 Magazine Street
New Orleans, LA 70130-3099
Phone(504) 589-7266
Fax(504) 589-3223

MARYLAND STATE OFFICE
City Crescent Building
10 South Howard Street, Fifth Floor
Baltimore, MD 21201-2505
Phone(410) 962-2520
Fax(410) 962-4947

MASSACHUSETTS STATE OFFICE
Thomas P. O'Neill, Jr.
Federal Building
10 Causeway Street, Room 375
Boston, MA 02222-1092
Phone(617) 565-5400
Fax(617) 565-6557

MICHIGAN STATE OFFICE
Patrick V. McNamara Federal Building
477 Michigan Avenue
Detroit, MI 48226-2592
Phone(313) 226-3897
Fax(313) 226-6740

MINNESOTA STATE OFFICE
220 Second Street South
Minneapolis, MN 55401-2195
Phone(612) 370-3100
Fax(612) 370-3046

MISSISSIPPI STATE OFFICE
Doctor A. H. McCoy Federal Building
100 West Capitol Street, Room 910
Jackson, MS 39269-1016
Phone(601) 965-4719
Fax(601) 965-4995

MISSOURI STATE OFFICE
See *Kansas*

NEBRASKA STATE OFFICE
Executive Tower Centre
10909 Mill Valley Road
Omaha, NE 68154-3955
Phone(402) 492-3135
Fax(402) 492-3150

NEVADA STATE OFFICE
Suite 700
Atrium Building
333 North Rancho Drive
Las Vegas, NV 89119-6516
Phone(702) 388-6500
Fax(702) 388-6736

NEW HAMPSHIRE STATE OFFICE
Norris Cotton Federal Building
275 Chestnut Street
Manchester, NH 03101-2487
Phone(603) 666-7432
Fax(603) 666-7711

NEW JERSEY STATE OFFICE
Hudson Building
800 Hudson Square, Second Floor
Camden, NJ 08102-1156
Phone (609) 757-5096
Fax(609) 757-5373

NEW MEXICO STATE OFFICE
625 Truman Street, NE
Albuquerque, NM 87110-6443
Phone(505) 262-6269
Fax(505) 262-6604

NEW YORK STATE OFFICE
52 Corporate Circle
Albany, NY 12203-5121
Phone(518) 464-4200
Fax(518) 464-4300

NORTH CAROLINA STATE OFFICE
Koger Building
2306 West Meadowview Road
Greensboro, NC 27407-3707
Phone (910) 547-4080
Fax(910) 547-4015

OHIO STATE OFFICE
200 North High Street
Columbus, OH 43215-2499
Phone(614) 469-5536
Fax(614) 469-2432

OKLAHOMA STATE OFFICE
500 West Main, Suite 400
Oklahoma City, OK 73102
Phone(405) 553-7401
Fax(405) 553-7405

OREGON STATE OFFICE
520 Southwest Sixth Avenue
Portland, OR 97204-1596
Phone(503) 326-2671
Fax(503) 326-7509

PENNSYLVANIA STATE OFFICE
The Wanamaker Building
100 Penn Square East
Philadelphia, PA 19107-3390
Phone(215) 656-0508
Fax(215) 644-2667

PUERTO RICO AND CARIBBEAN
New San Juan Office Building
159 Carlos E. Chardon Avenue
San Juan, PR 09918-1804
Phone(809) 766-6287
Fax(809) 766-5522

RHODE ISLAND STATE OFFICE
10 Weybosset Street, Sixth Floor
Providence, RI 02903-3234
Phone(401) 528-5351
Fax(401) 528-5312

SOUTH CAROLINA STATE OFFICE
Strom Thurmond Federal Building
1835 Assembly Street
Columbia, SC 29201-2480
Phone(803) 765-5466
Fax(803) 253-3429

TENNESSEE STATE OFFICE
One Memphis Place
200 Jefferson Avenue, Suite 1200
Memphis, TN 38103-2335
Phone(901) 544-3268
Fax(901) 544-3697

TEXAS STATE OFFICE
1600 Throckmorton
P.O. Box 2905
Fort Worth, TX 76113-2905
Phone(817) 885-5591
Fax(817)581-7440

UTAH STATE OFFICE
257 Tower Building
257 East—200 South, Suite 550
Salt Lake City, UT 84111-2048
Phone(801) 524-5241
Fax(801) 588-6701

VIRGINIA STATE OFFICE
The 3600 Centre
3600 West Broad Street
P.O. Box 90331
Richmond, VA 23230-0331
Phone(804) 278-4530
Fax(804) 278-4615

WASHINGTON STATE OFFICE
Seattle Federal Office Building
909 First Avenue, Suite 200
Seattle, WA 98104-1000
Phone(206) 220-5235—ext 3272
Fax(206) 220-5247

WASHINGTON D.C.
820 First Street, NE
Washington, DC 20002-4205
Phone(202) 275-7471
Fax(202) 275-0779

WEST VIRGINIA STATE OFFICE
Kanawha Valley Building
405 Capitol Street, Suite 708
Charleston, WV 25301-1795
Phone(304) 347-7064
Fax (304) 347-7050

WISCONSIN STATE OFFICE
Henry S. Reuss Federal Plaza
310 West Wisconsin Avenue, Suite 1380
Milwaukee, WI 53203-2289
Phone(414) 297-3156
Fax(414) 297-3947

Special notice: If you plan to use one of the government-insured programs indicated in this chapter, I recommend that you find a local mortgage broker or mortgage banker to assist you. Make sure that you are dealing with a person who is absolutely up to date in this area of finance because these programs undergo constant change. One such person is Maxine Nealon, who is the Senior Underwriter for CFI Mortgage Corporation which is based in West Palm Beach, Florida. This firm is owned and operated by the Castoro family, and consists of 11 branches throughout the state of Florida. Maxine Nealon has, for the past ten years specialized in government loan programs. I owe her a special note of gratitude for her help in reviewing this chapter and providing me with current updates and changes in the programs. She can be reached through her 800 phone number: 1-800-898-4889.

Chapter 8

HOW TO GET LAND DEVELOPMENT AND CONSTRUCTION LOANS

The essence of real estate depends on the development of land and new construction. When this sector of the real estate market is not doing well in the marketplace, the entire real estate market is in trouble.

The following two loans are the foundation of real estate development. They are: the *land development loan* and the *construction loan*. Each of these loans is similar to the other in many respects, yet in some critical aspects each differs greatly. Each of these loans is generally tied to a third loan: the *permanent loan*.

The purpose of this chapter is to examine each of the three loan formats. The goal of this chapter is to illustrate how each loan is obtained and what you can do to maximize your ultimate end result to best fit your needs and goals.

THE LAND DEVELOPMENT LOAN

The land development loan is obtained by a property owner or developer for the specific purpose of development of that property. The name *land* in the term is the key that this kind of loan is unique to the development of vacant land, or redevelopment of existing properties that are first removed to create vacant land. In the process of development, this loan will be similar to the construction loan once development of the basic infrastructure has been completed and actual buildings begin to rise.

Land development has been one of the greatest areas for an investor to build wealth. However, taking a vacant tract of land and turning it into home sites, or industrial sites or whatever, is not as easy as it might appear. There are many different steps that frequently come up between the idea and the last sale of the last site. To illustrate this process, review the following example.

155

Follow a Land Development Project from Start to Finish

Oscar owned 224 acres of prime timber land about forty-five miles west of Boston, Massachusetts. The timber had not been fully cut in over thirty years, and except for one time about ten years ago when Oscar had all the soft wood culled out for pulp, no trees had been taken.

Due to the property's proximity to Boston and the nature of the surrounding area, Oscar decided he would develop the land into two-acre single family homesteads. He would then sell the sites to Bostonians who would like to have a retreat a short drive from the city. He was sure this was going to be a quick deal. After all, for years local real estate brokers had been trying to get him to do exactly this.

To help finance the cost of development, Oscar planned to sell most of the hardwood on the land. By being selective with the cutting he would, however, maintain a heavy growth on the property. With this in mind, he contacted several hardwood buyers who dealt with the furniture industry. They were all interested until they found out that Oscar wanted to be very selective in the cutting. This would increase the cost to remove the trees, and would require a longer cutting period for the amount of board feet that would be removed. This added expense to the hardwood buyer meant a lower price for Oscar. Yet the deal still looked good on paper, so Oscar moved forward.

Oscar got a good price for the hardwood, even though it was much less than he had hoped. Economic reality was beginning to set in, as Oscar realized that for this project he would need additional funds to develop the land to a stage where sales could start.

Oscar discovered that development of his land was going to be much more expensive than he originally anticipated. Higher development cost meant a greater need for funds. This translated into higher interest cost, and the bottom line would be the sales price for the home sites needed to be higher. Would the sites be too highly priced to sell? Doubt added another problem. To make sure the sites sold, a bit more infrastructure would be added. "Give them a good deal," the brokers said, "and you will succeed every time." This meant a higher price, or lower profit. Oscar found that the days of taking a tree farm, cutting some dirt roads through it, to sell off honesties was a day of the past.

PUTTING TOGETHER A PRESENTATION TO THE LENDER

Oscar reviewed what he needed in the way of funds.

1. Roadway costs $ 275,000
2. Powerline costs   48,000

3. Sales brochures		8,000
4. Interest on loan needed during selling time		62,000
5. Miscellaneous costs		65,000
6. Sales commissions and other sales costs		<u>150,000</u>
7. Total development cost not including the land		$ 608,000
8. Less the net from the timber sales		<u>75,000</u>
9. Cash needed		$ 533,000

At this point, the cost of the land has not been calculated into this transaction. Oscar has owned the land for over seventeen years, and his actual cost was only $50 per acre. A more realistic value of the land today would be $3,500 per acre. This matches the current sales of similar raw land in the area. To provide values in the project that relate to the profit from the development, and not profit from appreciation of the land, Oscar has set up a development corporation that will handle all development, sales, and the like. In essence, he has "sold" his land to that new company at $3,500 per acre, or a total evaluation of $784,000. This value would show Oscar an appreciated gain in the land of $772,800.

The sale to the new corporation could be accomplished by many different means. Each strategy could have a different result and/or benefit to Oscar and his family. In this situation, a good lawyer and CPA suggested Oscar establish a "tax free" exchange using the Internal Revenue Code 1031. This would allow Oscar to transfer his profit into another investment without having to pay any gains tax. By setting up this kind of situation, Oscar would get the most out of the federal and state tax laws. Chapter 12 will cover the *tax-free* and *tax-deferred* exchanges the IRS allows. Each of these strategies is legal when used properly.

Oscar reviewed his potential sales. From the 224 acres he expected to obtain 112 tracts at an average of 2 acres in size including the roadway access, which would be kept private and not become a public dedicated way. Oscar had decided to keep the roadways private for two reasons. First, he didn't want the public having access to the area; second, by keeping the roadways private, he didn't have to build a roadway to the local road department's specifications, which would have more than doubled the cost of the road.

Oscar looked at the market to determine what other similar product was available to investors in an attempt to price his tracts. He discovered that there was nothing around that would compare with his end product, especially when he took into account the beauty of the hardwood trees, which was very unique to his site. Nonetheless, there was other property available that people from Boston and surrounding towns could buy, so Oscar was determined that the maximum price he could ask would be $17,000 per two-acre tract.

The Economics of Oscar's Development

Gross sales: $17,000 per tract × 112 tracts:		$1,904,000
Less direct cost of sales		
Sales brochures	$8,000	
Miscellaneous costs	65,000	
Sales commissions and other sales costs	150,000	
Total direct sales cost		223,000
Net revenue from sales		$1,681,000
Less cost allocated to development of land	$368,000	
Less cost to Acquire the land	784,000	
Total acquisition and development		1,152,000
Anticipated profit		$ 529,000

How Much Does Oscar Need To Borrow?

First of all, he owns the land. This means there is no actual cash needed to pay off the land unless he wants to pull some cash out of the financing. We'll leave that alone for the moment. Of the marketing and sales cost, much of this is sales commissions, so a lot of that is built into the sales aspect of the transaction. As sales occur, commissions are paid. Interest, and the actual development cost, which would include up-front sales cost are all a part of the actual funds needed. Review the following:

1. Roadway costs	$ 275,000
2. Powerline costs	48,000
3. Sales brochures	8,000
4. Interest on loan needed during selling time	62,000
5. Miscellaneous costs	65,000
6. Sales commissions and other sales costs	150,000
7. Total development cost not including the land	$ 608,000
8. Less the net from the timber sales	75,000
9. Cash needed	$ 533,000
10. Gross sales anticipated	$1,904,000
11. Loan-to-value ratio (Line 9 divided by line 10)	27%

As the gross sales is $1,904,000 we might consider this the value of the project. That is, we might, but a lender will discount that by the actual cost of sales. The net revenue from sales is $1,681,000 and the loan-to-value ratio based on this sum is still very conservative at 31% loan to value. Provided you do not have to fund the actual land investment, the loan-to-value ratio is very lender friendly.

Loan needed	$ 533,000
Value	$1,904,000 to $1,681,000
Loan-to-value ratio = 27% to 31%	

If you consider the purchase of the land into the deal, then the loan needed would be increased by $784,000, which is the land value. This means that the loan needed would be $1,317,000.

Total direct sales cost	$ 368,000
All acquisition and development cost	1,152,000
Less revenue from sale of hardwood	75,000
Total funds needed	$1,445,000

To borrow the full amount (100% financing) would establish a loan-to-value ratio of:

Loan needed	$1,445,000
Value	$1,904,000 to $1,681,000
Loan-to-value ratio = 75% to 85%	

Remember, divide value (line 2) by loan needed (line 1)

The best result for Oscar, could be to take the majority of the land purchase out of sales, rather than out of the loan proceeds. This would allow Oscar to get some up-front cash from the initial sale of the land, as he profited from the future sales of the honesties. The actual percentage of up-front money that can be borrowed in the land development loan will depend on the lender, the interest rate, and the pay-back terms. The more that Oscar is willing to wait for a return of the capital investment of the land (either as developer or as seller of the land), the less risk the lender has, therefore the easier the terms of the loan.

As this example is a relatively simple land development loan, that does not require later construction loans, or permanent loans, there would be no need for Oscar to do anything else. However, if Oscar wanted to provide potential buyers end loan or permanent loans he could continue the example further. The same land development lender, or a local bank or savings and loan association would be a good source for these loans.

Oscar would contact these lenders, explain what he was about to do, and ask if they would preapprove the project. By doing this, a prospective buyer interested in obtaining such financing would apply to a single lender for that financing.

If Oscar wanted to build homes on these home sites, then he could take care of the middle step. This would be the construction financing which would allow individual homes to be developed. The construction phase of the project could be based on one home at a time, or several homes all at once. When homes were sold the buyer would take out the permanent loan (already set up, or through their own lending source), and the construction loan on the home sold would be paid off. The amount

Oscar owed on the total construction loan (assuming there were more than the one home to secure the loan), would be reduced by the *release price* of the home sold. This release price would be an amount stipulated by the lender, to which Oscar had already agreed when the loan was set up.

ULTIMATE SALES FIGURES

Each lender will look at the ultimate sales figures and make its assessment of a prudent loan-to-value ratio. Oscar's logical approach would be to be conservative in his loan amount and in the cost to develop and to sell. This would require him to anticipate a loan larger than he would hope he would need, if he didn't *draw down* or *draw against the loan*, (get the money from the lender as he needed it) to the full extent of the loan requested and approved. This way he would always have something in the bank as a pillow to fall back on, if plans and timing didn't work out right.

A review of Oscar's situation and how it was handled may give you some ideas of how you might have handled it differently. There is no doubt that the pattern could have been different, and the end results better suited to your own specific needs and goals. The lessons to be learned from Oscar's example is the need to examine all potential problems, and to look beyond the basic idea to find methods that get you to your desired location quicker, and with fewer problems.

A CONSTRUCTION LOAN

Along comes Bill, who is a general contractor of large office buildings in the Boston area. He wants to buy one of Oscar's lots so he can build a small home away from the big city. He makes his deal with Oscar and puts down $6,000 on the tract he is buying. He gets Oscar to subordinate his remaining interest to a construction loan to finance the cabin. Bill plans to replace the construction loan with a permanent loan from one of the savings and loans in the area as soon as he is finished building the cabin. That, at least, is his plan.

So far so good and there is no problem with Oscar. He gets sufficient money out of the down payment to release the development loan he has to pay off, and doesn't mind holding the balance owned on the land since Bill is paying good interest. Then the plan goes wrong. Bill discovers that he can't get a regular construction loan as long as there is secondary financing in the deal. Because he still owes Oscar $11,000 for the tract, the bank wants to see more equity put up to secure the loan. Even though they have the full value of the home site, they are apt to shy away from the higher leverage of the deal.

Bill comes up with a potential solution and gives Oscar a first mortgage in the amount of $11,000 against another property Bill owns. Now the home site purchased from Oscar is free and clear, and the lender approves the construction loan, and the permanent end loan. As long as Bill can build the home for what he thinks it will cost, he knows that once the job is completed he will be able to obtain a permanent loan for enough to pay Oscar the amount still owed to him.

THE COMBINED LOAN

The majority of all construction loans are combined loans. The combination of a construction and a permanent loan is in reality a circumstance where the lender advances the funds for the construction. When the property has been completed, the loan automatically converts to a long-term loan (either the same lender holds both, or two separate lenders are tied together). The ideal source for this kind of loan is the local savings and loan and other savings or thrift organizations, but as lending habits are quickly changing, these loans can be found from almost any lender.

The straight construction loan and the combined loan differ only in the effort it takes to nail them down. Combined loans are generally smaller than divided loans, where the construction loan is obtained from one source and the permanent loan is obtained from another source. For that reason, combined loans are often much easier to get when the amounts of the loan are modest with jumbo loans, of $500,000 or more it begins to make sense to look for two separate lenders. The extra cost and time to deal with double paperwork usually does not make good economics for the smaller loan amounts.

Fortunately, there are lenders for both, and often the same foundation source of money will fund both. For example, many insurance companies buy commercial paper from banks that support construction loans and at the same time buy long-term paper from savings and loan associations.

In this chapter, you will want to keep these factors in mind as we look at the ways in which you will deal with lenders to maximize your loan proceeds while minimizing your costs and interest.

WHY DEVELOPMENT AND CONSTRUCTION LOANS ARE IMPORTANT

These forms of financing are important because they form the basis for all new development. Very few projects will get off the ground unless the cost of development can be financed. It is necessary, therefore, for you to understand the workings of these types of financing and how to find lenders willing to look at your presentation.

The ability to provide for development loans is also important. If you are a real estate broker you will be able to sell properties when you know funds are available for specific projects. If you know in advance what lenders want to lend on, you will have a jump that may be sufficient to put you ahead of your competition. Naturally, this advantage will come as good news to your clients, both buyers and sellers. As a buyer or seller, this advantage will work to your favor too. Buyers find it much easier to invest in the kind of property that lenders like. To work against this trend, that is, to try to buy property the lenders do not like is clearly an uphill battle. Sellers of property that is in the lenders eye, will have a much easier time, and get top dollar than when lenders will not touch your property. You need to remember the condition of the market and risk. If the lender can get a good interest return without taking much if any risk, then he or she is apt to follow that line of action.

Before we get to the fine points for developing this advanced knowledge, let's examine the end loan or the permanent loan.

The Development or Construction Loan Usually Relies on the Permanent End Loan

The permanent or end loan is the final mortgage that will be placed on the property. This loan may have a term of twenty years or as long as forty years amortization schedule for pay-back. The longer the term of years of amortization the lower the constant payment. Keep in mind that lenders often quote loans on a long-term amortization schedule, but *balloon* the payment on a much shorter time period. Compare the following three loans:

The property is a triple net leased retail building. The price to the investor is $143,000 with the buyer putting $43,000 down. The annual NOI (all income less all operating expenses), is $17,160. In each of the three loan situations assume a loan origination fee of $3,000.

Loan 1: $100,000
Interest rate: 9% interest per annum
Amortized over 25 years
The monthly payments are: $839.17
Total payments to be made over the term: (25 × 12 × 839.17) is $251,751

Loan 2: $100,000
Interest Rate: 9% Interest per annum
Amortized over 10 years
The monthly payments are: $1,266.75
Total payments to be made over the term: (10 × 12 × 1,266.75) is $152,010

Loan 3: $100,000
Interest rate: 9% interest per annum
Amortized over 25 years with a balloon payment at the end of 10 years
The monthly payments for 10 years are: $839.17
Balloon payment at the end of the 10 years: $82,736.99
Total payments to be made over the term including balloon (10 × 12 × $839.17 *plus* $82,736.99) is $183,557.39

Reflect on these three loans for a moment. The first is the old style loan that was commonly made, and can still be found from some lenders. This kind of loan is more attractive to major institutional lenders who want to lock up a portfolio for a long term, and not have to deal with shorter-term loans. Security is the key, and the lender will often want a slightly higher interest rate than for a shorter loan term. Note that in the examples all three loans shown above are at 9%. In a real situation the actual parity between lenders and loans interest may vary. This kind of loan is good for borrowers as they can count on this loan until it self-amortizes. This means that as long as the monthly payments are met, the loan will eventually pay off sometime in the future. When other peoples' money (remember OPM), are paying off your debt, the key is that you do not have to reach into your pocket to meet those obligations. As the loan began as a loan-to-value percentage, and as income and expenses usually maintain a similar increase, your bottom line cash flow will increase in relation to the original investment. This loan has a constant rate of 10.07% of the original loan. As the investment property generates a net operating income of 12% of the purchase price, then the loan with a constant rate of 10.70% will allow very good leverage for the investor.

The net operating income is $17,160 which is 12% of the purchase price of $143,000. Deduct your debt service of $10,070 and you are left with a cash flow of $7,090, as you paid $43,000 down, plus an estimated loan fee and out of pocket of $3,000. Your actual invested capital is $46,000 and the $7,090 cash flow represents 15.413% of it (divide the cash flow of $7,090 by the invested capital of $46,000). Leverage from this financing has increased the NOI return of 12%, to 15.413%. This is good news for real estate investors, and is one benefit of a fixed-rate, long-term amortized loan. For many investors this is the best way to go, unless terms and conditions lead you to another loan.

The second loan is the kind of loan the lender might like to make. Shorter term, in this case ten years, but the lender might offer a term of five or seven years. The loan is self-amortizing and will pay itself off over ten years. If the income is sufficient, and the situation right for the investor, there is nothing wrong with this kind of loan. However, it is a very high constant rate of 15.2% of the loan amount per year. As the NOI is $17,160 there will be sufficient funds to meet the monthly loan payments, but just barely. At the end of the year the cash flow on this loan will be $1,960. Your cash flow return on the cash investment of $46,000 is 3.673%. Not very good and it is the effect of negative leverage. This may not be the wrong loan for you, if this kind of situation fits your overall needs. After all, this loan will pay off in only ten years, and if you wanted to put yourself into good financial shape at the end of ten or twelve years, just in time for retirement, or a kid in college, or whatever, then you can trade off cash flow for equity build up. There are some very good reasons why this loan can work for you.

The third loan is a middle-ground loan and gives the lender the short-term pay-out, and the borrower the leveraged income for the first ten years of the loan. Clearly at the end of the ten years the borrower will either have to pay off the loan, or make some other disposition of the property. The proper use of any of these three loan situations will depend on which fits your needs, and which is available. The disadvantage of a balloon mortgage is that the borrower may get caught with a property that is no longer in the lender's eye. Trends change, and it is possible that ten years from now, when that $82,736.99 balloon must be paid off, that the new loan to finance the payoff will either be very expensive, or not available at all.

Any of these permanent loans are made by commercial banks, savings and loan associations, credit unions, insurance companies, REITS, pension funds, and other sources. These loans are the pay-off for the earlier development and construction loan. While the borrower may have a commitment for the end loan, it is not placed on the property until construction is completed.

The timing works like this. Development and construction loans start with the actual development or building. The borrower takes down or is given advances from the lender as the money is needed. Interest begins to accrue on the amount of the loan being used. If the construction loan follows a development loan, then the development loan agreement must be fully met. In this situation there is apt to be a combination of construction and permanent loan to follow the development loan. While the permanent loan is the last in the sequence it has a major effect on the amount of the development or construction loan.

Development and construction loans are predicated on the amount of the final permanent commitment. If you are going to build 100 apartment units and you obtain a commitment from one or more lenders for a permanent loan, to lend $5,500,000, provided the final product meets the specifications of your submission, you will find the maximum development or construction loan available will not exceed the $5,500,000. In fact, it will generally be below that amount, depending on the size of the project and cost overrun averages for the area.

Because the permanent financing has such a profound effect on the nature and amount of development and construction funding you may obtain, we will look at the proper way to examine new developments.

NINE STEPS TO ACHIEVE MAXIMUM DEVELOPMENT AND CONSTRUCTION FUNDING

1. Feel out the market to see what permanent lenders favor. Once the lender's criteria and favorite categories of loans are understood, you can move forward to build or develop the kinds of investments where financing is available. For this example, if you find major permanent lenders are looking favorably at single-family homes in the $140,000 range, shopping centers located in new growing suburban areas, and mobile home parks that have a density no greater than six

sites per acre, then look for those kinds of projects in which to put your investment capital.

2. Smart developers follow big money. In the example shown in step 1, the favorites for lenders are single-family projects, shopping centers, and mobile home parks. There may be many other areas that will be open to funding, and it is natural for lenders to disagree on their favorite type of project. What is hot in one area of the country may be cool to cold in others. As with almost everything in real estate, you must look to the local aspect of the market and not national trends. "National trends" is a media concept, and not an investing concept. What goes on in your backyard will affect you the most, so pay attention to local trends first. National trends are important only in how the unsavvy investor or lender views the market. This can be a factor you may need to deal with when it comes to very large loans you need to get from lenders who look at the "big picture" first.

   If you have flexibility to move from one endeavor which is out of favor to another in vogue, you will do better in the long run than the investor who will only build warehouses, whether they can be financed or not. Our ideal investor has flexibility, and looks to either mobile home parks or single family projects as a potential.

3. Once you are armed with advance knowledge of the type of project a lender favors, you should look to the geographic areas that lenders prefer. Remember, in looking for the construction loan you are still concerned with finding the permanent lender. By dealing with local mortgage brokers, loan officers, and other loan officers, you will shortly discover that lenders tend to specialize in areas of a community. Because real estate is geographic, so are lenders. For one reason or other, which you will ultimately discover when you talk to the loan officers, certain lenders will favor specific criteria as to location, or even more specifically, certain precise areas of town. You will be surprised to find that many lenders maintain comprehensive statistics on the growth of areas in which they invest their funds.

4. You may not know which of the several types of projects to consider, or you may have narrowed it down to single-family homes. If you have picked one of several favored lender properties then you should start to look for the best location in town where the lenders are apt to lend the most. In a couple of days of talking to loan officers and/or mortgage brokers, you will be able to ascertain type of property and general location where the best loans can be obtained. Now you are ready to start putting your talents and this knowledge together. Real-estate brokers and salespeople, mortgage brokers, real-estate lawyers, and anyone else interested in the real-estate market should pay attention to this stage. Remember the term "Location, Location, Location" as the three most important criteria of real estate. As I have pointed out earlier this is not exactly the picture. The *key* is the importance of the location. This means that *use* of a location is the most important fac-

tor to value, when everything else comes together for *you*. Your goals must be the most important end result of any investment, and if you need financing, then the lender's goals must be considered if you expect to get a loan. If you are beginning to understand that real estate investing is a trade off between goals you are catching on. The concept is very simple. Work with the flow, not against it.

5. Okay, you have a lender-favored property in mind, you know the general locations of town lenders go top dollar. Now find a site that works for what you want to do.

    A site is selected and negotiations begin. The first rule of any real-estate investor (once you have reached this state) is to tie up the property. You will spend many hours leading up to this point in your investment strategy, so once you think you have found a property that works for you, in an area of town lenders like, and of an end use lenders favor, then tie it up. As I have mentioned before and will again, do not waste your time and effort, at this state, unless you can get the seller to agree to basic terms and conditions that should work for you. The should is the condition you need to work on, but if you have been doing everything according to plan, all you need is a reasonable due diligence period to check out the details of the property. With that information behind you a firm decision should be available to you. To move forward without having the seller firmly tied up can be a waste of time, money, and credibility.

    One method to tie up a property is to contract for option to buy. You put up a deposit pending some inspections, with the stipulation that if the inspections are okay (to your satisfactory approval) then you have a period of 90 days to act (buy) or not. Keep in mind that the actual time you might need will depend on local conditions, and lender preferences. If you must ask for changes in local ordinances, or zoning changes, then this will require a longer time period. This book will give you the proper strategies for you to follow.

6. When you have a loan commitment in your hand, you can nail down the development or construction lender. At times, the permanent lender will also make the interim loans leading up to the permanent loan. In this case, a combined package of construction and permanent loan can be arranged. But more often than not, there will be two different lenders on the large projects. Keep in mind, however, that on small projects requiring less than $500,000, the local savings and loan associations can compete favorably with other lenders by making a package development and permanent loan.

7. In most commercial projects where the investor is also a final owner, rather than a builder/seller, this stage would begin with negotiations on the terms of the construction loan. If, for example, you had a commitment for an end loan of $2,000,000, you would take this commitment to several commercial banks in

the area and shop for the best terms on the construction loan. Because the terms of the end loan may call for placement not earlier than 24 months from the present date to no later than 36 months, you would look to the longest take-out construction loan possible, or, in this case 36 months.

Many permanent end loans committed to income property projects have a floor loan amount and a maximum amount. The spread between the two sums is generally based on the break-even rent roll as projected. The lender will calculate the projected break-even rent schedule, then deduct a percentage the lender anticipates is reasonable for the market conditions. Based on the resulting net operating income, a floor or lowest loan amount available will be established. The maximum amount of the loan will be paid if a percentage of net operating income, as determined by the lender and agreed to by you, is met. There is generally a time period to allow you to meet rent roll. Fail at that goal and you will only get the lower amount of permanent loan. Because construction lenders look at all the terms of the permanent loan, any such variance in top or bottom loan amounts will force the construction lender to lend at the lowest of the two amounts. This spread in the two sums often leaves the builder short of loan funds to finish the job. This creates a gap in the transaction.

8. This is where "gap financing" comes in. This is another part of the development and construction loan process. The gap loan is a secondary form of financing that is used to literally fill the gap between the floor amount of the loan and the maximum, or the construction loan amount and the permanent loan. The source of these loans is often a mortgage banker or private party. At times commercial banks will take up the call here but these loans are often very expensive for builders and should be used only when absolutely necessary. The only redeeming factor on a gap loan is that it is usually for a short term. This means that even though the interest rate is high, it will not last for long.

9. With the end loan commitment obtained, the construction loan set, and the development loan tied down, the builder can now proceed with the expectation that he or she will not need any other financing. The project gets started, and as one loan is paid off by another, the progression of financing from development loan to end loan takes place.

There can be no denying the fact that the foregoing nine steps cover an ideal situation. All aspects of this development seemed to go smoothly. They often do, and when you are dealing with professional mortgage people all the way down the line you will usually have a smooth transition.

However, one clog in a long progression and a mess can occur. These clogs can appear with amazing speed and never seem to disappear. They take the form of title problems, legal hassles, attorney's errors, and nitpicking; fights over wording in legal descriptions (the legal direction and identity of each property is different), contracts, mortgage documents, or releases from mortgages; delays caused by documents lost in the mail, pages missing from loan commitment letters, or documents not properly signed or witnessed. There is no doubt that if things don't go right, it can be a mess.

Of course, the fact that all goes smoothly at first doesn't mean it will stay that way from the day construction starts until the day the end loan is placed. In the first place, the terms of the commitment must be met. That means that the building to be constructed must be exactly as the plans and specifications indicated when the commitment was issued. Any changes must be approved by the lender. This is where many loans have gone astray. A lender who wants to withdraw from a loan he or she committed to two years earlier when interest rates were 2 points lower than the current rate, will look very hard to see if there is a way to get out of it.

The construction lender gets very anxious about this type of talk from permanent lenders. The construction lender is in the project for a short time, he hopes, and enjoys the high interest rate he gets on the construction loan. But he is not ready to take over a project that fails to close on the end loan. If the end loan does not close because you did something wrong, you will have made an enemy.

GETTING A DEVELOPMENT OR CONSTRUCTION LOAN WITHOUT AN END LOAN

This was very popular at one time, and as you might suspect, due to its dangers, has lost the favor it once had. This type of financing gained support when the permanent market all but dried up. Builders, sensing that the money market was very tight on a long-term loan but still relatively soft in the construction money market, went out on a limb and started projects without effective end loans.

Not many lenders would make development loans without the end loan commitment first. Then, some of the big builders persuaded their banks to go with them on the idea that by the time construction of a big project was finished one, two, or three years later, the permanent market would be back in the swing of things and that type of money would be available again.

Other builders took advantage of commitment letters from mortgage brokers, bankers, and other sources, who in effect sold these letters to the builders. In essence, the commitment letter would state that an end loan was available. This would satisfy the construction lender and the loan would be made. However, these commitment letters were for throwaway loans. The terms of the end loan under many of these letters were so onerous that to take the loan would have been a financial disaster.

The idea was this: Pay for the letter to satisfy the construction lender that an end loan was available, then wait for better years ahead in the long-term end-loan market. As the best plans of mice and men don't always work out, the commitment letter format was not very effective. The permanent money market remained firm and the commitment letters were called to take out the construction loans. In some cases, the commitment letters were found to be worthless and projects got into trouble one after the other.

The lesson to be learned is simple and sweet. There are few reasons to obtain a construction loan without having an end loan. It is much better to have the end loan before you start.

WHY THE SIZE OF THE PROJECT DOESN'T MATTER

The size of the development or construction project is not the main criterion for understanding and using this form of financing. It is natural, of course, that in projects under $100,000 the local savings and loan association may compete favorably with a two-part loan, the construction loan that is replaced by the permanent loan. The combined package loan that most savings and loan associations and other lenders offer puts both aspects of the two separate loans into one document. Still, builders of single-family homes will operate with separate construction loans rather than have this combination package of end loan and construction loan as an automatic event.

USING THE DEVELOPMENT OR CONSTRUCTION LOAN TO MAKE MORE SALES

Putting the whole ball of wax together may be your role. If you are dealing in developable types of land, the redevelopment of urban areas, or in any type of real estate that calls for some form of development or construction, then you must have a working knowledge of this tool.

To be specific, the ability to package a deal will require a considerable amount of expertise in many areas. In some of these areas you need only have the sense to get someone else on your team. Planning and engineering, for example, will no doubt be beyond the scope of most salespeople. To be sure, moving from a listing to a sale can be an immense task for some salespeople on some properties.

Example: How One Broker Made a $4 Million Deal

Jackson had just listed a very interesting property in Fort Lauderdale. The site was about 15 acres of prime, business-zoned land located on a major highway. Its uniqueness was that it was the largest vacant property in the city that had deep water access to the Atlantic Ocean. The site was located in a high-income area of town and adjoined a major shopping center.

The drawbacks in marketing the property were the general economy and the price. The economy was still struggling to make a comeback and the price quoted by the sellers was eight dollars per square foot. The price was not high when compared to other smaller sites in comparable locations. In fact, smaller lots similarly zoned had sold for over $15 per square foot. However, the size of this tract and the fact that it could not be subdivided made prospective buyers scarce.

It was clear to Jackson that what was needed to entice an investor was an economic use. A use that could not be financed was not going to be productive, so Jackson had to find a use that could be financed. Therefore, Jackson tried to determine all the possible uses the site could be put to. He and others made a list of all the possibilities no matter how silly they sounded at the time.

Armed with this list, Jackson approached several lenders and mortgage brokers that he had dealt with in the past and presented the problem to them. He was not asking for money, only assistance in solving a problem. What were the possible uses for the tract which could be financed? Several new possible uses were added to the list by the lenders. Then Jackson put this question to each of them: "Of all the possible uses on this list, which is most financeable assuming that the economics work out?" Many of the suggested uses were eliminated. Some sound ideas were cast off as being overbuilt for the area or impractical for other reasons. The list was narrowed down to five possible uses that could be financed if the economics did work out.

Jackson knew that for the economics to work out, a conservative approach to development, income, and expenses would have to show the project to be profitable. Once he had some possible lendable projects, he went to work to see if the numbers would work.

One by one the projects failed to work out on paper. Then two concepts began to make economic sense. Jackson took his numbers to a mortgage broker. The mortgage broker went over the numbers and made some changes and suggestions, then sat back and agreed. It did look as though there were two types of projects that might work economically.

Jackson didn't stop there. He went to his builder and management friends and smoothed out the figures even further. With the refined projections, he returned to the mortgage brokers. Several brokers got excited about the two concepts. They could see the possibility of making a nice loan fee, so they in turn talked to several of their lenders. Before Jackson knew it lenders were hot to go. He knew that his job was now almost completed.

The result of Jackson's efforts was that the property was sold. He had developed two concepts that in turn attracted lenders and buyers' interest in the property. Interest that was prequalified, and able to recognize that the proposals were sound and feasible. What Jackson sold was not the land but the *concept*.

HOW TO INCREASE THE AMOUNT OF MONEY YOU CAN BORROW ON A DEVELOPMENT LOAN

It is possible to obtain 100% of the funds needed for the development and construction of many projects. In many cases, you can even include the land in this mortgage amount and enter into a development with little or no cash. Your ability to do this will depend on several simple factors. Experience by the way, is not necessarily one of these factors. The following list will outline the factors which must be developed in order to obtain the highest possible loan.

EIGHT FACTORS IN GETTING THE MAXIMUM LOAN

1. **Seek the lender's favorite type of project.** Follow Jackson's example of finding out what the lenders like and then go for that type of loan.

2. **Don't jump in too soon in asking for the funds.** Plan out your project. Some lenders will ask for a feasibility study if you move too quickly. Wait until you have done your own study. If you have done it well enough you may not need a feasibility study.

3. **Have the right numbers.** Don't take one person's advice on what rent you should be able to collect on a proposed office building until you have checked out the actual market as it now stands.

4. **Have the property tied up.** If you don't own it already, be sure you have some tie on it. You have a lot of work ahead of you, and unless you can hold onto the land you may end up with a commitment and then be unable to buy the property or have to pay more than you expected.

5. **When ready, act forcibly.** Bravado is important in asking for money, so have plenty of it (bravado is a nice word for guts). Don't, however, try to cover up lack of knowledge with smugness. Point out good features instead.

6. **Leave inexperience at home, yours or your client's as the case may be.** What is important is the project, the numbers, and ability. Note the word *ability* and not *experience.* The fact that it may be your first shopping center or strip store, or ten times larger than anything you have ever built is not important.

7. **Negotiate for more.** Your lender will usually offer less than you ask for. Hold firm if you can try to get what you feel you need. Remember, if you say you must have $500,000 you may then have to explain why you are willing to take $425,000.

8. **Offer incentives to the lender.** When the need for venture capital is overwhelming, you may have to resort to tradeouts with the lender. In order to increase the loan amount closer to 100%, you may often have to give the lender a percentage of the action. This can occur in many ways, which will be covered later in this chapter. Be careful, however, since the lender knows all the tricks and controls the purse strings.

HOW TO PUT TOGETHER A PRESENTATION
FOR A DEVELOPMENT LOAN

In Chapter 4, the basic loan presentation was outlined. This format should be used in all loan presentations that cover existing properties. Its adaptation so it can also be used for presentations on proposed projects will be covered in this chapter. In essence, greater detail must be included to cover the potential of the project. You cannot rely on past performance, which in the case of a new development does not exist.

The presentation itself will take on the aspects of a feasibility study. It is often thought that all feasibility studies ascertain the best use of a given site. However, this is only one type of feasibility study. More commonly, a lender may request that a study be made to indicate the potential for success a given project may have. The lender's reason for requesting this study is to use the data obtained to help the money managers come to a decision as to whether or not the money requested should be lent.

Unfortunately, the whole system of feasibility studies has gone somewhat astray. There is the classic story of a major lender from the northeast. This lender was presented with a well-planned hotel project that looked fantastic on paper. The developers were experienced, the designers were well qualified, and all the right things had seemingly been done. But the lender needed a third-party reference, so the loan was not going to be granted unless a feasibility study was made. At considerable cost, therefore, such a study was hastily ordered and sent to the lender as soon as it came off the press.

The loan was made. But after several years of development, and one failure after another, the project developers went into bankruptcy. The lender had to take the project into his portfolio and finish the construction. Some time later, a bright young lawyer in the lender's office read the feasibility study. The study had predicted that the project had merit and, based on the then-present statistics of competition, would be successful. However, the study continued, and there were over forty-seven similar ventures currently on the drawing boards, which would no doubt enter competition around the time of the proposed hotel development. The study went on to disclose the statistics, the number of projects and their locations.

The mistake in this situation is obvious. The venture under consideration was a hotel, and the existing hotels in the area would not be able to handle the demand for rooms that the future Disney World complex would provide. So, what else but a hotel would be a good idea? Unfortunately, what's good for the goose is not always good for the geese. The lender was anxious to make the loan, and once the study came in it was most likely glanced over and then filed. In reality, he had paid for a study that recommended that the project not be started in the first place.

HOW TO APPROACH A FEASIBILITY STUDY

In many respects, the feasibility study is similar to the loan request shown in Chapter 4. However, the differences are sufficient for you to follow a new outline. In Figure 8–1, I have provided an outline for you to use when compiling feasibility studies.

FIGURE 8-1 OUTLINE FOR A FEASIBILITY STUDY

I. The Project
   A. General description
   B. Site plan
      (1) Breakdown of project to square footage of improvements
      (2) Use of project
      (3) Stages to be built or developed
   C. Economics of project
      (1) Cost estimates
         a. builders' bid on other supporting data
      (2) Operating expenses
         a. during development
         b. marketing expenses
         c. preleased agreements (if applicable)
      (3) Cash flow, expense vs. income chart
   D. Feasibility of project
      (1) Economy of area
         a. aerial photo showing location of similar projects in competing area
         b. description of competing projects
         c. economics of competing projects
         d. future growth proposed and documented
         e. future demand on type of project (including supporting documents)
         f. summary of economics of competing projects
      (2) Opinion of use based on area economics
   E. Value of completed project
      (1) Estimated potential cash flow on finished project (if the property shows operational statement, 12-month estimate after project completed)
      (2) Market value based on cash flow (capitalized at current investor demand rate)
      (3) Value of existing projects of similar nature (refer to same projects covered in earlier description of competing projects)

II. The Property
   A. General description
   B. Legal description
   C. Locations
   D. Location sketch
   E. Aerial photo
   F. Location benefits
   G. Location drawbacks
   H. General statistics
     (1) Demographics
     (2) Average rent
     (3) Traffic count
   I. General site data
     (1) Legal
     (2) Size and square feet of land and site coverage
     (3) Use of site
     (4) Zoning
     (5) Utilities
     (6) Access
     (7) Sketch of lots sharing building location
     (8) Survey
   J. Land value
     (1) Estimated value of site
     (2) Comparable land sales and values

III. The Developer
   A. Name
   B. Address
   C. Occupation
   D. General data
   E. Net worth
   F. Supporting documents (not included, but will be on forms institution supplies)
     (1) Net worth statement
     (2) Schedule of assets
     (3) Schedule of liabilities

(4) References

(5) Position of employment

(6) Verification of salary

(7) Estimated annual earnings

(8) Credit report if applicable

(9) Other forms supplied for application

IV. The Loan Request (for End Loans)

    A. Recap value of finished product

    B. Recap development cost

    C. Add land cost to development cost

    D. Show relation to total estimated value and total cost to develop

    E. Amount of loan requested

    F. Terms and conditions requested (for construction or development loan)

       (1) Recap value of finished product

       (2) Recap development cost

       (3) Add land cost to development cost

       (4) Show relation to total estimated value and total cost to develop

       (5) Copy of end loan commitment

       (6) Amount of construction or development loan requested

       (7) Terms and conditions requested

V. Supporting Documents

    A. Full set of working plans (if available)

    B. Topography (if needed)

    C. Preleased documents (if applicable)

WHERE TO GO TO OBTAIN A DEVELOPMENT OR CONSTRUCTION LOAN

Many lenders will provide such funds, and for the most part all normal institutional leaders have involved themselves from time to time in this type of financing. However, some sources are better than others, depending on the size of the loan and the nature of the project.

I have provided a chart on pages 183–184 that illustrates the best lenders for the various situations which may appear. Keep in mind that much of this will have to do with the lending experiences of the lender. If the commercial bank has been burned with construction loans, they may not be ready to jump back into that market. Nonetheless, commercial banks tend to be the better source for short-term construction funds.

Never forget the private money sources. These funds can be available when all other sources dry up. In essence, they are costly monies to borrow, but can compete favorably in a very tight money market. When you have to borrow, the cost may be immaterial.

Examine the chart and use it only as a reference as to where to start first. The fact that savings and loans are not generally in the construction loan market will not mean that you should not ask them if all other avenues fail.

SEVEN POINTS TO REMEMBER IN NEGOTIATIONS WITH THE LENDER OR THE LENDER'S AGENT

1. DISTANCE REQUIRES MORE SUPPORT.   The farther you get from the lender in the chain of command, the more the decision to lend is based on the opinions of other people. This is human nature. The loan officer at a local savings and loan will act without having to check with as many people as the mortgage representative at a major insurance company a thousand miles away. Because of this, try to obtain as many outside opinions yourself. Then document them in your presentation. These outside statements of market conditions, rental proforma, expenses, and operating costs can be found without much effort. Fellow brokers, banks, property managers, owners of similar properties, and so on will often be glad to help. When you do get information from them, don't just refer to the facts, put a copy of the memo they sent you or the letter from the property manager in your report. This padding will become third-party support material that people who make the final decision can hang their hats on.

2. YOU CAN'T REALLY LOSE.   Do as much of the initial work as you can yourself. The first time you make one of these studies you will be amazed at how little you knew about the area, the project, and your perseverance. By the time you have finished the study, you will know more than much of your competition about this type of property and development. That is not a bad side-benefit, no matter what happens to the development. After you have gone through several such studies you will have the formula down pat.

3. CONTINUE TO EXPAND YOUR ABILITIES.   At first, there will be some aspects that you may need assistance with. If you are dealing with a mortgage broker, he or she can usually provide help. Brokers are often able to go over the numbers with you, and once they see a feasible project they will get excited as hell. If they can make the loan, then everyone will benefit.

4. BE READY TO NEGOTIATE FOR THE MONEY.   When money is tight, lenders will take advantage of the scarcity of funds to make as favorable a deal as they

can. This may mean they will demand a percentage of the action, which can take many forms. The most usual are shown here:

a. *An override.* This form of percentage of the operation is based on the lender receiving a preset percentage of all income that exceeds certain amounts. For example: A $10,000 loan on a shopping center has a provision that the lender will receive 10% of gross income on excess of $2,000,000. Once the loan is satisfied, this provision does not continue.

b. *Land ownership.* The lender takes title to the land and leases it to the developer. The lease may be reasonable, and in essence the lender becomes a partner in the venture. The loan covers the development of the land. Once the loan is paid off, the land lease still goes on. This way the lender continues to benefit even though the loan has been satisfied.

c. *Coventure.* This can take many forms. The percentage of coventure will depend on the lender and the deal. It is not uncommon that a lender will put up all the money and then take 50% of the venture. Usually, only builders of outstanding reputation can get these deals. However, when money is flowing, these builders can make deals without having to give up a percentage to a lender, or at most very little.

5. DON'T TAKE "NO" FOR AN ANSWER.   For the most part, you are dealing with very conservative people. They take lending the money of their employers very seriously. Therefore, you may get a "no," especially if you approach the lender prematurely. So, if you think you have a hot item, hang it on the possibility of getting the money. However, do not be overly pushy.

6. BOUNCE RIGHT BACK FROM A DEFEAT.   Nothing should keep a good guy down for long. When you have made your most fantastic presentation for the greatest project you have ever thought of and on the hottest site in town, and can't get a lender to sound interested, try to find out why. One mortgage broker I have dealt with in the past may smile if he is very excited. The rest of the time he speaks of doom as though it came two hours ago. He tells me this is his way of maintaining his sanity in the business he is in. From your point of view, negativism can sound like lack of interest. If one mortgage broker or lender gets to you in this way, go on to another. Always be ready to accept the fact that your idea is not sound. And if it's not, find one that is.

7. WATCH OUT FOR TOO MUCH PRAISE.   This is the one thing that concerns me. If all I hear is good news about a project I am working on, I start to worry. (I call my mortgage broker friend from item 6 and know he will have something bad to say.) You need to find someone you can count on to cut the project you are working on to ribbons. You won't get ahead riding the crest of disinterested praise.

FINE-TUNE YOUR FINESSE IN THE USE OF CONSTRUCTION AND DEVELOPMENT LOANS

There are many techniques that you can apply to development and construction loans to make them easier to obtain and to keep down their overall costs. The goal of most of these techniques is: Buy the property right. Thus far in this book, I have emphasized the need for proper attention to your own goals and abilities. When you are able to approach the "buying" moment with the end result in mind, you will be far more successful at attaining your desired goal.

However, from a practical viewpoint, things don't always work out that way. Keep your long-range goal in sight, of course, but if you are watching your comfort zone correctly, you will find it too difficult to pass up "bargain" property, even though you may see no benefit from the property that would blend with your goals.

Later, as you are proven right about the "bargain," you may want to develop the property. At this time, the need for development of construction money may arise. If you try to take this potential need into account, no matter how remote it may be, you can be successful at obtaining your needed financing without excess cost.

You need to look at many factors in any transaction where there will be a future need for development or construction loans. Begin with the following eleven factors.

ELEVEN KEY FACTORS TO WATCH FOR IN EXISTING FINANCING

Make a chart of all of the existing financing on the property and make sure you have all the answers to these questions.

1. WHAT IS THE TERM OF THE LOAN? This is important simply because it is the most basic of all elements of the mortgage. Some mortgages seem to have a term of one set of years due to a statement in the mortgage document that looks like this: "And the mortgage will be paid out over a 25-year amortization schedule." At this point, you might think you have a 25-year term . . . but three pages later there is a paragraph that has this phrase or something like it imbedded in the fine print: " . . . and at the call of the lender, to be given at any time at the option of the lender following the seventh year with a ninety-day notice, the loan is to be due and payable in full." This loan could be good for only seven years.

2. WHAT IS THE EXACT DATE OF THE LAST SCHEDULED PAYMENT? This can be a minor issue. However, sometimes mortgages are so devised that this date is never specifically shown. When a property is closed, the people taking care of these details often don't have the necessary equipment on hand (a math table and calculator) to show the amortization properly. Therefore, there can be a difference between a stated amount that should retire a loan within the desired and thought-to-be term between the parties at hand. When a third party enters the picture, there is a sudden remembrance of the incorrect math that set up a mortgage that will take

another five years to pay out. This can be absolute death to any refinancing ideas since the amount to pay off the mortgage at any given moment will also be incorrect.

3. IS THERE A BALLOON ANYWHERE IN THE PAYMENT, AND HOW MUCH IS IT?   Much the same is true with balloon payments as with other terms in the mortgage. The words used might not be the words you are accustomed to. For example, "ending the 50th quarter of the formation of the lien, its full and complete satisfaction to the mortgagee is herein demanded." Interpretation: A balloon payment is due at the end of 150 months. This might make what would look like a subordinate mortgage useless.

4. WHAT IS THE INTEREST CHARGED?   There are many ways to increase interest without the mortgagee realizing what is happening. Penalties, increases due to "adjustments to the All Items Index as published by the United States Government," would be just one way. If any such provisions exist, make sure you know what they are and how they can affect you.

5. DOES THE INTEREST CHANGE AT ANY TIME? IF SO HOW AND WHEN? Most modern mortgages have provisions that will limit the long-term obligation of the lender if you sell to someone else. In the mid-1970s and early 1980s, lenders began to enforce provisions that gave the lender the right to change the interest rate charged when a property was sold or leased on a long-term lease. Many property owners tried to get around these provisions, but most failed in the attempt.

6. CAN YOU PREPAY PRINCIPAL WITHOUT PENALTY? IF NOT, WHAT IS THE PENALTY?   This single element has ruined many potential new loans, which can of course include construction and development loans. One very good rule to follow is: Don't accept a loan that has a penalty for any prepayment, and if you are buying a property that has a mortgage with that kind of provision either get it removed (you don't care if the seller has to "pay" to have it removed) or build the penalty into your offer.

7. IS THERE ANY SUBORDINATION AVAILABLE IN ANY OF THE FINANCING? IF SO, WHAT, WHERE, WHEN, HOW MUCH, AND FOR WHAT?   Subordination is that event where the mortgagee has agreed to a provision that would permit some lien not yet in existence to be placed above the position of the mortgage, or if there were existing liens that were behind the rank of the mortgage, to move ahead. This increases the risk in all loans, and while warranted some of the time and essential for many investors, the provision itself may not provide what you think. When buying a property with the idea of future development and the seller is holding paper, try to get the seller to agree to allow new financing above that mortgage. For example, you could state that new financing and the remaining balance owed to the seller would not exceed a specific percent of loan to appraised value of the property.

8. WILL THE MORTGAGE PERMIT THE SECURITY TO BE CHANGED? This is a sliding mortgage technique that would allow you to move the security for the note to another property. In Oscar's sale to Bill, had Bill made this kind of provision with Oscar he would have been able to shift the mortgage to another property. The advantage to this is it will "free and clear" the specific property on which you plan to place a construction or development loan. This makes the task of getting good terms that much easier.

9. CAN YOU SELL OR REPLACE ANY OF THE ASSETS OF THE PROPERTY FREELY? Sometimes an existing loan will have a chattel as additional security. This has the effect of locking in different assets such as furniture, fixtures, equipment, and so on. Sometimes the chattel is so poorly drafted that it will not allow for replacement of the item. This requires careful attention if you plan to remodel a property completely and throw out all the old equipment and furniture.

10. IS THERE A RELEASE OF PROPERTY FROM THE MORTGAGE? IF SO, WHAT, HOW, WHAT PATTERN, WHAT CONDITIONS, WHAT PAYMENT? In the development of a property or construction on part of a property you have just bought or currently own, you must have the right to separate that property from any other mortgage prior to placing a new first mortgage on the property. If the underlying mortgage does not have provisions that allow releases, you must attempt to have the mortgage modified. Otherwise, you will be faced with having to pay off a mortgage at the very moment you might need available every penny from the construction loan; or worse, because of the added economic drain you may not be able to get the financing at all.

11. IS THE LENDER LOCAL, A PERSON, OR AN INSTITUTION? Where the lender is based has become critical. The more remote the home office is from the branch office, the more difficult it will be to get facts straight. It is unfortunate that in an age of computer data it has become impossible to communicate from Florida to California to get the current pay-off or terms to a specific mortgage and feel you have the right data. When it comes time to ask for any modification of any mortgage, you will find that the private party will be the best to deal with. He may extract some penalty or ask for some benefit given in exchange for what you ask, but that is far better than going to Federated Federal Savings and Loan only to find out that they have sold your mortgage along with several thousand others to an insurance company located in Mexico City. Buying any real estate that you plan to develop or on which you are going to build requires your attention to these eleven factors whenever there is existing financing or the seller will be holding the financing. Remember the following phrase: "Assume that your future goals are unknown—plan for everything." By this, I

mean that you should anticipate the need for as much flexibility as possible. It will not do you any good later on if you have overlooked one of these eleven factors.

Another element to the development and/or construction loan is your credit. This is something about which you can plan and improve. All lenders want you to have good credit and to provide them with good business references. The lender must be able to "check" on your credit and your references and credit checks cannot be performed unless you leave some history of credit. And the idea is to leave good history. References should be cultivated, and they should know that they are your references. To build good credit and excellent references, follow these steps:

TEN STEPS TO IMPROVED CREDIT AND EXCELLENT CREDIT REFERENCES

1. OBTAIN SEVERAL CREDIT CARDS AND USE THEM. Credit cards are not as difficult to obtain as some people think. Start with local shops, oil companies, bank cards, and so on. Work up to one or two cards that you use most of the time, taking advantage of the "credit payment plan" offered for a month or two. Then pay off the balance. Once you have done that with your bank card (or American Express or another similar card), write and ask for an increased line of credit. Find out the maximum credit offered and work up to that. Always pay early, since you want to build a history of responsibility.

2. MEET YOUR COMMERCIAL BANK PRESIDENT. Make sure that he or she knows you. Keep in touch with this person and inquire about what loans are available. Start with a small loan, even if you don't need the money. You can pay it back early, and the small cost will be worth the effort since it will build more good history into your credit check.

3. DO BUSINESS WITH PEOPLE ON A REGULAR BASIS, AND MAKE SURE YOU KNOW THE OWNER OR MANAGER OF THE BUSINESS AND THAT HE OR SHE KNOWS YOU ARE A REGULAR CLIENT. If the business has "charge accounts," get one, ask for the maximum line of credit, and always charge, then pay early.

4. TELL EVERYONE YOU DEAL WITH FROM ITEM 3 ABOVE THAT YOU ARE GOING TO BE TAKING OUT A LOAN SOON AND THAT YOU WOULD LIKE TO USE THEM AS A CREDIT REFERENCE. Ask them to respond to any inquiry as promptly as possible since it may mean the difference between your getting the loan and not getting it.

5. WRITE A SHORT PERSONAL REFERENCE LETTER. It should touch on those aspects that are critical to the potential loan, as well as give your personal background: where you live, who your wife and kids are, what school you went to, and so on. Everything in this personal reference letter should be positive.

6. GIVE THIS LETTER TO THOSE PEOPLE WHO MAY BE CALLED ON TO BE YOUR CREDIT REFERENCES. This letter will also improve your relationship with these people as they will find out things about you they didn't know.

7. BUILD A LIST OF CREDIT REFERENCES. This list should include all your business contacts indicated in item 3 above as well as your CPA, banker president friends, professional associates, and so on. It should not be a Christmas card list, but a solid and impressive list of known business people in your community. If you do not know any such people, go to the library and get a copy of the local social register book. Make a list of people you recognize, and make a point of meeting them. References must be cultivated, for if you neglect them, they will be worthless.

8. ADD THE LIST OF CREDIT REFERENCES TO YOUR REFERENCE LETTER. Update them each time you can add something important to the list. Each new person sees that he or she is in good company on your list.

9. GET A LETTER OF RECOMMENDATION. This is a letter from your selected reference that tells whom it may concern that you are a highly trustworthy and honest person who is respected in your community. Get this letter by sending your "public relations package" to this person and asking for a letter of introduction or recommendation because of an upcoming business deal with important people out of town (the big lender in far-off lands). Your P.R. package is made up of your personal reference letter, your list of references, and a sample letter of introduction. In your letter, mention that you know their time is valuable, so you have enclosed a short sample letter indicating what you need. It is important here that each sample letter you send is different and as personally oriented as possible. The sample letter should give the impression that it has been written specifically by that person. For example. "As State Representative from Florida, I can introduce and recommend Mr. Cummings with the clear conviction that he is one of the leaders of the South Florida community. Having served with him on a number of local committees. . ." It is important to be specific and that each letter be different because it is likely that the letter will be returned to you exactly as you wrote it.

10. GET A NEW LETTER FROM THE SAME PERSON EVERY COUPLE OF YEARS. If there has been a change in your biography or reference list, send it along, and attach to your new sample letter a copy of the last letter. Make the new letter a little more favorable than the last. Obtaining the maximum loan at the most favorable terms is now a matter of good planning and sound business practice. If you are to succeed at both, you should start to fill in any of the missing blanks in your plan. Learn the things you don't know, improve on those you do. And remember, when it comes to loans, a full, complete package wins out in the long run.

Loan Sources

Lender	Land development loan	Construction loan	Package: Development and construction	Package: Development, construction, and permanent
Commercial Banks	Bank policy varies as to local situation. Development loans must generally be backed by high credit or take out from end loan. Rare to find loans which exceed one million dollars except from majors.	The ideal place to look when an end loan is already committed. Loan will be set at a rate depending on the project. Often very competitive.	Are available from some commercial banks. The end loan commitment will be a major factor here.	Long-term lending will vary from bank to bank. Rates and years to pay back may not be as good as other lenders.
Savings and loans			Some possibility here. Depends on bank policy, situation, and type of project, but very rare.	Ideal for single family or condo-type development. S & Ls may bring in other S & Ls to combine funds to make big deals.
Insurance Companies	Some companies have been very active in this area in the past, primarily when the project is land sales rather than continued development. Good source. Funds are not limited, but prefer over $500,000.	Rare, but some companies have made such loans in the past. Better to look elsewhere.	Rare	For big projects this may be a good source. The lender often gets a piece of the action on this type of loan. Rates and closing costs may be lowest from this source.

Loan Sources *continued*

Lender	Land development loan	Construction loan	Package: Development and construction	Package: Development, construction, and permanent
REITS	When REITS have money they will look at almost anything. Some look only to the short-term loan (the development or construction loan). Others like the long-term loan. As of this writing, however, REITS have lost the potency they had in the early 1970s. But that is likely to change and they should make a comeback. Make friends now as they may well become the best source again, for all forms. They prefer the larger loan, and have made some of the biggest.			
Pension Funds	Don't like high-risk deals, so won't be in this field except for closely connected loans.	Same as development loan	Same as development loan	Are becoming effective lenders in this area. Try them for deals over $500,000. Like proven track record.
Mortgage Bankers	Yes. Depending on the banker, funds are often available for good, sound developments that have end loan take out already committed.	Same as development loan	Same as development loan	Can fund many moderate-sized deals. Beyond that they will seek coventure funds. Can be expensive money, but often available when others are dry.
Credit Unions	Credit unions, like the REITS, vary greatly. They have growing masses of funds like the pension funds, but like to lend first within their own circle. Yet, their managers will often allocate percentages to long- and short-term lending. They can be good for developments within their own area: teachers credit unions lending to a textbook publisher and the like.			

Chapter 9

HOW TO USE
BLANKET MORTGAGES

Definition

A *blanket mortgage* is any mortgage that has more than one property as security to the debt.

Example

Janette wanted to borrow $150,000 to purchase a studio for her art class, but the lender she was talking to told her the loan amount was too great for the value of the property. She told the lender that she would add to the security of the mortgage a first position on a vacant lot and a second position on her own home. The lender was satisfied that the loan-to-value ratio was well in his favor and the loan was made.

The blanket mortgage often is mistaken or confused with the wraparound mortgage. They are two very distinct tools that have some similarity, but serve to achieve different goals. As stated above, blanket mortgages are mortgages where the security to the loan is more than one property. This means that there is one lender, and one loan that needs to be repaid, but the borrower has given the lender two or more properties to secure that loan. The wraparound mortgage, which is the major subject in Chapter 10 is a mortgage on one or more properties that wraps around other mortgages. In the wraparound mortgage, the mortgagor generally pays on one mortgage amount, while there are actually several mortgages, often each with different terms and conditions.

The purpose of this chapter is to make you comfortable with some of the many different ways the blanket mortgage is used. I want you to know how to use the blanket mortgage to your advantage as either a buyer or seller.

185

Any basic form of mortgage, including a wraparound, can be used to encompass more than one property. The moment more than one property is security for the mortgage, you have a blanket mortgage. For example, an investor I knew owned three duplexes that were side by side. He wanted to refinance the mortgages on two of them, but found it was to his advantage to refinance all three under one mortgage. The resulting mortgage was a blanket mortgage.

As you read through this chapter, you will see the many advantages of the blanket mortgage. There are drawbacks as well, and these will also be examined.

WHO CAN UTILIZE THIS MORTGAGE?

The criterion for using a blanket mortgage is easy enough. You must have at least two parcels of property. It helps if they are adjoining, but this is not necessary. It is usual to have a blanket mortgage on two or more properties that are either adjoining or in the same area. A home and a lot, an apartment building and a warehouse, or vacant land and a duplex are some of the many combinations of dissimilar properties which can be combined in a blanket mortgage. Some mortgages of a blanket nature can include dozens of properties.

Most investors seeking to obtain maximum leverage will find the blanket mortgage helpful in obtaining the highest yield on their invested capital. Since maximum financing is one of the benefits that is attained from its use, let's look at this as well as the other benefits that can be derived from the blanket mortgage.

WHAT CAN BLANKET MORTGAGES DO?

1. PROVIDE MAXIMUM FINANCING.   Generally, if you can include more than one property as security for a loan, it is possible to borrow in excess of the value of a part of the total security. With this in mind, blanket mortgages can provide 100% financing for new ventures and throw off cash to boot. In the refinancing of several properties, the combined effect of the security can make the package presented to the lender more secure and thereby increase the amount to be lent.

2. ALLOW THE MORTGAGOR TO OBTAIN BETTER TERMS AND CONDITIONS ON THE LOAN.   It follows that if the loan is more secure, then you have room to bargain for better terms. Of the terms to be considered, the interest rate and annual payment will be most important. If you can decrease the percentage of the loan-to-value ratio, thereby decreasing the lender's risk, you will find the terms should ease considerably. For example, Simon, a local investor, wanted to purchase a ten-unit apartment house fairly priced at $145,000. The property had a low first mortgage of $30,000. The seller indicated he would hold up to $20,000 in a second mortgage,

and wanted cash above that. Simon discovered that within the new money market, the best he could come up with, after mortgage cost, was $102,000. This left him short the difference needed to buy the property, even if the seller held the $20,000 paper. The best terms available from a local savings and loan association were 24 years at 9 $^3/_4$ % with four points closing.

However, he did own a small lot that was across the street from the apartment house. It was free and clear and he hoped to build on it one day. Its value was $35,000.

He went to the bank again and offered to put the lot up as additional security on the loan. The lot was appraised at the $35,000 value. Thus, a total value of $180,000 was created. The bank was told a 72% loan-to-value ratio, or a $129,600 mortgage, was all that was needed. This ratio was lower than that which the bank was willing to lend, so they gave in on the terms. A 27-year mortgage at 9 $^1/_2$% was obtained. Points came to only 3% instead of 4%. Simon was able to have provisions put into the mortgage that would enable him to release the lot once the principal was reduced by $26,000. This would enable him to build at a future date without having to pay off the entire amount of the first loan.

Simon ended up with the ten units with no cash down, since the seller held the balance of the paper against the property.

3. CONSOLIDATE PROPERTIES FOR REFINANCING. Some investors have put together a considerable array of properties over the years. Mortgages have different payment schedules and termination dates. Sometimes it is feasible to add several properties to a refinancing package of another property to provide a larger base and reduce the overall loan-to-value ratio. In this type of blanket mortgage, the properties should be similar types of realty when dealing with institutional lenders. However, private lenders may not care.

Another local investor, Aston, had nearly a dozen small warehouses across town. Each of them was fully rented and none had a mortgage greater than 50% of its value. Two of the larger warehouses had mortgages that were at very high interest rates as compared to the present market. Aston decided to refinance them all under one blanket mortgage. He obtained an excellent commitment from one of the local savings and loan associations in the area, and another almost equally good from a local commercial bank.

I had the opportunity to see Aston just before he made his deal with the savings and loan. In looking over the package, I discovered he had two warehouses that had 5 $^1/_2$ % loans. While these loans were low in ratio of loan-to-value, their term was still 14 years to go. (They must have been FHA or VA in origin.) I suggested he keep these loans and let the lender hold second position on those two warehouses. This would lower the overall payment and probably not affect the amount of money lent.

The savings and loan did not go along with that idea, but the commercial bank did. The total loan was far in excess of the payoff of the existing financing, and Aston withdrew from the property nearly $175,000, which was not taxable.[*] His annual payment increased only $5,000 over his previous debt service on the earlier financing.

4. LOCK IN THE PROPERTY.   This can be an advantage as well as a disadvantage. If you were Aston and had ideas of selling some of the warehouses in a few years, you would have to have release provisions as a part of the mortgage terms. Some lenders will go along with this, but others won't. However, if you are selling property, the features of the blanket mortgage can be made to work for you if you are asked to hold paper. You can have the buyer include other properties which will become security to the transaction. This becomes both a buyer and a seller provision, depending on the circumstances and point of view.

5. LOCK IN OTHER ASSETS.   There is no reason why the blanket mortgage should be limited to real estate. As in the above situation, the buyer or seller can offer or require other assets to be pledged as security. A liquor license, for example, may be tied to a bar in this way. Stocks or other collateral can be given as additional security via the blanket aspects of the mortgage.

In both of the above shown examples, the assets can be pledged by the mortgagor or a cosigner. For example: Walters wanted to buy a home that had existing financing of $50,000 and $40,000 in equity. He had no cash to put down, but did have a father-in-law anxious to see his daughter move out of the guest house and into her own home. The father-in-law offered a second mortgage on his own home as additional security to the seller. In the end, the seller took a blanket second on the home being sold, with a second position on the father-in-law's home. The total equity was more than enough and this saved the deal.

WHERE TO GET BLANKET MORTGAGES

Not all lenders will consider a situation that calls for a blanket provision in the mortgage. However, the big lenders, such as insurance companies and REITS, have made such loans. Also, many of the more local lenders, such as commercial banks and mortgage bankers, will frequently lend with blanket provisions. The whole idea of blanket provisions is to make the loan more secure, and virtually all lenders will make blanket loans given the right circumstances.

The best place to look for money when you are willing to offer additional property as supplemental security is to the seller. The increased equity gained by virtue of this form of financing often can sway the seller into holding large amounts of paper.

---

[*] Funds obtained in a mortgage loan that do not exceed the basis (book value) of the property are not considered to be income, and therefore are not taxable as such.

Other private sources, such as investors, private lenders, and mortgage brokers, also like the blanket mortgage and should not be overlooked.

WHEN TO USE A BLANKET MORTGAGE

When you are considering the use of a blanket mortgage, reexamine the five things it can do:

1. Provide maximum financing.
2. Provide a stronger position for negotiating the terms and conditions of the loan.
3. Consolidate properties for refinancing.
4. Lock in the property.
5. Lock in other assets.

Situations that call for blanket financing require the satisfaction of one or more of the above five items. Since items (1) and (2) are rather general, it is important to remember that there are many different forms of financing that can accomplish these two desired goals. But when the best form for the borrower is unacceptable to the lender, then a blanket mortgage may be the answer.

Providing maximum financing may not be worth the cost or the disadvantages that result from both excessive leverage and overextension. Because of this, the use of blanket mortgages must be compared to the other alternatives. Once you have a basis for determining which form is the most advantageous to you, then you can proceed to see if you can work out the transaction on those more favorable terms.

HOW TO DETERMINE THE ACCEPTABILITY OF A BLANKET MORTGAGE

The acceptability of a blanket mortgage can be seen from both sides of the transaction. As in all forms of mortgages the effect may differ from transaction to transaction and from buyer to seller. Unless you can pinpoint what makes the blanket mortgage acceptable, you may not know when to use it.

Blanket Mortgages as Seen from the Buyer's Point of View

The buyer must understand that in order to use this form of financing, it is necessary to encumber more than one piece of property. If the transaction itself contains these separate properties, there may be no reason to hesitate, providing the buyer can obtain releases that may be necessary (such as purchasing four lots from one seller). It is usual for the buyer to add security to the blanket mortgage from property already owned.

The majority of blanket mortgages do occur with this extra outside security as a part of the transaction. The buyer uses equity in other property to assist in new financing. To some degree it is seen in pyramiding and other forms of high leverage and extension buying. Nonetheless, the buyer must understand the disadvantages, as well as the advantages, of this format, and must weigh these in determining whether it is wise to use a blanket mortgage.

DISADVANTAGES OF BLANKET MORTGAGES FOR BUYERS

1. These place a burden on other properties. Whenever a second property is pledged as additional security on a blanket mortgage, that property is in jeopardy if the mortgage falters.

2. These can make a separation difficult or impossible. Of course, this will depend on the terms of the blanket mortgage. But to some degree, the mortgagor is hampered in his or her ability to sell the other properties. A buyer can, however, purchase the property subject to the blanket mortgage, and if the principal of the mortgage is less than the amount of financing held there is no disadvantage.

3. Assets can be locked in. This works as both an advantage and a disadvantage. In this instance, the combined effect of tying two or more assets together can cause unforeseen hardships in the future if the mortgagor needs to separate those assets.

You can see that the main disadvantage is the combining of other properties with the inability to separate them when or if the need arises. With this in mind, you can then look to the blanket mortgage as a useful tool when the criteria which follow can be met.

BUYERS' CRITERIA FOR BLANKET MORTGAGES

1. Other conventional forms of financing do not generate the viable financing required to meet the cash requirements of the buyer.

2. Other properties exist which have sufficient equity that will be accepted by the seller or mortgagee as additional security to arrange the financing required.

3. Total income generated from all properties covered with the blanket mortgage is sufficient to meet the payout requirements of the debt service to be created. A reasonable leeway should provide for a drop of income before the break-even is reached. This will depend on the situation of course. Some transactions may be approached with a deficit, the mortgagor coming out-of-pocket for a time until new income from the property can be generated (as in the case of a new development, construction, or other income-increasing methods).

4. The mortgagor can project that he or she will not need to separate the properties from the mortgage in the relatively near future. Even if he or she has release provisions, they will no doubt be costly, so it may be dangerous to enter into a blanket mortgage if it is anticipated that early separation will be necessary. This will not be the case if the mortgagor is anticipating a complete refinancing of the property, and has confidence he can recast the mortgage and obtain separation in that way. Nonetheless, the risk remains and it may be costly to obtain separation.

In summarizing the blanket mortgage from the buyer's point of view, if the buyer can meet the four criteria and understands the disadvantages of this form, he or she can use the mortgage.

Blanket Mortgages as Seen from the Seller's Point of View

Like the buyer, the seller and other mortgagees should know all the ins and outs of the blanket mortgage. Yet because this format is designed to increase the security, the advantages are more often weighted in the seller's and the mortgagee's favor. However, disadvantages do exist.

DISADVANTAGES OF BLANKET MORTGAGES FOR SELLERS AND OTHER MORTGAGEES

1. The blanket mortgage may cause overextension of the property. This in turn could lead to the mortgagor failing to make payments. The seller can always look to the properties held as security, but to move into a foreclosure can be most unpleasant, costly, and to no one's ultimate benefit—if there is a choice. The mortgagee can take all precautions to see that this does not occur, but when the buyer is into the property with no cash, or at best very little, then the security may be dependent on what occurs with the other property.

Example

Curtis bought a 15-unit apartment house that had a fair market value of $200,000 and a good first mortgage of $140,000. He gave the seller a blanket second in the amount of $60,000 on the 15-units that also covered (by a first mortgage) a lot he owned across town. The value of the lot was estimated to be $30,000. The seller felt secure that he had $90,000 of equity covering his $60,000 second mortgage.

As it turned out, the lot was worth only about $10,000. Curtis milked the apartments for a few years, got behind on his mortgage payments, and then walked away from a foreclosure. The seller had to step in and rescue the 15 units from the first mortgage, and spend several thousand dollars as well to repair them.

2. Blanket mortgages generally reduce the cash at closing. This happens because the blanket aspect is used to supply additional security to a mortgage greater than the seller is willing to hold otherwise. The effect is to reduce the amount of cash he or she will receive. All things being equal, this in itself is not a disadvantage, but merely a characteristic of this form of financing. However, all things are rarely equal, and equity rarely equals cash.

The other advantages in blanket mortgages are of a more technical nature, and have to do with the possible legal terminology used in the document itself. I have found that most lawyers are able to draft a blanket mortgage which will adequately protect their clients. I suggest, however, that you never have the lawyer for the seller draw up the mortgage for both parties (or the other way around for that matter). Most lawyers will not do this, but I have seen some who will do exactly that. Each party should have separate legal representation for this and all mortgages.

Criteria for mortgagees holding blanket mortgages

Sellers Hold	*Third-Party Loans*
1. Must have strong motivation to sell or hold the blanket mortgage. It is possible that the blanket is sold, and more than provides the security. Usually, the overwhelming motive is the need to be relieved of superior debt, or is sick to death of the property.	1. Is the security good, sound, and acceptable?
2. The security checks out. The combined equity which secures the blanket mortgage should be well over the principal amount of the mortgage itself. This will vary, depending on the type of property and the existence of superior mortgages. Do not rely on the value as stated by the buyer or agent. Seek an independent appraisal, or at least ask the advice of other realtors in the area.	2. Are the terms of the loan good, sound, and acceptable?
	3. Is the return on the mortgage good enough, nonusurious, and acceptable?
3. Some cash can be a part of the deal. All buyers should put some cash into a transaction. Of course, the amount will depend on many factors. But it does have a solidifying effect.	4. Is the mortgagor good, sound, and acceptable?

HOW TO USE THE BLANKET MORTGAGE TO HELP SELL YOUR PROPERTY

Blanket mortgages have a function as a sales tool in some types of transactions. If you are selling property from a large inventory within the same owner's portfolio, such as tract lots or other subdivided property, the seller can offer packages of lots or parcels to investors with the blanket mortgage. In this way, the buyers would have two or more pieces of land covered by one mortgage. The seller would agree to release some of the lots as the mortgage is paid down. The release would be the same kind that could be used in any form of financing that may provide for the division of a property. The actual wording of the release could be predetermined by the seller to afford him or her the maximum protection in this type of transaction.

The advantage to the seller in this type of mortgage is mainly the increased sales potential. The risk to the seller over other forms of financing is negligible, if the land in question is substantially worth the price. The buyer can compare the blanket mortgage to other forms of financing to see how it will affect him or her. In the following example, you will find one such comparison.

Example

McMoore was a land developer and had more than 50 lots remaining in his most recent subdivision. He was not a builder, so he preferred to sell the lots rather than get into the housing business. While homes were moving at a fair pace, he could not attract private buyers and home builders were not interested in his normal sales terms. McMoore had been selling his finished lots at about one a week and was asking $12,000 for each one. In the past, McMoore wanted and had gotten $3,480 down and was holding the balance for one year. Some buyers had paid cash, financing the paper with their own sources. McMoore's broker, who had sold him the raw land nearly three years previously, suggested that he make a quick deal for a sellout and move onto the next land development program they had been working on. The broker reasoned that if the proper terms were given, they would be able to get some home builders to buy the remaining lots. They came up with this plan: The lots would be put into groups of five. This meant they had 10 packages to offer to the local builders or investors. The average price per package was $60,000. The down payment, however, was $6,000, instead of the $17,500 which was based on the normal down payment McMoore had received in the sale of the other lots. The mortgage terms offered was interest only for three years at 8% per annum on the balance. This marketing of the package at 10% down was bound to produce the desired results. McMoore knew this and wanted to make sure he was secure in the transaction.

What McMoore did was to require that $12,000 be paid against the purchase price for a lot to be released from the mortgage. The releases were for the purpose of building homes for a later resale. So McMoore took a second mortgage position on the home back into the blanket as additional security. That second would be removed when the next lot was released, and a new second would be placed on the second home. This would continue until the first four lots were released. On the last lot, only the remaining $12,000 plus interest had to be paid. Each builder had three years to build before the balloon came due on the unpaid balance.

HOW THIS TRANSACTION LOOKED TO THE BUILDERS THAT BOUGHT THE PACKAGES

It was a good deal. McMoore had priced the lots fairly and the housing market was strong enough to warrant tying up the initial cash. McMoore had also made the down payment reasonable, so once the builders had invested the $6,000 they could move forward with preparations to build. They would arrange construction financing through local lenders to cover the cost of the home (plus a little overage). The excess of the loan, if any, would help pay off the lot. When they were ready to go, the mortgage to McMoore was reduced by $6,000 and the first lot was released.

The giving up of a second position to McMoore was no hardship to the builders. They knew that as soon as they sold the home they would merely move onto another one anyway. If they sold a new home from the model, they only had to pay down $12,000 cash and build on another lot. There was to be only one second lien at a time. In the meanwhile, the cost to carry the remaining lots was not overburdening them and they liked the idea.

The real key to this formula was simply the security for the seller. The blanket formula of holding all the unreleased lots into the mortgage was part of the security. The idea of adding the second mortgage on each new home as it was built, releasing the previous one, put the icing on the cake for the seller and didn't affect the buyer.

SUMMARY OF BLANKET MORTGAGES

The concepts inherent in blanket mortgages are also found in other forms of equity liens. If you remember that the ability to add other assets in order to bind the mortgage is the concept behind the blanket mortgage, then you can apply this idea to leases as well.

In the lease, the term used to cover this concept is *cross-collateralization*. The main use of the blanket lease is in the sale lease-backs. In this situation the seller of a property becomes the lessee to the buyer. If the seller holds a mortgage as a part of the sale (e.g., sale price: $150,000, seller holds $50,000 in paper and takes $100,000 down), the mortgage may be given as additional security on the lease. This has a very strong effect in securing the lease.

Blanket mortgages can be in any position on the scale of superior or junior liens. The mortgage can actually take different positions on the various properties it covers. Usually, however, the same position on all the properties is attained, but the fact that this is not necessary is most important.

It is always possible to hold individual mortgages instead of a blanket. From the seller's point of view, if the two mortgages are offered at the same term, interest rate, and principal, then the only advantage in the blanket would be the lock-in provision. This would, of course, depend on the situation and what assets or property the seller wanted to lock into the transaction.

Buyers will use this form of financing to cover a down payment. However, even the buyer can take the alternative route and offer secondary paper on the existing property. Usually, the blanket mortgage is used in circumstances when the buyer is looking for the combined effect of one seller-held mortgage that is supported by his or her equity in other property, other than an exchange of equity by virtue of paper offered on something else. It is a matter of negotiation. And it often sounds better to offer a blanket mortgage secured by the purchased property and the buyer's equity in a vacant lot, instead of a mortgage to the seller and a mortgage on the lot. Of course, if several additional properties are used to add security, the blanket mortgage is easier to work with.

Chapter 10

HOW TO USE
THE WRAPAROUND
MORTGAGE EFFECTIVELY

Definition

A *wraparound mortgage* is a new mortgage that has one or more properties as security to the amount of the loan, and the total amount of the loan is a combination of the new loan, and one or more existing loans. This type of loan is most frequently held by a seller, and is sometimes called a *purchase money wraparound mortgage.*

Example

Sam is selling a warehouse he owns for $250,000 to Bruce. Bruce wants to put $75,000 down, and somehow structure the financing so that his annual payments on the balance owed of $175,000 does not exceed $22,000 per year. The current market rate for new financing is around 9.75 to 10.75% per annum. Bruce is willing to accept such financing as long as there is at least ten years of fixed payments before a balloon would be due. There is the following existing financing on the property:

- A first mortgage in the amount of $50,000 that was the original mortgage Sam had when he purchased the property fifteen years earlier. This mortgage will amortize in full in eight more years at $706.83 per month. The interest rate on this mortgage is 8% per annum.

- A second mortgage in the amount of $90,000 that Sam obtained five years ago. This mortgage is at 8.5% per annum and will amortize in ten years with monthly payments of $1,115.85 per month.

196

Sam tells Bruce that he will create a purchase money wraparound mortgage in the amount of $175,000 that will have monthly payments of $1,822.68 ($21,872.16 per year), at an annual interest rate of 9.75% per annum. This mortgage will be in effect for ten years, at the end of which time, there will be a balloon payment of (approximately) $94,065.00

In this example, it will take 100% of the payment that Bruce makes for Sam to meet the obligations of the two existing first mortgages.

First mortgage of $50,000 has a monthly payment of:	$ 706.83
Second mortgage of $90,000 has a monthly payment of:	1,115.85
Total monthly payment	$ 1,822.68

This means that until the first mortgage is paid off, by the end of eight years, Sam will not get any money in his pocket. Then, for two years he will be able to put into his own pocket the portion that was previously going to the first mortgage. This is $706.83 per month x two years (24 months), or a total of $16,963.92. Then at the end of the ten year payment schedule that Bruce is obligated to, there is a balloon payment due of $94,065.00.

Sam ends up with:	
Payments for years 9 and 10 after first mortgage is paid off:	$ 16,963.92
Balloon payment (because second mortgage was fully paid off)	94,065.00
Total payments to Sam by the end of ten years	$111,028.92

Remember that the portion of the $175,000 mortgage that consisted of Sam's equity in the mortgage was only $35,000. ($175,000 less first mortgage of $50,000 and less second mortgage of $90,000 = $35,000).

This means that for a $35,000 investment, Sam would have a return of over $111,028.92. I can say, over that amount because I can assume that as Sam begins to collect the monthly payments in years nine and ten (of $706.83 per month), that he could put that money in a savings account and earn some additional interest.

The actual yield on the $35,000 invested by Sam in this mortgage was leveraged up by the spread between the existing mortgages (which were 8 and 8.5% per annum respectively). The simple approach to find the yield would be to assume that Sam didn't get anything until the end of the tenth year. The compound interest it would take to increase $35,000 to $111,028.92 would be approximately 12.24% per year. As Sam did get some of the return (almost half of the original $35,000), earlier, his real yield would be considerably higher. While Sam will end up with a leveraged return, Bruce has not been penalized. He got a mortgage that was at current interest rates, did not have to pay mortgage points to a lender, and was able to make the deal at a price and terms he was comfortable with.

Because wraparounds are misunderstood by many buyers, sellers, and real estate lawyers, the format of the mortgage is often used incorrectly. There are some very important factors about the wraparound that you should understand to insure that you do not use the wraparound incorrectly or in a situation that will not be beneficial to you. At the same time, you should not be detoured from using the wraparound when one of your advisors tries to steer you away from the technique, just because they do not understand the benefits of this tool. Often, as a buyer, you realize that the wraparound mortgage may enable you to purchase a property. However, the seller does not know or understand how the wraparound can help. In this circumstance you may have to assist that seller in making a proper and educated decision. This chapter will be of assistance.

For all of these reasons, you should become familiar with the wraparound mortgage. It has its easy and its tough elements, but once you understand how and why it works, you will find that it will facilitate many difficult transactions.

I have provided several examples of wraparound mortgages that demonstrate the major elements of the technique. As with all tools in this book, I frequently use a technique in conjunction with other forms of finance without reexplaining elements of a transaction contained in other chapters. I mention this because you will find examples of other wraparound transactions in other chapters where the wraparound was combined with financing strategies which are the subject of that chapter. To find all the different examples of where a wraparound has been used as a part of a financing package, please check the index.

This chapter will stay close to the mechanics of the wraparound. There is no simple way to explain some of its workings other than by example, and there is no simple way to calculate the yield except by following the method contained herein. Some hand-held calculators have programs to calculate wraparound mortgage yields. Unfortunately, not all of these programs are accurate. If you are using one such program, I recommend you check it by comparison to the example later on in this chapter.

As you know by now, there are several different kinds of yields available in wraparound mortgages. The average yield is the usual one that computers give, but that is not the most effective yield. When you get the average yield, you have found nothing useful. Let's take a look at another example of a wraparound mortgage:

Example

Bobby wants to buy Jeff's house for $120,000. There is an existing first mortgage on the house of $50,000, which is payable over 20 years at a fixed interest rate of 8.5% per annum, with monthly payments of $433.92.

Bobby offers Jeff a down payment of $25,000 and a second mortgage of $45,000 at an interest-only payment of 10% for 10 years with a balloon payment at that time, with assumption of the existing mortgage. Under these terms, Bobby would have a combined monthly payment between the two mortgages of $808.92.

Jeff counters by offering to take the $25,000 down payment and hold a $95,000 wraparound mortgage with a 10% interest-only payment for ten years with the principal amount of the mortgage coming due at the end of the ten years. In these terms, the payment Bobby must make is only $791.66. As this amount is less than the payment in his own offer, Bobby accepts Jeff's deal. Both sides have won.

As far as Bobby is concerned, the wraparound that Jeff is holding is really one mortgage in the amount of $95,000. However, from Jeff's point of view, there are three mortgages:

1. An existing mortgage of $50,000 that has a mortgage payment of $433.92 per month for 20 years.

2. The wraparound mortgage in the amount of $95,000, which Bobby pays to Jeff ($791.66).

3. The *seller's equity* in the wraparound mortgage is the difference between the existing and the wraparound mortgages.

The wraparound mortgage of $95,000 less $50,000 gives Jeff a difference of $45,000.

In reality, Bobby is paying as if he held the single $95,000 mortgage that was interest-only for 10 years. Jeff continues to make payments on the existing financing, and puts the leftover money in his pocket. Since he collects $791.66 and pays out $433.92, he has $357.75 left over each month for himself. That amounts to $4,293 per year, which appears to be only 8.59% per annum on the $45,000 difference.

However, since the wraparound mortgage paid by Bobby is interest only, while the existing mortgage is being paid off by Jeff, at the end of each year Bobby still owes Jeff $95,000. In the ten years Jeff will completely pay off the existing first mortgage, but Bobby still owes $95,000.

At the end of the first 12 months the original $50,000 mortgage is now paid down to $49,007, which would put another $993 in Jeff's pocket if the mortgage were paid off at that time. This would increase Jeff's cash in pocket to a total of $5,286 and his yield to 11.75% per annum.

Bobby won because he decreased his debt service, and Jeff won because he increased his overall effective yield on the wrap. Other things occur too, but there will be time to discuss those factors later in this chapter.

THE MOST IMPORTANT FACTOR ABOUT WRAPAROUNDS

If there is a single, most important factor about wraparounds, it would be that a wraparound mortgage is just a tool. Depending on your knowledge of the tool and your goals, it has a lot of uses, it can be the best thing for your situation, or it can do nothing at all to take you closer to your goals.

WHAT THE WRAPAROUND IS NOT

To get a good grasp of what the wraparound is, it might be helpful to see what it is not.

1. IS NOT A CURE-ALL FORM OF FINANCING.   This can be said of any technique in this book. Nothing will do everything, and nothing is so inflexible that some other technique may not work just as well depending on the people, the property, and your needs and goals.

2. IS NEVER IN FIRST POSITION.   The very nature of a wraparound mortgage causes the situation to contain existing financing on the property. It could be possible for a mortgage to be called "The First Wraparound Mortgage." Even though this term might be used wrongly, it could refer to a transaction that had more than one wraparound mortgage in existence on the same property.

An example of that is a property Al wants to buy. The current financing consists of a wraparound in the amount of $100,000 that consists of the wrap of $100,000, a first mortgage of $60,000, and a difference of $40,000. In addition to the wraparound mortgage, the seller placed another mortgage on the property several years ago in the amount of $25,000. This would be a "third" mortgage as the rank of mortgages at this point would be: (1) the existing first mortgage; (2) the wraparound; (3) the $25,000 mortgage. In this transaction, Al wants the seller to hold a fourth mortgage for $35,000. The seller could do exactly that, or he would have the following options that would involve new forms of wraparound mortgages.

The seller could		
1st wraparound:	$100,000	($60,000 first plus 40,000 difference)
3rd management	25,000	
New difference	35,000	
2nd wraparound	$160,000	

If the seller did this, Al would make one payment on the second wraparound of $160,000 as would be indicated by the terms of that mortgage. In turn, the seller would make payments on the first wraparound (which would include the first mortgage payment and the difference to the holder of that wraparound), and make the payment on the third mortgage, keeping the balance left over as the payment on the new difference.

Or the seller could create a wraparound mortgage solely around the third mortgage. In this case, Al would make two monthly payments: one on the first wraparound, and a second to the seller on a wraparound at a face amount of $60,000 ($25,000 + $35,000). Out of that payment by Al, the seller would have to meet the obligations of the third mortgage.

The seller could also take a fourth mortgage, which Al would pay in addition to the wraparound and the third mortgage.

3. IS NOT REQUIRED TO ENCLOSE ALL EXISTING MORTGAGES.   The foregoing example was a good illustration of that. This is important to remember because if you buy a property with a wraparound do not assume that there are not other mortgages you need to pay. One of the key elements of any real estate transaction is to know exactly what debt there is against the property you are buying. You will only know for sure by having a title search made by your lawyer, or a title insurance company or escrow company. Even then, as a part of the closing statement, the seller should warrant that there are no hidden loans that may surface later on.

4. IS NOT ALL THE SAME.   Since this is a technique and not a specific form that can be bought at a stationery store, you must recognize that this tool is very flexible, and will be different each time you see it or use it. No matter how similar one form of a wraparound looks, you have to be very careful with the exact terms contained within the document to make sure you understand what is expected of each party. I mention each party, because the wraparound has obligations to both the mortgagor and the mortgagee. Later, there will be more on this aspect of wraparounds.

ANOTHER EXAMPLE OF A WRAPAROUND MORTGAGE

Example: The Pallsen Study

Pallsen wanted to sell his large home and put a price of $155,000 on it. He had an old low-interest existing first mortgage in the amount of $75,000 that had twenty years remaining in its payout at an interest of only 8% per annum.

Along comes Beck, the investor, who offers to pay $35,000 down, assume the first mortgage, and let Pallsen hold the balance of $40,000 in secondary financing. Like many sellers, Pallsen balked at that, saying the risk was too high and the yield was too low. Beck reconsidered and countered with the following terms:

Price	$150,000	
Cash down	$ 35,000	
Wraparound	$115,000	(20-year payout at 10%)

Beck's broker presented the new offer. He explained to Pallsen what a wraparound was and went over the advantages to Pallsen in this offer.

The broker showed Pallsen how this wraparound would return a yield of over 13% over the term of the mortgage. Take a look at the illustrations the broker used.

PALLSEN'S WRAPAROUND MORTGAGE

In the transaction, Beck will make payments on one mortgage: the $115,000 wraparound. It will be set up with a 20-year amortization at 10% per annum. The total annual payment will be $13,317.55.

Pallsen will be required to set up a method of collection of that mortgage from Beck so that from Beck's monthly check, the payment required on the existing first mortgage can be made. The required payment on the existing first mortgage is $7,527.75, which is deducted from Beck's total annual payment of $13,317.55. This leaves $5,789.25 per year for Pallsen. This means that Pallsen will get a monthly payment of $482.44 for the 20 years (unless he sells the mortgage or uses it in exchange for another property). This payment, on the equity in the wraparound of $40,000, would represent a monthly payment based on a 20-year payout at 13.5%.

HOW WAS THE YIELD ON PALLSEN'S MORTGAGE CALCULATED?

This was a simple calculation on a wraparound mortgage. There was only one existing mortgage, and the wraparound was for the same term as the existing mortgage. In essence, by the end of the term (20 years) each mortgage would be retired. Beck would make one payment each month that would total $13,317.55 per year for 20 years. During this same time, Pallsen or any successor holder of that mortgage would pay the existing payments of $7,527.75 per year and would collect on the difference of $40,000 an annual total of $5,789.25. To find the actual effective yield on this wraparound for the total term of the mortgage (20 years), you simply need to find the constant rate on the payment toward the difference. As long as the terms of the existing mortgage and the wraparound are identical and no interim balloon occurs, the following is a quick math solution to the problem.

FIND THE CONSTANT RATE OF PAYMENT ON THE DIFFERENCE

STEP ONE.   Once you have the annual payment of $5,789.25, which you obtained by taking the total payment on the wraparound and by deducting the payment to the existing mortgage, you then divide that amount by the total amount owed on the difference (equity in the wraparound). The difference in this example is $40,000 and is found by subtracting the existing mortgage from the gross amount of the wraparound mortgage.

STEP TWO.   The sum of $5,789.25 divided by $40,000 equals 0.1447312.

STEP THREE.   Convert the answer, 0.1447312, into a percentage amount by moving the decimal two places to the right. The percentage is now 14.47312. This is the constant rate of payment for an amortizing mortgage with monthly payments.

STEP FOUR.   Look at Table A in the appendix under the 20-year column until you find a constant percent that comes closest to the 14.47312.

STEP FIVE.   Discover these two percentages, 14.273 followed by 14.488. These correspond to the different interest rates for that term of years.

PERCENT INTEREST	TWENTY YEARS
13.25	14.273
13.5	14.488

As the desired percent is more than that shown for 13.25% interest but slightly less than that for 13.5% interest, the actual effective interest yield on the difference for the full term of the wraparound would be about 13.45% per year. It is sufficient to come to an average interest rate at this point.

WHAT ALL THIS MEANS THUS FAR

If Pallsen were to hold onto this mortgage for the full 20 years, his effective yield would be 13.45% per year. This is, of course, based on his equity of $40,000 and a full term payout. As real insiders know, mortgages do not always run the full term. If Beck, for example, decided to sell the property in a few years, a new buyer may want to refinance to new terms from an institutional or other lender. This is very good news for any holder of a wraparound mortgage, because when a mortgage is paid off early, there can be substantial bonus to its holder. For additional information about such bonus, look to Chapter 15 that deals with buying mortgages at a discount. For the moment, take a look at the following example to get an idea about early payoff.

WHAT HAPPENS IF THE MORTGAGE IS PAID OFF EARLY?

A strange thing happens in wraparounds that gives the holder a bonus when the mortgage gets paid off early. Assume for a moment that Beck sells the property at the end of the first year and the new owner refinances the wraparound, paying off the amount then owed. To see what happens, let's first get the facts.

WHAT THE MORTGAGES LOOK LIKE
AT THE END OF THE FIRST YEAR

	The wraparound mortgage	The existing mortgage
Original amount	$115,000.00	$75,000.00
Annual payment	$ 13,317.55	$ 7,527.75
Term of years	20	20
Interest rate	10%	8%
End of which year	1	1
Remaining term	19 years	19 years
Amount still owed	$113,100.21	$ 73,412.81

This last amount is found by finding the *constant rate* for the remaining term, at the interest rate for the mortgage, and then dividing that rate into the annual payment.

If Beck paid off the wraparound it would cost him $113,100.21 out of which Pallsen would have to pay $73,412.81 leaving him a balance of $39,687.39 from the original $40,000 difference. At the end of the first year then, Pallsen would have gotten:

In monthly payments	$ 5,789.25
Payoff at the end of the year	39,687.39
Total paid to Pallsen	$45,476.64
Subtract original Principal amount	40,000.00
Net interest for that first year	$ 5,476.64

Actual effective yield based on an annual return for the first year based on a payoff of the existing mortgage and the wraparound at that time would be found by dividing the original principal amount of $40,000 into the net interest for the year. The sum of $5,476.64 divided by $40,000 equals 13.692% per annum.

The point to this illustration is that in a wraparound mortgage the general rule is that the actual effective yield will be higher if the mortgage is paid off early than if held to maturity. This mortgage yield went from 13.45% to 13.692% on the prepayment of the first year. The yield earned at the end of a first-year payoff in a mortgage such as described will be its maximum annual yield. Each year thereafter, the mortgage yield will move closer to the 13.45% per annum.

Later on in this chapter when I illustrate the Hodges Shopping Center example, you will see how existing mortgages are affecting the total wraparound balance and the relationship to the difference.

Keep in mind that in the Pallsen example everything was at its simplest. In the real life use of the wraparound, it is usual to have more than one mortgage and more than one term of years within the existing financing. These factors make the wraparound a rather complicated mortgage to calculate, so don't be surprised if you have to apply some extra thought to this chapter. It will be worth it in the long and profitable run.

THE TWELVE MOST COMMON USES OF A WRAPAROUND MORTGAGE

1. Use this tool as a method of leveraging a seller's position upward with the idea of increasing the effective yield earned on the mortgage. The ability to increase the return on funds mortgaged is the primary benefit of the wraparound.

2. Used to induce the seller to hold secondary paper. The benefits of the increased return may help a broker convince a reluctant seller to take treater paper, or any paper at all for that matter. Many transactions are saved simply because the sellers were made aware of the benefits of this tool.

3. When the existing financing is at a relatively low rate and the constant payment percentage is relatively low, the green flag is out that a wraparound is potentially viable. The key factor here is the constant rate, and the investor's goals. More about that later.

4. If the existing financing has any provisions that make prepayment difficult or costly, then the wraparound mortgage may provide an effective solution to the inability to economically obtain new primary financing. When there are several mortgages encumbering a property, there may be one or more with provisions that will create such problems. It is best to consider the wraparound when such conditions are present. Sellers unwilling to approach the wraparound should be made aware of the full impact of their present financing.

5. A nonassumption clause in the existing financing may be an indication that the wraparound mortgage can be used. Institutional lenders almost always use these provisions in their loans. When a property is sold, the buyer must make application to the lender to be permitted to assume the obligation. Some lending institutions have taken a harder stand than others, but most will allow the wraparound if the first is assumed. The lenders, however, generally reserve the right to adjust the interest rate when such a new assumption takes place.

   Nonetheless, a wraparound mortgage does not require the buyer to assume the existing financing. This is a key factor in the whole structure of the wraparound mortgage, and indirectly has created the difficulty for third parties to lend on the wraparound. When a buyer purchases a property and gives the seller a wraparound mortgage, the existing financing remains the obligation of the seller.

The seller makes the payments directly or causes them to be made on the existing mortgages. Some secondary financing which may be encompassed within the wraparound may have absolute provisions which would make the wraparound difficult if not in violation to contract terms.

6   The increase of cash flow is a definite benefit which can be accomplished by using the wraparound. Therefore, when the sale of a property is hampered by a low cash flow, look to it. In essence, there are only a few ways to increase cash flow. Assuming a status quo in all other factors, the increase of income will accomplish this. If this fails, a reduction of expenses will also increase the cash flow. A combined effect of increased income (via more rents, and so on) and lowered expenses often will solve the problem and make the wraparound unnecessary. Normally, however, the seller has already maximized income and minimized expenses. The resulting net operating income (NOI) can only show an increased cash flow based on lowered debt service. The yield resulting from the cash flow, based on the invested capital, must meet the investors demand rate (at the price the seller is willing to sell at). In the general marketing of an income property, the cash down is often based on the seller holding some paper, or with new financing necessary. The cash flow yield may be too low with new financing at high market rates, to warrant the investment. The wraparound can, and often does, solve this problem nicely.

7.   Tight mortgage markets bring out the best need for the wraparound. When you find you are trying to sell a property which cannot be financed due to the current market conditions, you must look to all the possible alternatives. The toughness of the market need only be relative to the overall rate on the existing financing. This means that if you have a property that has existing financing at very low rates, and the current market is a point or two above those rates, then you should examine the possibility of the wraparound. Of course, the complete inability to refinance for any reason within the economics of the deal will bring the wraparound into play more quickly and with more dramatic positive results.

8.   Refinancing costs can sometimes be a major problem, and this factor can be a good reason to look to the wraparound. The overall effect of placing a wraparound mortgage is less costly to administer than new financing. The seller need only charge whatever legal cost is involved in the preparation of the loan document, and this should not be much more than the cost of preparing a standard form for a secondary loan.

9.   Multimortgaged properties can often be very difficult to sell or market simply because of the number of mortgages present. If you have a property that has three or more existing mortgages, the wraparound can convert these into one. The buyer, after all, makes only one payment on the wraparound, even though the seller must direct payments out to the encompassed mortgages.

10. A short balloon in existing financing can create many difficulties in selling property. If the property is an income producer and the possibilities of refinancing it to cover the balloon payment are slim, then the wraparound can provide a solution. Naturally, the amount of the balloon must be considered. But if it is due to close and is not excessive, then the wraparound may work out.

11. Marketing a property with sound financing can bring about a quicker sale and less negotiating of the price. When a property has only a moderate extension of financing, that is to say a low ratio of the loan to value, the seller's equity will come under attack by buyers anxious to buy at a lower price. It is obvious that a home offered at $100,000 with an $85,000 mortgage leaves only $15,000 to negotiate with. Buyers expect some equity, and will haggle on only the upper limits of such a transaction. The broker utilizes this technique and obtains a commitment from the seller (or a third party lender for that matter), and quotes the wraparound mortgage in his or her presentations. This extending of the loan to value ratio will benefit the negotiations. As the buyer approaches the close of the sale, full ramifications of the underlying mortgages encompassed by the wraparound will, of course, be disclosed. The first examination, however, need only show the higher wraparound.

12. Buyers will look to the wraparound as a beneficial investing tool as often as a seller will see it as a selling tool. The buyers' benefits are in the overall comparison with the existing mortgage market, rather than in seller-held, conventional secondary financing. There are a few examples where the buyer will benefit from a wraparound, such as when the seller will hold a usual second mortgage for the same terms and rates. The seller will, however, hold a wraparound for longer, and often at lower rates than a usual second. Therefore, the buyer can benefit by approaching any situation that may call for refinancing and offer the seller terms only slightly less costly to the buyer in the general lending market. In this way the buyer obtains better terms from the seller than he or she could at an institutional lender, saves the points, and at the same time passes on to the seller the full benefits of the wraparound.

    If the primary reason for using the wraparound is to increase the cash flow on the income property for sale, there may be a sacrifice in some other area. The nature of the wraparound and its effect on the dollar amounts paid and received by the seller or lender should be clearly understood. In the first place, it is normal for the balance of the "difference" (mortgagee's equity), that is owed, to increase for a period of time. Remember, the word *difference* in wraparound terms refers to the amount of the total wraparound mortgage that is left whenever you deduct the then present amount owed to the existing financing. This amount is the equity the seller or mortgagee has in the total amount of the wraparound. A wraparound in the amount of $100,000 that encompasses a first and a second totaling $80,000 will have an original difference of $20,000. This term is not universal, and in some areas this amount ($20,000) is called the *wraparound difference,* the *lender's position,* or *new money* and as I have used, the *mortgagee's equity.* From this point on, I shall refer to this amount as the difference. This difference will not remain constant throughout the mortgage and normally grows in the early years. In essence, the equity or investment that the mortgagee has in this wraparound will grow as it earns interest, that is not paid, and then begin to decline as the principal is ultimately repaid. To best illustrate what happens to this difference, examine the following case history.

THE FUNCTION OF THE AMORTIZATION AND ITS EFFECT ON THE DIFFERENCE IN WRAPAROUND MORTGAGES

Example: The Hodges Case

Hodges sold a shopping center for $2,500,000. He received $350,000 down and held a wraparound for the balance. The wraparound was for a face amount of $2,150,000, and was payable over a period of 20 years at 9% per annum in equal monthly installments which totaled $235,532.50. The existing financing was a first mortgage ($1,200,000) at 7 1/2% with 19 years remaining. Annual payment was $120,492. There was a second mortgage in the amount of $700,000 payable over 15 years at 8%. The annual payment was $81,781.

	Mortgages	Face amount	Annual payments
	Wraparound	$2,150,000	$235,532.50
Less:	1st mortgage	$1,200,000	$120,492.00
Less:	2nd mortgage	$ 700,000	$ 81,781.00
Original Difference:		$ 250,000	$ 33,259.50

The foregoing calculation is correct only for the moment the wraparound is made. Each year the balances due on the mortgage will alter. The payment allocation to the difference will also change when the existing mortgages retire.

Here's what occurs at the end of the first year:

		Mtg. balance at start of first year	Total payment Principal	Interest	Balance owed at end of first year
	Wraparound	$2,150,000	$42,032	$193,500	$2,107,967
Less:	1st mortgage	$1,200,000	$30,492	$ 90,000	$1,169,508
Less:	2nd mortgage	$ 700,000	$25,781	$ 56,000	$ 674,219
Difference:		$ 250,000	($14,241)	$ 47,500	$ 264,240

What has happened is this: The balance owed on the wraparound has declined by the principal paid of $42,032. However, the existing mortgages have declined $56,273. The total owed or remaining as a principal balance on the wraparound is $2,107,967. If the mortgage were paid off by the buyer at that time and the existing mortgages satisfied, then $264,240 would remain to apply to the mortgagee or the seller. The original amount at the beginning of the year was only $250,000. The $264,240 is the difference at the end of the first year. This is ($14,241) greater than the original difference of $250,000. What happened shows up in the interest column. The interest on the wraparound mortgage is $47,500 greater than the combined interest on the first and second mortgages. This $47,500 is net interest earned by the holder of the mortgage, but since the holder received only $33,259.50 (see previous chart) the total principal amortized on the existing financing exceeded that amortized on the wraparound. The deficit ($14,241) had to be deducted from the total interest, then added to the balance owed. This constant adding of the deficit interest to the balance applicable to the difference will continue as the mortgage progresses.

The following is what happens in the second year.

		Mtg. balance at start of second year	Total payment Principal	Interest	Balance owed at end of second year
	Wraparound	$2,107,967	$45,815	$189,717	$2,062,152
Less:	1st mortgage	$1,169,508	$32,779	$ 87,713	$1,136,729
Less:	2nd mortgage	$ 674,219	$27,843	$ 53,937	$ 646,375
Difference:		$ 264,240	($14,807)	$ 48,067	$ 279,048

The holder of the wraparound still only gets the $33,259.50 cash left after the total payment is received less the existing payments on the first and second mortgages (see first chart). In this year, however, the balance applicable to the difference has grown to $279,048.

The reason for this build-up is not simply explained. It is a function of several factors that combine to create the major leverage to the difference. In the first place, leverage is present in the spread of mortgage rates. The interest charged on the wraparound is greater than the combined effect of interest charges against the total existing financing. You should be cautioned at this point not to jump to conclusions that all the underlying mortgages must have interest rates below that of the wraparound. It is the combined effect you must look at. In a multimortgaged property you may have one or more mortgages with greater interest rates than the wraparound and still have a build-up of difference owed.

Therefore, the function of the amortization on the balance applicable to the difference will generally be that the amount owed will grow each year until there is a satisfaction of at least one existing mortgage. Keep in mind, however, that this is not always the case, and the actual calculation to determine this factor must be done. To recap the amortization of the wraparound in this case study, I have provided a breakdown of the mortgages and the difference throughout the full term of the loan. This breakdown is necessary in the understanding of the effective yield gained on the wraparound and will be used in the larger analysis of this yield later on. The amortization of the mortgages shown in Figure 10-1 on page 212 gives the amounts owed at the end of the periods shown. Generally, you are dealing with amortizing loans which will have one constant monthly or annual payment that includes interest and principal. Because of this, neither the interest nor the principal payments in each period are equal to other previous payments. Therefore, the corresponding balances of each mortgage and the difference must be calculated for each period. In analyzing a mortgage, you can be fairly accurate with year-end totals. Only in this way will you know what the pay-off amount applicable to the difference is at any given point of time.

In Figure 10-1, each mortgage is shown with the principal balance outstanding at the end of each period. For example, at the end of 8 years the balance outstanding on the wraparound mortgage is $1,686,446 Column A, the 1st mortgage is $881,469 Column B, the 2nd mortgage is $452,777 Column C, and the difference has grown to $379,200 Column E.

THE EFFECTIVE RATE EARNED ON THE WRAPAROUND

This is the most difficult part of the wraparound to fully comprehend. The big question is simply this: What is the real (or effective) return to the holder of the wraparound?

In looking at the Hodges Shopping Center Analysis Sheet (Figure 10-1) on page 212, we can see numerous yields. At first glance we see that the seller will receive, after all payments on the existing financing, a balance of $33,259.50, Column H, for the time that the existing mortgage debt service remains unchanged. This amount of return, in cash, represents 13.30% of the original balance of the difference, Column I ($33,259.50 ÷ $250,000 = 13.30%). However, the balance of the difference does not diminish during the period of full existing debt service. And should the mortgagor pay off the wraparound before any of the existing debt is satisfied, the holder will obtain the full $250,000 plus a bonus of built-up interest which was earned but not received. This bonus is in addition to the interest of $33,259.50 received or retained. With this in mind then, until the outstanding difference drops below its original sum, we can treat the wraparound as an interest-only return to the mortgagee with the effective yield being this original 13.30% plus the bonus rate.

Therefore, when analyzing the wraparound there will be more than one rate which you must recognize. First, there is the rate on the retained cash. This represents that sum of money that is actually received net of payments on the existing financing less amortization of the difference. In Figure 10-1, the total cash received on the difference, Column F, is $33,259.50 for the term of the existing financing. This will increase when the second is retired. As there is no amortization of the difference during this period, the Retained Total, Column H, equals Column F. Since the original investment by the mortgagee is $250,000, and that balance owed remains at or above that sum during the term of the existing financing, then the retained cash is 13.30% for that period of time only. This rate becomes the capitalization rate of the difference.

In reference to Figure 10-1, you will notice that this annual payment of retained cash changes when the second mortgage is satisfied. All calculations on wraparound effective rates must be broken down to the periods of the existing financing. When there is no amortization of the difference, which generally will occur only in the first period, the cash received will equal the retained cash. In addition to the effective rate of 13.30% for the retained cash, a bonus also occurs. This bonus is earned but not retained. It cannot be accurately computed until the mortgagee benefits from that sum at some time in the future.

FINDING THE OVERALL EFFECTIVE YIELD OF A WRAPAROUND MORTGAGE

The first step in finding the effective yield of the bonus is to fill out the wraparound analysis chart (Figure 10-1). In looking at the amortization chart for the wraparound mortgage and the existing financing, you will be able to note the year in which the build-up of difference stops and amortization of that balance begins. This is significant since it establishes the year the bonus is benefitting the mortgagee. In the Hodges Shopping Center Case Study (Figure 10-1), this occurs in the fifteenth year. When there is a build-up or accrual of bonus, the change generally occurs when all or part of the existing financing retires. In some mortgages, the retirement of one mortgage is not sufficient to increase the payment to the difference.

Because the bonus amount is important, and because the data necessary to obtain an accurate effective rate of return is dependent on the Analysis Sheet (Figure 10-1), a brief discussion of how to fill out this sheet is in order. Examine the chart. Notice that there are columns A through J. These ten columns will accommodate a wraparound and three existing mortgages. If you have a situation where you have more than three existing mortgages, you need to add Dl, D2, and so on, for each additional mortgage.

Figure 10-1
Hodges Shopping Center Case Study Analysis

| | The wraparound principal balance | | | | Existing financing principal balance at end of period | | | | | |
| | A | B | C | D | E | F | G | H | I | J |
End of period	$2,150,000 Wraparound mtg. Yrs. 20 Rate 9% Payment $235,532.50	$1,200,000 1st Mtg. Yrs. 19 Rate 7½% Payment $120,492	$700,000 2nd Mtg. Yrs. 15 Rate 8% Payment $81,781	3rd Mtg. Yrs. ___ Rate ___ Payment ___	Difference $250,000 20 Yrs. varies	Total cash received on difference $33,259.50	Difference amortized	Retained interest	Annual interest rate	Earned but not retained bonus
0	$2,150,000	$1,200,200	$700,000		$250,000					
1	2,107,967	1,169,508	674,219		264,240	$33,259.50	0	$33,259.50	13.30%	$ 14,240
2	2,062,152	1,136,792	646,375		279,048	33,259.50	0	33,259.50	13.30%	29,048
3	2,012,213	1,101,492	616,035		294,416	33,259.50	0	33,259.50	13.30%	44,416
4	1,957,780	1,063,612	583,828		310,340	33,259.50	0	33,259.50	13.30%	60,340
5	1,898,448	1,022,891	548,753		326,804	33,259.50	0	33,259.50	13.30%	76,804
6	1,833,775	979,115	510,872		343,788	33,259.50	0	33,259.50	13.30%	93,788
7	1,763,283	932,057	469,961		361,265	33,259.50	0	33,259.50	13.30%	111,265
8	1,686,446	881,469	452,777		379,200	33,259.50	0	33,259.50	13.30%	129,200
9	1,602,693	827,087	378,058		397,548	33,259.50	0	33,259.50	13.30%	147,548
10	1,511,403	768,627	326,522		416,254	33,259.50	0	33,259.50	13.30%	166,254
11	1,411,897	705,781	270,863		435,253	33,259.50	0	33,259.50	13.30%	185,253
12	1,303,435	638,223	210,750		454,462	33,259.50	0	33,259.50	13.30%	204,462
13	1,185,212	565,598	145,830		473,784	33,259.50	0	33,259.50	13.30%	223,784
14	1,056,348	487,525	75,715		493,108	33,259.50	0	33,259.50	13.30%	243,108
15	915,887	403,598	0		512,289	33,259.50	0	33,259.50	13.30%	262,289
16	762,785	313,376	0		449,409	115,040.50	62,880	52,160.50	10.18%	199,409
17	595,903	216,387	0		379,516	115,040.50	69,893	45,147.50	10.05%	129,516
18	414,002	112,124	0		301,878	115,040.50	77,638	37,402.50	9.86%	51,878
19	215,729	0	0		215,729	115,040.50	86,149	28,891.50	9.57%	34,271
20	0	0	0		0	235,532.50	215,729	19,803.50	9.18%	

HOW TO USE THE WRAPAROUND MORTGAGE ANALYSIS SHEET

COLUMN A: The basic information needed which pertains to the wraparound should be filled in at the top. The term of years, annual interest rate charged, and annual payment of P & I are important for reference. At the *end of period O*, you should place the face amount or original balance owed on the wraparound. In the following years, as the column extends down the page, you can put the principal balances owed at the end of each successive year. This is a purely mathematical calculation which can be done easily with a two-memory calculator or can be obtained from an amortization schedule. It should be noted that the years shown are the end of that period, and in order to find the balance owed at the beginning of a year you need to look to the balance owed at the end of the previous year.

COLUMNS B, C, AND D: These columns contain the same type of information as Column A, except that they are for the currently existing mortgages. Most sellers will have amortization schedules for this information.

COLUMN E: This is the balance owed on the difference and the most important part of this computation. If there is no amortization of the difference, as will usually be the case in early years, this amount will grow. The total in this column represents the net payoff to the mortgagee at the end of any given year. This column will indicate when the difference peaks out and begins to amortize. Subtracting the original balance of the difference from the amount in this column at the end of any year will give you the amount of the bonus thus far accrued (to be shown in Column J).

COLUMN F: The total cash received on the difference is the amount of net cash left over after the existing mortgage payments are deducted from the payments received on the wraparound. These payments will remain constant for the separate periods of the existing financing. If you have only one existing mortgage that is satisfied before the end of the wraparound, you will have only two periods. This column is very easy to calculate and should present no difficulty.

COLUMN G: This column will contain amounts only for the years when the difference is declining. These amounts are found by looking at Column E. In Column E you have the amount of the difference as it increases and then declines. You need not be concerned with the increase in the Column G calculation, only the decline. The amount amortized is the amount of decline each year as seen in the reduction of Column E. When the total in Column E does begin to drop, deduct the end of the year amount from the previous year.

COLUMNS H AND I: It is generally best to do these two columns as one calculation. The Retained Interest and Annual Interest Rate are found as follows: The Retained Interest, Column F (total cash received on difference) less Column G (difference amortized). The result will be the interest portion of the total cash actually received. In most all instances of a wraparound, the amortization, Column G, occurs late in the term.

The annual interest rate is found by dividing the interest received by: (1) In the event of 0 amortization as seen in Column G, by the original balance of the difference; (2) In the event of amortization, by the amount of the difference at the start of that year (end of the previous year). You may have a very low annual interest rate when the total cash received in the early years is just above the existing mortgage payments. Therefore, a low annual interest rate is not unusual.

COLUMN J: This column need not be filled in completely. Its function is to show the amount of accrual of "extra lending." It represents the amount found in Column E (difference) less the original balance of the difference. You need only put in this calculation the year the difference peaks out. (The year before amortization begins on Column D, as shown in Column G. This amount you will show in Column J is the total bonus for that period. Generally, this is the only bonus you will have for a wraparound.

In the example given in Figure 10-1, you will note that on the line which corresponds to the end of the fifteenth year under Column E the difference peaks out at $512,289. Further review of the remaining pay-out of the wraparound and the existing financing indicates that the difference amortizes beginning the sixteenth year. The amount of the amortization, Column G, is simply found by subtracting the current year's balance from the previous year's balance. The retained interest total, Column H, is the total cash received, Column F, less the amount of amortization, Column G.

Bonus, Column J, is the accrual of the earned but not retained portion of the difference. Of course, it peaks along with the difference. This bonus can be deemed to become a benefit at the time the difference begins to amortize. In essence, the return to the mortgagee can no longer be treated as interest only, as was done as the difference grew. Instead, the annual interest rate must take into account the bonus. While the difference was growing, the annual interest rate was found by dividing the retained interest by the original difference. Now, as the mortgagee is receiving benefit from a new difference, the annual interest rates, for years when there is amortization, are found by dividing the retained interest by the balance of the difference owed at the end of the previous year. For example: At the end of the fifteenth year the difference was $512,289, Column E. During that year the difference had grown and there was no amortization. However, in the sixteenth year there was a reduction of $62,880 (see Column G) and the balance at the end of that year was $449,409 (see

Column E). A total of $115,040.50 was kept by the mortgagee. Of that amount, the $62,880 is principal reduction of the new difference (benefit) and $52,160.50 interest. The annual rate for this interest retained, Column I, is found by dividing $52,160.50 by $512,289. The result is 10.18%. In essence, for that year the mortgagee earned 10.18% on the mortgage of $512,289.

The following year shows a reduction of the difference by $69,893.00 and an interest retained of $45,147.50. The annual rate for the seventeenth year is 10.05% (45,147.50 ÷ 449,409). This calculation is carried out each year until the balance of the wraparound is satisfied. By doing these calculations, it is possible to complete the full analysis sheet and to proceed to the final calculation of the overall effective yield for the mortgage.

The first step is to arrive at the primary effective rate which occurs during the early years when the difference is growing. To make this computation easier, I have provided Figure 10-2. (This chart shows sections A and B of the necessary calculation.) The use of this chart is not as complicated as it may appear. Once Columns A through J of Figure 10-1 have been filled, with simple math, the use of the sinking fund table provided in this book and a small calculator will make fast work of the primary effective rate.

Figure 10-2 Primary Effective Rate Calculations When Difference Grows

Section A

(A)	Amount of original difference:	$ _____
(B)	Annual cash retained:	$ _____
(C)	Annual interest rate (Line B ÷ Line A) (state as decimal):	_____
(D)	Total new difference:	$ _____
(E)	Amount of bonus (D less A):	$ _____
(F)	% of bonus (Line E ÷ A) (state as decimal):	_____
(G)	Total years for period:	_____ # years
(H)	Total benefit at period (Line B × Years) + Line E:	$ _____
(I)	Average annual benefit (Line H ÷ Years):	$ _____
(J)	Average rate (Line I ÷ Line A) (state as decimal):	_____

Note: Primary effective rate (PER) will lie between average rate (Line J) and annual interest rate (Line C).

Primary Effective Rate Calculations When Difference Grows (continued)

Section B

Formula to Find PER (Shown Below)
Primary Effective Rate (% of Bonus* × 1 S$_N$) = Annual Interest Rate
*Shown as a Decimal

1.   Target _____Annual interest rate
2.   Less_____(A)
3.
4.   _____(B)

Interpolation

PER = _____ + _.01 × (A)_
                                      (B)

PER = _____

Taking the known facts from the Hodges Shopping Center Case study, Figure 10-1, examine how the primary effective rate for the first period was obtained. Note that the first period is the time the difference was still growing.

The question is stated as follows: If $250,000 is invested now and the investor receives $33,259.50 each year for 15 years, and at the end of the 15-year period has a return of his investment plus $262,289, what is the investor's effective rate of return? This data is found in the computations on the Analysis Chart (Figure 10-1). With this information, fill in and compute Section A of the Effective Rate Calculation.

Figure 10-3 Primary Effective Rate Calculations When Difference Grows

Section A

(A)	Amount of original difference:	$250,000.00
(B)	Annual cash retained:	$ 33,259.50 (Column F)
(C)	Annual interest rate (Line B ÷ Line A) (state as decimal):	0.1330 (13.3%)
(D)	Total new difference:	$512,289.00 (Column E at 15th year)
(E)	Amount of bonus (D less A):	$262,289.00 (Column J at 15th year)
(F)	% of bonus (Line E ÷ A) (state as decimal):	1.0492
(G)	Total years for period:	15 years
(H)	Total benefit at period (Line B x Years) + Line E:	$761,181.50
(I)	Average annual benefit (Line H ÷ Years):	$ 50,745.43
(J)	Average rate (Line I ÷ Line A) (state as decimal):	0.202982 (20.2982%)

To complete the primary effective rate calculation, it is necessary to complete Section B of the chart (Figure 10-4).

Since the following calculation requires an assumption to begin with, examine the relationship of the annual interest rate and the average rate. The annual interest rate shown is 0.1330 (or 13.3%) and the average rate is 0.202982 (or 20.298%). The primary effective rate will lie somewhere between these two.

The formula is: primary effective rate (PER% of bonus $\times$ 1 S_N) = annual interest rate. The calculation 1 S_N, is found in the sinking fund table provided in this book. Because the PER is unknown, make a guess at a rate slightly less than halfway between the annual interest rate and the average rate. In this case, use 0.16 (16%) as a starting point. In completing the formula you will look in the sinking fund table under the rate you assume to be correct for the period of years which in this example would be 0.16 (16%). Look at the 16% table for the fifteenth year. The resulting number represents 1 S_N for 16% at 15 years. The number shown in the table is 0.019358. From the previous Section A of this chart on Line F, the percent of the bonus has been found. That number, shown as a decimal, is 1.0492. The annual interest rate, also found in Section A on Line C is 0.1330. Now complete the formula with the first assumed interest rate as shown on Figure 10-4, Line 1.

Figure 10-4 Primary Effective Rate Calculations When Difference Grows

Section B

Formula to Find PER (Shown Below)
Primary Effective Rate (% of Bonus[*] $\times$ 1 S_N) = Annual Interest Rate
*Shown as a Decimal

1. .16 − (1.0492 × .019358) =   0.139689   Target: 0.13300 Annual interest rate
2. .15 − (1.0492 × .021017) =   <u>0.127949</u>
                                  0.011740 (B)   Less: <u>0.12795</u>
                                                           0.00505 (A)

3.

4.

Interpolation
PER = <u>0.15</u>+ (0.01 x 0.00505 (A))/ 0.011740 (B)
PER = 0.15 + 0.00430, thus PER = 0.1543 (PER = 15.43%)

The resulting annual interest rate on the assumed PER of 16% exceeds the target rate. The target rate is the actual annual interest rate of 0.1330. Therefore, it is necessary to reduce the assumed rate. Try 0.15 (15%). In the table, locate 15% at the fifteenth year. The corresponding number is 0.2017. Therefore, the second part of the calculation would appear as 0.15 − (1.0492 × 0.02017) = 0.127949.

The annual interest rate found with this assumed rate of 15% is less than the target rate. By subtracting the annual interest rate on this lower interest from both the target rate (actual annual interest rate) and annual interest rate on the higher interest (16%), you can obtain the basis for Interpolation.

---

(1) $0.16 - (1.0492 \times 0.01968) = 0.13989$ Target: 0.13300

(2) <u>$0.15 - (1.0492 \times 0.02017) = 0.127949$</u>   <u>0.127949</u>

0.01   0.011740 (B)   0.00505 (A)

$$\text{Primary Effective Rate} = \text{Lowest rate assumed} + \frac{\text{spread} \times \text{difference A}}{\text{Difference B}}$$

therefore

Primary Effective Rate = $0.15 + (0.01 \times 0.00505 / 0.011740)$

Primary Effective Rate = 0.1543 (stated as a % = 15.43%)

The Interpolation will approximate the effective rate once you have narrowed it down. In the lower tables, you can come very close to the actual rate and will not have to use a full point spread in your assumed rates. The formula for the interpolation is:

Primary Effective Rate Calculations When Difference Grows

Section A

(A)	Amount of original difference:	$250,000.00
(B)	Annual cash retained:	$ 33,259.50 (Column F)
(C)	Annual interest rate (Line B ÷ Line A) (state as decimal):	0.1330 (13.3%)
(D)	Total new difference:	$512,289.00 (Column E at 15th year)
(E)	Amount of bonus (D less A):	$262,289.00 (Column J at 15th year)
(F)	Percent of bonus (Line E ÷ A) (state as decimal):	1.0492
(G)	Total years for period:	15 years
(H)	Total benefit at period (Line B x Years) + Line E:	$761,181.50
(I)	Average annual benefit (Line H ÷ Years)	$ 50,745.43
(J)	Average rate (Line I ÷ Line A) (state as decimal):	0.202982 (20.2982%)

The primary effective rate for the case study, as of the end of the fifteenth year, is 15.43%. If the mortgage were to balloon on that date, there would be no further calculations. If the mortgage were to be paid off earlier than the fifteen years, the entire process would be computed on the balances and amounts applicable for the specific period of time.

Should the mortgage continue beyond the fifteenth year, the annual yield for each succeeding year would have to be added to the multiple of the effective rate thus far obtained and the years received. See these calculations on the consolidation section of the effective yield calculation.

Consolidation of Yield

Period of wraparound analyzed	Effective rate per period		No. of years rate earned	Rate × yrs.
	Annual interest rate	Primary effective rate		
1st		15.43	15	231.45
2nd	10.18		1	10.18
3rd	10.05		1	10.05
4th	9.88		1	9.88
5th	9.57		1	9.57
6th	9.18		1	9.18
7th				
8th				
9th				
10th				
11th				
12th				
Combined totals of rate × years: Total				280.29
Divide by term of years on wraparound: Effective rate				14.015%

The foregoing table gives you the effective rate of interest earned by the mortgagee over the term of the mortgage. This sum, 14.015% is the result of the leverage obtained over the existing financing. You can see that a balloon on the fifteenth year would have given an effective yield over those 15 years of 15.43%. The later years of this wraparound gave a higher cash flow return than the early years. However, the benefit or bonus return accounted for the majority of that cash flow. It would have been best to have obtained the full benefit at the fifteenth year.

HOW TO USE THE EFFECTIVE RATE IN SELLING THE WRAPAROUND CONCEPT TO A MORTGAGEE

Keep in mind that the majority of mortgagees you will deal with will be sellers. The wraparound is a prime tool for increasing return to a seller, and this fact alone can convince many sellers who are reluctant to hold paper to do just that. To see this point clearly, examine the case study again (Figure 10-1). A wraparound in the amount of $2,150,000 was created for 20 years at 9% per annum. The difference held by the seller was $250,000. Over the term of the loan the seller received a total annual yield of 14.015%. What this really means is that in order for the seller to have done as well with a conventional secondary loan, he would have to hold a fourth mortgage at the same interest rate or greater. A buyer asked to pay that kind of financing may balk at such a high rate. The leverage shown in the case study was not exceptional for the wraparound, and it is not uncommon for you to have much more dramatic results than that. Nonetheless, a 14.015% per annum return is not readily available and may be enough to motivate the seller. In third party lending this same advantage will hold true. The third-party lender comes in and uses the same benefit to increase this overall yield on new money lent. The technique you use in convincing a seller of the advantages of holding the wraparound, instead of normal secondary paper, will depend on your fully understanding this leverage. The seller may find it to his advantage to accept a little more or even a lot more paper in order to take this increased yield. Yet, there are also other advantages to the seller in holding a wraparound. All of these are discussed in the next section.

ADVANTAGES TO THE SELLER OR OTHER MORTGAGEE AND HOW TO CAPITALIZE ON THEM

1. EFFECTIVE YIELD INCREASES.   This is one of the most important advantages to the wraparound. Great leverages in annual return are commonplace in them. No form of secondary financing can be as productive in increasing yield for the lender.

2. DEFAULT NOTICE.   When a seller or other mortgagee holds a wraparound mortgage, the owner of the property makes one payment to the mortgagee. From this payment the mortgagee then causes the existing mortgage payments to be made. Because the new owner has no control over this act, his default will come at the level of the wraparound. In other words, if the new buyer falls behind in payments, the wraparound mortgagee is the first to know. Action to collect, and even foreclosure if necessary, can be made at an early date, well before the existing mortgages themselves become overdue or go far in arrears. Of course, the mortgagee can easily step in and pay down the existing financing with no difficulty in the wraparound.

This advantage is considerable. If the mortgagor is going into arrears, it is not unusual for the mortgage having the lowest priority to be the last to be paid. It is possible and quite common, for example, for a new owner of multimortgaged property in financial difficulty to let the last mortgage (the third or fourth mortgage held by your seller) to go unpaid. In the meantime, this mortgagor may keep the first mortgage current for awhile, then slip into problems. But if the seller-held mortgage is sizable, the mortgagor may keep that one current and let the first mortgages go into default. Even with provisions that lenders are to notify the other mortgagees of any default, this may not occur until a bad situation has advanced into a most impossible default.

The wraparound solves this problem nicely. Point out the priority of a fourth mortgage to your seller and show him the possibility of not knowing about economic problems the new buyer is having until it is too late. With the wraparound he still has the same position against the property, but he gets all the money and makes the payments himself.

3. THE SELLING TOOL WORKS FOR THE SELLER. When you are marketing a property and have the ability to provide what appears to be an excellent mortgage, at terms under current rates and years longer than those available at local lenders, you have a good advantage in selling the property. This advantage goes to the seller. It is important to remember that you need not offer alternatives. A buyer may well understand the leverage of the interest on the existing mortgages and may not want to have that advantage pass on to the seller or some other party. In this event, he or she may ask the seller to hold secondary paper at a nominal interest rate and take over or assume the existing mortgages at their lower rate. The fact that the seller will hold a wraparound, however, should become the new financing offered. Hence, the comparison that a buyer must make is not between the wraparound and normal assumption of the existing mortgages and secondary paper, but between the terms offered on it and the conventional terms available at local lenders. The wraparound will compete favorably in almost any market, providing the existing financing can be wrapped around. In marketing a property with the wraparound, you will find it easy to make this comparison: "Mr. Buyer, we have provided terms which are far better than those currently available at the local lenders. This fact, the ease in closing on the property due to this mortgage, and no points are to your advantage." So, while this is a seller's advantage it is a buyer's advantage as well.

4. MAINTAIN INSTALLMENT SALE. The wraparound mortgage has a most important use that has nothing to do with leverage on rates or even its use as a marketing tool. When a property that has a very low basis is sold, there is a capital gain circumstance that can often be costly. If the owner of the property for sale has mortgages above the basis, simply to receive a sale, with no money down, can cause tax to be due. For example: Barkley owned a sizable office building for nearly twenty years. The current basis is only $50,000 even though the fair market value is over $500,000. He had placed new financing on the property a few years ago and currently owes $300,000 on it. He had a buyer willing to pay $500,000 with $100,000 down. Barkley determined that he would have a $425,000 adjusted gain in the sale and over $140,000 in capital gains tax. To make that sale would require him to come out-of-pocket over $40,000, plus fees, commissions, and other closing costs.

A wraparound mortgage was established in the amount of $400,000, payable over 20 years at a nominal interest rate. As Barkley was still on the mortgage and the buyer did not assume the liability, he was not relieved of that amount of debt. The income that came in over the term of the wraparound allowed Barkley to maintain an installment sale since he did not receive more than 30% in any year. The capital gains tax was still there, but now it was payable over the term as though a normal installment sale had taken place.

ADVANTAGES TO A BUYER OF PURCHASING WITH A WRAPAROUND

1. THE BEST TERMS IN TOWN.   The wraparound is so flexible that a high effective yield can be passed on to the mortgagee even though the buyer has a better rate and years than available elsewhere. The buyer saves on points, and when given no alternative of closing with assumption of the existing financing and the seller holding normal secondary paper, he or she will choose the wraparound. Of course, the wraparound can also offer better terms than assumption and secondary paper. If the existing financing has a low interest rate, but also a short term to go, the annual payment may be just about as high as the buyer can pay or the property can stand. To place on top of that a second mortgage of even the most modest annual payment may be more than either the buyer or the property will pay. The wraparound has the capability of having a very low retained interest on the difference. The build-up of the bonus and its later recoupment and greater yield are most unique to this form of financing. This factor can save many transactions that have a short balloon in one of the existing mortgages by having that mortgage amortized out of the total wraparound and carrying forward the new difference to a later year.

Many buyers are cash flow conscious. They don't really look to the term of the mortgage. A 20-year mortgage is just 10 years less than a 30-year mortgage. When an investor is looking at how much cash he or she gets now on the down payment, then the wraparound can keep the debt service at a more constant level, and often much lower than other forms of mortgages.

2. INCREASE CASH FLOW.   Because the wraparound can provide a lower total annual payment (even though over a longer term) than a combination of existing financing and secondary financing, the advantage to a buyer in the case of income property can be considerable. A property with a NOI of $20,000 and existing debt service of $15,000 provides a cash flow of $5,000. If the investor demands a 10% cash flow yield he or she can pay $50,000 cash to the existing financing. However, the seller may want $60,000 to the existing financing. If the combined cash down and balance owed is within the fair market value range and the seller is firm on the price, the wraparound can provide the answer. The question to answer here is: What total amount of wrap-

around, at what interest rate, for how long, will cover the existing mortgage and its constant annual payment? Assume that the amount is $100,000 at 8% for approximately 10 years, and as the annual payment is $15,000 the constant annual payment is 15%. Also assume that the investor will pay up to $45,000 cash down.

To find J, refer to annual constant percentage tables. Begin at same rate shown in Line I. Find constant nearest to but no greater than constant rate shown in Line G. Check years and find actual annual payment by multiplying constant rate found in column by amount of wraparound in Line C. Increase interest in increments of less than 1%, maintaining the same number of years or more as indicated on Line H, and a constant not more than that shown on Line G.

Any of the possible terms shown would offer a total debt service that would not exceed the maximum amount available for debt service (Line F). With a wraparound on these terms, the minimum cash flow yield demanded by the investor would be met, and at the same time the seller would have obtained the total asking price desired.

The seller would no doubt look to the maximum interest rate which would still offer the annual payment as shown. The 10% over 14 1/2 years would give the seller a greater overall effective yield than 8% over 12 years. The buyer would look to the smaller amount if he or she had a choice. When using this method, it is important to make sure that the annual payment on the existing debt service is met for the entire term of that mortgage. In a wraparound with only one existing mortgage, it is only necessary to keep the rate at or above that charged on the existing mortgage to accomplish this. If, however, you have a wraparound that encompasses several mortgages, using the highest rate on any existing one and the maximum terms on any other (even if they are not the same mortgage) will also accomplish this. It is possible to use an interest lower than the maximum rate on one of several existing mortgages, providing that the annual payment on the wraparound does not fall below the combined annual payment on the existing mortgages and the unpaid balance of the wraparound is equal to or larger than the declining balance of the existing financing. This will involve looking at the entire mortgage however, and if the first method (maximum rate and maximum years) is used this will automatically be accommodated.

A.	Minimum price	$160,000
B.	Maximum cash to invest	$ 45,000
C.	Amount to be held as wraparound	$115,000
D.	NOI	$ 20,000
E.	Cash return demanded (Line B × rate demanded)	$ 4,500
F.	Amount available for debt service	$ 15,500
G.	Constant annual payment percentage (Line F ÷ by Line C)	13.479%
H.	Minimum years possible (total years of remaining pay-out on existing mortgage)	10 years
I.	Nominal rate on highest existing mortgage	8%
J.	Possible terms	

	(1)	(2)	(3)	(4)
Nominal rate	8% (same as I)	8 3/4%	9 1/2%	10%
Years	12 years	12.5 years	13.5 years	14.5 years
Constant shown	13.270%	13.471%	13.450%	13.353%
Annual payment	$15,260.50	$15,491.65	$15,467.50	$15,355.96

3. EASE OF PAYMENT.   In multimortgaged property, nothing can be more annoying than to have to make several payments to different lenders each month. Keeping track of the amortization of each is a problem. With the wraparound however, the buyer has only one payment to make and can look to one amortization schedule. The form of payment is very important, as this is the area where most objections arise. Because the buyer does not directly make the payments on the existing mortgages, he or she may be most concerned that those payments will in fact be made. There have been many cases of wraparounds where the buyer faithfully made the monthly payment, only to find that the seller collecting payment did not pay any of the existing mortgages. This is a nasty situation, and people that have experienced it have been needlessly hurt.

PAYMENTS SHOULD ALWAYS BE MADE TO AN ESCROW ACCOUNT

When you set up a wraparound mortgage it is imperative that the payments on it be made to an escrow agency, or collection agency. The agency would then make the existing mortgage payments, collect for taxes and insurance, and disperse the balance to the mortgagee. This makes the maintenance of the wraparound relatively easy for all parties concerned, and assures the mortgagor that the existing payments which should go to the existing mortgages are made. This escrow agency, either a commercial bank, savings and loan association, or other third-party service, should be paid by the mortgagee, but it is not unusual that this cost is shared by the mortgagor as well.

HOW TO PROTECT THE MORTGAGOR AND THE MORTGAGEE IN THE ESCROW AGREEMENT

The escrow agent will only do as instructed, so it is important that he or she has complete and comprehensive instructions. The factors that need to be covered in this escrow agreement will be:

1. HOW THE FEE IS PAID FOR THE ESCROW SERVICE.   The escrow agent will normally deduct his or her fee from the amounts collected. If the mortgagor is sharing this cost, his portion of the fee must be added to the total wraparound payment.

2. COLLECTIONS FOR TAXES AND ESCROWS COVERED IN THE WRAP-
AROUND OR EXISTING MORTGAGES.   A first mortgage may have a constant
monthly payment added each year to the amortization which accrues annual taxes,
insurance, and other assessments. It is imperative that these provisions be made a part
of the wraparound document, and that the escrow agent be instructed to make those
payments as well. In the event of a future assessment, or changes in taxes or insurance
that would alter this escrow collection, the wraparound should provide for those
changes and the agent instructed on how to notify the mortgagor of these additions
or subtractions to the total payment.

3. PREPAYMENT PROVISIONS.   Careful analysis of prepayment provisions in
existing mortgages should be made and incorporated in the wraparound. The holder of
the wraparound should provide an equal pro-rata reduction of both the existing financing as well as the wraparound for all prepayments. For example: If the outstanding balance at the time of the prepayment is shown to be 80% to existing financing and 20%
to the difference, then the prepayment of $20,000 would be divided by that ratio. The
80% would then be prepaid to the holder of the existing financing. Of course, the entire
100% is reduced from the wraparound balance, and new calculations would occur. The
prepayment in full is the same as a balloon with regard to the effective yield rate.

4. GRACE PERIOD.   There should be a shorter grace period on the wraparound
than on the existing financing. This will assist in notification of default ahead of due
dates on the existing financing. When there is a very short grace period on any of the
existing financing, it may be desirable to allow a build-up on one period to accrue in
the escrow account in order to advance the lead time on default on the existing financing. For example: If a second mortgage has a 10-day grace period, the mortgagee may
find it to his or her advantage to allow collections, less disbursements, to build up to an
amount equal to one period payment on that second. If it is a monthly payment, then
the grace period allowed to the mortgagee is now one month plus 10 days.

5. AUTOMATIC FORECLOSURE BY UNDERLYING MORTGAGES.   In a multimortgaged property, the first mortgage may have a provision which provides that it will
automatically be in default and become subject to immediate foreclosure in the event
that any secondary lender file foreclosure proceedings. There is no real justification in
this, but some lenders have this provision in their loans. It is far more important that
the inferior loans have this provision, in the event the existing mortgagee or superior
mortgagees file foreclosure. As the mortgagee in the wraparound pays the existing mortgages, he or she knows when a default will occur. However, since the mortgagee has the
ability to make the existing payments on the existing mortgages, he or she can keep
them current even though the wraparound goes into default. Should the mortgagee file

foreclosure proceedings against the mortgagor, and should the existing mortgage have this automatic foreclosure provision in their loan, they too may file foreclosure, even though they are current. In this event, the escrow agent must be instructed not to file such proceedings without obtaining an agreement from the existing mortgage lenders that they will not file as long as they keep current. Most lenders, even if they have this provision of automatic foreclosure, will go along with such a request.

6. MAINTAIN INTEGRATED ACCOUNTS.   The escrow agent should keep one account for the funds. The account should be in the name of the mortgagee. If the agent is a bank or other lending institution with savings accounts or checking accounts, then all the funds collected should be paid into that account. Then the agent will pay out the funds required for the existing financing. Have your lawyer draw up this escrow agreement. It is a very important part of the wraparound process and is highly recommended. Naturally, this is not a necessity, yet to have a wraparound without collections made by a third party can be less than prudent for the mortgagor.

THE WRAPAROUND CAN PRESENT UNIQUE PROBLEMS FOR THE THIRD-PARTY LENDER

When a wraparound mortgage is given to a third-party lender, such as a commercial bank or mortgage company, some unique problems occur. Take this situation as an example: Midwest Central Bank examines a potential lending situation that will involve a wraparound mortgage. They have concluded that by lending new money to a buyer of property and wrapping around the existing mortgage they will leverage their yield to above 12%. Assume that the new money they lend is $100,000. At the end of the first year of the loan they will receive their total investment of $100,000 plus $12,000. The mortgage they are wrapping around has a one-time payment (shown as follows).

		Face amount	Rate	Term	Due at end of term
(1)	Existing mortgage	$400,000	7%	1 Year	$428,000
(2)	New money	100,000	?	1 Year	?
(3)	Wraparound total	$500,000	8%	1 Year	$540,000

Total principal and interest return on wraparound, End of 1st year	$540,000
Less total pay-out, 1st mortgage	428,000
Total principal and return on new money	112,000
Less original principal on new money	100,000
Total return on new money	$ 12,000
Effective rate of return on new money at end of 1st year	12%

The third-party lender has lent only $100,000 in this transaction. The lender has not had any obligation to pay the original first mortgage of $400,000. If he or she makes the wraparound loan with the existing owner and original mortgagor on the existing mortgage, or a new owner that has assumed the first mortgage, he or she is advancing only new money with no liability on the existing financing. Courts have contended that in these situations the return to the lender is 12% and if the sum is usurious the loan is not valid.

In the wraparound mortgages we have concluded it is possible to leverage a yield much higher than the 12% shown in this example. Nonetheless, in many states a 12% return may be usurious. Therefore, this examination of return must be considered a major problem for the third-party lender. The real advantages for a third-party lender are the leverage and the increased yield. If in making these loans the courts determine that usury is present, the loan can be null and void and the lender face loss of the sum lent and have a penalty placed on him or her as well.

The face rate of the wraparound is only 8%, well below usury in most states. But since the lender has no obligation to pay the existing financing, no risk as it were, the actual yield can be considered the effective rate of return.

HOW TO AVOID USURY ON WRAPAROUND LOANS BY THIRD PARTIES

The actual answer to this is not clearly defined by the courts. However, it does seem that if the third-party lender can place him- or herself in the same shoes, so to speak, as a seller holding a wraparound, then this problem can be averted. To do this will require the lender to assume the full obligation of the existing financing being wrapped around. When the lender has liability against the existing loans, then he or she may well be in the same position the seller would be in by holding the wraparound.

It is hoped that in the near future this matter of possible usury on third-party loans will be more clearly defined by the courts. In the meantime, third-party lenders must accept the advice of their legal advisors on this matter. There are numerous cases which have occurred in various states that indicate the above solution is perhaps the answer. But states may vary in this regard, so it is best to take a close look at what has happened in your state.

HOW TO CALCULATE INTEREST EARNED FOR ANNUAL INCOME ACCOUNTING

It is necessary to know how to account for interest earned in the wraparound for income tax purposes. In essence, the interest earned on the wraparound mortgages will be the interest to be reported as income. Deductions of interest to be reported as income and deductions of interest paid against the underlying existing mortgages will offset that total interest as long as the tax laws permit deduction of interest.

Total interest collected at end of 1st year on a $500,000 existing wraparound at 8% per year	$40,000
less	
Total interest paid out on existing mortgage, assuming a $400,000 existing mortgage at 7% per year	28,000
Net difference:	$12,000
Income to be reported	$40,000
Interest deduction	28,000
Taxable	$12,000

Note: Watch tax laws that may limit or remove interest deductions on real estate mortgages. If your situation is affected by such laws, then your use of the wraparound may be reduced.

HOW TO TELL IF A SITUATION IS IDEAL FOR A WRAPAROUND MORTGAGE

There will be definite signs which should indicate to you if a situation is right for the use of the wraparound mortgage. Your ability to recognize these signs will aid you in reaching the conclusion that the wraparound will help achieve the goals of your client. Listed below are some of the primary signs that you will encounter. At times they will present themselves alone, while at other times in combination with each other.

Signs That Indicate the Need for a Wraparound

1. EXISTING LOAN CONSTANT ANNUAL PAYMENT PERCENTAGE RELA-TIONSHIP TO MAXIMUM LOAN POTENTIAL.   Take a look at the total annual payment of the existing mortgages. Then find the constant payment percentage this represents of the total loan potential. If this constant is below a normal loan constant, you have a prime candidate for a wraparound. For example: The total loan payment on three existing mortgages is $15,000 per year starting the first year. The property is priced at $225,000, therefore a normal loan may be 80% of that amount or $180,000. The $15,000 existing loan payment represents 8.33% of the total loan potential. A look at constants available in the market for new money may show as 11% annual constant to be reasonable. The spread of 2.67% in constants for the first year is tremendous. In fact, a spread of only 0.5% would be sufficient to warrant a further look to see if the wraparound would be desirable. If you find that the constant annual payment on the existing financing is higher than the present market constant, a wraparound may not be effective.

2. A FORCED WRAPAROUND.   If you have existing financing that cannot be assumed and a refinancing of the property is not possible due to market conditions or economic cost, then the wraparound sign is very strong.

3. REINVESTMENT GOAL OF THE SELLER.   The leverage gained on the yield may be most attractive to the seller, and could be a primary sign that the wraparound should be considered. Keep in mind that the constant spread indicated in the first item (previous) should be favorable for the leverage to occur.

HOW TO USE THE WRAPAROUND TO MAKE MORE SALES

You should have a good understanding for what the wraparound will do, should do, and can do. The ability to take this tool and apply it to the selling of property will depend on whether you can sell the concept to the parties involved. The proficiency with which you accomplish this will therefore depend on how comfortable you feel in dealing with this tool. I suggest that the first step is to take several properties you presently have listed and restructure the existing financing via wraparound to see what happens to their marketability. If you see that you can offer a property with better financing and increase the cash flow, you are on the way to having a better inventory and making more sales.

You will have only relative difficulty in selling this concept to the buyer. After all, this depends on the alternatives offered. If he or she can buy with the wraparound, instead of conventional financing, and the wraparound offers better terms than the present market, then the buyer will go with it.

The seller must also see the advantages it has to offer the buyer. This chapter has given you all the ammunition to make that part of the sale easier than it might have been otherwise.

The wraparound is a fine tool in the hands of the real estate broker or associate. It is most effective as a selling tool, and while third-party loans may become more frequent in the future, the major lenders will continue to shy away from this format. Do not let that aspect dismay you however, since the third-party lender has problems that are unique to the wraparound that the seller does not have. Unfortunately, however, the power third parties exert in the lending area has been to hold down wider use of the wraparound by sellers and brokers.

Remember: The wraparound is merely a tool. It has limitations and drawbacks. The return to the mortgagee is often postponed until the future, and though the yield is leveraged upward, the funds may not be available for use when they are needed. This factor should be considered as the major disadvantage to the wraparound from a seller's point of view.

Chapter 11

HOW A SALE-LEASEBACK WORKS FOR BOTH BUYER AND SELLER

Definition

A *sale-leaseback* is the sale of an interest in realty and the subsequent leasing back of that same realty.

Example

Frank owns a hardware store. He is doing very well with the business, but needs capital to expand. He owns the real estate as well as the business, so he decides to sell the property, land and building, to generate the needed capital, and to lease this property back.

The sale-leaseback is one of the best tools to use in generating capital from real estate, either to support a sales price, or when the actual use is more important than ownership. This form of financing starts as a sale. The seller then agrees to lease back the property being sold. Sometimes this leaseback can merely be a move to entice the buyer into the transaction. In its most effective use, the sale-leaseback is a technique that allows the seller to generate capital by selling the property, but allows the seller to maintain the use of the property.

The property being sold can be all of the property. This means it can be land and buildings, or it may be just the buildings or just the land. Each aspect of the sale-leaseback can have different long-range results, depending on what portion of the realty is sold and then leased back.

The goal of this chapter is to show you how to use this important technique, as both a buyer and a seller.

HOW TO STRUCTURE THE LAND LEASEBACK

The most basic of the sale-leaseback is when the land only is the subject of the lease-back. It is very common in many parts of the world to have leased land under many types of buildings. These land leases generally began with a sale to one party, who then leases the land back to the seller. Over the years the owners of the leasehold change, but the lease remains in effect. Naturally, all leases are unique and it is rare that any two leases will have identical terms and conditions. As with any contract, just about everything is open for negotiation. This gives both parties to the agreement flexibility in tailoring the terms and conditions to fit very specific goals.

In all leasebacks of the land, the fee simple title to the realty does not belong to the lessee. All the lessee owns is the leasehold interest. If the leasehold is later sold, the interest passed on is merely the remainder rights in the underlying lease. Keep in mind that some leases may contain provisions that limit this transferability, and it is possible that a new owner may not have all of the rights that the original lessee had. Also, if the previous lessee was in default, or in any way caused a breach in the lease contract, there may be no rights to be transferred.

Fee simple title is the absolute of any real estate interest. A leasehold interest is less than this, and can create difficulties for the lessee to obtain other or additional financing. Some lenders will make leasehold loans, provided the terms of the lease meet their lending criteria.

THE SUBORDINATION FACTOR IN A LAND LEASE

Subordination is an event where one person gives up certain rights to another. In mortgages this takes many different forms. A simple example is when a seller takes a purchase money mortgage (second, or wraparound), and allows the buyer to put a new first mortgage ahead of this secondary financing. In land leases, the lessor (owner of the land) agrees to subordinate the fee simple right to the land by allowing the lessee to pledge the title to the land as security to financing.

This can be an essential part of any land lease, because many lenders will not lend on leased land without the title being subordinated to the mortgage. For good reasons, many land owners are reluctant to lease land to someone who requires the title to be subordinated to new financing. Nonetheless, there are thousands of subordinated land leases in the United States and for the most part they are viable transactions. However, there can be substantial risk for a property owner to give up first position right to the title. This chapter will show you these risks and steps you can take to lessen them.

When a lessee decides to develop a property he or she is leasing, there will be five points to follow to obtain development funds:

1. Use all cash with no lien.
2. Obtain a loan without property as the security.
3. Find a lender who will treat the leasehold as a fee simple.
4. Obtain a loan with something else as security.
5. Get the owner of the property to agree to subordinate to the required financing.

Taking the first solution, many builders do just that. They build with their own cash. It may be they have leased the land with options to purchase, and so they build without having to lay out the cash needed to buy the land. They pay the nominal rent during construction, and later when the building is finished, obtain a mortgage, pay off the land by exercising an option to buy, and move on to another project. This is done in single-family housing where the builder can and does build the house quickly, and then sells it before many of the outstanding bills on it come due. In those cases, the overall cash outlay by the developer is not as great as if he or she had bought the land for cash.

The second situation requires the lessee to find a lender who will make the loan without taking the real estate (either leasehold interest or fee simple interest) as security. This kind of loan is possible to find, depending on the amount of the loan, and the strength of the borrower. It may be possible to pledge a chattel; that is, give the lender a lien right against something that is not real estate. This might be inventory, or other assets. Any such loans would have no lien against the real estate.

The third situation is more likely, if the lease warrants it. There are lenders who approach the leasehold interest as being similar to fee simple. In some areas of the world, a long-term lease of such a time period as to be beyond the normal life span of the building planned, may be accepted as being the same as completed ownership. Some leases that have been in effect for many years have such reasonable lease terms that it is less expensive to lease the property than it would be to buy it.

Example

One good example of this is a tract of land that is located under an ocean front hotel in Fort Lauderdale. The lease was originally a 99-year lease, initiated in 1961. At the time the lease was negotiated, the value of the property was around $250,000. The lessor, thinking he or she was very smart, set the rent at $30,000 per year. After all, 99 years at this rent would total $2,970,000. Now, with a long time still to go, the rent is still only $30,000 per year. The annual real estate tax on the hotel is over $100,000. Even without subordination, it would not be difficult to find a lender willing to take this leasehold interest as security for the loan. While this fixed lease term was not uncommon in the 1960s, most leases drawn today have provisions to index the payment to a cost of living.

The fourth solution is to put some other real estate up as security for a loan. This may be a combination such as a blanket mortgage where you would pledge your leasehold interest together with some other property. In a pyramid loan, which will be discussed in Chapter 13, the borrower is constantly generating capital from one property to buy or improve another.

The fifth solution is the principal topic of this chapter, subordination. When you can get it, the ability to raise capital is improved. Your chance of convincing the lessor that his or her risk is warranted may depend on your financial strength or the combined strength of you plus a coguarantor. The introduction of a coguarantor into the picture is what makes land leases popular for many different types of businesses that do not need to own their real estate. Fast food franchise restaurants, for example, are one of these kinds of businesses. While this is a risky business, the solid players are able to substantiate that it is worthwhile for a property owner to lease the ground to a franchisee, or an investor who is going to build for that franchisee. The Franchiser becomes a coguarantor to the lease.

LEASEHOLD VERSUS FEE SIMPLE VALUES

Unlike the creation of a normal lease, whether it is land or buildings, the sale-leaseback is unique. The previous owner, or fee owner, becomes the leasehold owner. It is this change of ownership which makes the sale-leaseback both dangerous and quite often rewarding.

A lease is accompanied by a rent, and the value of the lease is based on the ability of the lessee to pay the rent or the security he or she offers to support that ability to pay the rent. If the tenant, or lessee, fails to pay the rent, and the security is not sufficient to support the economic base of the property until another lessee can be found, the lease may then become worthless. Of even more consequence, it may cost the lessor money to get the tenant out of the property.

If the building is a single-purpose structure and the tenant not very strong, then the ultimate ability to pay the lease and the possible long delay in finding another tenant could reflect on the value of the fee simple. An existing lease runs with the land, and a new buyer accepts the tenant on the remaining terms of the lease. The property may be worth $100,000, but if there is a 20-year lease at $3,000 per annum the value is not $100,000, due to the effect of the rent return. Also, if the rent were $10,000, but the tenant is always late with payment, the value may not be substantiated.

ESTABLISHING THE LEASEHOLD VALUE

The terms and conditions of the lease establish the value of the leasehold. It is clear, for example, that two identical parking lots, side by side on leased land, will have values depending on the terms of the underlying land leases. The parking lot which has an annual rent of $1,000 will be of far more value as a leasehold than the one which has an annual rent of $2,000. In reverse, the owner of the lots will find the lease which returns $1,000 per year is less valuable than the one which returns $2,000 per year. What is shown here is the variable between value of the lease and value of the leasehold. It is important, then, to distinguish these two values in each sale-leaseback situation. The sale-leaseback creates both events: the previous owner of the fee becomes a tenant and now owns a leasehold interest, and the new buyer becomes a lessor and owns the property.

HOW TO DETERMINE WHEN THE LEASEBACK IS EFFECTIVE

The sale-leaseback is used in these situations:

1. When the use of the property has more value than owning the property.
2. To substantiate the value of the fee by creating a fixed return.
3. The need for capital makes the leaseback more economical than other forms of financing.

These three situations cover a lot of territory, and from a practical point of view, the latter two will be seen more often in real life. However, a quick look at the three gives some insight as to the use of the two aspects of this form: the value of the fee and the value of the leasehold.

WHEN THE VALUE OF THE USE EXCEEDS THE VALUE OF OWNING

When you own a property, you have all the usual rights, including expenses and the potential loss of value if the property declines in worth. If you have a long-term lease on the property your obligations are only those described in the lease. Often there is a value to the lease that is created by improvements made by the lessee, or the relative cheapness of the lease. This is called *leasehold equity.*

Example

You have a $10,000 a year lease on a property that is now worth $500,000. This rent is cheap to that value, so your leasehold equity is considerable. If money was worth 8%, the $10,000 lease would be a return on $125,000 in the bank. Subtract this amount from the real value of the property and your leasehold equity or value is somewhere around $375,000 depending on the term of the lease. If the lease terminated in a short period, the leasehold value would be less.

Example

A case history illustrates this point. Kayser had a small restaurant. He owned the land and building free and clear. He wanted to start another restaurant across town, but found he did not have sufficient capital to do this. Naturally, he looked to the normal forms of financing to raise this capital, so he visited the local banks and savings and loans. Even though his past record was good, he found that new restaurants are not easily financed because they are costly to start up. He did find that he could obtain new financing, up to a point, but the balance must be cash out of his pocket. Kayser counseled with his broker and discovered he could approach an investor to buy his present restaurant to create the new capital. His options on a leaseback showed he could set up a sale-leaseback on the land, or the buildings, or both. The final decision would depend on capital needed, on the value of the property, and the rent he was able to pay.

The value of the land was $135,000. This was based on other similar properties in the area. The buildings had been appraised at $200,000. The new restaurant Kayser was planning was expected to cost about $400,000.

Kayser was sure he could support an overall debt service of $35,000 to $45,000 in annual payments with ease, once the second restaurant was built and operating. At present, he was making a good living from the first restaurant by taking home around $90,000 per year. He expected to make the same, or more, from the second one.

If Kayser were able to sell his first restaurant for $300,000 and lease it back on a net-net lease (he has to pay all maintenance, taxes, insurance, and so on, as well as the lease payments), he should easily be able to borrow the remainder on the new property to finish the construction and provide working capital.

The broker knew that an investor would be inclined to buy the first restaurant since it had a good track record, and Kayser would be, after all, leasing the property back at a good return to the investor. That return, by the way, is subject to good, hard negotiation. There are many factors on which to bargain in sale-leaseback, and the buyer and seller can find much to negotiate on before the final transaction is signed and closed.

For Kayser, the value of owning has taken second place to the value of use of the property. As long as he has control of the restaurant, it may not make much difference if he owns or leases. His leasehold value becomes more apparent after he leases. In this case the leaseback was $30,000 per year, based on a sale at $300,000 as Kayser was netting $90,000 before the lease. The $60,000 he will net after the lease becomes the factor in establishing the economic value of the leasehold. As restaurants have an investor demand yield of about 15 to 20%, the leasehold value is from $300,000 to $400,000. (Invest $400,000 and get a $60,000 return means your yield is 15%). The investor has this leasehold value as additional collateral on the lease, as long as the business is good and Kayser can pay the rent.

HOW TO SUBSTANTIATE THE VALUE OF THE FEE BY CREATING A FIXED RETURN

In this event, Kayser might not want to build another restaurant at all. The fact of the matter could be that business is off, and for the past year the best he was able to take home was $40,000. In this situation, he may want to get cash out of the property for other reasons.

To substantiate the value of $300,000 on the sale, he agrees to lease the property back on a long-term lease. That pleases the investor, until the lease becomes worthless when Kayser goes off to another state to run a bar. Of course, the title to Kayser's new bar is in his wife's name.

This would not be a laughing matter to the lender who was pulled into the deal with the promise of making a great return on the sale-leaseback. When the seller becomes the tenant, the motives of the sale should be very carefully inspected. If the seller tells you that he or she needs the capital to make improvements, then it would be a good idea to tie the funds to that end use. This can be done through an escrow account set up with a lawyer or escrow or title company. They would release the money directly to the contractor doing the improvements, or to the seller when he produces paid bills.

HOW TO USE THE SALE-LEASEBACK WHEN OTHER FORMS OF FINANCING ARE MORE COSTLY

If the money market will support your financial needs at reasonable rates through more conventional forms of mortgaging, there may be no need to look elsewhere. However, due to any number of circumstances, a reasonable or sufficient loan may not be available.

Specialty types of real estate fall into categories that many lenders will shy away from, or at best they'll quote high interest rates and low loan-to-value amounts. The combined effect of insufficient restructure of existing debt and high constant payments on the borrowed funds may put the borrower in deeper trouble than that in which he currently finds himself.

During this same time when the money market is tight, interest rates tough, and loans low or nonexistent, there may be a solution via the sale-leaseback. Your ability to determine the effectiveness of the sale-leaseback will require you to examine the effect the two forms available have on the situation.

For example: Lloyd has a used car lot. He makes a good living from this business, but finds he needs cash to expand his inventory. He has approached a local lender and has found he can borrow only 75% of what he needs by placing a first mortgage on the property. Besides the insufficient sum of money available, there is a high point cost and interest is set at five points above prime.

On the other hand, a sale-leaseback may produce 100% or more of the cash needed at an overall interest rate that is lower than that charged by the lender. As Lloyd needs the property and has substantial records to show he can support the rent, he may, out of necessity, move in the direction of the sale-leaseback to solve his problems. He recognized that his ability to earn money on the input of new capital is greater than the cost of the land lease. As long as he has a prudent leaseback from his long-term growth, he will make this move.

Of course, he will be forced to look to some other form of financing, or capital seeking, if he cannot raise the money in the conventional money market. However, Lloyd should seek conventional sources as possible alternatives to his problem, if for no other reason than as a comparison to the sale-leaseback.

There Is a Risk in the Leaseback

There are valid reasons for the leaseback. But the risk involved, due to the value adjustments, requires buyers to be rather cautious of overstated values of the fee or of the leasehold.

It is possible for the seller to substantiate the value of the fee by creating the fixed return with a minimum of risk to the buyer. This can be accomplished with lease insurance. The insurance will cover the rent in default should the seller/tenant get into trouble. What could be a bad deal can become a "Triple A" transaction.

AS SEEN FROM THE PROPERTY OWNER'S POINT OF VIEW, THE VALUE OF ALL LEASES WILL DEPEND ON THE FOLLOWING EIGHT FACTORS

1. **The guarantor to the lease.** Who or what is he, she or it? What are the past record, financial backing, and motivation? Will they sign personally? Put up corporate backing, a coguarantor? If not, why not?

2. **The use.** Has it been successful? Is the operation well run, managed, and staffed? Is there a future for the present use? Does the use present unusual hazards to the property? Does the use limit the function and flexibility of the property?

3. **Lease conditions.** The term of years: too long or too short? Who pays taxes, utilities, assessments, repairs, maintenance, and other property costs? Is there a provision for increasing the rent due to cost of living increases? What other provisions can affect the future return to the owner (options, provisions for cancellations, and so on)?

4. **The performance.** What is the record of the lessee in making rent payments? In new leases, this is a big unknown and only time will tell. What do other landlords say about this tenant?

5. **The property.** Is the economic life of the property beyond that of the term of the lease? If so, the fact that a new tenant must someday be found or the same tenant enticed to stay can cause a problem in the future. Is the location suitable for the present tenant? Is the tenant suffering because of the property or the location?

6. **Fee versus leasehold.** There must be a real value in both. The greater the value in the leasehold, the greater the security for the lessor. In the sale-leaseback, this apparent value in the leasehold should be carefully examined.

7. **Has the title been subordinated to tenant financing?** The terms of such subordination can reduce the risk to the tenant, and at the same time generate considerable risk for the owner. Elements to be watchful for: Does the subordination extend to multiple events? If so, then future new financing can be even more risky than original financing. Can the tenant divide financing over separate parts of the property? This can create a nightmare for the owner of the fee simple.

8. **How salable or leasable is the facility if the tenant leaves?** This can be very important because all of the items, one through seven can come through very positive in favor of making the lease. Often a property is modified by either the owner or the tenant in such a way as to make the use undesirable to another owner or tenant without substantial reinvested capital. If this is the situation, then one or more of the first seven items must counterbalance this aspect.

The value of the lease depends heavily on the use and the user. Artificial value can be generated in the leasehold by the lessee. This artificial value is, in essence, a burden to the property and results from pushing this form of financing.

THE NEED FOR CAPITAL

Need necessitates action, and a need for capital is generally the reason for the sale-leaseback. There are many more favorable forms of financing, if they can be obtained in the market. For example, there is no real reason why a seller who wants to use the property should take a sale-leaseback transaction, unless the economics of accepting another form are onerous or unavailable.

However, this does not make the sale-leaseback the last resort, and it should not be considered as a step down from something not available or economically unsound. It can be highly advantageous to the seller. If the seller cannot borrow the necessary funds and he needs the use of the property for economic reasons, then the sale-leaseback can solve these problems.

ADVANTAGES AND DISADVANTAGES OF THE SALE-LEASEBACK

Here are the advantages and disadvantages as they apply to both the seller and the buyer:

The Seller

Advantages	Disadvantages
1. Allows the seller to retain use of the property.	1. A seller gives up many benefits of ownership of improvements and land.
2. Allows the seller to negotiate the amount of the rent by offsetting the sale price.	2. Future appreciation of land usually lost completely.
3. Often, the terms of the lease are more flexible in the leaseback.	3. Leasehold value has a shorter life than the property.
4. Can firm up the price and value.	4. A decline in leasehold value can be a total loss.
5. Gives flexibility to difficult transactions since the land and improvements can be separated.	
6. As the seller is the ultimate tenant, he or she has great strength in dealing on the leaseback.	
7. Can provide capital when all else fails.	

The Buyer

Advantages	Disadvantages
1. Can provide an excellent tenant.	1. Either the price or the rent will be to the seller's advantage; often both.
2. Offers some flexibility in price vs. rent negotiations.	2. Too hard a push on the seller may give you an investment without a tenant.
3. In the case of unsubordinated land: (a) low risk investment, (b) future recoupment of improvements, and (c) appreciation.	3. A leaseback by a nonuser may be a good sign that the income won't support the value.
4. If very carefully examined and secured, can offer an excellent investment potential.	4. May have to step into a large mortgage to protect his or her interest.

To these advantages and disadvantages you can apply most pro-and-con aspects of any lease. One thing is definite, however. The sale-leaseback is more complicated than it appears on the surface. It requires good, sound legal advice and possible tax consideration. A buyer should never enter into a sale-leaseback, unless there is absolute confidence that the transaction is beneficial to both parties. It is far too easy for the seller to boost the value of the property with this form of financing and take advantage of some buyer, not aware of the potential danger. Be sure you understand the pros and cons of the leaseback before you establish that transaction.

This form of financing has a place in real estate. It is used in commercial realty and other forms of development, land planning, and, of course, industrial realty. Lenders find it an ideal tool for securing their position in large development loans. Here the lender may take a land lease under a project he or she is financing, participating in the overall project to the degree that he or she will always own the land. In many cases, the developer may buy the land back in the future at an escalated price. Since the lender may not be extending more funds than he or she would have on just a development loan, the lender exercises a strong advantage over the seller.

Yet the seller may not fare too badly either, and can cash out ahead of the project and still own the improvements. The cost of carrying the land and paying the portion of debt service that applies to the land lease will never retire any principal, and the ratio of constant to remaining balance will increase faster than in a mortgage without a land lease.

Many public corporations find that ownership of real estate can be less attractive than the use of the property. This is generally a tax consideration and may not be actual long-term benefits. When a public company is trying to boost earnings, it often gets rid of depreciable assets that reduce those earnings on paper.

HOW TO SET UP THE SALE-LEASEBACK

When you are sure the sale-leaseback is the proper way to go, carefully examine the two values involved: The fee simple and the leasehold value.

There will be some flexibility in the adjustment of these two values. This adjustment may have tax-saving results. For example, if the seller has a low base it may be possible to set a price which is near that base, and reduce the rent the seller will pay in the leaseback to offset the reduced price. Remember, the lower the rent paid by the seller the higher the value of the leasehold. Naturally, you cannot reduce the price to a point that is below the market value just to save on taxes. However, there is usually ample room in which to work in order to provide some flexibility in these negotiations.

It may be in the seller's best interest to attempt to establish the lowest value on the sale to reduce gains tax. The rent paid later on the lower base can, over a few years, make up the reduced sales price. On the other hand, if the capital gained from the sale is not sufficient, then the higher price, even with the tax, may be more prudent. Because the sale-leaseback can justify a higher price, the spread in the low-to-high value will be greater than in a normal sale. This high value is said to be somewhat artificial and warranted only on the basis of the leaseback.

Negotiating a Lower Price

This occurs because the buyer recognizes that he or she is buying at a good price and can adjust income accordingly. The buyer should realize that reduced rent and soft terms for annual rent increases increase the value of the leasehold interest for the tenant. In relative terms, these terms may be required to get the tenant in the first place, and if that is the case, do not reduce the value of the property. However, very long terms that favor the tenant can have a great effect on future appreciation of the owner's interest. Yet, from the initial point of view, if the tenant has a high equity in the leasehold, the owner of the property will be more secure in the transaction. This can be a very important tradeoff in the negotiations of a long-term lease. For this reason early concessions that entice the tenant into the property can pay off later. In the sale-leaseback, the concessions are part of the negotiation in the transaction. Assume the seller (and soon-to-be tenant), is asking $500,000 for a property and he or she then wants to lease it back for $50,000 per year, plus taxes, insurance and maintenance. If you push to get higher rent that may look attractive from your yield point of view, all that does is reduce the leasehold value, and put the tenant in a position where he or she might start looking for another place to rent. A better approach would be to try to buy for less, but give the tenant an even better deal than he or she was offering.

One approach is to let the tenant have prepaid rent or discounted rent as part of the deal. For example, instead of the $500,000 asking, you offer $400,000 with the initial four years rent to be graduated, with the first year at $10,000, the second at $25,000, the third at $30,000 and the fourth at $35,000. Year five can have a cost of living adjustment to bring it up to around $50,000 or so. If you analyze this you will discover the end results to be much the same as if you had paid $500,000 with an annual rent of $50,000. However, now you get in for less gross price, and let the tenant have an easy time.

A buyer will find that the maximum security he can have on a leaseback is the lease insurance. This type of insurance is obtained by the tenant and insures the lessor in the event the lessee fails to pay his rent. It is not easily obtained, however, and is not used too often in sale-leaseback situations. But if the buyer wants the utmost in security, then this type of insurance will provide it.

If only the land is being leased and there is no subordination, the risk to the buyer is limited. If the price for the land is realistic and not inflated, then the buyer has a sound investment. There would be little reason to consider insurance with this type of transaction. In limited subordination, where the lessee has the right to put on a mortgage of limited proportions, the buyer will find his or her security waning. The amount of the mortgage, a percentage to the value of the property, will establish the value of the security. Should the leaseback carry full subordination, the risk to the buyer will be predicated on: (1) the success of the property, and (2) the ability of the lessee to pay the rent.

The buyer should realize that in the sale-leaseback the lessee may have made a profit, and may have no actual equity in the property or the leasehold. In this event, the loss to the lessee in a failure to perform on the lease may be small.

We have seen two values. The fee simple and the leasehold. In fact, there may be three values. The third value is the value of the business itself. A retail shop, for example, may have a business value not dependent on the exact location or improvements. If the lessee can move the business with ease and retain its value, the security to the buyer is reduced unless he or she ties the lessee into the lease more stringently.

The ability of the seller-tenant to move the business does not in itself reduce the buyer's security. However, unless the improvements are single purpose the new owner may find it difficult to rent the space should the leaseback tenant fail on the lease for some reason. The best security for the buyer in the sale-leaseback will always be extreme caution.

Sale-Leaseback Highlights

What it will do:	1. Generate cash.
	2. Provide terms on a lease to suit the lessee.
When to use it:	1. When value of use exceeds value of ownership.
	2. To substantiate value of fee.
	3. When borrowing to raise capital is not economically effective or available.
What to look for:	1. Seller who has successful use of property.
	2. A use that is potentially successful, but may need either time or capital or both.
Negotiating points:	1. Term of lease.
	2. Sale price.
	3. Other options, such as: (a) subordination, (b) recapture of ownership, (c) subdivision of property to separate lease (land or improvements).
Danger to seller:	1. Gives up advantages of ownership.
	2. Loses future appreciation of property.

Chapter 12

THE LAST LOOPHOLE TO BUILD WEALTH:

Real-Estate Exchanges

The whole idea of swapping something you don't want for something else is the magic of this century. It is kind of like a game of dice that always comes up seven, or taking one unopened box instead of another unopened box. It is American. It is everything you ever thought magic could be. Best of all, for the true insider real-estate investor it is a way to build wealth, beat the IRS at their own game, and change the Buyers Market, when you are a seller, into your own personal avenue to the bank.

Definition

If you enter into an agreement to trade a property you own, for all or part of the equity in another property, you have accomplished a real-estate exchange.

Example

Fred owns a residential lot in North Carolina that he purchased on a whim ten years ago and has not seen since. A local real-estate broker in North Carolina said the lot is worth around $55,000. What Fred wants to own is a small strip shopping center near his home in Naples, Florida. The center is on the market for $250,000 and is free and clear. The center is run down, but Fred knows that if he fixes it up, mostly cosmetic changes, he can improve the rent and double the value of the center in a couple of years.

Fred offers the seller the following: $195,000 cash plus the free and clear lot in North Carolina. Because the seller's primary goal has been reached, that is, to sell the center and get a lot of cash at the same time, the deal is accepted. Fred gives the seller the lot, and borrows the $195,000 plus fix-up money for the center, from a local savings and loan association. Fred has entered the ranks of real-estate exchangers.

Several interesting things could have been incorporated into this deal. First of all, Fred might have asked the seller to hold a small second mortgage (behind the new first Fred was going to get); this would have freed up additional capital for Fred to use on the fix up of the center, or to use elsewhere. Fred could have asked the seller to hold a land lease under the center, subordinated to a new first mortgage, which would have freed up even more capital.

THERE ARE DIFFERENT KINDS OF REAL-ESTATE EXCHANGES: SOME ARE TAX FREE

The Internal Revenue Service looks at real-estate exchanges from several different points of view. Under some circumstances the exchange takes place without any gains tax being paid on the transaction. Take a look at the following exchanges as defined by the IRS. An exchange where the IRS gives no preference or tax breaks would be any exchange of property that did not fit into one of the following two exchanges:

1. IRC 1034. The exchange where you sell one residence and buy another. This kind of exchange is rather simple. If you sell a primary residence that meets certain requirements which will be outlined later on in this chapter, and within a qualified time period, buy another home, it is possible that any gain you have in the initial sale will not be taxable at that time. You can use the IRC 1034 rules and benefits in a direct one-on-one exchange of one residence for another, and skip the sale and purchase steps. This works if the owner of the residence you want is willing to take your house. I will give you more on this in a couple of pages.

2. IRC 1031. This is the last loophole left to real estate investors. This type of exchange is the subject of this chapter, and specifically is a technique that every real estate investor should know and understand. Internal Revenue Code 1031 provides that under specific circumstances a real estate transaction may be closed whereby a capital gain will not be taxable at the time of the closing. In fact, if the deal is handled properly, any tax on the gain can be postponed indefinitely.

NOT ALL EXCHANGES PRODUCE TAX BENEFITS

Not every real-estate exchange is beneficial. This also means that not all such exchanges will produce tax benefits, even if the property in question would qualify for either the IRC 1034 or the IRC 1031 rules. To benefit from either 1034 or 1031 you must have a potential taxable gain in the event of a sale. If your home has not gone up in value, and you sell it, there is no taxable gain. If your investment property has gone down in value, and you have not depreciated the asset more than this decline in value, and you have not borrowed more than the depreciated basis, then there would be no gain. But take note, just because you might not have a taxable gain, does not mean that the exchange would be without benefits. There are other benefits from a real-estate exchange. This chapter will show you how to maximize those benefits.

Review the IRC 1034 Exchange

Keep in mind that Internal Revenue Code 1034 does not require you to make an actual property-for-property exchange, but in more general terms, this rule does apply to your swap of one home (your personal residence) for another. This actual transaction can be a one-on-one exchange, where Able takes Baker's property and vice versa. Or it can be a combination of exchanges where Able sells his home, then a short while later, buys a home from Baker.

To qualify under IRC 1034 the transaction must meet the following rules and restrictions.

IRC 1034: Your Present Principal Residence for Another

This provision of the Internal Revenue Code deals with the replacement of your primary or legal residence. This can be by way of a sale, or an exchange. The following are highlights to this type of transaction.

1.   The property that qualifies will be your *old residence* which is your primary residence at the time you consummate the transaction of either selling your existing residence or acquiring another. By law you can have only one legal or primary residence at any given time. If you own two or more residences you will have to chose which is your primary one. The time you spend in one or the other is not the primary criteria in this respect.

Normally the sale of the existing residence occurs before the purchase of the new residence. However, many people buy a new home prior to selling the old one. The rules of IRC 1034 allow you a time span of forty-eight months to make this election. This period of time is divided into twenty-four months prior to the sales date of your old residence or twenty-four months after you sell your primary residence to make this election. The point in time when this twenty-four months begins or ends, is called the sales date. There are several exceptions to this twenty-four month period (total of forty-eight months). These exceptions are for people who, after selling their primary residence, reside outside the United States, or who are in the U.S. military. These rules are not easily explained, and can undergo special extensions in the event of war and other military conflict. If you are about to sell your primary residence and go into the military or move outside the United States, then check with a good CPA to see how the rule may affect you.

2.   The *sales date* is the date you actually transfer title of your old residence to a buyer (or a new owner if you exchanged the property rather than sold it). This date should not be confused with the *contract date* which is the date you and the other party comes to a meeting of the minds to sign an agreement of sale or exchange.

3.   The *new residence* is the place you plan to call your legal or tax residence. Because of the twenty-four-month rule, you can buy this residence twenty-four months prior to selling your previous residence or twenty-four months after selling your primary residence.

A critical aspect with this rule that many people fail to consider is what happens if you currently own two or more residences, say, one in New York and the other in Florida, and you plan to sell your existing primary residence and move to the other one. If your primary residence is in New York, and you purchased the Florida second home more than twenty-four months prior to selling the New York home, then you will not be able to use the 1034 provision. This is significant if the Florida home cost you as much or more than the *adjusted sales price* of the New York property, because any gain on the New York property would be sheltered by the Florida property if it fell within the 24-month period. In any situation where you cannot meet the twenty-four months rule, you need to get good tax advice from your CPA.

There are steps you can take to save on taxes. For example, you make your technical move to the Florida residence sooner. Make the New York residence a secondary investment, which you rent out prior to selling. Or you enter into a lease-option with the prospective buyer. Done properly, you can shift this property from the category of a residence to an investment property. This will allow you to utilize an IRC 1031 exchange for some future investment to move your potential gain and avoid the tax on that gain at this time. Both the old and new residences may include a houseboat, a house trailer or mobile home, an apartment, either condominium or stock in a cooperative, and any of the aforementioned that is a part of something else.

4.   The time you make the election to take advantage of the IRC 1034 is the taxable year during which you dispose of your old residence. If you have not purchased a new residence by the time you need to file your taxes for that year, you should obtain an extension. If you use up your allowed extension-to-file time and still have not purchased a new residence, then you may be required to pay the gains tax, and to make adjustments once you actually acquire the new residence. If you fail to do that within the twenty-four months after the sales date (or extended period if you resided out of the U.S. or were in the military), then you lose the opportunity to use the 1034 for any tax benefits it might have for you.

5.   The adjusted sale price for 1034 transactions is slightly different from adjustments for regular real estate transactions and gains calculations. The adjusted

sale price is an important calculation in the final establishment of the new tax basis in the new residence. Most sellers overlook the requirements to this important rule, and thereby lessen the benefits this internal revenue code provides. In essence, there are certain expenses that can be deducted from the contract price to arrive at the price against which a gain or loss can be determined. To qualify for the allowed deductions, the fix-up expenses must meet these conditions:

- All work accomplished must occur no later than ninety days from the date you enter into a sales contract.

- The expenses must not be otherwise deductible in computing taxable income. This means that any expenses to fix up or improve the cosmetics and repair of the properties that would not be capital expenses which increase the tax basis, are included.

- Are not to be considered normal selling expenses, such as lawyers fees to handle the closing, and so on. *Note:* these fees are normal selling fees that are separate from fix-up costs.

Take note that the hardest of all of these is the ninety-days-prior-to-sale rule. This is nearly impossible for a seller to anticipate, and unless the actual work done follows the initial buyer's offer, timing this to within a ninety-day period is tough.

Example

TWO SEPARATE 1034 TRANSACTIONS: OLD HOMES FOR NEW HOMES It will be helpful for you to follow the step by step procedure to calculate the benefits and new tax basis of these two separate 1034 transactions.

THE FIRST TRANSACTION   Charles wanted to sell his home, which cost him $250,000 seven years earlier. During his ownership he made capital improvements to the home at a cost of $50,000. To get the home ready for a sale, he made some major fix-up improvements at a total cost of $25,000. He paid for the work on March 1.

On May 29 Charles enters into a contract to sell the home for $495,000. The contract provides that Charles pays the broker's commission of $30,000 and all other closing costs that will total an additional $15,000.

After traveling around for a few months, Charles finds a nice apartment he would like to purchase. It is on the market for $600,000.

THE SECOND TRANSACTION   Francis sold her Park Avenue apartment which had cost her $150,000 for $850,000. She moved to Florida to live in an apartment she had purchased 14 months earlier. The price of the Florida apartment was $250,000. She had no fix-up cost on the New York apartment, and paid a commission and closing cost of $75,000.

Table 12-1

IRC 1034 Tax and Basis Calculations	Charles' Deal	Francis' Deal
1. Sale price of old residence	$495,000	$850,000
2. Deduct fix-up cost if any	25,000	0
3. Deduct selling expenses	45,000	75,000
4. Adjusted sales price (1 less 2 and 3)	$425,000	$725,000
5. Original cost of old residence	$250,000	$150,000
6. Add any capital improvements made	50,000	0
7. Deduct any depreciation taken (business)	0	0
8. Tax basis of old residence (1 plus 6 less 7)	$300,000	$150,000
9. Sale price of the old residence, line 1	$495,000	$850,000
10. Deduct selling expenses, if any	45,000	75,000
11. Amount realized from the sale	$450,000	$725,000
12. Deduct tax basis of the old residence, line 8	300,000	150,000
13. Realized gain on the old residence	$150,000	$575,000
To find if there is a taxable gain at this time:		
14. Adjusted sale price of old residence, line 4	$425,000	$775,000
15. Deduct the cost of the new residence	600,000	250,000
If line 15 is greater than line 14 enter 0 on line 16:		
16. Taxable gain recognized from the sale	0	$525,000
If line 16 is zero skip ahead to line 23		
17. Total realized gain, line 13		$575,000
18. Deduct taxable gain from sale, line 16		525,000
19. Gain not allocated to new residence (17 less 18)		$50,000
20. Cost of the new residence, line 15		$250,000
21. Deduct gain not allocated, line 19		50,000
22. New residence tax basis (15 less 19)		$200,000
If the new residence cost more than old residence:		
23. Cost of the new residence, line 15	$600,000	
24. Deduct the gain on the old residence, line 13	150,000	
25. New tax basis of the new residence	$450,000	

For Charles, his new tax basis in the new residence is $450,000. While it is true that the apartment cost him $600,000, because he qualified for the application of IRC 1034 he does not have to pay the tax on the gain of his old residence. However, that gain is deducted from the price of the new residence. If Charles sells the new home without being able to take advantage of the 1034 again (which he could), his gains tax on the new residence would be calculated on $450,000. In essence, the IRS catches up if you eventually sell the residence. In the meantime, Charles has been able to avoid paying the tax at this time. The end result to this situation is the same as if the IRS has lent Charles the amount of that tax. That amount could be around $150,000. This loan is cash in Charles' pocket, which he does not have to pay back until he is ready to. In essence, the tax is paid to the IRS only when he chooses to sell the property. If Charles makes another exchange moving up again, he could transfer the gain onto another property. In Francis' case, she had a substantial taxable gain, but even that was softened by the use of the 1034.

Keep in mind that there may be other income tax stratagem that may work for your specific circumstance. The use of any single technique may be enhanced by sound economic planning. Be sure to let your CPA or other tax advisors know what your long-term plans are and incorporate those plans with your real estate and other investment goals.

THE BEST BENEFIT OF ALL IS THE TAX-FREE BENEFIT OF THE IRC 1031

The potential indefinite postponement of tax on a gain that comes with the IRC 1031 is limited to *investment property* or *property held for production.* This kind of transaction has the mistaken name the tax-free exchange. It is important that you understand that the IRC 1031 provisions can have that end result only if the technique has been properly used. The ultimate escape of any gains tax can work as long as you live, with proper planning. Of course, to be fully free of a gains tax, it is necessary for the owner to die while he or she still owns the property. The 1031 exchange cannot be used if you are selling or exchanging your personal residence.

Later on in this chapter, I will discuss the specifics of the 1031 provisions. For the moment, just keep in mind that this tax-free exchange is a viable tool for many investors to use. It is one of the best methods of moving equity and building wealth. However, exchanges are complicated and to use them properly will require care and study on the part of any buyer or seller who finds that his or her benefits are desirable for the situation at hand.

Not all exchanges you may consider or in fact accomplish will qualify for the 1031 provision. For some exchanges that would qualify, it may not be advantageous for you to use the 1031 provision either. It is all a matter of understanding the bottom line and the future you have in mind for that asset, the new asset, or your investment portfolio. For example, if you have very little or no gain at all in the property you want to dispose of, a 1031 provision has little or no effect on your transaction from your point of view. On the other hand, the other side of the deal may find the 1031 provision of postponing tax on a gain to be absolutely critical to the transaction. In fact, it is so critical to that investor, that without that benefit there would be no reason to make the deal at all.

In any exchange, you will find that the motives and goals of the two parties can differ. In addition, as exchanges often have more than two parties in the deal, the motives of three or more owners can be very different indeed. You should look to your goals first as always, and attempt to make the kind of transaction that works best for your situation. Any give-and-take in the format of the deal are items of the negotiation that should be counterbalanced by some other element of the deal.

If you can save money through postponing the tax, then you are ahead of the game by that amount. If you can entice a reluctant seller into a transaction by showing him or her how to save money through the 1031 provision, you may make a deal that would escape you otherwise.

THE BENEFITS OF THE 1031 EXCHANGE

The IRS Code 1031 says that if you make a *like-for-like exchange,* you don't have to pay the gains tax at the time of the exchange. This is true as long as you have done everything properly, have not received any boot, nor had net mortgage relief. Let me explain. "Like for like," in this context, simply means "investment for investment." You can't exchange part of your inventory as a builder for an investment, or part of your parking lot for an investment, and have a 1031 exchange. Investment for investment is the major thing for you to remember. The major benefit of the 1031 is its ability to postpone any gains tax, to the ultimate goal of avoiding it.

"Gain" on property is the sum of everything you get in a sale (or exchange) less your adjusted cost. Your taxable gain, if any, is found by using the Tax Calculations for 1031 Exchanges provided at the end of this chapter. In any sale or exchange, the primary number you will need is your *tax basis.* The tax basis on a property is like book value. When you buy a property, it has a value. You can add to the value by building something on the property. You can take away from it by certain deductions, such as removing part of the improvements, or depreciating the assets over the years as allowed by the IRS. In the tax law revision of 1986 the depreciation rules were revised drastically to reduce real estate as a major tax shelter for investors.

The tax law also revised the method calculations for adjustment of basis. In essence, when you depreciate a property you artificially reduce its value, and reduce the basis accordingly. In reality, of course, depreciation has little effect on actual value. The IRS allows depreciation to be treated as an actual expense (even though no money was spent) and, as such, in the year-end tax accounting it will reduce actual earnings or profits. As earnings are automatically reduced each year, you pay tax not on actual earnings but the reduced amount. Depreciation, as an allowable expense deduction for income producing and investment property, reduces the taxable income from that investment. This has the benefit of allowing you to shelter income because while the taxable income has been reduced, the actual income has not.

Table 12-2

Your taxable income (if no other calculations)	$30,000
You have a net operating income from a rental property of	$20,000
You have depreciation from that asset of	$30,000
Your real cash in pocket	$50,000

Real-estate losses are generally passive losses and will offset only passive income, as is shown in the above example. An exception would be an investor who owns, say, 10% or more of real-estate investments and who actively manages that property. He or she could then apply a passive loss against $25,000 of active income. Continually review the IRS revisions as more changes in the treatment of real estate are anticipated.

Example

If you earn $100,000 this year from a combination of sources, some active and some passive, but have depreciation of $100,000 from your active business which you manage and operate, your taxable earnings are zero. Of course, in this example, you actually received $100,000 in earnings and did not spend the depreciation of $100,000. As far as the IRS is concerned you did. You would have no tax to pay.

Along with the new depreciation schedules, there has been a change in the accelerated-depreciation rules. In short, now if you take any form of depreciation faster than straight line (27.5 years at straight line), that depreciation cannot be used to create capital gain, and the gain equal to the overage will be ordinary gain.

This means that if you had an apartment building worth $275,000 and a $20,000 lot and you depreciated that building on the straight line over the 27.5 years allowed, you would have $10,000 of depreciation each year. At the end of five years, your adjusted tax basis would be $225,000 plus the lot cost of $20,000, or a total tax basis of $245,000.

If you sold the building and lot for a total price of $345,000, you would have a gain of $100,000 and it would be taxable as income.

Table 12-3

Sales price:	$345,000
Adjusted basis:	195,000
Capital gain:	$100,000

Boot is the part of the exchange that will be taxable even in the best-set-up 1031 exchange. Boot is anything other than real estate. If you get $10,000, it is boot. If you get a gold watch, it is boot. A car, boat, airplane, diamond ring are all called boot and are taxable. You can qualify for a 1031 with receipt of boot, but you will still be taxed on the boot portion.

Table 12-4

How to Calculate the Amount of Boot	You	Other Party
1. Total debt on the property offered to exchange		
2. Less total debt on the new property		
3. Net relief of liabilities (cannot be less than 0)		
4. Less any cash paid		
5. Less any boot given		
6. Plus any boot taken		
7. **Net boot received in this exchange by:**		

USE THE ABOVE TABLE TO CHECK OUT THIS EXCHANGE: Hugh exchanged an office building to Mike. Mike gives Hugh a prime commercial vacant tract. Here are the details of the exchange: Hugh balances the exchange with cash and a $44,000 sailboat that Mike agrees to take.

Table 12-5
The Hugh and Mike Exchange Data

How to Calculate the Amount of Boot	Hugh	Mike
Property value	$600,000	$580,000
Existing debt	$110,000	Free and clear
Existing equity	$490,000	$580,000
Cash given by	$ 46,000	0
Boot given by	$ 44,000	0
Balanced equity	$580,000	$580,000
Original price paid	$400,000	$150,000
Capital improvements made	$ 50,000	0
Depreciation taken	$120,000	0
Adjusted tax basis	$330,000	$150,000

Table 12-6
Start by Calculating the Boot Received

How to Calculate the Amount of Boot	Hugh	Mike
1. Total debt on the property offered to exchange	$110,000	0
2. Less total debt on the new property	0	$100,000
3. Net relief of liabilities (cannot be less than 0)	$110,000	0
4. Less any cash paid	46,000	0
5. Less any boot given	44,000	0
6. Plus any boot taken	0	$ 90,000
7. Net boot received in this exchange by:	$ 20,000	$ 90,000

This is not the entire picture of the tax consequences of this transaction. To see this, look at the total transaction:

Table 12-7
How to Calculate the Tax Consequences of a 1031 Exchange

IRC 1031 Tax Calculations	Hugh	Mike
1. Total debt on the property you offer to exchange	$110,000	0
2. Deduct from above the total debt on the new property	0	$110,000
Net relief of liabilities (1 less 2, cannot be less than 0)	110,000	0
3. Deduct also, any cash you paid to the other party	46,000	0
4. Deduct also, value of any boot you give to the other party	44,000	0
Subtotal	$ 20,000	
6. Add the value of any boot or cash you get	0	$ 90,000
7. **Total boot received by you in this transaction**	$ 20,000	$ 90,000
Computation of realized gain		
8. Value of property that qualifies as 1031 like kind you receive	$580,000	$600,000
9. Add qualified deferred installments	0	0
10. Add value of any boot you received from the other party	0	$ 44,000
11. Add any cash you received from the other party		$ 46,000
12. Add the amount of the existing debt on your old property	$110,000	0
13. **Total consideration you received in this exchange**	$690,000	$690,000
14. Deduct adjusted basis in the property you gave up	$330,000	$150,000
15. Deduct any **cash** you paid to the other party	$ 46,000	0
16. Deduct any debt you assumed on the new property	0	$110,000
17. **This is the gain or loss you realized in this exchange**	$314,000	$430,000
18. **This is the gain recognized and taxable (lesser of 7 or 17)**	$ 20,000	$ 90,000
19. **Gain not taxed in this exchange—** **Subtract line 18 from the greater of line 7 or 17**	$294,000	$340.000

Net mortgage relief is something else to look for. When you exchange one property for another and they are both free and clear of any mortgages throughout the exchange, there is no mortgage relief in that there are no mortgages given up. However, when you deal with properties encumbered with mortgages, you need to look for the situation referred to as *net mortgage relief.*

Assume you have a property worth $100,000, and you owe $55,000 against it. If you exchange for a property worth $45,000, making an even swap (your equity for theirs) you will be relieved of $55,000 of mortgage obligation. You now own a $45,000 property without mortgages. You have had an exchange without any boot, but you have a recognized gain of $55,000 (the amount of the mortgage). You will have a taxable exchange if the mortgage relief is greater than your realized gain by the amount of the mortgage relief. If there is any gain at all, and you have net mortgage relief, you will have some tax in this exchange. Review the calculations in the previous table.

The reason for this should be simple to understand. Assume for a moment that today you own the same $100,000 property and it is free and clear. You go down to the local savings-and-loan and borrow $55,000 in cash, which you put into your pocket, tax-free. A day later you make the exchange shown above, getting a free-and-clear $45,000 property. As you now have net mortgage relief, you may have a tax because you have already received the $55,000 cash without paying any tax on that revenue.

CALCULATING THE TAXABLE GAIN IN EXCHANGES

Smith and Greenwald are our two owners. Smith owns 100 acres of land. Its value is $200,000. He owns this land free and clear of any mortgages and his tax basis is the $100,000 he paid for the property. The other $100,000 in value is appreciation of more than 12 years of ownership. Greenwald owns a 15-unit apartment house. Its value is also $200,000, and it, too, is free and clear. Greenwald's tax basis is $140,000 (he paid $180,000 but has taken $40,000 in depreciation). Smith and Greenwald make a trade with no cash paid between them and no mortgages swapped or assumed. It is a one-on-one exchange.

Table 12-8
The Smith and Greenwald Exchange Data

	Smith	Greenwald
Property value:	$200,000	$200,000
Tax basis:	$100,000	$140,000
Existing debt:	Free and clear	Free and clear

In the second exchange, the two parties are Jones and Blackburn. Jones owns 100 acres of land valued at $200,000 with a first mortgage of $50,000. Jones's tax basis is $100,000. Blackburn owns a 15-unit apartment house valued at $300,000. His tax basis in the apartment house is $125,000 and he owes $200,000. Jones has an equity of $150,000, while Blackburn has a $100,000 equity. In order to make the exchange, Blackburn must balance his equity with Jones's. He will do so with a $50,000 cash payment to Jones.

Table 12-9
The Jones and Blackburn Exchange Data

	Jones	Blackburn
Property value:	$200,000	$300,000
Tax basis:	$100,000	$125,000
Existing debt:	$ 50,000	$200,000
Cash paid by:	0	$ 50,000

Table 12-10 shows the tax calculations in these two exchanges. In examining this table, you will notice that in the Smith and Greenwald exchange there will be no resulting tax, as the recognized gain for both Smith and Greenwald was zero. But look what happened to Jones and Blackburn.

You can use the numbers of your own exchanges in place of those shown in Table 12-10 to see just where you will stand in the case of a potential tax. The tax, of course, will be calculated on the taxable-gain portion by using the current calculations. As these are apt to change from year to year, consult your tax accountant for the current method.

Table 12-10 Calculations of Taxable Gain Exchanges

	Jones	Blackburn	Smith	Greenwald
Value of property received	$300,000	$200,000	$200,000	$200,000
Add				
Cash received	50,000	0	0	0
Other boot received	0	0	0	0
Mortgage relief	50,000	200,000	0	0
Subtotal	$400,000	$400,000	$200,000	$200,000
Subtract				
Tax basis at time of exchange	$100,000	$125,000	$100,000	$140,000
Amount of mortgage assumed	200,000	50,000	0	0
Amount of cash paid	0	50,000	0	0
Amount of other boot given	0	0	0	0
Gain realized	$100,000	$175,000	$100,000	$ 60,000
To compute taxable gain				
(1) Total mortgages relieved	$ 50,000	$200,000	$0	$0
(2) Less total mortgages assumed	200,000	50,000	0	0
(If 2 is greater than 0 put 0 amount)	0	$150,000	$0	$0
Less cash paid	0	50,000	0	0
Subtotal	$0	$100,000	$0	$0
Plus cash received	50,000	0	0	0
Recognized gain	$ 50,000	$100,000	$0	$0
Taxable gain is the lower of gain realized or recognized gain. Note below calculation shows the gain which is not taxed by virtue of the exchange				
Gain realized	$100,000	$175,000	$100,000	$ 60,000
Less taxable gain (Recognized)	50,000	100,000	0	0
Gain saved	$ 50,000	$ 75,000	$100,000	$ 60,000

MOVE INTO THE ADVANCED STATE AND LOOK AT THE STARKER EXCHANGE

The Starker Exchanges are a very special area of the IRC 1031. This is an exchange technique whereby you can find a buyer for your property, then go out and find what you want to own, and still qualify for the benefits of the 1031 exchange.

Starker Exchanges are very different to any other kind of exchange, and are full of pitfalls that can turn a potential savings of would-be tax liability into a nightmare of audits and future penalties. I can say this, not because this is the normal trend for Starker Exchanges, but because too many quasiprofessionals have entered this specialized area of IRS manipulation, and are making a mess of things for their clients.

Definition

A Starker Exchange begins when the first party initiates the exchange by entering into an agreement to sell a property he or she owns. This first party follows a very strict set of rules (which I will describe shortly) that allow this party to actually deed title in the normal way it would be transferred by a sale. However, the proceeds of the sale, that is the purchase money, must be kept away from the seller, pending the ultimate purchase of a *replacement property.* This replacement property will become the exchange property, which will hopefully meet the full test of the rules and regulations of the Starker 1031.

The advantages of using a Starker exchange technique is that it can put you firmly into the shoes of a buyer. Consider this: You have been looking for a direct one-on-one exchange for some time and the only thing that has come around is five hundred acres in the Sinai. You have identified a dozen properties you would like to buy, and you have been offering to exchange your property for those properties to no avail. Suddenly someone comes along and wants to buy your property. If there is a way that you could accept the deal, despite the fact that the offer is only 80% of what you have been asking, you know that you could take that cash and buy exactly what you want. Only, if you were to sell, Uncle Sam would eat you alive in taxes.

However, if you could keep in tact the opportunity to shift your $3,000,000 in gain to some other investment or *like kind property* you would save on all that tax. This is where the Starker Exchange comes into play. The IRS, after losing a couple of tax cases, has established some parameters that allow you to sell now, and exchange later. Take a look at how these rules and regulations work.

THE RULES AND REGULATIONS OF THE STARKER EXCHANGE

1.   The tax benefits only apply to that portion of the property you give up and the property you take that qualifies as like kind property. As has been stated earlier, the idea of like kind property is not its quality or category, but the intent of ownership. As

long as the property (not just real estate), is owned for investment purposes or for use in trade or business, then the IRS says you meet the test. There will be some gray areas in this test, but for the most part, any real estate investment you own that is not your personal residence, that you exchange for some other real estate that will not be your personal residence will qualify. This statement assumes that you are not a real estate developer who is building or developing properties to sell or exchange. Those kinds of property are inventory, and would not qualify as an exchange for an investment property. Keep in mind that when you make an exchange, you can qualify as the giver and receiver of like kind property, even if the other party does not. A simple example of this would be if you exchanged a vacant lot you owned as an investment for a home you planned to rent out. The developer who may have built the home most likely would not qualify, but you would.

2.   You must follow the time rules exactly as they are prescribed. This is the area where most people go wrong in trying to accomplish the Starker. Before I show you these rules, keep in mind that the most important factor in the calculation of the time periods and deadlines you need to follow is the date you transfer title to your old property. This date is the actual closing date when you hand over the title to your old property. It is not the date you enter into a contract to sell. The sales contract can be ten years earlier, for all that the IRS seems to care. They are only interested in the actual day of the month of which year you deed your property to someone else. Here are the rules:

- You must identify a potential property you are going to acquire within 45 days of the date you transfer your deed to a buyer.
- You must take title to the replacement property within 180 days from the date you transfer your deed of your old property to a buyer.

Sounds simple, right? The problem is the first 45 days. You can identify several properties, just in case one or more of them don't work out. Today, this is more often the rule than the exception. By the time you go through due diligence, and discover all the lies the seller told you about the property, you can start eliminating one property after the other pretty quickly.

3.   You cannot have access to the money paid to you for your property when you sold it. This violates the whole 1031 exchange process, so you have to be very careful that you set up the procedure correctly. The way the IRS sees this, if you have the money in your hot hands, then no matter what you do with it, the whole deal is off, as far as tax benefits are concerned. This means you have to use a qualified intermediary or facilitator to hold the money, and act on your behalf to contract for and close on the replacement property.

4.   Avoid intimacy in these dealings. This means you should not use your best pal as the intermediary, or even your life-long lawyer for that matter. Keep everything at arms length and follow the book from start to finish. To follow the book means not this book, because rules and regulations that have anything to do with the IRS are not etched in stone, and are subject to interpretation by courts. Also, the IRS has a nasty habit of changing things around just when you have properly memorized the routine. The clear and safe method to proceed with anything that has to do with the IRS is to discuss the situation with your CPA or other favorite tax advisor from time to time and most certainly, just before you actually enter into any contract.

DO YOU REALLY WANT TO USE A STARKER?

My personal experience of dealing with IRC 1031 is that there will be little reason for you to actually enter into a Starker Exchange. The technique works and is necessary when you have a property that you truly need to exchange, and there is a ready and willing buyer who will not wait for you to find another property to exchange. In those very few opportunities, you will have to decide within a short period of time if you are going to let this buyer slip away, or take a shot at using the Starker.

You can use the Starker and be very successful. You can find the right property within those first 45 days after you transfer title and hope you can close on it. Many investors, including some of my clients, have used this technique successfully. You should play the Starker very carefully. All the caution your lawyer or CPA might give you is well founded. This does not mean you should completely avoid using the Starker, as in its right moment it can save you a deal, and a lot of potential tax payments.

However, a safer route to follow is the simultaneous multiple exchange. This is an exchange that just does not happen unless you get what you want. In this situation, there is more than one party in the game. You might end up giving your property to A and ending up with property from D. Players B and C are in there somewhere, and each ends up with someone else's property. When multiple exchanges are taking place, play it safe, and close all at once.

Be very careful of being pulled into a Starker when the Starker should not have been used at all. Recently a friend of mine recounted such a situation that happened to him. A prospective buyer for half interest in a property he owned came along. His lawyer, and just about every other advisor he spoke to, told him that he needed to do a Starker Exchange, and that is exactly what happened. Only, of all the properties he picked out in that critical 45 days after transfer of half interest, none worked out. Zap, the IRS nailed him quick for a lot of money. There was no need for the deal to have ever been classified as a Starker. All he had to do was tell the prospective buyer (after all, he was only buying $1/2$ interest, and the two of them were going to develop the property later) to wait until he found the right property to buy. This could only have benefitted the buyer, who would have had a free ride during that wait.

A QUICK REVIEW OF WHAT EXCHANGES DO

Because of the nature of exchanges, there will be at least two property owners who are affected. Keep in mind too that as exchanges are generally transacted through brokers there may also be two or more brokers in the transaction.

It is important that you pay close attention to the four key benefits that are the mainstays of exchanges. I will expand on these benefits and get into the fine points, as well as some creative twists to this fine tool later in this chapter.

Exchanges usually affect three or four parties, the owners of at least two properties and the broker(s) (although there are rare instances in which two owners exchange properties without broker involvement). Therefore, the results of the exchange itself can be seen from at least two points of view. It is important that both points of view be analyzed briefly, as this will help establish the proper attitude toward the exchanges attempted.

WHAT THE EXCHANGE CAN DO FOR THE PROPERTY OWNER: FOUR KEY BENEFITS

Any exchange situation should be approached with a simple question: "Will the exchange solve or move you closer to a solution of the problem at hand?"

To be able to answer this question, you must have a clear understanding of the problem. It is crucial to know where you want to go when it comes to exchanges. If the answer to the question stated above is "No, it does not solve my problem or move me closer to a solution," then, obviously, the exchange should not be attempted.

THE KEY BENEFITS OF EXCHANGING

1. TAX-FREE BENEFIT.   Under the tax changes of 1986, capital gains tax calculations that existed prior to the change were eliminated. As of 1987, the previous exclusions which were allowed to reduce the taxable portion of a "capital gain" were removed, and all gain is to be reported as "earned" income. The 1031 provision allows, under circumstances I will outline in detail later on in this chapter, for the tax basis of the old property to be transferred to the new property. When there is a taxable gain, the actual gain is moved to the new property and is not taxable at the time of the exchange of the old property. It is possible that this gain will never be subject to a gains tax at all. The present tax laws of IRC 1031 allow exchanges of like kind property to avoid the payment of income tax at the time the transfer takes place. This

has been referred to as "tax-free benefit," but this is really a misnomer. The tax is merely *deferred* until ultimate sale of the received property. Should the device of exchange be utilized time after time, the tax on the gain continues to be put off until a final sale. Upon death, of course, other taxes come into play. New tax laws for estates carry forward the old basis, which will have an effect on the later sale. Nonetheless, the tax-law benefit has many applications and is one of the major reasons for exchanges. The law provides for the transfer of basis from the old property to the new property. Some tax may be due at the time of the transfer, but this will depend on a number of factors and will be covered later in this chapter in the discussion on the method of transferring the basis.

An exchange will be considered to be tax free (IRC 1031) when two or more properties are exchanged that are like property. The term like kind property has caused much consternation in real estate circles. Like property is the intent of use more than the physical characteristic. So, to be specific, *like kind property is any real interest that is held for use in a trade or business or held as an investment and was not acquired for a resale.*

To simplify this definition, any property which is owned by a nondealer can be exchanged for any other kind of property to be used in the same category as the old property, as long as either property is not a residence, and qualifies otherwise for a 1031 like kind property. For example, Roland owns several vacant lots which he used for outdoor storage of his equipment. There is no question that an exchange of one of these lots for another lot (to be used for storage) in another town would meet the like for like portions of the law.

Another lot, however, also owned by Roland, has not been used for several years. He did not sell it because he decided it would be a good investment and would increase in value in the future. He exchanges this lot for an apartment building. Because the apartment building can be construed as an investment, the exchange will meet the like kind property test.

There have been countless combinations of exchange in realty. In every instance, the like kind property test must be met for the exchange to have the deferment of tax at the time of the transfer. It is important for you to realize that this test need not be met by both parties, nor does it have to be met at all for exchange to be beneficial. The advantage to the exchange, from a tax angle, will depend greatly on the situation and the individuals.

2. INCREASED DEPRECIATION.   Because investment and business property can be depreciated, there are times when exchanging is used with the primary reason being to increase the amount of depreciation the owner is currently obtaining. This advantage is available because of the tax deferment ability, but has special significance to many transactions. The value of the depreciation itself may be taken into consid-

eration if the client needs a tax loss. Depreciation, by the way, is the old term for the declining value of an asset. For typical IRS illogical reasoning, the term was changed to MACRS, which is the acronym for Modified Accelerated Cost Recovery System. This system is designed to bring all depreciation calculation to a standard format. This system thus establishes the term of years for which certain assets can be written off, or cost recovered.

The system provides for two separate lists of years, the shortest being The General Depreciation System (GDS), and the Alternative Depreciation System (ADS). Understand that this book is not a tax guide, and that although I touch on many different aspects of real estate tax, mostly as these aspects affect different financing techniques, the information I provide in that context may or may not apply to your specific situation. All IRS tax codes can be, and often are, very complex. There are many possible cracks in the rules that might be modified, or changed by some other rule or code. What I am telling you now, and frequently throughout this book, is to get a good tax advisor who knows real estate tax rules, and hope they guide you down the right path.

Take a look at the basic MACRS as it applies to rental and investment real estate.

Table 12-11
Modified Accelerated Cost Recovery System (MACRS) for Residential Rentals

Item Covered	GDS Years	ADS Years
Appliances	7	12
Carpets	7	12
Furniture	7	12
Roads, and driveways	15	20
Shrubbery	15	20
Residential rental buildings or structures and components thereof	27.5	40

Depreciation is calculated against the portions of the investment that meets the above category. There are rules that cover items not mentioned above, which this book will not deal with. The chart shown above covers the majority of depreciation for rentals.

Land is not a depreciable item, so must be excluded from the tax basis (book value) of the property you are dealing with. Every year that you deduct the calculated depreciation from your preadjusted taxable income, you reduce your tax basis in that property by the amount of that depreciation.

What this means is this. If you have an income of $25,000 before depreciation, and a tax basis from the previous year of $400,000, and your depreciation is $15,000, then your taxable income (assuming no other additions or deductions) would be $10,000. Your tax basis at the start of the next year would be reduced by the $12,000 so your new tax basis would be $388,000. The significance of this is, if you sold the property and netted after cost of sale $400,000 the IRS would be able to tax you on that $12,000 deduction because your gain (whatever it is) has increased by $12,000.

This is the entire essence of *tax shelter*. Take the deduction now if it works for you. Get the *interest-free* loan from the IRS, and pay it back when you are ready. But do this only if this is the right thing for your overall master plan. You don't have a master plan? Then go back to the chapter that deals with setting your goals and work on it.

Lets take a look at what happens in an exchange vs. a sale and purchase with respect to this depreciation matter. If you have not gotten the overall picture yet, don't worry; if this concept was easy, more people would be doing it.

AN EXAMPLE OF AN EXCHANGE VS. SALE AND PURCHASE FOR EFFECT ON DEPRECIATION

Keaster owns 100 acres of land and an old farm building which he has been leasing out along with the land. His base in the entire property is $45,000, since he paid $60,000 nearly ten years earlier and depreciated the building to nearly zero. The value is $250,000 and he has a small $15,000 mortgage balance. Keaster exchanges his equity for a large apartment house worth $900,000 and having a first mortgage of $650,000. Keaster's new base is increased by cash paid plus the difference between the two mortgages. The subsequent depreciation will then be calculated on that base, less an allocation for the land.

What would have happened if Keaster had sold the farm and then bought the apartment house? Look at the two examples of this case study: (1) the exchange as it actually took place, and (2) the results from a sale and later purchase of the apartment house

The amounts shown are net sums, and brokers' fees are not shown at this time.

In comparing the two situations, you will see several important tax consequences. From the depreciation point of view, the exchange produces the new annual depreciation of $20,218 which amounts to 134% of the new investment (the cash portion of the exchange) paid to the other party ($15,000).

The sale followed by the purchase of the apartment complex required $86,750 new investment cash to close, and generated $26,181 of new annual depreciation or 30% ratio depreciation to cash.

The end result of these two different events is that Keaster is the owner of the apartment house in either case. However, if he sells, then purchases, he has to come up with $86,750 dollars in cash, whereas in the exchange he only invests an additional $15,000. The difference between these two amounts, interestingly, is the amount of tax that has to be paid on the gain of the farm. From a depreciation point of view, the immediate result is not overwhelmingly in favor of the sale/purchase deal as Keaster only increases his annual depreciation (on a 27.5 year depreciation term), by around $6,000 per year.

Keaster is likely much better off, as you would be, to take that cash (which he would have to already have in the bank anyway to do the sale/purchase), and buy an additional property, or to use it to improve the apartments.

Table 12-12

The Exchange	
Current depreciation:	$0
Current equity:	$235,000
Existing mortgages:	$ 15,000
Net market value:	$250,000
Exchange equity of $235,000 for	
Apartment house (shown below):	
Net market value:	$900,000
Existing mortgages:	$650,000
Equity (apt):	$250,000
Less equity (farm):	
Cash to pay:	$235,000
	$ 15,000

Adjustment for New Base	
Old base in farm:	$ 45,000
Less mortgage amount on farm:	$ 15,000
Plus new mortgage on apt. bldg.:	+ $650,000
Plus cash paid at closing:	+ $ 15,000
New base:	$695,000
Ratio of value: land vs. bldg.	
(20% land vs. 80% bldg.)	
New base:	$695,000
Land:	$139,000
Building:	$556,000

Average Rate (Estimated) Depreciation	
Straight line 27.5 years:	$ 20,218
Cash paid in transaction:	$ 15,000
Equity in apt. bldg.:	$250,000

A Sale and Then a Purchase	
Current depreciation:	$0
Current equity:	$235,000
Existing mortgages:	$ 15,000
Net market value:	$250,000

Table 12-12 (continued)

Assume a sale at this price:	
Calculate tax due at the close of the transaction.	
Sales price:	$250,000
Less base:	$ 45,000
Gain:	$205,000
(Estimated gains tax based on a 35% maximum rate.)	
Tax:	$ 71,750
Total proceeds from closing:	
Cash received by seller:	$235,000
Less capital gains tax:	$ 71,750
Net cash to seller:	$163,250

Sellers Now Want to Buy the Apt. House

Price of apt. house:	$900,000
Less total mtg.:	$650,000
Cash required:	$250,000
Cash from sale of farm:	$163,250
Additional cash needed:	$ 86,750
New base:	
Depreciation base	$900,000
$900,000 x 80% =	$720,000

Average Rate of Depreciation

Straight line 27.5 yrs.	$ 26,181
Cash paid in transaction:	$ 86,750
Equity in apt. bldg.:	$250,000

The cash required to end up with the same property differs greatly, the reason being the tax which must be paid in the sale. Keaster had no tax to pay at the time of the exchange, so his adjustments in arriving at new basis did not reflect the addition of taxable gain.

3. EXPANSION OF THE MARKET.   If you have a property which is difficult to move for one reason or another, then exchanging may provide an increased market. The key to this is to determine what you plan to do with the proceeds of the sale. If you intend to reinvest the money, or a major portion of it, in more real estate, then the exchange will not only be the extension of the market, but a tax saver as well. There are many dealers in the exchange market who will take property in trade just to make a move. These people are generally brokers or associates that have taken property from previous exchanges as a part of their fee.

The expansion of a market is important. There are many investors locked into large capital gains who cannot sell their investments without having to pay the tax. These investors look for exchanges to move their equity or to increase depreciation. It is not important that you may not want what they have. Often, their property is highly marketable for cash; *they* just can't sell at a price that would give them a beneficial return after they pay the tax due. But you can make the trade and then *you* can sell their property.

This points to one of the major motivations of a property owner who truly needs to make an exchange. Look at this simple, but very common problem.

Example

Bob owns a property he purchased nearly twenty-five years ago. It is a vacant tract of land, which cost him $15,000. Bob has taken the annual taxes as an investment expense, and made no improvements to the lot. His tax basis is still $15,000. After all this time, the land is now worth $600,000. If his selling expenses were $50,000, he would have a potential taxable gain of $535,000. Unless he had some losses to offset that gain in a year of sale, he might have to pay $175,000 in tax. This would leave him with only $375,000 to reinvest. See the following calculations:

Sales Price:	$600,000
Less selling fees and costs (estimated):	50,000
Less estimated income tax:	175,000
Total to reinvest	$375,000

If Bob wanted to reinvest in a property that gives him a 10% return on that amount of cash he would be left with $37,500 cash flow.

On the other hand, if he could exchange into an investment without having to pay the tax, and could get a return of 10% on the full value of the property, he would have an investment of $600,000 and would have a cash return of $60,000 per year.

Which of these two circumstances would you choose?

4. CASH-OUT. This occurs when the owner of a difficult-to-sell-or-finance property exchanges it for another property that is easy to sell or finance. Cash, not the property received in the exchange, is the motivation and the benefit. Ruth owns a vacant lot, the value of which is $100,000. Ruth needs cash, but cannot sell or finance the vacant property. So she exchanges it for a free and clear home. The home is easily financed, and once she has raised $70,000 on it she puts it on the market at $85,000. The $15,000 down payment and reduced price is apt to produce a buyer, whereas the same reduction on the lot would not.

For a cash-out, the easiest property to exchange into is a free and clear home up to $150,000. This home becomes prime cash-out potential for Exchangers.

Investing in real estate is best done with some sort of plan. The desire to start here and end there may require more than one step or move. Exchanging should be considered as a part of the steps in a dance. Or would you prefer to sit this one out?

Six Reasons People Avoid Real-Estate exchanges

1. Because they don't understand the benefits of exchanges. It is human nature to avoid something you don't understand. But remember this about your "comfort zone;" it works both for you and against you. As a real-estate investor, you must strive to expand all those areas that can increase your profit potential, and one such area is that of real-estate exchanges. When you know the techniques of this kind of investing, you no longer can use this excuse. But in dealing with people ignorant of exchanges, you will have to go slowly to avoid giving the "sharpie" look to what you are doing.

2. Because they believe that one party to an exchange gets the raw end of the deal.   I won't say this doesn't happen from time to time, but it can happen in anything you do. How many sellers feel they got the most they could? How many buyers feel they paid the lowest price possible? Any prospective buyer or exchanger who says that he or she will make one offer and it will be a take-it-or-leave-it offer is being very shortsighted. After all, if the seller said, "Okay, I'll take it." that buyer would forever wonder if he or she hadn't offered too much.

The more you know about exchanges, the more you will recognize that for some people an exchange is more beneficial than a sale. Some sellers will accept in an exchange a property they would not have purchased (given a wide selection and the cash to make the purchase), because the exchange was offered to them and the cash was not.

Your use of exchanges will show you that both sides of the exchange can and most often come out smelling like a rose. The biggest proof of this is that most exchanges occur between members of the real-estate profession, brokers and salespeople exchanging real estate in their own portfolios with other brokers and salespeople. These exchangers form clubs and networks where they deal with each other. The slipshod or shifty dealer is quickly recognized and is "dealt" out.

3. Because they believe that people who exchange set two prices: one for exchange and a real one for cash (which is much lower). Now this point is often true and is to me one of the drawbacks of the exchange side of investing, unless you know how to deal with it. The basic reason for setting prices this way is that most people don't understand that since exchanges can save you tax money, the exchange should be at a lower value than what the sale would have to be to end up at par after paying the tax. After all, I'd rather have a $40,000 lot in exchange (if I wanted the lot) than $45,000 in cash and a $12,000 tax to pay. Other people set higher prices on exchanges than on cash sales out of defense. Personally, I like to quote one price and then stick to it like glue to glue. However, you can easily counter the double standard of pricing by never asking someone the value of the exchange, but, instead, always asking what the price is for sale. Work from that evaluation every time.

4. BECAUSE THEY BELIEVE THAT IF YOU ARE GOING TO EXCHANGE, YOU MUST END UP WITH EXACTLY WHAT YOU WANT.   This is a downright silly misconception about exchanges as a comparison to a sale. When you sell your property, it is unlikely that you will end up with the exact terms you had hoped for. If you truly understand your goals, you will have an easier time with this negative view of exchanges. A clear view of your end goal will enable you to see when the exchange is taking you closer to that goal. When it comes to real-estate exchanges, you need to recognize the benefit in another property as it is compared to what you are trying to get rid of. Of course, often the first step to this process is to recognize that a property you own is not taking you closer to your goal in the first place. If the potential replacement property does not have any benefit for you, or in any way move you closer to your goal, then that is not an exchange you should consider. Remember: *any exchange that moves you closer to your goal is a good exchange.*

5. BECAUSE THEY CAN'T ACCEPT THE CONCEPT OF TAKING SOMETHING THEY DO NOT WANT AS AN INTERMEDIATE STEP TOWARD THEIR GOAL.   The professional exchanger will frequently go through a multiple exchange to end up with a beneficial exchange. For example, if I want to acquire a duplex, I might offer the owner of the duplex some cash (which I'll get from refinancing the duplex) as the first part of the deal. To balance off the equity I could offer some vacant land out of my Armadillo Ranch near Naples, Florida. If the duplex owner doesn't want my vacant land, the deal could hit a snag right there. But it probably won't if I explain that he doesn't have to keep the vacant land, that we can exchange it for something he does want or is willing to take if he will allow me the time for the extra legwork. I tell him I will still put up the cash part of the deal, so now all he needs to do is take that cash, and the vacant land, and acquire what he wants.

If he agrees to allow the deal to be tied together (binding us both to the exchange if I can dispose of the vacant land for him by bringing in something he will take), then I can work out the rest of the deal. He might say he would take a vacant lot, but only if it was in the Florida Keys. I might find a lot he would take, but that owner doesn't want the vacant land in Naples, Florida. I keep going until I find someone who will fit the slot and make the whole jigsaw go together.

I'm not sure what the world record of legs to an exchange is, but I know of one that had more than 25 different steps before it was finally put together. Patience is an essential factor to successful exchanges.

6. BECAUSE PEOPLE BELIEVE YOU HAVE TO OWN SOMETHING TO MAKE AN EXCHANGE.   The answer to this is simply that *you can exchange property you don't even own.* How?

What you are going to do is this: Find out if the seller of the property you want will take another property as part of his or her "sale." You get some specific information as to what that seller would take, even if it is only for a small part of the overall deal. Remember, if the seller will tell you that he or she would take something else for 10% of the deal, if all the other terms and conditions are okay, the seller might take 30 to 40% (or more) in this other kind of property. Now you locate something that is similar to or exactly meets that requirement and borrow it for a while until you make the deal.

Let's say you are interested in buying a small office building you have located in your town. The property is offered at $300,000 and has an existing first mortgage of $110,000 and second mortgage of $55,000. You know you can refinance the building, generating around $210,000 net after mortgage costs.

The seller started the negotiations saying he wanted all cash to the existing financing, but in the end game agreed to take a minimum of $100,000 cash and hold some paper. The seller confided to you (or your agent) that he needed the cash to buy some vacant land on which to build some apartment buildings.

Armed with this knowledge, you now see a possibility of finding some apartment land and making an exchange. You search around for a few days and find a tract of land that is zoned for business and commercial use, but can also be used for apartment sites. The property has not sold as a business site because it is a poor site for that kind of use, but it's ideal for apartment construction. The property owner will sell the land for $75,000 on easy terms.

The fact that the land is not labeled "apartment property" (it's zoned for business) causes many investors to forget that labels in real estate mean very little. It is what you can do with the land that is important, not the specific category of the zoning. Most zoning (get to know yours) comes in grades: business, industrial, commercial, residential, and so on, in varying orders of classification. In many parts of the world the building regulations permit a "down use:" for example, the right to build apartments on a business-zoned property, but not the right to build a business on apartment land.

You have found an owner of some vacant business land who can't sell it, but wants to sell it. You then offer him a "soft deal" that ties up the land so you can make your exchange on the small office building you wanted in the first place.

Example

You set this exchange up by telling the owner of the land that you will buy the land giving him $5,000 down and a $70,000 second mortgage on the office building across town. You tell the owner that you are about to refinance the office building and it will have a new first mortgage of $215,000. You set the interest on the second mortgage lower than the market rate because the seller of the vacant land would rather have some cash coming in than keep the cash-eating land.

You now go back to the seller of the small office building and tell him that you will do the following:

1. Give him $25,000 cash.
2. Take over his existing financing, subject to your obtaining the new financing mentioned.
3. Give him the apartment land (which can also be used for commercial and business use as a bonus). The value of this land is $100,000.
4. Give him a personal note signed by you in the amount of $100,000.

If he accepts this, you will then apply for the loan you want of $215,000, which, less $5,000 in loan costs, will net you $210,000. You will use this to pay off the existing mortgages on the small office building, a total of $165,000 (a first of $110,000 and a second of $55,000). This will leave you with $45,000.

But wait, you have to pay the seller of the land $5,000, so that also comes out of the $45,000, leaving you with $40,000. You then take another $25,000 from that and give it to the office-building owner. You end up owning the small office building and have $15,000 left over for fix-up or for further negotiations if this deal didn't fly on the above-described offer. In short, you have another $15,000 to play with to make your cashless deal work.

Even if you had not been able to increase the value of that vacant land, you were putting yourself in a far better economic position than by trying to buy the office building with the usual financing. The landowner, after all, was willing to take soft paper, which enabled you to maximize your leverage of the office building with some mortgage at below-market value.

HOW TO FINESSE YOUR WAY INTO GREAT EXCHANGES

Every time you buy real estate, there are four things you should do to ascertain whether the seller can be enticed into this kind of transaction.

1. GET TO KNOW THE GOALS OF THE SELLER. In the previous example, knowing that the seller wanted to build apartments was what started you off on this tangent.

2. TAKE A QUICK LOOK AROUND THE MARKETPLACE TO SEE IF YOU CAN HELP THE SELLER MEET THE DESIRED GOAL. Sometimes the seller has picked out exactly what he or she wants to buy. If you can find out what it is and then talk to the owner of that property, you might find you can still do the "soft paper" deal shown in the previous example. You do not want to be hunting for pie in the sky, however. Some sellers set unrealistic goals, and since even they won't find them, why should I spend my time looking for them?

3. TIE UP THE "BORROWED PROPERTY" BEFORE MAKING THE OFFER TO THE SELLER OF WHAT YOU WANT.   You must have control of a property before offering it in an exchange. If you have only a loose deal based on a handshake, it may not survive to the closing. Remember, good intentions are offset by many things, and greed is the number-one cause of death of real-estate deals.

4. UNDERSTAND THAT "IDEAL" DOESN'T EXIST, SO DON'T OVERLOOK OTHER ALTERNATIVES.   Perhaps the seller would build office buildings instead of apartments. If there aren't any apartment sites you can tie up to use in an exchange, try something else. Any property owner can and will take something in exchange. As long as you can "buy" a property on soft paper and move that paper onto the property you are going to buy, you have something to exchange. In this way you can generate a "cash" equivalent of property equity. You might tie up a North Carolina lot by agreeing to give the owner $20,000 (full price) in a soft mortgage on the $75,000 duplex you are buying. If you can give the seller of the office building the $20,000 lot as your total down payment, then you've just made another cashless deal.

PITFALLS OF THE BORROWED-PROPERTY EXCHANGE

Of the usual pitfalls, the most common is not having good control of the property you are dealing with. Another pitfall is that using a property you do not own is that by making a cashless deal you might end up taking on greater debt than the property will support. Becoming debt heavy is something you need to watch out for. Using a soft mortgage deal as a part of the total financing structure will aid you in the economics of the buy, but that may not be enough to give you breathing room in your financing. You must watch your proforma carefully and not kid yourself about what you and the property can produce.

REAL-ESTATE EXCHANGES ARE PRIME OPTIONS FOR BUYERS AND SELLERS

The fortunate thing about real-estate exchanges is that you will have the opportunity to use them as both a buyer and a seller. Your ultimate benefit, of course, is not to be a buyer or seller when using exchanges but to be an exchanger.

Where You Find Other Players Who Are Likely to Want to Exchange

Because you need to have at least two parties to make an exchange, it is helpful if you know where to get started. Understanding the motivations of why people will take your property as all or part of a deal is the first step in finding those people. Take a look at the seven primary motivations why people will accept an exchange.

THE SEVEN MOTIVATIONS TO ACCEPT AN EXCHANGE

1. Must sell, but no buyer has come forward.
2. Has a tax problem that can be softened or eliminated with an exchange.
3. Has a zero investment in the property that he or she does not want.
4. Wants out and is in over his or her head, either financially or emotionally.
5. Is an aggressive investor who understands the technique of exchanges.
6. Has nowhere to go, no place to turn, and wants to save face.
7. Can be motivated, or turned on to your property; in essence, sold on the idea of owning what you now own.

THE BEST SOURCES FOR PEOPLE WHO MEET THE SEVEN MOTIVATIONS

1. Local real-estate brokers who specialize in exchanges.
2. Real-estate lawyers.
3. Tax advisors who specialize in real-estate tax law.
4. Sellers of property that have been on the market for a long time.
5. Anyone who might have offered you a deal you turned down.
6. Any owner of a property you want to own.

PUT THE EXCHANGE TECHNIQUE TO WORK

Using an Exchange as a Buying Tool

When you learn the motivation of the seller, you often realize that the exchange might be your way to do one or both of the following things:

1. **Get rid of something you don't want to keep.** If the seller of what you want is highly motivated, he or she is apt to be willing to take as part or all of this equity something you have in exchange.
2. **Motivate the seller because of tax benefits.** The seller hanging on the fence might be motivated by the tax savings you can show him or her through the exchange you are offering.

Using an Exchange As a Selling Tool

As a seller, there will be times when you have to dig deep down to the bottom of your soul and come up with some powerful tricks. After all, not all real estate will sell itself; sometimes you have to find a taker for your property, as that is often the start of a deal.

Offering your property, or part of your equity, for an exchange will broaden your market. There are buyers out there trying to find what you have, only they don't have money. Try to show them how to make a cashless deal that will solve your needs.

In finding "takers" for your property, you generate additional options for yourself: "Give me your property, take 80% of your value in cash, and all you have to do is take this lot for your remaining equity."

If I accept this deal, I now have cash and a piece of land, which I can keep, exchange, or offer out on the same basis. I could even hold a new first mortgage myself and take something for 20% of the lot's equity. I have gone from trying to get rid of 100% of a problem to end up with 80% cash, and a much smaller problem.

I've made million-dollar exchanges in which only a small portion of the transaction was property taken in exchange while the majority of the deal was cash and mortgage. One such exchange arose out of my need to sell a large tract of oceanfront land I controlled in the Vero Beach area. My marketing program simply didn't produce a buyer, no matter what I did. Then I decided to open the property up for exchange. The exchange was neither the most desirable nor the most practical thing to do because of my partners in the ownership of the property. Nonetheless, I knew finding a *taker* was essential.

Shortly after placing the land on exchange, the offers began to come in. A large villa in Spain, an orange grove in Ocala, Florida and other proposals that didn't get to the writing stage were just a few of the offers made. Then an offer to take some vacant land as a major part of the exchange was presented. The land was free and clear of mortgages and there would be some cash to balance the equity in the oceanfront land. This offer came from a highly qualified "buyer" who thought of himself as an exchanger. Through heavy and long negotiations for more than four months (nothing else was happening on the property anyway), the deal was concluded. The exchanger saved face by reducing the amount of vacant land he would give me, and increased the cash and mortgage portion of the deal. He decreased the amount of the vacant land, and we got cash and mortgage for the balance. What started out as an exchange with no cash ended up as a lot of cash and very little exchange.

When you find a taker for your property, you have the choice of moving on your own property or moving off the exchange property. For example, if I offered you a small duplex as part of a deal to buy your motel, you might say: "I'll take the deal if I can find a buyer or other exchange for your duplex, as I don't want it."

If I'm motivated to take your motel, I'll sit still for a while and let you go in both directions at the same time. I can't stop you from making a deal without me if someone else comes along to buy or exchange for your property. I'm at the mercy of your intent to try to move off my duplex onto something else. I can, of course, try to find a buyer to take the duplex out of the picture and give you cash.

All sellers should investigate their opportunities and examine the value of an exchange. Even the seller who says "I can't exchange, because I need cash" might find that there are no buyers for what he or she has to sell and that the only way out is to exchange into something that is sellable.

THE MECHANICS OF MAKING EXCHANGES

There are several essential mechanical aspects of making exchanges. The first is the *balance of equities.* The others relate to *presentation* and the *maximizing of gains.*

Balancing Equities in Exchanges

All exchanges must have a balance of equities. There are three ways to achieve this balance:

1. THE CASH BALANCE. Assume that you own a duplex worth $75,000 and owe $50,000 in a first mortgage against it, so your equity is $25,000. You want to exchange for Peter's apartment building, worth (to you) $200,000. Peter has a first mortgage of $130,000 on the building, giving him an equity of $70,000. You want to make the exchange and will balance the equities with cash, as shown in Table 12-13.

In balancing equities with a mortgage, you add an additional mortgage to the property you are to take. In this case, you give Peter a $45,000 mortgage against the property you are taking from him, or some other property you already own.

Table 12-13
Cash Balance of Equities

	You	Peter
Property given up:	$75,000	$200,000
Less outstanding mortgages:	− 50,000	− 130,000
Equity:	25,000	70,000
Cash balance (who gives cash):	45,000	0
Balance of equities:	70,000	70,000

2. THE MORTGAGE BALANCE.   If you don't have enough cash to balance the equities, you might try a mortgage balance, as shown in Table 12-14.

Table 12-14
Mortgage Balance of Equity

	You	*Peter*
Property given up:	$75,000	$200,000
Less outstanding mortgages:	− 50,000	− 130,000
Equity:	25,000	70,000
New mortgage owed to:		(45,000)
Balance of equities:	25,000	25,000

3. THE COMBINATION BALANCE.   In the combination, you might give Peter $10,000 in cash and $35,000 in the form of a mortgage. Or you would augment your equity by adding other properties. Nothing will keep you from offering Peter the duplex, a gold watch, and seven partridges in a pear tree in addition to some cash and a mortgage.

THE PRESENTATION: ALL THE MARBLES

The key to all exchanges is the presentation to the other party. Does this sound familiar? It should, because so much of your success in real-estate investing depends on the tone set at the time the original offer is presented, and how well the pressure of the deal is both maintained and accepted.

If you are dealing with a real-estate broker who has not dealt in exchanges, you are apt to have some problems from the very start. For the same reason, however, it is very difficult for you to make your own exchanges. So your first step is to acquaint yourself with someone knowledgeable in exchanges in your area. I'd suggest a call to the local board of realtors, or a look in a newspaper for a real-estate-exchange column, or just call several brokers and ask them whom they would recommend you talk to. Since having the best representation won't cost you any more commission than the worst, and the worst can be more expensive in the long run, try to find the best *in your area*. I stress this last part because finding a great buy 1,000 miles away won't do you a dime's worth of good.

SEVEN THINGS TO AVOID IN ANY EXCHANGE PRESENTATION

1. NEVER ASK THE OTHER PARTY WHAT THE EXCHANGE VALUE IS OF THEIR PROPERTY.   You only want to know the sale value. Some sellers believe that there should be two values. Namely, a sales price that is more reasonable than the exchange price. This is shortsighted because if the exchange can actually save you money (by

reduced taxes), and get you closer to your goal faster than waiting out the poor buyer's market, then the exchange is worth more to you. However, because it is normal for sellers not to understand this, expect there will be this double standard, and deal with it by not stressing actual values, but point out the benefits that the seller is gaining.

2. NEVER PRESUME THE OTHER PARTY WILL TURN DOWN ANYTHING. Only soothsayers are good at presumption, and even so, look where they are. The first person who is apt to lead you away from the potential of an exchange could be the seller's broker or salesperson. I can tell you from more than thirty hard-fought years as an educator to the real estate profession, that most salesmen and -women are not versed in any form of creative financing. Some states, such as Florida and California (and others), have continuing education that touches on some of the current tax laws, and other financing techniques, but only a slight touch. The salesperson who tells you "I know Mr. Seller would not take your lot in Hilton Head as a part of the deal," can only say this truthfully if that salesperson is actually the seller. You should take the position that no one knows exactly what anyone will do until faced with the opportunity to make an informed decision. It is easy for a seller to condition the salesperson by making statements like, "I want all cash, or nothing." Salespersons can believe this if they want, and if they do, they are likely to lose sales that could have come together otherwise.

It is much easier for you to make your offer the way you want to do it. Sellers may not want your lot in Hilton Head (or whatever the property), but might just see that the rest of the terms to your deal take them out of their darkness and into the light of their desired goals.

3. AVOID TOO MUCH TALK. Simply put in writing, in a professional offer format, the concept that: "I want to buy your property, Mr. Seller, and I'll give you five acres of pine woods and ten thousand dollars as my deal." Sounds much better this way and won't upset a never-before exchanger. Far too many transactions fail because one or more of the parties talks too much. One of many good examples is what happened to a very good friend and major property owner who was very anxious to sell an oceanfront hotel he owned. He was a super guy who had made a lot of money in real estate. He knew everything about everything, and proceeded to let you know that every chance he got. He would simply talk people out of wanting to buy his property. What the prospective buyers did not recognize was that all this talk was his way of trying to cover up his anxiousness. Too bad he did not see the ultimate sale of the oceanfront hotel, but his estate did.

4. NEVER PRESENT AN OFFER WITHOUT DOCUMENTATION FOR THE OTHER PROPERTY IN THE EXCHANGE. Have some back-up package on what you are offering, too. If you let your broker go off to present your offer without a pack-

age, you will lose the edge. When you are ready to start making offers for property that will involve an exchange of one of your own properties, make sure that you have a professionally drafted presentation on the property. If you have never done this before you may want to *list* the property for sale and or exchange with a qualified real-estate broker who knows about exchanging. Keep in mind that in the initial offer to exchange, the owner of the property you want may not know anything about your property other than a geographic location. Photos, descriptions of the area, examples of value from recent sales or other offered property in the area, and so on all helps build your case.

5. DO NOT GIVE UP.   Be persistent in your offers. Make them until you are blue in the face, but don't be too conciliatory too quickly. "Look, Mr. Seller, I'm very interested in your property and will keep coming back to you if I can think of something to make this deal work." No genuine seller will want to turn you down too flatly, as you are demonstrating that you are a *taker* for their property. Given the right set of circumstances you might end up a buyer.

There is a tricky balance between this item and number three above. You can be persistent, however, without lots of talk. The idea is that as long as the property is on the market, you can let the seller know that you have continued interest. If the seller did not react positively to your first offer, try to find out why. Often the seller only needs to be educated to the benefits of the exchange.

6. NEVER BE TOO SET ON WHAT YOU WILL DO.   Exchanges are a new, wide-open game for many people. You might be turned on by an offer for an around-the-world cruise on the QE 2 as part of a deal, and who in the world would have thought of that? Options that are opening up to you will be exciting. Live with them for a while. The exchange business is a two-way street. Today you initiate the offer, whereas tomorrow someone else is offering you something. This will happen as the local real-estate brokers who deal in exchanges find out that you are a potential player. You may have made an offer through a local exchanger-broker only to have his or her seller reject your offer. Suddenly that broker is bringing you other possible deals. Keep your eyes open. Several positive events happen. First of all, when you find another possible taker for your property, that now gives you something else to exchange. This is the key to dealing in multiple exchanges. Assume you made an offer to the owner of a motel you want to buy, and he or she turned down your vacant commercial lot. Later a person with a nice home wants to exchange it to you for your vacant commercial lot. Instead of saying, "I don't want the darn house," think, "I wonder if the motel owner would take the home instead of my lot." The only way to find out might be to tie up the home by signing the exchange subject to your making another exchange (or sale) within a reasonable time.

7. NEVER CLOSE DOORS TOO HARD.   It is all right to ease them closed: "I'll say no to this, as it doesn't solve my problem, but I do appreciate your interest and I hope we can work something out." The real estate community in any town can be very small. What you do gets around pretty quick, and how you treat others in the market will come back to you. Be courteous and respectful of sellers and their salespeople and you will find that keeping the door open, even if only a crack, pays off. The seller you deal with today may become a buyer of another property of yours in the future.

GETTING INTO EXCHANGES

The only way to get into exchanges is to make exchange offers. You don't make exchanges by sitting on your rear waiting for someone to come around and ask *you* if you want to exchange. The best way, I believe, is to find an exchange-minded salesperson and then go through a learning process with him or her. All investors who expect to make profits over a long haul, and to reduce or eliminate as much risk as possible, will be continually learning. I know that I feel slighted if I don't learn something every week I am in business. Fortunately, I never feel slighted, as I usually learn something every day. All that learning doesn't always keep me out of trouble, but it sure keeps me from being bored.

THE PITFALLS OF EXCHANGES

Frustration is the enemy of the exchanger. There is a lot you can get frustrated about when it comes to exchanges. You will be dealing with people who think you are out to take them, or at best, will pretend they don't understand anything. You will have to deal with double-pricing situations, with hotshot salespeople who will tell you that a five-story building is a seven-story high-rise. You will get turned on only to find that what was described as a beautiful home by the sea just washed out at a high tide.

But, as Elbert Hubbard once said, "There is no failure except in no longer trying." When it comes to exchanges, you have to keep trying. Your day and the right deal will come along.

From an economic point of view, you need to watch your tax laws and your own tax situation when it comes to the exchange at hand. It is possible that you will be better off making a sale and then purchasing, accepting the tax liability in that year, rather than allowing your old basis to carry over to the new property. You see, if your old basis in that $200,000 investment property is only $25,000 you would have a $175,000 gain in that year. Even with a 20% maximum tax on gains, you would have a $35,000 tax to pay. However, if you also had a major loss in the same year, say $175,000 worth, you might prefer a sale in which your losses would offset the gain. You could then step up your basis in a new property, beginning fresh rather than passing along a $200,000 value with only $25,000 of basis.

Establishing Existing Tax Basis and Calculating New Tax Basis

If you have owned a property for a long time, it is likely that you do not have an accurate calculation for the tax basis of that property. This is because most people do not record all the capital expenditures they make to a property. This is important because if you sell, and perhaps if you exchange that property, you can have a tax liability based on the gain you have. That gain, as I have already discussed, will be the adjusted sales price, less your current tax basis.

The following chart will assist you in keeping track of your tax basis, and help you calculate your new tax basis in the event of an exchange.

Table 12-15
Checklist for Annual Tax Basis Adjustments

How to Calculate Annual Tax Basis Adjustment	*Dollar Amounts*
1. Original price you paid for the property.	
2. Any capital improvements made this year.	
3. Less any allowed depreciation or loss.	
4. Less any partial sale (use adjusted sales price).	
5. Less any improvements you removed.	
6. Your new property tax basis at year end.	

Note that in the above checklist, there can be a fine line between what is a capital improvement, and what is a replacement or repair. Because you can deduct repair and maintenance cost from income for investment properties, you may want to discuss the potential of shifting from capital improvement to repair. Talk this over with your CPA or other tax advisor to see how this might apply to your specific property and situation. Your personal residence is treated differently by the IRS. You cannot use a loss on your personal residence against investment income. Because of this, you generally want to capitalize rather than expense. This means that when you add onto your home, that cost is added to the tax basis, and will reduce the amount of gain you may eventually have when you sell or otherwise dispose of the property. This goes for replacements too. If you replace all your kitchen appliances with new ones, what you have actually done is get rid of the old ones (sell off for nothing or get some small trade-in value), at the price you originally paid for them, and replaced them with newer more expensive ones. The net result is that you have increased your tax basis by the difference.

This points out the need to have a value for everything in the residence which you may eventually replace. When you purchase an existing home or apartment or other residential property, you should establish a value for all the items in the house. You can easily accomplish this by having an inventory list with values that the seller agrees to, or have an independent evaluation of all of these items prior to closing. When you ultimately replace the items then the capital improvement works for you.

Depreciation is a tax break that is given to investment property and not residential property. However, if you have a co-use of the residential property, you may have the right to depreciate some of the property. For example, if you have a business office in your home, or otherwise use part of your property for some business use, then you may be allowed to deduct not only a depreciation for that part of the property, but some of the expenses that go to the upkeep of that portion of the real estate or other residential category. For most people this is not as attractive as it might first appear. The depreciation portion may not be that much to worry about when you consider the potential for an IRS audit on that point. Also, the amount that you depreciate the value of the property will increase the gain tax if and when you sell or otherwise dispose of the property.

When you close on an IRC 1031 exchange, you will want to establish your new tax basis. The calculations are easy if you use the following checklist. Please note, some of the amounts used in this checklist are found in the 1031 Tax Calculation Checklist shown previously. It will be necessary to calculate portions of that checklist first.

Table 12-16
Calculations to Find New Basis in the New Property Following an Exchange

1. Sale price or value of the old property.
2. Deduct allowable fix-up expenses.
3. Deduct selling expenses.
4. **Adjusted sales price.**
5. Add any cash you paid to the other party at closing.
6. Add mortgages you assume on new property.
7. Add gain recognized (see line 17 of the 1031 tax calculations shown earlier in this chapter).
8. Subtotal.
9. Deduct cash you received at the closing.
10. Deduct other taxable boot you received at the closing.
11. Deduct any loss which might be recognized.
12. **Tax basis of all property you received at closing.**
13. Deduct value of boot you received at closing.
14. **This is the new tax basis of your 1031 property.**

My suggestion is that you don't try to be an expert on tax ramifications, unless that is your business of course. Hire the services of a professional in tax law and taxes. It is important that you give your advisors as much factual information about yourself, your goals, and any other property you might be considering. Make sure they understand what you want, and that they are experienced in all of the investment techniques covered in this book. Recognize that when your lawyer or CPA gives you quick negative advice about using a creative technique it might be because they are not well-versed in the field. It has been my sad experience that many lawyers and accountant types are not as up-to-date on some of these creative strategies as they should be. It is a simple fact of life that when an advisor does not know or understand something, they are likely to advise against it. I can assure you that some very smart lawyers who were also owners of the property in question were giving themselves the wrong advice.

One of the basic reasons you should have as much knowledge about what works in this business is that you will find that you must help the other party along in the process of getting the deal done. Of course, you have to be careful about teaching the other party anything. This can be viewed wrongly, and after all, no one likes to deal with a smartalecky investor.

When you find a seller who will approach an exchange as a beneficial move on his or her part, or a seller who will take an exchange as a part of the deal, you are on your way to building equity for yourself prior to the deal and making a cashless transaction. You can do this *even if you don't own the property you are going to exchange.* In fact, you can make more exchanges at greater profit if you don't own the property in the first place.

SOME FINE POINTS OF EXCHANGING: HOW TO IMPROVE YOUR ABILITY TO MAKE MORE BENEFICIAL EXCHANGES

1. BE ON THE LOOKOUT FOR EXCHANGES WHEREVER YOU GO. Whenever you talk to owners or prospective buyers of real estate, ask them if they have anything they would like to exchange. Sometimes a buyer will suggest a piece of property you have not been talking about and the seller is always a prime candidate for the tool.

2. LEARN TO NEGOTIATE WITH OTHER EXCHANGERS. You will benefit from their experience, or at least will become comfortable in the language they use. It is a good idea to write up several hypothetical deals for practice before you sit down with your clients. If there aren't any advanced exchangers around to talk to, don't worry. See your attorney and have him or her go over one of the standard exchange forms with you so you will be able to use it properly. Tell your attorney that you are going to make some big deals (you will if you try), and that as your business improves your attorney's will too.

3. DON'T GET HUNG UP ON THE MATH OF THE EXCHANGE. First of all, it is not hard. You only have to follow the sequence, as shown in this chapter, to get at the right answers. Much of the time you will have help. When it comes to calculating the tax on the gain, you will have to pass that task on to the client's accountant anyway. The tax samples shown here are only estimates. You will never be able to arrive at the exact tax unless you have considerable knowledge of the client's other

income. Whenever you do show a tax consequence, be sure to point out the assumptions you made. Once you have the client's accountant working with you, he or she will do the rest of the calculations. Keep in mind that in math, there are different ways of arriving at the same solution. Don't be quick to tell the accountant that he or she has figured it out wrong, unless you see the calculations and know what assumptions were used.

4. USE EXCHANGES IN OTHER PARTS OF FINANCING. This is a tool to be used for finding solutions to your clients' problems. You can and will find ways to mix this form with others. For example, it is possible to take a property and break it up into land and buildings. Once values are set, you can sell part and exchange the other. Sale and lease backs can be intermixed into exchanging. A property can be sold, leased back, and the leasehold later exchanged for some other property. The possibilities are many.

5. DON'T BECOME A PROFESSIONAL EXCHANGER. There are a few people who have made that transition successfully. I am of the opinion, however, that exchanging is just one way to skin the cat. If you rely on this format alone and are unwilling to consider the possibility that you or your client should not exchange, then you will not be objective in your service. Be flexible.

6. TAKE THE UPPER HAND. You can become experienced in exchanging in a very short time. Try to read more about the topic. Articles often appear in some of the major real estate publications. Look for these new ideas used by others. Watch for changes in the law that affect exchanges.

The Bottom Line: Remember Your Goals

Real-estate exchanges, of any kind, are simply other tools you can use. They work well in all kinds of markets, and can help you move closer to your goal. Remember, any exchange that takes you closer to your goal, can be a good exchange.

Chapter 13

HOW TO USE
PYRAMID FINANCING

In the world of creative financing, one of the best methods to quickly build wealth is through the use of pyramid finance. This method is used widely and can be combined with other techniques outlined in this book. The term *pyramid* should not be confused with the old-time sales pyramids that are illegal. The finance pyramid is where you start small, and as you expand your equity, you use that equity as the security for a down payment or investment funds for more property. The finance pyramid works so well in many instances, that the primary pitfall is the potential to overleverage your investment.

Definition

Pyramid financing is where you pledge the equity on a property you own (or have under contract), as security for another investment.

Example 1

You have a vacant lot you are holding on to with the idea of building a new home one day. You purchased it for $50,000 with a small down payment ten years ago. You owe $15,000 on the lot and estimate its value to be $100,000. You want to buy a small apartment building that you feel you can buy for $130,000. There is an existing first mortgage of $70,000, and you have $10,000 cash. You offer the seller the following:

1. You will assume the existing first mortgage of $70,000.
2. You give the seller $5,000 cash.

3. You offer the seller a second mortgage on your lot in the amount of $55,000 at terms you can afford to handle.

If the seller's primary goal is to get rid of the apartments, and he or she does not need a lot of cash, then this deal might work well. There are some very good tax benefits to a seller in this kind of situation if he or she has a sizable gain in the apartment complex. You save part of your cash to negotiate if it becomes necessary to improve your offer.

Example 2

In the same basic situation the seller only has an existing first mortgage of $40,000 on the apartment complex. This gives him greater equity than you can come up with unless he takes a second mortgage on the apartment complex. The pyramid works well here too. You offer to pay his price of $130,000 as follows:

1. You will get a new first mortgage in the amount of $80,000, pay off the existing $40,000.
2. You will pay him cash at closing of $40,000.
3. You will give him a second mortgage on your lot of $50,000.

In this deal the seller gets a lot of cash, and you get to save most of your $10,000. You would have some loan expense on the first mortgage.

This Is an Advanced Technique

There is no investment strategy that requires a greater confidence in one's abilities than pyramiding, so if you have doubts about your ability to use this technique properly, don't use it until you have gained more knowledge of your abilities, your goals, and the marketplace in which you are about to invest.

Pyramiding has an element of risk that will be discussed in detail. As was mentioned at the outset, the greatest risk is in getting too deep in debt too quickly. As a short-term loan, however, the pyramid is at its best. By short-term financing, consider that if the two examples shown above are an interim step to your building up the equity in the apartments you acquire, to then make a quick profit on their sale, then the added debt would be worthwhile. Just be sure your plan is a sound one. In this kind of situation the real risk in using the pyramid is that you will spend a lot of time to put the deal together only to have the seller reject it in the end. If you are a seller to another party using the pyramid, you must be overly cautious and follow my guidelines in this chapter to ensure that you are taking prudent care of your investments.

Remember, Most Financing Works Best in a Rising Economy

Pyramid financing works best in a rising economy where property values are going up. This is, of course, the situation where virtually all financing will benefit the borrower. If you consider that property values go up, generally because the income potential has increased, then the more you have locked into low interest rate for payback, the greater your return will be in succeeding years. By low interest all that is necessary is for the rate to be less than the demand you want on your investment. For example, if you can borrow at 10%, and the property is capable of paying a return of 14% of your initial investment, then you are in very good shape as income goes up. As you become confident in your knowledge of your comfort zone, you will begin to see properties where you can quickly and often inexpensively increase value in a very short time, when the added value can result in increased income, or profit can warrant the high leverage. In this situation use this method of financing when it produces the best repayment terms of all other alternatives available to you.

THE MECHANICS OF PYRAMID FINANCING AND WHY IT WORKS SO WELL

When you use the pyramid you will often maximize the amount of debt you own. However, because you are mortgaging another property, (separately or in addition to the purchased property), you will not be reducing the loan-to-value ratio on the investment property.

Example 3

You purchase a $2,000,000 office building with the following terms:

1. You assume the existing debt of $500,000.

2. You borrow from another lender $500,000 with a second mortgage on the office building, and pay this to the seller. The total loan-to-value ratio in the combination of the first and second mortgage is 50%. This is a favorable loan ratio for a second loan to be placed at reasonable terms.

3. You give the seller a second mortgage of $1,000,000 on a shopping center you own that is worth $3,000,000 and the existing financing is only $300,000. The seller of the office building takes this second position because that too is a reasonable loan-to-value ratio of 50%.

Each of the loans in question represent a reasonable risk to the mortgagee (the lender), because the loan-to-value ratio as it relates to the specific security, is within the normal risk range. This presumes the above values to be accurate. However, many lenders insist that their mortgage documents contain a provision that limits the borrower to a first mortgage position, or a specific loan-to-value ratio.

A PYRAMID RESEMBLES A BLANKET MORTGAGE

When either of these provisions are contained in the existing mortgage, the pyramid may be the only way to obtain the secondary financing. Take note that the pyramid is much like a blanket mortgage, without the cross-collateralization effect that is essential in blanket mortgages.

Example 4

I buy your free-and-clear home and give you $20,000 cash and a first mortgage on a vacant lot I own in Texas as the balance, and I have used a simple pyramid. If that same transaction included the home and the lot as security in a mortgage, the financing method is no longer a pyramid but a straight blanket mortgage.

THE PYRAMID CAN BE USED IN CONJUNCTION WITH A BLANKET MORTGAGE

It is possible, however, for you to use a pyramid that incorporates a blanket form as well. Therefore, remember that you can use the advantages of the blanket as a seller to secure the mortgage with additional security. In this situation, I might buy your home, give you $15,000 cash (less cash, but a more secure mortgage) and a first mortgage for the balance with a lot in Texas and a lot in North Carolina as security. The combined effect of more than one property makes the pyramid also a blanket. It would be helpful for you to review the advantages and disadvantages of the blanket mortgage in Chapter 9 to see how this additional twist might make the pyramid system work even better.

WHY SELLERS LIKE PYRAMID FINANCING OVER SECOND MORTGAGES

There are several reasons why the pyramid works better for the investor than conventional financing and even better than normal seller-held financing. Let's look at a case study and take it apart to examine these different attributes.

Example 5

Ryan is just getting started in real-estate investing, and does not have much cash to invest. He owns a small home he bought for $55,000 four years ago. At that time, he obtained a first mortgage for $45,000 and invested $10,000 cash. An estimate of the value of this home today is $75,000. Ryan has paid down his mortgage to the point where he now owes $42,000. This gives him an overall equity of $33,000 ($75,000 − $42,000 = $33,000). The most cash he can come up with is around $20,000.

Ryan wants to buy an income property. He has found a nice four-unit apartment building that he can buy for $110,000. He is sure that with some minor fix-up he can increase the rents substantially. There is no mortgage on this apartment building, and the seller has indicated that he would hold some financing. The seller wants a sizable down payment if he or she is going to hold that secondary financing.

Ryan offers the seller the following terms:

1. A purchase price of $100,000.

2. A cash down payment of $75,000. Ryan knows this sum can be obtained from a local savings and loan association.

3. A second mortgage on Ryan's own home for the balance of $25,000.

This kind of offer will have a very strong chance of success for the following reasons:

- The amount of cash down is more than the seller thought he or she was going to get. That is in the seller's favor, and he or she may drop the price because of that.

- As the seller will not have to hold the second mortgage on his or her own property, the seller will feel relief that he or she is not financing 100% of the transaction. Sellers like the idea of being out of the deal.

- This is where the *greener grass* concept comes into the picture. Because the second mortgage is *not* on the seller's property, the seller does not feel as though he or she is taking a big risk. After all, if the seller held a second behind the $75,000 first, then Ryan would have purchased the property with zero cash down. That is a clear 100% loan-to-value ratio.

Ryan sets the terms on the second mortgage he will give the apartment building owner. Since this mortgage is private there will be no lending institution involved. This means that for that $25,000 there will be no closing costs, points, or the like associated with the mortgage, only state stamps on mortgages, recording costs, and preparation fees that will apply. Of course, Ryan will have all the normal cost to get the loan from the savings and loan association.

In the presentation of his offer to the seller, Ryan says: "In addition to the $75,000 cash, I will give you a $25,000 mortgage against this home (showing a photo of the home), which is where I live." Ryan would continue to explain the terms of the $25,000 mortgage. "I know the $75,000 will be of interest to you, Mr. Seller, and this second mortgage will pay back to you $177 per month for the next 120 months and then balloon in full at $25,000. That would total return to you on this mortgage of nearly $60,000 in all if you were to invest the payments to you at 9% per annum."

THE GRASS LOOKS GREENER ON THE OTHER SIDE OF THE FENCE

This statement is true in all forms of investing and financing. People from New York City think prices in Florida are low, people in Florida think prices in South Carolina are low, and so on. The pyramid thrives because of the natural human trait that causes most people to look at something else and believe it is better than what they have. "Here, I'll give you this beautiful box. Now, I'll tell you what, if you give me the box back, plus ten dollars, I'll give you this bigger box." This is real. Because we often look at what other people have and wish it were ours, and often are glad to get rid of what we have to get theirs, this fuels the whole aspect of the pyramid. This very human syndrome also works wonders for the real-estate exchanger.

Once Ryan has outlined the basics of the deal and the seller shows interest by agreeing (at least in principal) to accept the price of $100,000 and the amount of cash down, the rest of the deal is simply formality. The mortgage is presented almost as though it were already in place: "In addition, I'll give you a $25,000 mortgage against my own home." This positive approach shown should be applied in every kind of transaction where you are creating an exchange. The essence is, "I'll give you the mortgage instead of the cash." Some novice investors wrongly turn this into a negative statement. "You wouldn't take a second mortgage of $25,000 instead of cash, would you?"

"Heck no."

It is important to remember that one should never make a comparison between two events or circumstances when only one is available. Sellers fall into this trap by making a direct comparison with the actual terms of a contract as they would compare to what the seller wants. Ryan offered a price that was acceptable, a lot of cash (from the bank of course), and a second mortgage. He did not give the seller the option of taking cash instead of the mortgage. Buyers fall into this trap too, and get hung up on what they want. Ryan wants to purchase this property for the above-stated terms. If there is no flexibility in his negotiations he might have the property slip by. If he did not know about the pyramid he might try to get the seller to hold the second against the property being sold. Sometimes this works, but when the loan-to-value ratio is close to or at 100%, the normal secondary mortgage usually is not acceptable.

Once the deal seems to be workable between the parties, the details should be discussed. Of course, the method of payment of the mortgage will not work in all situations. If the seller felt a need to cash out the mortgage more quickly, the 120-month payment (ten years) would be a bit long. On the other hand, if the seller had a seven-year-old child (or grandchild) the mortgage would provide a nice annuity to set up an education fund for the child. The $177 per month for 120 months with a $25,000 balloon will indeed total about $59,400 if set in an interest-bearing account at 9% per annum. This $25,000 mortgage is really an interest-only payment at 8 1/2% per annum and would leave some room for betterment. If Ryan had done some homework on the seller, he might have had his own stockbroker show how these payments into a mutual fund, or insurance annuity could turn out. The idea in all negotiations is to get the other party to focus on the parts of the deal in which you have room for modifications to the terms.

The advantage to this pyramid transaction is easy to follow:

1.   Assuming the deal is sound, Ryan could go to an institutional lender and borrow the $75,000 without any problem. As long as there is no second mortgage on the property, which in this case there is not as the second mortgage is against another property (Ryan's home), the lender will not be bound by any rules or limitations on lending with the presence of secondary financing. The advantage here is that Ryan will get a better loan than if he were trying to get the maximum loan on the property, or if he did want to get a maximum loan he could pocket some additional cash if he wanted to.

2.   By using the grass is greener approach, the second mortgage that is at a lower than market interest rate may be accepted. After all, the seller is out of the property, has pocketed a bundle of cash, and can go about his or her business collecting from Ryan on the second mortgage. All Ryan has to offer the seller is a better return than if the seller had invested the cash himself in triple A-rated bonds or a good money market. It is important to remember that the seller may have some additional benefits in this transaction. If the seller were to have a taxable gain from the sale, the portion of the sale proceeds that are deferred, that is, paid over a period of years, would fall under the tax break provisions of the *installment sale*. The IRS allows any seller the opportunity to spread the tax on the gain over the period of time that the money is actually received by the seller. This is a very important IRS rule that has a major effect on a seller's reinvestment return. As you can demonstrate the benefit to the seller by holding secondary financing of any kind, you should know how to calculate this benefit. Later in this chapter I will explain this and other benefits you can use in selling the seller on taking your offer. But first, lets look at the benefits to the buyer.

HOW THE BUYER BENEFITS BY USING THE PYRAMID

1. Circumvents existing mortgage limitations to secondary financing.
2. Reduces debt service.
3. Increases yield on cash invested.
4. Gets a *yes* from the seller.

5. Gives you flexibility.
6. Can put cash in your pocket.
7. Is a great *cashless investing* technique.
8. You can purchase two properties at the same time.

Take a look at each of these buyer's benefits separately.

Circumvents Existing Mortgage Limitations to Secondary Financing

When the existing financing on a property is being assumed by the buyer, you need to be careful of all the terms contained in both the mortgage and the mortgage note. Many lenders insist that the loan be limited to or prohibit the future existence of any secondary financing on the property that secures their loan. The idea behind this is that the lender does not want to have the property overleveraged to the point that additional financing increases the total loan-to-value ratio above the initial percentage when the loan was made. This does not matter what position the loan is, as a second mortgage that you want to assume, may contain this same kind of provision, even if the first mortgage does not. When you encounter any kind of secondary loan prohibition this may affect any kind of secondary lien being created against that property. This would likely rule out wraparound mortgages, regular secondary financing, and blanket mortgages, as all of these forms generally cause a direct lien against the same property that secures the existing loan or loans in question.

The pyramid takes care of this situation because the security for the loan is another property. Keep in mind that it would be okay to use a blanket mortgage or wraparound mortgage as long as the combined security did not include the new investment.

Reduces Debt Service

This is a relative benefit of course, and while an ideal benefit, may not always be available. Any time you can move some of the financing you need to obtain to a less expensive kind of financing then you will benefit in the long run.

Example 6

You need $100,000 in total financing and the market rate from institutional lenders is 9% interest per annum. In addition to paying the annual interest on that $100,000, you would owe, at the closing of the loan, all the loan costs that would be applied against the $100,000. By getting the seller to take $25,000 of the deal at 7% interest per annum you improve your overall position by reducing your annual cost. While a 2% savings on the $25,000 may not seem much, you also save on the loan origination cost. In real estate, every penny counts.

Increases Yield on Cash Invested

As you contemplate using the pyramid, you should take into consideration that while this is one of the very best *cashless investing* techniques available to the smart buyer. Because you are introducing soft terms to a transaction while at the same time reducing your cash invested, your overall yield of cash on cash is increased. Clearly, in the Ryan case, he invested none of his own cash in the initial purchase. Any cash that he now spends can be directed 100% to the improvement of the property. Improvements which Ryan knows will increase his cash flow.

Gets a Yes from the Seller

Once you know that you want to tie up the property the next step is getting the seller to agree to a price and terms that work for you. Keep in mind that the very initial price and terms that you both agree to may not be the final terms of the deal. You must first be in control of the property in such a way that the seller is bound, but you are not. In the purchase agreement you spell out the terms and conditions you want. You present the agreement and negotiate the fine points to a point where the seller will say yes. That is your goal at this point of the game. It is important that those terms and conditions be very accurate to the deal as you want it to end up. However, as you will have a due diligence period whereby you can make inspections and investigate the property, its zoning, city rules and regulations, and so on, you will have the unilateral right to back out of the deal unless you find everything as presented, or as you expected it to be. That gives you a later opportunity to go to the seller to renegotiate the deal. This needs to be done carefully because you must stay in control all the time. If you let the deal expire then the seller has an out, and he or she may take it. Getting the yes then is critical, and the pyramid goes a long way when secondary financing is needed.

Can Put Cash in Your Pocket

The prospect of buying a property and ending up with cash in your pocket is very possible when you use the pyramid. That is the good, the bad is you will end up with more than 100% of the purchase price being debt. A quick example of how easy this can be accomplished follows:

Example 7

In the Ryan purchase, suppose that he offered the seller $100,000, with a cash payment of $65,000 and a second mortgage on his house of $35,000. Only, instead of borrowing just $65,000 from the local savings and loan association, he borrows $80,000. After paying the closing costs on the loan he will still end up with cash in his pocket. This cash can be used to benefit the new purchase, or can go to work in another transaction.

Is a Great Cashless Investing Technique

As long as you have real equity in one property, you can use that equity as a source for pyramid mortgages for other transactions. The biggest advantage in using this technique is that it allows you to keep the property you own, rather than having to sell it or use it as a direct exchange. This is important to the greener grass syndrome that works. By keeping the property you demonstrate that you feel it has value. "Take this second mortgage on my home," has a very sincere feeling about it. Sellers would rather take the mortgage than the property.

You Can Purchase Two Properties at the Same Time

This is a technique I don't recommend a novice real-estate investor do right away, Yet it works in many situations and can be exactly the tool you need to close the right transaction. This kind of transaction requires that you identify two or more properties you want to purchase. You are sure of the market, and what you can do with these properties. They are in your comfort zone and you are ready to pick them up. The only problem is you want to maximize your investment cash to the fix-up and not the actual purchase of the properties. What you do is get control over one of the properties, then springboard into another.

Example 8

Suppose you do not own any property at the moment, but you do have $30,000 cash, and a lot of talent in being able to fix up a property. You have spent a lot of time looking for properties and have found two you think will work well for you. In fact, because they are very near each other, you can maximize your time by working on both of them at the same time. *Property A is* a three bedroom home with a separate detached garage that has an apartment over the parking area. Selling price will be $125,000, and there is an existing mortgage of $50,000 that is due now.*Property B is* a five bedroom home that needs a lot of cosmetics and landscape work. Selling price will be $105,000. There is an existing mortgage of $70,000 that can be assumed.

You offer seller A the following terms:
1. You will pay off the existing first mortgage that is due.
2. You will give seller A $25,000 cash at closing.
3. You will give the seller 50,000 second mortgage on property B.

You offer seller B the following terms:
1. You will assume the existing mortgage.
2. You will give seller B $10,000 in cash.
3. You will give seller B a $25,000 second mortgage on property A.

To accomplish this double transaction you would go to a local lender and show how you were going to improve property A. Your plans show how you will convert this home and garage into a five unit apartment complex that would be easily worth $200,000. All you want to borrow is $100,000. Why, that's a 50% loan-to-value ratio for the finished product. You agree to let the lender hold back $25,000 which you will use for fix-up. Out of the $75,000 left, you will be able to pay off the existing first mortgage and give the seller $25,000 cash at closing. You will balance the deal with seller A by showing him or her your plans for property B that you are going to turn into a beautiful law executive office.

Now lets look at deal B. Because the bank is holding the funds needed to fix up property A you don't need all your cash for that. So, you take $10,000 of your $30,000 in cash and give it to seller B, and give him or her a second position on property A. You show how that property will be worth $200,000, and that you have allocated the funds to do that work. You are off and running, and still have cash left over.

HAVE YOUR CAKE AND EAT IT TOO: THE REAL BENEFIT OF THE PYRAMID

The strategy of pyramiding is to use equities from other properties as acquisition capital for new investments. This allows you to move into new real estate transactions with a minimum cash payment. Because you use equity as a basis for the transaction, you retain ownership of the previous property and at the same time gain another.

Any property owner with equity can go into the marketplace and find someone who will take that equity as security for the property being sold. Generally speaking, there will always be properties available, because there are always owners who are highly motivated. These sellers will do anything that offers an opportunity to relieve themselves of what they own. While many of these situations would fall into the category of distressed properties, sometimes it is the owner who is distressed and not the property. Many investors make a lot of money looking for prime properties of distressed owners. This strategy works for virtually any kind of investing, and is not restricted to real estate.

PYRAMIDING IS A RISK THAT CAN BE WORTHWHILE

You should not get the impression that pyramiding is to be avoided, as there are many situations that are acceptable for all parties. It is only necessary for you and other participants in a pyramid to be aware of the risks involved. Without a doubt, pyramiding is one of the highest leverage forms of financing available to the broker or his client. There will be times when the risk is well worth the possible gain.

Because every real estate property is unique it is very difficult to evaluate in exact value terms. Comparative values can give you a good guide, but unless a lot of research and study is made, two exact buildings, situated across the street from each other can vary in value depending on very subtle differences. When you purchase a property that is distressed, it is likely that through cosmetic improvements the apparent equity can be increased in a very short time. This new equity, or surplus over what you have invested, becomes the power behind the pyramid. In a rising market, this value may have the promise of rising further, adding to the "security" of the potential junior mortgage to be used in the pyramid.

HOW TO BUILD A FORTUNE IN A HURRY BY PYRAMIDING EQUITY

The amount of risk you take when using the pyramid depends on the amount of equity you start with. If you purchase a property with $5,000 down, and spend another $5,000 in cosmetic fix up, your invested equity is $10,000. If you have no contingent liability to the debt on the property, that is to say, if you defaulted on the existing debt you would only lose the property, then this $10,000 is the total possible capital risk you have. If you establish an apparent equity in this property of $20,000, that does not increase your risk any as you still have invested only $10,000. Keep in mind that if you are personally obligated to the existing debt and you get into economic difficulties your risk is greater than the capital invested.

The best way to explain pyramiding is to go through a detailed example. I have chosen an extreme example because it points out the many aspects and benefits of this exciting tool.

HOW ONE INVESTOR STARTED HIS PYRAMID WITH $30,000 AND ENDED UP WITH $510,000

Example 9

Blackburn owned an apartment building worth $90,000. Against this value there was a first mortgage of $60,000 and he had a real equity of $30,000. His desire was to buy more properties, but he was limited by the capital he had to invest, only $30,000 in cash. While he could live without the income from his investments, he could not invest more cash than the $30,000. Blackburn's long-range plan was to build as much equity as possible, sell out, and retire to a ranch in Montana. Everything he had was dedicated to this goal.

Within Blackburn's comfort zone, he located several interesting apartment houses of varying sizes. Each needed some improvements to increase the income, but

Blackburn believed that these repairs would substantially increase the value. The first property was a ten-unit building for sale at $100,000. The property had a recent first mortgage of $70,000.

Blackburn offered to buy the apartment house for the full price of $100,000. However, he did not want to invest cash. He offered to assume the first mortgage and give the seller a second mortgage of $30,000 secured by Blackburn's original apartment house. This offer was accepted and closed. Now in ownership, Blackburn added $8,000 in cash from his bank account to improve the property.

With the improvements made, the rental income was quickly improved and the fair market value of the ten units increased to $130,000. It took Blackburn six months to accomplish this build-up of value, and at the end of this period the first apartment house had also increased in value by $5,000 due to an overall improvement of the market. Blackburn now had:

- a first apartment house ($95,000 value, against the total mortgages of $90,000 leaving an equity of $5,000)
- a 10-unit apartment house worth $140,000 with mortgages of $70,000 (equity in the ten units was $60,000 plus a remaining cash amount of $22,000).

THE NEXT STEP: MOVING INTO ANOTHER TRANSACTION.   Next Blackburn found a 20-unit apartment house also in need of repair. The estimated cost for repairs was $15,000. Although the seller was asking more, Blackburn believed he could buy the property for $180,000. There was a mortgage of $100,000 on the property.

Blackburn went to his banker and told him he would like to borrow a net of $140,000 on the 20-unit complex. (An additional $4,000 was needed for closing costs to cover the lending expense, and so on; so the total loan required was $144,000.) Blackburn explained to the banker that he would spend $15,000 on the property after the closing, and with this improvement the property should be worth over $220,000. He showed the banker a pro forma he and his accountant had worked out, indicating the rental potential after the minor improvements and repairs.

The banker agreed. Blackburn then offered the seller the following:

- $25,000 cash
- a second mortgage on the 10 units of $55,000 to equal the seller's $80,000 equity
- $100,000 to pay off the existing financing

The total cash needed in this transaction was: $25,000 to the seller, $100,000 to pay off the existing mortgage, $4,000 for closing costs, and $15,000 for improvements ($25,000 + $100,000 + $4,000 + $15,000 = $144,000).

Blackburn had made the transaction totally out of the new loan proceeds, and therefore did not have to touch his remaining cash in the bank.

WHAT THE PYRAMID LOOKED LIKE AFTER TWELVE MONTHS.   At the end of twelve months, the three properties were worth more and the picture looked like this. (The reduced mortgage amount is due to principal payments made).

Property	Present value	Total mortgages	Equity
1st apartment house	$100,000	$ 86,000	$14,000
10-unit complex	$130,000	$125,000	$ 5,000
20-unit complex	$220,000	$144,000	$76,000
Totals	$450,000	$355,000	$95,000
Plus $22,000 in cash			

In each of the above transactions, Blackburn had to be sure that the income from each property would cover the debt service being placed on it. Because the second mortgages are always from the previous purchase, Blackburn did not attempt additional pyramid transactions until there was income to support the new second to be used as part of his subsequent acquisitions.

Blackburn did not stop here, however, but continued to do the same thing on a larger scale.

BLACKBURN PYRAMIDS INTO A MINIWAREHOUSE.   Blackburn found an old industrial building which would convert nicely into a miniwarehouse and storage facility. He knew he would have to put all his remaining cash into the renovations, but the deal looked promising. He outlined the plan to his accountant who confirmed that the numbers were correct. Blackburn moved forward. Here is what happened.

Blackburn offered the owner of the warehouse complex the following.

- a second mortgage of $75,000 secured by the 20-unit apartment house
- to assume the existing mortgage on the industrial building of $325,000

He then went to the bank holding the mortgage on the building. He got them to extend the loan by the amount of interest for one year and at the same time put a one-year moratorium on principal payments. He told the bank he was going to put another $22,000 into the property and presented them with a detailed pro forma prepared by his accountant showing how he expected to double the present revenue within twelve months. Since the bank was concerned about the future of the present loan, they liked Blackburn's idea and decided to work with him.

At the end of another year, Blackburn had increased the value of the warehouse to $550,000, with the promise that in a few years it would exceed $600,000.

IF YOU SUCCEED ONCE, WHY NOT TRY AGAIN.   Because of his luck in the last venture, Blackburn did the same thing across town. He bought an even larger industrial complex which had been vacant for over two years and put $100,000 into remodeling the buildings.

HOW DID HE GET THE $100,000?   The complex was on the market at a rock-bottom price of $1,025,000. Blackburn knew his bankers would lend up to $750,000 since the existing loans on the property were only $225,000. Blackburn was able to show the bankers his success rate in turning property around. This success impressed the bankers.

Blackburn went to the owners and explained what he wanted to do. He offered them a deal which, after much negotiation, ended up as follows:

$370,000	Cash paid to the owners
255,000	Pay-off of existing mortgage
150,000	Second mortgage secured by the miniwarehouse
$775,000	Total thus far

Blackburn then offered the owners the following terms:

Annual payments of $24,000 on a land lease under the complex's property to be held by the sellers. The land lease was to be subordinated to a first mortgage not to exceed $750,000. The land could be purchased by Blackburn at any time within the next twenty years, or the lease would continue for a total of forty years. Blackburn and the sellers agreed that any loan proceeds over the amount to be paid on the purchase price must go into improvements on the property. This amount was agreed to as being slightly over 8 $1/2$% of the $275,000 remaining value of the land. The option to buy the land during the twenty years was at a flat $290,000. As an additional kicker for Blackburn, the rent did not start until twelve months after closing. The transaction went as follows:

$ 370,000	Cash paid to the owners
255,000	Pay-off of existing mortgage
100,000	Improvements
15,000	Paid as loan cost
10,000	Legal and other closing costs
$ 750,000	Amount borrowed from Blackburn's bank
275,000	Value of land Blackburn leased
$1,025,000	Full asking price

At the end of twelve months, with the new complex fully rented and doing well, Blackburn's overall financial picture, due to increases in value and principal reductions, looked like this:

Property	Market value	Mortgages	Equity
1st apartment house	$ 105,000	$ 83,000	$ 22,000
10-unit complex	$ 135,000	$ 122,000	$ 13,000
20-unit complex	$ 230,000	$ 215,000	$ 15,000
Miniwarehouse	$ 575,000	$ 475,000	$100,000
Industrial complex	$1,110,000	$ 750,000	$360,000*
Totals	$2,155,000	$1,645,000	$510,000

*Buildings only

In very few years, Blackburn had built his net worth from $60,000 to $510,000, with only equity and $30,000 in cash to work with. At this point he was generating a cash flow of about $55,000 per year. (All values used were based on the positive cash flow being just over 10% of the equity.) At this stage in Blackburn's plan, he could retire to Montana to live out his life punching cows, or stay in the pyramiding game a bit longer.

HOW TO SET UP THE MOST PROFITABLE PYRAMID

There are two major factors to keep in mind when you approach pyramiding:

- Pyramiding is highly risky
- The property taken in the pyramid should have the potential to substantiate the risk

Once these cautions are clear in your mind, you are ready to go to work to make use of this high-leverage financing tool.

THE SIX KEY STEPS IN BUILDING A STRONG PYRAMID.   In keeping with the step-by-step procedure, follow these six steps to pyramiding:

1. Review your goals. Then work toward these ends.
2. Outline your risk equity and/or cash.
3. Substantiate your equity by appraisals or *pro forma*.
4. Look for property that has not reached peak income potential.
5. Make an offer.
6. Do not move on until the new property will support new pyramiding by carrying a secondary loan.

Suppose you want to build an estate, and you determine that to build this estate quickly you can risk going into the pyramid program. The next step is to establish the value of the equity on which you plan to build. In Blackburn's case, he started with a $30,000 equity plus $30,000 cash. (Cash is not always a requirement, but some may be needed to improve the properties being acquired.)

An appraisal of one sort or another would be helpful to show the real equity in the property with which you plan to start. Appraisals generally work to the owner's advantage since it is rare for a property to sell for a price over the appraisal, and market value often lies somewhere below that appraised value. The appraisal, therefore, will give a value above the actual marketable sales price in the majority of cases. If you know that the market will support a higher price than that given by the appraiser, then be ready to support that price with hard facts. If you do not want to spend the time and money to hire a qualified appraiser, you have a couple of options to follow. The easiest is to check the tax appraisal on the property as it is, and then compare that appraisal with other similar, but already fixed up properties. Both of these comparative appraisals will go a long way to substantiate your value. You can also make your own appraisal by following the techniques that professional appraisers follow. The quickest way to accomplish this is to call on every similar property that is listed by a real estate broker until you find one or more that have professional appraisals to substantiate the offered price. Get a copy of all such appraisals you can, and use them as a guide to make your own. In both of these situations you will find that a visit to the Property Records department of your county will be helpful in finding out new information. Remember, all public data on property is available. Very quickly you can find out what every similar property has sold for, often going back several years. Your real estate broker can be helpful in working out this information.

Armed with this appraisal, the equity for the pyramid will be apparent. This equity will determine the amount of a second mortgage to be secured by it.

One of the best sources for properties that may be available for pyramid buying will be the local exchange group. In essence, the pyramid buyer is exchanging a mortgage in one property for equity in another. If you don't have an exchange group in your area you may find your job more difficult, but not impossible.

In either case, start with what you would like to buy and what you are capable of managing or developing into a winner. It may be possible to work out a transaction that blends the pyramid into a normal transaction. We saw how Blackburn was able to use the pyramid and give the seller cash by refinancing the existing mortgages. Look to the combination of as many forms of financing as possible to meet the goals you have set.

HOW TO PRESENT THE PYRAMID OFFER TO THE SELLER

Once you have located one or more properties that seem to be worth considering, make an offer on each one. Follow these tips in the presentation of the offer.

What Not to Do

> *"Mr. Owner, I notice you have an apartment house on 2nd Street that has a 'For Sale' sign in the yard."*
>
> *"That's right."*
>
> *"I was wondering, you wouldn't be interested in taking a mortgage back on another property instead of cash down, would you?"*

It is obvious that this type of approach is not professional or effective. However, because this *is* the approach that many buyers *do* take, a brief analysis is needed. First, very few sellers know what kind of transaction they will accept until they actually accept one. Second, a negative approach (you *wouldn't* be interested, would you?) will invite a negative reply.

HOW TO PRESENT THE OFFER

Follow these key steps in presenting pyramid offers:

1. **Have all the data about the security on the property being used to leverage up in the pyramid.** A survey, appraisal, income statements (if the property is an income producer), comparable sales values, and photographs are helpful. Be ready to take the seller over to the property if he or she wants to see it.

2. **Begin the presentation in a positive mood.** If you know you are going to make the deal, you will begin with an edge.

3. **Don't become defensive when the seller rejects the idea.** It is normal for a seller to be skeptical and even negative about something he or she does not understand. It is a natural reaction to what the seller wants, and most times you will get a first reaction that is negative.

4. **Agree with the seller that the offer does not satisfy his or her desire to receive cash instead of the mortgages.** But then restate the objection in a softer tone. "Mr. seller, as you say, it would be better to get cash, but there are some aspects that deserve careful consideration." At this point, you should talk about the property being used as security for the mortgage. Go over some of the material you have brought for this purpose. From time to time, mention what you plan to do with the new property. If cash has to be spent to upgrade it, say: "And I will be investing additional cash too." This may show your sincerity and close the deal.

5. **Call on your very best closing techniques; the rest is up to you.** When it gets down to this stage, there are no guidelines to follow. You must play it by ear the rest of the way. Some sellers will have to sleep on the offer. Don't get pushy here, since pyramiding may be a very new concept to them. Other sellers may go to the dotted line right away.

HOW TO USE PYRAMIDING AS A SALES TOOL

There are times when a property is difficult to sell because of the low mortgages it carries. A free and clear property may be extremely difficult to sell unless there is some form of financing available, either from the seller or from other sources.

When a combination of the following factors is present, the pyramid can be used to benefit the seller.

THE SELLER'S CHECKLIST TO SEE IF PYRAMIDING CAN AID A SALE

1. The seller's equity presents a problem in the sale. This will occur in many situations where a high equity and minimal existing financing require a high capital investment on the part of the buyer.

2. The seller cannot or will not hold purchase money financing to facilitate the ultimate sale.

3. The conventional financing market does not offer effective refinancing of existing financing. This may be the major stumbling block in the sale of the property in the first place. If the property is an income producer, a high interest rate and a high constant rate may not be absorbed in the net operating income to offer a respectable yield to the investor.

4. The seller wants to reinvest in more real estate. This factor makes the seller a buyer, and the pyramid program can be examined in detail to see how it can be used to satisfy all four of these criteria.

In a situation that involves a seller and where all four of these criteria can be met, you can then move into a pyramid.

The objectives of the pyramid for the seller are to help make the property more salable, and at the same time reinvest the equity into more real estate. To follow this, I am presenting an example that shows a step-by-step application of these principles for the seller.

Example 10

Bristow was the owner of a retail complex that consisted of seven shops. He is one of many investors that likes to build and own with a high-equity position. In this case, he had built the complex with his own cash and had no mortgage at all.

Over the years, he realized that his attitude toward real estate investing was not giving him the desired leverage on his capital. Thus, he wanted to sell the retail complex and build a larger one by using the capital from the first.

He discussed this with his accountant and then with me. When I examined his property and his situation, I realized that his conservative approach would make the sale difficult. First, he needed to realize most of his equity to move ahead with his plan. Second, he therefore could not hold much paper, if any, at all. To test the third item on the checklist, calls to the local lenders were made. These indicated that while there was money available for mortgages on the present complex, they would be costly and could hurt the ultimate value since the constant rate was high.

The fourth item on the checklist was already met, as the seller was indeed ready to reinvest. There were numerous options to follow in a marketing plan. The property could be put on the market with new financing, but I felt that the loss of value, due to the cost of the money alone, would make this choice secondary if we could come up with another solution. To be specific, the value of the property was determined to be $250,000, based on the fact that the NOI was $25,000 and a 10% capitalization rate was felt to be warranted in this situation.

Commercial money was available at 9 3/4% per annum, over 17 years. This created a constant rate of 12.07%, or $22,631 per year (P & I) on the maximum loan of $187,500 (75% of the value). On top of this, the loan cost would be approximately $8,000.

With a NOI of $25,000 and a deduction of the annual debt of $22,631, a cash flow of only $2,369 would remain. If the investor wanted a 10% return, the total capital payment would have to be $23,690. But as $8,000 of that would go to the cost of the loan, the seller would receive the $187,500 plus $15,690, or $203,190. Thus, with conventional financing the seller would get only $203,190 for a $250,000 value. A loss of over $46,000 was too much to take without further study.

HOW THE PYRAMID GOT THE SELLER THE FULL $250,000 VALUE

I knew if financing could be put on the property, that would provide a 10% constant, at no cost to the ultimate buyer or seller, the overall value of the complex could be sustained.

In counseling with the seller, I ascertained that he wanted to buy a vacant tract of land where he could build another, larger complex. He did, in fact, have several locations in mind, even though he had not negotiated on any of them. His conservative nature had kept him from buying until he sold. One site was a three-acre tract that was well suited for his needs. It was on the market for $210,000, a very fair price, and was free and clear of any debt.

My first approach was to see if the owner would consider an exchange for the shops. An offer was presented in the normal exchange procedure. He would not exchange. Yet, I learned that he only wanted a secure return and would sell with a very low down payment and hold paper for the balance. However, this would not solve my investor's problem, as he needed the land free and clear to obtain a development loan and had to sell his property.

A PYRAMID WAS STRUCTURED.   We presented the seller of the three acres with a contract that would allow Bristow to meet his needs, if all went well. The offer was structured as follows:

- The owner of the three acres was to receive $10,000 cash
- A first mortgage in the amount of $190,000 on Bristow's shops as the full price for the land. The mortgage was set up on these terms: 8% per year, interest only for the first three years, then an amortized pay-out over the remaining 25 years with a balloon on the fifteenth anniversary of the closing. The closing was to occur upon the sale of the retail complex, providing this sale could be accomplished within sixty days

HOW THE PYRAMID HELPED SELL THE RETAIL COMPLEX

In an instant, the retail property now had a $190,000 first mortgage that offered an investor who would ultimately purchase the shops a mortgage with excellent terms and potential for return. That the interest rate on the mortgage was only at 8% for the first three years meant that the annual debt service on the $190,000 would be $15,200. This would leave a cash flow of $9,800. If the property were to sell for $250,000, the down payment of $60,000 would show a 16.33% yield. This provided excellent leverage for those three years.

At the end of the interest only period, the annual debt service would go to a 9.27% constant, or $17,613. If there were no improvement in the NOI (which was projected to go up), the cash flow would be $7,387 or a 12.3% yield on the original investment of $60,000. The balloon did not hamper the sale of the property, as the time period allowed ample opportunity for future refinancing of the loan prior to its balloon. On this basis, the sale of the units was rather easy and was accomplished well within the 60-day period.

The investor who ultimately did purchase the shops did well, and so did Bristow who sold the retail complex for its full value of $250,000. He took $10,000 of the $60,000 he received on the sale and paid that over to the seller of the three acres. Then, the $190,000 mortgage was established to the benefit of all the parties involved. Bristow now proceeded to develop a larger complex on the three acres that he owned free and clear.

FINE POINTS IN FINALIZING THE PYRAMID

The pyramid can be used in many different ways to produce a foot in the door, as well as "the final close" to a purchase or sale you are trying to accomplish.

Some highly creative aspects of the pyramid come into play when you begin to use it in connection with other techniques that either have been discussed thus far or will be covered in the book later on. To give you an overview of some of these combinations and a preview of things to come, take a look at the following four examples of very creative uses of the pyramid.

Remember that the pyramid used value in another property as a security for debt you will place on a property you are trying to buy. This is the natural *grass is greener on the other side of the fence* aspect that occurs in this technique that makes it so powerful and effective.

THE DISTANT PYRAMID

The distant pyramid is where you double up on the use of the pyramid concept to the extent that two sellers are involved, each taking the other property as security for a second mortgage on the purchase of their property. In this creative look at the pyramid, you will actually buy two properties more easily than one. Earlier in this chapter I gave an example of how this would work. Here is a more detailed example of a distant pyramid.

Example 11

Alex wanted to buy a 10-unit apartment building. He had approached the seller with several different techniques, each using a low down payment offer, and each offer was turned down with the same reply from the seller: "Look, son, I'm not going to finance any buyer that doesn't have equity to back up his offer." The seller you are dealing with may not put it that bluntly, but the end result might be the same. The fact of the matter is that many sellers balk at the very idea of holding financing on their own property simply because they remember how much they paid for that property. After all, if they paid $20,000, how can they justify holding $80,000 in secondary financing on that same property, even if they are selling for $300,000.

While Alex was fooling around with this apartment building, he found a strip store complex that he liked and felt would be a good investment. He made several offers on that property and found the same kind of response from that seller.

Alex decided to offer the apartment seller a second mortgage on the strip store as security for that part of the contract. At the same time, he offered the strip store seller a second mortgage on the apartment building as a part of that purchase offer.

Each owner would be taking a mortgage position against the other property. In each situation, Alex was careful to word the contract so as not to be misleading. He made sure that each seller knew that the second mortgage was to be on a property "that I am in the process of buying," and Alex covered himself with an "out" provision that both transactions were to close at the same time or the deal would be voidable at Alex's option. Another example of a distant pyramid is shown in the following example.

Example 12

Steve had been working his comfort zone for about six months. He had made a list of all of the properties that he thought would be good deals if he could buy them. Like Alex, Steve made several offers on several properties at the same time, but knowing the power of the pyramid he discovered that he could start right out with the pyramid to his best advantage.

One such deal involved these following two properties:

1. A three-bedroom home that Steve wanted to move into. He felt it would be a great home for his growing family. The seller was asking $125,000, and except for a small $38,000 loan there was no other debt.

2. An older home down the street that was on a lot zoned for multifamily properties. Steve was sure that he could convert this older home and the two-story separate garage that went with it into five apartments. The price Steve thought would be the "right" price was only slightly less than the seller was asking, $95,000. But Steve anticipated that he would have to spend $25,000 to make the changes he needed to convert the property into apartments.

Here's how the deal progressed. Steve began with an option on the older home. He went to the seller and offered him $90,000 cash for the home, subject to Steve being able to arrange new financing on the property within 75 days, with a closing to follow that by 30 days. As the deal offered was all cash, the seller accepted the deal.

At this point, Steve had the older home tied up and was free to negotiate from a position of strength on the three-bedroom home he wanted for himself.

He offered that seller a straight pyramid deal:

- Price: $125,000
- Cash at closing: $90,000
- Second mortgage on the to be 5-unit apartment house: $35,000

Steve showed this owner the sketch of how he was going to remodel the older home, and an estimated value of that property once the work was completed of $160,000. Steve agreed to put into the agreement that he would not place a first mortgage greater than $100,000 during the life of the second mortgage. With this provision, the seller accepted.

Steve then went back to the older home seller and said he needed to change the contract slightly. He could pay only $70,000 cash at closing and asked if the seller would take a second mortgage on the beautiful three-bedroom home down the street in the amount of $20,000 to balance out the deal.

The seller balked, and to sweeten the deal Steve agreed to pay an additional $5,000 and increase the price to $95,000. The way that deal now looked was:

- Price: $95,000

- Cash at closing: $70,000

- Second mortgage on the three-bedroom house down the street: $25,000

The next step for Steve was to go to two or more different lenders on each property. He was careful not to present both property deals to the same lenders since he assumed that the loan officers wouldn't understand what he was doing and wouldn't approve it. He wanted to get the best new first mortgage he could on the three-bedroom home and the $100,000 maximum loan that he had agreed he would not exceed on the older home.

In usual circumstances, Steve could obtain a $104,000 loan on the three-bedroom home, and if his figures on value were correct, a total of $100,000 plus on the home to be remodeled.

What Steve Needed to Close and What He Would Get

	On the 3-bedroom home		*On the older home*	
Needed:				
Cash down	$ 90,000		$ 70,000	
Closing cost	1,700		1,800	
Fix-up	3,000		25,000	
Miscellaneous	1,000		1,000	
To carry debt*	5,000		5,000	
Totals:	$100,000	Plus	$112,000	= $212,700
Could get:	$104,000	Plus	$100,000	= $204,000
Would have to add out of his own pocket				= $ 8,700

I have included extra cash to pay both mortgage payments while repairs are being made on the older home, so that Steve can begin to generate income from the newly remodeled and now rented apartments. If Steve didn't need that income, he could buy the two properties without any cash down out of his own pocket.

WHAT WORKS WELL TWICE MIGHT BE BETTER THRICE

Example 13

It would stand to reason, thought Brad, that if you could buy two properties with a pyramid without using any of your own cash, then three properties would be even easier. He tied up three separate properties using the pyramid.

1. Property A was a vacant lot on which he was going to build. It was offered at $50,000, and Brad offered:

    * $5,000 cash

    *   A $45,000 second mortgage on property B

2. Property B was a strip store that Brad wanted to fix up and remodel. He was going to turn it into a medical complex to complement the demand for such services in the area. The price was $470,000. He felt that he would need another $35,000 for remodeling of the center. His offer was as follows:

    *   A new first mortgage of $350,000, a third on property C for $50,000

    *   A land-lease set at a value of $70,000, which Brad could buy any time over the next twelve years at that same amount. The annual rent was to be $6,300

3. Property C was an apartment building that consisted of 15 units near the beach. The owner was operating it as an annual apartment building, but Brad knew that if he converted it to seasonal units, putting into the building a hot-shot young couple he knew could take care of the property, he could increase the income substantially. The price was $400,000, and he offered the sellers the following deal.

    *   A $300,000 wraparound mortgage to wrap the existing financing of a first mortgage of $265,000

    *   A second mortgage of $35,000

    *   A first mortgage on property A of $30,000

    *   Plus $65,000 cash

To accomplish this, $105,000 cash was required to close on all three properties. If Brad could show that property B would be worth $575,000 due to the new income projection, he might be able to borrow up to 80% of that amount, or $460,000 (an increase of $110,000 over his original mortgage on that property of $350,000). Even with some added expenses for that mortgage, Brad could buy these three properties without using any of his own cash.

Brad could have extended this concept even further by bringing in another property and so on, but the more properties you have in any transaction, the greater the difficulty in closing the whole transaction. Therefore, even though it might be tempting to bring in additional properties in pyramid transactions, it is best to keep the new deals to a minimum. However, it wouldn't matter how many second or third mortgages you offered on properties you already owned as part of the package.

PYRAMID TRANSACTIONS OFFERING LAND LEASES

Several examples shown thus far have included Land Leases as a part of the financing package. In the previous example Bryan owned several different properties, all of which were producing more income than was needed to support the expenses and current debt service that was on the property. This gave Bryan a positive cash flow that increased the value of the property substantially over his original cost. He wanted to remove some of this equity, but wanted to keep the cost of the new debt at a minimum.

One of the best ways to keep the cost of debt at a minimum is to use the land lease format. However, the major problem to overcome in using a land lease is how do you deal with the question of subordination of title. If the property you want to buy already has existing financing on the property that lender would require that the land be subordinated to the lease. This is essential for the lender because lenders want to protect their position in the event of a default. As you are buying the property improvements and leasing the land the land owner remains the previous mortgagor. The lender would have to agree to an unsubordinated situation, which is unlikely, or to get the land owner to subordinate his or her interest to the lender. This puts the land owner in a position that can be risky, depending on the amount of the debt he or she is subordinating to. Because of this, many property owners balk at giving a subordinated land lease.

The pyramid land lease is a potential answer to this problem. Remember, when sellers have a potential large gains tax to pay in a sale, the land lease can be a very motivating factor. So, on one hand the seller wants to take a land lease, and on the other is frightened of the risk.

To solve this problem you give the seller land under another property and lease that back. If you can demonstrate that the loan to value ratio is reasonable, then the land lease you offer can be more attractive to the owner than the land under his or her own property you are buying.

UNDER EVERYTHING IS LAND

There are many people who believe that ownership of the land is the best, and better than holding a mortgage is holding actual title to the land.

There is no argument from me about that, and as long as the lease is favorable to my needs I will take a land lease just as I would cash; in fact, sometimes quicker, for reasons that I will explain.

Bryan got to a point in a negotiation on a small office building where he needed to move some of the seller-held debt to another property so he could overmortgage the property he wanted to buy to generate the cash to make the transaction. He looked over his inventory of real estate and discovered that in several situations he could create extra debt without hurting himself or the property.

BRYAN CREATES A LAND LEASE

Example 14

Bryan had a 12-unit apartment building. It was throwing off a net operating income of $46,000. From this, he had existing debt service of $31,000 (which represented annual payments on $305,000 of mortgages). The office building he was trying to buy was offered at $275,000 and was free and clear. The seller demanded a minimum of $150,000 cash down and said he would hold a first mortgage for the balance. That wouldn't work for Bryan, so he "created" a land lease on his apartment building. He sat down with his lawyer and had a simple, but effective lease drawn up. It had provisions that I will show you later on in this chapter, and an annual rent of $11,250 per year. In addition, it had an option to buy the underlying land for $125,000 any time within the first twelve years of the lease, which was a forty-year lease.

Bryan then offered the seller the $175,000 cash he wanted and the land under his twelve-unit apartment building subject to lease. In essence, Bryan was offering to give the seller of the office building the twelve units at the end of the forty-year lease if Bryan had not bought out the land prior to that time. In the meantime, the seller would have full ownership of the land. Bryan put in several other provisions that we will discuss now.

THE LAND LEASE CHECKLIST

1. *Do* provide for an option to buy back the land. Try to keep it at the same set price you have established as the value of the land at the start.

2. *Do* have the land lease extend more than thirty-five years, or at least ten years plus the option term past the longest term of an existing mortgage. Assume that the longest mortgage was fifteen years, and your option to buy back was twelve years. You would then have a total of 10 + 15 + 12, or 37 years. The reason for this is you may want to refinance the mortgages that are on the property prior to the termination of your option to buy. You would need a minimum of ten years beyond that new mortgage term to have a lease in effect for most lenders to approve the loan. As you might wait until the end of the first option to buy the land back to decide if you want to keep the land lease instead of buying it back (twelve years), you would need that term plus a similar term for a new mortgage, or an additional 12 + 15 years. Longer would be good, but you anticipate buying back the land within your first refinance term or letting someone else worry about that as you may sell the property within a short time.

3. *Do* allow for a refinance during the term. If your land lease is subordinated to the existing financing only, you would not be in a position to refinance the property once the existing financing has been paid off. So provide for additional refinancing, but be ready to limit the amount to some percentage of the value of the land and buildings, say, 80% of the lender's appraisal of the land and improvements.

4. *Do* make sure the document is a land lease and not a mortgage. Your lawyer should make sure that this is the case. If you are using this technique to take advantage of the tax laws that fit your circumstance, and the document that says "land lease" is deemed by the IRS to be a mortgage, it could be a costly mistake.

5. *Do not* have a required pay-back agreement, where you must buy back the land. That is one of the first IRS red marks that suggest that the land lease is really a mortgage.

6. *Do not* have your rent payment increases tied to a cost-of-living index, or any other index that has no known future value, unless you: (a) can time the increases to come into effect following a date on which you believe you could exercise an option to buy the property; (b) can limit the effect of any future index by obtaining credit for payments of rent against the purchase price, or by having only a percentage of the increase of the index apply; or (c) have no other choice and are ready to take the risk that the cost-of-living increases will not decrease the lease's benefit to you.

7. *Do not* make your offer with the idea that the land lease is something that will be established or negotiated. You might flex a bit on its ultimate value, but never on the terms of the lease.

Bryan had created a lease that had an annual payment of 9%, which at the time was better than he could do with a second mortgage or in any institutional first-mortgage situations. The seller took the land lease because there is that feeling that some people have about that sort of thing.

THERE ARE PROBLEMS, OF COURSE

Land leases can cause lots of problems for both sides of a deal. Generally, the problems come from three major areas.

1. **The carelessness of one or more of the parties to leave something important out of the lease.** Remember that memories are meaningless when it comes to what was intended to be included in a contract that looks bad to one side later on. If the contract isn't absolutely clear, you will absolutely have problems.

2. **The subordination dilemma.** If you are on the receiving side of this deal, you should know that for this to work for the investor the land lease would have to be subordinated to the existing and possibly future financing. This means that the "position of lien" has been subordinated (given up) to allow the mortgages to come ahead of the actual ownership of the land in the event of a default on the mortgages. Should such a default occur later on, the owner of the land may find him- or herself having to take over a mortgage to get his or her own property. If the investor has run the property into the ground, there may not be income available to support the mortgage, and value may have eroded as well. Keep in mind that this problem would be similar to that of a junior mortgage holder.

3. **The time problem.** I have seen investors actually let a land-lease option to buy slip past and expire because they "forgot" when it was coming up. You cannot rely on your lawyer, your banker, or your accountant either.

Despite these kinds of problems, there remains a world of flexibility in land leases and pyramids.

In a general summary of the pros and cons of pyramids, there are a number of elements that I have covered that should be repeated and remembered.

1. *Pyramids work on the greener grass theory.*
2. *Pyramids can be the box behind the silver curtain.*
3. *Sellers will hold something they "see" as valuable that isn't theirs.*
4. *You can pyramid off real estate you own or don't own.*

In going into a pyramid program, you should review some of the general advantages and disadvantages.

There are two factors that create a risk in pyramids that can bring a swift end to your economic house of cards.

- The ability to pay the increased debt service
- The danger of having greater debt than value

As you can see, both of these factors are related. If the buyer extends his or her value-to-equity ratio to the point where there is no real equity at all, the overleverage may cause all of the cards to come tumbling down. We've seen this effect in other improperly used techniques.

What are the advantages and disadvantages? First, remember that there are two different parties involved. The buyer's goals and motivations will generally be greatly different from those of the seller. Each party should look at the end result of the transaction from his or her own position and needs.

The Buyer: The Person Who Generally Instigates the Pyramid

Advantages	Disadvantages
1. Expands holdings.	1. Possibility of overleverage.
2. A low-cost financing tool for reinvestment.	2. One failure and the whole pyramid can fall.
3. Establishes good "selling" terms.	3. Buyer limited to fewer sellers.
4. Fantastic estate builder.	
5. As the interest paid is apt to be on an "exchanged" mortgage, the interest would be deductible.	

The Seller: The One Who Feeds the Pyramid

Advantages	Disadvantages
1. Creates a sale.	1. Sale generates paper, not cash.
2. Tax advantages, due to spread of gain on the sale to the terms of the mortgage taken.	2. Paper may not be secure.
3. Provides long-term income.	3. Another remote transaction could have a great effect on this security.
4. Secured by other property with visible results.	4. Paper is flexible in terms.

The seller in the pyramid is generally a person highly motivated to sell. He or she considers and later accepts the offer for paper because it is the best deal offered. If you were to compare the pyramid offer to an all-cash offer of the same value, there could be no question as to the better, less risky transaction. However, this is not a proper comparison. The seller wants to sell and has a plausible offer. Hence, it may be worthy of acceptance and better than holding onto the property.

HOW TO MAKE THE TRANSACTION WORK

The pyramid can be a very safe and profitable way to finance new acquisitions if used conservatively. This means the amount of real equity transferred via a mortgage should be kept at a low to moderate amount. In most cases, the total debt service on the property should not exceed 80% of the net operating income of that property. In very stable income properties this percentage may be extended to 90%. There should be a 10% or greater buffer between income and expenses. In taking over a new property, the buyer should consider out-of-pocket expenses to bring the income up, and this out-of-pocket must be taken into account before the transaction is completed. It should be figured into the total price or at least accounted for in later expenditures. If the buyer is able to generate this needed out-of-pocket cash from additional financing on the acquired property, then the total debt should be reasonable and not overleveraged.

The market conditions themselves will provide some limitation to this over-leverage, as it will be difficult for the buyer to obtain excessive financing on marginal properties. But the domino effect of the total pyramid can build up quickly if you are not careful.

The seller should exercise caution in any transaction that does not involve cash. However, that caution should not mean a pyramid transaction is not worth considering. To the contrary, the property being sold may not be saleable by any other method.

The Installment Sale: Another IRS Benefit

Earlier in this chapter I mentioned that the Internal Revenue Service allows a seller to delay payment on gains. Two methods mentioned earlier are the IRC 1031, which is the tax-free exchange that works well for investors who are able to plan ahead and work toward a major investment goal. The other method outlined was the IRC 1034 which is the home-for-home transaction where you either sell or exchange your home, ending up with another home. This has some limited use, and both of these two methods have their specific rules and regulations that must be followed. The installment sale is a method of accounting for the receipt of a gain in a sale.

Definition of an Installment Sale

An *installment sale* is any sale where you are not paid all the proceeds of the sale in any given tax period. If there is a taxable gain as a result of the sale, you are allowed (not required) to spread the gains received in a prorata basis over the terms of the installment sale. Simply put, if your gain equaled 50% of the total contract price, then one-half of each dollar you get would be gain, and taxable as such.

Example 15

In 1985 you purchased a property for $100,000. You put $20,000 down on the property, and the seller held a purchase money mortgage for the balance of $80,000. In 1997 you sold the property for $190,000. At that time your loan balance was $40,000. While you owned the property your depreciation on the property totaled $15,000 and you made no improvements.

The terms on your sale are:

- Zero down payment
- Three installments of $50,000 due over three annual payments

How to Calculate an Installment Sale on the Above Transaction

First—Find Gross Profit

Selling price	$190,000	
Less adjusted tax basis	85,000	
Gross profit	$105,000	Amount of taxable gain

Second—Find Contract Price

Sales price	$190,000	
Less mortgage relieved of	40,000	
Contract price	$150,000	Amount of sales proceeds

Third—Establish Ratio/Gain to Proceeds

Divide gross profit
by contract price
$105,000 ÷ $150,000 = 70%

In this example, 70% of the total amount of sales proceeds equals taxable gains. Every time you would get a payment of $50,000, 70% of that or $35,000 would be taxable gain; the rest, $15,000, would be return of part of your original invested capital or mortgage amortization. Any interest that would also accompany the annual payments would be taxable as return on investment and may be treated separately as a return on a long-term capital investment.

There is some fine-tuning you need to know about when calculating the installment sale. The most critical aspect to watch out for is the situation that occurs when you are relieved of a mortgage that exceeds your basis. This frequently happens when people own property for a very long time and depreciate the asset down to a low level, then somewhere along the time of ownership obtain new financing. If in the above example you would have had a loan outstanding of $90,000, or greater, you would have mortgage in excess of tax basis. The IRS calculates that this excess mortgage is capital you have already pulled out of the property. While that was not taxable at that moment, it will be taxable at the time of the sale, even though you may not get cash at closing.

Sellers can benefit using the installment sale, by spreading a large taxable gain over several years. Because this is very positive tax planning, buyers should point this out to a seller every time the buyer is trying to use secondary-seller-held financing as a part of the purchase price and terms.

Chapter 14

HOW AND WHEN TO USE A DISCOUNT SALE + BUY-BACK

Everyone likes to find a bargain. One of the best ways to find them in real estate is to look for people who need capital, want to keep their property (use or right to recapture), and offer them a discount sale.

A discount sale, as it applies to real estate, is a sale at a drastically reduced price in relation to the supposed value. The principal ingredient in this technique is that the seller has an option to buy back the property at a future date. This technique is most often used when there is no reasonable financing available for the property, and the seller has a use for the property. When financing is hard to find at reasonable terms, the property owner may find that a sound economic strategy is to sell the property and retain a buy-back at a later date. The seller may combine this technique with a leaseback as well. The advantage of the discount sale-buy-back or leaseback is the seller can generate capital while retaining interest in the property. If the property being sold is vacant land, which is often the subject of a discount sale, the seller can have the added advantage of getting capital out of the property without having the obligation of meeting debt service.

Example 1

You have been sitting on a vacant tract of land that you believe is in the path of progress, only progress is taking longer than you had anticipated. You estimate the value is around $400,000, but there are no takers at that price. Even if there were, you want to hold out for the big bucks that will come when the new highway this property will front is completed. Your immediate problem is you could use some cash out of this property for your business. You quickly discover that no one wants to loan anything on the vacant land at rates that are reasonable. You decide to offer the land at a bargain sale to generate the needed cash. To give yourself protection on the up-side, you take an option to buy the land back within 6 years at a substantial increase. In essence, you agree to sell the land for the tax appraisal, which is $250,000, and have an option to buy it back within the next six years at $443,000. If you do your math correctly you will realize that the actual cost to you to buy the property back is a 10% compounded interest. If the property value sky-rockets, as you hope it will, the actual value six years from now could be much more. If not, you had the use of the $250,000 for that same period.

BE CAREFUL OF THE IRS

The Internal Revenue Service may look closely at a discount sale with a careful eye to see if it has been contrived as a method of reducing possible tax on a gain. Of course, the sale may never come to its attention, but don't count on that because it may very easily examine such a transaction at some time in the future. The three-year statute of limitations on audits of past income tax returns will not hold if there is reason to believe that fraud was committed. If the discount sale was accomplished to evade tax, fraud may be claimed. Be sure that you properly document any possible discount sale, or for that matter, any sale where you have a buy-back or leaseback as a part of the transaction. To help you ascertain if there is any danger follow the checklist that I provide for you. If you can answer "no" to all of the questions, then you should be able to justify the use of a discount sale. In using this checklist, however, it is wise to check with your tax advisor to see whether he or she thinks that the discount sale may create a future tax liability.

CHECKLIST TO DETERMINE WHETHER A DISCOUNT SALE CAN BE USED

All questions must be answered "no." Even one "yes" answer may raise doubt as to the acceptability of using a discount sale as a method of selling a property.

1. Is the buyer a relative of the seller?
2. Is the buyer a close business partner or associate of the seller?
3. Does the seller owe the buyer money or any special favors?
4. Is the sale price below the assessed value of the property?
5. Is the sale tied to other terms or conditions involving other property?
6. In the event of a leaseback by the seller are the terms of the lease unreasonable for either party based on the market area?
7. Is there a mandatory recapture provision where the seller must become a buyer at a future date?

8. Is there reason to believe that the seller does not need immediate cash or other financial relief?

9. Are there buyers at a higher price, with reasonable terms?

10. Have similar properties been sold above the sale price within a reasonable time-span?

11. Has the seller taken a large long-term capital gain in the same year?

12. As a broker or salesperson and listing agent, are you the buyer?

Assuming you have answered "no" to all the above questions you can now pro-ceed with the discount sale as a method of helping your seller accomplish his or her goals. If you have answered a "yes" to any of these questions, then you need to look at the situation surrounding that question. A "yes" to questions 5, 6, & 7 will almost automatically cause the IRS to sharpen its pencils and bring out its spy-glasses. For example, if you sold the $400,000 property for $200,000 and leased it back for $20,000 per year, with a mandatory buy-back in ten years at $400,000, then IRS will call this transaction a mortgage and not a sale. This may not affect you at all, but could create problems for the buyer who will be treated as a lender. The overall return might be usurious in your state if this were treated as a loan. Of course, the IRS could con-sider that the low lease terms allowed you to escape a capital gains tax, and attack the sale by giving a value to the leasehold interest as well as the cash portion of the sale.

The discount sale has a real function. It can often be the only solution, short of financial disaster, for some clients and some properties.

A DISCOUNT SALE GENERALLY MEANS CASH

A sale at half the value may, after all, be the only cash price you can get due to mar-ket conditions. Because the reason for a discount sale is usually the need to produce immediate cash, it is generally associated with the "cash sale."

If you are in need of immediate cash, and are not in a position or are willing to borrow the required sum of money, and the sale of a real property becomes the only suitable solution, you may find yourself looking to the discount sale to satisfy his or her needs. To raise cash in a tight mortgage market may automatically direct you to the discount sale. Keep in mind that the value of any property is relative to time and place. If you own property at the wrong place at the wrong time, options available to you diminish quickly.

From the buyer's point of view, a purchase at a bargain price is more appealing than buying at a market price. Of course, the all-cash requirement may limit the quantity of buyers who would offer on the property. But you might be surprised to discover the number of possible buyers who come out of the woodwork when a "steal" is offered.

If you are the seller, the viability of the transaction depends on what problems you are trying to solve. If your most critical need is for cash, then you can raise cash with more ease by utilizing the discount sale. Often, the need for cash is overshadowed by the necessity to "get out" or to be released from financial burdens of existing financing, which you are unable to support.

Example 2

Roscoe owned an apartment lot suitable for ten units. In a good rental market the lot might bring $125,000. In fact, a few years ago this price may have been attainable. However, times are now tough and rental properties are overbuilt and have high vacancy factors. Roscoe has been hurt by the decline in the economy and is in need of some ready cash. The property cannot be sold at its past value. Some prospective buyers have indicated a willingness to pay $80,000, but only with a very low down payment and long terms on seller-held paper. Since Roscoe needs cash immediately the broker recommends the discount sale as a method of solving the problem.

Roscoe sells the lot for $60,000 cash. Because of the obvious "steal" at this price, a buyer was found almost overnight. But the discount sale has a buy-back option, so Roscoe retains the right to repurchase the lot within the next thirty-six months for $85,000. If he fails to do so the option is lost forever.

The discount sale solved the immediate cash need Roscoe had, and at the same time offered him an opportunity to buy back the property in the near future if the market reversed itself. Should the value return to the lot within the thirty-six months, or increased values make the lot worth more than the supposed $85,000, then Roscoe will profit.

The buyer of the lot will have a limited gain should Roscoe recapture the lot within the thirty-six months. Yet, his gain could be respectable and above the interest yield available to him or her from a savings deposit. For this reason, the bottom line for the buyer is the recapture. He may gain much more if Roscoe cannot or will not recapture within the thirty-six months. There are several ways that Roscoe could sweeten this deal, if it was necessary. I will touch on this later on in the chapter.

LEASEBACK, BUY-BACK, RECAPTURE OF OPTION: A NECESSARY PART OF THE DISCOUNT SALE

Leaseback, recapture, or option: one of these methods is almost always used in conjunction with the discount sale to provide for future gain to the seller. It is this trade-off of values that allows the seller to give the buyer a secure position in the property. This secure position is what attracts money to this kind of deal.

How can these methods be useful? First, accept the fact that the discount sale offers the most potential when the market for the type of property being offered is not at a peak, or when you need to retain the use of the property. After all, when there is a demand for what you are offering you need not offer a discount. When the sale of apartment lots is down and not many buyers are around, it may be necessary to seek drastic measures in order to sell. Of course, the poorer the market the greater the discount required to make the buy a "steal." If you need to retain the use of the property, or anticipate a strong increase in the value of the property over the next few years, then the right to retain use or future buy-back rights are important. Without one of these future values in your hand, the only reason for a discount sale is if there is absolutely no other remedy to your problem other than letting the property go at whatever the market will bring.

At times, the discount by itself is still not enough to entice a buyer. You may have a floor price under which you cannot go. As the seller you may have financial obligations to pay off or may simply be unwilling to sell below a fixed price. Many sellers have lost all their equity in a property rather than drop the price to a level at which the property would sell. It is a hard fact of real estate investing that market price often has very little to do with actual value. Keep in mind that what you have paid for a property and have invested in it may be your value. Market value is what someone else is willing to pay for that property.

In the discounted sale, the seller generally wants to retain either existing use, or a future benefit, or both. A discounted sale combined with a leaseback of the property (with or without a later option to recapture the property) is not uncommon. In such a situation the seller will arrange to lease the property from the new buyer for a period of time. This is the same as a sale and leaseback, but with a discount on the sale. The basic difference would be that the terms of the leaseback would reflect the reduced price on the sale.

If the seller has a use for the property and can produce income to pay the lease, the reasons to leaseback the property may be sound. With the discount off the sales price and additional income (in the form of rent), the transaction may entice a buyer, and the transaction proceed to close. The amount of the lease payments can usually be lower than an economic return on the price, as the buyer is looking at the discount as the major incentive for buying. This is another flexible aspect of this form of financing. You can negotiate different time periods of the lease, amount of the lease, and discounted prices. The variance on any one could be advantageous to one party and not the other. A balance of these variations may be necessary in the negotiations on this kind of transaction.

The Recapture Allows the Seller to Recoup Value

With a recapture clause in the lease, the seller may, at a later date, buy back the land at a price fixed in the contract or at a price adjusted by other agreements.

The most common extra provision used with the discount sale is the option to buy back. Because the seller is taking a reduced price, he or she may want to buy back at a future date. This future price may be considerably higher than the price the property was sold for in the first transaction. Consider this case:

Example 3

Aston owns 200 acres of farmland outside the city in a growing area. Land nearby has sold for $1,500 per acre. Based on this information, the current value of the land should be $300,000. The tax assessment on the property is $100,000. Aston wants to get some cash to buy a yacht and spend a year or two at leisure. He paid $50 per acre twenty years ago and presently has no use for the farm site. The current market conditions indicate that there are not many buyers ready, willing, or able to buy this land today, or in the very near future. Aston had a loss on the sale of a business property that year of around $80,000 and could take a gain without creating a taxable situation that year. His accountant advised him that if he could take advantage of the loss he would be ahead of the game.

DISCOUNT SALE EQUALS A STEAL

At what price then do the 200 acres become a "steal?" When you can answer that question to the highest dollar amount you have the probable discount price. In this case it was $500 per acre. Remember, the discount sale may require all cash to suit the client's needs. If the $100,000 which can be generated by the discount sale is more than Aston needs, then he may back off and sell only a portion of the property at a discount and hold onto the rest. However, as Aston needed the $100,000 he proceeded to market the property with this in mind.

In the future, Aston's 200 acres may skyrocket in value due to a new subdivision nearby or for some other reason. If the value should go to $3,000 per acre, some of the new value of $600,000 could be recouped if Aston had taken an option to buy back the land at the time he sold it.

An option to buy back, however, is normally not granted for a long period of time, except in leaseback and recapture situations. The reason is simply that the option is one sided, and the new owner does not want to be locked into the property for a lengthy period of time without being able to sell. As Aston felt the land would appreciate greatly within a few years, he negotiated for a short option at a lower recapture price rather than a long option at a high price.

Aston settled for a five-year option to recapture the land at $162,000. This would give the new owner a $62,000 profit, less his carrying cost if Aston buys the land back at the end of that time. If the land went to $600,000, Aston could buy it back at $162,000 and have a potential profit of $438,000, plus the original $100,000 he received from the first sale. Had Aston made the decision to sell the property for its top value of $100,000, that would have been the maximum top dollar he would have received, less the tax.

RECAP OF THE TRANSACTION

Aston had land similar to that which had sold for $100,000. To get a quick sale, he took a discount and sold it for $100,000, but with an option to buy back within five-years at $162,000.

Three years later, Aston realized that a new subdivision nearby had opened up this farmland and that it could be sold for as high as $400,000. So, with time on his side (he had twenty-four months before the option came due), he put the land on the market. He knew that he could exercise his option to recapture the land if he got a buyer.

A year later a buyer came along, and Aston sold his option to him for $260,000. The new buyer exercised the option for $162,000. Aston sold the option rather than exercise it because the buyer wanted the extra time, another twelve months before he had to pay off the $162,000 to recapture the land.

ADVANTAGES OF A DISCOUNT SALE

There are four basic advantages of the discount sale:

- Cash in a hurry
- Fast closing
- Action in a bad market
- Very flexible

The discount sale can be used effectively in these situations:

- Seller needs cash in a short time
- Market is difficult
- Property is difficult to sell
- Seller needs a fast transaction
- Fast cash-out for an exchange is needed

The discount sale is a seller's and a broker's tool, but can be used by an astute buyer as well. The buyer can go into a transaction offering a reduced price. The later buy-back can become a negotiating point. It can follow many avenues and can be very flexible.

The discount sale and buy-back option offer the seller more possibilities for return when the property has the promise of fast appreciation. In the event of a property valuation decline, the seller simply does not use the option and walks away from the property.

DISADVANTAGES OF A DISCOUNT SALE

Many things can go awry in planning a discount sale. It may be that the price is reduced too low, or the terms of the buy-back are too high or for too short a period of time. The value in appreciation may not warrant the buy-back and the seller may have lost out on part of the gain. Many things can and do go wrong, but this is more often a fault of the planners and not of events. You cannot fit the discount sale format into all situations. In those cases where there is a three-fold increase in the value of the property the year after the option is dropped, the planning was obviously wrong.

Just because the discount sale is highly effective, the buyer should not rush out to use this tool until he or she has looked at all other possible options. An overzealous broker can sell a lot of property with the discount method, but not always to the benefit of the seller.

A discount sale holds considerable risk for the seller if the market value of the property does not appreciate to cover the pick-up cost, or if his or her situation changes and he or she cannot exercise the option when the time comes. The amount of risk the seller is taking depends on the amount of the discount and the probability of appreciation. A reduction from $100,000 to $60,000 with a likelihood that the value will go to $200,000 in three years, is less risky than a reduction from $100,000 to $75,000 with little hope of an appreciation in value to $150,000 within four years.

Because of this risk factor, the discount sale can be used by the buyer with a certain degree of effectiveness. It is normally the seller who is telling the buyer how great the value of this property will be in a few years. In essence, the buyer turns that around and says: "I'll give you part of your price now, and if you are right about the future, you can buy the property back at a reasonable price and make a lot more later." When the seller has been pushing how the $100,000 lot was going to jump to $800,000 as soon as the new bridge was finished, the buyer's offer to pay $60,000 for the lot now, and let the seller have several hundred thousands of dollars later (if the property exceeds the seller's buy-back price), can suddenly change the seller's confidence in the increase of value.

Review the Discount Sale from the Seller's Point of View

The following guide will be helpful in reviewing the discount sale from the seller's point of view.

1. Keep in mind that the discount sale is effective when:
   a. Fast cash is needed.
   b. The seller has no other acceptable way to get the cash.
   c. A fast closing is needed.
   d. The property is very difficult to sell.
   e. A cash-out for an exchange is needed.
   f. The seller knows the value will increase substantially.

2. If one or more of the six preceding factors is not present, the discount sale will probably not be the best form to use.

FINE POINTS IN THE DISCOUNT SALE

Since the seller is in a give-and-take situation by virtue of the discount on the price, he is able to negotiate terms not normally possible on the later buy-back, or leaseback and recapture. However, the buyer knows that the longer the time period of the option the less value the discount has, unless there is another counterbalance. It is possible to structure these counterbalances to provide some protection to the seller for a longer time, without unduly burdening the buyer.

Example 4

You have offered the seller $50,000 as a discount price for a lot and are now attempting to negotiate the terms of the buy-back option. The seller wants a seven-year option to buy back, which you feel is a very long time for the discount sale in question. However, a number of factors can be brought into play to make it feasible.

1. THE FUTURE PRICE TO BE SET AT A PREDETERMINED BASE PRICE, WITH AN APPRAISAL TO BE MADE AT THE SEVENTH YEAR.   If the appraisal price is lower than the predetermined price then no further adjustment is taken and the seller can either recapture or not. If the appraisal is higher than the predetermined price, then an adjustment to the predetermined price could apply. The amount of the adjustment would be a negotiating point. For example, you set a price that would be good any time during the seven years for the recapture to be no less than $100,000. At the end of seven years the appraisal suggests the value is $150,000. If you and the seller have agreed to a 20% increase of the overage, then the seller's recapture price would be $110,000. (The base recapture price of $100,000 plus 20% of the $50,000 overage; $100,000 plus $10,000 = $110,000).

2. GIVE THE BUYER THE RIGHT TO "BUY OUT" THE OPTION WITH A PAYMENT TO THE SELLER.   This provision will allow the buyer, for a sum of money, to null and void the option. It is possible that the buyer may want to sell or even

develop the property, and with the option over his head that may not be practical. The sum of the buy-out is normally at least the balance to the discount plus some profit. If the value was $100,000 and the discount sale was at $50,000, the buy-out may be at $45,000. However, this is a highly negotiable point, and could be set on an annual scale, or a formula. For example, in addition to the seller's right to recapture the property any time during seven-years for $100,000 you have the right to buy back the recapture during the first three years (or any other time that suits you), for $45,000. If you take a good look at this, you will see that this is much like buying the property for $95,000 with a deferred payment at zero interest over three years. This term may not affect you, but the seller might have to impute interest in that payment. As long as you have run the details of any such transaction past your tax advisor, you should be okay.

3. FIRST RIGHT OF REFUSAL.   This may be all the seller can get, or may run with the property for a period of time after the option to buy back has expired. For example, you give the seller a very short buy-back recapture option, say for one or two years. Then the seller can have a first right of refusal for another five or so years. Be cautious about giving anyone a first right of refusal, as unless you are very clear in the terms of how the right is to be exercised, your hands can be substantially tied in trying to sell the property. For example, if the seller had a two-year option to buy, then a five-year first right, you would spell out clearly the terms of that first right. Such terms might be as follows:

After the second anniversary of the closing, the seller shall retain the right of first refusal to meet any terms of a sale of the subject property. Should the owner of the property elect to sell the property and receive a bona fide offer, the owner would provide a copy of said offer to the seller who would then have a period of five working days to match the exact terms of said offer. The seller, after matching the exact terms of the bona fide offer, would have a period of 30 days of inspection time of the subject property. At the end of the 30 days, the seller could elect to proceed to close under the exact terms and conditions of the bona fide offer, or elect to withdraw.

Terms such as the above would clearly tie your hands if you were the owner of the property, for a period of at least 35 days. A prospective buyer offering you a bona fide transaction may not want to wait that period. Worse than that, if the seller did not elect to meet the terms of the offer, and the buyer proceeded with his or her own due-diligence period, only to come back to you and want changes in the agreement, you would be forced to go back to the seller to give him or her another shot at the first right of refusal.

Another hazard of first right of refusal is what happens if the bona fide offer is an exchange? This can truly complicate events, and to anticipate this, it would be a good idea to include wording that covered that potential problem.

Should the bona fide offer contain an exchange of property or boot, the offer will also contain a purchase price which would allow the original seller to match under the provisions of the first right of refusal. As the owner of the property has accepted the property or boot as a part of the bona fide offer, nothing shall prevent the seller in negotiating the price of said property or boot with the party making the bona fide offer.

4. ESCALATING OPTION OR LEASE PRICE.   The seller may agree to a series of higher prices in future options to buy back. The same may occur in the lease payments. This and other long-term options or provisions are used in vacant and other nonincome-producing properties more often than in income-producing property. Buyers should remember that if they make the buy-back terms too difficult, there may be no incentive for the seller to actually want to recapture the property. This is important if the property includes buildings that need to be maintained. An excessive buy-back may encourage poor maintenance of the structure.

A Review of the Discount Sale

The discount sale is viable when viewed as a technique to raise quick money, at reasonable interest rates, for relatively short periods of time. There are many problems that the seller must understand and check out prior to using this kind of technique. The following are some of the pitfalls that await the user of the Discount Sale.

PITFALLS TO WATCH OUT FOR WHEN USING THE DISCOUNT SALE

FOR THE BUYER

1. Is the price truly a discounted price, or have the values been manipulated to appear to be a discount?

2. Has the leaseback term been contrived to entice the buyer into "too good of a deal?"

3. Are there sufficient future benefits to encourage the seller to recapture the property at the increased price contained in the terms of the transaction?

FOR THE SELLER

1. Will the seller's capital gains tax be excessive? If so then the IRS may red flag this transaction and open both sides up for an IRS Audit.

2. If the market is headed down, there may not be a future benefit in the option to recapture.

3. Is there sufficient time to plan for the recapture of the property?

Chapter 15

WHEN, WHY, AND HOW TO DISCOUNT A MORTGAGE

The ability to increase the yield on a mortgage by buying it below face value is a great way to make money quickly and safely. The concept of mortgage discounting is widely used in the world of finance from institutional banking to government loan programs as well as applicability to the private sector as well. This chapter is designed to show you why a discounted mortgage will give its new holder a greater yield, and the specific techniques of how and when to discount the mortgage to get the highest possible yield.

Definition

A *discounting of a mortgage* occurs when the holder of the mortgage sells the note to either the maker or a third party at an amount less than the current amount owed. This current amount would be the combined total of outstanding principal plus unpaid interest owed. The result is that the buyer would, upon satisfaction of the note at its contract rate and terms, receive a greater yield than the original holder.

Example 1

Frank sold his home four years ago and took back a second mortgage in the amount of $50,000. The mortgage called for interest only payments at 10% payable annually for ten years, with a balloon payment of the outstanding principal due at the end of the tenth year. The loan has 6 years remaining and Frank needs some cash to make another investment. Bob comes along and says he will give Frank $40,000 cash for the outstanding loan. In taking this offer, Frank has discounted the second mortgage to Bob. Bob is now getting $5,000 per year (the interest only payments of 10% on the face amount of the loan), which is a 12.5% yield based on the interest. But remember, when the loan is paid off in seven years or sooner, there will be another $10,000 bonus because the payoff is based on the original face amount of the loan, which was $50,000. As Bob only paid $40,000 that bonus jumps the average yield up. The real bonus would come if the mortgagor of this second mortgage wanted to refinance his first mortgage 12 months after Bob purchased the mortgage. The payoff would be one year of interest, $5,000, plus the hold face amount of $50,000 or $55,000 in all. This is a return of $15,000 (interest plus bonus) on the $40,000 investment. The actual yield in this example would be 37.5% interest.

WHEN A MORTGAGE SHOULD BE DISCOUNTED FOR CASH

A mortgage should be discounted whenever the need for cash, or the yield which can be obtained with the cash, exceeds the return on the mortgage. Naturally, there are other alternatives, such as obtaining a loan against the mortgage or seeking the funds elsewhere. These alternatives, which may be highly desirable solutions in normal circumstances, may not work quickly enough or produce the desired results as effectively as a discounting of the mortgage.

The cash discount is a sale of the paper at a reduced price to enable the buyer to have an overall yield greater than the contract rate on the mortgage. This cash sale of the paper can occur at any time after the mortgage is written and up until the date it is satisfied. A mortgage which has some maturity is considered to have a performance record, and hence may have a lower discount than if it had no record of payment. Mortgages discounted in the early years will generally have an additional penalty for this lack of seasoning. This will depend on the type of mortgage and the position in rank and the overall total loans to value. For example, if the property was worth $200,000 and there were three mortgages against the property totaling $180,000, this establishes a 90% loan-to-value ratio. If the mortgage to be discounted was a third mortgage for $40,000 the risk in buying this loan is much greater than buying a first mortgage of $40,000. In either event however, the total loan-to-value ratio is such that the property owner may be overleveraged and the absolute creditworthiness of the mortgagor needs to be carefully reviewed.

It is obvious that a second mortgage will not be as saleable as a first mortgage on the same property. Therefore, it may require a greater discount. Yet, a third mortgage on one property may be more marketable than a first mortgage on another property. The loan to value ratio is important throughout this ranking process. If a property is valued at $100,000 and there is a first mortgage of $40,000, the loan ratio is 40% and the equity ratio is 60%. That same property with an additional loan (second) of $20,000 would have a loan ratio of 60% to value and the equity ratio of 40%. Therefore, the loan-to-value ratio is crucial and the remaining equity ratio essential to determine the risk factor to the mortgage.

Example 2

Castile had taken back a third mortgage when he sold his home nearly two years earlier. The mortgage now has ten years to go and the unpaid balance is $10,500. The contract rate is 8 percent and the monthly payment to amortize the balance is $152.88. Castile wants to sell the mortgage at a price that will give an investor 10% on the invested capital. This means that the investor could pay no more than $9,639 to have that yield. The first potential investor looked at the discounted price and was interested. He asked Castile what the loan percentages and equity percentage ratios were. Castile wasn't sure what the investor meant, so they figured them out together. The estimated value on the property was $60,000. The mortgage represented 17.5% of the total value and the superior financing totaled $42,500 or 70.8% of the value. This meant there was a total of 88.3% financing and 11.7% equity. The investor decided that with only 11.7 % equity between the mortgage and foreclosure, he needed a minimum of a 12% return. The mortgage would have to sell for $6,993 to show a 12% yield. Castile decided to keep the mortgage, since his need for cash would not generate a 12% return.

However, later in the same year Castile found a small apartment building he could buy if he could pay cash to the existing mortgages. The apartment building should throw off nearly 13% cash. He tried to get the owner of the building to take the mortgage as part of the transaction. Failing that, he went back to the investor and discounted the mortgage to come up with the cash to buy the apartments. Castile now had a greater use for the cash than the present return generated from the yield on paper.

Example 3

In the previous example, Castile made an attempt to exchange the mortgage rather than discount it. This can be a very good way to move off mortgages, and there are several ways that Castile could have sweetened the deal for the seller of the apartment building he wanted to buy to entice him into taking the mortgage as a part of the deal. Remember, the face amount of the loan outstanding was $10,500, and the closer Castile could get to that amount, the better off he would be owning the apartment complex. How could Castile sweeten the deal? One way would have been to offer additional collateral to improve the security on the loan. He could do that by giving the new holder of the mortgage a second or third position on the apartments he was buying. Take a look at the following to gain a better insight at using discounted mortgages in exchange.

WHEN SHOULD A MORTGAGE BE DISCOUNTED IN EXCHANGE?

Castile attempted to get the owner of a property he wanted to buy to take paper he held. This was a step to exchange the paper at its face amount. Later in the negotiations Castile tried to make the paper more attractive by discounting the face amount, but the apartment owner had a need for cash that overshadowed the yield any reasonable discount could generate. While Castile failed in the exchange of the paper, he was at least on the right track in trying to better the buying power of the paper by using it as a part of a transaction rather than discounting it.

When an investor attempts to buy a property it is wise to offer as a part of the total transaction any paper being held, especially if the paper has a yield less than the expected return on the property being purchased. Yet, even though the yield on the paper is greater than the overall yield, the leverage gained in the purchase terms may make the use of the paper desirable.

Example 4

Redding, an investor, offered to buy a strip store. he had $75,000 in cash and $50,000 in paper he was holding on a vacant piece of land he had sold the year before. The strip store had a first mortgage of $300,000 and an annual debt service of $33,000. The NOI of the store was $45,500, or a cash flow of $12,500 on a total offering of $125,000 cash to the mortgages. The $50,000 in mortgages Redding was offering would yield nearly 12%. Nonetheless, Redding was most interested in the strip store because of yields other than just the cash flow. In the first place, the tax shelter boosted the yield as did the principal build-up. Appreciation was that added bonus that he was not getting in the mortgage.

First Offer: Adjusted Price with Firm Face Value on Paper

Price	$95,000
Cash	$80,000
Mortgage in exchange	15,000
Total	$95,000

Second Offer: Adjusted Price and Discounted Value of Paper

Price	$90,000
Cash	$80,000
Mortgage in exchange	10,000
Total	$90,000

There are two ways to discount a mortgage in an exchange. The first is in adjusting the total price offered, still showing the mortgage at its face amount. The second is adjusting the price and showing the mortgage at a discounted value.

Example 5

Rosenblum wanted to acquire a vacant parcel of land to build on. The asking price was $100,000. Rosenblum had cash and, in addition, a $15,000 mortgage he was holding from the sale of another property. He decided he would not pay more than $80,000 cash plus his mortgage.

It would appear that the proper method would be the first offer. After all, it is argued, the higher price is the best way to go. This may be true in many circumstances. However, if this is the maximum which can be offered, that is $80,000 in cash and the balance in the paper, and the face amount of the paper is $15,000, then there is little room for negotiation.

Therefore, I suggest that in the offering of paper in exchange for a part of the transaction that the paper be generously discounted right at the start. If the above $15,000 paper yields 8% at its face amount, and assume that if discounted to $10,000 it will yield 16%, you have removed the primary argument of the value of the paper before the seller can settle in on that portion of the negotiations. If he were to counter at a higher price, you could merely remind him that in fact there was another $5,000 in face value in the paper anyway.

In Rosenblum's situation, he knew the maximum he wanted to pay for the property and that he wanted to use the paper as a part of the transaction. Generally, sellers will absorb part of a bigger deal in old paper, thereby removing the paper from the buyer's portfolio.

HOW TO DETERMINE THE AMOUNT OF A DISCOUNT

This is a two-part problem. The first is the market condition. What amount of discount is necessary to make the paper saleable? The second part of the problem is the actual computations to arrive at the discount.

HOW TO ANALYZE THE MARKET FOR A DISCOUNTED MORTGAGE

To some degree, it is the old story of how long must your legs be? The answer, of course, is long enough to reach the floor. In the discounting of mortgages the amount of the discount must be sufficient to market the paper. Investors dealing with the purchase of paper look to a demand rate that is generally greater than the yields on the property securing the paper. If the mortgage is a first mortgage and there is a low loan-to-value ratio, the discount will be reduced as the risk is lessened. On the other hand, if the mortgage is a second or third mortgage and the total loan-to-value ratio is high, equity is therefore low and the discount must be increased.

The motivation of the seller of the paper must be considered as the most important factor. If the seller must have cash, then he has little choice but to increase the discount until the paper sells. But if his need for cash is limited to a portion of the mortgage, he may be able to borrow the needed funds by placing the mortgage up as security for the loan. The interest paid on such a loan can be greater than the yield offered in the discount, and yet the total cost is less than if the mortgage were discounted.

When you deal in the discount mortgage market it is a good idea to establish a few buyers for such paper. You need to have a list of such investors on hand in case you need one. It seems that the need arises when time is short, and an attempt to find a buyer then can be difficult. The investors will dictate the amount of discount needed from their point of view. Unless you are able to dispose of the paper through other means, the general market will be your only hope; and it sets the terms.

If you already know of a few buyers for mortgages, and you plan to offer a mortgage you hold as a part of a purchase or exchange, you may be able to let the new holder of the mortgage cash out of the paper by having a ready buyer for the mortgage. This seller may actually take a bit less than you would have, just to have the cash. When you make your offer, you can say, "This $15,000 mortgage will pay out at a fair interest rate, but if you want to convert it to immediate cash, here is a possible buyer at $10,000. However, I'd recommend you keep it as it is a good investment at $15,000." This strategy allows you to maximize your paper when using it as a part of another transaction.

HOW TO FIND THE DISCOUNT

Constant annual percent tables are provided in this book. These tables have many uses, one of which is an easy way to arrive at the discount amounts for mortgages. The method of finding the discount is explained in the example that follows.

Example 6

Williams needed cash and had a mortgage to sell. The principal amount was $50,000 over fifteen years at 8% annum. The monthly payment was $478. Once the pertinent data is given, the next step is to find the current constant annual percentage of the mortgage. The monthly payment is $478, therefore twelve times, that would give the annual sum of $5,736. The annual sum of payments is then divided by the face amount of the mortgage (that amount still unpaid) and this gives the current constant annual percentage ($5,736 ÷ $50,000 = 0.1147). This should be stated as a percentage (in this case 11.47%). This represents the percent of the total annual payment in relation to the outstanding balance for the years remaining. With the constant annual percent known, the remaining calculation is quite simple. In this example, assume the yield the investor demands is 12%. We know the mortgage has 15 years to go. Find the constant annual percentage which corresponds to 12% for 15 years. Turn to the table of constant annual percentages in the appendix of this book.

In the table of constant annual percentages you would look in the 12% interest column for the 15 years. The answer would be 14.40% (some tables may vary based on the full calculations made[*]). Now complete this formula:

Constant annual percent divided by the demand rate constant = Discounted percentage

$$11.47 \div 14.40 = 79.65\%$$

To apply these results multiply the face amount of the mortgage by the discounted percentage ($50,000 x 79.65% = $39,326). The $39,326 is the value of the mortgage to an investor demanding a 12% yield. To find the percentage of the discount, subtract the discounted percentage from 100% (100% − 79.65% = 20.35% discount).

Mortgage Discount Sheet When Demand Rate Is Known

1. Face amount of mortgage (Present balance owed) $_____
2. Contract rate   _____%
3. Payment (monthly ___, quarterly ____, semiannually ____, annually ____; check one). $_____
4. Constant annual percent annual adjustment of line 3 divided by line 1   _____%
5. Demand rate   _____%
6. Term of years of mortgage   _____ years
7. Constant at demand rate. (Find by looking in demand rate column for number of years)   _____%
8. Line 4 divided line 7 = Discounted value %   _____%
9. Discount percent (Subtract line 8 from 100)   _____%
10. Amount of discount (Line 9 × line 1) $_____
11. Amount to be paid at discount $_____
    a. Line 1 less line 10 or as check
    b. Line 1 × line 9 or as check

[*]Use Table A. Note that examples shown are rounded off so that 11.817 would become 11.82 in the table.

When you are computing a mortgage that has payments which are other than monthly or does not have equal payments over the term, this method of arriving at the discount will cause errors. However, when the payments are equal but not monthly you can still compute the constant percent for that mortgage by using the table for payment at a given rate.

Example 7

Assume a mortgage is paid semiannually at 8% over 15 years. To find the constant annual percentage, look in a table for semiannual mortgages at 8% for 15 years. The semiannual payment is $57.83 for each $1000 of the mortgage, or $2,891.50 twice a year for a $50,000 mortgage. This totals $5,783 per year or a constant semiannual percentage (per annum) of 11.57%, whereas the monthly constant was 11.47%. To find the constant rate, take the payment ($57.83), multiply it by 2, and move the decimal to the left one place. Since this mortgage is payable semiannually, you need to take the demand rate from the same table. As the demand rate is 12%, look under 12% for 15 years. This indicates a $72.65 semiannual payment per $1,000. Multiply the payment by 2 (72.65 x 2 = 145.3) then move the decimal to the left one place (14.5). The end result is the constant annual percentage of the demand rate based on a semiannual payment. The formula can now be completed as in the first instance. However, remember that different payment schedules at the same contract rate and term of years will have different constants.

Mortgages with unequal payments require rather complicated calculations. However, it will be possible to obtain an estimate for such mortgages by totaling the payments received on a mortgage with equal principal plus interest. This will provide an average constant. The following calculations are for a $10,000 mortgage.

Estimate Constant Annual Percent for Mortgages with Constant Principal Plus Interest on the Unpaid Balance

Assume $10,000 mortgage, $1,000 per year plus interest at 8% per annum. 10-year payment.

Step 1: Compute total interest for term of loan

Formula: Principal Amount × (Term + 1) × Rate ÷ 2
$10,000 × (10 + 1) × .08 ÷ 2 = $4,400
Total interest paid: $4,400

Step 2: Add principal amount

Interest:	$ 4,400
Principal:	$10,000
Total:	$14,400

Step 3: Divide by years (term of loan). This gives the average annual payment.
$14,400 ÷ 10 = $1,440

Step 4: Divide average annual payment by original principal amount of loan and convert to a percentage.
$1,440 ÷ 10,000 = .1440
Converted to % = 14.40%

This results in the constant annual percent for the mortgage: 14.40%.

In this example, assume the demand rate is 12% as in the other examples. Because we have adjusted the payment of the mortgage to show an annual average payment of $1,440, you can use the annual payment table for 12% to find the demand constant. Using the table you will find $176.98 is the annual payment for $1,000 for 10 years at 12%. It is not necessary to multiply this by 2 as with the semiannual payment; merely move the decimal one place to the left: 17.7% (rounded off).

Complete the formula: 14.4 ÷ 17.7 = 81.35

The 81.35% is the discounted price of the mortgage in this estimate (81.35% x $10,000 = $8,135). Remember that this is just an estimate. It is not accurate because the constant annual percent is based on averages only.

HOW TO FIND THE INTEREST YIELD ON A MORTGAGE WHICH IS DISCOUNTED

It will be necessary from time to time to know how to calculate the yield on a mortgage that is offered at a discount. For example: Sterling has a $50,000 mortgage with 15 years remaining at 8%. The payment is $478 per month (same as Williams' mortgage mentioned earlier). Sterling is offering this mortgage for sale at a 20% discount. The purchase price of the mortgage is therefore 80% of the face amount ($50,000 × 80% = $40,000). What is the yield to an investor?

The following chart will assist in this calculation. Note that it is very similar to the previous discount chart but with one important difference: we do not know the demand rate.

The formula in this computation is:

Constant annual percent ÷ discounted value percent = Constant at yield rate

The chart has been worked out below. Review it and make your own by using it as a guide.

Yield on a Discounted Mortgage

A.

1. Face amount of mortgage (Present balance owed) — $50,000
2. Contract rate — 8 %
3. Payment (monthly___, quarterly___, semiannually___, annually___; check one) — $ 478
4. Constant annual percent adjustment (line 3 divided by line 1) — 11.47%
5. Discount rate (Known factor) — 20 %
6. Discounted amount ratio (100 less line 5) — 80 %
7. Constant annual percent of discounted mortgage (line 4 divided by line 6) — 14.33%

B.

_____

8. Find yield from tables:
   Locate closest constant rate at 15 years

	Constant rate found:	Corresponding yield:
A.	13. 64	11%
B.	14.40	12%
C.	_____	

9. Estimate yield at nearly 12%

_____

HOW SELLERS CAN USE DISCOUNTED MORTGAGES TO HELP THEM SELL THEIR PROPERTY

Given a standard set of circumstances, any buyer will pay more for a property on terms than he or she will pay if investing 100% of the price in cash. This conclusion is based on two major assumptions: (1) the buyer can earn a greater yield on his capital from the income of the property or from other sources than the cost of the financing, and (2) the buyer has the alternative of paying cash, such as obtaining financing from the seller.

The seller now has the opportunity to use this factor to best advantage. If the buyer wants to pay cash, there is no problem and the discounted mortgage aspect does not enter into the picture. However, to broaden the market, or to create a market for a property that is difficult to sell, the seller may offer reasonable financing.

Example 8

Robinson owns a 50-acre tract of land. It has been on the market for $20,000 per acre ($1,000,000) for nearly six months. His broker suggests that the terms he wants (50% down and short pay-out) are the major drawbacks. Robinson, however, needs cash for another venture and agrees to reduce the price to $18,000 per acre to move the property ($900,000), but he still needs 50% down. His broker examines the situation and proposes that Robinson keep the price at $20,000 per acre since it is reasonable for the market, but that he be willing to accept only 10% down. The balance of 90% will be broken into two mortgages: a first mortgage in the amount of $500,000 and a second in the amount of $400,000.

The terms are to run concurrently for fifteen years at 6% on the first at normal amortization with monthly payments and 8% interest only due on the second for the fifteen years. The broker then suggests that Robinson look to a discount of the first mortgage to generate the cash required.

The first mortgage will pay out at the rate of $4220 per month over the fifteen years. The mortgage is saleable if it will yield 10% in the general market, as it is only 50% of the total value and represents low risk. The broker calculates the sale price to be $392,600, so Robinson would clear this amount on the sale of the mortgage. He would also receive $100,000 down on the property and then have a total of $492,600 (before he pays his broker his fee). Also, he still is owed $400,000 which is earning interest at 8% per annum.

Had Robinson offered the property at $900,000, it is unlikely that it would have moved. Instead, the broker used creative financing to convert a difficult property into a more easily marketable one. The buyer needed only $100,000 down, and had a low-interest first mortgage and an interest-only second mortgage, both highly acceptable forms of financing for a buyer. Also, since the seller was offering the property with 90% financing, little room was left for negotiations by the buyer to reduce the price.

The buyer of the mortgage obtained a good yield at a fairly safe risk. In Robinson's case, the land was at a fair value so the risk was slight. Robinson came out better than he had thought in that the package produced a sale. Had he received 50% down at a price of $900,000 he would have had $450,000 in cash, whereas with the $100,000 price and the discount he had $492,000.

The tradeoff of a discounted mortgage, instead of lowering the price, will work in many areas of real estate. A free and clear property where the seller can use a first mortgage for the discount, as did Robinson, is best for such a transaction, but the secondary mortgages can be discounted as well.

HOW TO FIND INVESTORS WHO WILL BUY DISCOUNTED MORTGAGES

There are several markets for mortgages. The most organized is that consisting of mortgage brokers. These professional people make their living by placing and making mortgages. They deal with private investors as well as institutional funds and will act on their own behalf or as broker agents. Because they have daily contact with this field, they are a prime source for discounted mortgages.

Locating these sources is relatively easy. Most will be listed in your phone book. You can also obtain the names of others who are outside your area from your banking sources. The contact you make with them is important.

It should be noted that not all the mortgage brokers you may contact will be viable. Some don't have the contacts that others may have, or may find dealing with you uncomfortable. I presume that you will not be dealing as a mortgage broker and as a real estate broker at the same time. You should make your situation clear to the mortgage broker right away. Your interest in dealing with discounted mortgages is merely to help your client reach a desired goal. Unless you are licensed as a mortgage broker, you may not be entitled to receive a fee. The mortgage broker knows this and will be relieved that you also understand the situation. Those of you who may have both types of licenses already know how to get the cooperation of your fellow mortgage brokers. Therefore, I shall leave that topic alone.

Mortgage brokers are but one source. Trust departments and pension funds that may be located in your area are also candidates for good mortgages, and they like the idea of leveraging up on a discounted mortgage. These sources are found in your local commercial banks and insurance companies. The commercial bank is the best place to start and you might as well go right to the top: the secretary of the president. This astute person will direct you to all the right people. Often, a recommendation from the secretary to the person you want to deal with is more important than if the president himself called the trust officer and said you were on your way. How so? Follow this suggestion: meet and establish good rapport with the bank's president. This is essential to other dealings you will have in the community anyway. Go over some of the services that the bank offers. Does it have a trust department? If so, what type of trust services does it provide? Once you have had two or three meetings with this bank president, you will have made contact with his secretary. Be sure he or she knows who you are and that you are on friendly terms with the boss.

The day you want to sit down with the trust officer, give the president's secretary a call and ask the name of the trust officer in charge: "Is it a Mr. Rankin?" you might ask. Then ask if he or she would mind giving Mr. Rankin a call as an introduction for your appointment that day. The secretary usually will and may also have something nice to say about you.

Once you are with the trust officer ask about services. He or she will become a salesperson, giving you data about the department. Do not rush in to a trust officer you have never seen and confront him or her with a discounted mortgage you must sell by that afternoon or else blow a big deal.

Ask about the mortgage brokers the officer deals with in buying private mortgages for the trust account or pension fund the company represents. If he or she gives you some names remember them, but the important thing you have learned is that the bank does buy such mortgages. Ask the trust officer who approves such private mortgage purchases how you would go about presenting a package.

Private investors are numerous, although very difficult to cultivate. Earlier chapters have dealt with this private investor in mortgages. But to be somewhat repetitive, remember the private investor in mortgages is not greatly unlike the investor in real estate. They both recognize the advantage of realty as a security. However, the mortgage investor is willing to take a lower yield at a reduced risk than the real estate investor.

Some of your realty buyers may like to sink some of their portfolio into mortgages, so don't overlook your own buyers of real estate as possible investors. To some degree, this source comes out of your back pocket because you will not receive a fee for placing such an investment. But the sale of the mortgage may close another deal. Besides, passing a good mortgage at a high yield on to a past investor will be appreciated and the favor will be returned.

Look in the mirror. The person looking back at you may be a prime discounted mortgage buyer. It is not impossible that you may look to the mortgage as the total commission or at least a part of your fee. Sellers will often ask you to take part or all of a mortgage as your fee. Your ability to plan for this possibility and to have the mortgage discounted will depend on your willingness to take the paper.

If you approach the possibility of discounting a mortgage as part of a cash-out program for the seller, you should speak to him or her early and explain that at times your firm will buy mortgages as an investment or take the paper as all or part of the fee. Do this only if you are prepared or if your firm is willing to do it. The opposite is also necessary. Tell the seller that your firm is not in a position to take paper on such a discount, but you will do all you can to help dispose of the mortgage.

To avoid mention of one of these two possibilities will leave the suggestion up to the seller. Refusing to take the paper at that moment in time may cast doubts in the seller's mind about your earlier suggestions that he or she make such a transaction and hold such paper in the first place.

Don't Forget the Mortgagor

The mortgagor may be a prime buyer for a discounted mortgage. Naturally, in these situations the seller of the mortgage is the mortgagee. The seller may be holding paper from a previous sale or may be investor who bought a mortgage from you or someone else. Before you run off and seek out other investors, offer the discount to the person who makes the monthly payment. By giving a break in the payoff, he or she may become a good client later on. In any event, the buyer of the mortgage makes little difference to the mortgagee selling the paper; it is the cash that is important.

A REVIEW OF THE SOURCES THAT WILL BUY DISCOUNTED MORTGAGES

1. **Mortgage brokers.** For the broker who will not deal frequently with discounted mortgages, this source can be consistent and easy to approach.

2. **Trust funds and pension funds.** A little harder to approach, but one of the prime sources used by the mortgage broker. These sources are found at your commercial banks and insurance companies.

3. **Private investors.** Look first at your own realty investors. Some of these clients may like a good discounted mortgage. Other private investors will advertise in local papers or can be found through your bank or savings and loan.

4. **Real Estate Brokers.** Many brokers and salespeople will take a discounted mortgage as part of their commission. All you have to do is ask.

5. **The mortgagor.** Never overlook the person who writes out the monthly check that pays off the loan.

WHEN TO OFFER A PARTIAL DISCOUNT
TO THE MORTGAGOR

It may be possible to raise some quick cash by going to the mortgagor and suggesting a discount on the future payments if he or she will prepay some of the outstanding principal. I was involved in such a case some time ago.

Example 9

Emory was holding a $45,000 second mortgage on a business he had sold several years earlier. The mortgage had fifteen years remaining at 8 $1/2$% interest per annum. The annual payment was based on monthly payments of $443.25. The constant annual percentage on this mortgage is 11.82 (found in constant table under 8 $1/2$% at fifteen years). Emory needed a quick $15,000 and found that if he were to discount the mortgage the yield necessary would be 12%. This meant the sale price would be $36,936 (11.82 ÷ 14.40 × 45,000). Emory felt this was too great a discount to take in order to obtain the $15,000 needed.

He approached one of the local mortgage brokers to see whether he could borrow against the mortgage, but that did not produce any positive results. By the time Emory called me, he was at his wits end. "I need the cash by the end of the week," he said, "and it seems that the more I need it, the tougher it becomes to get it." Sounds very familiar, I know.

After counseling with Emory, I suggested we make the following proposal to the mortgagor. The mortgagor would prepay $15,000 on the outstanding mortgage. This would bring the unpaid principal balance down to $30,000. Based on this balance, the monthly amortization would be reduced to $295.50. As an inducement or bonus to the mortgagor, Emory agreed to reduce the interest rate on the mortgage to 6 $1/2$% rather than the 8 $1/2$% percent for its remaining term. This gave a new constant of 10.45 and a monthly payment of $261.25 instead of the $295.50. What this meant was that the mortgagor was obtaining a discount for the remaining balance by the prepayment of the $15,000. Over the balance of the term the mortgagor would save $6,165. The cost to Emory was not really the $6,165 however, as the reduction of the interest lowered his pretax income and converted future pay-back (the mortgage) into ready cash. A discounting of the mortgage would have caused a greater reduction of total earnings, and hence all parties benefitted.

There were many other ways to approach the benefit Emory had given the mortgagor, but this solution seemed to be the best for Emory. The mortgage, as it turned out, was paid off four years later when the property was sold by the mortgagor. No doubt the low interest on the second was somewhat instrumental in attracting a buyer, even though the property was refinanced anyway. The gamble Emory took in reducing the interest rate was well calculated. Had he reduced the principal amount in the discount, that sum would have been a lost item regardless of when the mortgage was paid back. The reduced interest was an expense to Emory only as long as the mortgage was in force. Emory knew that most mortgages had a maximum life span of seven to ten years in the type of business he had. The life span of mortgages is important in discounting. The early retirement of a mortgage will boost the yield to the holder when the face amount is discounted.

The bonus yield that comes when a discounted mortgage is paid off cannot be calculated except by experience in the loan market for the area. Some savings and loans and commercial banks will give you the statistics on their type of loan history, but many feel this is confidential information. Here's why:

Example 10

Assume that Emory had sold his $45,000 mortgage at a discount which would have yielded 12%. As we saw in the example the price would have been $36,936. Remember, the face amount on the mortgage is $45,000. If the loan were paid off at the end of the first year the new mortgagee (the investor who bought the mortgage from Emory) would have been paid approximately $48,800. As the investor paid only $36,936 for the paper, his return on his investment for one year would be $11,864 or a yield of 32.12%. Each year this bonus will decline, and by the fifteenth year the yield is down to the 12% discounted yield. The incredible bonus interest that comes with this early prepayment is one of the real advantages of the discounted mortgage and should never be taken lightly.

Examination of the total financing on the property may disclose a potential necessity for refinancing in which a mandatory prepayment of a mortgage may be imminent. For example: A first mortgage is offered for discount. It is a twenty-year mortgage at a moderate interest rate. Because of the term of years, the discount will be rather high. The mortgage broker examines the underlying mortgages and finds a large second mortgage which is interest only for three years with a balloon payment. The combined financing is less than 60% of the value and the second mortgage is nearly half that total. The mortgage broker concludes that the owner of the property will refinance all of the mortgages into one new first mortgage before the end of the three years when the second mortgage balloons. Not only is such a mortgage a good risk, but the discount and probable bonus will give an exceedingly high yield.

Another situation would be when the discounted mortgage is a second mortgage behind a low-interest-rate first mortgage that is nearly paid off. Such mortgages have a high constant rate and become prime candidates for refinancing even though the new interest rate would be higher. The constant rate for income property is often more important than the interest rate. Once the mortgage is refinanced, the second mortgage would automatically be paid off.

The combinations are endless. The motivation of the mortgagor is also important. Some mortgagors have a history of early prepayment. If you have this information, it's worth its weight in discounted mortgages.

Chapter 16

TWO PRIME
INSIDER TECHNIQUES:
Preferred Income Sweeteners
and
Options

This chapter is devoted to two very different investment and financing techniques; each of these two techniques *preferred income sweeteners* and *options*, has a different goal as its result. Like most financing tools, they can be used together and in combination with many other techniques discussed in this book. Each of these two techniques functions at a different level of the transaction. However, both work mainly because of the greed factor of other parties to the deal. This will become evident as you progress through this chapter. So, lets start with the first of these two techniques.

PREFERRED INCOME SWEETENERS

Preferred income forms of financing are often found in joint ventures or partnerships. Here an equity partner puts up all or most of the initial capital investment with a working partner or syndicator who has put the deal together. However, the technique works well in sweetening secondary financing.

Definition

When you bring in a partner or borrow money, you can offer the partner or lender a piece of the income as an incentive to his or her capital. One of the most effective methods to accomplish this is to offer a preference of income. This income comes off the top of net revenue, prior to any splits for the balance of the equity. A *sweetener* is anything you can offer another party to close the deal. Ideally you look for sweeteners that do not take away from your benefits. In the preferred income form of a sweetener, if your income pro forma is correct, then offering a partner or lender preference on their return does not diminish your return.

Example 1 Preferred Income Used in a Joint Venture

You invite a fellow investor to put $500,000 of his money in a project of yours. Together you borrow another $2,000,000 to acquire an apartment building you are going to manage. This debt has an annual debt service of $220,000 per year. You and the investor are 50/50 in ownership, even though the investor has put up all the capital to get the deal started. To entice this investor you agreed to give him 12% return on his invested $500,000. This investor insists that the 12% return be preferred. This means that he expects to get $60,000 of the income from the project before you get anything. The numbers are as follows.

Assume the project is a 100-unit rental apartment complex. Note income and expenses:

Gross rents collected	$ 600,000
Other income	50,000
Total income collected	$ 650,000

So far this looks like a normal kind of partnership split. However, assume that this property was a turn-around property and that the income for the first couple of years was not projected as high as that indicated above. You can see what would happen if the NOI for the first year was only $280,000:

Net operating income	$ 280,000
Less debt service	220,000
Cash flow	$ 60,000
Less preference income to partner	60,000
Balance	$ 0
You take your share	0
Balance to be divided equally	$ 0

The investor insisted on the preference income because he wanted to be sure that if there was any income at all, he would have first shot at it.

Example 2 Preferred Income as a Sweetener to Entice the Seller to Hold a Mortgage

You want to buy a strip store and keep the existing financing in place. However, to do this you must get the seller to hold some form of secondary financing. The price for the center is $1,500,000. The existing first mortgage is $900,000 and you have $300,000 cash to invest. You ask the seller to hold a second mortgage for the difference, of $300,000 and you offer interest only at 8% per annum. He balks at this and asks for

10% per annum. In your own mind you are ready to go to 9% anyway, but why not give yourself some edge in the deal? After all, the seller has been telling you how good the income is in the center and how rents are scheduled to go up in a few months. You tell him that you will offer him 9% interest on the mortgage for every year that the net operating income of the center equals the revenue the seller promises it will do.

REDUCING RISK IS THE NAME OF THE GAME

One of the primary rules of smart investing is: Reduce your risk. I have referred to this idea often and thus far you have seen many different techniques that allow you to accomplish exactly that. If you were the investor in the above example, you would have substantially reduced your risk in this transaction by taking a preferred position against the income. Remember, you can reduce your risk in a variety of ways, and risk is relative to your knowledge and ability. While one man's risk might be another man's fun, investment capital leans to the safer side of any transaction. As the investor, this chapter will give you the real insider techniques on how to get the maximum benefits from preferred income transactions. As the entrepreneur to a deal, looking for added capital, this chapter will help you obtain needed funds to complete the transaction.

Example 3 Tradeoffs: Reduce the Risk by Reducing the Yield

"I will pay your price if you accept my terms." This works for any savvy buyer since the buyer knows the alternatives available to make the terms fit the price he or she is willing to pay. What happens is this: You find a property you want to buy. You then approach the seller with the news that you are interested in buying and will pay a reasonable price. The seller views reasonable price in different terms than you do, but let us not argue at this stage of the game. You look the seller in the eye and say, "Tell me your price, Mr. or Ms. Seller. If I can work it out, I am interested in buying." Everything that happens from that moment on is a series of tradeoffs. The first place you generally look to make tradeoffs is with the seller. Remember, the seller has a goal in sight and might be willing to settle for something less than full attainment of the goal. If by selling the property most of the goal is reached, then the seller's motivations make him or her the initial candidate for a preferred deal.

Example 4 Preferred Purchase: A Sweetener to the Seller

One of my early clients taught me about this kind of transaction. It is a magnificent way to get down to the nitty-gritty in any deal. Specially where the seller is telling you, "I would love to keep this property but I need some cash." Mind you, this kind of transaction is based on a sizable amount of cash going to the seller. Remember that the cash invested may not be your money. Frequently the "cash" can be obtained from other sources, but from the seller's point of view cash is what is going to talk. Note the preferred purchase transaction in the next example.

Example 5 Preferred Income to Reduce Buyer's Risk

Charles owns a beautiful office building in downtown San Francisco. It is fully rented, or nearly so, and Charles has a nice suite of offices in the building. He has a proforma showing the income and expenses, and projects that within a year or so, when he can increase the rents in the building, the investment will provide a very good return to a prospective buyer. But Charles has some other opportunities and cries out to his broker that he needs some cash.

Now, buying an office building is one thing, but assume that you aren't in the business of managing office buildings. You like the idea of the rent and the income and the tax shelter, but the idea of management isn't to your liking. Besides, you live in Chicago.

In this deal, Charles reports the following:

Price	$4,500,000
Mortgages	3,050,000
Cash to buy	$1,450,000

The debt service on the existing $3,050,000 mortgage is $320,000 per year. Charles reports that the operating expenses and taxes and the like total another $380,000 per year. Gross revenue at the moment is $850,000.

If these figures were correct and you paid $1,450,000 cash for this deal, and all the numbers Charles gave you were correct, you would be making the cash flow shown below:

Gross revenue	$ 850,000
Operating expenses	380,000
Net operating income	$ 470,000
Debt service	320,000
Cash flow	$ 150,000

This is 10.3448% on your invested capital. This is not bad, because you have lots of other benefits going along with this deal. There is ample tax shelter and lots of future equity build-up. If the rents can be increased and costs held down, there is even appreciation. Not a bad deal at all.

Except that Charles has overestimated on the pro forma a little. The expenses are probably low by $30,000 to $60,000, and there is no vacancy factor accounted for. There is a maximum of around $60,000 in income at risk here, although that's being conservative from the buyer's point of view. But the property is a very nice building and you would like to own it.

Example 6 Offer a Preferred Purchase Deal

You offer to buy 50% of the building and will pay $800,000 cash for that opportunity. This represents approximately 55% of the $1,450,000 down payment to buy 100% of the building. This is a premium to Charles, and all you want is the following:

- To be preferred (to receive from the top of the cash flow), 12% on your cash invested. Based on a cash investment of $800,000 your preference income would amount to $96,000. The seller takes the next equal amount, and everything else is split 50/50

- All or most of the depreciation. This is a negotiating point; depending on the deal and the motivation of the seller, you might end up with the building and the seller with the land (land is not depreciable)

- When you sell or refinance the property, you will share in the proceeds on a 50/50 basis only on the assumption that your share is at least $800,000.

- There are other points you could have asked for, such as the right to buy out the seller's interest. This could be at a time in the future with a formula you present now. Or you might be satisfied with an agreement of a first right of refusal. You might find that as the loan is paid off, and the value increases. This may enable you to be able to buy out the partner through funds obtained in refinancing the property.

Example 7 Creative Build-Up of Investment

You could also have asked for the deficit (if any) of your preferred interest to build up and add to your investment. For example, say there is a bad year and the total cash flow is only $100,000. As you would get the first $96,000 you would get nearly the entire $100,000, and Charles would only get $6,000. If the income fell to a cash flow of only $86,000 then you would be $10,000 short of the amount you needed. If the agreement contained a provision to allow you to have a build-up on a deficit, then your invested capital for next year's calculations is now $810,000. You could even provide that any deficit would apply as purchase price paid in a buy out of Charles interest. Or, you could have it set up so that Charles actual interest in the property is reduced by a set percentage. This would go on until some defined point where the partner would see his share eaten up and would drop out of the picture.

Why would a seller accept a deal like this? Well, look at it from his point of view. He is getting $400,000 in cash and still has 50% of the deal. He might insist on having the management contract for the property. That would give him income, and as a nonpreferred owner, this gives him incentive to properly manage the property.

If Charles has confidence in the deal, he will quickly see that within a few years he is going to profit far more than if he had sold the property and taken the $1,450,000 cash to the mortgage. But note one very important aspect here: Charles isn't being given the choice of $1,450,000 or the preferred deal. He must choose between this preferred deal or his best offer (if any).

The buyer's advantage is easy to see. As the investor in this deal, you have purchased sound management and given it motivation to stay in place and do a good job. If you were concerned about Charles ability to manage the property, then you had best stay away from the deal unless it was so good that outside management could be found easily and quickly.

In making this kind of deal you might well find the seller suddenly changing his or her tune about how good the project is. "Well, I don't think the income will be *that* good" is the aftermath of some preferred presentations.

Big smart money uses the preferred deal to nail down solid projects with good management and a motivated seller who needs some cash. In the development business there are often good managers and developers who get cash-short on a new project and for construction overages or whatever. These deals make for the mainstay of the preferred deals, but they aren't necessarily limited to that kind of project.

You can buy a business or any small venture on this preferred plan. Whatever you buy that is income-producing has the potential of being financed in this way. If you are looking at a business, don't buy 100% of the deal, but instead keep the current owner in at a percentage of the deal. That way you can move into many varied deals without losing your flexibility.

USING THE PREFERRED INCOME TECHNIQUE AS A SWEETENER TO DEBT

Later on in another chapter I will discuss a technique called *percent of income.* That technique frequently is tied to leasehold interests, or joint ventures and can work somewhat like the preferred income. However, there are some differences you will find when you get to that chapter.

Using a preferred income technique as a sweetener to secondary financing works like this:

Example 8

You want to buy an income property that the owner tells you has a solid NOI of $50,000. As part of the deal you offer the seller a second mortgage in the amount of $150,000 over 15 years at 7% interest per year. The seller balks and cries on your shoulder that 7% is too low. You tell him or her that any year that the NOI exceeds

$55,000 you will pay an additional 2% interest on the unpaid balance of the mortgage. You can see that there are several elements that can be negotiated at this point; why not 3%, why not a floor of only $50,000, and so on. The idea is that you have moved the seller into negotiating for the sale, rather than deciding if he or she wants to take the deal.

HOW TO MAXIMIZE YOUR RETURN WHILE REDUCING YOUR RISK AS THE MONEY MAN

Whenever you are the source of funds in a preferred deal, you will find it helpful to review this chapter. The following checklist will be a big help.

THE MAXIMUM RETURN REDUCED RISK CHECKLIST: WHEN YOUR MONEY IS AT RISK

1. LOWER THE DOWN PAYMENT.   Once the deal is pretty well set, work on reducing the down payment. In general, negotiation follows a standard pattern. You make an offer that is usually lower than you will ultimately go, and the other side makes a counter that is usually higher than they will expect to end up. Once you have gone through a couple of offers and counteroffers you should have a pretty good understanding of where you expect the other side wants to end up. If you understand the techniques of negotiation as has been offered in this book, you know the importance of letting the other side of the deal win. This concept of winning is even more important in a preferred income deal because if the party you are dealing with is going to manage the property you don't want to start out with a partner who thinks you shouldn't deserve what the contract says you should get. However, having said this, you may offer as a final tradeoff to let the other side win a point or two, to give in, if he or she will reduce the up-front cash you were to invest. If, for example, instead of putting $800,000 up front, you invested that amount with $600,000 at closing, and two payments of $100,000 plus interest at 10%, you will have increased your yield (you get 12% on $800,000 remember), while at the same time you decrease your risk.

2. SPLIT THE DOWN PAYMENT INTO EQUITY AND DEBT.   The above example is a division of payments of equity over a period of time, but why not divide the $800,000 into a down payment of $500,000 and a straight second mortgage of $300,000? This second mortgage might be negotiated into a first mortgage on another property, if you had something else. The key here is that your return is still based on $800,000, and the yield of 12% (as in the previous example) remains at $96,000 even after you have paid off the $300,000 second mortgage.

3. TRADE THE DOWN PAYMENT: ALL OR PART.   Keep in mind that the seller might benefit from an IRC 1031 exchange. If this is the case, then a partial or full exchange of the needed equity of $800,000 might work to both your benefits. Never overlook the opportunity to get rid of a property that does nothing for you. Even if it is only a small part of a deal, this is your chance to have it be absorbed into the transaction. One of the brokers might end up with it as a part of a commission.

4. TIE THE YIELD TO A COST OF LIVING INDEX.   Nothing says that your yield has to remain fixed to any predetermined amount. If you can tie down 12% in early negotiations, and the seller wants something that you might be able to give up, ask to have your yield be indexed to the *All Items Cost-of-Living Index*. This is a standard index that is published by the United States Department of Labor and Statistics, and has been mentioned many times in this book. Your lawyer or real estate broker should know how to incorporate that into the transaction. The end result of this would be that if the cost of living went up 10% over a couple of years, your yield would also go up. Remember, no matter what income you get out of the transaction, it is only your share in preference. If there is sufficient income left over for the other partner or partners to get their equal share, then everyone ends up fine. You can remind the seller or partner of this when they balk at why your preferred income should go up.

5. GET OTHER COLLATERAL FROM THE SELLER OR PARTNER.   Even though a preferred income might be good, there are other things that can make the deal even better, and increase your return while lowering your risk. A motivated partner who doesn't have the extra capital it takes to do the deal, or the motivated seller, may be willing to give you extra security to bring you into the deal. Look to the transaction first to see if there are ways to get additional security from the other side. Will they stay on the debt? If you don't have to sign personally that is a benefit to you. Will they assign rents from other projects, or put up other property as security? All important ways to reduce your risk. In tradeoff you may allow this additional security to drop off the deal at a future date, or when the income reaches a much higher level of safety than it currently has been projected.

6. GET A BUYOUT PROVISION.   This is usually the most important, and often the most difficult provision of the deal to negotiate. Because of this, I suggest you do not even bring it up until the very end of the negotiations. Why? Because it is likely that they will bring it up first. Generally it is better to be working to an agreement than working against someone who doesn't want to even approach the subject. Buyout provisions do not have to be equally fair. In fact, because it is your money that is making the deal work in the first place, you should get the advantage of the

buyout provision. Some of the elements that can be negotiated have been shown in earlier examples in this chapter. For example, if there is any deficit in income off your preferred amount, that can apply against a buyout, or build up in your equity side of the deal. You might have a set buyout amount for a period of years, say, the right to buy the other side out of the deal based on fixed amounts at the end of certain years. Another method is to have a formula that follows an increase of a certain set percentage every year until the buyout is accomplished. One thing is sure, avoid getting into a situation where one side has the right to match the other's offer. This kind of a buyout works as follows: If I want to buy you out I can offer you an amount. If you decide to buy me out you get to follow the same formula that I offered you. This is a bad deal for you as the money guy.

BEFORE YOU GO TO THE MONEY PERSON REVIEW THESE SIX KEY FACTORS

1. HAVE CONTROL OVER THE TRANSACTION. This is the same advice I give to syndications or anyone else looking to generate a joint venture or raise money from potential partners. If you don't have the deal locked up, then you might as well go out on the street with a cardboard sign that reads "Might have deal, need money." Real estate is all about control. Brokers need exclusive listings or they cannot spend the time and money to sell the property, and if you are looking for partners of any kind, it is critical that you get the property tied up 100% before you go out looking for money.

2. REMEMBER, UNTIL THE DEAL CLOSES THERE IS STILL ROOM TO NEGOTIATE. This means that even though you have the deal tied up, you still have room to negotiate. As long as you have a reasonable due-diligence period to make inspections and review different aspects of the transaction, you can still get out of the deal. If you cannot, then you have not tied up the deal correctly. This out clause can be a simple right to approve the final inspection to your satisfaction. Sellers may not like your coming back to the bargaining table at the last minute, but if you discover something that makes you believe you need to renegotiate some of the terms, including the price, then do so. Later is often better than sooner, from your point of view. Sellers start to mentally spend the money and make other plans. In addition, while you are doing your due diligence you may be negotiating several other aspects of the deal. This could be a refinance of a mortgage, the purchase of secondary financing at a discount, or establishing new leases; any of these items may generate a reason to reopen negotiations.

3. KNOW HOW FAR YOU CAN GO WITH THE DEAL. This is very important because when it comes down to the nitty-gritty, many investors are likely more astute at the fine tuning of the deal than you might be. The more you know about how far the income will meet its projections the better off you will be. If you are out looking for

money you have already set yourself into the ranks of the lesser astute. The more astute already have the money, so you must learn from your mistakes and learn how they do deals. If you can find a good real estate broker who understands what it takes to make deals, rather than follow instructions, then you will be ahead of the game.

4. BE FLEXIBLE.   As with any real-estate negotiations, the more flexible you are, the more likely you are to make deals. Keep in mind that the majority of people buying and selling real estate are not professionals, nor are they loan sharks. They are likely to be just like you, and anxious to do a deal. Be as honest as you know how, and honesty will keep you out of more trouble than a Sherman tank.

5. OFFER THE OTHER PARTY AN OPPORTUNITY.   Any time you have something good to offer someone, make sure he or she understands that you are doing a favor. You are not asking for a loan, you are giving the chance to be a part of something good, and you have so much confidence in the deal you are willing to back that confidence up by giving preference of the income.

6. HAVE EVERYTHING READY FOR THEIR SIGNATURE.   The professional approach is to make sure that all bases are covered, and that the documentation of the presentation is clear and backs up what you have said about the deal. Then have the proper documents that would allow you to get a commitment from the money source. The better your preparation, the easier your task will be. A well-documented presentation shows that you are serious, and that if you get a "no," you are ready to move on to another source.

PITFALLS IN PREFERRED-INCOME TRANSACTIONS

As with anything you can do there are pitfalls that await you. Take a look at the most critical pitfalls from the point of view of the money source.

1. INACCURATE OR OVERLY OPTIMISTIC INCOME AND EXPENSE FIGURES. Income and expense figures are rarely correct, even when every item is properly accounted for. There are many reasons for this. Property owners let the business rent their car, pay their health insurance, pick up the tab for travel, and so on, all on the up-and-up, but not the way you might do it. Then, there are property owners who have been known to actually lie about what they take in, or spend. Many syndicators get so enthusiastic about what they are doing that they puff up the income numbers and downplay the expenses. If you are the seller who is given the opportunity to make a couple of extra interest points if the income comes in as you promised, be sure to ask yourself if the numbers you gave the buyer were correct.

2. NARROW-MINDED APPROACH TO COMPETITION.   Some income properties look good, but if you are going to invest your capital make sure that the competition is not about to overwhelm you. This is specially the case with people properties, such as motels, hotels, restaurants, apartment rentals, and so on. Lenders have been burned by not taking special care to see what else is in the market place *now* that will compete with this property, and what is on the drawing board for the near future. All of this can be checked, and is essential.

3. OVERVALUED PROPERTY.   Clearly, if you put up $500,000 as a down payment to existing financing of $2,000,000 to get a 50% interest, and the property is worth only $2,400,000 then you have overpaid, even if you get 18% preferred income. Whenever you are offered anything that looks good, be sure to find out just how good it is.

4. EXCESSIVE DEBT: HIGH LOAN-TO-VALUE RATIO.   Overleveraged transactions bring with them greater risk. This risk may be worthwhile, and you might find ways to help cover your exposure to that risk. But all real estate transactions need to have some breathing room. If all the cash goes into a deal that is running on the edge of the bank book every month, just to make mortgage payments, then more capital needs to be put into the deal. When you are asked to come up with the initial capital, and the other parties tell you they will supply additional funds, if and when needed, you may discover that, if and when the funds are needed the other parties don't have any funds. The greatest failure of any business is lack of proper capitalization.

THE OPTIONS

There are many different forms and uses of the option. It is found in almost every real-estate transaction to a certain degree, and has a use by itself that can put you into control, buy you time, and reduce your overall cost in any real estate deal.

Definition

Option, is defined as a choice. In real estate terms it is the right to buy, sell, or otherwise dispose of an interest in property at a specific or defined time, at specific or defined terms. The person who has the option controls the situation.

Example 1 An Option to Buy

You agree to give the seller $5,000 to allow you 12 months time to have your architect design a home for a lot. During that time you have the option to buy the property for $50,000, and apply the $5,000 against the purchase price. If you do not exercise your option to buy within that time you lose the $5,000.

Example 2 An Option to Lease

You sign up for a 12-month lease, and ask the owner to give you the right (option) to lease for another 12 months at the same terms. At the end of the first year's lease you have to notify the owner that you exercise your right to renew. If not, then you move out.

Example 3 Due-Diligence Approval

In your contract to purchase an ocean front hotel, you have a period of 60 days to make a series of inspections. These include review of employment contracts, current reservations, future reservations, maintenance records, and so on. At the end of the 60 days you have the option to close on the property or to cancel the deal.

OPTIONS PUT TIME ON YOUR SIDE

Buying with an option is an ideal way to put time on your side for a change. The option contract gives you the opportunity to put up some money that can build into a sizable equity in a hurry if you are right about the trends. If you are wrong, then you have kept your risk at a minimum. As you will discover in this chapter, you can use options that will absolutely reduce your risk to zero.

Two Basic Kinds of Options

There are several kinds of option agreements, but for the most part they fall into two categories: the *straight option*, and the *conditioned option*.

The straight option is, as the name would suggest, a standard type of agreement that simply gives one party a right to buy or lease a property at a set date in the future at a price agreed to. The time periods and the actual terms can be specific, set to a formula, tied to appraisals, based on income or any other kind or method of calculating price. The optionee (the person who has the option and is in control), may or may not have paid money for the option. Keep in mind that all options should have some kind of consideration, but the actual consideration does not have to be money. Note the following examples in which something other than money is the consideration to the option:

1. Buyer to undertake inspections; then gives the owner copies of the inspections.
2. Buyer to verify zoning; essential to ascertain if the property can be used to fit the Buyer needs.

3. Buyer leases with option to buy; the consideration is the lease.

4. Buyer promises to have lawyer draw up contract; the consideration is that the buyer spends money to create a future benefit to the property owner.

5. Buyer promises to make zoning change request; to suit the buyer's needs, and as an improvement to the property if the buyer does not exercise option to buy.

Each of these five items should spark your own imagination to think of other similar examples where you, as a buyer, can obtain control over a property, even if for a very short period of time.

All aspects of a contract are flexible and open to negotiation up until the contract is closed. The key to any negotiation is to be in control for as long as possible. Control means you have the right to buy (or lease or whatever), and the other side must go along with what the terms of the deal call for. However, as the optionee is in control with a choice, the optionee can elect not to exercise the option. This is critical because it reopens the door for more negotiation to fine-tune the deal.

Example 4 Using the Option to Renegotiate the Deal

You have a two-year lease on a home. The lease contains a provision that gives you the right to renew the lease for another two years at the same terms, or, at your option, you can buy the home for $150,000 any time during either term of lease. As with all options this puts you in control of this property to the extent that as long as you do not default on the lease, you know you can buy this property for $150,000. Keep in mind that the seller can sell the property subject to your lease and option, for whatever price the seller can get. But aside from that, the fact that your option is for $150,000 does not preclude you from coming back to the table and attempting to negotiate for a reduced price. After all, you have lived in the house for a year and some months now, and know exactly what needs to be fixed. You can negotiate from a very strong position.

Opening the door to negotiations is what the option is all about. By gaining control over a property you generally shut down the seller's efforts to try to sell or lease the property to someone else. As long as you play your cards right, that is, pick the right time to negotiate for an improvement in the deal, you might be successful.

WHEN DO YOU GO BACK TO THE NEGOTIATION TABLE?

The timing on opening up negotiations again depends on the transaction and the time period you have to work with. The most important factor is not to wait until time works against you. The key to this is to make sure you really want to buy the property. Once that decision has been made, then you can begin to make overtures to the seller that all is not as you would like it to be. Care must be taken that you do not relinquish control in the deal. The following is an example that occurred the same week that I was writing this chapter. Take a look at how one prospective buyer stuffed his foot in his mouth by accidentally giving up control.

Example 5 Losing Control of the Option

Mick and Jake were partners who tied up a 100-unit oceanfront hotel in Fort Lauderdale for just under $5,000,000 (subject to a cheap land lease). They had a long due-diligence period, which they insisted on because they lived nearly 2,000 miles away from the property. During the due-diligence period they came back to the negotiation table several times. Each time they would have their local lawyer send a letter to the seller with a statement that unless certain redress to the price and terms could be agreed to between the parties by a specific date they may be forced to exercise their right to withdraw from the agreement. The letter looked like a very strong demand that they were going to withdraw, but each time the date the letter specified approached, the seller caved in to the demands and reduced the price, gave in to interest terms, and so on, setting a pattern that only made Mick and Jake want to test some more.

Deposits eventually went hard (the point when they should be nonrefundable), and suddenly another letter comes in from the lawyer. This time the letter cited several problems that had come up and claimed the sellers had grossly misrepresented the deal, and demanded a refund of the deposits, and canceled the agreement. Somehow the lawyer made a mistake. What he meant to say was, "if you do not clear up this matter by a certain date, they may be forced to rescind the contract." Suddenly the seller had an out. Back in control, the buyer had to scramble. If he truly wanted out of the deal he was now going to have to fight for his deposit. If he wanted back into the deal, he was going to have to fight for that position. This was a prime example of going back to the well once too often, and at that, doing it incorrectly.

The Option Is No Guarantee of a Successful Conclusion to the Contract

In any option there is no guarantee the optionee will follow through and close. If the seller has been compensated by the option money for the time the property is taken off the market that might be okay. But usually the option money is not enough to make up for the lost time. Or worse, it might be that the time the seller gives up is a period when things happen that make the property less valuable. The buyer skips town, and no other buyers are around to take up the slack.

HOW TO NEGOTIATE THE BEST OPTIONS TERMS WHEN YOU ARE THE SELLER

Start with a Free Option

Sellers can use the Option as a tool to entice a prospective buyer or tenant. If you own a commercial tract of land and think it would be a great spot for a fast-food restaurant, you might be willing, or even excited, should a major fast-food restaurant come to you and ask for a 90-day free option to allow it to ascertain if your site was the best one. If you can understand this concept, take it one step further. Why not go out and find all the fast-food restaurants who are not in the immediate area and offer them a 90-day free look at your site. All you want is to make sure that they actually spend the time and effort to make a decision.

Get Paid for the Option

There is a point of time when you should not be expected to give the prospective buyer any more of a free look. At this point of time, which generally follows a reasonable due-diligence period, the contract should call for a deposit to go hard, and a timetable established that winds down to the actual closing:

> . . . and further, at the end of the 90-day period of due diligence, the buyer shall either give notice of intentions to close, under the provisions of closing as covered elsewhere in this agreement, or buyer may elect to continue the due-diligence period another 90 days, thereby retaining the option to purchase the subject property at the terms and price contained herein, by payment to the seller of $50,000. This $50,000 will be payment in full for this additional 90-day option and will not be refunded to the buyer should the buyer fail to close on this contract for any reason. Seller, however, will give the buyer credit for said $50,000 against the purchase price provided that the buyer close on this property no later than 30 days following the termination of the additional 90-day due diligence.

You can see that there are many different ways to negotiate in a transaction. It is important to both parties that there be a very clear understanding of the terms and conditions surrounding the option. Does the option money get to be applied as part of the purchase price? When is the buyer in default? Is there any other term in the agreement that might extend time periods, and cause dates to conflict? Very careful reading of a contract is essential. If it is not in plain language, as some lawyers seem to pride themselves in avoiding, then get the darn thing redrafted so that it is clear.

The Conditioned Option

Here the optionee has included in the contract some conditions that can cancel or change the contract. These conditions might be such that the price will change, or the time to buy will be increased or decreased; most importantly, the conditions may call for a full return of the option money if something doesn't occur (or does occur, as the case may be).

From the buyer's point of view the conditioned option is the least risky of deals. If you have an option agreement and can tie up a tract of land for a period of time, and because of some condition in the agreement (which you may control) you can get your option money back, you haven't risked anything.

THIRTEEN CONDITIONS USED IN CONDITIONAL OPTIONS INCLUDE:

1. *Soil test.* Your right to test and approve the subsoil conditions.
2. *Survey certification.* Your approval of the exact dimensions, and so on.
3. *Bering test.* A more detailed subsoil examination.
4. *Site plan approval.* Government approval of your planned development.
5. *Issuance of building permit.* Actual and final stage before building.
6. *Partner's approval.* A clear-out if your partner nixes the deal.
7. *Corporate ratification.* Similar to the above.
8. *Obtaining satisfactory financing.* Necessary in many deals.
9. *Government approval.* This covers a wide range of conditions.
10. *Prior sale of a third property.* When you need to sell something else.
11. *Prior development of a section 1031 exchange.* You have to develop an exchange before you can close.
12. *Preleasing of to-be-developed space.* Many lenders will demand this.
13. *Environmental inspections.* Many lenders insist on this.

Of these thirteen items, you can see that some can be simply accomplished and would not normally take a long time, while others can take months or in some cases, such as government approval, years. In all cases you (the buyer) have control over these items and can make sure the condition fails to be met.

The seller in the conditioned option contract will naturally object to tying up his land with the buyer having a full right to a refund of option money in situations where the buyer can back out of the deal. In essence, what has been created is a free option, with the money being not much more than good-faith deposit. Yet despite the fact that many sellers will object to such contractual agreements, many conditional agreements are made each day. Sellers try to limit the time for these conditions, realizing that the option is "free," and to provide for other safeguards to counterbalance the lack of security in the refundable deposit. Such counterbalances are in strict timetables, elements of past performance being a main criterion in the decision to go along with the condition if it is time consuming. In essence, if the optionee is genuine and can give the impression he or she is going to buy, his or her chances are improved in using a conditioned option agreement.

All the previous items used in the option contract can be conditions in the actual sales agreement as well, and when they are used in that form of purchase they convert the buy-and-sell agreement into a conditional option agreement.

USING OPTION AGREEMENTS

The scenario is as follows: A tight money market, high interest rates, and unrest in the real estate market. It is a growing buyer's market, and while the trends indicate that there is a turnaround somewhere down the road, you aren't sure when that is going to be. You have found a property that you want to buy. You know that the more you reduce your risk, the more profit potential you have in the future.

The price you feel you can get for the property is $100,000. The seller has been asking more, but that's what you want to pay. You find that current interest rates are around 15% in the prime market, around 12% in land sales.

Your first offer is a conditioned option agreement. You offer $10,000 option money for the right to buy the property for $100,000. You agree to give the seller $10,000 right away. As a condition of the deal you call for your unqualified approval of a subsoil test. You want to make sure that there are no subterranean conditions which will make building on this site very expensive. You allow for ninety days for this to be made. If you disapprove of the results, you get your money back and the deal is off.

If you approve the test, you have nine months in which to exercise the option to buy. All you have to do to exercise the deal is to sign the buy-and-sell agreement attached to the option and return it to the seller. You have sixty days to close on the deal after that. (By the way, when you close on the property the option money you paid is to be applied to the sales price.)

The soil test condition gives you three months to examine the property to decide if you want to go through with the deal. If you go ahead, you have another nine months to exercise the option to buy, and then another sixty days to close on the purchase. In all, you have one year and two months to make the deal. You paid $10,000 at the beginning, which is counted as a part of the purchase price. Even if the seller had insisted that the $10,000 not be counted at closing, you would have tied up the property for under 10% interest for those fourteen months.

WHEN YOU KNOW YOU ARE GOING TO BUY, USE THE OPTION

You can see that when you aren't sure about buying, the option gives you some time to make the final decision. It locks up the price and terms so that you know exactly what to base the decision on. But when you know you are going to buy, the option gives you added appreciation and reduces your carrying cost for the first year or so.

In the deal described above, you would have tied up a $100,000 property for fourteen months at no real cost in the long run. You would have gotten fourteen months during which time you didn't have to pay the real-estate taxes on that property and you got all the appreciation. As long as you don't need immediate title to the property, the option-to-buy deal is a great way to get a head start on appreciation.

USING THE OPTION TO SELL

The seller likes the option because he is a gambler. If you were a seller and you didn't have a buyer for your property and someone came along and said, "I'll give you money just to let me decide if I'll buy the property," you might be inclined to take the deal. After all, if the option fails to be exercised, you still have the property. In the meantime, the investor has paid you for the time which passed, during which you might not have sold the property anyway. Options work because people like to gamble and options are a safe way to risk little from the seller's point of view.

As a seller you can use the option to help entice a buyer into your hard-to-sell property. If a buyer will pay your price if you accept his or her terms, then you should be able to get a better price by offering better terms. In the case of a tough-to-sell property, you may have to resort to some very creative selling techniques. There is nothing wrong with being creative, and moving a dog in a tough market may call for all the creativity you can generate.

One of the problems of the real estate market is that there are times when value has little to do with the ability to sell something. The inability to finance a deal might cause a builder to shy away from your kind of land, or a potential user to decide not to buy your vacant building. Use the option to get interest, then sink the hook.

It's like anything else. If you can get someone's attention, then you can often create an environment that didn't exist before. In dealing with builders and developers, getting them involved is often the first step in making the deal.

A tough deal may need lots of good ideas and some hard work running around getting tenants, getting sites rezoned, and so on. The builder won't do that if he or she has to lay out heavy bucks to tie up the land. So offer an option.

When the potential buyer has an option, he or she will start thinking how it can make a profit. Once the would-be buyer starts thinking about making a profit, then the creative mind is working in your favor as well. The buyer will have to buy your land or building to make a profit.

The idea is to find a probable buyer for your property and establish some rapport. You can't walk into his office and say, "How do you do; by the way, I'll give you an option on my land." Sure this sounds fresh and creative, but also a little nuts.

A better approach is to have your broker make a presentation to the buyer. ("How would you like to buy Jack's land?") You will get feedback when you do that and you will see if there is any interest. One of the first signs of interest comes with the statement, "The price is too high." There is no reason to knock your price unless there is some interest (or he is just one of those guys who likes to knock everything).

Your broker can take this approach: "Mr. or Ms. Prospective Buyer, I understand your reasons for saying the price might be too high. But I feel that someone with your experience could put this site to its best use. The owner is so conscious of your ability that he'll/she'll give you a sixty-day option to buy this land. I know that if you truly become interested in this land you will profit by it."

Yet options are more of a tool than just this. In fact, over the past dozen years the option has evolved into one of the best methods of building a great amount of wealth. Move on through the remainder of this chapter to see just how attractive the option can be when used in the right circumstance by a knowledgeable investor.

USING THE OPTION TO FINANCE YOUR WAY TO A FORTUNE

As you have discovered thus far, there are many ways to use the option in real-estate investing and financing. The creative ways in which you use this tool will depend only on your full understanding of four elements of the option.

THE FOUR KEY ELEMENTS TO THE OPTION

1. The option is a one-sided event that gives one party control over some future event that the owner of the property does not have.
2. The option has a psychological effect on sellers and buyers alike depending on the circumstance and use of the tool.
3. Options can be used successfully by both the buyer and the seller.
4. Options are a promise of a future event, a box behind the curtain that holds a lure to the other party that can be more attractive than the known offer.

Using the option to your best benefit will depend on its placement in the right situation. Look at several examples of how you might use the option and win.

The Primary Option

The primary option transaction is a basic study in greed. In this technique, the buyer uses the option to keep the cost of the total financing at a minimum, while tying up the property for a period of time in which the buyer can back out of the deal without excess cost. As in all option transactions, the buyer holds the cards and all the aces.

The significance of this specific kind of option is the buyer knows ahead of the game that he or she is absolutely going to buy.

The advantage of the option in this case is purely as a delaying tactic to the usual costs of a closing: down payment, interest, costs, and so on.

The transaction follows this scenario: A seller is asking, say, $800,000 for the tract of land on which you want to build a strip store. You know that you will buy the land and are attempting to lessen the interest cost between now and the exact date you have to fund the construction project, and reduce your immediate cash outlay. To accomplish these ends, you make the following offer. You will pay the seller $30,000 cash within 90 days as option money to allow you to make a feasibility study of the specific site for commercial use. For this payment, you will be allowed 240 days in which to complete the study. If you are satisfied with the study, you can proceed to a closing, within a 60-day period or you can obtain an extension of the option period for an additional 180 days by paying another $50,000 to the seller. If you determine at the end of that time that the commercial venture is not feasible for any reason, the seller keeps the option money paid and you are released from any further obligation to that party. On the other hand, the contract indicates that if you determine that you want to purchase the property, you can proceed with the closing. At the closing, you will receive full credit against the purchase price for any and all option money thus far paid to the seller.

The end result of this transaction is ideal for the buyer, who has tied up the property for 390 days for only $30,000. The buyer can extend this time or can close. The $30,000 paid, as well as any additional option money, is applied toward the purchase price. Best of all, the actual closing, and interest that might have been otherwise due on any mortgages, is postponed during this same time. This interest would have exceeded the total option money paid.

OPTION TO BUY IN A LEASE TRANSACTION

In a sale lease, one of the most critical elements to the transaction is the option to buy the property, and if possible all sale leasebacks should contain the option to buy back.

Remember, options are absolutely one-sided. The best time to establish them is when you have control in the transaction. If you are leasing, insert a simple option provision in the lease if you can. If you are selling your own property and leasing it back, even the most hard-hearted buyer is apt to grant an option for you to buy back your own property at a more than generous profit to the buyer down the road. Keep in mind, this option may end up having no value to you if you overestimate the future growth of the area or that specific property. On the other hand, if things go as they have in the past, you might find that the sale of your option in the future is far more profitable than the sale of the property the first time.

Whenever you have a sale leaseback, the option to recapture the property is a benefit that you should attempt to negotiate into the deal. You may have no interest at the moment of ever owning the property, but times change and property values can skyrocket when future events create demands not deemed possible at present.

HOW TO WRITE THE OPTION

"The lessee herein has the option to purchase the subject property any time during the lease or its extensions for $1,000,000." It might be as simple as that, but most likely it will be far more complex. As in all contracts, it is important that you get it right, and that means get it done with a good real estate lawyer.

The following list should be reviewed by you and your lawyer when it comes time to draft the option agreement into the lease or sale-leaseback portions of the contract. Many of these items are business decisions you or the other party will have to make a judgment on. Since you should know more about the property and what you can do with it than your lawyer, that decision should be solely yours.

THE FIVE KEY ELEMENTS TO THE OPTION CONTRACT

1. THINK BEYOND WHAT YOU THINK YOU NEED. This is where most people overlook the option in the first place. "Well, for goodness' sake, I never thought about asking for an option." Well, now you will, right? You should attempt to put the options in every agreement you can whenever you buy or lease real estate. Remember, the worst that can happen is that the other party will want to remove it, giving you the opportunity to counteract by putting in another benefit to you. If you are leasing, ask for an option to renew the lease at the same terms, or to buy the property, or to have the first right of refusal if someone else wants to buy it. The option puts you in control. If you can get one for free, then jump at it.

2. USE THE OPTION AS A NEGOTIATING TOOL. Assume that you are trying to lease a home. The property owner is telling you that you can have a two-year lease. The price is okay, but you want to push for additional leverage or benefits in the deal. You say something like this: "Mr. Property Owner, as my wife and I plan to improve this property while living here, we would like to have the option to buy the home at the end of the lease. If we can establish a fair price to you at this time, we will put that amount in the lease. That will give us incentive to improve the property. Naturally, if I get transferred to California and we are unable to take advantage of the option, you will keep the improvements we do to the home."

There are several subtle elements here to help the property owner make up his mind to give you the option: improved property, fair price, incentive for the lessee to improve (and stay and pay rent on time), and best of all, the lessee might be transferred to California and lessor keeps all.

If you are leasing an office within an office building, ask for an option to buy the building. "Mr. Office Building Owner, as we may have to expand over the years, it is possible that we may need the whole building some time in the future. If that were to occur, I think it would be the time for us to own the building. We will sign your lease right now if you could give us an option to buy the building within the first ten years of our lease."

3. WATCH OUT FOR SELLERS OR LANDLORDS WHO TRY TO ENTICE YOU WITH THE OPTION.   There is a program called Shared Equity Transactions, which I describe in more detail in the chapter entitled "Fifteen Creative Deal-Making Techniques." This is a wealth-building plan that works on buyers' or tenants' motivation to own their own property.

The way the plan works is this: A real-estate investor will buy a property for $40,000 and then advertise that he will sell 50% of the equity for nothing down. When someone comes along, the deal is described as follows: The prospective buyer, who has nothing to put down, will move into the home (or apartment) and pay all actual costs. These costs might include (1) payments on a $55,000 mortgage, and (2) taxes, insurance, and upkeep of the house. The deal is that if the prospective buyer will stay in the house for five years, the house will then be sold, and the prospective buyer will get 50% of the net proceeds of the sale that exceed $60,000.

The actual numbers may differ, but the plan works by enticing the prospective buyer to believe there is equity in the home and that entering into a lease with this kind of option has value. It may have, but you should always know values prior to making that kind of contract. The people who teach the courses that instruct the real estate investor how to use the shared equity plans stress the "profit" that comes up front in the deal through increased value from the day the property was bought to the day it is leased under the kind of option explained (even if that was day two of the transaction).

Options offered to tenants that have unrealistic prices or formulas to arrive at a price have no value to the deal and should be viewed as the bait to the deal. Of course, you can keep the option in, but be sure you recognize what might be nothing more than an attempt to get you in the property. Make sure that you are not taking the lease for that reason alone.

4. KNOW YOUR OPTIONS IN THE NEGOTIATIONS.   Many people ask for an option, and when the sharp property owner puts in a paragraph that looks like an option they are satisfied. Here are some elements you can ask for in option provisions:

- *Option to extend your lease.* If your lease was for one year, ask for options to extend for additional years by doing something each year on the eleventh month. That something might be a notice to the owner, or payment of $50 or whatever you can put into the lease. If your lease provides an option to buy during the term of the lease that provision should also include extensions of the lease, so that your "option to buy" would not terminate simply because you extended the term of the lease.

- *Option to buy during the lease.* You can ask for, and some owners will agree, to give you credit for some or even all of the rent paid. This will be determined by the need of that property owner to get the place rented in the first place.

- *Options should have a specific price, or clear formula of establishing prices for new rent or purchase prices.* There are many different ways to approach this. A percentage of the cost of living, or the entire increase of a cost-of-living index can be used. However, there are several different indexes, so ask your lawyer about this format. I recommend that you remember the term *All Items Index* as that averages out the specific items index that can rise quicker than the average.

- *If all else fails, get a "first right of refusal."* This is an option triggered only when the owner has a bona fide contract from another party which is acceptable to that owner. You would have a period of time to accept the same terms. This is the weakest of all options, but gives you some control over the property.

- *Remember, when it comes time to take advantage of the option to renew your rent or buy the building, you don't have to do it as the contract says.* The option only binds the other party to those terms. "Mr. Property Owner, my option to buy is at $150,000. However, as conditions are not as attractive now as I had thought they might be, I don't feel the property is worth more than $125,000. I'll pay that now, or wait a couple of more years to see if I could afford the full price covered in my option."

5. USE OPTIONS AS AN ASSET WHEN BUYING OTHER PROPERTY. As a part of the deal, you can offer the seller of a property the same option you have with the office building owner. If you own property, you can use the option as a future benefit bonus in any transaction you want to move forward.

REVIEW THE CONCEPT OF GREED

I have never met a seller that didn't want to get the most he or she could out of the deal. Even the most practical thinker of the bunch truly wants to come out on top of the deal. This competitive nature of doing business in real estate can and frequently places the money ahead of just about everything else. This is not the right way to look at the transaction, and can most certainly get in the way of the deal coming together when both parties feel the same way about who is going to come out on top of the deal. The fact of the matter is that you can either go with the flow, or you can get caught in the riptide and drown.

Using greed as a tool to the transaction is what both the preferred income and the option do. Here, take this now, and it is yours; see how you came out ahead of me. The reality is that in a truly sound real estate transaction, where the numbers work for the buyer, the preferred income is protection, not extra money. Protection is good, of course, and being able to give up something that does not actually take money from your pocket is even better.

The best use of the option is, as has been stated, when you know you are going to buy. This is the time that you get the full benefits of gaining time without having to pay for it in the end.

Chapter 17

THREE SECONDARY FINANCING TECHNIQUES THAT CLOSE DEALS

Every real-estate investor hopes to be able to pull the magic technique out of the hat at the right moment. For some of us, that technique is there just when we need it. For others, they make the wrong gesture, and instead of a closed deal, what they end up with is a dead rabbit.

This chapter focuses on four unique forms of financing mentioned earlier, as adjunct techniques to other examples. They are as follows: *leasehold financing and land leases, percent of income,* and *coventures and syndicates.*

All the techniques are very important when used in combination with others. Each has a special benefit to offer you as a buyer or seller. When you are coming down the home stretch of closing your deal, no matter if you are buyer or seller or broker, knowing how and when to pull one of these three magic rabbits out of the hat can often mean the difference between making and not making a deal. The purpose of this chapter is to cover these three methods of financing. This will enable you to see how they are used, what they do to help you make more transactions, and when you can bring them into play.

LEASEHOLD FINANCING

Definition

A *leasehold* is the ownership of a right to use a specific property for a term of years for which the lessee pays rent. The tenant has a leasehold interest in the property or space. If he or she meets the terms of the lease that interest is real and can be pledged as security on loans.

Example

You have a 99-year lease on the land under your hotel. You want to remove the existing building and build a new hotel. You review the lease document to discover that the lessor is not obligated to subordinate the land to any financing. If the land owner were to subordinate his or her interest to a lender, then the lender would have a lien against the land ahead of the owner's rights. Without the subordination the lender could only lien your rights, which are those rights granted to you by virtue of the lease. These are your leasehold rights, and your leasehold interest would then secure any loan. You find a lender who understands that your leasehold interest for ninety-nine years is more than sufficient time for you to repay the loan. The rent you pay of $30,000 per year, without any increase over the term of the lease, is a bargain rent. This cheap rent gives you substantial leasehold equity in the property. This equity or value is what the lender takes as security for the loan. Of course some types of leasehold interests are more valuable than others. This value depends on the following factors:

1. THE TYPE OF PROPERTY LEASED.   Different properties will obviously have different values. If all other aspects are equal, the lease on an office building should be more valuable than a lease on vacant land. A lender looking at the possibility of making a loan on a leasehold will look very strongly to the value of the space or property. If the leasehold loan is for improvements in a boutique in a shopping center, the usefulness of that space for other types of businesses will be important. The economics of the property will be most important in the evaluation of real equity.

2. THE ANNUAL RENT OF THE LEASE.   The lease is the document that will create the actual value. The leasehold equity will become the security for the unsubordinated loan. Appraising the space or property finds property value. After you deduct the capitalized value of the rent from the value, the remaining amount is the leasehold equity. For example: F.P.A. Corp. has a 60-unit hotel on the beach. It is located on leased land. F.P.A. Corp. owns the right to use the property, for which it pays an annual rent of $26,500. Assume it had no financing and built the hotel with cash. The finished value of the building was $1,050,000 and the land, according to comparable values in the area, was $875,000. Therefore, the total combined value is $1,925,000. As F.P.A. Corp. pays $26,500 in rent, this amount can be said to represent a cost of a capital investment. Setting a capitalization rate of 10% on this cost would relate to an investment of $265,000. An 8% cap rate would increase the comparative investment to $331,250. See the computations that follow to determine the leasehold equity at 10% and 8% cap rates with a leasehold mortgage of $800,000. It should be clear that the cost of the lease, in terms of annual rent, must be capitalized to give an adjustment in the equity. The rate used may vary from property to property and from lender to

lender. It is a good idea to show the leasehold equity at two different rates and then take the lower rate in your loan package. In any event, the fact that F.P.A. Corp. is leasing the land at $26,500 per year, and the land has a current value of $875,000, is some indication that you will have excellent leasehold appreciation and equity. Yet, the leasehold equity must consider the improvements and their existing financing.

		10%	8%
1.	Annual rent on the lease of land	$ 26,500	26,500
2.	Capital investment of a cap rate to provide rent	265,000	331,250
3.	Combined value of land and buildings	1,925,000	1,925,000
4.	Less existing financing	800,000	800,000
5.	Gross equity before adjustment for a land lease	$1,125,000	1,125,000
6.	Less amount from line 2	265,000	331,250
7.	Total leasehold equity	$ 860,000	793,750
8.	Less capital investment	100,000	100,000
9.	Leasehold equity appreciation	$ 760,000	$ 693,750

3. THE PERIOD OF TIME REMAINING ON THE LEASE.   If the lease expires in one year, the leasehold equity will be that equity which can be substantiated economically over the remaining term of the lease. The hotel owned by F.P.A. Corp. on leased land will continue to have value, as will the land. F.P.A.'s leasehold value, however, will begin to decline at a point in time when the remaining term of the lease does not allow return of capital at a reasonable rate of return for that remaining period. For example: The hotel has a value based on the economic return. In most income properties this economic value is the more important of all value approaches, and should be close to or below the replacement cost evaluation. If the replacement value were lower than the economic value, it might be more prudent to build a new hotel. Nonetheless, this economic return may continue for twenty years in a reasonable projection. However, F.P.A. Corp. may have only ten years in which to enjoy the benefit of the leasehold if the lease expires at the end of that time. An investor interested in purchasing the leasehold from F.P.A. Corp. would analyze the yield only for the remaining term, giving little credit to the actual value of the property. A lender would look at the leasehold equity in the same way.

4. THE CONDITIONS AND PROVISIONS OF THE LEASE.   Each lease is a new ball game. There are many provisions or conditions which can make it desirable or undesirable. Rights to sublet, diversity of use, high maintenance costs and the like will be examined carefully by any lender prior to a loan. Because these terms are so important in possible financing, a lessee should make every effort to create a lease that will offer a good basis for leasehold financing.

5. THE USE OF THE PROPERTY.   Is the building a single-purpose structure or is it easily adaptable to other uses? Is the use economically sound or not? These are important factors to the lender, not only because he or she may end up with the building, but for the tenant to survive and the leasehold equity to be maintained the economics of the operation must be in the tenant's favor.

6. THE TENANT.   Of course, the lender will always take a good long look at the tenant. After all, it is the tenant that wants to borrow the money. All lenders are very interested in the person they lend money to.

7. OPTIONS AVAILABLE TO LESSEE.   Of all the items in a lease that can have effect on the leasehold value, the most critical are options that give the lessee rights to future benefits. These benefits can vary, and can include any of the following: Option to Buy, option to extend the lease, option to remove buildings without replacing them, option to recast debt to old levels or greater, option to obtain full or partial subordination at a future date or dates. When you negotiate a lease of any kind, the best time to ask for and get options is at the beginning. In some situations the lessor may not grant certain options because the option would not be practical. If you were leasing an office or space in a building, to have an option to buy the building may not be an advantage to you. However, being able to renew the lease for long terms at past rent levels could be a great advantage to you in establishing a leasehold equity.

These seven factors will be the main criteria which will create leasehold financing. Each factor is important on its own, but it is the combined effect of all seven that will provide a package that is financeable.

HOW LENDERS DEAL WITH SECURITY FROM LEASEHOLD EQUITIES

Leasehold financing is secured in two different methods: *subordinated fee* and *unsubordinated fee*. There is a considerable amount of money lent with the security established by either of these two forms of security. In general, however, the majority of the larger loans are on leasehold interests with subordinated fee. The situation of F.P.A. Corp. with its hotel on leased land is a good example. The land lease had a provision which enabled F.P.A. to obtain a first mortgage that would be secured by the improvements as well as the land. The owners of the land subordinated their interest to the lender on the first mortgage and took a second position. The lender could foreclose on both the improvements and the land if F.P.A. Corp. defaulted on the mortgage and the land owners did not step in to take it over.

Giving the lessee the right to give a mortgage right to a lender, by virtue of having the land owner subordinate that right to the lender, increases the land owner's risk. The tradeoff to this is that just about anything in a lease that increases the owner's risk will increase the leasehold equity of the tenant. In certain situations for certain leases, this aspect can help make for a good lease. After all, if the property owner wants to establish a steady long-term tenant, giving that tenant flexibility to grow and expand can be important. So important in fact, that the offer of subordination may actually entice a better tenant than would be available otherwise.

Many owners do not want to subordinate their land or other interests so that the leasehold owner can use their equity to obtain a loan. After all, when the land is subordinated, the lender will look to the real value of land and buildings without deducting the capitalized rent cost to arrive at a leasehold equity. If the owner does not subordinate the fee to the lender, then the financing must be made with unsubordinated fee.

The terms of the lease become most important here, if the lease is for a very long term; usually the term of the loan plus a sufficient remaining term allow the investor to benefit from a build-up of equity, say 150% of the mortgage life. And if the lease payments are not onerous; then the lender will look to these leasehold interests as though the tenant actually owns the property. This *fee simple* or ownership of the land is seen as a clear use of the land, and if all other factors work out, a loan can be made without the subordination.

There are some areas in the world where almost all the land is leased and most all real-estate financing is leasehold. Hong Kong and Hawaii are good examples of places where leasehold financing is rather prominent. In England it is not uncommon for whole towns to be situated on leased land. The rights of the tenants may filter back to the original owner through many different subtenants. One property that I know well in downtown London has over fifteen subtenants. The owner of the building pays a very high land lease to the most recent subtenant, who pays a lesser amount to the person he leases the property from who pays the person he leases the property from and so on, all the way back to a member of the Royal Family, whose original lease goes back several hundred years ago.

HOW LEASEHOLD FINANCING CAN BE A DEAL MAKER

The ability to pull apart a property to a fee equity and a leasehold equity can be a useful form of financing that can provide money making benefits to both the property owner and the tenant. I have discussed how a sale and leaseback can be one method for a property owner to raise capital while at the same time keeping the use of a property. This type of lease is generally the sale of a property tied to a leaseback by the seller, but may also be a sale with a lease that is obtained by the seller prior to or shortly after the closing of the sale. Because every property has different rights that can be sold or leased, it is possible to separate each of them so that some of these rights are sold, while others are leased or retained. Take a look at some of the rights that you may own when you own a vacant tract of land.

Property Rights That Go with the Land

Mineral Rights. Just because there is oil or gold under your land doesn't mean you own it. Often mineral rights were retained by some previous owner, or sold or leased to a third party long before you came along. But if your deed gave you these rights, then they are yours to keep, sell, lease, trade, or otherwise dispose of them, even if there is nothing down there worth anything. Remember, what might be there may not be valuable simply because no one has figured out a use for it yet.

Subterranean Rights. Not exactly the same as mineral rights, subterranean rights can allow you to dispose of space under your land for a tunnel, parking garage, wine cellar, or whatever.

Surface Rights. Generally surface and some subterranean and some air rights go together in one package; however, if what you own is an antenna that sticks up into the sky, and don't need the surface or subterranean part of the land, then those rights can be disposed of separately.

Air Rights. The acquisition or lease of air rights is big business. If you have a large parking area for your business, you are free to sell or lease or otherwise dispose of these rights as long as the use of them does not diminish your needed parking area. The construction of an office building or hotel over city parking, for example, is not uncommon in major cities.

Riparian Rights. When a property fronts on a body of water, there may be riparian rights that go with the land. These rights allow the owner of them to use the water or bottom to certain distances from shore. Local laws may govern that use, so the value of the riparian right will vary.

Water Rights. These may coincide with riparian rights, but generally are more extensive. If the land fronts on a large body of water, the land owner may have the right to lease areas of this water for certain uses. These uses may include mooring facilities for boats, docks, fishing piers, and so on. Generally these areas are public waterways, and the rights can be leased but not purchased.

Subdivision Rights. The right to subdivide the property is a very important right. This is a function of local rules and regulations more than a right that runs with the land. When you can subdivide a property this means you can divide it in such a way that you can dispose of each division separately. Some properties are zoned in such a way that the minimum size that a property can be will not permit further subdivision of the land. When this occurs, unless the zoning is changed, or the property rezoned, there could be more division of the property.

Any of these rights can be leased, sold or otherwise disposed. It may be feasible to sell the land, keep the mineral rights, and lease back the land and build on the land. You could sell the land, with or without the mineral rights with a leaseback on the land, then sell the building subject to a new subtenant lease. You could lease the riparian rights, lease the mineral rights, sell the land, lease back the land and build a building on it which you keep.

HOW TO USE A LEASE AS A FINANCING TOOL TO CLOSE DEALS

If you remember that financing is a shift of equity from one party to another, you can see that a lease can do that much in the same way as does a mortgage. There are, however, some very important differences between your selling a property and your leasing it. The important part of this is to take into consideration what is the best way for you to attain your goals. If you are a seller, you might find that you will attract more buyers if you package your property into two separate elements. You can, for example, sell the buyer the improvements subject to a land lease. Later in this chapter I will illustrate some of the benefits to both parties in such an example. By comparison of the benefits that come from selling or leasing you will be able to establish a method of the disposition that maximizes your benefits of the deal. As a buyer, you should know what advantages and benefits you can gain by leasing or by only buying. There can be substantial benefits depending on which method you use. Review the following list to see how you could choose which method works best for you.

ADVANTAGES AND DISADVANTAGES OF SELLING A PROPERTY

1. YOU MAY CREATE A TAXABLE GAIN.   If your adjusted basis is lower than the contract price of the property then you may have a tax to pay. It is important to know if you have any losses or other tax credits that can offset the taxable gain. If you do, you may want to take advantage of those losses while you can, and the sale, even with a potential taxable gain, might be the best way to go. If you have a taxable gain, and no losses to offset the gain, you might want to look to other options that could help reduce or eliminate the gain.

You sell a property for $750,000. Your adjusted tax basis (what you paid for the property adjusted for any improvements and depreciation) is $395,000. This means you will have a taxable gain of $355,000. Your tax is likely to be based on at least a 33% bracket, or a total of $117,150, or more.

2. YOU ESTABLISH A CAPITAL LOSS.   Selling a property at a loss is rarely a benefit, but there are times that cutting your losses by getting rid of a property is a smart move. Not all losses can be used to offset gains. At present the tax laws do not

allow you to apply a loss on the sale of your residence against other capital gains. This may change in the future, so before you sell your own home or apartment, double check all the current tax codes to see if there has been a change.

You bought a home five years ago for	$500,000
You added a pool, closed in the garage at a cost of	100,000
Your tax basis in this property is	$600,000
You sell for	540,000
Your loss is	$60,000
As this property is a home you get no benefit from the loss.	

3. YOU HAVE A TAXABLE GAIN BUT NO PROCEEDS TO COVER IT. This is not a nice situation to be in, and happens when your tax exceeds the amount of cash you are left with after the closing. Usually this occurs when there is a low down payment, and the seller has mortgaged over his or her tax basis. Because the IRS allows you to borrow money on property without having to pay any tax on that money, the extent to which that borrowed money exceeds your book value (adjusted tax basis) in the property will then be taxed. The fact that you spent that money five years ago is no consolation, as you may have to dig into your pocket to pay the tax.

You have a property that cost you $500,000
The present value due to its income is $750,000.
You have depreciated it 15 years and your adjusted tax basis is $100,000.
Two years ago you borrowed $550,000 and have spent all of it.
You sell the property for $750,000 at $200,000 cash to your mortgage.
Your gain is $650,000 and at 33 percent tax bracket your tax is $214,500.
After you pay the tax you are in the hole $14,500.

ADVANTAGES AND DISADVANTAGES OF LEASING A PROPERTY

1. AS YOU STILL OWN IT YOU HAVE NOT CREATED A GAIN OR A LOSS. There is, however, an income tax to be paid on the rent you earn from the transaction. Because you do not have a taxable gain in the disposition of the property when you lease it, it is possible that you will save considerably in the reinvestment potential by leasing the portion of the property that has the gain, and selling or leasing the nongain portion of the property. For example, you own a 10,000 square foot office building that you constructed five years ago on a lot you have owned for more than twenty years. When you purchased the lot it cost you $15,000 and for most of the fifteen years prior to building the office building you leased the lot to a nearby new car dealer as a place to store cars. Along comes a buyer for your office building who

offers you $750,000 net of any costs you might have in the sale and transfer, to buy the building and lot combined. You review your records and discover that your depreciated tax basis on the office building is $380,000. If you add your cost of the lot to that, your book value (adjusted tax basis) in the property is $395,000. You have a first mortgage which you took out to build the building and still owe $350,000. Review your potential tax liability:

You sell the building and lot for	$750,000
Subtract your adjusted tax basis	395,000
Your taxable gain	$355,000
Your tax bracket (assumption)	× 33%
Your estimated tax	$117,150

If you had gotten all cash in the sale you would be left with $282,850 after you have deducted the mortgage and the tax. ($750,000 less $350,000 = $400,000 less $117,150 = $282,850.)

You invest your cash at 10%; $282,850 × 10% = $28,285. This $28,285 is a comparable return from the reinvested cash left over after the sale.

2. YOU OFFER THE OFFICE BUILDING FOR SALE SUBJECT TO A LAND LEASE.   You do not take the above offer, instead of taking this offer, you decide to sell the building for $400,000 and give the buyer a ground lease on the lot at $35,000 per year. Here is how this deal turns out:

On the Sale of the Building:		
Sale price	$400,000	
Less adjusted basis in building	380,000	
Taxable gain	$ 20,000	
Tax bracket	× 25%	
Estimated tax	$ 5,000	
Cash you get at closing	$ 50,000	* Remember you owe $350,000.
Less the tax you pay	5,000	
Cash left over	$ 45,000	
You reinvest this at 10% interest	× 10%	
Interest you earn on the cash	$ 4,500	
On the Lease of the Land		
Annual rent	$ 35,000	
Add interest earned and rent	$ 39,500	* This is your total annual benefit.

You can quickly see that by using the land lease as a part of the financing package, you have increased your reinvestment potential from $28,285 to $39,500. The reason for this is the result of two factors. First you do not have to pay the gains tax, and secondly the tax you do pay is at a lower tax rate (assuming that the sudden gain of the sale would increase you to a higher tax bracket).

How the Buyer Benefits

Buyers benefit in several ways. First of all, in the above example, the land lease functions much like an interest-only mortgage. Because the buyer can not depreciate the land, and as the rent paid is an allowable deduction against income, the amount of invested capital, which is the lease payment, is a 100% tax deduction. The fact that the buyer does not have to come up with the cash to buy the land means that he or she buys the property with less invested cash.

HOW BUYERS USE LAND LEASES TO BUY PROPERTY OTHERWISE NOT FOR SALE

There are many property owners who are reluctant to sell because of the large tax liability they will have in a sale. By the time they pay the tax due, the remaining cash cannot be reinvested at a high enough rate to give them a reasonable benefit. If you were dealing with a seller who owned such a property, that seller may be unwilling to sell, or have an unreasonable price to cover tax liability. If you approach the transaction by offering a land lease you may turn around a difficult purchase into one that benefits both of you.

In many cases you will have to educate the seller to see where the benefits come from. Remember, this seller has priced the property at $900,000 to cover a $150,000 tax payment. The real value in benefits to the seller is only $750,000. If that is a more reasonable price, then you need to make an offer that gives the seller benefits worth the $750,000 without you having to pay that much for the property.

The ability to obtain new financing on leased land or on leasehold space in other buildings will depend on your contacts in the money market. It will also depend on the total combined effect of the seven factors shown in the earlier part of this section.

The rise and decline of the leasehold equity is, of course, the most important aspect of leasehold financing. The security offered by this equity, along with other risk reducers such as personal signature and guarantee on the note and pledge of other collateral or security, makes the leasehold mortgage a most interesting form of financing. Your ability to use this kind of financing in a future deal will depend on your clear focus to your goals. Everything you do in real estate investing should be directed toward this end. Your ultimate success, as I continue to reiterate, will be enhanced by your pursuit of your goals.

PERCENT OF INCOME

Definition

In real-estate financing, the sweetener percent of income is one of the most sought-after bonuses that institutional lenders look for. It is a simple giving by the borrower to the lender a percentage of the income derived from the investment. In application there are many different ways to express this sweetener, and many different terms and conditions that can be dealt with. This portion of the chapter is devoted to showing you the general concept, and how to use this aspect to your benefit, either as buyer, seller or lender

Example 1 Buyer

You want to buy Charlie's apartment complex. You have offered him nearly the amount he has been asking, $1,200,000 only he has turned down the offer because he will not hold a wraparound mortgage for $1,195,000. So back to your drawing board you go, and you come up with a new plan. You offer him $1,200,000 with 20% cash down, and his holding a wraparound mortgage for $960,000. The wraparound mortgage is for a reasonable interest rate and terms, each designed to be good for you, and to provide benefits for Charlie. The closing item is that you offer Charlie a bonus to the transaction of 5% of all revenue that exceeds his pro forma NOI. If he does not accept this deal as offered, at least you are now dealing in negotiations that will not cost you anything. If he puffed the NOI, then he will want to back off this kind of negotiations. This can be a clue to you that this project is not what it was presented to be. If he wants to fine-tune this kind of deal, then he is showing confidence in his pro forma.

Example 2 Seller

The buyer is balking at the deal, and you are grasping for something to close the deal. His last offer, which was well below your counter, was $900,000 cash down, with you holding a second mortgage of $2,000,000 at 9% interest per annum, over the existing financing of $45,000,000. You countered that you needed a minimum of $2,000,000 down. So there you are, $1,100,000 apart.

You counter again, this time pulling out all the stops in hopes of showing your confidence in the deal. You will accept $1,300,000 cash down, and will hold secondary financing of $1,600,000 at 6% interest per annum provided that for the term of the second mortgage you also receive a bonus of 15% of all income in excess of the NOI projected.

In following counters you may deal with both the time period and the actual interest bonus, but you are now back on track. Whatever the bonus you get, over and above the interest rate of the mortgage, is not out of the buyer's pocket. The project is paying that cost.

Example 3 Lender

You are Mr. Big Bucks and are used to getting high interest rates for your money. I come along and tempt you with a very interesting project and ask for your seed money of $50,000. You want 14% interest for your money. I offer you 8% and 20% of all NOI over and above my break even number. We set the term for the over-age at 20 years, even though the loan will be paid off in fifteen.

This form of percent taking is far more frequent than the sharing of actual own-ership. In this form of financing the lender will receive normal payment of interest and principal. But in addition to those payments, will also receive a bonus of all or part of the income above a set standard. For example: Insurance Company A loans all the money needed to build a major shopping center. The loan provisions indicate that they will receive a bonus of 20% of all income above a gross revenue of $2,500,000. Another lender, REIT B., has just financed a ten-story office building. The loan states they get a bonus of 3% of the gross income above $200,000.

Both these situations required the borrower to pay a percentage of the income on the project to the lender. These types of loans are very similar to rents under leases that require the tenant to pay a bonus or percent of the gross income. Sometimes the lender will look to these leases as a source of the bonus on the mortgage. If the tenants in a center average 3% overages on their leases (that is to say, the leases are set at 3% of gross income against a minimum rent), then once the base rent is reached by the calculation of the 3% of gross income, all income above that will earn the bonus of 3% to the land-lord. If the lender is participating in the income with the developer, then one method may be to split or in some way divide the over-ride of gross income on the leases.

Lenders usually have a cutoff on this revenue to assure that they do not exceed the usury for the area. For example, if the maximum interest which could be charged was 12%, then the total interest earned by the lender for that year could not exceed 12%. In most areas there is a difference in usury between private parties and corpo-rations, with the corporation having the highest chargeable interest. Because of this, most lenders wishing to participate in ownership or percentage of income will require the borrower to be a corporation. This will give them a higher amount of interest that they can receive and an additional buffer between earning and potential earning.

Offering a percent of the income on a property as an incentive to the lender to give good terms has its merit. If the base income passes through without any bonus to the lender, then only that income that may come because of improvement or appreciation in the property will go to him. And since the investment and cash flow are improved for the buyer, he or she also benefits from the transaction.

Using this same principle, it is possible to entice a seller to hold a good second mortgage on the sale of an income property. For example: Wilton wants to buy a small shopping center that Miles owns. Miles is asking $650,000 with $225,000 cash to his existing $425,000 mortgage. The existing cash flow based on the current debt service is $24,000. However, Miles is sure that the income will increase, as there are several vacant stores and rents will undoubtedly go up with new tenants. Wilton, however, demands at least a 12% return on his invested cash and can't quite see how to get it out of this center.

I took a look at the situation nearly four weeks after Wilton had given up on the Miles center. Wilton had come to me to see if I had anything else he might like to buy. During the several visits we made to other centers, he kept talking about Miles's center. I asked him why he was unable to put it together. "Miles won't take paper" was the reply. I spoke with the broker that had shown Wilton the Miles center and we agreed that if I could get Wilton back there and show Miles how a deal could be made, we would split the fee.

The first step was to go visit Miles with the other broker. I wanted to see how strongly Miles felt about the future of the center, and what his motivation was to sell. It turned out that Miles was motivated to sell because of an inability to cope with the problems of the center. He was not management oriented, and the tenants had quickly found that they could get what they wanted by bugging Miles to death. Yet, he did feel strongly about the future of the center and knew that if someone had the knowledge to manage it properly it would show a greater return than it presently did.

Based on this information, Wilton and I went over the income statement of the center. Wilton agreed that the income could be increased, but he had to be sure of a 12% return.

Example

Here is what Wilton did: He offered the full price of $650,000, since it was a fair price. He was to pay $150,000 cash at closing and give Miles a $75,000 second mortgage to make up the balance. The pay-out of the second mortgage was as follows: 10-year interest only at 7% per annum. At the end of the ten years the total outstanding balance would be paid (Wilton would refinance the first mortgage at that time). As an inducement, Wilton added the provision that Miles would receive an additional bonus of 25% of all cash flow above $24,000.

Aside from some minor changes added by Miles to clarify the term "cash flow," we were able to sell him on the contract. Wilton could not prepay the second mortgage without a stiff penalty so Miles is still collecting on it. The income is over the original estimate and the property is throwing off better than a $33,500 cash flow. Miles is receiving an annual bonus of $2,375 along with his interest only payment of $5,250, giving him a total yield of 10.17%. In addition, the income is apt to increase before the mortgage is paid off.

The use of percent ownership or percent of income as negotiating points will depend on their introduction at the right time. At times, the adversary in the negotiations brings these factors into the picture when you don't want them. A lender, for example, may want a piece of the action, but your client has not anticipated this possibility and has not allowed for such an eventuality. Many brokers do not know how to handle this type of situation and become confused by the lender's suggestion. Many lenders will look you right in the eye and tell you that they all want this kind of action. That may be true, of course. They may want it, but not all lenders demand it. Stick to your guns when you are unwilling to give up a piece of the action, but don't close the door. See what the lender is willing to do to get it.

COVENTURES AND SYNDICATES

These two forms of financing will be discussed together since they both involve some similar techniques. To some degree they can be the same thing, depending on your point of view. A coventure is a joint effort by two or more people who combine abilities or capabilities. In real estate, the coventure can take many forms. It may be a land owner who joins up with a developer. The land owner puts up the land and the builder his or her knowledge of building, and together they develop the land. Or, it could be two doctors who join forces to buy a lot to build a medical complex.

A *syndicate*, on the other hand, is generally thought of as a group of people who combine their monetary ability to buy land or other property for a mutually profitable end result. As you can see, the syndicate is a form of joint venture, even though not all coventures take the syndication route.

There are numerous legal forms of ownership for both types of investing and financing. Limited partnerships have been used for both coventures and syndicates and have special tax privileges which, to some degree, still hold up under the new tax laws. Investment trusts, corporations, professional associations, and partnerships all are legal forms of ownership which can be used in both of these creative forms of financing.

The purpose of this section of this chapter is not to make you an expert in coventure enterprises or syndications. This takes considerable study and knowledge. Instead, the brief passages on these topics are meant to spark your interest in these exciting fields.

What Coventures and Syndicates Can Do for You and Your Clients

There will be times when the price or size of a property you represent is beyond the capability of the average investor. When this situation presents itself, the solution may be to divide the ownership interest among several buyers. This division of ownership could take the form of a syndication and you would become the syndicator.

Remember, no matter which form of financing you use, your goals are the first factor to consider. If all parties are suited for a coventure, then this tool can be used satisfactorily. However, the coventure transaction will keep the seller in (if the seller is a coventure partner, of course) and this fact may not provide the desired results; but remember, any form of financing which will give reasonable results should be attempted.

Where Do You Find Partners for Coventures?

They are almost everywhere. The first step is to determine the probable use of the property. Once you know, or at least have some idea of, the use which would be economically feasible, you will know where to go to find a partner for the transaction. For example, if you represent the owner of a tract of land that is suitable for construction of a shopping center, you would look to developers of shopping centers as possible partners.

Your build-up of contracts in other areas will help. Mortgage bankers, mortgage brokers, architects, and general contractors all have leads that can direct you to someone actively looking for such a transaction.

What You Can Do to Make the Transaction More Appealing to the Possible Coventure Partner

This is the most important part of the process. Once you have a property and feel that the coventure is best suited for your seller, the move you make to entice the developer into the transaction may mean the difference between a deal that will work and one that will not. There are many ways to structure a coventure deal, and the actual transaction itself can vary from the original plan with just minor changes. Most sellers are not aware of the special clauses which are often inserted in such transactions. Many make the deal workable, others just complicate it. All are important, however. Some of the more important fine points are the following:

FIVE IMPORTANT FEATURES IN COVENTURES

1. THE PREFERRED RETURN.   Often, one of the partners will demand a preferred return on the investment. Either the seller or the other partners can request this, but it is generally the money partner who will prevail. The seller may offer this as an inducement to get big money investors. The preferred return, in essence, is a condition that allows the first percent of the income to go to this investor. The percent can be a set percentage, such as 12%, or some other percentage based on income gross. For example: Reynolds invests $100,000 into a coventure deal and is preferred 12% on his investment. This means he will get the first $12,000 of income. The

other partners then get the next $12,000 and the overage is split based on other provisions of the agreement.

2. THE GUARANTEED RETURN. This is much stronger than the preferred return and is not used too often. The same occurs as in the above situation, except that Reynolds will be guaranteed the return of 12%. What would happen if the income did not total enough to pay his return would depend on the balance of the terms of the agreement. However, a guaranteed return may constitute a security and should be used only in situations where the sellers can sell securities under the laws of the state in which they act and meet Federal Security Laws as well. It is best to seek the advice of a lawyer on this matter. This type of agreement is widely used outside the United States, and is seen in international real-estate transactions frequently.

3. ACCRUAL OF UNPAID BUT EARNED RETURN. This can be used with both the preferred return and the guaranteed return. Here, the investor will not be paid the amount of the preference or guarantee, either because of a lack of income from the project or desire not to receive the funds. The amount of his or her investment is then increased by the amount not paid, thus increasing later return. For example: Reynolds was not paid $12,000 this year because the income and expenses broke even. His total investment is now calculated at $112,000 and his preference or guaranteed income will be based on that amount, instead of the original investment of $100,000.

4.SUBORDINATE INTEREST. While either party can subordinate its interest, it is generally the seller who is called on to do this. The seller puts up all or a part of his or her equity in the transaction behind financing to be obtained. This will allow the coventure to benefit from the full equity and obtain the maximum mortgage available. This requires the party giving the subordination to accept higher risk, but may be warranted if the transaction is economically feasible.

5. LAND BANK. At times, the owner of a tract of land may be willing to carry the cost of the land while the coventure partner gets the development ready. In essence, the cost of carrying the land will become an additional expense for the owner, but land banking is sometimes essential for obtaining the other partner. It is usually used when the time needed to bring the property to development cannot be determined, or is already known to be such that immediate development will not be possible, and when the coventure partner does not want to hold land.

Your ability to use these features to make the coventure attractive for developers or investors will depend on your understanding of the area's and the investors' needs. For example, it would not be productive to look for a developer for a hotel if hotels cannot be financed or are in disfavor in your area for some reason. Also, the use of the property must be almost immediate. However, remember that the time it takes to develop a shopping center is much longer than the time it takes to build a strip store. Because of this, the time needed to begin construction will vary. A major center will take at least two years from the word "go" to the word "open."

What You Can Do to Become Involved with Syndications and Coventure Deals

The first step may be this book. It contains most of the tools used by both the syndicator and the broker to put together coventures. Study these tools and see how they can be used in these forms of financing. The application of all the aspects of financing will be no more difficult when dealing with a group of buyers for a syndication or a builder for a coventure than when dealing one-to-one with a buyer. The only difference may be the size of the commission, which might be greater in the syndication or coventure.

Ask your lawyer to help you with the syndication or to give you some information about the coventure deals he or she has put together. If you can read over some actual coventure and syndication prospectuses you will learn a great deal.

Be careful of the legal requirements in syndication. There are many laws which control the sale of securities and most syndications will fall within one or more of these laws.

DO NOT BECOME A PROFESSIONAL SYNDICATOR. This is the person who does nothing but syndications. He or she is generally not highly regarded in the industry and will syndicate anything to make a deal. However, this certainly does not hold true for all professional syndications. The best syndications are those knowledgeable brokers and associates who use syndications as a tool to build their own wealth. Remember, you should want to invest in real estate yourself if this is your profession. And what better way to do this than to bring in other investors to help you.

Look around your market area and see who is involved in syndicating. If you can locate several brokers, talk to them and see what they feel you could do to get started. Some will be candid and offer you help in this direction while others won't encourage competition.

Chapter 18

ELEVEN CREATIVE FINANCING TECHNIQUES THAT MAKE YOUR DEALS FLY

Creative financing is the art of developing a financing package that fits to best solve problems that exist and help take one or more of the parties closer to the desired goal. It is important that you remember that aspect because it applies to all financing techniques. The only difference, then, between so called creative financing and normal financing is the application of the tool. Most creative financing occurs in secondary mortgages or when the property owner or the seller (not always the same people) participates in the structure of the debt.

CREATIVE FINANCING IS FLEXIBILITY

If you go to a savings and loan association to borrow money to buy a house, they will approach that loan in one singular format. Its format. There is almost no deviation in how you will get the loan, and how its pay-back will be set up. Your flexibility is to negotiate some of the terms, pay off early, and not much more. There is nothing creative about this, nor is there much room for you to tailor this kind of loan package to fit something specific that is important to you. On the other hand, if you are dealing with a seller of a leasehold, and both are anxious to see you take over the property, then you have considerable flexibility to fit the debt structure to your desired goals. If you have noticed, I continually reference your goals as being the most important equation if you expect to maximize your end results. Without even the weakest of goals you will never know if you have reached a point in your life when you need to raise them, or start another direction altogether. The beauty of having clear goals is that if you don't reach them on schedule you can adjust the schedule, and that is not so bad. What is bad is not to have any goals at all.

I have already given you many financing techniques that are highly creative, and that serve different aspects of putting deals together. In this and other chapters to follow I will open up more doors to some very unique concepts in mortgage financing or techniques that can put you into the deal when all looked like it was going down the tube.

This chapter covers the following list of financing techniques:

1. Sliding mortgage.
2. Double finance.
3. Glue transaction.
4. Discounted paper.
5. Other people's property.
6. Shared equity.
7. Zero-coupon bonds financing.
8. Split funding.
9. Future rent.
10. Management interest.
11. Three-party blanket.

Each of these techniques has its own niche in real-estate financing, as well as its own specific kind of problems. While I don't intend to spend as much time on these techniques as I have other forms of financing in this book, by now you should have a good understanding of how to take a creative concept and apply it to your own specific problem, using, as a model, some of the other techniques thus far discussed.

I will follow the same pattern in each of the eight methods in this chapter and the five techniques in the following chapter to make it easier for you to assimilate the form of the technique and its problems. This form will (1) give a brief description of the technique, (2) give an example, (3) show several fine points to the method, and (4) show the pitfalls to the technique.

THE SLIDING MORTGAGE

Definition

The sliding mortgage technique occurs when you slide a mortgage from one property to another, removing that specific debt from a property you are buying or exchanging and replacing the security with some other form of asset or promise. This technique is a very good tool to use in several different kinds of transactions. One situation would be when you want to assume an existing mortgage because of its term, interest rate, or other provisions but at the same time you want to take out new financing. If you can move that mortgage over to another property you can accomplish that task, and often buy a property with zero of your own money. Another use of this technique is to have the right to slide a mortgage to another collateral. If you have purchased a property and at the closing gave the seller a first mortgage, if you could have the right to slide that mortgage to another property that was of equal or greater value in the future, you would have more flexibility with the purchased property.

Example 1 A Cashless Transaction

Donald has contracted to buy a small home for $65,000. The seller has agreed to the following:

1. A down payment of $25,000.
2. Donald to assume the existing debt, which consisted of a first mortgage of $28,000 payable over four remaining years at 10% interest, and a second mortgage of $12,000 payable over ten years interest at 8%. This second mortgage is held by the previous seller and was initially a 15-year mortgage.

Donald's plans are to tie up the property, give himself an "out" in case his plan fails, then go to the former owner of the property who is now holding this below-market second mortgage and offer to slide it to another property. If he were successful, Donald would then anticipate some minor fix-up of the home, refinance the transaction at closing, putting a new first mortgage on the home at maximum percent loan to value, pay off the existing first, give the seller his $25,000 cash, cover the cost of the transaction, and if all goes well pocket some cash at the same time.

THE DEAL PROGRESSES.   The small home appraises out at $74,500. Donald gets 80% financing, or a total of $59,600. The former owner of the home agrees to slide the mortgage over to a free and clear lot Donald owns, which he will sell, or build on, and that has a real, fair value of $30,500. To give the mortgagee a bonus, Donald pays him $500 principal against the amount owed on that loan. The former owner is no longer in a second position, has gotten some cash, and has strong value behind his loan so he has improved his situation.

The cash from the loan then goes as follows:

$25,000	To the seller
28,000	To pay off the first mortgage
500	To the former owner, now mortgagee on the lot
1,800	Loan and closing costs
4,300	To Donald's pocket (tax-free, too)
$59,600	

Donald has improved his position in several ways. He took a good mortgage with good terms and put it on a vacant lot that will help him sell the lot if he so desires. He has pulled out some of his equity from the lot without having to go to a lender and take out a mortgage. Many lenders don't like to make vacant lot loans either, so the deal worked several benefits other than getting Donald the home and cash in his pocket.

The lender came into the deal and made a usual 80% loan. From the lender's point of view it was a good deal. Everyone is happy.

To fine-tune this deal might be tough. But other deals might not be as clear as this and need some finesse. Getting the mortgagee to want to move to another security is not always easy. If they think they can block the deal by staying put and require you to pay them off, they sometimes will do exactly that.

Setting up a purchase to allow your mortgages to be slid to another security is one way of helping a prospective buyer to come along and take you out of a property when it is time for you to sell. After all, the seller in this example got what he wanted: cash.

Example 2 A Future Substitution of Collateral

You have made an offer to buy a vacant lot on which you think you may build a small office building in a few years. The seller has agreed to hold an $80,000 first mortgage for a period of fifteen years payable interest only for five years then interest plus a small principal payment so that at the end of the term there is a balloon of $50,000. The interest rate is only 7%, which was part of the seller's plan. You didn't negotiate too hard on the price because you got great terms. In this seller's case, as will happen with sellers who are looking to set up an income stream for a period of years, it would not be difficult to include a sliding mortgage provision in the contract. To do this you have your lawyer include in the offer (before you present it), something along the following, adapting the provision to fit your situation.

> . . . and furthermore, the mortgage will contain a provision that allows the mortgagor to slide the mortgage to a substitute collateral at any time during the term of the mortgage, provided that the mortgagor is current and not in default in this mortgage and that other provisions of this paragraph are met. The substitute collateral shall be the replacement security of this mortgage, providing that the substitute collateral meets the following criteria. (1) the collateral is real property located within the State of Florida, (2) has an appraised value equal to 150% of the outstanding principal of the mortgage, (3) has no secondary debt against the property, and mortgagee agrees not to place any secondary debt against the property. If there is a dispute by the holder of the mortgage as to the value of the substitute collateral, the mortgagor will present an appraisal made by a MAI registered appraiser to show the current market value of the property; if the holder of the mortgage continues to dispute the value, the mortgagee will have a period of 60 days to present his or her own appraisal made by another MAI registered apprais-

er. If the mortgagee's appraiser opinion shall be the deciding appraisal, and if the value shown by said appraisal does not equal 150% of the loan balance, the mortgagor may, at his option, slide the mortgage to the new collateral by reducing the outstanding debt to such a level as to not exceed the 150% of loan balance.

To establish slidable mortgages is not too difficult if you have the mortgage drafted in such a way. The mortgagee sees that he or she is in control by having a qualified appraiser show him or her the real value of the property. At the same time, as mortgagee, you have the right to pay down the mortgage if the appraisal was off, but still within your grasp to move the mortgage. It should be clear that if the mortgage was $50,000 that the value of the property need only be $75,000. If the appraisal presented by the mortgagee showed the property to be worth $60,000 then the maximum amount that the mortgage could be would be $40,000. Being able to slide a $40,000 mortgage at great terms to this other property may still be worthwhile to you.

Benefits to the Mortgagee to Sliding a Mortgage

1. If he or she holds a junior mortgage, it will become a first mortgage.
2. Will have a more favorable value-to-loan ratio.
3. May have a chance to renegotiate the terms of the loan.
4. Might be the term that entices the buyer to take the property.

Pitfalls in Sliding Mortgages

Not many pitfalls will occur for the investor other than the risk that he or she has overextended the capability of the property to carry the new debt. If Donald is able to unload his lot quickly, however, now that he has some attractive financing to assist that purchase, he will have made a very satisfactory transaction.

The big risk comes to the mortgagee that is allowing his or her mortgage security to be shifted from something he or she knows to something he or she doesn't know. Yet by being careful in this matter that problem can be safely covered. Donald by the way, as will you, knows of many other ways to entice the mortgagee to slide.

DOUBLE FINANCE

Definition

Double finance is simply the application of two or more techniques of finance to allow the buyer to maximize the financing and minimize the capital invested. In many situations, like Donald by using the Sliding Mortgage technique, he also refinanced with a conventional lender, obtaining more than 100% financing. The surplus went into his pocket, or to be used as a down payment for another property.

Example Two or More Techniques Combined

Frank needed $800,000 to purchase a strip store complex that consisted of 25,000 square feet of shops. He wanted to upgrade the center at an estimated cost of $100,000 and hoped to be able to buy the property and do the fix up with no more than a total cash outlay of $75,000.

To accomplish this, Frank used several creative tools to meet his objectives.

1. Frank knew that as in all financing techniques he had to have control of the property, so he went to contract with the seller giving himself a period of 90 days in which to establish all the financing required to close on the transaction.

2. Have a clear understanding with the seller on the terms. In this instance, those terms were the following:
   a. Price of $800,000.
   b. Price broken into two segments:
      (1) The improvements (at $600,000).
      (2) The land (at $200,000).
   c. The land would be optioned at $200,000.
   d. Frank would lease the land for $18,500 per year with increases in the rent as per a cost-of-living index every three years. The land lease would be subordinated to a new first mortgage not to exceed 80% of the appraised value of land and improvements.
   e. The improvements would be paid: $425,000 cash at closing, and the remainder of $175,000 in an exchange for some land Frank owns in a growing area west of town.

3. Make all the estimates of work needed to make the needed improvements prior to talking to any lenders about new financing.

4. Present the total package to the lenders. Frank knew that if he showed the improvements and how that would allow him to increase the rents substantially and thereby increase the value, the loan to Frank should be more than enough to take care of the cash requirements.

Frank knew he would be able to show an appraised value of $1,000,000 based on the improvements he plans. Based on this he would be able to obtain a new loan of $800,000.

A quick review of Frank's cashflow showed that he would need $425,000 to pay off the seller and $100,000 to fix up the property. This would leave Frank with $275,000 cash in his pocket. Even after the loan costs, he would have sufficient money to buy the land if he wanted. On the other hand, if the property could support the debt service, Frank might be better off taking the cash and buying more real estate.

Pitfalls in Double Financing

The pitfalls of double financing are the same as any overleveraged property. Frank might be correct in his assessment that once the center is fixed up he can get more rent, and afford a greater debt service. However, if he was cutting things short, and there was a delay in construction, or some unforeseen problem came up that caused the plan to go awry, then Frank might need to dig into his own pocket and meet the heavy debt payments. If he had already spent his bank roll then his house of cards may be on the way down.

How to Avoid the Pitfalls

1. Know and understand your own goals. Do they allow risk of other property and cash based on projections that require elements to happen over which you may have little control?
2. Have a long-range plan that fits your goals. Are you keeping to that plan? Does the plan have safeguards?
3. Learn money management. Start by watching each dollar spent and don't let your income drop below your cash outlay without knowing full well the reasons for it, and have some plan to reverse that situation.

THE GLUE TRANSACTION

A glue transaction is any financial transaction that occurs where the *glue person* puts up his good name and/or credit to a transaction and other parties put up the initial cash, or bring the deal together for a piece of the transaction. This is the basis of many joint-ventures where the money partners put up all the cash just to do a transaction with a glue person or glue entity. It is important to recognize that in the *glue deal* the money person or people come to the glue person and not the other way around.

Example 1 Glue Makes the Money Stick

Insurance companies often seek out top developers or investors in an area to become joint venture partners with. The insurance company puts up the money, and the developer does what he or she has been doing for years, only this time has a built in source for loans, plus a partner.

As you develop your knowledge of your comfort-zone area, you will begin to recognize opportunities for investment. As you add to that knowledge, the techniques of investing and financing found in this book and in other sources such as seminars, books, tapes, college courses, or night adult courses, you will begin to demonstrate that you are confident in your abilities in real-estate investing. Each time you find some area in which you are weak, act to improve in that area and remove that weakness. All of this can and will happen if you want it to, and if you understand that it is not an overnight process and that there is no single source, no key that can unlock your future without your direct and continual growth and action.

Example 2 Even Local Investors Benefit

Alex has done everything necessary to establish himself as an expert in the area. He has learned his comfort zone like the back of his hand, and has bought several properties in the area and turned them into gold mines. Alex's specialty and strength is in finding properties that are underused. He discovered early in his real-estate investing that if he could buy a home that was on a lot that would permit multifamily living, he would be able to convert the home into apartments, increasing the income potential, and increase the value by a greater ratio.

Alex knows that each time he converts a property from one use to another he improves the income potential. As income increases so does the value of the property. He is making the best of his investments and is building profits along the way.

All of Alex's success was going unnoticed by his friends and others in the neighborhood. Some of them had gone to some of those high-priced seminars that promised overnight success, but they ended up having to look in awe at Alex's success. One day one of them got a terrific idea. Why not let Alex help them make money?

This is the first step to a glue deal. Someone recognizes your ability, then comes to you. You don't go to him or her. If you do go to them first, it isn't a glue deal. It might be a syndication, or a joint venture, or whatever.

The Seven Rules of Value That All Glue People Follow

1. All real estate value is related to the actual or potential income[*] from a specific property.
2. Value goes up when the actual or potential income goes up; conversely, value goes down when the actual or potential income decreases.
3. If you can buy knowing ahead of time that the actual or potential income can be increased or is bound to go up, you ensure that there will be increases of value.
4. *Value* is based on a capitalization rate to income. That is, if the anticipated yield is 10% on actual cash invested and the net operating income is $10,000, the value would be $100,000.

---

[*] Income and all other benefits derived from the specific property.

5. Every dollar of increase in net operating income will increase value by the multiple of the capitalization rate. If the cap rate were 10% and income went up $2,000, value would go up $20,000.

6. *Profit* is the increase of equity above your investment. If you put $25,000 down on a property worth $125,000 that had a net operating income of $12,500 and you increased that income to $14,500, your value increases to $145,000 ($125,000 plus the $20,000 value increase as described in rule 5). In the beginning, your equity was $25,000. You increased income by 16% (16% of $12,500 equals $2,000). Your value went up the same percentage. However, your equity increased from $25,000 to $45,000. That is an increase of 80%.

7. Learn this kind of math. It works wonders to the pocketbook.

The Glue Contract

When this person contacts you, you will want to enter into an agreement; that is, of course, if you plan to go ahead with the deal. There are some specific elements that you will want to know and understand about the other people involved and the property in question. Most importantly, you have to decide who is going to be in control of the deal. You or them? Each answer will have different specifics to consider, and you will have to examine the total deal to make that judgment. To help you in coming to this decision and to set up the contract between you and the other people, follow this checklist.

CHECKLIST OF DO'S AND DON'TS OF THE GLUE PERSON

1. *Do* get to know *all* the other people involved, including wives and husbands alike. When you are in a joint venture of any kind, it can be the hidden partners (the spouses you didn't meet) who can make your life miserable.

2. *Do* try to get a feel for their objectives and goals. Keep in mind that one single property may not fill each person's objectives or goals the same, if at all. Will that cause infighting later on? Or will everyone be happy no matter what?

3. *Do* let it be known the moment you feel you want to do the deal that you expect to be compensated handsomely. Keep in mind that they are going to be more demanding later on than now, so if you don't get your piece of the action tied down up front, you may find it slipping away into that dark abyss called poor memory.

4. *Do* have the option to buy them out. Set a fair formula so they will always have a profit, then never take advantage of that agreement unless there is an absolute break-up of the group. Even then, you may want to pass any additional profits (if any) on to them.

5. *Don't* let people use your name in some deal over which you have no control. They will ruin your name far more easily than their own.

6. *Don't* stick with a sinking ship. If the deal is going sour and they won't get out, make sure you have had the foresight to build in an escape provision for yourself.

7. *Don't* help people obtain objectives or goals that are against your own principals. You don't need that kind of money, those headaches, and those sleepless nights.

8. *Don't* sign your name to a mortgage unless you have a majority control and interest in the property, have absolute confidence in your abilities, and the full understanding and potential of the property, and have an agreement that if any shortfall occurs in the income to meet the debt service, and the other people don't pay that shortfall that you can take their interest and sell their interest to cover that shortfall. In hard times, if you are the only one with money in your pocket you may have a hard time getting your partners on the phone.

9. *Don't* hesitate to enforce any penalties on your partners. That is only sound business, and if you try to struggle through it may put the whole project in trouble and your future as well.

10. *Don't* let this keep you from doing a glue transaction. They can be great, and if you approach each deal with the knowledge that you can make a profit doing something you know and love to do, and help others too, then why not? You will find that by taking on some partners you may be able to buy a larger property than you would have by yourself. This can allow you to grow in confidence and ability and take you to more and greater opportunities.

Pitfalls in Glue Transactions

Pitfalls in glue transactions occur mostly when you don't know much about your partners and/or their goals. As long as you follow the checklist and avoid overextending your own abilities or fail to get compensated properly for your time and effort, you should be okay.

DISCOUNTED PAPER

Definition

Discounted paper is notes or mortgages which you buy or create and use in a transaction at a discount. Generally this transaction is done to improve the sales potential of the property which is security for the to-be-discounted paper, or as a way to get the seller to reduce your down payment.

Example 1 Buyers Use Discounted Paper to Close Transactions

You want to buy a home but do not have the cash down the seller wants. You do own a small apartment building that is presently financed with a low (loan-to-value) first mortgage. You go to the seller and offer to give her a second mortgage on the apartment building you have been thinking of selling in the near future and you create such a mortgage in the offer, but it does not exist. In your offer you make reference to this second mortgage as follows:

> . . . said second mortgage having, at the closing of this transaction a principal balance outstanding of $15,300 and is payable at a term of 120 months remaining and is payable at 6% interest, plus principal in equal installments until fully amortized.

You offer the seller $5,000 cash and this second mortgage. This looks like you have offered a value of $20,300. But the seller of the house does some calculations on the math of that mortgage and tells you that the interest rate is so low that she cannot value the mortgage at the $15,300 rate.

You ask her if she would take the mortgage anyway if you increased your cash down by $2,000. In essence, discount the mortgage by $2,000. This would increase the return on the mortgage to just under 9% over the term of the loan. The seller agrees and you close on the deal.

The benefit to you is double. First you need only invest $7,000 of your own money in the new house, and you have put a great second loan on the apartment building which may now help entice a buyer.

Example 2 Good Financing on What You Buy and What You Want to Sell

Lou is interested in buying a condo so that he and his wife, and their little dog, can live close to his business a few blocks away. At the same time, Lou has decided he would like to sell a motel he owns on the beach. The motel is already financed with both a first and second mortgage. If Lou were to use the discounted paper as a technique in this deal, he would need to create a third mortgage on the motel at reasonable interest and pay-back terms, and then offer the mortgage to the seller of the condo as part of the contract. To make the mortgage more attractive, Lou would be quick to discount the mortgage so that it would give a better yield to the seller.

Lou would want to keep the terms and payback of the mortgage as light as possible because he has to make the payments until he sells the motel. If the terms are attractive, the mortgage may make the motel more saleable, and at a higher price too.

Since debt payments distract from the ultimate cash return of any investor, whoever buys the motel will want to keep the debt payments as low as possible, thereby increasing the cash return. If Lou creates a $75,000 mortgage that is payable over 15 years at 9% interest, the mortgage payment would be $760.69 per month, or $9,128.25 per year.

Lou makes his deal on the condo using this mortgage as part of that transaction, as though it were cash, but had to offer the seller of the condo an improved yield of 10%. In this case, the actual face value of the mortgage would be $75,000, but because of the discount Lou would only get credit for $70,788.75. You may want to review the chapter on mortgage discounts to learn the math to use in obtaining this discount. A quick review of what happened follows.

The mortgage Lou creates is for $75,000, 15 years, with monthly payments of $750.69 (see the mortgage rate Table A: under 9% for 15 years: 12.171; multiply this times $75,000 to get the annual total of the 12 monthly payments or $9,128.25; divide by 12 to get the monthly payment of $750.69).

The condo seller wants a 10% yield. To find the discount, you take the constant rate at the face amount (12.171 from the foregoing calculations), and divide it by the constant rate for the yield wanted. To find the constant at 10%, look at Table A under 10% for 15 years to find 12.895. Divide 12.171 by 12.895 to get the discount of 0.94385, which means that 94.385% of the face amount of the mortgage will be the discount needed to give a yield of 10%. Multiply the original mortgage of $75,000 by 0.94385 to get $70,788.75, which is the discount amount that Lou would get credit for at the closing on the condo.

Why would Lou do this? One reason is to make the deal without having to add that much cash to the condo deal. It might also have been that Lou was using this technique to be able to take cash out of the condo through new financing. However, one additional benefit occurs with the financing on the motel.

Lou might find that in the mortgage market, a third mortgage on the motel would not be available through normal sources. If Lou leaves the mortgage off the motel, all that does is increase his equity and gives a prospective buyer additional areas to negotiate with. In the end, it might reduce Lou's ultimate profit or price in the transaction. Also, to make the deal Lou might have to end up holding a mortgage like that himself, and that would put him back into the position of having to pay cash for the condo now. After all, the condo seller wants to satisfy his primary goal, the sale of the condo. If he is willing to take the paper at a discount, then let him.

Lou knows that a realistic third mortgage on the motel might be at a rate closer to 12.5% or higher. A $75,000 mortgage for 15 years at 12.5% would have an annual payment of $11,092.50, which is $1,964.25 more than the payment on the mortgage Lou has set up. Let's go back to the value rules for a second. Remember, if the cap rate the buyer wants when he buys the motel is (say) 10%, the added cash in the investor's pocket due to Lou's smart move with the condo seller would be $1,964.25, which is worth $19,642.50 in value. Lou traded the mortgage at a discount for less than $4,300 and gets back an extra $19,642.50 or so from the motel sale. He has accomplished this with no expense to himself in the long run. Since the seller of the condo is happy and Lou is happy, so would the buyer of the motel be who now has to invest less cash to make the motel profitable.

These are just a few examples of mortgage discounts as transaction makers. You will have to examine all other potentials that may present themselves. By rereading the chapter on mortgage discounting and by applying these concepts to other techniques, you will come up with many different methods of using this highly creative tool. You should always remember that the tradeoff (Lou's first discount to the condo owner) between the discount and the benefit of the good terms (the sale of the motel) should be designed to work in your favor.

Pitfalls in Discounted Mortgages

Remember the baker who thought a dozen was 13? Well, when it comes to the mathematics of finance, you have to be sure you are using proper math. When you calculate yields in mortgages, you will find that due to the multiples of cap rates or the kind of amortization schedule you are using, a small error in the formula is exaggerated with the end result you may get. I discovered just recently that a calculator I had been using was rounding off its built-in formula on amortization schedules to the point that in a sizable mortgage discount the end result could be substantially off. For that reason, I suggest that you use the following step to check if your calculator has built-in finance programs to see if you are getting correct answers to your math problems.

Solve this following problem using your calculator:

1. Calculate the monthly payment on a $150,000 mortgage payable over 30 years (360 months) at 12% per annum (1% per month). Write down the monthly payment your calculator shows you.

2. Now, go to Table A in the back of this book. Look for the constant rate that corresponds to 12% interest for 30 years. That constant rate is 12.343. Convert the constant percentage to a mathematical number by moving the decimal left so that you now have 0.12343.

3. Multiply that times the mortgage amount ($150,000 × .12343 = $18,514.50). The result, $18,514.50, is the annual total of the 12 monthly payments.

4. Now divide the annual total by 12 to get $1,542.87 as the monthly payment.

5. Compare this last answer with the answer on your calculator. If your calculator gave you anything more than a couple of dollars less than $1,542.87, then it is rounding off decimals to the extent that you are obtaining improper and potentially damaging information.

Take the calculator back to the shop where you bought it and get your money back. Or use it just to add, multiply, divide, and subtract. You can use the tables in this book to obtain more accurate information. Keep in mind that if you get an answer that is very close to the $1,542.87 it could be that you have a calculator that is carrying the problem to more decimal places than the table, in which case you are in good shape. You can find out by taking the monthly payment you get and working back to the constant rate. Assume you got $1,543.13 as your monthly payment from your calculator. Multiply that by 12 to get the annual amount, which is $18,517.56. Divide that by the amount of the mortgage ($150,000) to get your constant rate in a mathematical form, which would be 0.1234504 more or less. If your calculator shows 0.1234 or 0.12345, you have a good financial calculator and can work with it to obtain accurate calculations.

Using discounts properly will depend on your use of this kind of math. Do not rely on a banker or mortgage broker to come up with these calculations, for you may be getting wrong information if they have an old calculator that is rounding everything off.

OTHER PEOPLE'S PROPERTY: OPP

Some people say that the way to true riches is to invest as little of your own cash as possible and as much of other people's money as available. Buying real estate using other people's property, and not their *cash*, is a technique where you use an asset that isn't yours as security to acquire something of your own.

Definition

Using OPP would mean buying, exchanging or leasing property where you give as all or part of the equity in the transaction a property you do not currently own. This can be accomplished through mortgages, exchange, or barter. Unlike the concept of buying with OPM, which is other people's money, you can use other people's property as a method of acquiring the real estate you want to own. This works if you keep in mind that it is benefits that count, and any benefit can have the same importance to a transaction as its money equivalency. In fact, sometimes the benefit is more acceptable because it hits the hot button.

Example 1 Part Cash, Part Exchange

Dominic wanted to buy a vacant lot on which he planned to build a small apartment building. The price of the lot was $55,000. Dominic offered to pay $20,000 cash out of the apartment building's final draw on the construction loan. For the balance of $35,000 he agreed to give the seller a vacant lot in the Florida Keys. This was okay, only the Florida Keys lot was not owned by Dominic. Dominic had made a side deal with that owner to "exchange" for the lot, giving the lot owner one of the condo apartments to be built on the lot.

Example 2 Part Cash, Part Mortgage

Jane wanted to buy a home in Charleston. As a part of her deal, she offered the seller a second mortgage on a mountain home in the Beech Mountain area of North Carolina. Jane didn't own that home, her mother did. She had made a deal with her mother to take a piece of the action on the Charleston home when it was sold.

Example 3 Part Cash, Part Barter

Roger, a good handyman kind of investor, offered a two-week holiday every year for the next five years as part of an OPP transaction. The resort was actually a timeshare facility in the Bahamas. The owner of the property Roger wanted to buy would be getting a solid $15,000 to $30,000 value depending on how many people actually traveled. Of course, Roger didn't own the resort, but he had made a side deal with a friend who owned a large block of timeshare weeks at the resort. Roger's barter to this person was $20,000 worth of carpenter time.

In each of these examples, the buyer knew of someone who had something that could be offered as a part of another transaction. It is likely that you will have no problem finding someone whom you could use, if the opportunity came up, as an OPP part of the deal.

Of course, you can go out and find a few people right now who have property they would sell to you under the kind of terms that would work. These terms could range anywhere from their taking a second position in the property you buy, holding some other security, or just becoming a partner with you in the deal. Line some of these people up and have them ready and willing when the time comes.

Parents and relatives may not be the best place to go to get them to "lend you" one of their properties, unless you are ready to give up a piece of the action on the property.

For example, meet some rental apartment owners in your area that own and operate tourist types of rentals. They will have units that are vacant during specific times of the year as a natural course to their business. Those people will make deals with you. The best way to make an enemy out of a relative is to use that person or their assets to the point where you profit at their expense. If you deal with a relative, give him or her some added benefit. It might be the depreciation, or it might be a percent of the ultimate sale in the future.

Pitfalls in Using OPP Transactions

The biggest pitfall is not having the deal with the other property already worked out in advance. Have it up front, and have it in writing. Working on good faith, you are apt to go out and cut a deal with a seller only to find that your brother in-law now says, "Hey now, Charlie, I don't remember saying you could have that lot of mine up in Maine to use in buying that run-down fish cannery."

Make sure that the plus and downsides are covered. Never make an OPP deal without the other property owner understanding his or her risk. If it is slight or limited to some time use in the other property, be sure you spell it out.

SHARED EQUITY

In the history of real estate people have shared property together. Several dozen families in this cave, half a dozen in another. Families rent houses together, cohabit apartments, and in general have become comfortable with the idea of time-shared property. Using this as a basis for a form of financing, can become a good closing tool in certain deals.

Definition

In a shared equity transaction you "sell" your property to a tenant, who will get a percentage of the equity at the time of a future sale. Or you can be the tenant who goes to the owner to set up the deal whereby you improve the property for a future profit. In turn the owner gives you a reduced rent and you both profit in the future.

Example 1 Lock in a Tenant

You own a couple of rental homes that are just too far away for you to bother with them. You go to the tenants in each and offer them the same deal. If they will buy the property they are now leasing, you will let them close with zero cash down, and reduce their monthly payments at the same time. The real bonus is, that at the end of five years, or sooner if you both agree, the property will be put on the market and sold. The tenant will get 50% (this is open for negotiation by both sides) of the profit. Profit to be determined as all cash left over after the deduction of closing costs, the purchase money mortgage you established at the time of the sale. As one further condition to the transaction, each tenant must agree to fix up the property according to a very detailed list of improvements. You agree to pay for any items needed for the fix-up (to be added to the balance of the purchase money mortgage), and the tenant is to do all the work. Each tenant accepts the deal and you draw up the papers and close.

If this property is in a state that has Homestead exemption for the purpose of real estate taxes, the fact that the owner of the property now lives in the home will reduce the annual tax bill. As either you or the tenant was paying the bill before, this is a benefit from the deal.

Example 2 Lock up the Landlord

You have been living in a condominium apartment owned by Craig. It is an okay apartment but needs work. You are a salesman for a home decorating firm and have access to just about everything it would take to fix up this apartment. You go to Craig and show him a very detailed list of improvements, and the retail cost of the improvements plus labor to accomplish the fix-up. You also show Craig the potential sales profit a year or two from now when the apartment will be finished. You tell Craig that you will do all the work, and pay for all the materials if you are allowed to take the cost of the materials out of your rent. The labor part will give you a 50% interest in any profit that is above a price the two of you agree is the present value of the apartment. Your actual cost of the materials is about half of what the retail cost is, so you benefit there. Craig gets a good deal too, if you do a good job. His downside is some loss of rent, but if the apartment doesn't sell, and you move out, then he is left with a fixed-up apartment.

Example 3 Buy with Locked-in Tenants

Saul is going out and tying up properties that he wants to buy. He has been doing his homework and has found properties owned by motivated sellers on which he has negotiated excellent prices. One such property is a home that he can buy for $45,000. It needs a little work, and Saul plans to spend $500 on the property.

Thus far, the deal is that Saul is buying the property. Assume that he is able to spend the $500 to paint and fix up the property, get the seller to hold an unsecured note for $10,000, and get cash for the balance. Now Saul goes to the local savings and loan and gets a new first mortgage for $40,000. Based on an appraisal of $50,000, this loan would be approved. This gives Saul the cash to close with the seller, the money for the new mortgage, and the cash to fix up the property, with about $3,000 left in his pocket.

He advertises for a "nothing down deal," the buy-your-own-home-for-nothing-down kind of deal. Along comes a prospective buyer, who has no cash, and Saul says: "Move in now, pay everything in the way of debt service, and we will split the profit at a sale within four to five years away."

The "buyer" gets a contract that is much like a lease with option that says that at the end of the agreed term the property will be sold or that the "buyer" can take Saul out of the deal. Each party will get half of the equity of the sale or some formula that is established at the time of the lease transaction.

Saul might consider his equity to be only $500. "After all," he might say, "I just bought the home and I have a first mortgage of $40,000 and a seller-held note of $10,000." In this deal, the "buyer" would pay the debt on those two loans and get a percentage of any sale above $50,500 less the mortgage reductions.

Example 4 Pull Out Equity Lock in Tenant

Francisco owned a small condo for a couple of years and learned of the shared-equity kind of transaction. He put a maximum mortgage on the property to pull out tax-free cash and then proceeded to find a "buyer" who would come in with a price of $60,000. As Francisco had placed a $45,000 new mortgage on the property, and as the "shared equity" was based on the value of $60,000, the "partner" in the deal with Francisco would benefit only above the equity of $15,000 ($60,000 value less the $45,000 mortgage equals $15,000 equity). In essence, Francisco would be paid the first $15,000 above the mortgage at the time of the sale and then both Francisco and the "partner" would split the balance as would be agreed.

What Makes Shared Equity Deals Work

The motivation in these transactions seems to be the ability to entice "buyers" through the nothing-down concept. Property owners feel that a tenant who thinks she is building up equity will be a better tenant and that the long-range profit will be greater for both parties than if the comparison is to "rent only."

In Francisco's deal, he has already taken out the majority of the equity tax-free, and he likes the thought of keeping the tax shelter for a couple of years longer. In addition, and the real plus factor for Francisco, it would be unlikely that he could sell this condo for $50,000 in the current marketplace anyway.

Pitfalls in Shared Equity Transactions

Whenever you approach a technique with the idea of pulling the wool over someone's eyes, you are apt to have problems. While the shared-equity format can work nicely for both parties, most of the transactions I have seen have been based on the *dumber than I* concept. In this type of transaction, the temptation to "boost" the current values to above the current marketplace is great. Gullible buyers who are used to renting can be enticed to the deal. What sounds like lower rent really is not because the property owner is getting repairs at a cheap price. Also, because the tenant-cum-carpenter feels he is building up equity the rent becomes more steady.

Once the tenant moves in and begins to realize that he is paying more rent than everyone else in the building, or if there is a decline in the market and he sees values dropping or people offering to sell similar apartments at lower prices than his "base equity for participation," this "buyer" becomes very disgruntled.

Disgruntled tenants have been known to move to Texas in the middle of the night, taking with them refrigerators, carpets, drapes, sinks, ranges, and light fixtures, nailed down or otherwise.

Of course, you and Saul and the rest of the people doing shared equity deals might be giving your "buyers" the best deal in town. And if that is the case, your problems will be small ones.

ZERO-COUPON FINANCING

Definition

Zero coupons are a function that stock brokers and bond dealers are very familiar with. The essence of this kind of financial transaction on the stock or bond market is that the instrument sold is a note, bond or debt obligation that has an original face value, and that no payments are made against the debt for a period of years, then the debt balloons.

Example 1 Basic Zero Coupon Bond

Ace Corporation sells $5,000,000 worth of zero-coupon-debt obligations that are divided into certificates or debt instruments of $100,000 each. This means there are fifty of these separate obligations being sold. The obligation carries an interest rate of 10% per year, but no payments are made until the final payment when all debt and interest comes due at the same time, five years later. This payment would be the accumulation of all interest compounded for the five years and would total $161,105.10

In the marketplace, these kinds of investments either sell at a price that would give the holder the actual yield stated (10% in the above example), or a yield over or under that yield, depending on the quality of the debt and the interest rate demanded by the market.

ZERO-COUPON FINANCING IN REAL ESTATE

When this zero payment of interest or principal formula is applied to real estate it can have some very interesting results.

Example 2 Two Zero Coupons Put Cash in Buyer's Pocket

Brad had negotiated with Francis to buy her home, and they were very close to making a deal. Francis didn't need any cash, but didn't want to do a deal that wasn't secure for her. The price was agreeable to both parties: $300,000.

The property had a first mortgage that Brad could assume in the amount of $150,000. What was in question was the balance. Brad offered to give Francis a note that had a single payment at the end of fifteen years of $150,000. In addition, he would give her right now a zero coupon bond that would pay another $150,000 at the end of fifteen years. Francis didn't need the cash, so she took the deal by putting the note and the bond in the names of her three grandchildren for their college fund.

Brad closed on the deal by putting a new first mortgage on the home for $189,000. He paid off the existing $150,000, bought a fifteen-year zero coupon bond that would pay off at $150,000 for $35,000, and paid for the mortgage with the balance. Brad had no thought of keeping the house for fifteen years, so wasn't concerned about the other payment of $150,000 down the road fifteen years from now. He expected that appreciation in the property would ultimately give him a profit, plus pay off the amount owed Francis.

Francis didn't do all that badly. The total amount owed to her of $150,000 would turn into $300,000 at the end of the fifteen years. If she did not have a taxable gain in the property she would not have to worry about having cash out of the deal to pay off Uncle Sam. The income would not come in for 15 years, so unless she sold the debt to someone else, the interest would accumulate untaxed. Her actual yield on the $150,000 would be slightly less than 5%. While not high, she might not do better in savings, and the fact that the deal solved her problem had a certain value. She might have been ready to drop her price to a point that the outstanding would only be $100,000 so the $300,000 return was really a yield of 7.6%.

Fine Points in Using Zero-Coupon Financing

The first step is to learn everything you can about what the bond is and how it increases in value. To do this, you need to understand *compound interest*. This is interest that is added to the principal. The two factors that govern compound interest are time and interest rate. Time falls into two segments. How often does the interest get added to the principal, so that the principal becomes larger and more interest can be added? If it is annual, the interest is added at the end of each year and the next year would earn interest on the original principal plus interest on the previous interest added. Obviously, monthly is better than annual, and daily is better than monthly. The other time factor to consider is the total duration of the bond. If it is a ten-year bond, it doesn't get paid off until that time; a thirty-year bond pays off thirty years down the road, and so on. However, you can sell these bonds prior to that time and take the price someone is willing to pay at that time.

To sell or discount a zero payment real-estate debt is possible. The prices would fluctuate due to market demands as to the yield that investors would expect to earn based on the remaining time on the debt. If there are other higher paying forms of investments than the yield on the debt you want to sell, you may find that you have to take a big discount. If it is a long-term bond that you haven't held for too long, it is possible to lose money selling these forms of debt, over what you took it in for. On the other hand, if the yield is better than other investments, the face value owed may support a bonus if you sell the debt on the open market.

Some real estate debt is financed by institutional or municipal bonds. Some of these bonds are given tax-free status to entice investors to buy them, despite the low yield interest. These bonds are generally secured by a first mortgage or pool of first mortgages.

Pitfalls in Dealing with Zero Coupon Debt

The biggest pitfall is ending up taking a zero coupon bond as part of a sale without realizing what its actual "cash out" value is at any future date. Don't fool yourself by taking a thirty-year bond that will pay $200,000 ten years from now and think it is currently worth that. If you had to sell it right now, you would be shocked at what you would receive.

On the other hand, if you view the bond as additional security and don't mind sitting back and not getting any return for a while, there are situations in which this form of financing can be attractive.

You may discover that you will have a tax disadvantage taking back a seller a second party zero coupon bond. Under the 1986 income tax revisions, changes in installment sales reporting eliminate the advantages for most sellers in holding long-term mortgages. Review your circumstance with an accountant prior to accepting any mortgage when you sell a property. You may discover you have a tax to pay that is greater than your cash down.

The buyer has little to worry about as long as he or she understands what is going on. Too many people get caught up in the use of a technique without really understanding what is going on. Don't let that happen to you by using zero coupons incorrectly.

SPLIT FUNDING

Split funding is a psychological approach to payment. It gives the buyer the opportunity to say, "I'll pay you what you want as a down payment; only, I'll pay it when I'm good and ready to." Sometimes this works, sometimes it is good for the seller, not only the buyer.

Definition

Split funding occurs when the buyer splits the down payment, or purchase price into more than one payment, but where the total of all the payments never add up to more than the original amount. In essence, a payment over a period of time without any interest added in. Simply, a payment split into two or more increments.

Example 1 Basic Split Funding

The seller is asking $500,000 with $200,000 down. You start your negotiations by saying, "I'm okay with the $200,000 down. Will you hold a $200,000 first mortgage over 30 years at 8% interest with equal payments for the full term?"

The strategy is to move the seller's focus to the terms for the moment. As the seller believes you have agreed to the down payment part of the deal, the seller might soften on the balance. In any event, the negotiations will center around whether or not you pay on a $300,000 mortgage or a $250,000 mortgage. The terms will eventually sort themselves out.

Once you are set on that, you have the final draft of the agreement made. It contains a provision that now spells out the split funding of the down payment, something like the following:

> . . . and as has been agreed, the buyer will pay a down payment of $200,000 as follows: At closing there will be an initial payment of $100,000, and each year thereafter for a term of 4 years, an additional payment of $25,000 until the entire down payment of $200,000 has been met.

Will you have more negotiations over this kind of payment? You might, and you might not. The cost to the seller at this point, if money is worth 8%, would be a loss of interest of $20,000 before taxes. If the seller is in a 30% tax bracket, the cost to the seller is only $14,000 in total. Of course, cost is not the only criteria, as the buyer has now bought the property with only $100,000 down. If this is an income-producing property much of the annual $25,000 of split-funded down payments can be met by income. Very good for the buyer.

Example 2 Giving the Seller What He or She Wants

You have offered to Bob, a seller of a small office building you want to buy, a purchase price of $250,000. The terms of your offer consist of $25,000 down with your assumption of the existing first mortgage of $150,000. Bob will hold a second mortgage for the balance of $75,000 for seven years at 9% interest.

He objects, as would many sellers, to the low down payment and the high second mortgage. He insists on a $50,000 down payment.

Using the split funding method, you would meet his objection with a positive statement: "Okay, Bob, I'll pay the $250,000 price, I'll give you a $50,000 second mortgage for nine years at 9 1/2%. Now, instead of the $75,000 second mortgage it will only be $50,000. Okay?"

While he is beaming, you go on to explain the full details of your counteroffer. "Here's how we'll handle the down payment. We will 'split fund' the payment as follows: At closing, I'll give you $25,000 and at the end of eighteen months the second $25,000. Naturally I will be making payments on the second mortgage each month in addition to this split funding of the down payment."

What you did, of course, was agree to the $50,000 down payment only you won't pay it all at once. The net effect of this split fund is it will give you an opportunity to obtain some other financing during that eighteen-month period, or at least collect some income on the building to help make the payment. For Bob, it took that additional $25,000 out of the mortgage and got it into his pocket earlier.

How to Fine-Tune the Split-Funded Payment

There are several fine points to this example that you should look at now. First, I show no interest on the second $25,000 payment. This is a matter subject to negotiation between you and Bob. If you can get away with no interest, great. There is no law that says you have to show or provide interest on this kind of payment. From Bob's point of view, the IRS will assume that he received interest in that second payment and that the principal amount was less than $25,000 and the difference was an interest imputed into the deal.

Another factor that generally comes to play whenever you "give in" to the other side's demands is a counteroffer to even out the deal. In your split-fund counter, you have reduced the second mortgage to $50,000 but at the same time have extended the term to 9 years and reduced the interest to 9 1/2%. This tactic may do nothing but move Bob's attention to that factor and cause him to say: "Okay, but the mortgage has to be the same term and interest rate as before." On the other hand, you might end up with some compromise that is more in your favor.

Advantages in Split Funding on Closings at the End of the Seller's Tax Year

Split funding often works to the seller's advantage when it allows him or her to divide taxable funds over two separate tax years. If you discover that it is likely that you will close near the end of the seller's tax year, you can use this to your advantage. Keep in mind that the IRS allows you to establish tax year-ends other than December 31. If you were going to close around August 31 and you discover that the seller's year end is October 31, you might be able to show the seller the advantage of splitting the money into two or more taxable years.

MIXING THE SPLIT FUND WITH OTHER CREATIVE TECHNIQUES

If the assumption is that you will meet the obligation of this split-funded down payment from the property itself, you need to plan the purchase accordingly.

The following are two methods of getting cash out of a property you just bought. Each of these methods is described in more detail in other chapters in the book and is shown here only to illustrate the need for you to be as creative as possible in combining techniques.

Example 3 Split-Fund Split-Deal

You have just contracted to buy a one-hundred acre tract of land. The purchase price is $250,000. The down payment is $50,000 split into two payments. A payment of $20,000 is due at closing and the balance of $30,000 is due in 18 months. The balance is a first $200,000 mortgage held by the seller for 15 years at 9% per annum.

Your plan is to sell off some of the twenty acres so that you can generate sufficient cash to cover the balance owed on the down payment. You know from your homework that by breaking this twenty acres into smaller tracts you can increase the value of the sites on a per-acre basis and profit greatly.

However, you must be sure that you have set up the purchase money mortgage to allow you to obtain releases from the first mortgage to permit you to sell off some property. Keep in mind that when you have a mortgage secured by property you now own, that mortgage creates a lien on all of the property. When you anticipate or want the right to sell off some of the property you buy, you must make sure that you obtain an agreement from the seller in the very beginning that will allow you to release land from the mortgage. The following is an example of the kind of language you can use. Be sure that your lawyer drafts language that fits the exact transaction and tries to take into account your potential future intentions with respect to a sale of some of the land. The following language is more of a catch-all that can cover most eventualities.

> . . . and furthermore, as long as the mortgagor is current and not in default on any of the payments of this mortgage, the mortgagor will have the right to obtain partial releases of the security to the mortgage. These releases will be in increments of the land of no less than one acre, and will follow the following pattern:

The pattern of releases will be that the land will be divided into blocks of land consisting of no less than one acre. (Draw such a sketch that blocks out the land as you anticipate it might be developed or need to be released). If in the future this pattern proves to be impractical for reasons beyond the control of either party, then the mortgagee will not unreasonably object to a revised pattern provided that the intent of Exhibit A is followed, giving the benefit of any change to the mortgagee.

Releases of the land will be based on an accelerated price of 125% of the pro/rata per acre loan ratio. The per acre loan ratio is found by dividing the amount of principal plus unpaid interest outstanding by the remaining number of acres secured by the mortgage prior to a release. For example, if the total loan (principal plus outstanding interest) were $200,000 and 100 acres remained as security to the mortgage, then the per acre loan ratio is $2,000 per acre. As the release price is 125% of that amount, the *next release price* would be $2500 per acre. The mortgagor may make principal payments against the amount owned without taking the release those payments may provide. If the mortgagor has made payments without asking for a release from the date of closing or the date of a previous release, the mortgagor may accumulate all principal payments made and apply them to a release at a future date. If this occurs, the calculation as to release price would be made as though none of the principal payments had been made. All expenses to accomplish the release will be paid by the Mortgagor, and these expenses shall include but not be limited to: Recent survey of the actual property to be released, all cost to record, pay documentary and other transfer taxes as may be applicable and mortgagee's legal cost.

Be sure to have your lawyer draft the actual mortgage document, and don't just try to insert this previously shown paragraph into a standard mortgage. There may be conflicting wording in a standard mortgage that will destroy your ultimate plan. It is important to remember all the different aspects of a purchase money mortgage that can be inserted, such as right of substitution of collateral for sliding mortgages, subordination, assumption of the mortgage by a future buyer, and so on.

Fine-Tuning Partial Release from Mortgage Statement

There are many other provisions that could be put into a mortgage release statement, and many different forms of releases could be devised. The $2,500 payment in the foregoing example is what would be termed *above par* payment (125%) and would pay off the mortgage faster then the original schedule as you released land. The mortgage of $200,000 relates to $2,000 per acre in the beginning. If you made a prepayment to release 20 acres at the initial per acre price of $2,500 you would have to pay $50,000. This would reduce the amount of the mortgage to $150,000 and there would be 80 acres remaining as security to the mortgage. The loan to acre has dropped to $1,375 ($150,000 mortgage divided by 80 acres = $1,875.). The next release price is going to be 125% of that amount or a total of $2,343.75 per acre.

If the seller called for a 150% release, the release price would be 150% of the allocated value per acre of the face amount of the mortgage. Keep in mind that some lawyers would word a release to say 150% of the per acre purchase price per acre. This is not what you want.

Armed with the release provision, you could then anticipate that to meet your split fund and pay the release you would have to sell sufficient land to pay the $25,000 balance on the down payment, and (at 125%) a release of $2,500 per acre for the initial release.

How much would you need to sell? The total you need has to be $25,000 plus due interest (calculate 12 months before the next payment of the down payment at 9% is $2,250 plus you need the release price per acre of $2,500. Consider this a math problem. For each acre you sell $2,500 in the first release, has to go to the release from the mortgage. If you can get $5,000 per acre for small tracts, then you will have $2,500 left over from each acre to pay the portion of the down payment due. That is $27,250 and when you divide the amount due by what you have per acre to meet it, you will discover that you have to sell 10.9 acres ($27,250 divided by $2,500 = 10.9 acres.)

Proceeds from 10.9 acres		$54,500
To release from the mortgage		
(minimum of one acre increments)	$27,250	
To pay the split fund down payment	27,250	
Balance	$54,500	$54,500

By using the split fund with the split deal, you would have the flexibility to spin off some of the land to meet your other obligations as well. It is important to remember that whenever you buy a property that can be divided, you should attempt to allow for releases within the mortgages. If financing already exists on the property, you may not have the opportunity to change those mortgages, but you can ask for that as a condition to the transaction. Previous mortgages can be altered, and the prospect of an early payment or advance payment through releases may be attractive to mortgagees of mature mortgages.

Certain provisions that are critical in these circumstances would be:

1. **The release pattern.** You must allow flexibility to suit your needs or development plans. Sellers or mortgagees will want to ensure that the remaining property more than secures the mortgage balance owed. For this reason, sellers or mortgagees will want to keep the prime portions of the property under the mortgage umbrella.

2. **Where advance payments apply.** If you stated "any advance payment of principal will apply toward releases as well as the next scheduled payment" you will have an ideal method of payment for a buyer. In this format, you may take care of three years of scheduled payments with one release, and not have a principal payment for three years in so doing. The other side of this coin is the statement "and any advance payment in excess of the normal scheduled principal payments will be applied to the last payments due on the mortgage." This statement is the usual provision in mortgages, which simply means that if you make an advance payment you don't affect the mortgagee's schedule for regular payments except by accelerating the ultimate payoff of the mortgage.

3. **Penalty if the mortgagee doesn't give the release.** You might have a sale and not be able to deliver because the mortgagee decides that he or she isn't going to give you the release no matter what the mortgage says. A paragraph added by your lawyer could give you some protection in this event by allowing you to provide some incentive for the mortgagee to act according to the original agreement.

FUTURE RENT

Definition

Future rent is simply the obligation or the benefit (depending on which side of the payment you are) of rent for one or more periods that will take place some time in the future. Because this is both a benefit and an obligation, it is an ideal financing tool that can be used in many different ways. If you are a buyer, you can use this benefit as a part of the cash down, a benefit of prepaid rent at another location, and as a "free" option to entice you into the transaction in the first place. As a seller, you can hold out "free" future rent for other concessions, accept trade or barter in lieu of the future rent, and guarantee all or part of the projected future rent available to be passed on to the buyer.

Example 1 Part of Cash Down

The seller is insisting on $150,000 cash down for the office building you want to buy. The total price is $700,000 and there is a first mortgage of $200,000. The seller says she will hold the balance in secondary financing.

You split the deal into building and land lease, so that there is a $20,000 annual land lease payment. Assume you cap the land lease at 8%, so the $20,000 represents a value of the land at $250,000. At this point there is a total of $450,000 in financing arranged. The existing mortgage of $200,000 and a $250,000 (value) land lease. You now ask the seller to hold a second mortgage of $250,000 at 7.5% interest for the balance of the financing. This gives you a total of $600,000 in financing. Of the $150,000 down payment, you categorize $50,000 of this as prepaid rent.

You offer the prepaid rent when you get a tax break by calling part of the deal prepaid rent. There would be no other advantage, but when it works for you, it can allow you to offset current income against future obligations you pay now. Please note, this is a deal by deal situation and may not apply to your circumstances. Be sure you have a need for the extra expense, and that you are able to take advantage of it.

Example 2 As Prepaid Rent in Another Location

You are buying a home from Jake, and discover that he is looking for a place to store equipment he uses in his construction business. You just happen to own a warehouse that has some vacant space, so you offer Jake three years prepaid rent, worth $40,000 as your down payment on the home.

Example 3 Prepaid in the Same Property

This occurs if you pledge two years' free rent to the seller's son, in one of the apartments in the building you are going to buy, and get credit for it off the closing statement.

Example 4 As a Seller, You Agree to Take Part Rent

If you have a live buyer, to get him to close, you agree to reduce his down payment by taking two years prepaid rent for your own office space in the building you are selling.

Example 5 You Exchange Rent

You have several vacancies in a strip store you own, so you exchange the space for other benefits. To one tenant you take all of one year's rent for roof repair work on that and several other buildings you own. Another tenant gives you barter dollars for part of the rent. Another offers you merchandise for part of the rent, and so on.

There are many ways to use future rent as part of a real-estate transaction. It might be to pledge the rent of another property as security for a note or mortgage on the property you want to buy. Or you might offer the seller the right to stay on for a period of time as a tenant without paying any rent. It is important for you to think again in the area of benefits and not money. If you have something you have not been able to rent, or even thought about renting, why not offer that on your next deal. If one of those things you own is a mountain cabin, you could offer "free rent" in that facility for some period of time.

Nonetheless, the usual method of using this technique is to take rent you are getting as a security against a note or loan you want to obtain or offer to another party. In this way the seller of the property you want to buy doesn't have to have a need for the property for rent, only recognize that its rent is a value that can secure another note or mortgage.

Example 6 The Brownie Deal

Brownie got right down to the last straw in trying to make a deal with Roco. The only thing that was holding them apart was that Roco wouldn't take Brownie's unsecured note for $5,000 as part of the down payment. Brownie countered with the same $5,000 note, but added as a security all rents above the first $800 each month from a four-unit apartment building Brownie owned. Each apartment rented for $425 and so had a gross monthly rent of $1,700. Roco saw that his note would be secure providing that Brownie agreed not to put any additional financing on the apartment until the note was paid off. Brownie countered that he would agree not to put any additional debt that could not be covered (along with all normal expenses) for $800 per month. Roco felt that was reasonable and a deal was made.

Example 7 Another Future Rent

In another kind of future rent deal, Oscar offered the owner of a small home the right to stay in the home until Oscar's building plans were completed for the rental apartment building he wanted to build. Then, as the total price for the transaction, Oscar offered the sellers a lifetime right to rent one of the new apartments for $1 per month.

Oscar knew what he was doing, as he had calculated his yield on the amount of money it would have taken to buy the house just to get the lot. He also knew from the ages of the participants that it was a good investment to offer the life estate for $1 per month as on the actuarial calculation the apartment would be vacant within ten years. Oscar calculated that even if he had to give up the use of that apartment for twenty years, he was making a good decision.

The seller loved the idea, and told Oscar, "What a wonderful incentive to live another 100 years."

Pitfalls in Future Rent Deals

1. THE DEAL IS NOT PROPERLY DOCUMENTED.   If you are going to offer or take prepaid rent as a part of any transaction, make sure that there is a properly drawn lease that meets all the criteria that both parties understand to be the situation and have it agreed upon prior to the final closing of the deal. If there is no such lease predetermined and executed at the closing, then you are bound to have problems in the future.

2. Do not let the future rent benefit or obligation go too far in the future without indexing the value.   By this I mean that if you are giving up five years of future rent, make sure that a value is put on that future amount. If the lease has a cost-of-living index increase, and the increase bumps the annual rent above the amount which you have given (or gotten) credit for, then the overage is due in cash. Remember, if you are getting a future value today, without having to wait for it, then that is worth more now than in the future. On the other side, if you are having to pay for the future benefit (because you gave it up now), then you should have some benefit of that added value. For example, I sell you my home, but stay in the home for two years rent-free as a part of the deal. If two years rent is worth $4,000 per month, then that is a total of $96,000 over 24 months. If I prepay that by allowing you a reduction in the price of the home, then I have given you a value greater than $4,000 per month if you had to wait month after month for 24 months to get it.

MANAGEMENT INTEREST

Obtaining real estate through a management interest is where you agree to manage a property on the basis that you will receive an ownership interest in the property as part of the remuneration for your efforts.

Mike knew a couple of real estate investors who needed a tax shelter. He found a small 10-unit apartment building and tied it up on a contract. He then told these investors that if they took over his contract he would manage the building and take for that effort a 20% ownership in the building.

They went along with the deal, and for a while it worked out for all until some problems set in. Before we look at Mike's problems, let's look at another example.

Example Management for an Interest in Ownership

David was an expert at hotel management. He was asked to manage a property in the Bahama Islands by some offshore investors. He said he would if they gave him a 10% ownership in the property with an additional 5% for every year that he increases the net operating income by 5% or more. David also added that when and if his interest reached 50% he would have the right to buy out the other partners on a formula based on the income average for the past three years.

The owners calculated that for David to reach 50% ownership he would have to have eight years of growth and that the new operating income would have to increase by 80% or more. Based on that, they could afford to sell at the formula offered.

The key to this scenario was that David was an expert in hotel management. He knew that the property was currently poorly managed and that he could slowly build the business so that by the time he reached the end of eight years the place would just be ready for even bigger things.

Some property owners go out and try to find good employees by offering this same kind of incentive. The same basic idea works here.

FIVE KEY CONDITIONS TO HAVE IN A MANAGEMENT INTEREST AGREEMENT

1. SPECIFIC TERMS AS TO THE DURATION OF THE AGREEMENT AND HOW IT CAN BE TERMINATED. This is the toughest part of any such agreement. How does the current owner lock in the "employee" but not to the extent that if it is a bad relationship it can't be ended? On the other hand, the "employee" doesn't want to be doing everything according to the agreement, succeeding to the terms of the management interest pay outs, only to find that the owners want to eliminate him or her now that the property is running smoothly. These will be terms that will be discussed in such agreements:

a. **"Golden Parachute" provisions.** What happens if the company or property is sold? The new owner is not going to honor any such agreement that gives away interest to some other party. If you were that other party, you would want protection over and above your actual interest at that moment to the proceeds of the sale.

b. **Limitation of employment or competition trade areas.** If you leave or are fired for reason, the owners will want some kind of protection that you won't take all the clientele and go into business for yourself down the street. This is difficult to establish, but it is apt to come up.

c. **Calculations of interest, profits, and dividends.** If you don't have control and have a formula on which all your interest, share of profits, or dividends are calculated, make sure that you have a clear understanding of the accounting. Normal business expenses can also include salary to key people, and the other partners could legally be entitled to salaries that could eat up any profit and take away any bonus you thought you were going to get. Also, to arrive at a net operating income requires deductions from the gross income of all such operating expenses. You might find that unless you had set up things very clearly that gross goes way up, but net drops each year.

2. GET COPIES OF PAST YEARS' INCOME AND EXPENSE STATEMENTS. Base your future growth and formulas on known factors. Take into account that things are going to go up, that rent won't be the same, and that the phone bill will increase five years down the road. However, establish those patterns and follow them if you are on a formula percentage basis.

3. KNOW THE GOALS OF YOUR PARTNERS. If your partners are happy with a small operation, they might be frightened when you turn it into a big operation. Scared partners do things you can't anticipate.

4. BUILD A PERIODIC REVIEW INTO YOUR AGREEMENT.   This allows you to stop any problems you might have with your partners before they get out of hand. It is good for them, too, but a series of constantly positive reports makes it difficult for anyone to suddenly claim that he or she suspected that you were taking petty cash for the past six years.

5. DON'T PLAY AROUND WITH WHAT YOU ARE DUE.   If you meet the objectives of the contract, demand what you have coming. When it comes time to exercise your option to buy, remember that you can offer less, that the option is one-sided for you, and that you can take it or leave it or offer less.

Pitfalls in Management Interest Transactions

There are several pitfalls to watch out for:

1. Getting in over your head with a project you can't handle.
2. Not having everything in writing.
3. Not living up to the spirit of the agreement.
4. Giving cause to be fired when you are really doing a good job.
5. Getting tied down to a job you hate and people you don't like.

Each of these five pitfalls has its obvious counterpart. Use caution and good legal advice prior to entering into the agreement, and do your homework as to the people, the plan, and the future potential.

THREE-PARTY BLANKETS

Definition

A *three-party blanket* occurs when you add additional property to a mortgage that you don't own. This provides additional security to the lender, who is usually the seller of a property you are buying. Remember, a blanket mortgage is any mortgage that has one document (the mortgage and mortgage note combined) that is secured by two or more properties.

Example

Ruth wanted to buy a home in Tulsa. She offered the seller $168,000, which was slightly less than the $175,000 she was asking. The terms offered were: $25,000 cash down, $110,000 to assume the existing mortgage, and $33,000 second mortgage on a duplex that Ruth owned

The seller agreed to the price, but balked at the second mortgage on the duplex. "Not enough equity," he said.

Ruth tried several other tacks, but nothing worked. Then she asked her father if she could "borrow" some land that the family owned for a couple of years. What Ruth wanted to do was to add the land to the security of the second mortgage. Ruth offered her father a kicker of a percentage of the ultimate sale, and pledged her own equity in the house to her father should anything go wrong.

Ruth's plan was to move into the house and fix it up, refinancing the improved home and selling it for about $230,000. If all worked out as she hoped, there would be room for the kicker percentage that she offered her father, and little risk for everyone.

Bring in a Partner

The three-party blanket is a method of bringing in a partner who gets a small part of the deal, or some other kicker because he or she doesn't have to invest any cash. The advantage is to the seller as he or she is being appeased with additional equity in any paper he or she may hold.

Since the value or quality of the paper has been improved, other terms in the deal often can be counterbalanced to offset the kickers that Ruth and you may have to pay to get the "use" of the other property.

Notice that the end result is similar to what might happen with the OPP techniques (other people's property) also discussed in this chapter. The technique here is the use of the blanket mortgage in this method. You may wish to review the chapter on blanket mortgages also provided for you in this book.

This technique often is used with first-time buyers who need additional security to make their transactions work. Sellers being asked to hold paper are naturally reluctant to extend credit to "fresh" investors who are still wet behind the ears. In those situations, the buyer has to dig deep into a bag of tricks to find a technique that is acceptable to both the seller and to any third party he or she is going to find to help.

Pitfalls in Three-Party Blankets

If you were the third party and you allowed Ruth to use your land as additional security on her mortgage, and Ruth defaulted on her mortgage, you could be at risk for the mortgage in a foreclosure or risk action against your land to recover the amount owed on the mortgage.

Be very careful if you are the third party. Obviously, the solution is to weigh the risk against the kicker being offered. If you are to become a partner in the deal, have not put up any cash, have little risk in losing your security, and the gain potential is good, the whole transaction is sound.

This points up the prime benefit of using the third-party blanket as an investment tool. The person who comes out best often is in fact the person who put up the security in the transaction.

Like cosigners, which will be covered later, the one who helps someone else put a deal together often is the one who profits the most. Keeping this in mind, as the investor you have to make sure that bringing in a partner, even in the form of a third-party blanket, is worth the effort. Ask yourself this question: "Have I tried everything I could to buy that property without a partner, or do I need someone to share my lack of confidence in that property?" The answer to that question might surprise you if you are honest with yourself.

Chapter 19

FOUR TECHNIQUES WHERE YOU KEEP PART AND SELL PART

In this chapter, I will cover four creative techniques that give you methods to lock up deals you might miss otherwise. In each of these four techniques you keep part of the deal, at least for the time being, and sell part:

1. Landscape transaction.
2. Keep the plus, sell the negative.
3. Private timeshares.
4. Subdivide and sell or exchange.

Each of these techniques allows you to obtain the maximum benefit through 100% or more financing. Each technique is easy to use, and each has built-in flexibility to allow you to combine the technique with other methods of financing.

THE LANDSCAPE TRANSACTION

Of all the creative transactions you will read about, this is one of the best, when the situation fits. Naturally several criteria have to fit for the deal to make any economic sense, but when the parts fit you can benefit nicely.

Definition

A *landscape transaction* is when the prospective buyer can sell off landscaping from the property being purchased.

Example 1   Finding a Landscape Deal

You have been looking for some fixer-upper properties that are found in pleasant areas of town, but that have been run down. You know that this kind of property usually comes with a distressed owner. These properties often stand out like sore thumbs because of the overgrown landscaping, which hides the buildings and creates an overall distressed look to the property. A lot of plants and trees can actually do a property harm. The leaves clog gutter drains, accumulate on roof areas and rot. Roots crack foundations, and the dark damp conditions create mold, turn pools into penicillin ponds, stain drives, walks and patios, and so on. All this becomes a nasty situation when you see it. Yet it is also an opportunity.

You find such a house, and you take steps to get control. Remember, get control then spend the time, effort and money to analyze the situation and plan the next step. You enter into negotiations and after a couple of offers and counteroffers you arrive at a point in the process where you feel you have reached the best deal you can. At this stage of the game, the deal looks good. You have won points and the seller is satisfied. You actually *want* the seller to be satisfied. When a seller begins to *believe* he or she has sold and made a good deal doing it, he or she begins psychologically to spend the money.

You start down your checklist of things to do, and one of them is to find out if there is any green in all that green. In short, can you sell the landscaping for enough money to make it worthwhile.

Savvy real-estate investors never try to keep up on what plants or trees are worth at any specific time because that depends on the market. When you are dealing with mature plants and trees, the prices you can get can be very attractive. You might be surprised to find that some moderately sized trees can bring several thousand dollars from the right buyer. The key, of course, is knowing who the right buyer is.

You make a few phone calls, and within a few days have gotten some offers for all the mature landscaping around the house. You have your own landscaper give you an estimate of what plants you might want to keep, to enhance the property. Then you cut the best deal you can to sell or trade the unwanted landscape. Naturally you cannot deliver the landscape to a buyer until you close on the property. However, with careful planning you can make it a simultaneous deal separated by only a few minutes if your lawyer can schedule it that tightly.

Example 2   Finding the Right Buyer

You have just bought five acres of land which you plan to hold for a couple of years. The idea is to build a fast food restaurant on part of it, and resell or hold the balance. The land is full of trees, which the broker who has it listed tells you, "Should not cost more than $5,000 to clear off." You smile, and a fleeting thought runs through your mind, "Little does she know."

You get control of the property by negotiating until you have a binding agreement. You do not play too hard nose at this stage, and get through the negotiations rather quickly. I like to follow the pattern that if I think it is worth my time as an investor, there might be someone else who will come to the same conclusion. I need to beat those investors to the punch. So do you.

At this point you are in control. You have negotiated a 120-day due-diligence period to walk the property through your predevelopment checklist. This checklist will be very extensive and will include everything from checking environmental rules and regulations, to finding out the history of the property. If it were once a site for storage of waste oil products you can just about stop there and move on. One obvious step you will want to check out well is the potential value of the landscape. You or someone you hire, will make an inventory of what is potentially saleable. You list the type, size and condition of every potentially saleable plant on the property. If there are one or more really valuable trees on the site, take photos of them. Be sure to have a person standing next to it to give perspective to the size.

You make up the inventory list, without prices, and send it to a dozen developers in town who are building new properties. These might be homes, apartment buildings or commercial projects. All these need new plant material, and they are used to paying top dollar for quality stuff.

If that does not produce some quick phone calls, then you can call around to some better landscapers to discover if there is a potential market for the material. Quality material will sell. You can be sure of that.

Be Creative: Split Fund-Plant Transaction

Remember from Chapter 18 the split-fund technique. Tie this into the plant landscape transaction for some very creative financing. The plan is to sell crops or timber or plants on the property for sufficient cash to meet the obligations of the down payment owed.

This idea works well in farm or timber lands as you might visualize, but also in areas where the property may have an overgrowth of "landscape quality" plants. The deal is simple to set up provided you do your homework in advance. If the investment is farmland, you have to have a good understanding of the marketing of that type of produce. Buying farms that have groves or crops in the field is a very special kind of investing and generally not for the novice. Nonetheless, it is possible that you are buying the land for another reason and that the land just happens to be an old farm or grove. Why not capitalize on its potential to spin off some additional income one last time before you turn it into a subdivision?

Selling standing timber is easy to set up if there is a market in the area. There should be timber brokers, mills, and the like who could give you some help in this area. The state agricultural agent is a good source of information. You can find the agent by calling your state's Department of Agriculture.

A landscape deal requires a bit more finesse, since you might have a gold mine under your nose and not recognize it. Landscapers will pay a lot of money for the right kind of plants. If many "large style" developments are going on in your area, such as clubhouses, banks, shopping plazas, airports, hospitals, and so on, mature plants will be in demand.

SEVEN TIPS ON SETTING UP THE LANDSCAPE TRANSACTION

1. GETTING TO KNOW TWO OR MORE LANDSCAPERS IN YOUR AREA IS PART OF DEVELOPING YOUR COMFORT ZONE.   It is important that you obtain some basic information early about the cost in landscaping. You will find that maintaining shrubs and plants is one of the best ways to improve the value of a property. However, the larger and more mature the plant, the more costly it is. You can buy a small plant for $2.50 that will be worth $150 in a few years. Many landscapers have price lists that they provide to real estate developers and contractors.

2. BECOME A LANDSCAPE WHOLESALER.   It is easy for you to become a "qualified" buyer of wholesale products by incorporating or taking out a city occupational license as a "decorator" or "home repairer." Usually nothing more than a municipal fee of $25 or so is required for that title. Then if your state has a sales tax, contact the local sales tax office and get the forms and a tax identification number. This is required for businesses that will buy wholesale and sell retail. Then (depending on your state), it may apply the sales tax. That tax number is the key to the wholesaler that you have done the required steps to be able to buy at the below-retail price.

3. BUY A BOOK ON LANDSCAPING.   Get one that has photographs or illustrations of plants and check the values of those plants with the price lists. Always use the wholesale price since that is the maximum price you will get from a landscaper.

4. WHEN YOU FIND A PROPERTY LOADED WITH VALUABLE PLANTS, DO A THOROUGH EXAMINATION AND LIST THE PLANTS ALONG WITH THEIR SIZES. Go to a couple of landscapers to see if they are interested and at what price. It is possible that information alone could entice you to buy the property.

5. NEVER CLOSE ON A PROPERTY BASED ON THE VERBAL PROMISE FROM THE LANDSCAPER.   Tie up the property first, give yourself an out or two in the contract, and then get firm quotation from two or more landscapers. Make sure the prices are "in-the-ground" prices and that when they remove the plants they will fill any holes left.

6. IF YOU NEED PLANTS FOR THAT OR OTHER JOBS, CONSIDER TAKING SOME DEAL WITH THE LANDSCAPER IN TRADE FOR YOUNG PLANTS.

7. DO NOT OVERLOOK THE FACT THAT MANY OLDER HOMES LOOK BETTER ONCE THE LANDSCAPE HAS BEEN CLEANED OUT AND NEW SMALLER PLANTS HAVE BEEN PUT IN PLACE.   It could be that a complete change in the landscape around an older property can give it such an uplifting look that values can be increased overnight. By using your contacts with the landscapers, you will find that you can buy and also sell plants profitably.

Dealing successfully in landscape does not mean only tropical items or crops. Keep in mind that beautiful green grass can be turned into green cash too. The sod may be expensive, but if that five acres of yard is just sitting there waiting for the right person to sell it, why shouldn't you be that person?

KEEP THE POSITIVE AND SELL THE NEGATIVE OR VICE VERSA

By now you should be thinking about benefits you get or give up and not just the money part of the transaction. Every property you own or will ever own will have its problems and its benefits. As a real-estate investor you need continually to remind yourself if the benefits are worth putting up with the problems. The moment the problems win the agreement that is a time to consider making a change. As I have shown in previous situations, making a change does not automatically mean getting rid of the property. Oddly enough, as you will discover, you can obtain benefits by keeping the negative and selling the positive.

This chapter deals with dividing the positive and the negative of a property. You need to ascertain if there can be a division between the two. If this is possible you can sell one and keep the other. If you discover that you can make the division, then the next decision to make is which to sell and which to keep. The answer is not as obvious as you might think.

Definition

This form of financing is a shift of equity to another person. This equity, or value, is a divisible part of a property. As you can sell it, lease it, or exchange it, it is open game for you to use this in your real estate investment plan.

Example 1 Finding the Positive and the Negative Benefits

Remember: Every property has both a positive benefit and a negative problem. Review the following chart that shows some usual benefits and negatives. Keep in mind that you may have benefits that are not shown, and experience none of the negatives showed.

Type of Property	The Positive Benefits	The Negatives
Vacant lot	Appreciation, some income if it can be rented as a parking lot, storage field, u-pick it farm, and so on	Government and environmental problems, little income potential, taxes to pay, cleaning after trash is dumped, and so on
Strip stores	Income, appreciation, jobs, expenses, tax shelter	Vacancies, maintenance, management
Office building	Income, appreciation, jobs, expenses	Vacancies, maintenance, management
Rental apartments	Income, appreciation, jobs, expenses, tax shelter, place to live	Vacancies, maintenance, management
Your home	Place to live, appreciation	Maintenance, taxes, no income
Rental house	Income, appreciation, tax shelter	Maintenance, vacancies, taxes, management
Hotel or motel	Income, appreciation, jobs, paid, tax shelter, place to live	Management, maintenance, vacancies, expenses
Second home	Possible income, slight tax shelter	Maintenance, taxes, little tax shelter, little income, loss of value

EXPLANATION OF BENEFITS

Income Suggests that there would be rental income greater than the expenses it takes to own the property. These expenses would include real-estate taxes, interest on any mortgage, maintenance, management and a modest cap rate on your investment. (If you have invested $100,000 and money is worth 5% then 5% of your investment should be considered a part of the expenses.)

Appreciation The potential amount your property is going to increase in value. If this is not happening, or you cannot see an improvement in value, then the lack of appreciation will become a problem and not a benefit.

Tax Shelter Tax shelter is the benefit you get from buildings and other assets that are a part of those buildings when you deduct the allowed depreciation of those assets from income. As this reduces income tax, it is called a tax shelter. This benefit can come back to bite you if you do not plan for it properly. However, even if it becomes nothing more than an interest-free loan from the Government, that is worthwhile.

Jobs　　　Some real estate is a very good investment because it can give a whole family jobs, and wage income. Some of the best examples of this are hotels and motels, restaurants, large apartment rental complexes, farms and other similar agricultural ventures, office buildings, and other commercial buildings. This benefit is very real if you have a large family of hard workers.

Expenses　Another real benefit. Think of a whole family that owns and works at a restaurant. Wages, food, insurance, even cars to drive. Families that own and operate hotels and rental apartments even can get a place to live on the house. Another very good benefit when it fits your needs or goals.

EXPLANATION OF PROBLEMS

Maintenance　Some properties have greater maintenance than others depending on how many people are required to keep up with the task. This includes everything from fixing up, to plumbing, electrical, pool, yard, and so on.

Management　The number-one problem. Taking care of the tenants is only part of it; taking care of the employees another.

Vacancies　This is the major source of reduced income. Vacancies then relate to *loss of income*. The inability to get good tenants who will pay good rents puts the property into a downward trend. Lack of sufficient rents means reduced maintenance, which translates to reduced value. The biggest problem with vacancies is that it is very difficult for most income properties to operate at 100% occupancy. Because of this, the key to overcoming most of the other problems is to reduce the vacancy factor while at the same time bringing a better-than-average level of tenant into the property. This is the major problem to attack.

SIX CHOICES OF HOW TO DEAL WITH THE NEGATIVES

1. Dispose of 100% of the property.
2. Dispose of only a part of the property.
3. Net lease 100% of the property.
4. Sell and leaseback 100% of the property.
5. Sell and leaseback a part of the property.
6. Sell or lease part of the property and keep part of the property.

Generate Income from a Lost Benefit

Often we own property that has benefits that do not appeal to us. These benefits were not the principal reason we purchased the property, or we no longer need or have use for those benefits. The problem with this is that those benefits usually attribute to the cost of ownership of the property and now become a negative to the ownership of that property.

Example 2 Lease the Lost Benefit

One example of this is abundant in my home town, Fort Lauderdale. Many people want to live on deep water (any waterway in Fort Lauderdale that has access to the ocean). Some of the general reason of ownership on this kind of property is to enable you to tie your boat, or yacht right next to your home. If this was the reason to buy such a property, you might find, as do thousands of people in Fort Lauderdale every few years, that life owning a boat or yacht is not what they really thought it would be. They sell the boat, and are content to have the waterway behind the house. But they are paying for that waterway in the form of higher taxes. A deep water lot in a good area of Fort Lauderdale can start at around $350,000 and go up from there. A dry lot in the same area (if you could find one) would be well under half that. This added value can then cost the home owner anywhere from $2,000 to $5,000 just for the location on the water, every year in added taxes.

One solution to getting rid of this negative is to rent out the dock. In a city where dock space for large yachts is going at a premium, a dock capable of taking a boat over 45 feet in length would easily command an annual rent that would offset all or most all taxes. An added benefit to this is the beauty of having a $500,000 or more yacht behind your home, and to be invited out on it from time to time by your tenant.

Example 3 Lease, Sell, Exchange, Part of the Lost Benefit

If you own a second home it is likely you had a very good reason for buying it. Whatever that reason was at the time, it is likely that the ownership has many gaps of use. These are all lost benefits, which you can transfer into other benefits somehow. The mechanics of doing this can come through a lease, outright sale, or an exchange of those lost benefits for something else that will be useful to you. When you cannot lease the unused time, you might join a local barter club or organization. Two such organizations are ITEX and BXI, and each are national barter programs that are very good. Look in the yellow pages of your local telephone guide and you will discover several such organizations. I have found it easy to barter time in my second homes this way, gaining a wide range of other benefits that include scrip in local restaurants, Italian ceramic tile, carpets, professional services that include dentistry to plastic surgery, and on and on.

Selling the Negative Can Be the Answer

"For Sale: 50% interest in a Mountain Cabin." This is not a bad idea, and if you have a nice property there shouldn't be a problem in making this kind of sale. In fact, you might want to sell 25% to three people so that you keep the remaining 25%. This percentage can be divided by specific time during the year, much like a time-share apartment or resort, only with the major difference; the facility will get less use than the time share and will provide much more flexibility to the investor.

Sell Them Their Positive and Keep Your Positive

Some investors have discovered that they can add to their wealth quickly by looking for a property that is all positive to someone. When the investor locates this kind of property, he or she can then divide up the positives, keeping the benefit wanted in the first place and selling off the other positives. One of the best ways to sell them the positives while you keep your positive is by creating your own private timeshare.

PRIVATE TIMESHARE PROPERTIES

By constantly looking for the positive property, the investor will discover that if he or she sets up the transaction properly he or she can establish many such timeshare facilities. These do not have to be limited to real estate either; boats and airplanes can do nicely in this kind of transaction.

Setting up your own private timeshare property can be easy, fun, and profitable. It may be the very best way to increase your real-estate benefits without having to spend any of your own cash. The method I shall describe is one of the best uses of other people's money I know of. If you try it, you will find that there are many potential problems that the following tips will help you avoid.

FIVE TIPS ON HOW TO SET UP A PRIVATE TIMESHARE

1. LOOK FOR POSITIVE PROPERTIES. As I mentioned earlier, these are properties that have benefits that are extended throughout the year. These benefits might not appeal to everyone, but you will only sell that segmental benefit to the person who wants that specific use, so there will be little or no negative time for sale.

2. ANTICIPATE THE KIND OF MARKET YOU WILL BE SELLING TO BEFORE YOU TIE UP THE PROPERTY. If the property is in the mountains and one of the benefits to sell is ski time, you will want a property that is well located to ski areas. Even though you want the place for the cool summer nights and don't care about the proximity to the lifts, you need to consider the needs and benefits for the other owners.

3. MAKE OFFERS THAT TIE UP THE PROPERTY BUT GIVE YOU AN OUT. When buying a property for a syndication or private timeshare ownership, you will want to make sure that you don't get locked into a deal that you can't handle by yourself. One of the best ways to give yourself this out would be to make your offer subject to the full 100% subscription to the joint venture you are forming. Give yourself ninety days or more which begin after you have approved the inspection of the property. Don't forget to also allow yourself time to make the inspections without being rushed. Nothing beats honesty in this kind of transaction, and if the seller is anxious to make a deal he or she is apt to go along with you. After all, you are trying to buy his or her property.

4. HAVE ALL YOUR BASES COVERED.   This means anticipate every possible question that will be asked and have the right answer. The most important questions to deal with will center around the following: who is in control, upkeep, time periods, income potential, how to sell, and form of ownership. In the beginning you are in control. After that the group votes in a new person every year or so. You make the rules up front, so make sure you have a printed list of exactly how all this is going to work, and what penalties there are for those who don't come up with their share of expenses, and so on. The tougher the penalties are the better everyone will like it (because everyone thinks someone else will be the one to default). The same goes for upkeep; have it all down pat. Have a local company who will do the cleaning after every visit (to be paid for by the person who used the facility last. Let people shift their time around, but have a clear understanding of how that will work. As to income, it is important that you have a local company who will rent out the facility, but also line up a couple of barter organizations in your home town who will trade you and the other owners services and goods for time at the facility. How to sell and the form of ownership is something you need to discuss with your lawyer. The logical way is not to restrict the sale of time, but to require the owner to offer it first to the existing members. A first right of refusal generally works well.

5. HAVE A GOOD JOINT OWNERSHIP AGREEMENT DRAFTED BY A LAWYER.   Explain to the lawyer that you are going to do a joint venture form of private timeshare. Have the lawyer go over the specific kinds of forms of ownership you can use and make sure you're aware of the laws of the state where the property is located. In setting up the documentation, there are several important factors that you must attend to, as follows:

ELEVEN KEY ELEMENTS TO PUT INTO YOUR PRIVATE TIMESHARE AGREEMENT

1. A COPY OF THE PURCHASE AGREEMENT.   Don't try to hide any of these details from the others. They'll find out anyway.

2. DETAILED INFORMATION ON THE OBLIGATIONS OF ALL PARTIES WITH RESPECT TO THE MORTGAGE (IF ANY), AND ALL COSTS WHICH RELATE TO THE UPKEEP OF THE PROPERTY.

3. HAVE VERY STRICT PENALTIES FOR THOSE MEMBERS WHO DO NOT MEET THEIR OBLIGATIONS.   One way is to prohibit their use. Another would be to rent their time to help cover any unpaid bills. The ultimate penalty would be the sale of interest to cover the amounts due.

4. MAKE SURE YOU ARE IN THE DRIVER'S SEAT.   This is your deal, your property, your contract. You are "allowing" other investors to buy a part of your deal. One form of ownership you might consider would be a general partnership. Here you would be the general partner and all other investors would be limited partners. Another form available in some states would be a land or investment trust. Here you are the trustee and the other investors are beneficiaries of the trust.

5. GET PAID FOR YOUR WORK.   This means that you are in charge for the control over the property, and that you should get paid for your time. Don't try to be magnanimous about this because there will be things to do and times you don't want to do it. If you provide for payment you can hire others to help, but get paid and have it as a part of the deal from the very start.

6. PROVIDE FOR A FUND FOR THE REPLACEMENT OF FURNITURE AND FURNISHINGS.   This might be a small sum per person deposited into a money market account, but have it because you will need it sooner or later. On this same subject, be sure that all members know that if they break something they have to replace it. On the other hand, if something mechanical stops working, then that is the responsibility of the whole group.

7. HAVE A RESERVE FUND IN THE CHECKBOOK.   A good idea is to keep ahead three to six months of any expenses. This gives you a better night's sleep.

8. HAVE AN OPTION TO BUY BACK THE OTHER'S INTEREST.   This keeps you in control, and if they want to sell at any given time you could either buy then, or let them sell to someone else and retain that option. However, be flexible enough to let the option rise in value or to revert to a first right to buy so that the investor can participate in the appreciation of the property.

9. MAKE SURE YOU HAVE FULL AND AMPLE INSURANCE TO COVER ANY POTENTIAL CASUALTY OR LIABILITY.

10. HAVE A DO'S AND DON'TS LIST THAT SERVES AS THE RULES AND REGULATIONS FOR ALL THE OWNERS TO ABIDE BY.   The list should include the responsibility for nonowners who may use the facility.

11. DO YOUR HOMEWORK ON THE PROPERTY, THE AREA, AND BENEFITS OF OWNERSHIP FOR ALL TIMES OF THE YEAR.

Pitfalls to Timeshares

Timeshares are filled with traps that can attract even the smartest of all developers and will then cause them to lose their investment capital promptly.

The reason for this is the fantastic profit potential that the winner can take home if he or she hits the timeshare market right. The kind of timeshare I am talking about is the one you see that advertises itself as the "best resort in the Rockies," or "Orlando's Finest Timeshare Resort." It is the "hotel-minded" kind of place that caters to you during your week. These places are hard-sell, expensive properties that the developer sells for one week or more at a price of from $3,000 up to $20,000 per week depending on the place and the week.

In Orlando, Florida, the most "populated-by-time-shares" place in the world, a two-bedroom timeshare apartment could easily cost $12,000 per week during prime summer months. In addition to that initial cost, the upkeep and taxes for that same week could cost the owner as much as $295 or more each year (just for that one week).

If the developer sells his week fifty-two times, and the average price is around $10,000 per week, the gross price for the apartment is $520,000. I can assure you that the apartment would not have that resale value if you owned all fifty-two weeks. This fantastic price is buffered by the incredible cost to market. Timeshare developers will admit to as high as a 55% marketing cost and more in many cases. When you consider that the developer will "blow out" inventory when he or she gets down to the remaining 100 weeks, the actual cost to market could be as high as 60% on an average project. But that still leaves lots of room for unbelievable profits.

This is where the pitfalls begin. Those profits are all in the minds of the projectionist, and in reality the cost to develop and the cost to "create prospects," "carry the line," and "buy back bad paper" can eat up the best project and the developer with the deepest pockets.

The former president of the Florida Timeshare Council once said, "No one ever woke up and looked in a mirror and said to themselves that today was the day they were going to buy a timeshare." And he was so very right. To counteract this problem and to provide the salespeople (the "line" all prospects must "run") with fresh minds they can sell, the developers have to spend a lot of money in upfront advertising, direct mail, and prizes that get the prospects in the door. The cost to "carry the line" is very high. The best "line" will close one out of six prospects that walk in the door no matter what.

Most developers have lenders that finance these overpriced products so that the average buyer can get his or her holiday week for as little as $500 down (which the salesperson might lend him or her) and with payments as low as $99 per month. The problem for the developer is that most lenders require the developer to ensure the paper they are holding. This insurance takes the form of a "buy back of bad paper" agreement. Here, the developer promises to take back any units that the buyer defaults on, and then repays the lender for the balance of the mortgage. Sometimes this buy-back is only for the first few years of the total mortgage term, while other lenders force the developer to hang onto the deal until the final payments are made.

Developers often take this risk because they feel they are making sufficient profit to warrant some buy-back. However, this most precarious domino will topple the soonest. If a project goes sour, sales fall off, salespeople leave, sales get worse, those who have bought stop making payments, bad paper comes back to the developer, and the whole house of cards comes tumbling down.

The Resort Timeshare Is the Best of Two Worlds

The timeshare concept is best when the project is designed to provide the best possible comfort, benefits, and accommodations for the least possible cost. No one minds a reasonable profit going to the developer or to the general partner, but when greed enters into the picture, watch out.

The best way to avoid this pitfall is to examine the benefits you are looking for when you commit to a private timeshare. If your goal is to add to your real-estate ownership, to provide yourself with second-home benefits, to have added equity build up, and to do that through the private timeshare program, you will succeed.

If you want to profit by selling units in private timeshares and don't care about the other aspects of the deal, then you may succeed; most likely you will fall into the same pit that seduces half of the developers, who think timeshares are gold mines.

SUBDIVIDE AND SELL OR EXCHANGE

When you can tie up a property for a substantial period of time, it may be possible for you to spin off some of the property you have under contract in such a way that you close simultaneously on both contracts. This double-dealing can generate the capital or benefits you need to close on the property you are acquiring. As this is a technique to generate new capital, the end result is a neat way to finance a deal.

Definition

Subdivision: The act of subdividing a larger property into smaller properties; it is the essence of real-estate development. Whenever you take one property and break it into smaller parts, this is the act of dividing the property into separate legal descriptions. These separate legal descriptions allow the property to be properly described as independent tracts or lots. The end result creates a subdivision, which in general real-estate jargon is an area of specific geographic entity that has been divided by a uniform or common method. In most communities the actual procedure of making a subdivision requires very specific parameters be followed. West Lake subdivision, as an example of a name the developer may select, would be a tract of land. The developer would, in most communities, be required to have a surveyor and land-planning architect draw detailed maps showing the lots, or tracts with all streets, utility easements (if any exist or are required by the community), and other criteria that local ordinances demand. Generally the subdivision is broken up by lots and blocks, that is to say that each individual lot or parcel would be identified by being a specific lot number within a specific block. This description becomes what is known as the legal (description), such as, Lot 5 of Block 10 of West Lake subdivision. Where the local community requires that the subdivision be recorded in the public records, the legal description would include the plat book and page number where the subdivision was first recorded. Such subdivisions can be described by tracts, such as Tract 1, 2, 3 and so on, or Tract A, B, C and so on.

Example 1   Sell Off Some

You contract to buy a one-hundred-acre tract of land with a 180-day time period for due diligence. Your overall purchase price is $500,000 with $50,000 down, and the balance over a 10-year payout. The proposed mortgage will allow releases of land from the mortgage at $6,500 per acre. You anticipate that your land development costs will be $4,000 per lot.

While you are going through your studies, you have your surveyor draw up a subdivision of the tract into two-hundred half-acre lots. You contact a couple of builders and give two of them the opportunity to pick up twenty lots each at a bargain price of $12,000 per lot. This would be $240,000 from each builder, or $480,000 in total. The forty lots you are preselling will cost you $160,000 to develop. Your release price for these lots is $6,500 for each lot, or a total of $260,000. You need $50,000 to close on the deal. You will take in $480,000 from the developers, and pay out $470,000 and be left with $10,000 to cover the surveyor's bill.

Of the original 100 acres, you are left with 60, and as you have paid off $50,000, the original down payment, plus the release payment of $160,000, you only owe $290,000.

Example 2 Exchange Some

What if the whole idea of getting this subdivision was so that you could have lots that you could exchange to Bobby, who owns a shopping center you would like to get your hands on. This center is free and clear of any debt, and is worth $1,000,000. Bobby needs some cash, but really wants to get back into the single-home-building business where he had made a lot of money once. You have offered him 60 single family lots in West Lake subdivision worth only $18,000 per lot. You show him the plans from the two other builders who have twenty lots each, and are getting ready to put up model homes. These 60 lots have a value of $1,080,000 and a first mortgage of $290,000, and require $240,000 of development cost to finish. Your equity is $550,000.

You will give Bobby the equity in the 60 lots, $250,000 cash, and a second mortgage of $200,000 on the center, subject to your obtaining new first mortgage financing equal to 75% of the value.

You borrow $750,000 on the center, give Bobby $250,000 of that amount, and put aside $250,000 for some future venture elsewhere, and save the balance of $250,000 to cover your costs and fix-up money.

Four Key Points to Remember About Subdividing and Selling or Exchanging

Many of the different techniques covered in this book use exchanges from one person to another. You should remember that I stress the single element: benefit. This includes all exchanges, money, scrip, barter, sweat equity, paper, subdivided property, or whatever works best when the investor remembers and follows these four key points:

1. People want to feel that they have made a profit in their transaction.   No one wants to be told "You sold that too cheap" or "You idiot, that property was worth twice what you got." Yet that kind of talk comes easy from the very person who would not have offered you even that much. When you offer something of value to a person who can't sell a property, no matter how much that item might have cost you, no matter if it is your spare time waxing his or her cars or being his or her CPA for a year or doing five gold inlays, the element you offer has value. Best of all, that value allows the seller to say, "Boy, did I get my price" or "I got every penny I asked for."

Sellers will do almost anything to avoid loss of face. Therefore, when you come along and don't knock the price, but instead examine the benefits you are willing to give up for the benefits you will get, people will take bags of gems or envelopes full of stamps.

2. ALWAYS STRIVE TO BE HONEST, BUT AT THE SAME TIME REMEMBER THAT MEMORIES ARE SHORT AND PEOPLE WILL BELIEVE WHAT THEY WANT, THINK WHAT THEY FIND CONVENIENT, AND WANT MORE THAN THEY HAVE. You will sleep better at night if you know you did your best to present anything you offer in an exchange at a realistic value. Now that doesn't mean you have to offer a bargain or give away any secrets, but it does mean that you must allow the other side time to check values, to seek legal advice, to back out of the deal if they feel wronged.

3. MAKE SURE YOU HAVE GOT THE PROPERTY TIED UP FOR A LONG ENOUGH TIME TO WORK OUT THE DETAILS OF THE OTHER TRANSACTIONS. If you think you need 90 days, ask for 120 or 160. You never want to be in a rush (even if you need to hurry), because that is apt to tip your hand and a savvy buyer or exchanger may wait you out and pick up your project when you fall flat on your face.

4. BE SURE YOU HAVE THE TERMS IN YOUR ORIGINAL TRANSACTION THAT GIVE YOU THE RIGHT TO SUBDIVIDE, AND TO HAVE RELEASES TO MAKE IT WORK.   If this is your first deal like this make sure your lawyer knows exactly what you want to be able to do. The purchase money mortgage on the original deal must provide releases in such a way that you are not tied up in where or how the property is released. One very good technique at this point is to have a condition in your purchase money mortgage (to the seller of the initial property) where any pre-payment of principal counts against the next principal payments due. This simple phrase will do wonders to your payment schedule of a 10-year payout. For example, if your mortgage was $450,000 over ten years, at principal payments of $45,000 per year plus interest at 8% on the outstanding principal, your payment schedule would look like the following:

Period of Payment	Principal	Interest	Total	Remaining
1.	$45,000	$36,000	$81,000	$405,000
2.	45,000	32,400	77,400	360,000
3.	45,000	28,800	73,800	315,000
4.	45,000	25,200	70,200	270,000
5.	45,000	21,600	66,600	225,000
6.	45,000	18,000	63,000	180,000
7.	45,000	14,400	59,400	135,000
8.	45,000	10,800	55,800	90,000
9.	45,000	7,200	52,200	45,000
10.	45,000	3,600	48,600	0

If the mortgage allowed that any prepayment of principal counted against the next in line principal payments, if you released 40 acres with a payment of $260,000, your payment schedule would now look like the following:

Period of Payment	Principal	Interest	Total	Remaining
1.	$260,000	$36,000	$296,000	$190,000
2.	0	15,200	15,200	190,000
3.	0	15,200	15,200	190,000
4.	0	15,200	15,200	190,000
5.	0	15,200	15,200	190,000
6.	10,000	15,200	25,200	180,000
7.	45,000	14,400	59,400	135,000
8.	45,000	10,800	55,800	90,000
9.	45,000	7,200	52,200	45,000
10.	45,000	3,600	48,600	0

If the mortgage terms had not allowed the prepayment of principal to apply toward the next principal payment due, the above schedule would not appear this way. The normal way a mortgage is amortized is if you prepay principal, then the remaining balance is adjusted to account for the new amortization schedule.

The Pitfalls of Subdividing and Selling or Exchanging

What happens if you are counting on getting rid of the property through a sale or exchange and the market goes to pot? Or you overestimate your ability and underestimate the cost to subdivide? Or the city or the county impose moratoriums on such things as subdividing? These are some of the pitfalls that lie in the darkness for the developer.

Be careful of the laws in your state with respect to land sales. Florida and other states have very specific ideas of what a subdivision should consist of and what you have to do in order to meet the requirements of the state. These often can be very expensive requirements if you fall under the control of those government bodies.

Fortunately, even the most strict state will have a cut-off point at which you would not fall into their full or even partial control. Know exactly what that is before you get started.

Keep It Simple

The best way to do anything that involves other people is to consider their benefits as your own. Buy the property because you want the property. Let them in because they too can benefit from the property. No one will ever correctly say you asked too much or took too much and gave too little if you approach things that way.

Chapter 20

HOW TO USE HIDDEN BENEFITS TO BARTER YOUR WAY INTO REAL ESTATE

Real-estate investing is a simple matter of transferring benefits from one pocket to another. Yet most people who buy and sell real estate are never able to relate to this concept. One reason for this is that there is nothing more personal or valuable than the benefit that you obtain from what you own. You have probably heard someone who just had his offer rejected, say, "They think they own gold?" Well, that's exactly what many people think about what they own. The unfortunate aspect of this is that they often have this opinion without considering what the actual value of the "benefits" are.

BARTER: THE ANCIENT WAY OF THE NEW MILLENNIUM

Equating a benefit value to everything you own is possible. Your car gives you certain benefits that may include transportation to and from work. Your television set provides entertainment or keeps the kids occupied while you do something else. Real estate also provides benefits and these benefits vary from property to property and from person to person.

For example, take a person who owns a home. As long as the person lives in that home, the benefit derived by the investment is the basic use of the facility and the long-range appreciation of the asset. Real-estate benefits fall into two categories:

- The benefit of living space
- The ultimate appreciation of the asset

Both benefits are real, yet it is the anticipation of appreciation that makes ownership desirable. The home owner who sells his or her house transfers his or her benefit to another person. This new property owner may view the benefits differently, depending on the goals of the original owner. The seller takes his or her new benefit and moves into another position.

You must think of everything in terms of benefits. The connection of the success to your investing in real estate to your goals is a tight circle. If you overlook proper orientation to your goals, then you kiss a real success goodbye. If you know what you want and strive to get it, you succeed. However, knowing what you want is not a dollar goal, but a benefit-oriented goal.

You seek to get the benefits you want, and in so doing you get rid of the assets that do not provide the benefits you either want or need. To this end, it is critical that you recognize the benefits that you are deriving from your property. Are the benefits part of your goals, or are they lost? Do you own a boat that you do not use, or own a vacation cabin you have not seen in years?

With this idea in mind, you can relate to your ultimate goals. You can learn far more quickly which of your properties is not providing the goals or benefits you want or need. In making this determination, you can then decide to get rid of a particular property in exchange for another property that provides the desired benefits and sought-after goals.

Barter Things You Own That You Do Not Need

Bartering is neither new nor unique; it is one of the oldest forms of commercial enterprise, and has been mentioned in several chapters thus far. The exchange of goods, products, services, and promises for similar items has been going on for hundreds of years and will continue if people realize that others want what they have or have what they want.

Barter includes just about everything and every service of which you can think. From services as a bartender, CPA, lawyer, doctor or gardener, any item you have around the house, office, or backyard, is available for barter. Keep in mind that the chapter on real estate exchanges will go into the 1031 type of exchange and to get a full understanding of barter and exchanges that chapter would be worth rereading. Look at some examples of barter.

Barter of Products You Own or Can Get

Phillip wants to buy a condo from Ocean Development Company in Miami Beach, Florida. The drawback is he doesn't have the sufficient cash to make the down payment. However, he does have something to barter, if he'll only make a proper inventory of what he does in fact own.

Example 1 Finding What You Have to Barter

Assume for a moment that Phillip is a CPA. That ability has value, and that value is an item he could consider to exchange or barter to Ocean Development Company. If he had to offer his time, off hours, for a year or two, as the down payment on the condo of his dreams, and it was acceptable to the seller, another barter transaction will have succeeded.

On the other hand, Phillip may be a mechanic working for the local gas station. It could be that his hobby is gardening and that the backyard of his father-in-law's house, where he and his wife live, is filled with rare and unique plants, the kind of plants that developers look for when they decorate their condominiums.

If Phillip is lucky, he might find that his plants were more than enough to be his down payment. Chalk up a second barter deal that just succeeded.

BARTER YOUR WAY TO YOUR GOAL

As you head down the pathway to wealth and fame as a real estate investor, keeping your goals firmly in sight, you might have a very common hurdle to overcome. Bad credit. One of the hardest things for some investors to overcome is bad credit. Without good credit, getting loans can be absolutely out of the question. That is, getting loans from a bank. Getting a mortgage from a motivated seller who is more willing to get rid of a property that he or she cannot handle might be more important to them than your credit rating. But you still have to have something to put down. Okay, here is your predicament. Like many investors you have discovered that the biggest problem in buying is to come up with either super triple A credit or to have a sound and valuable down payment. You can almost always make a deal if you can give a down payment. Owning property starts the ball rolling. Once you own something solid, like real estate, you have equity. The more equity you have, the simpler your task is of getting a mortgage, or other needed financing. Therefore, one of the foundations of creative financing is the transfer of equity. Barter can help you create equity and make deals. Look at the following example.

Example 2 Realizing You Need to Get Closer to Your Goal

I own a vacant lot, free and clear of all debt, which is worth $15,000. My intrinsic benefit is a banking of $15,000, yet this benefit is not the same as a realized benefit. The lot does little for me unless I look at it either as an investment that I hope will increase in value or as a future building site. On one hand, if the area was booming and property values were going up each week, I would look to appreciation as the benefit. But it is important for me to make some judgment on this lot. Why do I own it? What do I want to get out of it? What are the benefits I hope to obtain from owning this lot? Can I swap it for that immediate benefit or another benefit closer to my goal?

Along comes Charlie, who offers me $11,000 cash. This now creates a scale to which I must weigh the benefit of the lot. Would $11,000 cash provide more benefit than the vacant lot? Or should I hold out for something else? Whatever the answer is, I should review my goals once again.

Then along comes Alex. In exchange for the lot, he offers me a 48-foot sailboat that has a mortgage of $60,000 against it. This presents another dilemma, another opportunity to examine the benefits I want versus the benefits offered.

Barter as a Pathway to Your Goals

You need to look at your assets as a route to your goals. Through barter and exchange, you can frequently go directly to GO and collect that desired benefit. That three-year-old car sitting in your driveway might be the down payment to get you into that duplex across town that in turn will help you attain a part of your desired goals.

Real-estate investors need to open their eyes to the potential of barter. It may be that barter will only be a clincher to a deal and not the total transaction itself. Professional deal-makers know the value of some final benefit to lock up a hard-to-close transaction.

An example of this is what I often call the "vacation on me" barter transaction. The goal of this type of closing technique is to be in a position to offer the seller something that guarantees your deal. The item here would be a vacation for the seller and his wife.

Example 3 Offer a Benefit

"Ms. Seller, you will notice that I have adjusted your counteroffer only slightly, giving in to the majority of your needs. To compromise those areas that were not possible, I want to offer you and your husband accommodations for seven nights, space available of course, in any resort in the world affiliated with the RCI organization. I have here a catalog of the several thousand such resorts located around the world."

RCI is the primary timeshare exchange network in the world. Timeshare properties are usually a condominium form of ownership that is divided into "week" segments. For example, the 23rd week of the year at Orlando International Resort Club would relate to my actual ownership and fixed use during my ownership of that week at that location. However, through RCI I can "bank" my week's use and swap it to another location at another time vis à vis other timeshare owners banking their weeks in the same manner. If I owned only one time share that was approved by RCI and I was a member of the organization, I could select to exchange my week for any other location for any time of the year and I could give you or another person that week's vacation. This simple act might be enough to close the deal.

But what about those thousands of you who don't own a timeshare week that you could so simply offer as a deal-maker? Don't worry, you can either obtain your own timeshare week, or at least obtain use of a week through barter. The key here is to know someone who has a timeshare week that you can borrow for a year.

Assume that you know me and that you feel that if you offered the seller a week's vacation somewhere you could tie down the deal. You could come to me and say: "Jack, I'll

- paint your car."
- supply carpets for your rental units."
- do your income tax calculations for two years."
- recover your living room sofas."
- give you 20 hours of tennis lessons."

And so on, so that you could obtain the use of one of my timeshare weeks to use it as a clincher to one of your deals. I might find that one of (a) through (e) was more of a benefit to me than the timeshare week. If so, I would make the deal with you, and you in turn could use that week as a deal-maker. This naturally is just a hint of the hundreds of such potential transactions you could do for yourself with other kinds of benefits. It might be that the "deal-maker" for your transaction would be a seven-day cruise to Jamaica, a mink coat, or a sapphire and diamond ring. Each of these "things" can be obtained through barter.

WHAT IS A BARTER CLUB, AND SHOULD YOU JOIN ONE?

In most cities, there exist what are called "barter clubs." They have names such as Barter Center, Exchange Club, or Interchange. These organizations act as clearing-houses for barter of all kinds by giving their members "credits" or barter dollars for the exchange made between members. In this way, I could get from you barter dollars for an item or service I trade to you. Later on, I could "pay" to someone else those barter dollars for an item or service I was to get in exchange.

The concept is very sound and works out great on paper. In fact, in some real situations barter clubs serve a good purpose and actually give their members a fair value for the cost, which usually is a cash payment to the club based on a percent of the trade dollars you spend or receive (or both). The benefit to owning barter dollars is the freedom to make one deal and to spend the credits in several places.

One such barter club that I belong to has members that offer every kind of service you can think of from acupuncture to Zebra rides. There are doctors, dentists, accountants, massage clinics, schools, auto repair, advertising, professional consultations of different needs, carpet sales, restaurants, vacations of various kinds and location, and so on. Each business barters their service or product for the barter dollars they will get, which they can then spend on other services or products available.

If you accumulated a bankroll of barter dollars, which you could very easily do by offering a service to the barter club members in your part time, you could use these "dollars" as part or all of a down payment on real estate you want to buy.

Join one of the local barter clubs that you find listed in your Yellow Pages under Barter, or Exchanges, or Trades. The two best known I've already mentioned in the previous chapter, are ITEX or BXI. Whether you have a professional service or hobby you could offer, or just some hard work, such as cleaning offices or waxing cars, put a top price on the service.

As you collect barter dollars, you are on your way to accumulating equity that you may be able to use in your real estate investing. However, there is a drawback to these barter clubs. The people who offer their services often have double standards. I'll wax your car or do your books or paint your car for this cash price, but for barter-dollars you have to pay more. While this might be realistic, in the long run it cheapens the value of the barter-dollar. Also, some people in the barter clubs get barter dollar heavy from one or two large transactions and then "dump" their dollars by buying anything they can get their hands on. This too, cheapens the value of the barter dollar.

HOW TO TELL IF A BARTER CLUB IS OKAY

1. If it has been in business for more than five years, that is a plus.

2. Will it give you a list of members prior to your joining? If not, forget about that organization.

3. Talk to some of the members. What do they tell you? Are they happy with the barter exchanges? If not, avoid the club.

4. Will the owner of the club give you references? If not, forget the club. If he or she does, check them out by calling the person directly. Ask questions such as: "How do you know this person?" "Have you dealt with the barter club?" "How so?" "Do you think my joining the club is a good idea?" Keep the person on the phone for a while. Even the best reference will start to tell you the nitty gritty after a while. Play it by ear, but if you are not comfortable with what you hear then forget that club.

5. Ask the Better Business Bureau if it knows anything about the club. If it does, it is apt to be through complaints. Get as much information on that aspect as possible.

Barter the Use of Your Home

One of the truly interesting things to do, is take a long holiday in some far-off land. Sure, this kind of trip might be very expensive, but it will not be if you swap the use of your home for the holiday. This is easier than you might think. There are a number of sources for such swaps, and most come with a track record of success. But with everything as important as giving up your home for another person's home for a month or two, be sure to check out references from satisfied customers. The following is a list of companies that arrange such exchanges.

Where to Go to Swap Your Home for a Long Vacation

INTERVAC
P.O. Box 590504
San Francisco, California 94159
(800) 756-4663

TEACHER SWAP
P.O. Box 454
Oakdale, New York 11769-0454
(516) 244-2845

HOME-LINK INTERNATIONAL
P.O. Box 650
Key West, Florida 33041
(800) 638-3841

AGENCY ALPHA INTERNATIONAL
Suite 13
11789 Montana Avenue
Los Angeles, California 90049
(301) 472-7216

LOAN-A-HOME
7 McGregor Rd.
Woods Hole, Massachusetts 02543
(508) 548-4032

INTERNATIONAL HOME EXCHANGE NETWORK
www.homexchange.com or
TRAVEL EXCHANGE CLUB
www.horizon.bc.ca/travex/home.html

Sweat Equity as a Barter Concept

Your own sweat can be one of the very best of the barter elements. Since this form of barter is actually a separate technique, I will treat it as such.

Make Deals with Your Promise to Perform as a Valued Service

The first-time investor can look to the sweat equity kind of transaction as one of the very best to enable that first transaction to be made with a minimum amount of cash passing hands.

In essence, sweat equity is your own work or labor that will be used to transform a property or provide value to the seller, or both. You will use this future or promised value as the down payment (all or part) in the transaction.

Why Sweat-Equity Transactions Work

Sweat-equity deals sometimes work because the seller is enticed to believe that if the intended work is not completed on time, or if the buyer cannot then get the financing needed to complete the transaction, the seller will end up keeping the property that has now been improved.

Other sweat equity transactions work because the sellers are very willing to sell on easy terms and need only be convinced that the transaction proposed by the buyer is "safe." The equity the buyer brings to the transaction is in fact real. It is work, time, and effort, all of which are expensive and have value. Of course, the key is to find the right transaction.

Look at the guides on the following pages that outline the steps in looking for a property that will fit the profile for a sweat-equity deal.

Property Profiles for Sweat-Equity Deals

You will want to look for properties that fit as many of these criteria as possible. While it is possible to find properties outside of this list, as this may be your first investment stick to the guide if possible.

1. Look for properties that are:
   a. not more than a one-hour drive from where you now live.
   b. in need of some repair or fix up.
   c. in an area that has properties of greater value.
   d. the kind of properties you would want to own.
   e. properties that you feel you can handle.

2. The first property you buy should be:
   a. an income-producing property.
   b. have at least three separate rental units, or be convertible into three such units or more.
   c. well constructed.
   d. not have any serious defects.

3. For you to get the best deal, find an owner who is:
   a. a successful and busy professional person (doctors make ideal sellers).
   b. unable to manage his or her own property.
   c. owner of other real estate.
   d. local or not, but lives far away.
   e. not in need of immediate cash.

4. Make sure you know what your sweat-equity abilities are by:
   a. being honest with yourself as to what you can do.
   b. trying to learn sweat-equity abilities if you have none.

5. You will find this property by:
   a. developing your comfort zone.
   b. looking for "For Rent" signs on neglected property.
   c. finding a real-estate broker you can relate to.
   d. making offers.

6. Before you buy you should:
   a. visit the property during all hours of the day and night.
   b. get a good understanding of the rental market in the area. Know what is for rent, what is not rented, and the prices and comparisons of rentals.
   c. know and understand the zoning restrictions.
   d. know and understand the subdivision restrictions if any.
   e. make sure that you can deliver your sweat equity offered.
   f. have a good real-estate lawyer.

Example 1 The Johnson Sweat-Equity Case

Robert Johnson worked as a manager of a supermarket. His wife was a secretary for a real-estate office. They lived in a small one-bedroom apartment that was about twenty minutes from both their jobs. They had a little cash saved. Mr. Johnson could work different shifts at the supermarket and was more flexible with his free time. They took stock of their sweat-equity abilities.

Robert's Sweat-Equity Abilities

1. Good at painting.
2. A green thumb, so good at gardening.
3. Minor carpentry.
4. Strong.
5. Flexible with his time by working night or weekend shifts at the supermarket.
6. Willing to learn other tasks that will help own real estate.

Helen's Sweat-Equity Abilities

1. Good at color selections.
2. Can sew.

3. Also good at gardening.

4. Knows where and how to buy things right.

5. Willing to learn other jobs.

6. Free weekends and evenings.

7. Very supportive of her husband's ideals.

You can see that the Johnsons are moderately equipped in the sweat-equity department. If it isn't on their list, we will assume that they are going to have to seek outside help. Therefore, if it requires plumbing or electrical or anything beyond simple carpentry, extra help will be needed. That means added expense, so when the Johnsons look for a property they want to avoid properties that require work outside their major advantages. If you are an expert in electrical wiring of homes and other kinds of real-estate improvements or are a plumber, you would look for those properties that could be improved with those specific talents.

WORKING THEIR COMFORT ZONE: THE SEARCH FOR A PROPERTY

The Johnsons had been studying a geographic zone that was near where they lived. It was a nice residential area that had a mix of different kinds of real estate. They were looking for a small apartment building or a large, older home that was in an area that was properly zoned to allow multifamily residences that they could convert to apartments.

They searched the area by using two methods. They had taken up riding bicycles as a form of exercise, so whenever they could they would ride their bikes through this area. They didn't just ride their bikes in a haphazard route, however; it was always carefully planned out, and a small map of the area and note pad accompanied them on their nearly daily trips in the area.

What they wanted to do was to become so familiar with this section of town that they would have a mental picture of each property, street, and opportunity when it came up. This process took time. As they would ride through the area and locate for-sale signs or any change in the status quo, they would make note of it.

If the for-sale sign was by a broker, they would have Phyllis, a real-estate saleswoman they had met and liked, check it out. Phyllis was their second method of searching for their future investment. They had met Phyllis after talking to several salespeople at several different offices and felt comfortable that she understood their needs.

They soon began to know everything about the area possible. They started to get a feel for the streets and the neighborhood. They began to make value assessments based on elements that often are missed by the people who live in the area. Why is this street nicer to live on than another? Or what makes this building a better investment because of what is going to happen in the near future?

That last bit of news was the result of going to the monthly city council meetings where they learned that two blocks away a new government center was to be built that would employ nearly 300 people. The impact to the area would include demand for rentals and increased traffic. The opportunity might not last too long as sooner or later the information would sift down to all property owners. They also discovered that very few people ever showed up at these meetings. Once they looked around the room and guessed that the majority of the people were lawyers, a few interested neighbors of the areas being discussed at the meetings, and several real insider real-estate investors. Just like they were becoming.

They Found the Ideal Property

The sign said, "For rent." It was on a property that they had noticed was going downhill for several months. An old beat-up pickup truck had been left in the front yard, the lawn was in bad shape, and in general the house was showing a lot of wear and little loving care.

When they called the number, they were told they had reached "Doctor Funt's office."

As it turned out, Dr. Funt had owned this property for nearly five years, renting it out for most of that time. The last tenant had turned out to be a deadbeat, however, and left in the middle of the night, taking with him anything of value that wasn't nailed down. The Johnsons said they simply wanted to see the inside of the home and did not get into any negotiations with the doctor at this time. They didn't even ask if the property was for sale.

After spending about an hour looking through the home, Robert and his wife realized that all that was needed was cleaning, paint, new carpets, new drapes, a new lawn, and attendance to the shrubs. The home would be well worth their effort if they could buy the property on terms that worked for them. The real ace for them was the separate garage which, due to the zoning, could be converted to an apartment and rented out.

The Sweat-Equity Plan

The Johnsons did their homework. They made a long list of all the items that needed repair, cleaning, paint, and so on. The list was very complete, and alongside each item was an estimate of the time needed to repair, clean, paint, and so on.

Next, there was a separate list of material needed. This list was equally as complete and the prices for the material were estimated with the help of a salesman at one of the local builder supply stores in the area.

THE OFFER TO THE OWNER

Armed with this proposal, the Johnson's met with Dr. Funt and proposed that he sell the home to them on the following terms:

1. A purchase price that was reasonable. Johnson suggested $70,000. This was nearly $15,000 more than Dr. Funt had paid for the property five years earlier according to the records down at the county records office.

2. That the Johnsons would repair, clean, paint, and fix up the house according to the detailed proposal that Robert Johnson had prepared.

3. All Dr. Funt had to pay for were the materials, which would cost around $4,000.

4. At the end of the fix-up period, the Johnson's would have 120 days to obtain a new first mortgage on the property of at least $60,000.

5. Dr. Funt would hold a second mortgage for $10,000, plus the material cost of $4,000 ($14,000 total mortgage). The mortgage would be interest only for 7 years at 9% interest per annum, payable annually.

Dr. Funt thought about this for a while and then rejected the proposal. The Johnsons let it rest for a few days and then got back in touch with Dr. Funt, asking him to meet them at the house. There they went over each repair that they would make to the property. They stressed the condition of the home, and the time needed to put it into shape.

Robert Johnson reminded Dr. Funt that in the proposal to buy the home the transaction was conditioned on the Johnsons finishing all of the work. If they didn't do so within 90 days, Funt could keep the house with the work done thus far. To show additional good faith, Johnson also agreed to pay half of the material cost up front.

Johnson also reminded Dr. Funt that the property would need most of the work done anyway just to get it rented again, so the doctor couldn't lose. He would get a fair value for the home, or he would get a lot of work done at little or no cost to him.

A couple of days later, the doctor signed the deal that was drafted by the Johnsons' lawyer. The Johnsons went to work, and by the time they had finished the home looked like a million dollars.

A savings and loan appraised the property for $110,000 and agreed to lend up to $88,000. To soften the terms of the loan, Robert Johnson took only $75,000. He gave $60,000 to Dr. Funt, paid off the $2,000 he owed the building supply house, paid $750 to his lawyer for the work and closing costs, and paid $2,250 back to the savings and loan for their points and costs. This left him with $10,000 in his pocket and a beautiful home.

The Johnsons had succeeded, their equity was because of their sweat . . . and their brains.

THE FIVE CRITICAL ELEMENTS OF A SWEAT-EQUITY PROPOSAL

1. Put everything down in the contract; exactly what you are expected to do and what you will get because of it.
2. The "option" for you to buy the property must be very specific.
3. Be sure to give yourself ample time to complete the work and to get the financing. Check with your local lenders to know how long the financing may take. Double that time.
4. Start looking to improve your position right away with your new property. Can you sell it or exchange it prior to having to close on it, making a profit along the way? Keep your options open.
5. Perform on the deal. A thousand things can come up that you didn't count on. But do everything you can to fulfill your deal. Future deals will count on it.

There Are Many Forms of Sweat Equity

Sweat equity has many faces and can be used in many different kinds of transactions. Your sweat equity can come via a three-way deal. You might barter your future work to me for something I'll give you now that you exchange with Dr. Funt. Also, as in all kinds of exchanges and barter you can swap your sweat equity for a note or mortgage. In this way, you can then exchange or swap the mortgage to the seller instead of your sweat equity. This technique would be useful if your specific ability was not needed for the property, but you still needed to create equity from some source other than money.

Of course, you might just as well learn how to print your own money, called *scrip*. In fact, this method of adding to the deal is used all the time and can be very helpful to you in closing many kinds of transactions.

HOW TO CREATE YOUR OWN LEGAL CURRENCY: SCRIP

Scrip comes in whatever shape, color, and form you print it. It can look like Monopoly money or play cash or it might resemble the currency from some foreign government—just as long as it doesn't look like U.S. currency. Scrip can be for specific values as you decide, and it is good for whatever specific item or service you can provide.

Example 2 Restaurant Scrip

If you own a fried-chicken restaurant, you could print up a couple of thousand dollars' worth of your own money in $10 increments and use this cash as part of your down payment on your next real-estate investment.

Example 3 Fishing Scrip

Or, if you own a fishing boat you could print up scrip in $200 increments to be applied to fishing trips. Or, if you could borrow your father's Cadillac from time to time (paying for gas, oil, and a small rental, of course), you could print up scrip in $100 increments to be applied against your nightly limo service.

The opportunities to create your own scrip are endless, as you will discover. In each instance, the concept of dealing with scrip is a deal closer and not necessarily as the total deal. Nonetheless, there will be transactions that can be made with your using scrip as your total payment to the seller.

Example 4 Fried-Chicken Scrip

The owner of the fried-chicken restaurant, Charles, printed up $5,000 of his own scrip in $10 bills. He indicates on the scrip that it must be redeemed by a specific date and that it cannot be used to pay tips or tax and that no change will be given against the scrip. To ward against counterfeiting, Charles signs each bill with his fountain pen and marks each bill with an invisible pen (visible only under ultraviolet light).

Charles did all of this because he had seen a small duplex that he wanted to buy. He had made an offer several weeks earlier, but was turned down because he didn't have enough cash to put down. The seller of the duplex was asking $55,000 for the property. He had a small mortgage of $25,000 and wanted $30,000 cash above the mortgage.

Armed with his scrip, Charles went back and offered to buy the duplex for $50,000 with $35,000 cash and $15,000 in scrip at his restaurant. The seller countered: $40,000 cash, and $10,000 in scrip. Charles knew that he could swing this deal now by putting up the $10,000 in scrip and borrow the balance from a local savings and loan.

Example 5 The Kitchen Sink

Ellis owned a kitchen appliance store. He too wanted to use scrip to buy real estate. So he printed up scrip in $250 denominations and indicated on the scrip that it had to be redeemed within twelve months, and that it was not good on any red-tagged sales items during that time.

Ellis had found a property he wanted to buy. It turned out to be owned by a local real estate investor who owned a lot of different kinds of properties. Some of these properties included rental apartments. Ellis knew that this seller would have use of kitchen appliances sooner or later, so this seller fit nicely into Ellis' plans.

This points out the advantage of knowing something about the seller prior to making the offer. Once you know the seller can use the kind of scrip you have, you have the edge in making this type of transaction. Ellis' offer would be a simple $10,000 in kitchen appliance scrip as the down payment on the desired property. The deal may require other techniques to be used in addition, such as outside financing or additional seller-held financing, or some other highly creative technique provided for you in this book.

WHAT IF YOU DON'T OWN A RESTAURANT OR APPLIANCE STORE

There are several ways to create scrip. Having your own business helps, but it is not the only way to use this very effective tool. In essence, there are two basic methods of generating your own scrip from outside sources. In my book *$1,000 Down Can Make You Rich*, I discuss these two methods as "Watered Scrip," and "Commissioned Scrip."

Watered Scrip That Comes from Others at a Discount

The basic element to understand here is that you will acquire from other people credits against their services or products. You will print up the scrip that they agree to honor, and you will buy it from them, either at a discount or by using paper you create against things you now own or are about to buy.

The people who own the businesses must be shown that the scrip you are going to create will bring them business they don't already have, which in turn will generate more business that will be on a cash basis. Scrip business then has an advertising value that accounts for the discount to you. Also, by offering to buy future business now you can frequently get a substantial discount for that alone. Couple these factors with the idea that you aren't going to pay money for the scrip, and the idea becomes very attractive for you. Best of all, since you are going to tailor the scrip to the transaction, you will have a higher success rate in real estate transactions. You can go out and get the kind of scrip that will fit the deal.

BUYING SCRIP ON YOUR TERMS.   You say to Mr. Furniture Store Owner, "I'll give you a $10,000 second mortgage against a five-unit apartment building I'm buying if you will sell me $12,000 in scrip good only in your store." Or. . . "Mr. Schultz, I'll give you an option to buy my five-unit apartment building, good for one year, for $5,000 worth of hotel scrip in New York City." Or. . . "Mr. Marks, I'll give you a two-year lease in the garage apartment for you or one of your clients if you will give me $12,000 in scrip good for meals in your chain of restaurants." Or. . . "Mr. Hennington, I'll give you $12,000 in scrip for meals in Mark's restaurant chain if you'll give me $14,000 in scrip good for cars on your used car lots."

In each case, you want to offer something of value for scrip at a greater face value. The difference between the two is your profit for doing the transaction, but it comes to you at no real cost to the other side of the scrip transaction. The furniture store owner has a markup of products and may want to move off some furniture. The owner would want to make sure the scrip didn't apply to sale merchandise, so the $2,000 profit you make in the scrip versus second mortgage trade is warranted. By the way, it is possible that the owner would take your second mortgage and use it as a down payment on something if he or she was unable to swap furniture for the property he or she wanted to buy.

COMMISSIONED SCRIP.   Unlike the watered scrip that you "buy" at a discount, the commissioned scrip is scrip that you establish through some third party and then redeem as cash, less your commission.

This kind of scrip doesn't have the benefit of allowing you to exchange a long-term pay-back as you can if obtaining watered scrip by giving a three-year mortgage on the five-unit property you are going to buy. However, it does have a very strong impact on a transaction and can help you close transactions that need this kind of kicker. You will get a discount nonetheless and frequently get up to a year or so to pay for the scrip.

Example 6 Commissioned Scrip Transaction

Assume for a moment that you are attempting to buy a vacant tract on which you will build a small strip store. The owner of the site is asking $200,000 for the site and you have offered $175,000.

The negotiations have gone on for a week or so and the seller is agreeing to the following terms in his most recent counteroffer to you:

Price: $185,000
Cash down: $50,000
Terms on the balance: Cash within 18 months with interest at 12% per annum. If you want to build right away, the mortgage would have to be paid off at the time you took out a construction loan.

Most of this is acceptable to you as you are going to build right away, only you hate to put up the $50,000 now as you are going to mortgage 100% on the project. In dealing with the seller, you discover that the seller likes to travel, so you come back with this following proposal:

Price: $185,000
Down payment: $70,000, made up of $20,000 cash and a ticket on QE 2 Around the World Cruise that leaves in 14 months with a double deluxe outside cabin for two that has a value of $50,000. The balance is as the seller wants.

If the seller takes this transaction, you will have made a good deal as you have met the seller's terms but you only have to put up $20,000 cash plus a deposit on the cruise of around $1,500. In around 10 months, when the cruise has to be paid off in full, you will not have to pay the full $50,000 price because you will have made an arrangement with a travel agent to become one of their salespeople. In essence, you get a commission on the cruise.

Back up a moment. There are certain things you can buy that you wouldn't get until some time in the future. Cruises and other vacations of almost any kind are prime examples of closing kickers that you can offer any seller. If the seller likes to travel, he or she is apt to bite at that offer, even though they may not have spent that much money on themselves.

You can see that you didn't have to own the travel agency to make the deal work. Whenever you acquire scrip that you will redeem in the future, you will have a discount built in through the commission. However, if you follow the tips in this chapter, there are other discounts you have to take into account that add to your profit in the transaction. All of these profits require that you set up the scrip transaction properly, so look at the checklist that will aid you in commission scrip deals.

CHECKLIST ON HOW TO MAKE PROFITABLE COMMISSION SCRIP DEALS

1. Never enter into a commission scrip deal until you know exactly how much scrip you will need and for what specific product.

2. Do, however, look for the kinds of products that will generally be useful and begin to make contacts in those areas. Meet the owners of these prime scrip products and services.
    a. Travel agencies.
    b. Kitchen and other building and home appliances and products.
    c. Lumber yards.
    d. Jewelry stores.
    e. Restaurants.
    f. Resorts (best through timeshare resorts).
    g. Legal services.
    h. Accounting services.
    i. Used car lots.
    j. New car agencies.
    k. Auto repair shops.

3. Have a firm agreement with the owners of the businesses that you are doing business with. Make sure the agreement covers these following items.
    a. The name and address of the business or businesses honoring the scrip.
    b. The term for which the scrip shall be good (ample time).

    c.   What the scrip includes and excludes.

    d.   A statement that if the business is sold the liability of the scrip shall continue, or the scrip will be bought back for cash.

    e.   A penalty if the scrip is not honored. If you have to then redeem the scrip for cash yourself, you won't get the commission, so you should be owed that commission from the original party.

    f.   How and when you are to redeem the scrip and for what price, less what commission.

4. Check on the transaction from time to time to see if any scrip you may have traded is being turned down.

No matter what you do, there is apt to be a problem or two if you try to cut your deals too tight. Remember, the dealer in the product or service has to see a benefit. They are dealing in business for a profit and if you hit them for too much commission or don't redeem the scrip on time, the rest of your deal can fall apart. Also, remember that scrip and barter transactions work best when they are offered later on in the transaction and not right up front. They are kickers that close deals that you are getting close to, but just can't seem to nail down. You will find sellers who are willing to take scrip as the total down payment or outright purchase, but those transactions are far more difficult to find and make.

HIDDEN BENEFITS YOU NEED TO DO HOMEWORK TO FIND

Other kinds of kickers that you can use as deal makers often are overlooked because you don't spend the time or homework needed to find out what might turn the seller on.

Take a look at your potential kickers, keeping in mind that a kicker is any form of benefit that you can give or lend to the seller as part of the deal or as a bonus to entice him or her to make your deal.

The following is a list of your assets:

- You have your home
- You own a cabin in North Carolina
- You are an excellent tennis player

Just looking at those assets you could offer a prospective seller some or all of the following:

- A holiday in North Carolina for two weeks
- A holiday in North Carolina for two weeks for the next three years
- A quantity of tennis lessons

Each of these assets has a flexibility, and each has value that doesn't cost you anything other than some time or some inconvenience. Keep in mind that as you could offer the holiday in North Carolina to the owner of the sailboat, who could in turn provide sailing lessons to the seller you are dealing with, the opportunities are endless.

KICKERS USING THE TAX LAWS

There frequently are kickers that are of little or no benefit to you, but are cash in the pocket of the other party. For example, take the tax laws that you can work to your profit.

If you want to buy a property and are very close to making the deal, but no matter how much you try to close the transaction you are still a few thousand dollars apart, the depreciation kicker often works wonders. Let me set the stage of a transaction that is already filled with several different creative tools but still hasn't closed.

Example 7 Looks Like a Tax Break

Frank is the seller, and the property is a duplex that you want to buy. The price you and Frank have finally agreed on is $75,000. The terms that are agreeable to both parties are:

Price: $75,000
Cash to Frank from a mortgage to be obtained by the buyer: $40,000
Plus, as a part of the deal: $5,000 in scrip at Mark's restaurant chain
Plus, as a part of the deal: $15,000 in the form of a second mortgage on a property you are buying down the street.
Plus, as part of the deal: $5,000 cabin on a two-week cruise for two to Alaska.

We are still $10,000 short. Frank wants that in cash, and you want to give him a second mortgage on the duplex in that same amount. To close the deal, you go back to Frank and suggest that he take the scrip, the second mortgage, the cruise, but not deed you the property for one year. In the meantime, he can get the new mortgage to which you will be a cosigner, with an agreement from the bank that when the property is transferred to you Frank's name will be taken off the mortgage. In this way, Frank has everything in the deal and still has the property, only it's still $10,000 short.

You agree to rent the property for the exact cost of the mortgage and other fixed costs just as though you owned the property. At the end of the year, you will give Frank $2,500 cash and a second mortgage for the remainder of $7,500.

The benefit is you get the property. You save interest on the mortgage for one year (that might have been $1,000), and you therefore have a net cash payout of $1,500 at the end of one year. The balance owed to Frank is as you had originally wanted.

Frank gets the depreciation for twelve months plus the potential that at the end of the year something will have happened to you and he'll keep the house as well as the scrip, the cruise, and the second mortgage. Most importantly, however, you are able to offer to Frank something that doesn't cost you anything. In fact, if you had to add the interest back into the deal that you had saved on the mortgage, you still benefit.

SUMMARY OF BARTER, SWEAT EQUITY, SCRIP, AND KICKERS

In general, all these techniques are sound financing tools that can be used from time to time in making deals work for you. As I've mentioned several times, do your homework to try to fit the transaction to the seller, but don't worry if you make a cold offer when time or circumstances don't allow any homework. The worst anyone can ever do is turn you down. And one thing all real-estate investors know if they are ever to succeed in the game is if you aren't turned down from time to time you aren't making enough offers.

Beware of the Pitfalls of Barter Deals

The biggest pitfalls in barter, sweat equity, scrip, or kickers is knowing who you are dealing with, and then being sure to back up everything with good sound contracts. This means that you will have to have good legal representation in this area.

People get into trouble in barter by not checking values carefully, or, if the barter is through a barter club, by getting in too deep and building up too large a bank account. Barter dollars can be difficult to spend, and if the club folds they are impossible to get rid of.

Sweat equity is most likely the best single tool for the investor who has a strong back, good business mind, but little cash. It is hard to make too many errors if you are careful with your fix-up expenses. The worst area that gets sweat equitors into trouble is not having enough time to do the work promised. They start out thinking that they can do everything in days, only they get the flu or get transferred or a million other things come up. Be very careful of these kinds of problems.

Scrip has a mountain of problems if you are careless or don't document the deal properly. If you are dealing with a restaurant that is sold or goes out of business, your scrip is like bad checks. The people you gave scrip to will come back looking to you for redemption (some might even look for vengeance).

Kickers have few problems as long as you can deliver and as long as you don't tie yourself up with a commitment that you don't want to have to honor later on. For this reason, it is a good idea to have a "cash" value on all kickers that you can pay off if you want to or have to.

Chapter 21

THE FIVE STAGES OF EVERY REAL-ESTATE TRANSACTION

There are five fundamental stages of every real estate transaction. These stages begin with the idea that you want to invest in or sell real estate and conclude with the actual closing of the deal. These stages occur for every buyer, and every seller, and each side of the deal will have a different opinion and point of view of everything that happens. This chapter will approach each of these states and attempt to give you a good idea what to expect, from either side of the fence, and give you tips on how to deal with some common problems and pitfalls that occur. These stages are as follows:

1. Laying the foundation to buy.
2. Selecting a property to buy.
3. Negotiating to win.
4. Offering/contracting to buy.
5. The closing.

Each of these stages has its own start and finish. While some stages may appear to overlap, what is really happening is that you have moved too quickly into the next stage, without having completed the earlier one. This creates a gap, that often appears as indecision or purchaseitus. This is when doubt creeps in and you have to move back a step or two to either decide that you need to end the process, and move onto another property or buyer, or move forward. Not all transactions are smooth events. There is the potential for considerable human drama. After all, the purchase or sale of real estate can be the most expensive transaction you will ever undertake (except getting married, or being divorced). Everything may be moving along nice and smooth. Then the storm can come crashing in and in a second the whole thing seems to fall apart. It is in those moments you see your dream disappear.

Each of these stages has people involved: you, of course, your real estate broker and sales agent, the other party to the contract, your lawyer, the other party's lawyer, the CPA, the closing agent, the escrow agent. Each takes time and adds to the complexity of the transaction.

Buying and selling real estate for a profit is not a one-person job. No highly successful investor has ever done it all alone. There simply isn't enough time. Once the money begins to build up, the time it would take for some simpler tasks will best be left to others you can hire. It becomes a matter of priority as your wealth grows, not a matter of your not being able to do the job yourself. Wealth does have its rewards.

LAYING THE FOUNDATION TO BUY

Without the proper foundation you will have a random chance at success. Granted, there are people who do have success at things they do and they have no foundation at all. You can read about them or you have known people like that. What did you say when you learned about the guy down the street who sold his house for twice its value because he was the key piece to a redevelopment of that block? "That lucky son of a gun."

That is right, he was lucky, and many other investors will be just as lucky due to no act of their own. They just happened to make a buy that turned into a small pot of gold. Unfortunately, for every one of these lucked-out investments, there are dozens of not so lucky ones. Buying real estate is just not an absolutely guaranteed deal. Not everything you buy is going to go up in value fast enough (if at all) to cover the cost of holding on to it. Not every property will produce a profit; not every apartment building will be fully occupied and become a money machine. Losing your shirt investing in real estate is possible for you no matter how much you know.

In fact, some smart boys lose their shirts. Not every investment I have made has turned out the way I wanted it to. I have taken a few high flyers that could have turned out like a diamond mine, but instead developed into a latrine. The risk in these investments was higher than you can absorb; I thought I had overcome it. Still, some can thwart the best laid plans of men and women, or time.

So the occasional high flyer (risky deal) should be left to the big player who can anticipate and afford the potential loss. Building your wealth in real estate will not always be an uphill ride. There will be times in even the most conservative investment when you may have to pull in the belt a notch or two to counteract temporary setbacks. Setbacks, such as high unemployment in your area (which does nasty things to rental projects), or city projects such as new roads that will have a future benefit, but meanwhile can cause you to lose tenants in your strip store because of the repaving for twelve months.

Being able to bend with these elements of the game is all part of the road to success. If it were easy, it would not be so rewarding when you got there. Success is simply attained. Not easily, just simply. It requires only your dedication and persistence.

The development of your foundation is, of course, up to you. Some of you will get it in the school of hard knocks. That is, you will experience a bit more failure early in your learning, and if you hang in, the success will come later. Hard knocks, by the way, are really a misnomer. If you succeed, you will look back on all your failures as important stages in your success. You cannot simply have success without failure. This is the most important part of your total foundation for success.

People who are failures in life find a reason why each failure was not their fault. People who succeed found out what they did to cause each failure, and did not do it again. The successful embrace failure, as it is essential to advancement and success. Into every real-estate investor's life a little rain must fall.

I've given you all the basics you need to know to get ready. Applying them is up to you. The six elements of success: knowledge, enthusiasm, motivation, perseverance, clear goals, and no fear of failure, are within you if you pull it together and make them work for you. You can be a little success or a big success depending on your balance of elements. You will find the balance, or you will simply find that real estate is not your thing.

Finding a Salesperson

There are two categories of real-estate brokers and salespeople. There are realtors, and brokers who are not realtors. Let me explain it this way. The National Association of Realtors is a nationwide professional organization, the largest of its kind. The members of the realtors' association, to join, must agree to be bound by a series of rules that govern their activities in many ways. They have their own internal professional standard code, and a strict self-policing of that code and its enforcement. The realtors make up the majority of the brokers dealing in real estate. Yet not all brokers are in fact realtors. No state law requires the holder of a real-estate license to be a realtor.

As a realtor I feel the major benefit to an investor in dealing with a fellow realtor is the benefit of a wider access to the product than the nonrealtor. There may be other reasons to choose realtors. The National Association of Realtors would be quick to point out that realtors stick to a more strict code of ethics, but while that may be true, I have known many fine and qualified brokers and salespeople who did not become realtors.

Yet, because your interest is in finding the best selection of property for your invested capital, look first among the realtors in your neighborhood. Try to find a sales agent with whom you can develop rapport; someone who will put his or her total knowledge at your disposal that you will profit from. It is your interest that you want this person to have at the top of his list.

The best way to find this ideal sales agent is to look for them. Ask around in your own circle of friends to see if they will recommend someone. The good sales agent usually has a wide range of satisfied clients who are that salesperson's best source of new clients. Let your friends know you are looking for a good real-estate sales agent and very soon you will have several names from which to choose.

Of course, that may not produce a person you feel you can work with. The importance of your having rapport with this person cannot be overestimated. He or she might be the best sales agent in town, but if you cannot get along with him or her, then seek out someone else.

Visit several real estate offices and ask to speak with a broker. Tell the broker that you are planning to invest in real estate and you feel you need to meet several sales agents. Say you want to find one you can work with over the years. If the broker is smart, he or she will discuss your needs with you and introduce you to one or two sales agents he or she feels would be right for you. If not, then try another office.

It is a good idea for you to explain to the salesperson that you want to find a sales agent you can work with and you do not want him or her to spend any time for you until you are ready. The sales agent will appreciate the fact that you want to find one sales agent to deal with and will respect that. There is nothing worse for a real-estate sales agent than to be working with a client who hasn't told him or her about the other sales agent from a competitor's office with which he or she is currently working. They waste a lot of time and effort in the real-estate business because of this.

Ask questions and expect answers that show to you that the sales agent is knowledgeable about the area and can be of help to you. If you do not get a good feel for the setup, then do not waste your time or the salesperson's; move on. The time you spend in searching out a sales agent to work with will pay off benefits later, and you will be glad you were cautious.

The Kind of Real-Estate Salesperson You Do Not Want

- *The salesperson who doesn't ask you questions.* This shows this salesperson does not know enough to find out what your goals, needs, and time requirements are. If the salesperson does ask questions but they are disjointed and unrelated to your goals, the time you have spent was for nothing. Move on.

- *The salesperson who talks and does not listen.* (The worst thing any salesperson can do!) Some do it because they feel they must impress you. Giving you a brief history of him- or herself is okay for the salesperson or his or her office, but you are there to have your problems solved; your goals met. He or she has to listen to do it effectively.

- *A salesperson who is in a rush to make a sale.* The first sign of this is when he or she wants to take you out to see a property before he or she has found out sufficient data about your needs. This is a common trait with real-estate salespeople and may be a sign of lack of confidence. Understanding your needs is important, so he or she will save time by showing you property that is closer to your needs.

- *The salesperson you are uncomfortable with.* It does not matter why, she smokes and you cannot stand smoke, or the accent of his voice, or his hairstyle, or the funny mole on the side of her nose. If you are uncomfortable and cannot get rapport, move on.

EIGHT TRAITS OF TOP REAL-ESTATE SALESPEOPLE

1. They listen.
2. They are prompt.
3. They ask pointed and direct questions aimed to help you shape your goals so that they will understand what they are.
4. They are constantly learning. Real estate is a profession that demands constant update and learning.
5. They are enthusiastic about their ability to solve your problem.
6. They display self-confidence.
7. They look successful.
8. They know the techniques of the trade that will enable you to make more deals.

Once you have a real-estate salesperson on your side and you have been candid with him or her about your financial position, you are ready to move onto the second stage of the transaction.

SELECTING A PROPERTY TO BUY

We have said much already about this stage. You know that the selection of real estate is very important because it sets the theme of the kind of real-estate investing you are going to do. If this is to be your first buy, then you will seek a living investment; that is, one you can live in yourself. That might be a single-family property or an apartment complex. Whatever it is, you will make the proper selection by following the many suggestions I have given you in this book.

Ten Key Factors in Finding the Property You Will Ultimately Buy

1. Stick close to your backyard.

2. Do not get beyond the scope of your ability, but know what that ability is.

3. Be willing to stretch yourself to the maximum limit of your economic capability.

4. Remember that risk is relative, and you can ease, reduce, or even remove risk by knowing as much as possible about the area, the market, and the property.

5. In building wealth you must look for property you can improve. The top of the heap has no place to go but down.

6. Have property inspected for problems by qualified people. The cost is nothing in comparison to the benefit of knowing the real condition of the property.

7. Recognize that if you like it and can afford it, this is one of the most important parts of buying real estate.

8. Do not overanalyze a deal. If it is really good, by the time you have decided to buy it someone else will have bought it. Besides, the likelihood is your long-range projections will not be accurate anyway.

9. Trends are generally clearly visible if you know where to look for them.

10. History repeats itself in real estate, so to know what is going on, look back to the past.

In reality you do not select the property you are going to buy, but instead you select property you would like to own. The time between wanting to own it and actually owning it has yet to come. It is highly possible that once you begin negotiating to buy, you will change your mind about the property in the first place. Price and terms the seller is willing to take can be the deciding factors. Or, as you continue to progress in the selection process you might start negotiating on one parcel of land or one building only to find another which suits your goals better than the first. In that event, simply break off negotiations and go on to the second property.

Sellers should recognize that a savvy buyer will not be bound to a deal until the deposit is placed and the contract fully executed on all sides. The highly motivated seller, then, should keep in mind that a bird in the hand is worth a whole flock in the bush (in real estate that is the way it goes).

Naturally, it depends on the status of the real-estate marketplace. If it is a seller's market, that is, if the demand to buy is greater than the supply to meet that demand, then the sellers sit in a good position. They will usually have several potential buyers out there, so the prices are firm and terms not as easy as in other markets. There is a danger here, however. If you are a seller and it may be a seller's market, it could well be that your property is not in that market at all. Real estate is not one marketplace; it is many. There is the single-family-homes market, but even that is divided into different strata. Then there are vacant lots, acreage, office buildings, hotels, and so on. Not all markets are up at the same time, and fortunately not all are down at the same time either.

When you enter the market to buy, the condition of that market will affect the method in which you negotiate; obviously, if it is a seller's market for the kind of property you want to buy. When you cannot be detoured to buy another kind of property, then you cannot be too standoffish in your attempts to bring the price down or to get better terms in the negotiations. If you do, you are apt to lose the deal to a less finicky buyer.

In a buyer's market, the conditions are such that there are more sellers than there are ready and willing buyers. This is more often the case in vacant land and acreage, as there is a lot of that kind of property. However, even this can become a hot item in a local area and then switch overnight from a buyer's market to a seller's market.

A buyer's market might be the ideal time to buy a property, but this is not always the case. You have to look to your own reason for buying and decide based on your own goal. If you want to use the property right away, or you anticipate the need for immediate income, a seller's market could be your best market. The buyers' market might have been created because of a recession or a slowdown in the growth of the area. These conditions might work against your goals, and buying at this time might not suit your needs. Price is a function of the use of a property, so as the need for the use (in the marketplace) goes down, so will the price.

Hotel sites in an overbuilt area will be a buyers' market. However, unless the buyer can find another use for the site or wait out the overbuilt condition, the purchase of that site at this time may not be prudent. Waiting until the time is right to build and pay more might be wiser. Builders and developers have long since recognized the fact that in a developmental program the cost of the land is only a fraction of the total picture anyway. It makes no economic sense to buy cheap and have the risks of holding for a long time when only an increased price (when compared with the total picture) will produce a ready and set property. You should remember this as well.

Now it is time to move into the third stage of the deal.

NEGOTIATING TO WIN

There are six key factors in negotiating and winning. These are:

1. AVOID PERSONAL CONFRONTATION DURING THE ACTUAL OFFER. This is essential to successful negotiating. The buyer will do far better if he has a mediator, a broker or sales agent, between him and the seller, at least when the offer is presented. Every professional arbitrator, negotiator, politician, salesperson, broker, lawyer, and judge knows that placing the two parties (buyer and seller) face to face is not in the best interest of the best deal.

Here is why. A buyer attempting to make the best deal for himself is going to press the transaction. If that pressure is direct and face-to-face the seller can and generally will react in a defensive way.

Buyer: "Mr. Seller, I realize you want $150,000 for this property, but the most I am prepared to offer is $95,000, and that is a good price."

Seller: "Well, you can take that $95,000 offer and stick it." As you can see, negotiations have broken down. Another example of the same kind of thing happening:

Or

Buyer: "Mr. Seller, if it weren't for the blue-and-pink drapes in this house, which I'll have to replace, I would be offering more, but whoever picked those colors out had to be nuts."

Seller: "My wife picked them out, and if you don't like those colors then you don't have to buy this house. In fact, I don't think I want to sell to you."

And so on. I could continue giving you examples of what can happen. Now, granted, there are those rare people who can sit down and make a deal face-to-face with the seller. However, it is too risky, I think. Saying the wrong thing in such an encounter and ending up with a seller who doesn't like you is far too easy, who will not be reasonable from that moment on.

Good salespeople who know the art of negotiation can deal with a difficult seller (or when we turn things around with a difficult buyer) without compromising your interest in the deal. The salesperson can absorb (as he or she should) the heat of the negotiations so the other side of the deal can vent his or her frustrations at the broker and not at you.

2. REVIEW YOUR GOALS BEFORE MAKING THE OFFER TO BE SURE THE PROPERTY FITS IN THE SCHEME OF THINGS.   There is no sense in starting on a negotiation that will end with a property not suited for your goals. A simple review of those goals will put you back on the right track. You will find on occasion that what has happened is that emotion has become an insider to the deal and has, at least temporarily, replaced your goals or at best clouded those goals from clear sight. Watch for that, because once you get away from the goals and let emotion run wild with the deal, you will find yourself rationalizing away the best part of your plan.

3. TRY TO LEARN SOMETHING ABOUT THE OTHER PARTY'S GOALS.   If you know what the seller (or buyer) is really attempting to accomplish, then you might have a better way to help him or her reach a goal. One example that comes to

mind involved a client of mine interested in selling a lot he owned in a subdivision west of Fort Lauderdale. A prospective buyer made an offer through another office. My client rejected the offer and countered $5,000 higher. The would-be buyer balked and said he would think about it. As he and the other broker were about to leave my office, he asked me what the seller was going to do with the money. "He wants to get a summer home in North Carolina," I said.

"Hell," the buyer said. "I am a builder in Asheville. I have several homes I will trade."

The story did not end there. The owner of the lot never ended with a home this client had, but an exchange was made in which the builder from North Carolina did participate, and he did get the lot he wanted. The seller of the lot got what he wanted because of the North Carolina builder.

Learning the true reasons for a sale or the real use to which the money is going to be put can be next to impossible sometimes. Your broker or salesperson will have to dig a little to find out what he or she can, and sometimes you are well into the negotiations before you find even anything that resembles the truth.

Yet it is simple and should be clear to you that the more you know about the other party to the deal the better you can come out on top of the negotiation. In fact, knowing more about the buyer is more important for the seller than the other way around. Best of all, the seller can find out information about the buyer once the negotiations start. Sellers being asked to hold secondary financing, for example, can rationally and logically ask for and usually receive financial information on the buyer. References and the like are a good source of data on the buyer, and most buyers attempting to buy hard will be forced to give up some of this information. You should be careful about relying on such references, however, as a buyer would not give you the name of someone who would badmouth him or her. However, you can get leads from a reference on where else to go to get more information about a person, so they are highly useful in that sense.

4. BE FLEXIBLE IN THE NEGOTIATIONS, BUT FIRM AT THE SAME TIME. Does this sound like a contradiction? It is not. The idea is to decide where you want to be flexible and where you want to be firm. If the deal is all cash, then you are closing the options you are giving the other party and the only place where there is any flex left is in the price. This is, in my opinion, a bad stand for a seller, as it places him or her in the tightest of all boxes to make a deal. Naturally, this stand must be taken at times when cash is the only way out, and there is no way to generate that cash from some outside source. But the fact of the matter is there are so many options open to buyers to give a seller cash and yet keep their own out-of-pocket cash investment at a minimum that it is folly to assume that all cash to one party means all cash paid by the other.

Financing from a third party can usually be found in one form or other to help the deal along. Remember "I'll pay your price if you accept my terms." Or, said another way, "I can't budge on the cash down, but I can work out the terms," or "I know I can get the best terms to suit my deal if I'm flexible in the price."

You will see a clearer path in the decision on where you want or need to be firm by having a good understanding of your goals, of course, but it is more than just that. The property and its ability to sustain a profit while it produces income is very important. You don't want to overburden the transaction with heavy debt that can't be sustained unless a miracle happens, just because you are getting the price you were willing to pay.

5. REMEMBER THERE ARE OTHER FISH IN THE SEA. I've seen buyers go into deep depression because they lost out on a property they wanted to buy. Losing deals will happen to you if you plan to buy and sell real estate. There will be other investors who have snookered you out of a great deal, and other times it will be turned around. Yet, crying over spilled milk won't get you anything. Move on to the next deal. Be careful, however; you might act a little quicker the next time out of fear of losing the next deal, so watch out for this overreaction.

6. SELLERS SHOULD BE CAREFUL ABOUT HOLDING OUT TOO LONG. There is a time and place for holding out for a better offer. In typical hindsight I'll tell you that the time and place is only when you get a higher offer. Unfortunately, many sellers turn down offers that are never bettered. It might be possible that the seller will get a higher price some time in the future by holding out longer, but you must consider the time element. If you are a tough seller and yet you really want to sell, keep in mind that as you hold on to a property you are losing the potential from the reinvestment of that capital. Not selling at $100,000 because you are sure you will get $110,000 is okay if you get the $110,000 within a reasonable time. If you had to hold on to the property for twelve months or more, the chances are you have lost ground rather than come out ahead. This depends somewhat on your motivation, of course, and what you might have done with the money from a sale. Remember, time is the key factor to profit.

These six factors will help give you some edge in the negotiation of the contract. You win, however, in every transaction that takes you closer to your goal. Naturally, the real win is viewed from the nineteenth hole. The fifth-quarter viewpoint of the game is always the easiest, and most investors look back at every transaction to decide if they have won or lost. While this might give the investor a more satisfactory view of his or her analysis of winning or losing, it does provide the investor with the rationalization of that win or loss. This is natural, however, even though it will distort the true win or loss. The seller says, "You should have negotiated a little harder, because I would have taken much less than you paid."

In retort the buyer says, "That's okay, because if you would have held out for more I was ready to give you double what I actually paid."

Your viewpoint on winning should be tied to what it is you want to accomplish. Your flexibility in the negotiations will be very important to keep alive all possibilities to achieve what you wanted in the first instance. Try to keep personalities out of the picture by avoiding direct confrontation with the other party. If you have a broker or salesperson, let him or her become the buffer in nailing down the best deal for you. Remember, of course, that this salesperson or broker will have to see the transaction from three vantage points: yours, the other party's, and his or her own. As long as you keep track of your own interest and help point the salesperson in that same direction, you won't have to press the deal; the enthusiastic and knowledgeable salesperson will do that for you.

You have progressed well along in the buying or selling process if you have a contract. As a buyer you haven't made up your mind sufficiently unless you are at that stage, and as a seller nothing happens until there is an offer which can generate a contract. Thus, on to the next stage.

OFFERING/CONTRACTING TO BUY

How you present your offers is an essential part of the negotiation process. There are four basic forms of offers: verbal; letter of intent; standard form agreement; lawyer-drafted agreement. Not all are effective for each situation. Some may not be useful at all.

Verbal

It should be noted that in the transfer of real estate the contract must be executed in writing to be legally enforceable. This doesn't negate the use of the verbal offer, however, as with some people their word is as good as their bond. I've seen many deals hammered out in verbal terms with nothing written down until everything had been agreed to. This is not unusual or uncommon. However, for each deal worked out in such methods I've seen a hundred fall into one hassle or other as one of the parties lapses into forgetfulness as to what was exactly said, and the closing never occurs.

Frequently a buyer will instruct his salesperson, "See what the seller will take." This is generally followed by the salesperson asking the seller what is the lowest price the seller will take. These tactics generally don't produce any beneficial results and the salesperson won't find out the real facts in this maneuver. Most sellers don't know what they will take until a plan is presented to them that suits their goals (at that moment).

For the buyer to tell the seller (directly or through the salesperson) that he or she would like to buy the property and would the seller take, say, $100,000 is equally unproductive. If the seller was foolish enough to answer the question "Yes," the likelihood is that the offer will be $90,000 or less.

Thus, while there is a time and place for verbal offers, most sellers won't respond as effectively to a verbal offer as they would to a cash deposit and written contract. "Here's my offer, Mr. Seller, and here's a big check to show I'm real."

The Letter of Intent: A Written Verbal Offer

What happens in the letter of intent is that the broker or the buyer himself will write a letter to the seller. This letter states that the client (buyer) is interested in buying the seller's property on the basis of terms outlined in detail or in some loose form in the letter. The basics only are discussed, and the buyer leaves out much of the detail that would constitute a contract. One such letter of intent is shown below:

Mr. Bradford J. Williams
President
Westmoreland National Insurance Companies
New York, New York

Re: Letter of Intent to Acquire Ocean Side Apartments

Dear Mr. Williams:

This letter is to indicate to you the intent of our prospective purchaser THE WORLD DEVELOPMENT COMPANIES N.V. from Aruba, Netherlands Antilles, to enter into an agreement for the purchase of the apartment complex your company owns known as OCEAN SIDE APARTMENTS which is located in Hollywood, Florida. We have been informed by THE WORLD DEVELOPMENT COMPANIES N.V. that their legal representatives in Miami will draft the purchase offer and have it in your offices within five days from the date of your acceptance of this Letter of Intent. They are prepared to place $200,000 deposit with the offer.

The terms which would be acceptable to THE WORLD DEVELOPMENT COMPANIES N.V. are as follows:

1. A purchase price of: $5,750,000.

2. A cash down payment (of which the deposit is a part) of $2,000,000.

3. The balance of the purchase price would be held by the sellers as a first mortgage over 27 years term at a variable interest rate to be 2 points below prime as of the first of each month.

4. Closing to occur within 45 days of approval of the various inspections to be made. These inspections will include:

    (a) Structural of the buildings.
    (b) Electrical of the buildings.
    (c) Mechanical of the buildings.
    (d) Plumbing of the buildings.
    (e) Examination of the leases.
    (f) Examination of payment records.
    (g) Inspection of the maintenance records of the buildings.

5. In the event there is no approval given of these items within 15 days from the date the agreement of sale is completed, the sales agreement will be null and void and each party released from further obligations to the other.

6. Each party understands and agrees that there will be other terms and conditions in the final purchase agreement, but the first five terms outlined herein are the basic terms being agreed herein.

It is understood that the prospective purchasers will proceed immediately with the legal document if you agree to the basic terms in this Letter of Intent. It is understood also that this letter is not to be construed as a contract and only in the approval and execution of the final document of sale will there be a bona fide contract.

Your approval of this letter in the proper place indicated below will demonstrate your interest to proceed on this matter and your approval in principle of the price and sale terms indicated herein. Furthermore your approval will acknowledge that as seller your firm would be obliged to pay our fee at closing of title; said fee is Three Hundred and Fifty Thousand Dollars.

I have enclosed a packet of information on THE WORLD DEVELOPMENT COMPANIES N.V. which I'm sure you will find highly informative. You will find ample references to check on, and I'm confident you will be impressed with the credentials of these prospective buyers.

Very truly yours,

Jack Cummings,
Cummings & Regas Inc.
Real Estate Consultants

Approval
I HAVE READ THE LETTER OF INTENT AND DO HEREBY ACCEPT THE TERMS OF THE SALE AS OUTLINED. THIS ACCEPTANCE SHALL NOT CONSTITUTE A CONTRACT, BUT MERELY AN AGREEMENT TO ACCEPT THE PRICE AND TERMS BASED ON THE SATISFACTORY APPROVAL OF A FULL AND BONA FIDE CONTRACT

CONTAINING THOSE TERMS. OTHERWISE, THIS APPROVAL SHALL AUTOMATICALLY BE WITHDRAWN WITHIN ____DAYS FROM THE DATE BELOW.

Date:_____

_____

Bradford J. Williams

There are many items in this letter of intent which could be altered or made less specific, of course, and each letter of intent will be different. The idea is to simply indicate what you want to do and to proceed from there. These letters of intent aren't much more than verbal offers, but they do start things rolling. A more impressive way to present a letter of intent and at the same time make sure you have the attention of the seller is to put a deposit with the broker and have him mention that deposit in the letter: ". . . and the prospective buyer has placed a deposit of $10,000 in an escrow account as a statement of good faith. This deposit will become a part of the total cash down at closing."

Many large transactions use the letter of intent format to get moving, as it enables the buyer and seller to negotiate without having the considerable cost of having their lawyers draw full contracts. However, this shortcut works only in some instances, usually in cases where the broker has a good standing with the seller.

As a realtor I never hesitate to use the letter of intent if I know the buyer is sincere. In fact, I recommend using the letter of intent in many situations. But in cases where I know the seller will react more positively to the more formalized and customary form of offer, I shy away from the letter of intent.

The Standard Form of Agreement

There are many forms of "standard" deposit receipt contracts or buy and sell agreements used by the real estate profession. These agreements are easy to spot, as they will have a notice of who the printer is and in many cases a statement showing the forms are approved by the local lawyers' association and/or were formulated by local realtors' associations. These forms will differ slightly around the country and may vary with the kind of real estate being bought and sold.

Condominiums, for example, generally require some different terminology to take care of the special items of interest in that kind of real estate. There will be the usual attention to the condo association, the recreation lease (if any), and the percentages of ownership of the common area. Vacant land also differs in the contractual needs as compared to improved real estate. A contract dealing with vacant land often can be far simpler than one dealing with the sale of a residence.

To see how the standard form works to your advantage, you need to understand some of the selling philosophy that surrounds its use. The form is simple and covers nearly every aspect of the transaction in common, easy-to-understand verbiage. If you are dealing with a board-of-realtors-approved standard form, you will have a form which is up-to date on the needs of the area. It should have conditions which protect both the buyer and the seller and spell out in detail the important aspects of the deposits and defaults and the like. The magic that works for you as buyer or seller is the simplicity of the form. Nothing will frighten a buyer or seller faster than a twenty-page lawyer-prepared contract, even though the lawyer's agreement might be exactly the same, only spread out over more pages and in a different kind of type.

As a buyer you want the salesperson presenting your offer to be able to concentrate on the deal and not on the form of the agreement. As a seller you want your salesperson to be able to get the buyer in the heat of the moment to make the offer that might solve your problem and generate a sale.

To give you an idea of what one of these standard forms looks like, I've provided a copy of a contract form I often use. This form can be used for any sale, although it does have some provisions which are superfluous to transactions involving vacant land. There is ample room for the buyer or seller to add additional terms or provisions, and you can, of course, alter any of the standard provisions.

The form shown on the next pages has been filled out as though I were buying a $100,000 waterfront home. The property has existing financing of $50,000, and I am asking the seller to hold some additional paper. See what other "buyer" techniques you can spot.

Deposit Receipt and Contract for Sale and Purchase

Jack Cummings et al.   ,of _3015 North Ocean Blvd., Fort Lauderdale, Florida 33308_ (PH _(954) 561-0687_) hereinafter called the Buyer, and _Hank Bigdeal_   of _Boca Raton, Florida_   (PH _____ n/p_) hereinafter called the Seller, hereby agree that the Seller shall sell and the Buyer shall buy the following described property UPON THE TERMS AND CONDITIONS HEREAFTER SET FORTH AND CONTINUED ON REVERSE SIDE OF THIS CONTRACT.

1. LEGAL DESCRIPTION of real estate located in _Broward_ County, Florida.
   Tax Folio No. _14-869-2770_
   Lot 11 plus East ¹/₂ Lot 12, Block H, Rio Mar Sub. Plat Book 1, page 105, Broward County.
   STREET ADDRESS: _1235 South East 15 Street_
   PERSONAL PROPERTY INCLUDED: _Carpets, drapes, kitchen appliances. The built-in bar._   The pool table in den. Master bedroom furniture.
   Seller represents that the property can be used for the following purposes: _Single-family residence._

2. PURCHASE PRICE IS: $100,000.00
   METHOD OF PAYMENT:
   Deposit herewith........................... $ 5,000.00
   Additional deposit to be paid upon
   acceptance of Contract by both parties
   on or before _____ 19_____ $ 5,000.00
   All deposits to be held in trust by *Cummings & Regas Inc.*
   Time is of the essence as to additional deposit.
   Principal balance of first mortgage which Buyer shall
   take subject to _____ $ 50,000.00
   Interest 9 $1/_2$%; Method of payment *monthly*
   Other: *Seller to hold a Second Mortgage in the amount of* $ 25,000.00
           for a term of 10 years. Payments to be interest
           only for the first 3 years, annual payments
           Beginning the 4th year, monthly amortization
           Interest to be 10%.
   U.S. Currency, certified or cashier's check on closing and
   delivery of deed (or such greater or lesser amount as may be
   necessary to complete payment of purchase price after credits,
   adjustments and prorations). Said funds to be held in escrow
   pursuant to provisions of Paragraph R on reverse side of this
   contract .... $ 15,000.00
   TOTAL $100,000.00

3 SPECIAL CLAUSES: (See page 4 or addendum attached, if any) This offer
   is subject to the Buyer's unqualified approval of a Subsoil Test to be completed at his expense. Said test to be made within 30 days of acceptance of
   this offer and approval made (or not) within 10 days after that. If not
   approved for any reason this contract shall be null and void.

4. This offer shall be null and void unless accepted, in writing, on or before
     March 1 , 199__

5. CLOSING DATE: This Contract shall be closed and the deed and possession
   shall be or before the 1st day of ___*June*___, 19____, *unless extended by
   other provisions of this Contract or separate agreement.*

WITNESS: Executed by Buyer on _____ 19___ Time:____
X_____   *Jack Cummings*_____ (SEAL)
X_____   _____ (SEAL)
                              Buyer

ACCEPTANCE OF CONTRACT AND PROFESSIONAL SERVICE FEE:
The Seller hereby approves and accepts the offer contained herein and recognize
  Cummings & Regas as Broker(s) in this transaction, and agrees to pay, as a

fee __7 %__ of the purchase price, of the sum of ___*Seven Thousand*___ Dollars ($7,000) or one half of the deposit in case same is forfeited by the Buyer through failure to perform, as a compensation for service rendered, provided the same does not exceed the full amount of the agreed fee.

WITNESS: Executed by Seller on _____ 19___ Time:_____
X_____   ____*Jack Cummings*_____ (SEAL)
X_____   _____ (SEAL)
                                              Seller

Deposit received on _____ 19___ to be held subject to this Contract; if check, subject to clearance.

By: ___*Cummings & Regas*___ By:
      Broker or Attorney

BE ADVISED: When this agreement has been completely executed, it becomes a legally binding instrument. The form of this "Deposit Receipt and Contract for Sale and Purchase" has been approved by the Broward County Bar Association and the Fort Lauderdale Area Board of Realtors, Inc.

Standards for Real-Estate Transactions

A. EVIDENCE OF TITLE: The Seller shall, within ___ days (17 banking days if this blank is not filled in), order for Buyer a complete abstract of title prepared by a reputable abstract firm purporting to be an accurate synopsis of the instruments affecting the title to the real property recorded in the Public Records of that county to the date of this Contract, showing in the Seller a marketable title in accordance with title standards adopted from time to time by the Florida Bar subject only to liens, encumbrances, exceptions or qualifications set forth in this contract and those which shall be discharged by Seller at or before closing. The abstract shall be delivered at least 15 days prior to closing. Buyer shall have fifteen (15) days from the date of receiving said abstract of title to examine same. If title is found to be defective, Buyer shall, within said period, notify the Seller in writing, specifying the defects. If the said defects render the title unmarketable, the Seller shall have ninety (90) days from receipt of such notice to cure the defects, and if after said period Seller shall not have cured the defects, Buyer shall have the option of (1) accepting title as it then is, or (2) demanding a refund of all monies paid hereunder which shall forthwith be returned to the Buyer, and thereupon the Buyer and Seller shall be released of all further obligations to each other under this Contract.

B. CONVEYANCE: Seller shall convey title to the subject property to Buyer by Statutory Warranty Deed subject to: (1) zoning and/or restrictions and prohibitions imposed by governmental authority; (2) restrictions, easements and other matters appearing on the plat and/or common to the subdivision; (3) taxes for the year of closing; (4) other matter specified in this Contract, if any.

C. Existing Mortgages: The Seller shall obtain and furnish a statement from the mortgagee setting forth the principal balance. method of payment, interest rate, and whether the mortgage is in good standing. If there is a charge for the change of ownership records by the mortgagee, it shall be borne equally by the parties to the transaction. In the event mortgagee does not permit the Buyer to assume the existing mortgage without a change in the interest rate, terms of payment or other material change, the Buyer at his or her option may cancel the Contract and all monies paid on the purchase price shall be refunded to him or her and the parties shall be released from all further obligations. Any variance in the amount of a mortgage to be assumed from the amount stated in the Contract shall be added to or deducted from the cash payment or the purchase money mortgage, as the Buyer may elect. In the event such mortgage balance is more than three percent (3%) less than the amount indicated in the Contract, the Seller shall be deemed to be in default under the Contract. Buyer shall execute all documents required by mortgagee for the assumption of said mortgage.

D. New Mortgages: Any purchase money note and mortgage shall follow the forms generally accepted and used in the county where the land is located. A purchase money mortgage shall provide for insurance against loss by fire with extended coverage in an amount not less than the full insurable value of the improvements. In a first mortgage, the note and mortgage shall provide for acceleration, at the option of the holder, after thirty (30) days default and in a junior mortgage after ten (10) days default. Junior mortgages shall require the owner of the property encumbered by said mortgage to keep all prior liens and encumbrances in good standing and forbid the owner of the property from accepting modifications, or future advances, under a prior mortgage. Buyer shall have the right to prepay all or any part of the principal at any time or times with interest to date of payment without penalty and said payments shall apply against the principal amounts next maturing. In the event Buyer executes a mortgage to one other than the Seller, all costs and charges incidental thereto shall be paid by the Buyer. If this Contract provides for Buyer to obtain a new mortgage, then Buyer's performance under this Contract shall be contingent upon Buyer's obtaining said mortgage financing upon the terms stated, or if none are stated, then upon the terms generally prevailing at such time in the county where the property is located. Buyer agrees diligently to pursue said mortgage financing, but if a commitment for said financing is not obtained within _____ days (15 banking days if this blank is not filled in) from the date of this Contract, and the Buyer does not waive this contingency, then either Buyer or Seller may terminate this Contract, in which event all deposits made by Buyer pursuant hereto shall be returned to him or her and all parties relieved of all obligations hereunder.

E. Survey: The Buyer, within the time allowed for delivery of evidence of title and examination thereof, may have said property surveyed at his or her expense. If the survey shows any encroachment on said property or that the improvements located on the subject property in fact encroach on the lands of others, or violate any of the covenants herein, the same shall be treated as a title defect.

F. INSPECTIONS: 1. Buyer shall have the right to make the following inspections at Buyer's expense, subject to the provisions of paragraph 4 below:

a) Termite: The Buyer shall have the right to have the property inspected by a licensed exterminating company to determine whether there is any active termite or wood-destroying organism present in any improvements on said property, or any damage from prior termite or wood-destroying organism to said improvements. If there is any such infestation or damage, the Seller shall pay all costs of treatment and repairing and/or replacing all portions of said improvements which are infested or have been damaged.

b) General: The Buyer shall have the right to have a roof, seawall, pool, electric and plumbing inspection made by persons or companies qualified and licensed to perform such services. If such inspection reveals functional defects (as differentiated from aesthetic defects), Seller shall pay all costs of repairing said defects.

c) Personal Property: The Seller represents and warrants that all appliances and machinery included in the sale shall be in working order as of the date of closing. Buyer may, at his or her sole expense and on reasonable notice, inspect or cause an inspection to be made of the appliances and equipment involved prior to closing. Any necessary repairs shall be made at the cost of the Seller and, unless otherwise agreed by the parties, the Buyer shall by closing be deemed to have accepted the property as is.

2. Escrow for Repairs: If treatment, replacement or repair called for in subparagraphs a, b, and c hereof are not completed prior to closing, sufficient funds shall be escrowed at time of closing to effect same.

3. Reinspection: In the event the Seller disagrees with Buyer's inspection reports, Seller shall have the right to have inspections made at his or her cost. In the event Buyer's and Seller's inspection reports do not agree, the parties shall agree on a third inspector, whose report shall be binding upon the parties. The cost of the third inspector shall be borne equally between the Buyer and Seller.

4. Limitation and Option Clause: Seller shall be responsible for all costs of the above treatment, replacement or repairs up to _4 %_ (or 3% if this blank is not filled in) of the purchase price. In the event the total costs of items to be accomplished under subparagraphs a, b, and c exceed this amount, then either party shall have the option of paying any amount in excess and this Contract shall then remain in full force and effect. However, if neither party agrees to pay the additional amount above the applicable percentage of the purchase price, then, at the Seller's or Buyer's option, this Contract may be canceled by delivery of written notice to the other party or his or her agent, and the deposit shall be returned to the Buyer.

5. Time for Inspections: All inspections described in Paragraphs 1 (a) and (b) above shall be completed on or before five days prior to closing.

G. INSURANCE: The premium on any hazard insurance policy in force covering improvements on the subject property, shall be prorated between the parties, or the policy may be canceled as the Buyer may elect. If insurance is to be prorated, the Seller shall, on or before the closing date, furnish to the Buyer all insurance policies or copies thereof.

H. Leases: The Seller shall, prior to closing, furnish to Buyer copies of all written leases and estoppel letters from each tenant specifying the nature and duration of said tenant's occupancy, rental rate, advance rents or security deposits paid by tenant. In the event Seller is unable to obtain said estoppel letters from tenants, the same information may be furnished by Seller to Buyer in the form of a Seller's Affidavit.

I. Mechanics Liens: Seller shall furnish to the Buyer at time of closing an Affidavit attesting to the absence of any claims or liens or potential lienors known to the Seller and further attesting that there have been no improvements to the subject property for _____ days immediately preceding the date of closing. If the property has been improved within said time, the Seller shall deliver releases or waiver of all mechanics liens, executed by general contractors, subcontractors, or suppliers and in addition a Seller's mechanics lien Affidavit setting forth the names of all such general contractors, subcontractors, and suppliers and further reciting that in fact all bills for work to the subject property which could serve as the basis for a mechanic's lien have been paid.

J. Place of Closing: Closing shall be held at the office of the Buyer's attorney or closing agent, if located within Broward County; if not, then at the office of Seller's attorney, if located within Broward County.

K. Documents for Closing: Seller's attorney shall prepare deed, mortgage, mortgage note, bill of sale, affidavit regarding liens, and any corrective instruments that may be required in connection with perfecting the title. Buyer's attorney or closing agent will prepare closing statement.

L. Expenses: Abstracting prior to closing, State documentary stamps which are required to be affixed to the instrument of conveyance, the cost of recording any corrective instruments, intangible personal property taxes and the cost of recording the purchase money mortgage, if any, shall be paid by the Seller. Documentary stamps to be affixed to the note or notes secured by the purchase money mortgage, if any, or required on any mortgage modification and the cost of recording the deed shall be paid by the Buyer.

M. Proration of Taxes (Real and Personal): Taxes shall be prorated based on the current year's tax, if known. If the closing occurs at a date when the current year's taxes are not fixed, and the current year's assessment is available, taxes will be prorated based upon such assessment and the prior year's millage. If the current year's assessment is not available, then taxes will be prorated on the prior year's tax; provided, however, if there are completed improvements on the subject premises by January 1st of the year of closing, which improvements were not in existence on January 1st of the prior year, then the taxes shall be prorated to the date of closing based upon the prior year's millage and at an equitable assessment to be agreed upon between the parties, failing which, requests will be made to the county tax assessor for an informal assessment taking into consideration homestead exemption, if any. However, any tax proration based on an estimate may, at the request of either party to the transaction, be subsequently readjusted upon receipt of tax bill and a statement to that effect is to be set forth in the closing statement. All such prorations whether based on actual tax or estimated tax will make appropriate allowance for the maximum allowable discount and for homestead or other exemptions if allowed for the current year.

N. Prorations and Escrow Balance: Taxes, hazard insurance, interest, utilities, rents, and other expenses and revenue of said property shall be prorated as of date of closing. Seller shall receive as credit at closing an amount equal to the escrow funds held by the mortgagee, which funds shall thereupon be transferred to the Buyer.

O. Special Assessment Liens: Certified, confirmed and ratified special assessment liens as of the date of closing (and not as of the date of this Contract) are to be paid by the Seller. Pending liens as of the date of closing shall be assumed by the Buyer.

P. Risk of Loss: If the improvements are damaged by fire or other casualty before delivery of the deed and can be restored to substantially the same condition as now existing within a period of sixty (60) days thereafter, Seller may restore the improvements and the closing date and date of delivery of possession herein under provided shall be extended accordingly. If Seller fails to do so, the Buyer shall have the option of (1) taking the property as is together with insurance proceeds, if any, or (2) canceling the Contract and all deposits will be forthwith returned to the Buyer and the parties released of any further liability hereunder.

Q. Maintenance: Between the date of the Contract and the date of closing, the property, including lawn, shrubbery and pool, if any, shall be maintained by the Seller in the condition as it existed as of the date of the Contract, ordinary wear and tear excepted.

R. Escrow of Proceeds of Sale and Closing Procedure: The deed shall be recorded and evidence of the title continued at Buyer's expense, to show title in Buyer, without any encumbrances or changes which would render Seller's title unmarketable, from the date of the last evidence and the cash proceeds of sale shall be held in escrow by Seller's attorney or by such other escrow agent as may be mutually agreed upon for a period of not longer than ten (10) days. If Seller's title is rendered unmarketable, Buyer's attorney shall, within said ten (10) day period, notify Seller or Seller's attorney in writing of the defect, and Seller shall have thirty (30) days from date of receipt of such notice to cure such defect. In the event Seller fails to timely cure said defect, all monies paid hereunder by Buyer shall, upon written demand therefore, and within five (5) days thereafter, be returned to Buyer and, simultaneously with such repayment, Buyer shall vacate the premises and reconvey the property in question to the Seller by Special Warranty Deed. In the event Buyer fails to make timely demand for refund, he or she shall take title as is, waiving all rights against Seller as to such intervening defect except such rights as may be available to Buyer by virtue of warranties contained in deed. In the event the transaction is not consummated because of an uncorrected or unwaived defect in title, the Seller will be deemed to have defaulted under this Contract. Possession and occupancy will be delivered to Buyer at time of closing.

If Seller provided Escrow Disbursement insurance or if Buyer executes a Disclosure and Consent Statement, then disbursement of closing proceeds shall be made to Seller immediately upon closing. The broker's professional service fee shall be disbursed simultaneously with disbursement of Seller's closing proceeds. Payment shall be made in the form of U.S. currency, cashier's check, certified check, unless in the event a portion of the purchase price is to be derived from institutional financing or refinancing, the requirements of the lending institution as to place, time, and procedures for closing and for disbursement of mortgage proceeds shall control, anything in this Contract to the contrary notwithstanding.

S. ESCROW: The party receiving the deposit agrees by the acceptance thereof to hold same in escrow and to disburse it in accordance with the terms and conditions of this Contract. Provided, however, that in the event that a dispute shall arise between any of the parties to this Contract as to the proper disbursement of the deposit, the party holding the deposit may at his option: (1) take no action and hold all funds (and documents, if any) until agreement is reached between the disputing parties, or until a judgment has been entered by a court of competent jurisdiction and the appeal period has expired thereon, or if appealed then until the matter has been finally concluded, and then to act in accordance with such final judgment; or (2) institute an action for declaratory judgment, interpleader or otherwise joining all affected parties and thereafter complying with the ultimate judgment of the court with regard to the disbursement of the deposit and disposition of documents, if any. In the event of any suit between Buyer and Seller wherein the escrow agent is made a party by virtue of acting as such escrow agent hereunder, or in the event of any suit wherein escrow agent interpleads the subject matter of this escrow, the escrow agent shall be entitled to recover a reasonable attorney's fee and costs incurred, including costs and attorney's fees for appellate proceedings, if any, said fees and costs to be charged and assessed as court costs in favor of the prevailing party.

T. ATTORNEY FEES AND COSTS: In connection with any litigation arising out of this Contract, the prevailing party whether Buyer, Seller or Broker, shall be entitled to recover all costs incurred including reasonable attorney's fees for services rendered in connection with such litigation, including appellate proceedings and post judgment proceedings.

U. DEFAULT: In the event of default of either party, the rights of the nondefaulting party and the Broker shall be as provided herein and such rights shall be deemed to be the sole and exclusive rights in such event; (a) If Buyer fails to perform any of the covenants of this Contract, all money paid or deposited pursuant to this Contract by the Buyer shall be retained by or for the account of the Seller as consideration for the execution of this Contract as agreed and liquidated damages and in full settlement of any claims for damages by the Seller against the Buyer. (b) If Seller fails to perform any of the covenants of this Contract, all money paid or deposited pursuant to this Contract by the Buyer shall be returned to the Buyer upon demand, or the Buyer shall have the right of specific performance. In addition, Seller shall pay forthwith to Broker the full professional service fee provided for on the reverse side of this Contract.

V. PERSONS BOUND: The benefits and obligations of the covenants herein shall inure to and bind the respective heirs, personal representatives, successors, and assigns (where assignment is permitted) of the parties hereto. Whenever used, the singular number shall include the plural, the plural the singular, and the use of any gender shall include all genders.

W. SURVIVAL OF COVENANTS AND SPECIAL COVENANTS: Seller covenants and warrants that there is ingress and egress to subject property over public or private roads or easements, which covenants shall survive delivery of deed. No other provision, covenant, or warranty of this Contract shall survive the delivery of the deed except as expressly provided herein.

X. FINAL AGREEMENT: This Contract represents the final agreement of the parties and no agreements or representations, unless incorporated into this Contract, shall be binding on any of the parties. Typewritten provisions shall supersede printed provisions and handwritten provisions shall supersede typewritten and/or printed provisions. Such handwritten or typewritten provisions as are appropriate may be inserted on the face of this form or attached hereto as an addendum. The date of this Contract shall be the day upon which it becomes fully executed by all parties.

The form of this "Deposit Receipt and Contract for Sale and Purchase"
has been approved by the Broward County Bar Association and
the Fort Lauderdale Area Board of REALTORS®, Inc.

Notice:

Jack Cummings is a Registered Real Estate Broker and is dealing as a principal, and any profit or loss from a subsequent disposition of the Real Estate in this agreement is of no consequence to the Seller herein. This does not waive the rights of Cummings & Regas Inc. to collect a commission herein.

This agreement is shown simply as a sample of what is used in my part of the country. Not all brokers here use this kind of agreement, some opting for simpler agreements. Personally, I find this standard form to be adequate for almost all improved-property deals, although I prefer to see sellers use a form which has the real estate being sold in an "as is" condition rather than have repair conditions for damage and the like. However, to a buyer the provision of repairs is attractive.

If you are the seller in the transaction you must take a very special look at any contract that has a condition that you repair items not working or any damage. I've seen many arguments over this lead to the filing of legal actions. The buyer wants anything and everything that might be determined to be in need of repair fixed by the seller, while the seller will have a different point of view. Inspections are important, but often there is a narrow line on many items. Sure the roof isn't new, but just because it is old doesn't mean it needs to be replaced, or even repaired, for that matter.

My suggestion to sellers is to either remove the repair-or-replacement part of the agreement, or count on having to spend up to the total maximum percentage of the price for that repair or replacement and take that into consideration on the counteroffer. Buyers should realize, too, that sellers will look at the offer this way and should anticipate the removal of these provisions; see the sample agreement provisions F (1–5). A good way to counteract this is to play the removal.

When you make an offer to buy a property you should anticipate the seller making a counter to you. It is rare that sellers accept the first offer. This will, of course, depend a great deal on the market and your salesperson, but in the majority of instances anticipate a counter. To focus the attention of the seller on one item that you are flexible about (but he or she doesn't know that), then, will be wise. You do this by anticipating what factors of the deal are crucial to him or her or difficult in his or her situation. The inspections might be one area which you might be willing to bend on. If the total maximum exposure the seller would have in the deal due to the percent of price applicable to repairs was $5,000, then you might reduce your offer by that amount and be ready to drop that entire section as long as you had the right to make the inspections and approve of them. In that way you could firm up a deal and if you found the suspected problem was nonexistent then you won. If the needed repairs were extensive, then you could opt to negate the deal and renegotiate for better terms, or walk away from the deal.

You win by letting the other side win too. A smart buyer will put in some term or other that can be taken out of the offer as a face-saver for the seller. One good way to accomplish this is in the terms. The buyer offers a deal which calls for the seller to hold a second mortgage at 10% for eighteen years. The salesperson presents the offer that way and the seller balks at the terms. A counter which the salesperson feels would be acceptable is returned to you. The price is the same, the interest rate the same, only now the second mortgage has a ten-year balloon. You win because you anticipate paying off the mortgage within that time anyway, through a refinance of the total mortgage structure.

Sometimes it can be simple things like asking the seller to include some furniture, or to close within three months, when you didn't want the furniture or were ready to close much sooner.

As a seller you don't want to play around with the offers and counteroffers that much. That is the advantage of being a buyer. However, because you might be the seller, keep in mind that the way in which you offer the property for sale is in essence your first offer. It is here that you can provide your "room to play," and can anticipate the first offer to be less than your offer for sale.

You will keep your negotiations as a seller to a minimum by offering good terms that have some flexibility for that buyer who wants to dicker with you to win a point.

The Lawyer-Drafted Agreement

Important deals might require this agreement, but there's a good argument against its use. I've successfully sold to happy sellers and buyers properties in the millions-of-dollars price range with the simplest of standard forms. On the other hand, I've had twenty-page lawyer-drafted documents on some of the simplest deals that caused nothing but problems. Why?

If you are a seller and along comes a buyer with a high-priced lawyer and he or she presents you with twenty pages of legal language, what are you going to do? Go to your lawyer, if you see any merit, or throw the thing into the wastebasket.

Let's assume you go to your lawyer. What happens now? Your lawyer has to spend time reading each and every word, looking for deviations from the standard form she's familiar with. Also, to show that she's looking out for your interests, she will want to change a word or two, or a page or two, or rewrite the agreement.

Now you have a situation that can get out of hand. The two lawyers start to tear apart each other's agreement, and time seems to go on and on, with the heat of the moment cooling down and the deal lost.

Real-estate salespeople know and understand well the emotions of the buy-and-sell situation. As a buyer or seller I want my salesperson to have everything going for the deal. I know enough about what I want to look out for my interest as long as the legal aspect is taken care of. So in those events when I feel I need a lawyer's advice, or a client of mine wants to have her lawyer draft an agreement, I suggest the use of the standard form with changes or additions to protect where needed.

Most lawyers will go along with that when the contract can accommodate the deal. This will be the majority of the transactions, if the lawyer will acquiesce in allowing the standard form to be used. Some lawyers, however, wouldn't use a standard form under any circumstances. My advice from the realtor's point of view and as a buyer and seller of real estate is to keep it as simple as you can. If you have the best lawyer in town and you are comfortable with her advice, then you should listen to her advice and act based on that. It is rare, however, to find a lawyer ready and willing to come out in the middle of the night to draft an agreement and then stand by to work on the counter, as your salesperson is doing, to nail down the deal.

Every buyer or seller should have the opportunity to seek out legal counsel if the deal warrants it or he or she feels it is needed. The buyer has more time to do that before the negotiations get to the point of the offer; the seller should know where he or she is going once the property is offered on the market, before the first offer rolls in.

Make the deal subject to your lawyer's approval. This is a salesperson's touch to nail down the deal even though there is an out. It is important to keep the emotions hot. You are the buyer and you make an offer the seller might be inclined to go along with. "I'll go along," he tells the salesperson. "But while the price and terms seem okay, I don't know how this part in the offer about my holding a wraparound mortgage will affect me. I want my attorney to review this before I sign."

The salesperson, knowing that you, the buyer, might have a change of heart the next day or the seller might have a different point of view after taking the unaccepted offer to his lawyer (as well he might), will opt to get an acceptance subject to the approval of the lawyer the following day.

Two things take place in this kind of situation that are important. First, the seller relaxes in the deal. He does want to sell, and so far everything seems okay. He only wants the lawyer to check it over to see if it is a proper and correct deal. So he accepts the deal subject to the lawyer's review of the contract and approval thereof. The second and most important aspect is the mental release of the property. Sellers frequently hold on to property in their minds, not wanting to let go. If a salesperson can get this mental release to take place, then the problems seem to melt away. As both of these events benefit the buyer and now there is a contract that has been approved by both the buyer and the seller, all that must occur is the approval by the lawyer. Of course, the lawyer can still nix the deal, and sometimes that is exactly what happens. However, it won't occur often, and when it does, usually it is for good reasons.

Keep in mind as a buyer or seller that there are times when you will need a lawyer-drafted contract. It is always a good idea for you to have a lawyer you can relate to who understands your goals, to use as a sounding board and adviser for any transaction. Do keep in mind the psychology of the deal and try to keep it simple. Smart lawyers know this and will often use the simplest form possible to get across the most complicated transaction.

A Word About Contracts

Throughout this book, I've mentioned several items about contracts that I want to repeat as a general caution.

1. Watch out for verbal offers. Talk is cheap and memories as convenient as the other party wants them to be.

2. Beware of returned drafts of offers that have been fully retyped except for a slight change that zings you hard; a neat technique whereby your offer appears to be accepted, but what has happened is the offer was changed.

3. Shy away from the standard form that isn't standard at all. Some brokers, lawyers, and investors have developed their own contracts. They look exactly like the standard form I've included in this book except they won't have the name of the authority (Board of Realtors, and so on). Also, they might have some standard-looking phrases that are very one-sided and don't work to your benefit. A protection to you is to deal with a broker or salesperson who will give you a copy of his or her standard form, which you can have your lawyer check over in advance of a deal. If the form is approved, you don't have to worry about the little things and can concentrate on the importance of the sale.

4. Never be insulted by an offer or a counteroffer. Too many deals are lost by sellers who are insulted at a low offer. As a salesman, I tell my sellers that buyers often want to test the market. Making low offers isn't an insult, it is simply a buyer, interested in the property, looking to be educated. Don't feel that as a seller you have to counter on an offer that is very low. The best counter to a very low offer is often no counter at all other than a "Thank you, Mr. Buyer, but you had best check around. You'll find the price we are offering is a good price as it is."

THE CLOSING

In real-estate terms, the closing is the stage where buyer and seller perform under the terms and conditions of the contract. The buyers put up the money, and execute all documents required of them, and the sellers sign the deed(s), execute all the documents required of them, and transfer title in return for the buyer's money or other consideration.

However, there is a period of time between Stage 4 and the successful conclusion of Stage 5 that is often the most precarious period of all. It will be after the execution of the contract when the buyers begin their due diligence, that the sellers are in the limbo of not knowing for sure that they have a sale. Emotions can run wild during this period, and sellers get back-out-itus, and buyers get gastro-paid-too-much-itus. Deals can crumble because of the smallest issue that has, at its foundation, a much larger issue.

I have broken down this period of time, that starts on the execution of the agreement to sell (lease, or exchange) to illustrate some of the tips and traps that will help you get to the closing in one piece.

THE FOUR DIVISIONS OF THE CLOSING STAGE
1. Due-diligence period.
2. Preclosing period.
3. Transfer of title.
4. Postclosing.

Review each of these time periods.

Due-Diligence Period

In most real-estate transactions the buyer has a period of time to conduct inspections and studies to ascertain the condition of the property and, depending on the type of property being acquired, a multitude of other determinations. Listed here are some of the different aspects of a property that a buyer may want to check out prior to closing and taking title. While the following list appears to be very comprehensive, there will be items that are very unique to a property you want to buy that is not shown in this list; equally, there are many items on the following list that will not apply to your specific deal.

Items to Check Out Prior to Closing

Advance Deposits. Any property or business that takes in advance deposits will require a detailed check of these deposits. Buyer will get a credit for the amount taken in by the seller.

Advance Reservations. It is possible that there are advance reservations without deposits. If the buyer wants to honor these reservations, or if the contract requires the buyer to honor them, then a detailed list must be shown.

Asbestos. One of the most important items to check for, and is generally part of an overall environmental check. If you are planning any remodeling, this can be one of the most critical aspects to look out for. Having to remove asbestos can be very expensive, if possible at all.

Bar Licenses. Any business or property that has a bar, will have a bar or liquor license. Know exactly what the rules and cost are in making a transfer, in operation with the new license. If the old one has past violations there may be fees the seller should pay to allow the buyer to even operate.

Bill of Sale. When there are personal property items being transferred in the sale, it is customary and highly recommended to have a bill of sale signed by the seller. Values should be put in the bill of sale if the buyer anticipates future depreciation of these items.

Boilers. Heating systems and hot water systems are expensive to repair so you want to make sure that everything is working prior to taking title.

Building Codes. Does the property meet all the current building codes? How does it stand up when you apply new building codes that have been approved but have not gone into effect yet, or building codes about to be approved?

Business Records. Sellers want to limit your review of their business records, particularly if you are presently a competitor. The reason is clear: What if you opt not to close, and you have seen all their secrets. Buyers want to see the records for obvious reasons; to check up on what the seller said about how wonderful the business is. Somewhere there is a middle ground.

Catch Basins. Water catch basins are important when the heavy weather comes around. If you are buying during the dry season, you may want to have a tanker of water dumped in the area to check things out.

Code Violations. A city, state or federal building code violation can be a minor event, or a very expensive major catastrophe and might be the reason the property is for sale. Check for possible future violations that are going to occur as soon as the new law (passed last week), goes into effect.

Computer Apparatus. Property where there are computers as a part of the personal property should undergo careful computer analysis. Are they all outdated, old, or not working properly?

Condition of Title. There are many factors that contribute to a bad title. Some can be cleared up quickly; others can take years to sort out. You do not want to take bad title to any property.

Dedicated Easements. Often you cannot see the easement that runs across the property. If there are some, and you can get them released, then that is great. If you cannot, and the easement is for a potential gas line to run down the middle of your property, you may find your use greatly restricted.

Deed Restrictions. A previous owner or developer may have imposed a restriction in the deed. This may or may not be clearly evident by looking at the actual deed. Often a deed will have a phrase something like this: " . . . and further restricted by those deed covenants that are recorded in the Plat Notes of West Lake Subdivision, Page 7 or Plat book 1084 of the Property Records of Clay County, Georgia." If you look up those covenants (another name for conditions or possibly restrictions), you might discover that they are very restrictive. So much so that you would not want to own the property.

Drainage. Drainage, good or bad, may not affect the property in its present use, but unless you know how it is, you may not know if you can build the office building you want to construct without major land work.

Dry Wood Rot. In areas where this can be a problem, (which is just about everywhere), you want to make sure the problem is not extensive or expensive.

Electrical Appliances. Do they work?

Electrical Wiring. Is it up to code, proper for the present codes, not the past codes? Do you require greater amperage? Three phase?

Elevators. All elevators must be inspected prior to your closing.

Emergency Alarms. Do they meet code? Do they work as they are supposed to?

Employment Contracts. Are you locked into keeping employees? Can you fire them? Should the seller be obliged to pay severance cost? How much "sick or vacation time" has been built up that you might get stuck paying for?

Encroachments. Does anything on or under the property you are buying wrongly cross over the setback line or property line of a neighbor. Are there any on property violations of setbacks? Does your septic tank sit in the neighbor's back yard? These are all possible hidden events unless you have them checked out.

Environmental inspections. Only qualified companies or individuals should be hired to do this. You will want to know if there are any problems. An old fuel oil tank for a boiler no longer present could have been leaking into the ground for the past thirty years. If so, and you close on the property, you might be in for a horrible surprise and expense.

Escalators. Just like elevators, must be inspected prior to closing.

Estoppel to Mortgages. The mortgagee will let you know in this estoppel letter that the mortgage payments are current and there is no violation or default at present.

Estoppel to Leases. The lessee will sign the letter indicating that he or she knows the terms of the lease and that the termination date (contained in the letter) is correct. Will also attest to any violations or late charges or penalties due. Lessor will give you an estoppel of leases showing all leases, start dates, termination dates, rent charged, penalties that can be imposed and other important data.

Fire Inspection. A good idea to have this included in any inspection to make sure that all is as it should be. If there are past violations you will discover this in the final report on the inspection.

Fire Retardation Equipment. Does it meet the code? Has it been properly inspected and refilled or serviced? Does it work?

Fire Alarms. Do they meet the code? Do they work?

Gas Appliances. Do they meet the code? Do they work?

Gas Lines. Are they properly installed? Do they meet the code? Do they work?

Grease Traps. Used in restaurants and other facilities that generate a grease residue (usually when cooking items or dishes are washed). Are they properly installed? When was the last cleanout? Do they meet code? Do they work well?

Gutters. Often an essential part of keeping water out of certain areas (as per drainage). Do they work? Are they in need of repair?

Incinerator. Do they meet code? Are they properly installed and ventilated? Do they work?

Inside Lights. Do they all work? Are they adequate for your needs?

Inventory . Detailed lists of inventory can be an essential part of buying a business or a property where the inventory is critical. A hotel or motel, restaurant or bar are obvious examples. But in some properties, such as rental apartments, having a clear understanding what belongs to the property and what might belong to tenants is very important. Inventory needs to be visually checked, once with the list, and later just prior to closing to make sure things are as they were several weeks earlier during the due diligence period. Often the first inspection can be accomplished with a video camera. Instead of listing each item in a three hundred room hotel, one very slow scan of a typical room, followed by two hundred ninety-nine faster scans is an ideal way to keep everyone honest.

Kitchen Appliances. Important items in homes to restaurants. Do they stay? Do they work?

Landscape Material. When landscaping is important, make sure that it is included in the contract. I have seen people remove some beautiful plants just prior to closing.

Lease Contracts. If you are buying a property where there are potential lease contracts of any kind make sure you are given the current copies to review. Leases can be to tenants, or leases of items that the landlord pays for such things as ice machines, television sets, furniture, and so on.

Legal Description. This is very important. Is the property you think you are buying the property that is described in the contract. Sellers need to make very sure that they are not selling more than they want to, just as much as buyers want to be sure they are not paying too much for too little.

Liens. There are many different kinds of liens that can be placed against the property, or against the seller of the property. You want to make sure that none of these liens that can jeopardize your ownership will survive the closing. If they cannot be cleared up right away, make sure that sufficient funds are withheld from the seller to take care of the lien.

Liquor Licenses. Just because there is a liquor license at the property now does not mean that you automatically get one at closing. Each area of the country has different laws about this so make sure you have this covered in the contract. If you are buying a bar or a restaurant with a bar, or a hotel with a restaurant and bar, then this is a very important item.

Maintenance Records. Things might look fine, but how well has the property been cared for? If the seller had a crash fix-up to sell the property is one thing, but if the property has detailed records on how everything has been meticulously maintained, that is better.

Mechanical. Does everything that is not electric or gas work as it should?

Mortgages of Record. Just because the seller says he or she only owes $100,000 on a first mortgage does not mean there are not other mortgages recorded against the property. You will want to know all you can about the title, and this includes mortgages and other lien possibilities.

Operational Licenses. When buying a property that includes a business, make sure that you are clear on what is necessary to get the operational license. Often the city must make an inspection of the property prior to issuance of the operational license. If there are code violations or the zoning is not proper you may not get an operational license even though the seller's use was grandfathered in. Grandfathered use is dangerous. This occurs when there has been a change in zoning or some other rule or regulation (city code or ordinance), that no longer permits certain uses or businesses in the area. However, existing uses may be allowed to stay, as long as there is not a change of ownership or some other change. Along you come and you want to double the size of the building to expand the daycare center. Sorry, grandfather use, and you cannot do that.

Outside Lights. Do they work? Are they sufficient for your needs? Do they meet code?

Parking Garages. Are they sufficient for your needs? Do they meet code?

Parking Pavement. Is it in need of repair? Does it meet code? Are parking spaces properly spaced? Is the landscape adequate for the current code?

Pending Assessment. Cities often assess properties to cover the cost of city improvements. Just because there is no actual assessment charged to the property, is it common knowledge to everyone but you that next year the city will zap all the property owners in an area, including you after you have closed on a property there, a hundred thousand dollars? Check it out.

Pending Condemnation. A new roadway has been approved, but the road right-a-way team has not gotten to your area yet. But everyone knows it is coming; everyone but you. Check with all road departments (city, county and state) to make sure that there are no such pending events (roads, bridges, special right-a-way widening, tunnels, municipal expansion, down-town authority, and so on).

Personal Property. All items that are not considered realty should be listed or lumped into a common description and there should be a bill of sale at closing giving you title to those items.

Plumbing. Checking the plumbing is a usual part of any property inspection, and should be specially important when the building is over ten years old. Sometimes the older properties will have copper plumbing, which is a real bonus.

Pool. Swimming pools, or decorative ponds should be inspected from pumps to diving platforms.

Pool Equipment. Do they work? Do they meet code?

Property Boundaries. This is a very important item no matter how large or small the property. A visual check with a survey is good, but unless you know what to look for you might make a mistake. Always check the boundaries to be sure the distances match what the survey says they should be. Look for benchmarks or surveyor marks nailed into the street, or along retaining walls. A good idea is to always ask for a recent survey.

Radon. A gas you cannot see or smell and is radioactive. Easy to test for. If present you need to find out why, and if it can be eliminated and prevented from returning. If not then move on.

Restaurant Licenses. The same situation as liquor licenses. Check out what you need to do to transfer or get anew. Make sure you know the cost, and if there any seller violations you may get stuck with fixing prior to issuance of your new license.

Road Right-a-Ways. Just because the road is there does not mean that it is not planned to triple in width in a year or two. Make sure you know what the immediate plans are. Road plans generally extend five to ten years into the future so you can check out that far, at least.

Roof. Part of the usual inspections. Is the roof in good repair, does it leak, is it up to code? All simple items to check. If there are any problems make sure you have this covered in the contract.

Sea-Wall. When the property abuts a waterway of any kind there may be a sea wall or other kind of retaining wall to hold back the land to keep the water from washing it away. How sound is the wall? Does it meet code? Is there washing out going on under the wall? These are expensive items to fix.

Security Alarms. Does the alarm work? Is it up to code? When was it last inspected?

Security Devices. Do they meet your requirements? Do they meet code? Do they work?

Septic Tanks. When was it pumped out last? Does it work? Does it meet code? Does the drain field encroach on other property? Where is the drain field anyway?

Soil-Bearing Tests. If you are going to build on a property you may want to know how stable the subsoil really is. Local code may require you to have a subsoil test. Did you ask if the seller had a recent one? He or she might have done one and that is why the property is for sale. If not, you might want to pay for one yourself.

Squatters' Rights. Not much of a problem anymore, but worth checking out. If the property is remote, or large and remote, this can be critical. A squatter can take your property legally if they live on it, or otherwise demonstrate that they are acting as though it is theirs, pay taxes on it, and have it for a period of years (see your state's laws on this).

Structural. Part of the normal property inspection. This will let you know that everything seems to be correctly built, and that the building meets code.

Sub-Soil Conditions. What is under the ground that could be important to you. Muck, a sink hole, oil (tank), minerals that you can get title to. Be sure to have your agreement questioned if there are any problems in this area.

Survey. A recent survey should show encroachments, all easements, right-a-ways, and other potential boundary problems. If the seller gives you one, and you discover that the survey was not accurate then you may have a case against the seller. Most title insurance will not insure against any claim that would have been revealed (either the claim or the reason for the claim) with a recent survey.

Tax Liens. If the seller has not paid taxes, there could be a tax lien against the property. If any exists it can be paid off at the closing. However, the seller may contest the claim, as the seller could for any claim. If that is the case, then your lawyer can discuss with you options you might have to set aside funds from the seller's portion of the deal to cover that, or for the seller to buy a bond to cover the lien while he or she takes the case to court.

Tax Assessment. Every year the property will be assessed for ad valorem taxes. These taxes are collected by the county tax collector and are generally a total of various community and state charges against the property. Every now and then a special assessment is levied in addition to the annual ad valorem tax. Past due and unpaid taxes are the seller's responsibility unless the contract says otherwise.

Telephone. Is there any? Does it work?

Telephone Equipment. Is it sufficient for your needs? Does it work? Is it owned or leased? If leased, review the contract. Can you cancel the lease?

Tenant History. Helpful but not always provided. Ask for it in the contract.

Termite. Inspect for this pest and damage from them. Sellers can have a preinspection and obtain an insurance policy against infestation and damage.

Utility Easements. What kind are there? Where do they go? Can you remove them?

Wall Siding. Condition, code compliance matters are most important.

Water Leaks. Often you will see stains from water leaks. Are they current leaks? Always double check the stain to the possible cause. If the roof is the problem then double check the roof.

Yard Setbacks. Virtually every building code will have a prescribed setback for buildings and yards. If the building does not meet those codes it could be because a previous modification was allowed by the city. If that is the case then you may not have a problem.

Zoning Does it allow what you want to do on the property? What are the restrictions in this zoning?

Preclosing Period

This period comes toward the end of the due-diligence period. This is the time that the buyer is discovering what is wrong with the property. This is the time that the buyer may want to renegotiate the contract to take into consideration the problems that have been discovered.

The current approach to selling real estate is to sell it "as is." This means that whatever the problems, the buyer will close on the property taking title to it without warranty to any condition of the real estate or personal property covered by the contract. This covers the seller from potential liability later on if a warranty fails to meet a future test.

The "as is" situation is not always good, however, because it almost insists that the buyer have a long period of "free time" to check out the property to be able to make a learned opinion of the condition of the property.

Residential property, such as homes and apartments often have a more practical approach to this situation. The buyer can make inspections, and if there are any problems the seller is obliged to pay for the repair or correction of the problem up to a certain percentage of the purchase price. This percentage is a matter of negotiation (often 3 to 4% shown in the agreement). If the actual cost of the repair or correction exceeds that then the seller can spend the additional money, or if not, the buyer can get out of the deal. This kind of transaction is safer for the seller than the buyer, because the buyer knows that as long as the seller is willing to pay the required amount to fix or correct the problem, the buyer will have no option except to close, or lose his or her deposit (if any).

If the deal is an "as is" or the cost to fix or correct a problem is greater than the amount the seller is willing to pay to fix, then the buyer is almost guaranteed to attempt to renegotiate the deal. Sellers had best be ready.

Transfer of Title

This is the actual closing date. This is usually scheduled to take place at a lawyer's office, but can be anywhere the parties agree to. Usually the buyer picks the place, but that is a matter of convenience, and should be stated in the contract to keep from having a problem with this later on. What is important is to understand that it is not necessary for the two parties to actually come together for this process to work. In fact, it is usually better that the buyer and seller go to the closing separately. Let the lawyers or closing agents deal with the paperwork, and as long as everything has been properly attended to ahead of time, closings can be smooth events.

There are times, however, when closings are far from smooth events, and the following tips will help you avoid the rough waters of turbulent closings.

To have a smooth closing do the following:

1. Insist on the closing agents having a preclosing meeting to make sure all the paperwork is properly drawn.
2. Ensure that each party knows exactly what is going to be expected of them. Who is to sign, who is to bring the check or cash, and so on.
3. Plan to close early in the week rather than later in the week. If there is a last minute hitch and the scheduled closing was a Friday, then everything is on hold until Monday. Start on a Monday or Tuesday.
4. Make sure you understand the contract from top to bottom.

Postclosing

When you have closed there is still a relationship between you and the seller. There may be tax bills that will have to be adjusted in the near future, and a smooth transition of ownership might be added if you and the other side stay friendly.

When the seller has taken back secondary financing, your relationship to the seller may be rather long standing. It is a good idea to be as prudent as you can with any payment to a former seller, because seller's are quicker to call you in default and actually foreclose than a third party lender.

The best thing about the postclosing period is that you can sit back and smile to yourself. You started out with an idea to buy, and persisted all the way from that moment until present. Now it is time to turn back to your goals and to make the most of this new investment.

Chapter 22

THE FOUR MOST ASKED QUESTIONS ABOUT REAL-ESTATE FINANCING

Over the past 30 years I have appeared on hundreds of radio and television talk shows. This exposure along with the lecture and speaking engagements I have conducted has allowed me the opportunity to keep track of hundreds of questions dealing with just about every possible aspect of real-estate investing. In my book, *The Real Estate Investor's Answer Book*, published by McGraw Hill, I have provided over two-hundred such questions along with answers drawn from my years of experience as a realtor and as an investor. This chapter will give you four of the most important questions asked of me during this 30-year period that pertain to the subject of real-estate finance.

The following should help you maneuver around some of the most common problems.

QUESTION 1:
IF I DON'T HAVE GREAT CREDIT, HOW CAN I QUALIFY FOR A MORTGAGE WHEN I BUY PROPERTY?

The answer to this question will depend on the reason your credit is not so good, and your ability to meet the financial obligations of the debt. But first, are you sure about the status of your credit? Many people have better credit than they might think. Just because you might have been turned down for a credit card, or have had a problem in the past over a delinquent bill, does not automatically mean your credit has gone down the tube.

Check Your Credit

Everyone has the right to check their own credit report. In most states you can do this relatively easily, and if you have just been turned down for something due to a bad credit report you will be able to get a copy of that report free. The first step in this process is to ascertain if a credit report was actually obtained, and which company issued the report.

You may be turned down for something without knowing that a credit report has been obtained, and that there is something on that report that the person who asked for the report did not like. If you have applied for a job, a credit card, to buy something on time, to rent a car, apartment, furniture, a television set, or just about anything that will require you to meet some financial obligation, a credit report may have been obtained on you.

If you are told that you cannot get the job, card, or rent something, ask why you are being turned down. If the answer is because we checked your credit, that may or may not be true. It is easy to simply say, "Your credit is bad." In any event, ask which company issued the report, as that is your right to know, then call that company and discuss the situation. Generally you are entitled to a free copy of your report if you have been turned down because of that report within the past 30 days.

When you get the report the first things you will want to double-check is if the report is actually about you. It is possible that an error has been made in the request for the report. If your social security numbers and birthdate match the ones on the report then double-check the items that are shown on the report. If there is something wrong, such as a history of late payments, or outstanding bills going back several months or longer, or judgments, or whatever, make sure that those are items that were caused by you. It could be that your expouse ran up all those bills on your credit card without you knowing it, and as the bills go to the house, where you no longer live, you have been in the dark about this. Or one of your kids has signed your name as coguarantor to an account at the local video store and there is an outstanding balance of $4,000 you owe for back charges on video rentals. Or, the name on the account is yours, but the charges the report says you owe could not possibly be yours.

You can challenge any item in the report directly with the report company, however the best method is to contact the store or source of the obligation such as the store or business or landlord that says you are a deadbeat and find out what the problem is. It could be something old that you took care of some time ago, but has never been picked up as having been paid or satisfied. Try to get the problem resolved as best you can.

When all fails in getting the credit agency to correctly report your credit, then you can resort to an agency that deals with fixing your credit. Naturally, they cannot remove or fix valid problems that are showing up, but when there is a mistake or some other wrongly reported credit item, one of these doctors to your credit report can be a big help. They will charge you for this service, of course, so you might want to shop around to find the best deal in town.

The credit agency and the doctors to your credit report will be found in the local yellow pages of your phone book, under credit. By the way, the three major national agencies that issue credit reports are TRW, Merchants, and Equifax. You will find 800 phone numbers that serve your area and if you call you are likely to get a voice-mail type of system with recorded messages that can walk you through some of the steps I have just mentioned.

Find Property Where Your Credit Is Not in Question

If you have followed this procedure and the end result is that you really do have bad credit, not all is lost. The next part of the equation is to answer the question, can you meet the obligations to pay on a mortgage? Your credit might be in the toilet because you refuse to pay on something you do not owe or feel you do not owe, but until you do, or go to court to get a proper satisfaction of the situation your credit report is going to show that you have not met your financial obligations. But you have money, and can make the payment. So, what do you do?

Find a property where good credit is not some criteria you will have to meet. Where do you find this kind of property? Just about everywhere. You see, it is not the property that is going to check your credit, it will be the seller or an existing mortgagee that would get into that act. Some sellers are so motivated to sell that they are so anxious to get rid of the property that the question of your credit may never come up. Some mortgagees are so anxious to get rid of a property owner who has not made a payment on the mortgage for several months, that the thought of a new person taking over the payments sounds good, no matter what.

Assume Existing Debt

Often you can take over existing debt without having to fill out an application of assumption. This may be a mortgage from a previous seller, or some other kind of private loan that is on the property. It might even be possible to get the seller of the property to agree to stay on the existing mortgage because you know you would not pass the credit report. Often it is better to be up-front with the seller. There are creative ways that you can acquire property without having to ever deal with your credit.

Creative Financing Can Provide an Answer

If you want to buy a home, but your credit is not very good you might try leasing the property with an option to purchase. You can tell the seller that you want to build up a good credit in the area before going for a new mortgage or to assume the existing mortgage. If the seller will lease the property to you, then you can work to cure your credit while at the same time you have a leasehold position that can give you equity and boost your credit rating. Some sellers might balk at this kind of arrangement, but if you are genuine and are prepared to pay something "down" only call it an option payment to purchase the property, then most sellers will come around. A lot has to do with the motivation and the market.

Get a Cosigner

This is an easy answer if you have someone who has good credit and is willing to lend that to you. Many investors have found that a good way to buy single family fixer-upper homes is to find a partner who is a good handy person, who will live in the property while paying "rent" that is actually a part of the investment in the property. The "tenant" might be you, bad credit and all, and the investor a person with good credit, but no time or willingness to fix up the property for resale. The deal is this: you pay just like you would if you rented the property, only you get a piece of the action when the property is put on the market a year or so later after you have fixed it up. You move in, and use your sweat equity to fix the property up. Later it is sold, and after the money person has gotten back the original investment, which may not be much, you two split the profits.

Do Not Let Bad Credit Be an Anchor Around Your Neck

There is nothing worse than living with bad credit. If you have it now, make yourself a promise that you will solve that problem as soon as you can. The quicker you can go from a negative to a positive the better your chances for a future as a real-estate investor. If you are truly up to your neck in debt, the best solution may be to talk to a good bankruptcy lawyer. This can help get you back on the positive side of your finances, and there is no negative stigma to bankruptcy. Some of the most wealthy real estate investors in America have found out that their bankruptcy was their road to success.

QUESTION 2:
WHAT ARE THE DIFFERENT KINDS OF MORTGAGE PAYMENT SCHEDULES, HOW ARE THEY CALCULATED, AND HOW DO THEY AFFECT ME?

True, this is not one single question, but a mixture of several questions that all deal with the same problem. Repayment schedules vary and each has a unique benefit that may be advantageous to you, or not. The key is for you to know what each payment will require you to do, and what options you might have to choose another form of pay-back.

The basic repayment schedules that are used in mortgages:

1. EQUAL CONSTANT PAYMENTS OF INTEREST AND PRINCIPAL COMBINED, SO THAT THE ENTIRE AMOUNT OF THE DEBT WILL BE PAID OFF AT A FUTURE DATE.   Each month the payment remains the same. This is the usual format of a bank or savings and loan mortgage that is self-amortizing.

You buy a new home and borrow $100,000 from your local bank. The payment schedule is set to amortize over a period of 20 years in 240 equal monthly installments at 9% interest per annum. This would be calculated by looking in the appendix under interest Table A at 20 years and 9% interest. This would give you a constant payment indicator of 10.797 which represents the annual constant rate that would be the total of 12 equal monthly installments. You then find the monthly payment by dividing that number by 12.

To find the monthly mortgage payment multiply the beginning mortgage amount of $100,000 by the constant rate of 10.797. ($100,000 x .10797 = $10,797. Remember, when you multiply by an interest you move the decimal two places to the left.) This gives you the total annual payment. Divide this annual total by 12 and you end up with $899.75 which is the monthly payment that will, over 20 years pay both the principal and interest due on this mortgage.

The constant rate is very important as this is often a number bankers and lenders will talk about. The appendix of this book covers the use of these tables and how you can find a great deal about the mortgage payments and amounts due.

2. EQUAL PAYMENTS OF INTEREST AND PRINCIPAL COMBINED, WITH ONE OR MORE BALLOON PAYMENT IN THE FUTURE.   The balloon payment can be all or partial payment of principal in one or more lump sums. Generally a balloon payment is one that requires the full payment of principal outstanding to be paid off earlier than the payment schedule would completely amortize. Monthly payments are always the same until the balloon. This mortgage starts out exactly the same as the payment schedule in the previous mortgage, except that instead of going the full course to amortize all the outstanding principal, the mortgage will balloon at a date in the future. For example, if the mortgage starts out with a 20-year amortization schedule the lender may insist that the full payoff take place at the end of 10 years. This sudden payoff is a balloon payment. You can calculate the amount of a balloon by looking at the constant payment rate if you know the interest being charged and the number of years remaining. If the previous example were to balloon at the end of the tenth year, you would take the constant rate for a mortgage that is at 9% interest for ten years (the time remaining). Look in the appendix under Table A and you will find the constant rate is 15.201 (10 years at 9%). Divide the total annual payment by that amount. $10,797 divided by .15201 and you will get $71,028.22 which

represents the balance of principal that would still be owed after the end of the tenth year. If you were to pay off the loan at this date that would be the balloon payment amount.

3. EQUAL PAYMENTS OF PRINCIPAL, PLUS INTEREST ON THE OUTSTANDING BALANCE.   Each month the amount of the payment due will change. This mortgage is different from the first two payment schedules and is rarely used in institutional mortgages, but can be common in privately held loans, or foreign-generated loans. In this payment schedule there are equal principal payments with interest added. For example, say the amount of the loan was $120,000 to be repaid over 120 monthly installments of equal principal plus interest on the outstanding balance at 9% per annum. First you would divide the loan amount of $120,000 by the number of payments, which in this example is 120 payments. The monthly principal payment would be $1,000. To that amount you would then add interest which would change every month. See the following schedule for the first five monthly payments so you can see how this works.

Principal	Interest	Total	Amount still owed after payment
$1,000	$900.00	$1,900.00	$119,000
1,000	892.50	1,892.50	118,000
1,000	885.00	1,885.00	117,000
1,000	877.50	1,877.50	116,000
1,000	870.00	1,870.00	115,000

4. PAYMENTS OF INTEREST ONLY.   No principal payments until one or more dates in the future when principal payments are made. As long as the payment is sufficient to meet the annual interest due, each month would be the same. If the amount of the loan was $120,000 and the interest rate was 9% per annum, an annual payment of interest would be $10,800. Normally interest-only payments are made on a schedule throughout the year; these can be monthly at $900 per month, or quarterly (three months at a time) at $2,700 per quarter or to any other schedule. As only interest is being paid there would be no reduction of the principal amount during the term of this loan. At a specified date the schedule would change to either some other payment schedule or the principal amount would be due and payable.

5. PAYMENTS OF ONLY PART OF THE INTEREST DUE, SO THE UNPAID INTEREST IS ADDED TO THE PRINCIPAL.   The amount owed grows until paid or another form of pay-back starts to take effect. Each month can be the same, or adjust to a formula. This is a deficit payment plan, only not all the interest is actually being paid so the amount owed will grow larger each month as the unpaid interest is added to the principal amount. This mortgage is much like the interest-only schedule, except that not all the interest due is actually paid. This creates a deficit that is added

back to the principal amount, and the calculation of interest will be made on the larger amount each period. The following schedule illustrates how this works. Assume the mortgage amount at the start is $100,000, and interest is calculated at 12% per annum. The actual payment to be made is $500 per month.

Interest Due	Actual Payment	Deficit	New Principal Owed
1,000.00	$500.00	$500.00	$100,500.00
1,005.00	500.00	505.00	101,005.00
1,010.05	500.00	510.05	101,515.05

As you can see, the fixed $500 payment is short more interest each month. This kind of payment schedule is rarely used as a full schedule. However, it could function this way with a balloon payment due in the future. This kind of payment schedule can be very useful at the start of a repayment program to give the buyer some relief in meeting debt obligations and is better for the lender than a complete moratorium of payments as will be shown in the zero payment shown below.

6. ZERO PAYMENT MADE.   Principal owed grows quickly as interest that was due is added to the previous amount. This is a compounding effect on the debt owed. In this schedule there is no payment made at all and all interest would add to the principal owed. Each month's interest would then be calculated on the growing principal amount owed. Remember, when you calculate interest, you must move the decimal two places to the left, then divide the result by the period of the year you are calculating. If the amount of the principal is $100,000 and the interest rate is to be calculated at 9%, you would multiply $100,000 by .09 and would get the total interest due on that amount for one year which would be $9,000. If you are calculating a quarterly payment, you would divide that by four to get $2,250. Interest due for a monthly payment would be found by dividing the annual amount by 12 ($9,000 divided by 12 = $750.00).

7. ADJUSTABLE RATE MORTGAGE.   The interest rate charged changes to a fixed schedule or a formula. Usually each period between changes in the rate has the same monthly payment. This kind of mortgage is very popular with lenders. In this schedule the interest changes from time to time, both up and down. The usual adjustments occur once a year and are tied to an easy-to-ascertain rate, such as the quoted rate (or average over the past three months) for United States Treasury 90-day notes, or some other clearly identifiable rates. Keep in mind that any such rate can be used, including setting the price of gold at an amount, then any increase or decrease will cause the interest rate to adjust by the same percentage of rise or fall in the price of gold. While this kind of rate adjustment is not usual, I mention it to show you that

almost anything could be used. Borrowers must be very cautious when giving a mortgage on adjustable rate terms. Insist on the following:

- Annual adjustments only
- A cap on the maximum rate increase in any given adjustment period
- A total cap on the highest rate that can be charged no matter what
- Use the same formula for both rise and decrease in the adjustment index

8. GRADUATED RATE MORTGAGES.   The interest rate charged starts at one rate and graduates up or down as the payment progresses. Generally this kind of mortgage starts with low interest rates and moves to higher interest rates. Each period between adjustments generally has the same monthly payment.

9. REVERSE MORTGAGE PAYMENT.   Here the lender makes payments to the mortgagor until the total amount together with compounding interest needs to be repaid. At that time the repayment schedule can be one of the earlier schedules. The initial payments made to the mortgagor are usually a set equal monthly payment, but can allow for some extraordinary lump payments to cover emergencies.

QUESTION 3:
IS THERE SOMETHING *SPECIAL* I CAN DO TO GET A MORTGAGE?

There is a saying that if you don't need the money they will gladly lend it to you. Bankers are notoriously stingy about lending money. However, they are in that business, and unless they make loans they soon go out of business. Once you understand several things about lenders you will discover that there is a right way and a wrong way to deal with them. If you follow all the tips I am about to give you, your chance at getting a loan will be greatly improved.

First of all, lets take a look at the loan officer or other person who is attending to your request for a mortgage. This individual and others like him or her are responsible for keeping their employer in business. This means that the loans that are made should be good loans that will not go into default. Every time a loan officer brings in a loan that goes sour, that loan officer gets a big fat red X next to his name. Too many big fat red X's next to your name and loan officers go looking for another job. With this in mind, it is essential that everything the borrower does attempt to alleviate the loan officer's natural caution to avoid getting another big fat red X.

This means then, that from day one, the borrower has got to give the best impression possible that the loan will be repaid and never go into default. How do you do that? Take a look at the following chart of what to do and what not to do.

1. Begin by getting to know the lender.　When you have already established some rapport with a lender you will find that everything goes much smoother than if you walk in one day and ask for a million-dollar loan. Because this is so important, look at the following five items that will help you establish the right pattern to successfully obtain a loan.

- Introduce yourself to the President of the Bank (or other lender).

- Explain that you are a real-estate investor who is planning to make several investments in the area and would like to know about their lending policy. Let the President spend some time selling you on his bank and their services.

- Meet the President's secretary. Make sure he or she will remember you when you meet her or him by talking about something of interest. This is easy to do if you are observant. A photograph or some other clue on the desk can be the entry; giving a compliment will also help.

- Call the secretary a few days later and ask a question. Be thankful for the attention you got when you visited the President a few days earlier.

- Drop the secretary a note. Mention you will call in a few days and would like to know which loan officer would be proper for you to deal with for the kind of loan you need.

- Call and ask the secretary to please introduce you to the loan officer. This is the key. When the President's secretary takes the time to introduce you to a loan officer, it is as though the President has actually done the inviting. A very good start with this loan officer.

2. Have a loan request presentation that looks highly professional.　Look at the Outline for a Loan Request contained in this book (Chapter 5). Follow this outline as closely as you can, making sure that all the supporting material is typed, and that photos, drawings and other graphics used are neat and accurate. Go to a good quick print facility (Office Depot for example), and make several copies and have them bound with a title page behind a clear cover.

3.Whenever you meet with the loan officer be sure to dress the part of a successful businessperson.　No matter what your business or job, you are asking this guy to stick his neck out for you and he wants to be sure he isn't going to get a big fat red X. If you bring your spouse along, make sure he or she dresses the part as well.

4. Always be a few minutes early to every meeting.

QUESTION 4:
WHAT SHOULD I DO IF I WANT TO HOLD SECONDARY FINANCING ON A PROPERTY I SELL?

There are eight steps you should take prior to entering into any agreement where you hold secondary financing when selling a property.

1. DOES NEW OR EXISTING FINANCING ALLOW FOR SECONDARY FINANCING? Many new mortgages contain limiting conditions to additional financing on a property. It is possible that the existing financing, if from an institutional lender, or from a private party using an institutional mortgage form, also limits possible secondary financing. If this is the circumstance, any additional loans will have to be secured by other property.

2. DOES THE SALE TAKE YOU CLOSER TO YOUR GOAL(S)? This is always one of the most important aspects of a transaction. Are you accomplishing all or at least part of what you started out to do? The real answer to this must be found. Mind you, the truth might hurt, but it is better that you do not start rationalizing to yourself when it comes to your goals. It is at moments like this, right before you sign the sales agreement that will require you to hold financing, that you might discover the real truth that the goal you were aiming for was not the right goal. Be sure to check the bottom line math of the deal too. Have you calculated all the cost that will be generated as a result of this transaction? Will you have sufficient cash left over after you pay all those expenses? Will you end up selling the property and have to dig down deep to pay off things like closing costs, recording fees, stamps on deeds and/or mortgages, and your lawyer's fee, commissions, and do not forget your gains tax to Uncle Sam? As I have mentioned in this book several times before, it is possible to walk away from the closing owing more money than you get.

3. CHECK OUT THE BUYER. After all, you are going to rely on this person to make payments to you. You should run a credit check on the person, any related corporations, and have a detailed information sheet filled out that gives you names of references, the buyer's addresses, phone numbers, social security number, a driver's license number, as well as a recent balance sheet of assets and liabilities. Why do you want all of this? Just in case you have to go to court, the more past information you get, the easier it will be to collect. To run a credit check look in the yellow pages of your local telephone book under the heading "Credit;" you will find several companies that can, for a modest fee, run a credit check on your prospective buyer.

4. Can you improve the security to the debt?   One of the best ways to do this is to lower the amount of the mortgage. This is, of course, a negotiation factor at the time you are entering into the agreement. There are several approaches to this. One good way is to cut as hard a deal you can on getting the maximum price possible. Don't be hard-nosed about the amount of the secondary financing at this point. If the buyer wants you to hold $50,000 and you don't mind, then let that issue alone for the moment. However, do provide a condition in the agreement that you have the right to run a credit check, including checking references, and subject to your approval, without qualification, of this check, you will agree to the secondary financing. The buyer will insist on a time limitation, so on the last day of that time period you tell the buyer that you will approve the second mortgage terms, but only if the amount is reduced to, say, $100 dollars (or something more agreeable).

The following list suggests other possibilities of improving your security to the secondary financing you are being asked to hold, that generally do not show up in most mortgage forms. Remember, a mortgage is a contract, and like any contract you can have terms and conditions that are unique. The only limitation is that everything contained in the contract must be legal.

- A personal guarantee. Buyers like to let the properties be the sole liquidated damages in the event of a default. Hold out for personal signature and guarantee.

- Get a cosigner. If the buyer has dubious credit, then get additional guarantees on the note.

- Get additional security. Does the buyer own other property or stock or something valuable? Then get the buyer to pledge all or part to the security of your loan.

- Make sure you do not subordinate to additional financing unless you fully understand the added risk you put yourself into.

- Have a very defined default clause in the mortgage. Unless your lawyer is well versed in real-estate law, you might find a common place general generic mortgage document that might be more suited for the buyer than the seller.

- Have the right to inspections of the property. This will allow you to make sure that your asset is being well cared for.

- Insist on notice of payment of every other debt obligation, including real-estate taxes. You do not want to discover that every debt except yours is in default.

- Have penalties for past due payments built into the mortgage and allow it to be your option to accept the penalty or to accelerate the payments and call the mortgage due.

- Be sure that the mortgage allows you to collect lawyers' fees and collection fees if you have to use legal means to collect on past due payments.

- Do not allow simple assumption of the mortgage by someone else. This can happen when your buyer later on sells to someone else. That other person may not be as good a credit risk. You can protect yourself by having a provision that the mortgage *is not assumable*. Nothing is wrong with this. If the buyer wants to sell, there is always the opportunity to modify the agreement if a new buyer comes along that you would approve.

5. MAKE SURE YOU UNDERSTAND ALL THE TERMS OF THE NOTE AND MORTGAGE. Sounds simple enough, but this is absolutely critical. Have your lawyers read the documents to you aloud and slowly. Stop any moment there is anything you are unclear about and make sure you understand every word. You will be surprised how few people ever do this with documents they sign. Also, you might be surprised to discover that your lawyer is going through a learning process too, and may find something disagreeable in what was just read.

6. REVIEW AND UNDERSTAND YOUR OPTIONS IF THERE IS A DEFAULT OF ANY KIND. Okay, what do you do if the monthly payment is late? Do you know? Most likely you do not; in fact, most people do not know, so the time to learn this is *prior* to signing the contract that will put you into a position of having to deal with this potential problem. In general there is a procedure that will be covered by laws of your state. You can generally obtain a booklet on the rights of mortgagors and mortgagees from the State Government Printing Office. To find this, call the general printing office in the State Capital and ask. If there is nothing, then ask your top notch real-estate lawyer who is a part of your investment team. The procedure usually includes these following steps.

a. When the mortgage payment is past the grace period, send a registered letter that calls attention to the fact that the payment is past due. This letter may state that if the payment, plus penalties (state what it is as provided for in the mortgage), is received by you no later than a reasonable date (usually no greater than 30 days), then you will not proceed legally to accelerate the mortgage or foreclose.

b. Second notice can follow in seven days as a courtesy if there is no reply to the first letter.

c. Now you turn things over to your lawyer to start foreclosure.

7. MAKE SURE THE NOTE AND MORTGAGE CLEARLY REFLECT THE DEAL. A standard form mortgage and note will not clearly reflect the deal, nor will a computer-driven note and mortgage from some other transaction. This should be cleared up when you and your lawyer read through these documents together.

8. Make sure the mortgagor lives up to obligations 100%.   First of all you must consider that you did not go into this deal willing to be lenient if the buyer is late on the payments to you, or stops making them. As long as you know what to do when the payment is late, then be ready to act. This is not a matter of being tough. It is a matter of being a good business person.

Chapter 23

HOW TO KEEP THE WOLF FROM THE DOOR
Dealing With Foreclosure

There may not be any huffing or puffing to blow your door down, but when a lender turns nasty and the collection agencies start calling at all hours, and you can even feel the hot breath over the phone line, you can feel the cold shivers of foreclosure creeping up to your front door. Well, take two aspirins and get a good night's sleep. Things are not as bad as you might think. Sure, you might be headed for bankruptcy, but there are far worse things that could happen.

Like "bankruptcy," the word "foreclosure" has a ring of failure about it. In financing, foreclosure is the one thing that investors and borrowers alike seem to fear. The fact of that matter is, however, that neither foreclosure nor bankruptcy are the evil monsters that most borrowers believe them to be. Lenders, on the other hand, have good reason to be fearful of their consequences.

WHAT IS FORECLOSURE?

In essence, the act of foreclosure is the legal process which is begun by a mortgagee or lien creditor to gain title to property owned by the mortgagor. The foreclosure of the interest of the mortgagor is to defeat that interest or redemption of equity so that the mortgagee may have title to the property without any obligations to or interference from the mortgagor. The reasoning behind the law is usually to protect both the mortgagee and the mortgagor.

We all remember the stories of the banker calling on the widow who was two days behind in the monthly mortgage payment. The sinister banker would twirl his waxed mustache and then boot the widow out onto the dusty front steps. To many, this is foreclosure at its worst hour. Yet, this is not foreclosure at all. How about the widow? She pledged the equity in her ranch on a moderate percentage loan to value, and now just because she is behind in the payment is she to lose everything? I think not, and the courts would agree. Today, even with all the inequities and problems in the foreclosure laws, they are still much more protective of the mortgagor's rights than is generally believed.

In essence, no mortgagor, by right of most foreclosure laws, can be deprived of interest or equity redemption which may exceed the amount of the debt (plus cost and outstanding unpaid interest, of course) without due process of law. The laws that deal with foreclosure, while different for many states, generally agree that the right of this possible redeemable equity should be retained by the mortgagor. The purpose of this chapter is to take a close look at foreclosure, to see if it is such a terrible animal, and if so, whom does it bite the hardest? An in-depth look at how to avoid foreclosure will be examined, and some sure-fire steps for moving from possible foreclosure to positive cash flow for income properties will be provided.

BEFORE FORECLOSURE THERE MUST BE A DEFAULT IN THE MORTGAGE

The language used in mortgages to describe default and to pinpoint when default occurs will vary. Some mortgages will provide a grace period for payments. This "grace period" is a period of time that comes after the actual date the payment is due, and is generally a matter of ten to fifteen days. During this time period the mortgagee allows the mortgage to enter a period during which the payment is due but actual default has not occurred. These grace periods can be long or short, or there may be none at all for that matter. Even without a grace period, a mortgagee will generally allow a reasonable time for default since notice and legal actions that precede foreclosure would take time, and if the mortgage were brought current prior to a foreclosure being filed, the matter could be mute.

Everyone who seeks to borrow money should understand that the lender expects the funds to be repaid. The absence of personal liability on the note or mortgage does not lessen the lender's desire to be repaid, even though it may reduce the obligation for repayment from a legal point of view. In a loan where security is pledged and the borrower gives a mortgage to the lender to evidence the security, the lender will look to the mortgagee's loss of the security as the primary basis for the loan to be repaid. If the loan is not repaid, the security may or may not compensate the lender for the problems he or she must go through to collect the amounts due. This happens when the value of the property is no longer sufficient to cover the amount of the loan.

The lender's rights, or ability to collect beyond the security, are seriously hampered, even when there are personal signatures guaranteeing the note. Lenders often find it difficult to collect beyond the security, as there are numerous ways a borrower can be insulated from action greater than a security to the loan. The recovery of an amount greater than the actual security occurs when values drop and the sale of the security generates an amount below the combination of principal, interest and cost that is due. This fear of a potential deficiency is why most lenders want personal guarantees on the loan to cover them past the value of the security. Courts sometimes do not look favorably on deficiency judgments against borrowers on primary loans, and almost never on purchase money financing held by sellers. There are both pro and con arguments to the controversy of course, and the situation in your state may vary from Florida; it is a good idea to have a good understanding on how the courts in your state are likely to go prior to putting your name as a personal guarantor to a friend's loan.

When there has been a breach in the contract between the lender and the mortgagor, the mortgagee has the right to accelerate the payments. This means that the lender calls for a full and complete repayment of the amounts due. When the borrower does not comply, the next step is usually that the lender will seek foreclosure as a means of collecting funds. Or, can sue in a court of law on the debt (the note), attempt to attain a judgment against the mortgagor, and then execute the judgment on property owned by the mortgagor. With a judgment against the note, the lender is not limited as to what property to go against, and may look for property that has a much greater value than the amount of money owned.

Foreclosure then is a process that must be preceded by a default. It is not the only process of remedy the mortgagee can seek to collect on the unpaid mortgage. Because default must come first, the simplest way to avoid a foreclosure is to never go into default. This may sound obvious, but isn't. It is possible to obtain many concessions from the mortgagee for allowing the mortgage to slip into actual default under the terms of the contract (note and mortgage) without default being claimed. These concessions will be discussed in detail later on in this chapter. You should know that many mortgagees will do almost anything to stop a property from going into foreclosure. Highly institutionalized lenders will generally work with the average borrower. Private lenders, on the other hand, have a tendency of acting quicker to foreclose, as they either want to take over the property or to protect the possible advance of loss should the payments continue to go unpaid.

Once a default occurs, and the lender does not agree to an extension of the grace period, or to enter into a modification of the mortgage, the mortgagee is in a position to call on his or her rights to foreclose. Prior to the actual foreclosure, however, there is generally a period of foreclosure assertions. That is, the mortgagee threatens to foreclose unless the mortgage payment is made. This preforeclosure period is a maze of typical first, second, and final notices, then letters from the lawyer, and so on; all steps lenders take to avoid having to file foreclosure. Finally, there's the nice phone call from the executive vice-president in charge of collections at the bank to ask if you are having problems.

It is during this time that deals can often be made that would curl your hair. But never count on that last ditch transaction to save the whole ball of wax. Foreclosure proceedings have a tendency of being drawn-out affairs that can be most unpleasant. Dealing with the respective parties during this period of actual foreclosure is often far more difficult than when the property was only on the verge of going into foreclosure. The preforeclosure period is when the mortgagee hopes or believes that the mortgagor will still make the payments. But when the mortgagor does not make the payments, the mortgagee realizes he or she must now make good the threats to foreclose.

FORECLOSURE AS SEEN BY THE LENDER

The attitudes taken by lenders, of course, will vary. The majority of all foreclosures are made by institutional lenders, so let's look at foreclosure from their point of view. Once the mortgagor knows how the lender looks at this final stage of the lending cycle, he or she will have some understanding of what to expect. Most institutional lenders (as well as many noninstitutional lenders) divide the foreclosure action into four periods:

1. The collection period.
2. The preforeclosure period.
3. The foreclosure.
4. The postforeclosure period.

Depending on the size of the lender and the staff available, a standard operating procedure is designed to take care of these four periods. (An outline of this procedure follows.) Note that the institutionalized approach to this very critical event is impersonal. The people involved have very little actual knowledge of the person who borrowed the money or the property pledged as security.

The Collection Period

1. Check calendar to see if payment arrived on time; if not, make note to follow-up within three days.
2. If follow-up indicates payment still overdue, then send out courtesy reminder that payment is due (first notice).
3. Continued late payments will be followed five to seven days after the first notice with another notice, indicating the date which terminated the grace period (second notice).
4. Follow-up calls to insure the borrower is aware the grace period has terminated. (third notice).

5. If the payment is 30 days past due, an inspection is generally ordered to determine if the property has been vacated or if there are other problems.

6. If the property appears not to have been vacated, a registered letter is sent from the legal department advising the borrower that his or her loan is in jeopardy of being foreclosed (fourth notice).

7. No response to the registered letter within seven days will cause the matter to be placed in the preforeclosure period.

The Preforeclosure Period:

1. A notice is sent to the collection department to the effect that no payments on this loan will be processed without approval, since the loan has gone into default.

2. A second letter may be sent to the borrower asking for a conference to discuss the status of the loan and to see if anything can be done to avoid foreclosure (fifth notice).

3. The lender now prepares for the possible foreclosure:

    a. Note and mortgage are reviewed and sent to legal department.

    b. Records are examined; insurance and other matters pertaining to the maintenance of the file and the property are checked.

    c. A field report is made showing the status of the property (occupied, maintenance of property, and so on).

4. A review of the situation is made by the proper authority and a decision is reached on the basis of the alternatives given or proposed by the borrower. If none are offered or they are not plausible, then foreclosure is filed.

The Foreclosure Period

1. An appraisal of the property is made.

2. Accounting and collection departments prepare the status of the loan, total unpaid balance and other costs, indicating the bottom line needed by the association for their bid at auction, and the top line to cover their total cost bid by others.

3. The file and report are reviewed by the foreclosure panel and the top bid the association plans to make is decided; authorization is given to the officer or trustee of the association to make the bid as stated.

4. The sale takes place; the property is purchased either by the association or by another party who makes a higher bid.

The Postforeclosure Period

1. If the property were purchased by someone other than the lender, then the funds received are processed and the loan closed.

2. If the lender purchased the property, then the appropriate departments process the property and files to account for the change in ownership.

3. The property is then turned over to the proper department for marketing.

These four periods described above vary from lender to lender. A foreclosure of a second or junior loan would require a slightly different procedure. If the first or superior mortgages are not joined in the foreclosure and the foreclosure was made subject to those loans, then the junior lender would make sure the superior loans were kept current during the entire process. Once the junior lender has made a successful bid on the property, he or she would take the necessary steps to assume the existing superior loans or give notice that he or she is the new owner.

It has been stated earlier that the lender will generally do all possible to prevent the property from going into foreclosure. Of course, there is a limit to how far he or she will or can go. Nonetheless, if the borrower has shown good intentions in the past and has not been late in making payments, the lender will go a long way to keep the loan from foreclosure.

Why Lenders Avoid Foreclosure If at All Possible

In almost all states, the foreclosure process is often long and burdensome. The time element is the most costly of all, since much can happen to the value of the property while the foreclosure grinds to the eventual sale or redemption of equity. At best, it is not a simple event. At worst, years can pass before the final document is filed and title is granted to the winning bidder at the foreclosure sale. Many arguments have been made for changes in the law and a speeding up of the process. Also, the law often seems to protect the less scrupulous mortgagor more than the one who attempts to do his or her best to pay back the monies owed.

If the property is an income producer, the mortgagor can slip behind in his payments, wait out the preforeclosure period, and prolong that by attempting to work out a settlement or payment plan. Then, in the end he or she will let the lender foreclose, knowing that without any debt service during this period of time he or she can milk the property until the lender can either foreclose or have a receiver or trustee appointed to operate it until the foreclosure is complete and settled.

Seasonal properties are most vulnerable to this type of "milking," and lenders are most cautious about lending in these areas when the equity is either vague or slight. Even then, the loan can be in jeopardy in a hurry since a milked hotel can drop 20% in value over the season. Goodwill can be destroyed and the property itself left in disrepair. Hotels and other volatile properties that depend on limited times of operation (e.g., amusement parks and recreational facilities) will generally have mortgages that have strong default provisions. These provisions, however, do not always provide sufficient security to prevent "milking."

The speed with which the mortgagee can remove the mortgagor's control of the property will vary. In some states this removal can be accomplished in a relatively short time, while in others the time required will be longer. It may be possible for a mortgagor to claim that the mortgage interest is usurious or other aspects of the loan are onerous, and hence request the loan to be set aside. Such actions may cause the entire matter to go to court. But in the meanwhile, the mortgagor may be left in control of the property. Because the matter of foreclosure is a legal one, lawyers can often find many ways to delay the process. Lenders know this, of course, and while they may ultimately win the case, it may be only a paper victory.

It is often thought that the only type of property immune to the effect of mortgagor control is vacant land. Today, however, vacant land can become a victim of the timekeeper as well. In many communities there are movements to change zoning. Usually, zoning changes have considerable effect on the value of property. Since most zoning changes affect vacant land, they can make the land gain as well as lose value. Most rezoning provisions allow for a time period of adjustment. They usually permit an owner to file for building permits under the old zoning by a cutoff date. However, it is obvious that if the land is in the midst of a foreclosure this would not be possible. And once the foreclosure sale occurs the value of the land may be less than the amount of the mortgage.

In most office buildings and other income properties, where the gross income is gained from rents collected from tenants in the building, the mortgagee will have assignments of the leases. These assignments will permit him or her to step in and collect the rents in the event of a default. The owner and mortgagor may still have physical control of the building, but he or she no longer has control over the income from the property. The mortgagee will generally deduct from those rents the payments due and turn over the balance to the mortgagor while the foreclosure is proceeding. Keep in mind that once the mortgage has gone into default and a foreclosure has been filed, the only redemption may be for the mortgagee to pay off the entire loan and not just to bring the payments up-to-date.

FOURTEEN OPTIONS AVAILABLE TO LENDERS AND BORROWERS WHEN A MORTGAGE DEFAULT OCCURS

1. **The lender agrees to wait for the payment or payments.** This is the usual first step option that lenders will hope works. The mortgagor can insure that the lender will go along with this option by presenting a good case on his or her own behalf. However, if this is the third or fourth time in the past six months that the borrower has fallen behind, promises to come forward may fall on deaf ears.

2. **The borrower brings the mortgage current for interest but holds up on the principal portion of the payment.** This option occurs when the lender begins to flex some muscle, but the borrower doesn't have the ability to come up with the full amount of money to meet the principal and interest payments due.

3. **A partial payment of interest is made.** This might be all interest or a combination of all the interest due plus some outstanding principal. The deeper you go in these options the stronger the lender is pressing the borrower.

4. **A lump sum of interest and principal is made and the mortgage is adjusted to change the overall terms to provide relief for later payments.** This option is taken when both parties agree that something needs to be done to stop a chronic situation of late payments. This can work to the benefit of the borrower, especially if interest rates have gone down. Borrowers can simply attempt to refinance the loan to a longer term at lower interest rate, pulling out sufficient cash to bring the past due payments current.

5. **The mortgagor turns over all income, less operational expenses gained on the property, for application against the debt service.** This is the lender's option to get into control of the property without having to go through actual foreclosure. This is not a good move for the borrower and if the lender is pushing this option be sure to get a good real-estate lawyer.

6. **The lender agrees to refinance the loan to provide needed capital to bring the project back to its feet.** This is the option, but what is missing here are the conditions which the lender will insist on. If options one through five have been approached, and now the lender is moving toward option six it is likely because the lender is not in as strong a position as they would like to be in the advent of a foreclosure. Perhaps they do not have personal guarantees and now want to see if they can get that by offering more money.

7. **The lender advances funds on a secondary loan to cover the debt service.** This is a possibility that will follow the similar caveats as shown in option six.

8. **The mortgagor adds additional security, the loan is extended into a blanket mortgage, and additional cash is added by the lender to cover the debt service.** The lender is looking to improve their position. This might be an okay situation for the mortgagor, but the mortgagor needs to be careful.

9. **The mortgagor can give up partial ownership in favor of the lender for a reduction of the debt.** This is not a likely option if the lender is a bank or savings and loan association, but private or large institutional loans might go this direction.

10. **A portion of the property can be deeded over to the lender as a partial or full satisfaction of the debt.** As with option nine, this is more of a potential with private or very large institutional loans.

11. **The mortgagee allows you time to try to sell your interest in the property to someone else.** This is another last ditch effort to keep from going to the foreclosure stage. The problem here is to what degree the lender will participate in this situation. Suppose you find a buyer and the lender will not let the loan be assumed by that buyer. This is not as viable an option for the mortgagor as it looks, unless the mortgagee is truly a nice guy.

12. **Seek secondary financing from another lender.** This is more often than not the borrower's option to seek a source of funds to pay the amounts due.

13. **A deed in lieu of foreclosure (often called voluntary deed) is granted by the mortgagor to the lender and the debt is satisfied.** The next to last step has arrived. Failing in this the lender is sure to move to the last stage.

14. **Foreclosure.** Not the end of the world, but the start of the legal action that might lead up to a sale of the security on the court house steps.

The first twelve of these options can occur alone or in combinations. The willingness of the lender or the mortgagor to enter into any of these options will depend on the nature of the property and the history of the mortgagor. If the property is not worth the mortgagor's efforts to pull it out of default or he has a history of going into default in the past, then the matter may be mute and the lender may look to only the last two options.

The deed in lieu of foreclosure is a most attractive way out for the lender in many situations. The borrower may also look to this as a way of saving face in the community or meeting his moral obligations if all else fails, especially if the impending foreclosure suit does not appear to offer the opportunity for the mortgagor to gain in overage at the sale. After all, by the time the property is about to go into foreclosure, most mortgagors have tried almost everything to sell it so the market has been tested to some degree. Of course, if the mortgagor is behind in the payments by a wide margin, the cost to bring the property current, just in past due interest alone, may make the sale preforeclosure difficult. More on this aspect later.

A deed in lieu of foreclosure is a way the mortgagor can get out from under the mess of foreclosure and allow the mortgagee to enter the property without a long battle. If the property has several mortgages, all in default, and the first mortgage holder takes the property back by deed in lieu, then that mortgagee is assuming the obligations of the junior mortgagees. In foreclosure and a forced sale, the junior mortgagees would have to either protect their interest by bidding in above the first mortgagee or hope other buyers bid in sufficiently to cover their position. Often, this will not happen. Hence, the first mortgagee must decide if the junior mortgagee will in fact protect his or her interest by bidding in or attempting to obtain a deed in lieu him- or herself, thereby assuming the existing mortgage or foreclosing subject to the superior mortgage and keeping that mortgage current. Frequently, the circumstances do not favor the first mortgagee allowing the property to foreclose if he or she can obtain a deed in lieu him- or herself, even if that means the mortgagee is assuming the junior mortgages.

If the property is seasonal in nature and the season is just around the corner, the mortgagee may pay the mortgagor to sell the deed in lieu of foreclosure. The fact that the mortgagor is behind in payments and owes the mortgagee money, does not mean that the mortgagor has any equity in the property. To avoid the cost and time of foreclosure and the loss of seasonal income, the payment to the defaulting mortgagor can expedite the end result and perhaps allow him or her to receive some cash out of the mess.

WHAT A MORTGAGOR SHOULD DO TO HOLD OFF FORECLOSURE

When all good planning and hope fails, and the cash just isn't there for the next mortgage payment, there are several things the mortgagor can do to hold off foreclosure.

STEPS TO HOLD OFF FORECLOSURE: THE PREVENTIVE MEASURES

1. DEVELOP A GOOD PAY-BACK RECORD. THIS MEANS MORE THAN JUST PAYING ON TIME.   Whenever possible, get in the habit of paying early. Mortgages, credit card payments, and the like all fall into this category. If you have never borrowed large sums of money before, you have no real credit rating with the banks on your pay-back ability. One client of mine has never had to borrow money, but he has made it a practice to borrow up to $50,000 at once from one of the commercial banks in the area. He does this on his own signature and asks for the money for six months, but he pays it back in less than a month. The total cost to him is not much since he manages to get interest on the amount borrowed from another bank. He says he doubts the bank would ever turn him down now if he really needed money. I don't recommend that you follow this lead, but a loan every once in a while will establish a good credit rating if you pay the money back promptly or early.

2. DON'T ATTEMPT TO OVEREXTEND THE LOAN-TO-VALUE RATIO. Remember, the best way to keep from going into default is to be able to afford the debt service in the first place. Naturally, few investors would be able to carry all or at least a major portion of the debt service, so look to a prudent demand rate and safe mix of extension and leverage. When you buy, try to take into account the possibility of a reduced income, look at the break-even point, and be ready to risk some capital.

3. KNOW YOUR ABILITIES.   This means staying away from investments you know nothing about unless you are sure you can rely on your advisors and/or partners. Most bad real-estate investments are really good investments, but are made by underexperienced investors. Don't look across the fence and think the grass is greener on the other side. Those investors who are experts in their field make their jobs

look easy. In fact, however, some areas of real estate are very difficult and take years of training and experience to understand and master. In Florida, as I am sure it is elsewhere, bars, lounges, motels, and restaurants are the big thing. Investors often feel that anyone can run a bar, lounge, and so on. Wrong!

4. GET TO KNOW THE LENDERS YOU ARE DEALING WITH. It is a good idea to be on speaking terms with them. Keep an account at all banks or savings and loans where you borrow. Drop in every now and then and talk to the officers about anything except foreclosure. If you are on friendly terms with them when you are making your payments, that rapport will carry over to a pre-foreclosure period if it should ever come along.

What to Do When Default Is on the Way But Has Not Yet Occurred

1. IF YOU KNOW YOU WON'T BE ABLE TO MAKE THE NEXT PAYMENT ON TIME, THERE ARE TWO THINGS YOU CAN DO. First, if the payments are over short periods, such as monthly or quarterly, it is a good idea to call the bank or savings and loan president and let him or her know you have a problem. This is just to inform him that you are concerned about your inability to pay on time. Second, if the payments are over long periods, such as semiannually or annually, you may not want to give prior notice that you may be late: Lenders who wait for long time periods between mortgage payments have a tendency to become very nervous when informed that a payment for which they have waited a whole year may not be in on time. These lenders will think the worst right away and may start planning what they will do the very moment the payment is not in.

2. THE RAPPORT BETWEEN THE MORTGAGOR AND THE MORTGAGEE IS VERY IMPORTANT. The record of past performance is likewise crucial, since a poor record will cause the lender to be most unsympathetic to tales of economic problems. Keep in mind that lenders have heard every story that exists, so keep the sob stories to a minimum, even if they are true. Remember, honesty usually works best when all else fails.

3. IF YOU THINK YOU WILL BE DELAYED IN MAKING YOUR NEXT PAYMENT, SEND THE LENDER A LETTER OUTLINING VERY BRIEFLY YOUR INABILITY TO MAKE THE PAYMENT ON TIME. If there is a good reason for the delay, state it. If not, then merely say that you will be unable to make the payment on time but that you hope to have the money before the grace period is up.

4. REVIEW YOUR SITUATION AND LOOK AT ALL THE POSSIBLE ALTERNATIVES YOU MAY BE ABLE TO USE TO SOLVE YOUR PROBLEM. The fourteen options listed previously are open to you. Look at each one and play with the figures to see if any are plausible.

What to Do When Default Comes and You Have No Real Prospect of Pulling Out Without Help

1. THIS IS THE TIME FOR YOU TO MAKE THE DECISION TO HOLD ONTO THE PROPERTY OR TO ATTEMPT TO MAKE A SETTLEMENT WITH THE LENDER WHICH WILL ALLOW YOU TO BACK OUT.   By now, you may have tried to sell your interest but to no avail. Many mortgagors hang on too long, even when the property is not worth the effort or aggravation. The time to settle on a deed in lieu will depend on the property of course, but you should make that decision early in the default rather than wait until foreclosure is already filled, since it may be too late by then. On a very large property, however, your lawyer may advise you that if you do hang on you may be able to pull the loose ends together.

2. ASSUMING YOU DECIDE TO TRY TO KEEP THE PROPERTY, THIS IS A GOOD TIME TO SIT DOWN WITH THE LENDER AND WORK OUT A DEAL WHICH WILL GIVE YOU TIME OR RELEASE YOU FROM THE BURDEN OF THE DEBT SER-VICE, PERHAPS BY SOME ALTERATION OF THE MORTGAGE.   Sitting back and ignoring the lender's letters will not help your situation at all, and could show a lack of good faith on your part. If you are willing to cooperate, this probably will work to your advantage.

3. HAVE A PLAUSIBLE PROGRAM WHICH YOU FEEL WILL WORK.   You may need help in putting this program together, so seek it. If you are representing a client in such a predicament, then you will do all you personally can to find a solution and will speak to those contacts you feel can help as well.

4. IF THERE IS EQUITY IN THE PROPERTY, AND YOU HAVE A REASONABLE SOLUTION WHICH WILL SOLVE THE PROBLEM BUT THE LENDER REFUSES TO GO ALONG, YOU MAY WANT TO LOOK TO BANKRUPTCY AS ANOTHER ALTERNATIVE. A Chapter 11 bankruptcy, for example, if acceptable in your situation, would hold off foreclosure and permit a settlement of the economic problems. This avenue is a good one to follow when there are a large number of unsecured creditors, because the bank-ruptcy court may tend to be lenient to protect the rights of these creditors. It is not uncommon for very large sums of debt to be settled by the courts for fractions of the actual amounts owed. This possibility should be considered. Don't feel that bankrupt-cy is something you should avoid, especially if it is your only chance to protect all the creditors. Remember, if the first mortgage forecloses and the market sale does not pro-duce an overage above it, then those creditors may be wiped out. The bankruptcy, how-ever, may allow a partial settlement as a minimum for those creditors.

APPENDIX

HOW TO USE THE CONSTANT TABLES
SHOWN IN THE APPENDIX

We live in a world of computers and sophisticated calculators and often rely so much on their use that when it comes to relatively simple math we have to stop and think twice or more, before attempting to multiply $1,554.56 by 12. In an attempt to bring you back to the numbers, I have provided two comprehensive tables that will work wonders for you and your pencil and paper even if you don't happen to have a calculator handy. Armed with a less-than-ten-dollar calculator you and these tables will be able to calculate everything you need from discounts of mortgages, to finding balances owed, payment schedules, interest rates charged, and more.

The first step is to understand how to read the tables. There are two such tables. Table A is to be used for the usual mortgage calculation where the mortgage calls for monthly payments. Table B is for mortgages which have but one annual payment. In each table the mortgage must be amortizing of principal and interest, rather than a mortgage which may be interest only, or have set payments of principal each month plus interest on the balance. In the amortizing mortgage the monthly payment will be the same throughout the life of the mortgage. Yet within that payment the amount allocated to principal and the amount charged as interest will change each month. This occurs because in the early years of the mortgage the amount of interest charged against the amount owed is much greater than in the later years, as the mortgage is continually reduced.

Example: Equal Monthly Payments of Principal and Interest Combined

If a loan was $100,000 for a 25-year period at 12%, amortized then over a total of 300 payments, the monthly payment would be $1,053.25 per month. Of this payment the amount of interest for the first payment would be $1,000 and only the balance of $53.25 would be principal. On the other hand, the last payment would also be a total of $1,053.25 but the allocation to interest would be only $10.43, and the amount of principal reduction to the mortgage would be $1,042.82. Sometime during this 25-year term the amount charged against interest and the allocation to principal were equal.

In a mortgage of 25 years at 12% as indicated above, where the amount borrowed is $100,000 the loan officer of the lending institution would ascertain the monthly payment you would have to pay by using a table such as Table A. By looking under the year column (25) and moving down the page to the interest rate of 12%, you would find the number 12.639 which would be the constant rate for that mortgage at the day it was to begin.

The interest is 12% as shown earlier, but the charges which would reflect both interest and principal payback would be this slightly higher amount of 12.639%. By multiplying the gross loan outstanding by the constant rate ($100,000 × 12.639%) we would end up with an annual amount of $12,639. To get the monthly payment simply divide that amount ($12,639) by 12 to end up with $1,053.25 per month.

It is critical that you remember that these constant tables are an annual percentage figure. To get the monthly payment you would use Table A only (as Table B is for single annual payments per year). Always divide the annual payment by 12 to end up with the correct monthly payment of principal and interest.

Take Note of Where to Place the Decimal Point

When doing a math problem with a percentage amount, remember to move the decimal point two places to the left (the same as dividing by 100). For example, in the multiplication of $100,000 by the constant for 12% interest at 25 years you found the constant rate to be 12.639%. In the actual multiplication you would have used $100,000 times .12639 to end with $12,639.

If you have a calculator that will multiply by percentages you would not have to move the decimal over to the left. If you aren't sure about your calculator then do this following problem:

1. Make sure your calculator is cleared.
2. Multiply $100,000 by .12639

3. Check the results: It should be 12,639 (or 12,639.00).

4. Now divide $100,000 by 12,639. The answer should show as 7.912018 or 7.91202. If the results you get in check 3 or 4 differs from what is shown here, your calculator is rounding off short of what you need to properly compute problems using these tables.

Example: Finding the Constant Rate When Term and Interest Are Known

To check out the table, follow along with this exercise. Find the constant rate for a mortgage that is 30 years long at 15% interest, with monthly payments.

1. Look for the 30-year column in Table A.

2. Go down the page for the 15% interest indication.

3. Make note of the constant rate: 15.173.

With this information you could multiply the math number of .15173 times any loan amount (for that rate and duration) and divide the annual amount by 12 to get the monthly rate. For example, $100,000 loan, times .15173 = $15,173 divided by 12 = $1,264.42 rounded up from a slightly larger number.

Example: Find the Interest Rate When Term and Payment Are Known

Find the interest rate for a mortgage of $80,000.00 over 22 years, with 12 payments per year with a payment of $805.80 per month. In this situation you will use the table to help you establish terms on a mortgage to suit a transaction you are working on. You might have discovered that there are existing mortgages on a property you want to buy that will be fully paid off in 22 years. You want the seller to hold a mortgage for the balance of the deal for that term. She wants $80,000 to make the deal. You can afford a monthly payment of $805.80. What's the interest rate?

Example: Find the Interest Rate When You Know the Years and Amount Owed

1. Arrive at the annual payment by multiplying the monthly payment by 12. ($805.80 times 12 = $9,669.60).

2. Divide the annual payment by the loan amount owed that day. ($9,669.60 divided by $80,000 = .12087) *Note*: It is important here that you make sure your calculator will write at least three numbers to the right of the decimal

point. If you round off at 12.01 then you will not have a very accurate number to work with. Either get a new calculator or divide by a smaller number, for example 800, and omit the next step.

3. Take the number you have ended up with (step 2) and move the decimal over two places to the right, .12087 will become 12.087.

4. Go to Table A and find the 22-year column.

5. Go down that column until you find the constant rate of 12.087% or the closest possible rate. You will notice that 12.087% is a constant rate for 11% interest.

Example: Find the Mortgage Amount When Term, Interest and Payment Are Known

This is a rather common problem that comes from different circumstances.

You may be working with a seller who doesn't know the amount he or she owes on a mortgage. The seller can tell you the payment (make sure it is principal and interest only and that it does not include taxes and insurance, and so on), knows how long it has to run, and even the interest rate. It has 20 years to go, the monthly payment is $805, and the interest rate is 10.5%. Okay. Are you ready for this one?

1. Get annual payment again ($805 times 12 = $9,660.00).

2. Go to the 20-year column at 10.5% interest and see the constant rate which would be: 11.670%.

3. Divide the annual payment by the constant. ($9,660.00 divided by .11670 = $82,776.35, rounded up from a slightly larger number.)

Example: Find Term of Years When You Know Amount Owed, Interest Rate and Payment

When you are negotiating on a deal, you may find that the flexibility of a mortgage term might bring the payment into reach. In this situation you might be fixed at having to pay off a $90,000 mortgage at 12.5% interest, with only $970 per month available from the current income of the property to support the added debt service. You and the seller agree to set the mortgage so that the $970 will pay out the mortgage. But what is the term?

1. Get the annual payment again ($970 times 12 = $11,640).

2. Divide the annual payment by the amount of the loan owed that day ($11,640 divided by $90,000 = .12933).

3. Move the decimal place over to the right two places (.12933 then will become 12.933).
4. Go to Table A, and look at the interest rate charged in the mortgage (In this case 12.5%). Move along the line until you find the same or closest rate to match the number you found in line three above. This is the rate you will try to match. (However, you will not find that rate exactly). Under the 27.5-year column you will find 12.923 constant at the 12.5 interest rate, and at the 27th year 12.951 constant. The answer you need would fall between these two time periods. As a buyer you might try to settle for a 27-year payout at $970 per month, or 27.5 years at the 12.923 constant rate. As a seller you'd opt for the $970 for 27.5 years, or the 12.951% constant for the 27 years.

Example: Discount of Mortgage

When you are dealing with mortgages at a discount, you will find that almost any problem which you can think of dealing with mortgage discounts can be ascertained using the constants.

Look at this question: When I sell my property, if I take back a second mortgage that is for $50,000 payable over 10 years in equal monthly payments calculated at an amortization of principal and interest, with interest at 10%, and I want to sell the mortgage, what price will I get?

Now this is a very good question. A $50,000 second mortgage, 10 years in monthly payments at 10%. Buyers of mortgages usually want a discount to increase the yield of the mortgage for that buyer. For example if the buyer of the abovementioned mortgage wanted a 15% return rather than the 10% rate on the mortgage, he or she would have to buy the mortgage at a discount price that would accurately provide that yield.

To begin with, find the constant rate for the mortgage as it now stands. To do this, look in the ten-year column of Table A, and go down to the 10% interest rate line. You will find a constant rate of 15.858%. This indicates an annual payment (the total of 12 monthly payments) of $50,000 times .15858 or $7,929. This relates to a monthly payment of $660.75.

Now find the constant rate the buyer of the mortgage (at a discount) requires. The same number of years is in effect, so go to the ten-year column, and go down to the 15% line. The constant rate for this yield is 19.360%.

The relationship between these constants is as follows: If you take the constant of the existing contract rate (10% interest, and a constant of 15.858%) and divide that by the constant for the desired rate (15% interest desired, and a constant rate of 19.360%) and move the decimal two places to the right, you will end up with the percent of discount needed to discount the mortgage to permit the desired yield.

Existing constant which is *15.868* = .8197 converted
Desired constant is 19.360
To a percent would then be: 81.97%

Multiply this percentage of discount by the face amount of the mortgage at the day of the discount, and you will have the amount the buyer would pay under these circumstances to obtain a yield of 15% on a mortgage that has a contract rate of only 10% interest.

Amount of the mortgage times discount percentage = Price
$50,000 × .8197 = $40,985

This same mathematical sequence can be turned around to find any part of this type of problem as long as you have sufficient data to close the circle.

Example: Find the New Yield of a Discounted Mortgage

Charles may own a mortgage with six years to go of $35,000 payable monthly at an interest rate of 11% interest per annum. He might offer it to you at a price of $25,000. Would it be a good deal? You would want to know your yield (as well as much more about the security, the mortgagor, and so on) before you said yes to his offer.

Here's how you find the solution to the above problem.

1. Find the constant at the contract rate in Table A. Go to the six-year column at 11% interest. You will find a constant rate of 22.841%.

2. Find the discount percentage. To find this, divide the price of the mortgage ($25,000), by the face amount owed at the day of the discount ($35,000).

   Price of mortgage /Amount owed or $25,000 / $35,000 = .7143 or 71.43%.

3. Now take the constant rate found in step one (22.841%) and divide that by the discount percentage (71.43%).

   Existing constant rate / Discount percentage or 22.841 / 71.43 = .3198 or 31.98%.

4. This new percentage (31.98%) is the new constant rate for the discounted mortgage. If you then look down the sixth-year column until you find a rate equal to or close to this new rate, it will correspond to the yield on that mortgage. In this case, you will find 31.958% under the six years' column at 24.5% interest. In essence at $25,000 the purchase of this $35,000 mortgage would yield you over 24.5% interest should the mortgage go to its full term.

Mortgages rarely go the full term, however, and whenever you have purchased a mortgage at a discount, and that mortgage pays off sooner than the contracted term, a bonus will result.

Example: Review of a Discounted Mortgage Transaction

If you paid $25,000 for that mortgage which has a face value of $35,000, and you held the mortgage for one year and the mortgagor then paid the mortgage off, you would get the following:

1. One year's payments of $7,994.35.
2. At the end of the year there is still an outstanding balance on the mortgage of $30,640.26. This is found by taking the constant rate for the mortgage for the remaining term (five years) at 11% interest (26.091%) and dividing that into the annual total payment ($7,994.35). $7,994.35 / .26091= $30,640.25 is the payoff amount at the end of year one. This little step can be most useful in other financing problems as well.
3. Add the total payments gained, and the payoff. $7,994.35 + $30,640.25 = $38,634.60.
4. Subtract the amount paid to buy the mortgage: $25,000.00. Return of other than principal: $13,634.60.
5. Divide by the number of years you held this mortgage.
   $13,634.60 /1 = $13,634.60 (this mortgage might have been held longer).
   This amount is your average return of interest per year.
6. Divide the average return ($13,634.60) by the price you paid for the mortgage to get the average yield actually earned.
   Average return / price you paid or $13,634.60 / $25,000.00=.5454 or 54.54%.
   This indicates that you have actually averaged a 54.54% yield on this mortgage. Remember. The contract rate is still only 11%.

By playing around with the constants in these few problems I've provided for in this section of the book, you will find many new ways to use the constant formulas to solve your specific problems.

Notes

1. Calculations will result in slight error if mortgages calculated are less than annual payments. However, the error will not be sufficient to warrant that the table does not need be used.

2. A constant annual payment percentage is that percentage which when multiplied by the loan balance will give an amount representing the annual payment of principal including interest. The table given will allow the user to take the interest rate to be paid, locate the term of years, and determine the constant annual percentage. This percentage multiplied by the principal owed will give the total annual payment which, in the case of Table A, is made up of 12 monthly installments. It is important to remember that the constant interest rate changes each year whereas the amount paid does not. This is due to the fact that the principal owed and years remaining diminish each successive year of the loan.

Table A
Constant Annual Percents Expressing the Sum of 12 Equal Monthly Payments Needed to Amortize a Principal Amount for the Term of Years Shown

% INTEREST	YEARS							
	.5	1	1.5	2	2.5	3	3.5	4
8	204.694	104.387	70.969	54.273	44.266	37.604	32.853	29.296
8.25	204.836	104.523	71.104	54.409	44.403	37.742	32.992	29.436
8.5	204.991	104.666	71.244	54.548	44.542	37.882	33.133	29.578
8.75	205.139	104.805	71.381	54.685	44.680	38.021	33.273	29.720
9	205.287	104.944	71.518	54.823	44.819	38.160	33.414	29.863
9.25	205.433	105.083	71.656	54.960	44.957	38.300	33.555	30.005
9.5	205.578	105.220	71.793	55.098	45.095	38.440	33.696	30.148
9.75	205.729	105.361	71.931	55.236	45.235	38.580	33.838	30.292
10	205.879	105.502	72.070	55.375	45.375	38.722	33.981	30.436
10.25	206.021	105.639	72.207	55.512	45.513	38.862	34.123	30.579
10.5	206.171	105.779	72.345	55.652	45.653	39.003	34.266	30.724
10.75	206.318	105.918	72.484	55.790	45.793	39.145	34.409	30.869
11	206.464	106.057	72.622	55.929	45.933	39.286	34.552	31.015
11.25	206.615	106.199	72.762	56.069	46.075	39.429	34.697	31.161
11.5	206.766	106.340	72.902	56.210	46.216	39.572	34.842	31.307
11.75	206.911	106.479	73.040	56.348	46.357	39.714	34.986	31.454
12	207.060	106.620	73.179	56.489	46.498	39.858	35.131	31.601
12.25	207.204	106.758	73.317	56.628	46.639	40.000	35.276	31.748
12.5	207.356	106.900	73.458	56.769	46.782	40.145	35.422	31.896
12.75	207.503	107.040	73.597	56.909	46.923	40.288	35.568	32.044
13	207.654	107.182	73.738	57.051	47.066	40.433	35.715	32.193
13.25	207.800	107.322	73.877	57.191	47.209	40.578	35.861	32.342
13.5	207.946	107.461	74.017	57.332	47.351	40.722	36.008	32.491
13.75	208.099	107.605	74.158	57.474	47.495	40.868	36.156	32.642
14	208.248	107.746	74.299	57.616	47.639	41.014	36.304	32.792
14.25	208.396	107.887	74.440	57.758	47.782	41.159	36.452	32.943
14.5	208.544	108.028	74.580	57.900	47.926	41.305	36.601	33.094
14.75	208.691	108.168	74.720	58.041	48.070	41.451	36.749	33.245
15	208.841	108.310	74.862	58.184	48.214	41.599	36.899	33.397
15.25	208.991	108.453	75.004	58.327	48.359	41.746	37.049	33.549
15.5	209.141	108.595	75.145	58.470	48.504	41.893	37.199	33.702
15.75	209.287	108.735	75.286	58.612	48.649	42.040	37.349	33.855
16	209.435	108.876	75.427	58.755	48.794	42.188	37.499	34.008
16.25	209.587	109.020	75.570	58.900	48.940	42.337	37.651	34.162
16.5	209.738	109.163	75.713	59.044	49.087	42.486	37.802	34.317
16.75	209.885	109.304	75.854	59.187	49.233	42.634	37.954	34.471
17	210.035	109.447	75.997	59.331	49.379	42.784	38.106	34.626
17.25	210.182	109.588	76.138	59.475	49.525	42.933	38.258	34.781
17.5	210.331	109.731	76.281	59.619	49.672	43.082	38.411	34.937
17.75	210.483	109.874	76.425	59.765	49.820	43.233	38.564	35.094
18	210.632	110.017	76.567	59.909	49.967	43.383	38.717	35.250
18.25	210.780	110.159	76.710	60.054	50.115	43.534	38.871	35.407
18.5	210.931	110.303	76.854	60.200	50.263	43.685	39.025	35.564
18.75	211.078	110.444	76.996	60.344	50.411	43.836	39.179	35.722
19	211.228	110.588	77.140	60.490	50.559	43.987	39.334	35.880
19.25	211.381	110.732	77.285	60.637	50.709	44.139	39.490	36.039
19.5	211.530	110.875	77.428	60.783	50.857	44.291	39.645	36.198
19.75	211.679	111.018	77.572	60.929	51.006	44.444	39.801	36.357
20	211.827	111.161	77.716	61.075	51.155	44.596	39.957	36.516
20.25	211.976	111.304	77.860	61.221	51.305	44.749	40.113	36.676

Table A (*continued*)

% INTEREST	\	\	\	YEARS	\	\	\	\
	4.5	5	5.5	6	6.5	7	7.5	8
8	26.535	24.332	22.534	21.040	19.780	18.704	17.774	16.964
8.25	26.677	24.475	22.679	21.186	19.928	18.853	17.925	17.117
8.5	26.821	24.620	22.825	21.334	20.077	19.004	18.078	17.271
8.75	26.964	24.765	22.972	21.482	20.227	19.155	18.231	17.425
9	27.108	24.910	23.119	21.631	20.377	19.307	18.384	17.580
9.25	27.252	25.056	23.266	21.780	20.528	19.460	18.538	17.736
9.5	27.396	25.202	23.414	21.930	20.679	19.613	18.693	17.893
9.75	27.542	25.349	23.563	22.080	20.832	19.767	18.849	18.051
10	27.687	25.497	23.712	22.231	20.985	19.922	19.006	18.209
10.25	27.833	25.644	23.861	22.383	21.138	20.077	19.163	18.368
10.5	27.980	25.793	24.012	22.535	21.292	20.233	19.321	18.528
10.75	28.126	25.942	24.162	22.688	21.447	20.390	19.479	18.689
11	28.274	26.091	24.314	22.841	21.602	20.547	19.639	18.850
11.25	28.422	26.241	24.466	22.995	21.758	20.705	19.799	19.012
11.5	28.570	26.392	24.619	23.150	21.915	20.864	19.960	19.176
11.75	28.719	26.542	24.771	23.305	22.072	21.023	20.121	19.339
12	28.868	26.694	24.925	23.460	22.230	21.183	20.284	19.504
12.25	29.017	26.845	25.078	23.616	22.388	21.344	20.447	19.668
12.5	29.168	26.998	25.233	23.774	22.548	21.506	20.610	19.835
12.75	29.318	27.150	25.388	23.931	22.707	21.668	20.775	20.001
13	29.470	27.304	25.544	24.089	22.868	21.831	20.940	20.169
13.25	29.621	27.458	25.700	24.248	23.029	21.994	21.106	20.337
13.5	29.772	27.612	25.857	24.407	23.190	22.158	21.272	20.506
13.75	29.925	27.767	26.015	24.567	23.353	22.323	21.440	20.676
14	30.078	27.922	26.172	24.727	23.516	22.488	21.607	20.846
14.25	30.231	28.078	26.331	24.888	23.679	22.654	21.776	21.017
14.5	30.385	28.234	26.490	25.049	23.843	22.821	21.945	21.189
14.75	30.538	28.391	26.649	25.211	24.008	22.988	22.115	21.361
15	30.693	28.548	26.809	25.374	24.173	23.156	22.286	21.535
15.25	30.848	28.706	26.969	25.537	24.339	23.325	22.457	21.709
15.5	31.004	28.864	27.130	25.701	24.506	23.494	22.629	21.883
15.75	31.159	29.022	27.292	25.865	24.673	23.664	22.802	22.058
16	31.316	29.182	27.454	26.030	24.840	23.834	22.975	22.234
16.25	31.473	29.341	27.616	26.196	25.009	24.006	23.149	22.411
16.5	31.630	29.502	27.780	26.362	25.178	24.178	23.324	22.589
16.75	31.787	29.662	27.943	26.528	25.347	24.350	23.499	22.767
17	31.945	29.823	28.107	26.696	25.518	24.523	23.675	22.946
17.25	32.104	29.985	28.272	26.863	25.688	24.697	23.852	23.125
17.5	32.263	30.147	28.437	27.031	25.859	24.871	24.029	23.305
17.75	32.422	30.309	28.603	27.200	26.031	25.046	24.207	23.486
18	32.582	30.472	28.769	27.369	26.204	25.221	24.385	23.668
18.25	32.742	30.636	28.935	27.539	26.377	25.398	24.565	23.850
18.5	32.903	30.800	29.103	27.710	26.550	25.574	24.744	24.033
18.75	33.063	30.964	29.270	27.881	26.724	25.752	24.925	24.216
19	33.225	31.129	29.438	28.052	26.899	25.930	25.106	24.401
19.25	33.387	31.294	29.607	28.224	27.075	26.108	25.288	24.586
19.5	33.549	31.460	29.776	28.397	27.251	26.287	25.470	24.771
19.75	33.712	31.626	29.946	28.570	27.427	26.467	25.653	24.957
20	33.875	31.793	30.116	28.743	27.604	26.647	25.837	25.144
20.25	34.039	31.960	30.287	28.917	27.781	26.828	26.021	25.331

Table A (*continued*)

% INTEREST	YEARS							
	8.5	9	9.5	10	10.5	11	11.5	12
8	16.252	15.623	15.062	14.559	14.107	13.699	13.328	12.989
8.25	16.406	15.778	15.219	14.718	14.268	13.860	13.491	13.154
8.5	16.562	15.935	15.378	14.878	14.429	14.024	13.656	13.321
8.75	16.718	16.093	15.537	15.039	14.592	14.188	13.822	13.488
9	16.875	16.252	15.697	15.201	14.756	14.353	13.988	13.657
9.25	17.033	16.411	15.858	15.364	14.920	14.519	14.156	13.826
9.5	17.191	16.571	16.020	15.528	15.085	14.686	14.325	13.997
9.75	17.351	16.733	16.183	15.693	15.252	14.855	14.495	14.168
10	17.511	16.895	16.347	15.858	15.420	15.024	14.666	14.341
10.25	17.672	17.057	16.512	16.025	15.588	15.194	14.838	14.515
10.5	17.834	17.221	16.677	16.192	15.757	15.365	15.011	14.690
10.75	17.996	17.386	16.844	16.361	15.928	15.538	15.185	14.866
11	18.160	17.551	17.011	16.530	16.099	15.711	15.360	15.043
11.25	18.324	17.717	17.180	16.700	16.271	15.885	15.537	15.221
11.5	18.489	17.885	17.349	16.872	16.444	16.060	15.714	15.400
11.75	18.655	18.052	17.519	17.044	16.618	16.236	15.892	15.580
12	18.821	18.221	17.690	17.217	16.794	16.414	16.071	15.761
12.25	18.989	18.391	17.861	17.390	16.969	16.591	16.251	15.943
12.5	19.157	18.561	18.034	17.565	17.146	16.771	16.432	16.126
12.75	19.326	18.732	18.207	17.741	17.324	16.950	16.614	16.310
13	19.496	18.904	18.382	17.917	17.503	17.131	16.797	16.496
13.25	19.666	19.077	18.557	18.095	17.682	17.313	16.981	16.682
13.5	19.837	19.251	18.733	18.273	17.863	17.496	17.166	16.869
13.75	20.010	19.425	18.910	18.452	18.044	17.680	17.352	17.057
14	20.182	19.601	19.087	18.632	18.227	17.864	17.539	17.246
14.25	20.356	19.777	19.266	18.813	18.410	18.049	17.726	17.435
14.5	20.530	19.953	19.445	18.994	18.594	18.236	17.915	17.626
14.75	20.705	20.131	19.625	19.177	18.779	18.423	18.104	17.818
15	20.881	20.309	19.806	19.360	18.964	18.611	18.295	18.011
15.25	21.058	20.488	19.987	19.544	19.151	18.800	18.486	18.204
15.5	21.235	20.668	20.170	19.729	19.338	18.990	18.678	18.399
15.75	21.413	20.849	20.353	19.915	19.526	19.180	18.871	18.594
16	21.592	21.030	20.537	20.102	19.715	19.372	19.065	18.790
16.25	21.771	21.213	20.722	20.289	19.905	19.564	19.260	18.987
16.5	21.952	21.396	20.908	20.477	20.096	19.757	19.455	19.185
16.75	22.133	21.579	21.094	20.666	20.288	19.951	19.652	19.384
17	22.314	21.764	21.281	20.856	20.480	20.146	19.849	19.583
17.25	22.496	21.949	21.469	21.046	20.673	20.342	20.047	19.783
17.5	22.679	22.134	21.657	21.237	20.867	20.538	20.245	19.985
17.75	22.863	22.321	21.847	21.430	21.061	20.735	20.445	20.187
18	23.048	22.508	22.037	21.622	21.257	20.933	20.646	20.389
18.25	23.233	22.696	22.227	21.816	21.453	21.132	20.847	20.593
18.5	23.419	22.885	22.419	22.010	21.650	21.331	21.049	20.797
18.75	23.605	23.074	22.611	22.205	21.847	21.531	21.251	21.002
19	23.792	23.264	22.804	22.401	22.046	21.732	21.455	21.208
19.25	23.980	23.455	22.998	22.597	22.245	21.934	21.659	21.415
19.5	24.169	23.647	23.192	22.794	22.445	22.137	21.864	21.622
19.75	24.358	23.839	23.387	22.992	22.645	22.340	22.070	21.831
20	24.548	24.032	23.583	23.191	22.847	22.544	22.276	22.039
20.25	24.738	24.225	23.779	23.390	23.048	22.748	22.483	22.249

Table A (*continued*)

% INTEREST	12.5	13	13.5	14	14.5	15	15.5	16
8	12.680	12.397	12.136	11.896	11.674	11.468	11.277	11.099
8.25	12.847	12.565	12.306	12.067	11.846	11.642	11.452	11.276
8.5	13.015	12.734	12.477	12.239	12.020	11.817	11.629	11.454
8.75	13.184	12.905	12.649	12.413	12.195	11.994	11.807	11.633
9	13.354	13.076	12.822	12.587	12.371	12.171	11.986	11.814
9.25	13.525	13.249	12.996	12.763	12.549	12.350	12.167	11.996
9.5	13.697	13.423	13.172	12.940	12.727	12.531	12.349	12.180
9.75	13.870	13.598	13.348	13.119	12.908	12.712	12.532	12.365
10	14.045	13.774	13.526	13.299	13.089	12.895	12.717	12.551
10.25	14.220	13.952	13.705	13.479	13.271	13.079	12.902	12.738
10.5	14.397	14.130	13.886	13.661	13.455	13.265	13.089	12.927
10.75	14.575	14.310	14.067	13.844	13.640	13.451	13.278	13.117
11	14.754	14.490	14.249	14.029	13.826	13.639	13.467	13.308
11.25	14.934	14.672	14.433	14.214	14.013	13.828	13.658	13.500
11.5	15.115	14.855	14.618	14.401	14.202	14.018	13.850	13.694
11.75	15.297	15.039	14.804	14.588	14.391	14.210	14.043	13.889
12	15.480	15.224	14.991	14.777	14.582	14.402	14.237	14.085
12.25	15.664	15.410	15.179	14.967	14.773	14.596	14.432	14.282
12.5	15.849	15.597	15.368	15.158	14.966	14.790	14.629	14.480
12.75	16.035	15.785	15.558	15.350	15.160	14.986	14.826	14.679
13	16.223	15.975	15.749	15.543	15.355	15.183	15.025	14.880
13.25	16.411	16.165	15.941	15.737	15.551	15.381	15.225	15.081
13.5	16.600	16.356	16.134	15.932	15.748	15.580	15.425	15.284
13.75	16.790	16.548	16.329	16.129	15.946	15.780	15.627	15.488
14	16.981	16.741	16.524	16.326	16.146	15.981	15.830	15.692
14.25	17.173	16.935	16.720	16.524	16.346	16.183	16.034	15.898
14.5	17.366	17.130	16.917	16.723	16.547	16.386	16.239	16.105
14.75	17.560	17.326	17.115	16.923	16.749	16.590	16.445	16.313
15	17.755	17.523	17.314	17.124	16.952	16.795	16.652	16.521
15.25	17.950	17.721	17.514	17.327	17.156	17.001	16.860	16.731
15.5	18.147	17.920	17.715	17.530	17.361	17.208	17.069	16.941
15.75	18.344	18.120	17.917	17.733	17.567	17.416	17.278	17.153
16	18.543	18.320	18.120	17.938	17.774	17.624	17.489	17.365
16.25	18.742	18.522	18.323	18.144	17.981	17.834	17.700	17.579
16.5	18.942	18.724	18.528	18.350	18.190	18.045	17.913	17.793
16.75	19.143	18.928	18.733	18.558	18.399	18.256	18.126	18.008
17	19.345	19.132	18.939	18.766	18.610	18.468	18.340	18.224
17.25	19.548	19.336	19.146	18.975	18.821	18.681	18.555	18.440
17.5	19.751	19.542	19.354	19.185	19.033	18.895	18.770	18.658
17.75	19.956	19.749	19.563	19.396	19.245	19.110	18.987	18.876
18	20.161	19.956	19.772	19.607	19.459	19.325	19.204	19.095
18.25	20.367	20.164	19.983	19.820	19.673	19.541	19.422	19.315
18.5	20.573	20.373	20.194	20.033	19.888	19.758	19.641	19.535
18.75	20.781	20.583	20.406	20.247	20.104	19.976	19.861	19.757
19	20.989	20.793	20.618	20.461	20.321	20.195	20.081	19.979
19.25	21.198	21.004	20.831	20.677	20.538	20.414	20.302	20.201
19.5	21.408	21.216	21.046	20.893	20.756	20.634	20.524	20.425
19.75	21.618	21.429	21.260	21.110	20.975	20.854	20.746	20.649
20	21.829	21.642	21.476	21.327	21.194	21.076	20.969	20.874
20.25	22.041	21.856	21.692	21.545	21.414	21.297	21.193	21.099

Table A (*continued*)

% INTEREST	YEARS							
	16.5	17	17.5	18	18.5	19	19.5	20
8	10.934	10.779	10.635	10.500	10.373	10.254	10.142	10.037
8.25	11.112	10.958	10.815	10.682	10.556	10.439	10.328	10.225
8.5	11.291	11.140	10.998	10.866	10.742	10.625	10.516	10.414
8.75	11.472	11.322	11.182	11.051	10.928	10.813	10.706	10.605
9	11.655	11.506	11.367	11.237	11.116	11.003	10.897	10.797
9.25	11.838	11.691	11.554	11.426	11.306	11.194	11.089	10.990
9.5	12.023	11.877	11.742	11.615	11.497	11.386	11.283	11.186
9.75	12.210	12.065	11.931	11.806	11.689	11.580	11.478	11.382
10	12.397	12.255	12.122	11.998	11.883	11.775	11.675	11.580
10.25	12.586	12.445	12.314	12.192	12.078	11.972	11.872	11.780
10.5	12.777	12.637	12.507	12.387	12.274	12.170	12.072	11.981
10.75	12.968	12.830	12.702	12.583	12.472	12.369	12.273	12.183
11	13.161	13.025	12.898	12.781	12.671	12.570	12.475	12.386
11.25	13.355	13.220	13.095	12.979	12.872	12.771	12.678	12.591
11.5	13.550	13.417	13.294	13.180	13.073	12.975	12.883	12.797
11.75	13.747	13.615	13.494	13.381	13.276	13.179	13.089	13.005
12	13.944	13.815	13.695	13.583	13.480	13.385	13.296	13.213
12.25	14.143	14.015	13.897	13.787	13.686	13.591	13.504	13.423
12.5	14.343	14.217	14.100	13.992	13.892	13.799	13.713	13.634
12.75	14.544	14.419	14.304	14.198	14.100	14.009	13.924	13.846
13	14.746	14.623	14.510	14.405	14.308	14.219	14.136	14.059
13.25	14.950	14.828	14.717	14.613	14.518	14.430	14.349	14.273
13.5	15.154	15.034	14.924	14.823	14.729	14.643	14.562	14.488
13.75	15.359	15.242	15.133	15.033	14.941	14.856	14.777	14.705
14	15.566	15.450	15.343	15.245	15.154	15.071	14.993	14.922
14.25	15.773	15.659	15.554	15.457	15.368	15.286	15.210	15.141
14.5	15.982	15.869	15.766	15.671	15.583	15.503	15.428	15.360
14.75	16.191	16.080	15.978	15.885	15.799	15.720	15.647	15.580
15	16.402	16.292	16.192	16.100	16.016	15.938	15.867	15.801
15.25	16.613	16.506	16.407	16.317	16.234	16.158	16.088	16.024
15.5	16.826	16.720	16.623	16.534	16.453	16.378	16.309	16.247
15.75	17.039	16.934	16.839	16.752	16.672	16.599	16.532	16.470
16	17.253	17.150	17.057	16.971	16.893	16.821	16.755	16.695
16.25	17.468	17.367	17.275	17.191	17.114	17.044	16.979	16.921
16.5	17.684	17.585	17.494	17.412	17.336	17.267	17.204	17.147
16.75	17.901	17.803	17.714	17.633	17.559	17.492	17.430	17.374
17	18.118	18.022	17.935	17.855	17.783	17.717	17.657	17.602
17.25	18.336	18.242	18.156	18.078	18.007	17.943	17.884	17.830
17.5	18.556	18.463	18.379	18.302	18.233	18.169	18.112	18.059
17.75	18.776	18.685	18.602	18.527	18.459	18.397	18.341	18.289
18	18.996	18.907	18.826	18.752	18.686	18.625	18.570	18.520
18.25	19.218	19.130	19.050	18.978	18.913	18.854	18.800	18.751
18.5	19.440	19.354	19.276	19.205	19.141	19.083	19.031	18.983
18.75	19.663	19.578	19.502	19.433	19.370	19.313	19.262	19.215
19	19.887	19.803	19.728	19.661	19.599	19.544	19.494	19.448
19.25	20.111	20.029	19.956	19.889	19.829	19.775	19.726	19.682
19.5	20.336	20.256	20.184	20.119	20.060	20.007	19.959	19.916
19.75	20.562	20.483	20.412	20.349	20.291	20.240	20.193	20.151
20	20.788	20.711	20.642	20.579	20.523	20.473	20.427	20.386
20.25	21.015	20.939	20.871	20.810	20.755	20.706	20.662	20.622

Table A (*continued*)

% INTEREST	YEARS							
	20.5	21	21.5	22	22.5	23	23.5	24
8	9.938	9.845	9.757	9.674	9.596	9.521	9.451	9.385
8.25	10.127	10.035	9.948	9.867	9.789	9.716	9.647	9.582
8.5	10.318	10.227	10.142	10.061	9.985	9.913	9.845	9.781
8.75	10.510	10.420	10.336	10.257	10.182	10.111	10.045	9.982
9	10.703	10.615	10.532	10.454	10.381	10.311	10.246	10.184
9.25	10.898	10.811	10.730	10.653	10.581	10.513	10.449	10.388
9.5	11.095	11.009	10.929	10.854	10.783	10.716	10.653	10.593
9.75	11.293	11.209	11.130	11.056	10.986	10.920	10.858	10.800
10	11.492	11.409	11.332	11.259	11.191	11.126	11.066	11.009
10.25	11.693	11.612	11.535	11.464	11.397	11.334	11.274	11.219
10.5	11.895	11.815	11.740	11.670	11.604	11.542	11.484	11.430
10.75	12.099	12.020	11.947	11.878	11.813	11.753	11.696	11.642
11	12.304	12.226	12.154	12.087	12.023	11.964	11.908	11.856
11.25	12.510	12.434	12.363	12.297	12.235	12.177	12.123	12.072
11.5	12.717	12.643	12.573	12.509	12.448	12.391	12.338	12.288
11.75	12.926	12.853	12.785	12.721	12.662	12.606	12.554	12.506
12	13.136	13.064	12.998	12.935	12.877	12.823	12.772	12.725
12.25	13.347	13.277	13.211	13.150	13.093	13.040	12.991	12.945
12.5	13.560	13.491	13.426	13.367	13.311	13.259	13.211	13.166
12.75	13.773	13.705	13.643	13.584	13.530	13.479	13.432	13.388
13	13.988	13.921	13.860	13.803	13.750	13.700	13.654	13.611
13.25	14.203	14.138	14.078	14.022	13.970	13.922	13.877	13.835
13.5	14.420	14.356	14.298	14.243	14.192	14.145	14.101	14.061
13.75	14.638	14.576	14.518	14.465	14.415	14.369	14.327	14.287
14	14.856	14.796	14.739	14.687	14.639	14.594	14.553	14.514
14.25	15.076	15.017	14.962	14.911	14.864	14.820	14.780	14.742
14.5	15.297	15.239	15.185	15.135	15.089	15.047	15.007	14.971
14.75	15.519	15.462	15.409	15.361	15.316	15.274	15.236	15.201
15	15.741	15.685	15.634	15.587	15.543	15.503	15.466	15.431
15.25	15.965	15.910	15.860	15.814	15.771	15.732	15.696	15.662
15.5	16.189	16.136	16.087	16.042	16.000	15.962	15.927	15.894
15.75	16.414	16.362	16.314	16.270	16.230	16.193	16.159	16.127
16	16.640	16.589	16.543	16.500	16.461	16.424	16.391	16.361
16.25	16.867	16.817	16.772	16.730	16.692	16.657	16.624	16.595
16.5	17.094	17.046	17.002	16.961	16.924	16.890	16.858	16.830
16.75	17.322	17.275	17.232	17.193	17.156	17.123	17.093	17.065
17	17.551	17.505	17.463	17.425	17.390	17.358	17.328	17.301
17.25	17.781	17.736	17.695	17.658	17.624	17.592	17.564	17.538
17.5	18.011	17.968	17.928	17.891	17.858	17.828	17.800	17.775
17.75	18.242	18.200	18.161	18.126	18.093	18.064	18.037	18.012
18	18.474	18.433	18.395	18.360	18.329	18.300	18.274	18.251
18.25	18.706	18.666	18.629	18.596	18.565	18.538	18.512	18.489
18.5	18.939	18.900	18.864	18.832	18.802	18.775	18.751	18.729
18.75	19.173	19.135	19.100	19.068	19.039	19.013	18.990	18.968
19	19.407	19.370	19.336	19.305	19.277	19.252	19.229	19.208
19.25	19.642	19.605	19.572	19.543	19.516	19.491	19.469	19.449
19.5	19.877	19.842	19.810	19.781	19.754	19.731	19.709	19.690
19.75	20.113	20.078	20.047	20.019	19.994	19.971	19.950	19.931
20	20.349	20.315	20.285	20.258	20.233	20.211	20.191	20.173
20.25	20.586	20.553	20.524	20.497	20.473	20.452	20.432	20.415

Table A (*continued*)

% INTEREST	24.5	25	25.5	26	26.5	27	27.5	28
				YEARS				
8	9.322	9.262	9.205	9.151	9.100	9.051	9.005	8.961
8.25	9.520	9.461	9.406	9.353	9.303	9.255	9.210	9.167
8.5	9.720	9.663	9.608	9.557	9.508	9.461	9.417	9.375
8.75	9.922	9.866	9.812	9.762	9.714	9.669	9.625	9.585
9	10.126	10.070	10.018	9.969	9.922	9.878	9.836	9.796
9.25	10.331	10.277	10.226	10.177	10.131	10.088	10.047	10.008
9.5	10.537	10.484	10.434	10.387	10.343	10.300	10.260	10.223
9.75	10.745	10.694	10.645	10.599	10.555	10.514	10.475	10.438
10	10.955	10.904	10.857	10.812	10.769	10.729	10.691	10.656
10.25	11.166	11.117	11.070	11.026	10.985	10.946	10.909	10.874
10.5	11.378	11.330	11.285	11.242	11.202	11.164	11.128	11.094
10.75	11.592	11.545	11.501	11.459	11.420	11.383	11.348	11.315
11	11.807	11.761	11.718	11.678	11.639	11.603	11.570	11.538
11.25	12.024	11.979	11.937	11.897	11.860	11.825	11.792	11.761
11.5	12.241	12.198	12.157	12.118	12.082	12.048	12.016	11.986
11.75	12.460	12.418	12.378	12.340	12.305	12.272	12.241	12.212
12	12.680	12.639	12.600	12.563	12.529	12.497	12.467	12.439
12.25	12.901	12.861	12.823	12.788	12.755	12.724	12.695	12.667
12.5	13.124	13.084	13.047	13.013	12.981	12.951	12.923	12.897
12.75	13.347	13.309	13.273	13.240	13.208	13.179	13.152	13.127
13	13.571	13.534	13.499	13.467	13.437	13.409	13.382	13.358
13.25	13.797	13.760	13.727	13.695	13.666	13.639	13.613	13.589
13.5	14.023	13.988	13.955	13.925	13.896	13.870	13.845	13.822
13.75	14.250	14.216	14.184	14.155	14.127	14.102	14.078	14.056
14	14.478	14.445	14.414	14.386	14.359	14.334	14.311	14.290
14.25	14.707	14.675	14.645	14.618	14.592	14.568	14.546	14.525
14.5	14.937	14.906	14.877	14.850	14.825	14.802	14.781	14.761
14.75	15.168	15.138	15.110	15.084	15.059	15.037	15.016	14.997
15	15.399	15.370	15.343	15.318	15.294	15.273	15.253	15.234
15.25	15.632	15.603	15.577	15.552	15.530	15.509	15.490	15.472
15.5	15.865	15.837	15.811	15.788	15.766	15.746	15.728	15.711
15.75	16.098	16.071	16.047	16.024	16.003	15.984	15.966	15.950
16	16.333	16.307	16.283	16.261	16.241	16.222	16.205	16.189
16.25	16.568	16.542	16.519	16.498	16.479	16.461	16.444	16.429
16.5	16.803	16.779	16.757	16.736	16.717	16.700	16.684	16.669
16.75	17.039	17.016	16.994	16.975	16.957	16.940	16.925	16.910
17	17.276	17.254	17.233	17.214	17.196	17.180	17.165	17.152
17.25	17.514	17.492	17.472	17.453	17.436	17.421	17.407	17.394
17.5	17.752	17.730	17.711	17.693	17.677	17.662	17.649	17.636
17.75	17.990	17.970	17.951	17.934	17.918	17.904	17.891	17.879
18	18.229	18.209	18.191	18.175	18.160	18.146	18.133	18.122
18.25	18.468	18.449	18.432	18.416	18.401	18.388	18.376	18.365
18.5	18.708	18.690	18.673	18.658	18.644	18.631	18.619	18.609
18.75	18.949	18.931	18.915	18.900	18.886	18.874	18.863	18.853
19	19.189	19.172	19.157	19.142	19.129	19.118	19.107	19.097
19.25	19.431	19.414	19.399	19.385	19.373	19.362	19.351	19.342
19.5	19.672	19.656	19.642	19.628	19.617	19.606	19.596	19.587
19.75	19.914	19.899	19.885	19.872	19.861	19.850	19.841	19.832
20	20.156	20.141	20.128	20.116	20.105	20.095	20.086	20.078
20.25	20.399	20.385	20.372	20.360	20.349	20.340	20.331	20.323

Table A (*continued*)

% INTEREST	YEARS							
	28.5	29	29.5	30	30.5	31	31.5	32
8	8.919	8.879	8.841	8.805	8.771	8.738	8.706	8.676
8.25	9.126	9.087	9.050	9.015	8.982	8.950	8.919	8.890
8.5	9.335	9.297	9.261	9.227	9.194	9.163	9.134	9.106
8.75	9.546	9.509	9.474	9.440	9.409	9.379	9.350	9.323
9	9.758	9.722	9.688	9.656	9.625	9.596	9.568	9.541
9.25	9.972	9.937	9.904	9.872	9.842	9.814	9.787	9.762
9.5	10.187	10.153	10.121	10.090	10.061	10.034	10.008	9.983
9.75	10.404	10.371	10.339	10.310	10.282	10.255	10.230	10.206
10	10.622	10.590	10.560	10.531	10.504	10.478	10.454	10.431
10.25	10.841	10.810	10.781	10.753	10.727	10.702	10.679	10.657
10.5	11.062	11.032	11.004	10.977	10.952	10.928	10.905	10.884
10.75	11.284	11.255	11.228	11.202	11.177	11.154	11.132	11.112
11	11.508	11.480	11.453	11.428	11.404	11.382	11.361	11.341
11.25	11.732	11.705	11.679	11.655	11.632	11.611	11.591	11.572
11.5	11.958	11.932	11.907	11.884	11.862	11.841	11.821	11.803
11.75	12.185	12.160	12.135	12.113	12.092	12.072	12.053	12.035
12	12.413	12.388	12.365	12.343	12.323	12.304	12.286	12.269
12.25	12.642	12.618	12.596	12.575	12.555	12.537	12.519	12.503
12.5	12.872	12.849	12.827	12.807	12.788	12.770	12.754	12.738
12.75	13.103	13.081	13.060	13.040	13.022	13.005	12.989	12.974
13	13.335	13.313	13.293	13.274	13.257	13.241	13.225	13.211
13.25	13.567	13.547	13.527	13.509	13.492	13.477	13.462	13.448
13.5	13.801	13.781	13.762	13.745	13.729	13.714	13.700	13.686
13.75	14.035	14.016	13.998	13.981	13.966	13.951	13.938	13.925
14	14.270	14.252	14.234	14.218	14.204	14.190	14.177	14.165
14.25	14.506	14.488	14.472	14.456	14.442	14.429	14.416	14.405
14.5	14.742	14.725	14.709	14.695	14.681	14.668	14.656	14.645
14.75	14.980	14.963	14.948	14.934	14.921	14.908	14.897	14.887
15	15.217	15.202	15.187	15.173	15.161	15.149	15.138	15.128
15.25	15.456	15.441	15.427	15.414	15.401	15.390	15.380	15.370
15.5	15.695	15.680	15.667	15.654	15.643	15.632	15.622	15.613
15.75	15.934	15.920	15.907	15.895	15.884	15.874	15.865	15.856
16	16.174	16.161	16.149	16.137	16.127	16.117	16.108	16.100
16.25	16.415	16.402	16.390	16.379	16.369	16.360	16.351	16.343
16.5	16.656	16.644	16.632	16.622	16.612	16.603	16.595	16.588
16.75	16.898	16.886	16.875	16.865	16.856	16.847	16.839	16.832
17	17.140	17.128	17.118	17.108	17.099	17.091	17.084	17.077
17.25	17.382	17.371	17.361	17.352	17.343	17.336	17.329	17.322
17.5	17.625	17.614	17.605	17.596	17.588	17.581	17.574	17.568
17.75	17.868	17.858	17.849	17.840	17.833	17.826	17.819	17.813
18	18.111	18.102	18.093	18.085	18.078	18.071	18.065	18.059
18.25	18.355	18.346	18.338	18.330	18.323	18.317	18.311	18.306
18.5	18.599	18.591	18.583	18.575	18.569	18.563	18.557	18.552
18.75	18.844	18.835	18.828	18.821	18.815	18.809	18.804	18.799
19	19.089	19.081	19.073	19.067	19.061	19.055	19.050	19.046
19.25	19.334	19.326	19.319	19.313	19.307	19.302	19.297	19.293
19.5	19.579	19.572	19.565	19.559	19.554	19.549	19.544	19.540
19.75	19.825	19.818	19.811	19.806	19.800	19.796	19.791	19.787
20	20.070	20.064	20.058	20.052	20.047	20.043	20.039	20.035
20.25	20.316	20.310	20.304	20.299	20.294	20.290	20.286	20.283

Table A (*continued*)

% INTEREST	32.5	33	33.5	34	34.5	35	35.5	36
8	8.648	8.621	8.595	8.570	8.546	8.523	8.501	8.481
8.25	8.862	8.836	8.811	8.787	8.764	8.742	8.721	8.701
8.5	9.079	9.053	9.029	9.006	8.983	8.962	8.942	8.923
8.75	9.297	9.272	9.249	9.226	9.205	9.184	9.165	9.146
9	9.516	9.492	9.470	9.448	9.428	9.408	9.389	9.372
9.25	9.737	9.714	9.692	9.672	9.652	9.633	9.615	9.598
9.5	9.960	9.938	9.917	9.896	9.877	9.859	9.842	9.826
9.75	10.184	10.162	10.142	10.123	10.104	10.087	10.071	10.055
10	10.409	10.388	10.369	10.350	10.333	10.316	10.300	10.285
10.25	10.636	10.616	10.597	10.579	10.562	10.546	10.531	10.517
10.5	10.863	10.844	10.826	10.809	10.793	10.778	10.763	10.749
10.75	11.092	11.074	11.057	11.040	11.025	11.010	10.996	10.983
11	11.322	11.305	11.288	11.272	11.258	11.243	11.230	11.218
11.25	11.554	11.537	11.521	11.506	11.491	11.478	11.465	11.453
11.5	11.786	11.769	11.754	11.740	11.726	11.713	11.701	11.690
11.75	12.019	12.003	11.989	11.975	11.962	11.950	11.938	11.927
12	12.253	12.238	12.224	12.211	12.198	12.187	12.176	12.165
12.25	12.488	12.473	12.460	12.447	12.436	12.424	12.414	12.404
12.5	12.724	12.710	12.697	12.685	12.674	12.663	12.653	12.644
12.75	12.960	12.947	12.935	12.923	12.912	12.902	12.893	12.884
13	13.197	13.185	13.173	13.162	13.152	13.142	13.133	13.125
13.25	13.435	13.424	13.412	13.402	13.392	13.383	13.374	13.366
13.5	13.674	13.663	13.652	13.642	13.633	13.624	13.616	13.608
13.75	13.914	13.903	13.892	13.883	13.874	13.866	13.858	13.851
14	14.154	14.143	14.133	14.124	14.116	14.108	14.101	14.094
14.25	14.394	14.384	14.375	14.366	14.358	14.351	14.344	14.337
14.5	14.635	14.626	14.617	14.609	14.601	14.594	14.587	14.581
14.75	14.877	14.868	14.859	14.852	14.844	14.838	14.831	14.826
15	15.119	15.110	15.102	15.095	15.088	15.082	15.076	15.070
15.25	15.362	15.353	15.346	15.339	15.332	15.326	15.321	15.315
15.5	15.605	15.597	15.590	15.583	15.577	15.571	15.566	15.561
15.75	15.848	15.841	15.834	15.827	15.822	15.816	15.811	15.807
16	16.092	16.085	16.078	16.072	16.067	16.062	16.057	16.053
16.25	16.336	16.329	16.323	16.317	16.312	16.307	16.303	16.299
16.5	16.581	16.574	16.568	16.563	16.558	16.553	16.549	16.545
16.75	16.826	16.819	16.814	16.809	16.804	16.800	16.796	16.792
17	17.071	17.065	17.060	17.055	17.050	17.046	17.043	17.039
17.25	17.316	17.311	17.306	17.301	17.297	17.293	17.290	17.286
17.5	17.562	17.557	17.552	17.548	17.544	17.540	17.537	17.534
17.75	17.808	17.803	17.799	17.795	17.791	17.787	17.784	17.781
18	18.054	18.050	18.045	18.042	18.038	18.035	18.032	18.029
18.25	18.301	18.296	18.292	18.289	18.285	18.282	18.279	18.277
18.5	18.548	18.543	18.540	18.536	18.533	18.530	18.527	18.525
18.75	18.794	18.790	18.787	18.784	18.781	18.778	18.775	18.773
19	19.042	19.038	19.034	19.031	19.028	19.026	19.024	19.021
19.25	19.289	19.285	19.282	19.279	19.277	19.274	19.272	19.270
19.5	19.536	19.533	19.530	19.527	19.525	19.522	19.520	19.518
19.75	19.784	19.781	19.778	19.775	19.773	19.771	19.769	19.767
20	20.032	20.029	20.026	20.024	20.021	20.019	20.017	20.016
20.25	20.280	20.277	20.274	20.272	20.270	20.268	20.266	20.265

Table A (*continued*)

% INTEREST	YEARS							
	36.5	37	37.5	38	38.5	39	39.5	40
8	8.461	8.442	8.424	8.406	8.390	8.374	8.358	8.344
8.25	8.682	8.664	8.646	8.629	8.613	8.598	8.584	8.570
8.5	8.905	8.887	8.870	8.854	8.839	8.824	8.810	8.797
8.75	9.129	9.112	9.096	9.081	9.066	9.052	9.039	9.026
9	9.355	9.338	9.323	9.308	9.294	9.281	9.268	9.256
9.25	9.582	9.566	9.552	9.538	9.524	9.512	9.499	9.488
9.5	9.810	9.795	9.781	9.768	9.755	9.743	9.732	9.721
9.75	10.040	10.026	10.012	10.000	9.988	9.976	9.965	9.955
10	10.271	10.258	10.245	10.233	10.221	10.210	10.200	10.190
10.25	10.503	10.490	10.478	10.466	10.455	10.445	10.435	10.426
10.5	10.736	10.724	10.712	10.701	10.691	10.681	10.672	10.663
10.75	10.971	10.959	10.948	10.937	10.927	10.918	10.909	10.901
11	11.206	11.195	11.184	11.174	11.165	11.156	11.147	11.140
11.25	11.442	11.431	11.421	11.412	11.403	11.395	11.387	11.379
11.5	11.679	11.669	11.659	11.651	11.642	11.634	11.627	11.619
11.75	11.917	11.907	11.898	11.890	11.882	11.874	11.867	11.860
12	12.156	12.146	12.138	12.130	12.122	12.115	12.108	12.102
12.25	12.395	12.386	12.378	12.370	12.363	12.357	12.350	12.344
12.5	12.635	12.627	12.619	12.612	12.605	12.599	12.593	12.587
12.75	12.876	12.868	12.861	12.854	12.847	12.841	12.836	12.830
13	13.117	13.110	13.103	13.096	13.090	13.084	13.079	13.074
13.25	13.359	13.352	13.345	13.339	13.333	13.328	13.323	13.318
13.5	13.601	13.595	13.588	13.583	13.577	13.572	13.568	13.563
13.75	13.844	13.838	13.832	13.827	13.822	13.817	13.812	13.808
14	14.088	14.082	14.076	14.071	14.066	14.062	14.058	14.054
14.25	14.331	14.326	14.321	14.316	14.311	14.307	14.303	14.299
14.5	14.576	14.570	14.565	14.561	14.557	14.553	14.549	14.546
14.75	14.820	14.815	14.811	14.806	14.802	14.799	14.795	14.792
15	15.065	15.061	15.056	15.052	15.048	15.045	15.042	15.039
15.25	15.311	15.306	15.302	15.298	15.295	15.291	15.288	15.286
15.5	15.556	15.552	15.548	15.545	15.541	15.538	15.535	15.533
15.75	15.802	15.798	15.795	15.791	15.788	15.785	15.783	15.780
16	16.049	16.045	16.041	16.038	16.035	16.033	16.030	16.028
16.25	16.295	16.292	16.288	16.285	16.283	16.280	16.278	16.276
16.5	16.542	16.538	16.535	16.533	16.530	16.528	16.526	16.524
16.75	16.789	16.786	16.783	16.780	16.778	16.776	16.773	16.772
17	17.036	17.033	17.030	17.028	17.026	17.024	17.022	17.020
17.25	17.283	17.281	17.278	17.276	17.274	17.272	17.270	17.268
17.5	17.531	17.528	17.526	17.524	17.522	17.520	17.518	17.517
17.75	17.779	17.776	17.774	17.772	17.770	17.768	17.767	17.765
18	18.027	18.024	18.022	18.020	18.019	18.017	18.016	18.014
18.25	18.275	18.272	18.270	18.269	18.267	18.266	18.264	18.263
18.5	18.523	18.521	18.519	18.517	18.516	18.514	18.513	18.512
18.75	18.771	18.769	18.768	18.766	18.765	18.763	18.762	18.761
19	19.020	19.018	19.016	19.015	19.013	19.012	19.011	19.010
19.25	19.268	19.266	19.265	19.264	19.262	19.261	19.260	19.259
19.5	19.517	19.515	19.514	19.513	19.511	19.510	19.509	19.508
19.75	19.766	19.764	19.763	19.762	19.760	19.759	19.759	19.758
20	20.014	20.013	20.012	20.011	20.010	20.009	20.008	20.007
20.25	20.263	20.262	20.261	20.260	20.259	20.258	20.257	20.257

Table B
Constant Annual Percents for Loans with Annual Payments
*To be used only in the event of 1 payment
made annually or semiannually*

% INTEREST	1	1.5	2	2.5	3	3.5	4	4.5
6	106.001	71.692	54.544	44.261	37.411	32.522	28.859	26.014
6.25	106.250	71.901	54.735	44.441	37.584	32.691	29.025	26.177
6.5	106.501	72.112	54.926	44.622	37.758	32.860	29.190	26.340
6.75	106.751	72.323	55.118	44.803	37.932	33.029	29.357	26.504
7	107.001	72.533	55.309	44.983	38.105	33.198	29.523	26.669
7.25	107.251	72.744	55.501	45.164	38.280	33.368	29.690	26.834
7.5	107.500	72.954	55.693	45.345	38.454	33.538	29.857	26.999
7.75	107.751	73.166	55.885	45.526	38.629	33.709	30.024	27.164
8	108.000	73.376	56.077	45.708	38.803	33.879	30.192	27.330
8.25	108.251	73.588	56.270	45.890	38.979	34.050	30.360	27.497
8.5	108.501	73.799	56.462	46.072	39.154	34.221	30.529	27.664
8.75	108.750	74.010	56.654	46.254	39.330	34.393	30.698	27.831
9	109.001	74.221	56.847	46.436	39.506	34.565	30.867	27.998
9.25	109.250	74.432	57.040	46.618	39.682	34.737	31.036	28.166
9.5	109.501	74.644	57.233	46.801	39.858	34.909	31.206	28.334
9.75	109.750	74.855	57.426	46.984	40.035	35.082	31.377	28.503
10	110.001	75.067	57.619	47.167	40.212	35.255	31.547	28.672
10.25	110.250	75.278	57.812	47.350	40.389	35.428	31.718	28.841

% INTEREST	5	5.5	6	6.5	7	7.5	8	8.5
6	23.740	21.882	20.336	19.031	17.914	16.947	16.104	15.361
6.25	23.901	22.043	20.496	19.190	18.073	17.107	16.263	15.521
6.5	24.064	22.204	20.657	19.351	18.233	17.267	16.424	15.682
6.75	24.226	22.366	20.818	19.511	18.394	17.428	16.585	15.843
7	24.389	22.528	20.980	19.673	18.555	17.590	16.747	16.006
7.25	24.553	22.690	21.142	19.835	18.718	17.752	16.910	16.169
7.5	24.717	22.853	21.305	19.997	18.880	17.915	17.073	16.332
7.75	24.881	23.017	21.468	20.161	19.043	18.078	17.237	16.497
8	25.046	23.181	21.632	20.324	19.207	18.243	17.401	16.662
8.25	25.211	23.346	21.796	20.489	19.372	18.408	17.567	16.828
8.5	25.377	23.511	21.961	20.654	19.537	18.573	17.733	16.995
8.75	25.543	23.676	22.126	20.819	19.703	18.739	17.900	17.163
9	25.709	23.843	22.292	20.985	19.869	18.906	18.068	17.331
9.25	25.876	24.009	22.458	21.152	20.036	19.074	18.236	17.500
9.5	26.044	24.176	22.625	21.319	20.204	19.242	18.405	17.670
9.75	26.211	24.343	22.793	21.486	20.372	19.411	18.574	17.840
10	26.380	24.511	22.961	21.655	20.541	19.580	18.744	18.012
10.25	26.548	24.680	23.129	21.823	20.710	19.750	18.915	18.183

Table B (*continued*)

% INTEREST	YEARS							
	9	9.5	10	10.5	11	11.5	12	12.5
6	14.702	14.115	13.587	13.111	12.679	12.287	11.928	11.599
6.25	14.863	14.275	13.748	13.273	12.842	12.450	12.092	11.763
6.5	15.024	14.437	13.911	13.436	13.006	12.614	12.257	11.929
6.75	15.186	14.600	14.074	13.600	13.170	12.780	12.423	12.096
7	15.349	14.763	14.238	13.764	13.336	12.946	12.590	12.264
7.25	15.512	14.927	14.403	13.930	13.502	13.113	12.759	12.434
7.5	15.677	15.092	14.569	14.097	13.670	13.282	12.928	12.604
7.75	15.842	15.258	14.735	14.264	13.838	13.451	13.098	12.775
8	16.008	15.425	14.903	14.433	14.008	13.621	13.270	12.948
8.25	16.175	15.593	15.071	14.602	14.178	13.793	13.442	13.121
8.5	16.342	15.761	15.241	14.773	14.349	13.965	13.615	13.296
8.75	16.511	15.930	15.411	14.944	14.522	14.139	13.790	13.471
9	16.680	16.101	15.582	15.116	14.695	14.313	13.965	13.648
9.25	16.850	16.271	15.754	15.285	14.869	14.488	14.141	13.825
9.5	17.021	16.443	15.927	15.463	15.044	14.664	14.319	14.004
9.75	17.192	16.615	16.100	15.637	15.220	14.841	14.497	14.183
10	17.364	16.789	16.275	15.813	15.396	15.019	14.676	14.364
10.25	17.537	16.963	16.450	15.989	15.574	15.198	14.857	14.545

% INTEREST	YEARS							
	13	13.5	14	14.5	15	15.5	16	16.5
6	11.296	11.017	10.759	10.519	10.296	10.089	9.895	9.714
6.25	11.462	11.183	10.926	10.687	10.465	10.259	10.066	9.886
6.5	11.628	11.351	11.094	10.856	10.635	10.430	10.238	10.059
6.75	11.796	11.519	11.264	11.027	10.807	10.602	10.411	10.233
7	11.965	11.689	11.435	11.199	10.979	10.776	10.586	10.408
7.25	12.135	11.860	11.607	11.372	11.154	10.951	10.762	10.586
7.5	12.306	12.033	11.780	11.546	11.329	11.127	10.939	10.764
7.75	12.479	12.206	11.954	11.721	11.505	11.305	11.118	10.944
8	12.652	12.380	12.130	11.898	11.683	11.483	11.298	11.125
8.25	12.827	12.556	12.306	12.076	11.862	11.663	11.479	11.307
8.5	13.002	12.733	12.484	12.255	12.042	11.845	11.661	11.491
8.75	13.179	12.911	12.663	12.435	12.223	12.027	11.845	11.675
9	13.357	13.089	12.843	12.616	12.406	12.211	12.030	11.862
9.25	13.535	13.269	13.025	12.799	12.590	12.396	12.216	12.049
9.5	13.715	13.450	13.207	12.982	12.774	12.582	12.404	12.238
9.75	13.896	13.633	13.390	13.167	12.960	12.769	12.592	12.427
10	14.078	13.816	13.575	13.353	13.147	12.958	12.782	12.618
10.25	14.261	14.000	13.760	13.539	13.336	13.147	12.972	12.810

Table B (*continued*)

% INTEREST	YEARS							
	17	17.5	18	18.5	19	19.5	20	20.5
6	9.545	9.385	9.236	9.095	8.962	8.837	8.718	8.607
6.25	9.717	9.559	9.410	9.270	9.138	9.014	8.896	8.785
6.5	9.891	9.733	9.585	9.446	9.316	9.192	9.076	8.966
6.75	10.066	9.910	9.763	9.625	9.495	9.372	9.257	9.148
7	10.243	10.087	9.941	9.804	9.675	9.554	9.439	9.331
7.25	10.421	10.266	10.121	9.985	9.857	9.737	9.624	9.516
7.5	10.600	10.447	10.303	10.168	10.041	9.922	9.809	9.703
7.75	10.781	10.629	10.486	10.352	10.226	10.108	9.997	9.891
8	10.963	10.812	10.670	10.537	10.413	10.296	10.185	10.081
8.25	11.146	10.996	10.856	10.724	10.601	10.485	10.375	10.273
8.5	11.331	11.182	11.043	10.913	10.790	10.675	10.567	10.465
8.75	11.517	11.370	11.231	11.102	10.981	10.867	10.760	10.660
9	11.705	11.558	11.421	11.293	11.173	11.060	10.955	10.855
9.25	11.893	11.748	11.612	11.485	11.367	11.255	11.150	11.052
9.5	12.083	11.939	11.805	11.679	11.561	11.451	11.348	11.251
9.75	12.274	12.131	11.998	11.874	11.757	11.648	11.546	11.450
10	12.466	12.325	12.193	12.070	11.955	11.847	11.746	11.651
10.25	12.660	12.520	12.389	12.267	12.153	12.047	11.947	11.854

% INTEREST	YEARS							
	21	21.5	22	22.5	23	23.5	24	24.5
6	8.500	8.400	8.305	8.214	8.128	8.046	7.968	7.894
6.25	8.680	8.580	8.486	8.396	8.311	8.230	8.153	8.079
6.5	8.861	8.763	8.669	8.580	8.496	8.416	8.340	8.267
6.75	9.044	8.947	8.854	8.766	8.683	8.604	8.528	8.457
7	9.229	9.132	9.041	8.954	8.871	8.793	8.719	8.648
7.25	9.415	9.319	9.229	9.143	9.062	8.984	8.911	8.841
7.5	9.603	9.508	9.419	9.334	9.254	9.177	9.105	9.036
7.75	9.792	9.699	9.610	9.526	9.447	9.372	9.301	9.233
8	9.983	9.891	9.803	9.721	9.642	9.568	9.498	9.431
8.25	10.176	10.084	9.998	9.916	9.839	9.766	9.697	9.631
8.5	10.370	10.279	10.194	10.113	10.037	9.965	9.897	9.832
8.75	10.565	10.476	10.391	10.312	10.237	10.166	10.099	10.035
9	10.762	10.674	10.591	10.512	10.438	10.368	10.302	10.240
9.25	10.960	10.873	10.791	10.714	10.641	10.572	10.507	10.446
9.5	11.159	11.074	10.993	10.917	10.845	10.777	10.713	10.653
9.75	11.360	11.276	11.196	11.121	11.050	10.984	10.921	10.862
10	11.562	11.479	11.401	11.327	11.257	11.192	11.130	11.072
10.25	11.766	11.684	11.606	11.534	11.465	11.401	11.340	11.283

Table B (*continued*)

% INTEREST	YEARS							
	25	25.5	26	26.5	27	27.5	28	28.5
6	7.823	7.755	7.690	7.629	7.570	7.513	7.459	7.408
6.25	8.009	7.943	7.879	7.818	7.760	7.704	7.651	7.600
6.5	8.198	8.132	8.069	8.010	7.952	7.898	7.845	7.795
6.75	8.389	8.324	8.262	8.203	8.147	8.093	8.041	7.992
7	8.581	8.517	8.456	8.398	8.343	8.290	8.239	8.191
7.25	8.775	8.712	8.652	8.595	8.541	8.489	8.439	8.392
7.5	8.971	8.909	8.850	8.794	8.740	8.689	8.641	8.594
7.75	9.169	9.108	9.050	8.994	8.942	8.892	8.844	8.798
8	9.368	9.308	9.251	9.196	9.145	9.096	9.049	9.004
8.25	9.569	9.510	9.454	9.400	9.350	9.301	9.256	9.212
8.5	9.771	9.713	9.658	9.606	9.556	9.509	9.464	9.421
8.75	9.975	9.918	9.864	9.813	9.764	9.718	9.674	9.632
9	10.181	10.125	10.072	10.021	9.974	9.928	9.885	9.844
9.25	10.388	10.333	10.281	10.231	10.184	10.140	10.098	10.058
9.5	10.596	10.542	10.491	10.443	10.397	10.354	10.312	10.273
9.75	10.806	10.753	10.703	10.655	10.611	10.568	10.528	10.490
10	11.017	10.965	10.916	10.870	10.826	10.784	10.745	10.708
10.25	11.229	11.178	11.130	11.085	11.042	11.002	10.963	10.927

% INTEREST	YEARS				
	29	29.5	30	35	40
6	7.358	7.310	7.265	6.897	6.646
6.25	7.552	7.505	7.460	7.101	6.857
6.5	7.747	7.702	7.658	7.306	7.069
6.75	7.945	7.900	7.857	7.514	7.284
7	8.145	8.101	8.059	7.723	7.501
7.25	8.346	8.303	8.262	7.935	7.720
7.5	8.550	8.508	8.467	8.148	7.940
7.75	8.755	8.714	8.674	8.363	8.162
8	8.962	8.921	8.883	8.580	8.386
8.25	9.170	9.131	9.093	8.799	8.611
8.5	9.381	9.342	9.305	9.019	8.838
8.75	9.592	9.555	9.519	9.241	9.066
9	9.806	9.769	9.734	9.464	9.296
9.25	10.020	9.984	9.950	9.688	9.527
9.5	10.236	10.201	10.168	9.914	9.759
9.75	10.454	10.420	10.387	10.141	9.992
10	10.673	10.640	10.608	10.369	10.226
10.25	10.893	10.860	10.830	10.598	10.461

Table C
Annual Sinking Fund Tables Wraparound Yield Calculation for 6–30 Years

YEARS	6%	6¼%	6½%	6¾%	7%	7¼%	7½%	7¾%	8%	8¼%	8½%
1	1.000000	1.000000	1.000000	1.000000	1.000000	1.000000	1.000000	1.000000	1.000000	1.000000	1.000000
	.485437	.484848	.484262	.483676	.483092	.482509	.481928	.481348	.480769	.480192	.479616
	.314110	.313341	.312576	.311812	.311052	.310293	.309538	.308784	.308034	.307285	.306539
	.228591	.227745	.226903	.226064	.225228	.224396	.223568	.222742	.221921	.221103	.220288
	.177396	.176513	.175635	.174760	.173891	.173025	.172165	.171308	.170456	.169609	.168766
6	.143363	.142463	.141568	.140679	.139796	.138918	.138045	.137177	.136315	.135459	.134607
	.119135	.118230	.117331	.116439	.115553	.114674	.113800	.112933	.112072	.111218	.110369
	.101036	.100133	.099237	.098349	.097468	.096594	.095727	.094867	.094015	.093169	.092331
	.087022	.086126	.085238	.084358	.083486	.082623	.081767	.080919	.080080	.079248	.078424
	.075868	.074982	.074105	.073237	.072378	.071527	.070686	.069853	.069029	.068214	.067408
11	.066793	.065919	.065055	.064201	.063557	.062522	.061697	.060882	.060076	.059280	.058493
	.059277	.058417	.057568	.056730	.055902	.055085	.054278	.053481	.052695	.051919	.051153
	.052960	.052116	.051283	.050461	.049651	.048852	.048064	.047288	.046522	.045767	.045023
	.047585	.046757	.045940	.045137	.044345	.043565	.042797	.042041	.041297	.040564	.039842
	.042963	.042151	.041353	.040567	.039795	.039035	.038287	.037552	.036830	.036119	.035420
16	.038952	.038158	.037378	.036611	.035858	.035118	.034391	.033678	.032977	.032289	.031614
	.035445	.034668	.033906	.033159	.032425	.031706	.031000	.030308	.029629	.028964	.028312
	.032357	.031598	.030855	.030126	.029413	.028714	.028029	.027359	.026702	.026059	.025430
	.029621	.028880	.028156	.027447	.026753	.026074	.025411	.024762	.024128	.023507	.022901
	.027185	.026462	.025756	.025067	.024393	.023735	.023092	.022465	.021852	.021254	.020671
21	.025005	.024300	.023613	.022943	.022289	.021651	.021029	.020423	.019832	.019256	.018695
	.023046	.022360	.021691	.021040	.020406	.019788	.019187	.018602	.018032	.017478	.016939
	.021278	.020611	.019961	.019329	.018714	.018116	.017535	.016971	.016422	.015889	.015372
	.019679	.019029	.018398	.017784	.017189	.016611	.016050	.015506	.014978	.014466	.013970
	.018227	.017595	.016981	.016387	.015811	.015252	.014711	.014186	.013679	.013187	.012712
26	.016904	.016290	.015695	.015119	.014561	.014021	.013500	.012995	.012507	.012036	.011580
	.015697	.015100	.014523	.013965	.013426	.012905	.012402	.011917	.011448	.010996	.010560
	.014593	.014013	.013453	.012913	.012392	.011890	.011405	.010938	.010489	.010056	.009639
	.013580	.013017	.012474	.011952	.011449	.010964	.010498	.010050	.009619	.009204	.008806
	.012649	.012103	.011577	.011072	.010586	.010120	.009671	.009241	.008827	.008431	.008051

YEARS	8¾%	9%	9¼%	9½%	9¾%	10%	10¼%	10½%	10¾%	11%	11¼%
1	1.000000	1.000000	1.000000	1.000000	1.000000	1.000000	1.000000	1.000000	1.000000	1.000000	1.000000
	.479042	.478469	.477897	.477327	.476758	.476190	.475624	.475059	.474496	.473934	.473373
	.305796	.305055	.304136	.303580	.302846	.302115	.301386	.300659	.299935	.299213	.298494
	.219477	.218669	.217864	.217063	.216265	.215471	.214680	.213892	.213108	.212326	.211548
	.167927	.167092	.166262	.165436	.164615	.163797	.162984	.162175	.161371	.160570	.159774
6	.133761	.132920	.132084	.131253	.130428	.129607	.128792	.127982	.127177	.126377	.125581
	.109527	.108691	.107860	.107036	.106218	.105405	.104599	.103799	.103004	.102215	.101432
	.091499	.090674	.089857	.089046	.088241	.087444	.086653	.085869	.085092	.084321	.083557
	.077607	.076799	.075998	.075205	.074419	.073641	.072870	.072106	.071350	.070602	.069862
	.066610	.065820	.065039	.064266	.063502	.062745	.061997	.061257	.060525	.059801	.059085
11	.057715	.056947	.056187	.055437	.054696	.053963	.053240	.052525	.051819	.051121	.050432
	.050397	.049651	.048914	.048188	.047471	.046763	.046059	.045377	.044697	.044027	.043366
	.044289	.043567	.042854	.042152	.041460	.040779	.040107	.039445	.038793	.038151	.037518
	.039132	.038433	.037745	.037068	.036402	.035746	.035101	.034467	.033842	.033228	.032624
	.034734	.034059	.033396	.032744	.032103	.031474	.030855	.030248	.029651	.029065	.028490
16	.030951	.030300	.029661	.029035	.028420	.027817	.027225	.026644	.026075	.025517	.024969
	.027673	.027046	.026432	.025831	.025241	.024664	.024099	.023545	.023003	.022471	.021952
	.024815	.024212	.023623	.023046	.022482	.021930	.021391	.020863	.020347	.019843	.019350
	.022309	.021730	.021165	.020613	.020074	.019547	.019033	.018531	.018041	.017563	.017096
	.020102	.019546	.019005	.018477	.017962	.017460	.016970	.016493	.016028	.015576	.015134
21	.018149	.017617	.017098	.016594	.016102	.015624	.015159	.014707	.014266	.013838	.013421
	.016415	.015905	.015409	.014928	.014460	.014005	.013563	.013134	.012718	.012313	.011920
	.014870	.014382	.013909	.013449	.013004	.012572	.012153	.011747	.011353	.010971	.010601
	.013489	.013023	.012571	.012134	.011710	.011300	.010903	.010519	.010147	.009787	.009439
	.012251	.011806	.011376	.010959	.010557	.010168	.009792	.009429	.009079	.008740	.008413
26	.011140	.010715	.010305	.009909	.009527	.009159	.008804	.008461	.008131	.007813	.007506
	.010140	.009735	.009345	.008969	.008606	.008258	.007922	.007599	.007288	.006989	.006702
	.009238	.008852	.008481	.008124	.007781	.007451	.007134	.006830	.006538	.006257	.005988
	.008423	.008056	.007703	.007364	.007040	.006728	.006429	.006143	.005868	.005605	.005354
	.007686	.007336	.007001	.006681	.006373	.006079	.005798	.005528	.005271	.005025	.004789

Table C (*continued*)

YEARS	11½%	11¾%	12%	13%	14%	15%	16%	17%	18%	19%	20%
1	1.000000	1.000000	1.000000	1.000000	1.000000	1.000000	1.000000	1.000000	1.000000	1.000000	1.000000
	.472813	.472255	.471698	.469483	.467290	.465116	.462963	.460829	.458715	.456621	.454545
	.297776	.297062	.296349	.293522	.290731	.287976	.285257	.282573	.279923	.277308	.274725
	.210774	.210003	.209234	.206194	.203205	.200265	.197375	.194533	.191738	.188991	.186289
	.158982	.158194	.157410	.154314	.151284	.148315	.145409	.142564	.139778	.137050	.134380
6	.124791	.124006	.123226	.120153	.117158	.114236	.111390	.108615	.105910	.103274	.100706
	.100655	.099884	.099118	.096111	.093192	.090360	.087613	.084947	.082362	.079855	.077424
	.082799	.082048	.081303	.078387	.075570	.072850	.070224	.067690	.065243	.062885	.060609
	.069126	.068399	.067679	.064869	.062168	.059574	.057083	.054690	.052395	.050192	.048079
	.058377	.057677	.056984	.054290	.051714	.049252	.046901	.044657	.042515	.040471	.038523
11	.049751	.049079	.048415	.045841	.043394	.041068	.038861	.036765	.034776	.032891	.031104
	.042714	.042071	.041437	.038986	.036669	.034480	.032415	.030466	.028628	.026896	.025265
	.036895	.036282	.035677	.033350	.031164	.029110	.027184	.025378	.023686	.022102	.020620
	.032030	.031446	.030871	.028668	.026609	.024688	.022898	.021230	.019678	.018235	.016893
	.027924	.027369	.026824	.024742	.022809	.021017	.019358	.017822	.016403	.015092	.013882
16	.024432	.023906	.023390	.021426	.019615	.017947	.016414	.015004	.013710	.012523	.011436
	.021443	.020944	.020457	.018608	.016915	.015366	.013952	.012662	.011485	.010414	.009440
	.018868	.018397	.017937	.016201	.014621	.013186	.011885	.010706	.009639	.008676	.007805
	.016641	.016196	.015763	.014134	.012663	.011336	.010142	.009067	.008103	.007237	.006462
	.014705	.014286	.013879	.012354	.010986	.009761	.008667	.007690	.006820	.006045	.005357
21	.013016	.012623	.012240	.010814	.009545	.008416	.007416	.006530	.005746	.005054	.004444
	.011539	.011169	.010811	.009480	.008303	.007265	.006353	.005550	.004846	.004229	.003690
	.010243	.009896	.009560	.008319	.007231	.006278	.005447	.004721	.004090	.003542	.003065
	.009103	.008778	.008463	.007308	.006303	.005429	.004673	.004019	.003454	.002967	.002548
	.008098	.007794	.007500	.006426	.005498	.004699	.004013	.003423	.002919	.002487	.002119
26	.007210	.006926	.006652	.005655	.004800	.004069	.003447	.002918	.002467	.002086	.001762
	.006425	.006159	.005904	.004979	.004193	.003526	.002963	.002487	.002087	.001750	.001467
	.005730	.005482	.005244	.004387	.003665	.003010	.002548	.002121	.001765	.001468	.001221
	.005112	.004881	.004660	.003867	.003204	.002651	.002192	.001810	.001494	.001232	.001016
	.004564	.004349	.004144	.003411	.002803	.002300	.001886	.001545	.001264	.001034	.000846

	21%	22%	23%	24%	25%	26%	27%	28%	29%	30%
1	1.000000	1.000000	1.000000	1.000000	1.000000	1.000000	1.000000	1.000000	1.000000	1.000000
	.452489	.450450	.448430	.446429	.444444	.442478	.440529	.438596	.436681	.434783
	.272175	.269658	.267173	.264718	.262295	.259902	.257539	.255206	.252902	.250627
	.183632	.181020	.178451	.175926	.173442	.170999	.168598	.166236	.163913	.161629
	.131765	.129206	.126700	.124248	.121847	.119496	.117196	.114944	.112739	.110582
6	.098203	.095764	.093389	.091074	.088819	.086623	.084484	.082400	.080371	.078394
	.075067	.072782	.070568	.068422	.066342	.064326	.062374	.060482	.058649	.056874
	.058415	.056299	.054259	.052293	.050399	.048573	.046814	.045119	.043487	.041915
	.046053	.044111	.042249	.040465	.038756	.037119	.035551	.034049	.032612	.031235
	.036665	.034895	.033208	.031602	.030073	.028616	.027231	.025912	.024657	.023463
11	.029411	.027807	.026289	.024852	.023493	.022207	.020991	.019842	.018755	.017729
	.023730	.022285	.020926	.019648	.018448	.017319	.016260	.015265	.014331	.013454
	.019234	.017939	.016728	.015598	.014544	.013559	.012641	.011785	.010987	.010244
	.015647	.014491	.013418	.012423	.011501	.010647	.009856	.009123	.008445	.007818
	.012766	.011738	.010791	.009919	.009117	.008379	.007701	.007077	.006405	.005978
16	.010441	.009530	.008697	.007936	.007241	.006606	.006027	.005499	.005017	.004577
	.008555	.007751	.007021	.006359	.005759	.005216	.004723	.004277	.003874	.003509
	.007020	.006313	.005676	.005102	.004586	.004122	.003705	.003331	.002994	.002692
	.005769	.005148	.004593	.004098	.003656	.003261	.002909	.002595	.002316	.002066
	.004745	.004202	.003720	.003294	.002916	.002581	.002285	.002023	.001792	.001587
21	.003906	.003432	.003016	.002649	.002327	.002045	.001796	.001578	.001387	.001219
	.003218	.002805	.002446	.002132	.001858	.001620	.001412	.001232	.001074	.000937
	.002652	.002294	.001984	.001716	.001485	.001284	.001111	.000961	.000832	.000720
	.002187	.001877	.001611	.001382	.001186	.001018	.000874	.000750	.000644	.000554
	.001804	.001536	.001308	.001113	.000948	.000807	.000688	.000586	.000499	.000426

INDEX